WHAT DO YOU THINK?

Percentage of people who believe . . .

Apes and humans do not have a common ancestry	**47%**
Global warming exists	**82%**
The assassination of Martin Luther King, Jr., was part of a larger conspiracy	**58%**
It is morally wrong to use human cloning technology in developing new treatments for disease	**53%**
Some form of intelligent life exists in outer space	**55%**
Journalists have been trying to scare and alarm people with their coverage of hurricanes	**24%**
A nuclear power plant to generate electricity should be built in their community	**36%**
Religion plays too small a role in most people's lives today	**69%**
UFOs exist	**34%**
Miracles happen	**82%**

THiNK

VICE PRESIDENT AND EDITOR IN CHIEF **Michael Ryan**

EDITORIAL DIRECTOR **Beth Mejia**

SPONSORING EDITOR **Mark Georgiev**

EXECUTIVE MARKETING MANAGER **Pamela Cooper**

DIRECTOR OF DEVELOPMENT **Nancy Crochiere**

EDITORIAL COORDINATOR **Briana Porco**

EDITING, DESIGN, AND PRODUCTION MANAGER **Melissa Williams**

PROJECT MANAGER **Bonnie Briggle, Lachina Publishing Services**

COVER DESIGN **Andrei Pasternak**

INTERIOR DESIGN **Maureen McCutcheon**

ILLUSTRATION **Lachina Publishing Services**

PHOTO RESEARCH **David Tietz, Editorial Image, LLC**

SENIOR MANUFACTURING SUPERVISOR **Tandra Jorgensen**

LEAD MEDIA PROJECT MANAGER **Ron Nelms**

SUPPLEMENTS **Southern Editorial**

CREATIVE AND PRODUCTION ASSISTANCE **Jasmin Tokatlian, Rachel Castillo**

COMPOSITION **Lachina Publishing Services**

PRINTING **Worldcolor**

Front cover photo: © Digital Vision/Getty Images. Back cover photo: © Johannes Kroemer/Digital Vision/Getty Images. Inside flap photo: Courtesy of Alyssa Boss, who the author would like to thank for her support during the writing and production of this book.

Library of Congress Cataloguing-in-Publication Data

Boss, Judith A.
   Think: Critical thinking and logic skills for everyday life / Judith A. Boss, 1/e.
   p. cm.
   Includes index and biographical references.
   ISBN-13: 978-0-07-740705-6
   ISBN-10: 0-07-740705-9
1. Critical thinking. 2. Logic I. Boss, Judith A. II. Title.
B105.T54M66 2010

160—dc22   20080412556

THiNK

BRIEF CONTENTS

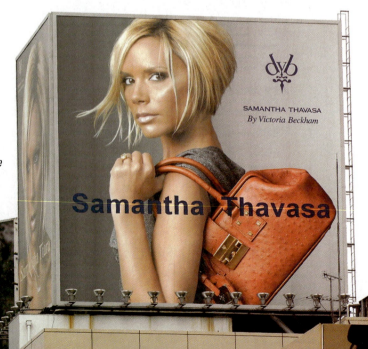

Features

CRITICAL

Nazi war criminal Adolf Eichmann was tried in Israel in 1960 for crimes against humanity. Despite his claim that he was just following the orders of his superiors when he ordered the deaths of millions of Jews, the court found him guilty and sentenced him to death. Was Eichmann an inhuman monster? Or was he, as his defense lawyer claimed, just doing what many of us would do—following orders from our superiors?

To address this question, social psychologist Stanley Milgram of Yale University conducted, between 1960 and 1963, what has become a classic experiment. Milgram placed an advertisement in a newspaper asking for men to take part in a scientific study of memory and learning.[1] Those chosen to participate were told that the purpose of the experiment was to study the effects of punishment on learning—and that their job was to administer electric shocks as punishment when the learner gave a wrong answer. The participants were instructed that the shocks would be given at the direction of the experimenter and would range in intensity from 15 volts to 450 volts. In fact, no shocks were actually being administered, but the participants didn't know this.

THINKING
WHY IT'S IMPORTANT

Think FIRST >>

- What are the characteristics of a skilled critical thinker?
- What are the three levels of thinking?
- What are some of the barriers to critical thinking?

As the intensity of the shocks "increased," the learner (actually an actor) responded with increased anguish, screaming in pain and pleading with the participant delivering the shocks to stop. Despite the repeated pleas, all the participants administered shocks of up to 300 volts before refusing to go on. In addition, 65 percent continued to deliver shocks of 450 volts simply because an authority figure (a scientist in a white lab coat) told the participants to continue. Most who continued were clearly disturbed by what they were doing. However, unlike the participants who refused to continue, they were unable to provide logical counterarguments to the scientist's insistence that "the experiment requires that you must continue."

How could this happen? Were the results of Milgram's study some sort of aberration? As it turns out, they were not.

Several years later, in 1971, the U.S. Navy funded a study of the reaction of humans to situations in which there are huge differentials in authority and power—as in a prison. The study was administered under the direction of psychologist Philip Zimbardo, who selected student volunteers deemed psychologically stable and healthy.[2] The volunteers were randomly assigned to play the role of either guard or prisoner in a two-week prison simulation in the basement of the Stanford University building in which the psychology department was located. To make the situation more realistic, "guards" were given wooden batons and wore khaki, military-style uniforms and mirrored sunglasses that minimized eye contact. The "prisoners" were given ill-fitting smocks without underwear and rubber thongs for their feet. Each "prisoner" was also assigned a number to be used instead of a name. The "guards" were not given any formal instructions; they were simply told that it was their responsibility to run the prison.

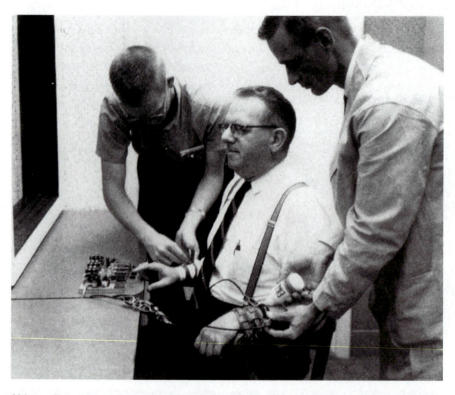

Milgram Experiment   Scene from the Milgram experiment on obedience. The "learner" is being hooked up to the machine that will deliver bogus electric shocks each time he gives a wrong answer.

2 • THINK

The experiment quickly got out of control. "Prisoners" were subjected to abusive and humiliating treatment, both physical and emotional, by the "guards." One-third of the "guards" became increasingly sadistic, especially at night when they thought the cameras had been turned off. "Prisoners" were forced to clean toilets with their bare hands, to sleep on concrete floors, and to endure solitary confinement and hunger. They were also subjected to forced nudity and sexual abuse—much like what would happen many years later at Abu Ghraib prison in Iraq. After only six days, the Stanford prison experiment had to be called off.

These experiments suggest that many, if not most, Americans will uncritically follow the commands of those in authority. Like the Milgram study, the Stanford prison experiment demonstrated that ordinary people will commit atrocities in situations where there is social and institutional support for behavior that they would not do on their own and if they can put the blame on others. Milgram wrote:

> Ordinary people, simply doing their jobs and without any particular hostility on their part, can become agents in a terrible destructive process. Moreover, even when the destructive effects of their work become patently clear, and they are asked to carry out actions incompatible with fundamental standards of the majority, relatively few people have the resources needed to resist authority.[3]

What are these resources that people need to resist authority? Good critical-thinking skills are certainly one. Those who refused to continue in the Milgram study were able to give good reasons for why they should stop: for example, "it is wrong to cause harm to another person." In contrast, those who continued, even though they knew what they were doing was wrong, simply deferred to the authority figure who was making unreasonable demands of them.[4]

Although most of us may never be in a situation in which our actions have such grim consequences, a lack of critical-thinking skills can still have negative consequences in our everyday decisions. When it comes making to personal, education, and career choices, we may defer to our parents or cave in to pressure from friends rather than think through the reasons for our decisions. When major life decisions are not carefully thought out, there can be long-lasting consequences, such as dropping out of school or choosing a career in which you are ultimately unhappy. Besides giving us the tools to avoid bad decisions, effective critical-thinking skills have been found to contribute to higher self-esteem, better relationships, and an enhanced sense of well-being—all qualities that give us the confidence to make good decisions for ourselves rather than simply defer to others. In addition, because critical-thinking skills are transferable across disciplines, improving these skills can have a positive impact on our success in college. In this chapter we'll be looking at some of the components of critical thinking as well as the benefits of developing good critical-thinking skills, both in terms of our personal growth and our participation in a democratic society. We'll conclude by examining some of the barriers to critical thinking. Specifically, we will

- Define *critical thinking* and *logic*

- Learn about the characteristics of a good critical thinker

- Distinguish between giving an opinion and engaging in critical thinking

- Explain the benefits of good critical thinking

- Relate critical thinking to personal development and our role as citizens in a democracy

- Identify people who exemplify critical thinking in action

- Identify barriers to critical thinking, including types of resistance and narrow-mindedness, to critical thinking

At the end of the chapter, we will apply our critical-thinking skills to a specific issue by discussing and analyzing different perspectives on affirmative action in college admissions.

> These experiments suggest that many, if not most, Americans will uncritically follow the commands of those in authority.

WHAT IS CRITICAL THINKING?

Critical thinking is a collection of skills we use every day that are necessary for our full intellectual and personal development. The word *critical* is derived from the Greek word *kritikos,* which means "discernment," "the ability to judge," or "decision making." Critical thinking requires learning *how* to think rather than simply *what* to think.

Critical thinking, like logic, requires good analytical skills. **Logic** is part of critical thinking and is defined as "the study of the methods and principles used in distinguishing correct (good) arguments from incorrect (bad) arguments."[5] Critical thinking involves the application of the rules of logic as well as gathering evidence, evaluating it, and coming up with a plan of action. We'll be studying logical arguments in depth, in Chapters 5 to 8.

critical thinking A collection of skills we use every day that are necessary for our full intellectual and personal development.

logic The study of the methods and principles used to distinguish correct or good arguments from poor arguments.

opinion A belief based solely on personal feelings rather than on reason or facts.

Critical thinking provides us with the tools to identify and resolve issues in our lives. Critical thinking is not simply a matter of asserting our opinions on issues. **Opinions** can be based on personal feelings or beliefs, rather than on reason and evidence. As a critical thinker you need to be willing to analyze and provide logical support for your beliefs. We are all certainly entitled to our own opinions. Opinions, however, are not necessarily reasonable. While some may happen to turn out to be correct, opinions, no matter how deeply and sincerely held, may also be mistaken.

Uninformed opinions can lead you to make poor decisions in your life and act in ways that you may later come to regret. Sometimes uninformed opinions can negatively impact society. For example, even though antibiotics kill bacteria and have no effect on cold viruses, many people try to persuade their doctors into prescribing them for cold symptoms. Despite doctors' telling patients that antibiotics have no effect on viral infections, studies show that about half of doctors succumb to patient pressure for antibiotics for viral infections.[6] Such overuse of antibiotics makes the bacteria more drug resistant and has led to a decline in the effectiveness of treatment in diseases where they are really needed.[7] This phenomenon has been linked to the

SELF-EVALUATION QUESTIONNAIRE

Rate yourself on the following scale from 1 (strongly disagree) to 5 (strongly agree)

1 2 3 4 5   There are right and wrong answers. Authorities are those who have the right answers.

1 2 3 4 5   There are no right or wrong answers. Everyone has a right to his or her own opinion.

1 2 3 4 5   Even though the world is uncertain, we need to make decisions on what is right or wrong.

1 2 3 4 5   I tend to stick to my position on an issue even when others try to change my mind.

1 2 3 4 5   I have good communication skills.

1 2 3 4 5   I have high self-esteem.

1 2 3 4 5   I would refuse to comply if an authority figure ordered me to do something that might cause me to hurt someone else.

1 2 3 4 5   I don't like it when other people challenge my deeply held beliefs.

1 2 3 4 5   I get along better with people than do most people.

1 2 3 4 5   People don't change.

1 2 3 4 5   I have trouble coping with problems of life such as relationship problems, depression, and rage.

1 2 3 4 5   I tend to sacrifice my needs for those of others.

1 2 3 4 5   Men and women tend to have different communication styles.

1 2 3 4 5   The most credible evidence is that based on direct experience, such as eyewitness reports.

Think Tank

THE MORE YOU KNOW, THE HARDER IT IS TO TAKE DECISIVE ACTION.

ONCE YOU BECOME INFORMED, YOU START SEEING COMPLEXITIES AND SHADES OF GRAY.

YOU REALIZE THAT NOTHING IS AS CLEAR AND SIMPLE AS IT FIRST APPEARS. ULTIMATELY, KNOWLEDGE IS PARALYZING.

BEING A MAN OF ACTION, I CAN'T AFFORD TO TAKE THAT RISK.

YOU'RE IGNORANT, BUT AT LEAST YOU ACT ON IT.

CALVIN AND HOBBES © Watterson. Distributed by Universal Press Syndicate, Inc. Reprinted with permission. All rights reserved.

"ALL OR NOTHING" THINKING

DISCUSSION QUESTIONS

1. Discuss Calvin's claim that seeing the complexities of knowledge is "paralyzing."

2. Think back to a time when you felt, as does Calvin in the cartoon, that life is easier if you can think in dualist terms of black and white rather than "seeing the complexities and shades of gray." Referring back to this and other similar experiences, what are some of the drawbacks of making decisions or taking action on the basis of all-or-nothing thinking? Be specific.

emergence of new, more virulent strains of drug-resistant tuberculosis. In addition, the incidence of some venereal diseases such as syphilis, which was once treatable by penicillin, is once again on the rise.[8]

The ability to think critically and to make effective life decisions is shaped by many factors, including our stage of cognitive development, the possession of good analytical communication, and research skills and such characteristics as open-mindedness, flexibility, and creativity.

Cognitive Development in College Students

Becoming a critical thinker is a lifelong process. Education researcher William Perry, Jr. (1913–1998) was one of the first to study college students' cognitive development and their style of understanding the world.[9] His work with college students has gained wide acceptance among educators. Although Perry identified nine positions along the developmental continuum, later researchers have simplified his schemata into three stages: dualism, relativism, and commitment. These three stages are represented by the first three questions in the self-evaluation questionnaire in the Think Tank feature.

Stage 1: Dualism. Younger students such as freshmen and many sophomores tend to assimilate knowledge and life experiences in a simplistic, "dualistic" way, viewing something as either right or wrong. They see knowledge as

existing outside themselves and look to authority figures for the answers.

This dualistic stage is most obvious when these students confront a conflict. Although they may be able to apply critical-thinking skills in a structured classroom environment, they often lack the ability to apply these skills in real-life conflicts. When confronted with a situation such as occurred in the Milgram study of obedience,[10] they are more likely to follow an authority figure even if they feel uncomfortable doing so. In addition, a controversial issue such as affirmative action, where there is little agreement among authorities and no clear-cut right or wrong answers, can leave students at this stage struggling to make sense of it. We'll be studying some perspectives on affirmative action at the end of this chapter.

When researching on an issue, students at the dualistic stage may engage in **confirmation bias**, seeking out only evidence that supports their views and dismissing as unreliable statistics that contradict it.[11] The fact that their "research" confirms their views serves to reinforce their simplistic, black-and-white view of the world.

Students at this stage may also be unable to recognize ambiguity,

confirmation bias At the dualistic stage of research, seeking out only evidence that supports your view and dismissing evidence that contradicts it.

Connections

How do you determine if the statistics found in the results of a scientific experiment are credible? *See Chapter 12, p. 393.*

conflicting values, or motives in real-life situations. In light of this, it is not surprising that young people are most likely to fall victim to con artists, financial fraud, and identity theft, despite the stereotype that the elderly are more vulnerable to scam artists.[12] Because many young people lack the critical-thinking skills needed to resolve many real-life conflicts, people at this stage of development are also more likely to experience what psychologists call "problems with living."[13]

Students are most likely to make the transition to a higher stage of cognitive development when their current way of thinking is challenged or proves inadequate. During the transition they come to recognize that there is uncertainty in the world and that authorities can have different positions. Some educators have called this period of disorientation and doubting all answers "sophomoritis."[14]

Stage 2: Relativism. Rather than accepting that ambiguity may be unavoidable and that they need to make decisions despite uncertainty, students at the relativist stage go to the opposite extreme. They reject a dualistic worldview and instead maintain that all truth is relative or just a matter of opinion. People at this stage believe that stating your opinion is the proper mode of expression, and they look down on challenging others' opinions as "judgmental" and even disrespectful. However, despite their purported belief in relativism, most students at this stage still expect their professor to support his or her opinion.

Having their ideas challenged, grappling with controversial issues, encountering role models who are at a higher stage of cognitive development, and learning about their limits and the contradictions in their thinking can all help students move on to the next stage of cognitive development.

Stage 3: Commitment. As students mature, they come to realize that not all thinking is equally valid. Not only can authorities be mistaken but also in some circumstances uncertainty and ambiguity are unavoidable. When students at this stage experience uncertainty, they are now able to make decisions and commit to particular positions on the basis of reason and the best evidence available. At the same time, as independent thinkers, they are open to challenge, able to remain flexible, and willing to change their position should new evidence come to light.

As we mature and acquire better critical-thinking skills, our way of conceptualizing and understanding the world becomes increasingly complex. This is particularly true of older students who return to college after spending time out in the "real world." Unlike people at the first stage who look to authority for answers, people at the third stage accept responsibility for their interactions with their environment and are more open to challenges and more accepting of ambiguity.

HIGHLIGHTS

COGNITIVE DEVELOPMENT IN COLLEGE STUDENTS

Stage 1: Dualism There are right and wrong answers. Authorities know the right answers; those who don't are frauds. If I work hard and learn everything they say, I too will know the right answers.

Transition to Stage 2 There are some uncertainties and different opinions, but these are temporary. Authorities are working on these problems to get to the truth, even though they may not know the answers for a long time.

Stage 2: Relativism When the authorities don't have the right answers, everyone has a right to his or her own opinion; there are no right or wrong answers. In some cases, authorities don't give me the right answers; instead they want me to think about things in a certain way and support my opinion.

Transition to Stage 3 All thinking is contextual and relative but not equally valid. But if everything is relative, how can I know whether I'm making the right choices?

Stage 3: Commitment I should not just blindly follow or oppose authority. I need to orient myself in an uncertain world and make a decision or commitment to a position that is based on evidence and well-reasoned arguments.

Adapted from Ron Sheese and Helen Radovanovic, "W.G. Perry's Model of Intellectual and Ethical Development: Implications of Recent Research for the Education and Counseling of Young Adults," paper presented at the annual meeting of the Canadian Psychological Association (Ottawa, Ontario, June 1984).

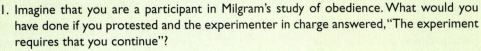

1. Imagine that you are a participant in Milgram's study of obedience. What would you have done if you protested and the experimenter in charge answered, "The experiment requires that you continue"?

2. College professor Stephen Satris maintains that the relativism of the second stage of development is not a genuine philosophical position but a means of avoiding having one's ideas challenged. Student relativism, he writes, "is primarily a method of protection, a suit of armor, which can be applied to one's own opinions, whatever they may be—but not necessarily to the opinion of others.... It is an expression of the idea that no one step forward and judge (and possibly criticize) one's own opinion."[15] Do you agree? Support your answer.

3. Most college students do not make the transition to the third, or commitment, stage of cognitive development. Why do you think this is so? Discuss ways in which the curriculum and college life in general might be restructured to encourage cognitive growth in students.

4. Today, more people are returning to college after having children and/or having worked for several years. This phenomenon is especially prevalent in community colleges, where about half the students are now older than age 25. Discuss whether there are differences in how students of different ages in your class think about the world.

5. The first three questions on the "Self-Evaluation" in the Think Tank feature represent the three stages of cognitive development. Which stage, or transition between stages, best describes your approach to understanding the world? What are the shortcomings and strengths of your current stage of cognitive development? Develop a plan to improve your skills as a critical thinker. Put the plan into action. Report on the results of your action plan.

CHARACTERISTICS OF A GOOD CRITICAL THINKER

Critical thinking is not a single skill; rather, it is a collection of skills that enhance and reinforce each other. In this section we'll be discussing some of the more important skills for effective critical thinking.

Analytical Skills

As a critical thinker, you need to be able to analyze and provide logical support for your beliefs rather than simply rely on your opinions. Analytical skills are also important in recognizing and evaluating other people's arguments so that you are not taken in by faulty reasoning. We'll be studying logical argumentation in more depth in Chapter 2 and in later chapters.

Effective Communication

In addition to analytical skills, critical thinking requires communication and literacy skills.[16] Communication skills include listening, speaking, and writing skills. Being aware of your own communication style, as well as of cultural variations and differences in the communication styles of men and women, can also go a long way toward improving communication in a relationship. We'll be learning more about communication in Chapter 3 on "Language and Communication."

Research and Inquiry Skills

Understanding and resolving issues requires research and inquiry skills such as competence in gathering, evaluating, and synthesizing supporting evidence. For example, in researching and gathering information on what would be the best major or career path for you, you need first to identity your interests and talents and then evaluate possible majors and careers in the light of these interests and talents. Research skills are also important in understanding and moving toward a resolution of a complex and divisive issue such as affirmative action in college admissions.

Connections

How do scientists identify a problem and develop a hypothesis for studying a problem? *See Chapter 12, p. 378*

Inquiry and gaining greater insight requires asking the right questions, as Milgram did in designing his study of obedience. While most people were asking what sort of twisted monsters the Nazis were or why the German people allowed Hitler to have so much power, Milgram asked the more basic question: How far would ordinary citizens would go in obeying an authority figure? Despite the fact that experiments such as Milgram's were declared unethical by the American Psychological Association in 1973 because of long-term psychological distress suffered by many of the participants, his scientific experiments still stand as classics in the field.

method of doubt A method of critical analysis in which we put aside our preconceived ideas and beliefs and begin from a position of skepticism.

As critical thinkers we need to avoid confirmation bias and the tendency to selectively see and interpret data to fit into our own worldviews, a practice that often leads to stalemates and conflict in personal as well as in political relations. Our research should also be accurate and based on credible evidence. We'll be learning more about researching and evaluating evidence in Chapter 4.

Sorting through the various claims and evidence involves discernment and tolerance for ambiguity on the part of the critical thinker. Too many people defer to others or fail to take a position on a controversial issue simply because they are unable to evaluate conflicting views. As we mature, we become better at making decisions in the face of uncertainty and ambiguity. Effective decision making includes setting clear short-term and long-term goals in our lives and developing a realistic strategy for achieving these goals. Critical thinkers also build flexibility into their life plans so that they can adapt to changes, especially since most of us haven't had sufficient experience to finalize our life plan during our first few years of college. We'll be discussing the process of developing a life plan in more depth later in this chapter.

Open-Minded Skepticism

Critical thinkers are willing to work toward overcoming personal prejudices and biases. They begin with an open mind and an attitude of reflective skepticism. The point is not simply to take a stand on an issue—such as What career is best for me? Is abortion immoral? Does God exist? What should be the role of women in the family?—but rather to critically examine the evidence and assumptions put forth in support of different positions on the issue before coming to a final conclusion. In doing so, effective critical thinkers are able to balance belief and doubt.

First put forward by French philosopher and mathematician René Descartes (1596–1650), the **method of doubt** suspends belief. This method of critical analysis, which has traditionally been preferred in fields such as science and philosophy, begins from a position of skepticism in which we put aside our preconceived ideas. Descartes wrote regarding the rules for using the method of doubt:

> The first of these [rules] was never to accept anything as true if I did not have evident knowledge of its truth: that is to say, carefully to avoid precipitate conclusions and preconceptions, and to include nothing more in my judgments than what presented itself to my mind so clearly and distinctly that I had no occasion to doubt it.[17]

It is especially important that you be willing to adopt a position of doubt or skepticism when critically examining your own cherished beliefs and the claims of author-

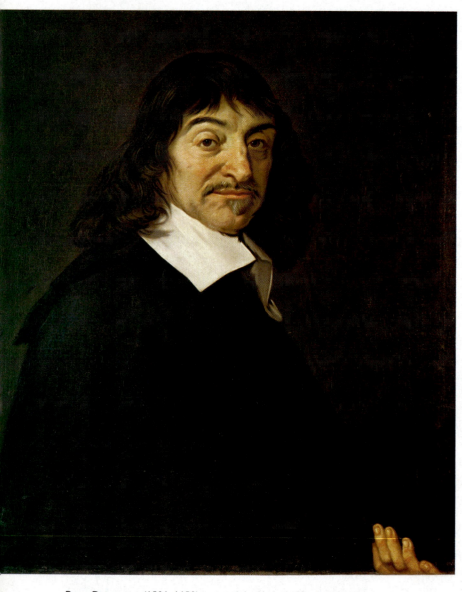

Rene Descartes (1596–1650) proposed the Method of Doubt in which we never accept anything as true without evidence and reason to support our conclusion.

The Aftermath of Hurricane Katrina, New Orleans. *Thousands of people who were driven from their homes sought refuge at the Dome where, because of lack of foresight on the part of the government, they endured squalid conditions without adequate sanitation and water.*

ity figures. Albert Einstein (1879–1955), in developing his theory of relativity, used the method of doubt regarding the generally accepted belief that time is "absolute"—that is, fixed and unchanging.

The **method of belief**, in contrast, suspends doubt. Becoming immersed in a good book, movie, or a play often involves what English poet Samuel Taylor Coleridge (1772–1834) called the "willing suspension of disbelief." This approach is also productive when we are discussing issues on which we hold strong views and are not as open as we should be to opposing viewpoints. In dialogues between people who are pro-choice and pro-life, for example, a pro-choice critical thinker, in order to compensate for his or her biases, should be genuinely open to believing what the pro-life person is saying, rather than start from the traditional position of doubt. This task requires empathy, active listening skills, and intellectual curiosity.

Creative Problem Solving

Creative thinkers can view problems from multiple perspectives and come up with original solutions to complex problems. They use their imagination to envisage possibilities, including potential future problems, and to develop contingency plans to effectively deal with these scenarios.

When staff members of the U.S. Department of Homeland Security put together a handbook of possible disaster scenarios, they failed to foresee the possibility of civil unrest and social breakdown following a disaster, as well as the inability or unwillingness of first responders, such as police, to show up for work. Because of lack of preparedness for such occurrences, hundreds of people died who might have been saved and thousands of others were left homeless and living in chaotic and squalid conditions for weeks and months after Hurricane Katrina struck the Gulf Coast in 2005. Fortunately the problems were corrected before two other potentially devastating hurricanes—Hanna and Ike—struck the Gulf coast in the fall of 2008.

Creativity also involves "a willingness to take risks, to cope with the unexpected, to welcome challenge and even failure as a part of the process to arrive at a new and deeper understanding."[18] Instead of giving up when times are difficult or resources lacking, creative critical thinkers are able to make creative use of available resources. In 1976 when he was only 21, Steve Jobs built the first Apple personal

Connections

Why is having an open mind important in the sciences? *See Chapter 12, p. 373*

method of belief A method of critical analysis in which we suspend our doubts and biases and remain genuinely open to what people with opposing views are saying.

computer in his family's garage. His innovative idea of user-friendly software changed the way people perceived computers and heralded the age of personal computing. He later went on to introduce the iPod, which revolutionized portable music players.

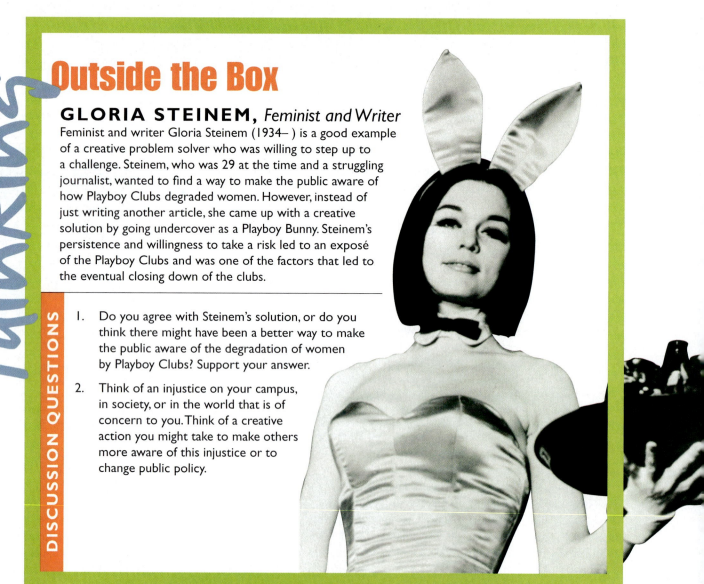

Creative thinking is an increasingly sought-after skill in the business world.[19] Because young people are usually less invested in traditional ideas and ways of doing things than are people who have been working in a field for years, they tend to be more open to new ideas. Being able to recognize creative solutions to a problem and to generate and communicate new ideas requires not just creative thinking but also being open-minded, confident, intellectually curious, and an effective communicator.

Attentive, Mindful, and Curious

Critical thinkers are intellectually curious. They are attentive and mindful to what's going on around them and to their own thoughts and feelings. The Buddhist concept of the "beginner's mind" is closely related to the Western concept of the critically open mind, or mindfulness. Zen master Shunryu Suzuki defined the beginner's mind as "wisdom which is seeking for wisdom." He wrote:

> The practice of Zen mind is beginner's mind. The innocence of first inquiry—what am I? . . . The mind of the beginner is empty, free of the habits of

Thinking Outside the Box

GLORIA STEINEM, *Feminist and Writer*

Feminist and writer Gloria Steinem (1934–) is a good example of a creative problem solver who was willing to step up to a challenge. Steinem, who was 29 at the time and a struggling journalist, wanted to find a way to make the public aware of how Playboy Clubs degraded women. However, instead of just writing another article, she came up with a creative solution by going undercover as a Playboy Bunny. Steinem's persistence and willingness to take a risk led to an exposé of the Playboy Clubs and was one of the factors that led to the eventual closing down of the clubs.

DISCUSSION QUESTIONS

1. Do you agree with Steinem's solution, or do you think there might have been a better way to make the public aware of the degradation of women by Playboy Clubs? Support your answer.

2. Think of an injustice on your campus, in society, or in the world that is of concern to you. Think of a creative action you might take to make others more aware of this injustice or to change public policy.

Opinion Force, Violence, and Aggression	Men	Women	Difference
		Percent	
Support military against Iraq	55	35	20
Want stricter gun control laws	45	70	25
Favor the death penalty over life in prison for capital murder	62	38	24
Compassion			
Budget surplus should be spent on social programs, not tax cuts	49	64	15
Government should provide health insurance	35	41	6
Government should see to good jobs/standard of living	20	29	9
Government should increase spending for the homeless	52	63	11

Good critical thinkers respect diversity and are willing to consider the perspectives of others, even if they initially conflict with their own opinions.

the expert, ready to accept, to doubt, and open to all possibilities. . . . If your mind is empty, it is always ready for anything; it is open to everything. In the beginner's mind there are many possibilities. . . .[20]

Like the beginner's mind, good critical thinkers do not reject, without sound reasons, views that conflict with their own. Instead, they respect diversity and are willing to consider multiple perspectives. One of the recent breakthroughs in neuroscience is the discovery that the brains of Buddhist monks who meditate regularly—a practice that involves being mindful, open, and attentive to what is going on in the present moment—are neurally much more active and more resilient in neuroplasticity than are the brains of people who do not meditate.[21] Many large corporations, including some Fortune 500 companies, are currently encouraging their executives to take meditation breaks on the job, since it has been found to improve their performance.[22]

Collaborative Learning

Critical thinking occurs in a real-life context and anticipates the reactions of others. We are not isolated individuals—we are interconnected beings. As critical thinkers we need to move beyond the traditional, detached approach to thinking and develop a more collaborative approach that is grounded in shared conversation and community. Physicist, feminist, and developmental biologist Evelyn Fox Keller uses the term *dynamic objectivism* to define a "pursuit of knowledge that . . . recognizes difference between self and other as an opportunity for deeper and more articulated kinship."[23]

The failure to take into account context and relationships can lead to faulty decisions that we may later regret. An example of this type of faulty reasoning is the tendency of many individuals to neglect both feedback and complex-

ity. Because of this, they tend not to fully and accurately consider the other side's response. In a relationship we may do something in an attempt to get our partner to pay more attention to us—for example, threatening to leave a boyfriend if he doesn't stop spending so much time watching sports with his male friends—only to see this backfire, losing the relationship altogether because we failed to consider how the other person might react.

To use another example, military planners in developing strategies sometimes fail to con-

Did You Know

The ancient Greek thinker Socrates (469–399 BCE) spent much of his time in the marketplace of Athens surrounded by his young followers. He used this public venue to seek out people in order to challenge their traditional beliefs and practices. He did this by engaging hitherto unreflective people in a type of critical thinking in which his probing questions provoked them into realizing their lack of rational understanding and their inconsistencies in thought.

sider what the enemy might do in return to minimize the effectiveness of these strategies. During the War of 1812, a group of politicians in Washington, D.C. decided the time had come to add Canada to the United States. Their military strategy failed primarily because they did not adequately assess the Canadian response to the U.S. mission to annex Canada. Instead of greeting the American invaders as liberators from British rule, Canadians regarded the war as an unprovoked attack on their homes and lives. In addition, many Americans, especially New Englanders, were totally opposed to the war. Rather than uniting Canada and the United States, the War of 1812 gave rise to the first stirring of Canadian nationalism (and even provoked a movement in New England to secede from the United States).[24]

Good critical thinkers adopt a collaborative rather than an adversarial stance, in which they listen to and take others' views into account. Let's go back to the boyfriend example. Rather than accusing our boyfriend (or girlfriend) of not spending enough time with us, a good critical thinker would express his or her feelings and thoughts and then listen to the other person's side. Critical thinkers carefully consider all perspectives and are open to revising their views in light of their broader understanding. Using our critical-thinking skills, we might come to realize that his friends are very important to him. Perhaps we are being insecure and need to spend more time with our own friends, giving our boyfriend more space. Maybe we can find a solution that meets both our needs. For example, the guys can bring their girlfriends or another friend along once or twice a month to watch the games with them.

EXERCISES 1–2

1. Watch the Milgram film *Obedience*. Discuss ways in which the participants in the film demonstrated, or failed to demonstrate, good critical-thinking skills.

2. Identifying good role models in your life can help you come up with a picture of the person you would like to be. Think of a person, real or fictional, who exemplifies good critical-thinking skills. Make a list of some of the qualities of this person. Discuss how these qualities help the person in his or her everyday life.

3. As much as possible, adopt the stance of the Buddhist "beginner's mind." Be attentive only to what is happening in the now rather than dwelling on the past and future. After one minute, write down everything you observed going on around you as well as inside of you (your feelings, body language, etc.). Did you notice more than you might have otherwise? Share your observations with the class. Discuss ways in which sharing this practice might enhance your effectiveness as a critical thinker.

4. Working in groups of four to six students, select an issue about which the group is evenly divided into positions for or against it. Each side should adopt a stance of belief and open-mindedness when listening to the other side's position. After the pro side presents its views for two minutes, the anti side takes one minute to repeat back the pro's views without interjecting their own doubts. Repeat the process with the anti side presenting their views. Discuss as a class how this exercise helped you to suspend your biases and to actively listen to views that diverge from your own.

5. Discuss the results of your self-evaluation questionnaire, found on page 4, with classmates or someone else you feel comfortable talking to. Brainstorming plays an important role in the development of critical-thinking skills. Sharing ideas and being open to those of others broadens our perspective. Discuss steps you might take or have already taken to work toward or overcome some of your weaknesses.

6. Referring to the self-evaluation questionnaire on page 4, share your strengths and weakness as well as your plans for improving your critical-thinking skills with others, whether friends, family, or in class.

CRITICAL THINKING AND SELF-DEVELOPMENT

Critical thinking is not just about abstract thought. It is also about self-improvement and your whole development as a person. Working on your self requires that you be reflective and honest with yourself and others about your biases, your strengths, and your limitations. Are our expectations realistic? Do we have a well thought out plan and goals for our life? People who are inflexible in their thinking may be unable to adapt to changing or novel circumstances and may instead get caught up in rules and conventional ways of thinking that are inadequate to resolve the situation.

Living the Self-Examined Life

"The unexamined life is not worth living," Socrates said. Often we flounder in college because we have not taken the time to learn about ourselves or develop a plan for our future. The lives of too many people are controlled more by circumstances than by their own choices. Good critical thinkers, in contrast, take charge of their lives and choices rather than opting for the security of fitting into the crowd. In addition to being rational thinkers, they are in touch with their emotions and feelings. We'll be looking more at the role of emotion in Chapter 2.

Age Differences in Depression

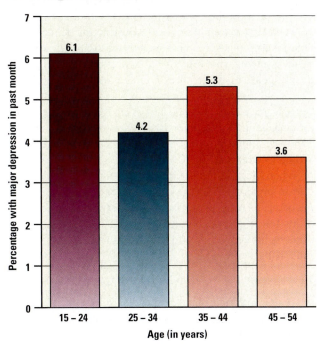

Some psychologists and psychiatrists believe that irrational beliefs and poor critical-thinking skills contribute to many of the "problems of life," such as depression, rage, and low self-esteem.[25,26] While depression often has a biochemical component that needs to be treated, poor critical-thinking skills can aggravate or even be a major factor in some types of situational depression where a student feels overwhelmed and unable to cope or make a decision in a particular set of circumstances. In a 2003 survey by the American College Health Association, more than 40 percent of college students reported that at least once during the past year they felt "so depressed, it was difficult to function."

Although by no means a cure-all, improving critical-thinking skills, whether through a class in critical thinking or therapy, has been shown to help people deal more effectively with their problems.[27] Rather than view the problems in our lives as being out of our control, we should— so cognitive psychologists in particular counsel us—develop strategies for taking charge of our lives, develop realistic expectations, and commit ourselves to acknowledging and developing the skills to resolve our problems.

Connections

How can participation in civic life improve your critical-thinking skills and enhance your personal growth? *See Chapter 13, p. 426 and p. 434.*

What marketing strategies should you be aware of so as to avoid being an uncritical consumer? *See Chapter 10, p. 320.*

Developing a Rational Life Plan

American philosopher John Rawls (1921–2002) wrote that in order to get the most out of life, everyone needs to develop a "rational life plan"—that is, a plan that "would be chosen by him with full deliberative rationality, that is, with full awareness of the relevant facts and after a careful consideration of the consequences. . . . Someone is happy, when his plans are going well and his more important aspirations are being fulfilled."[28]

In drawing up our life plan, we make a hierarchy, with our most important plans at the top, followed by a list of subplans. We should also organize our activities according to a schedule when they are to be carried out, although the more distant a goal is, the less specific the plan will be. Of course, we can't predict everything that will happen in life, and there will be times when circumstances hinder us from achieving our goals. Think of a life plan as being like a flight plan. Airplanes are off course about 90 percent of the time because of such factors as weather, wind patterns, and other aircraft. The pilot must constantly correct for these conditions to get the plane back on course. Without a flight

your life direction. Start out by listing short-term goals, or those that you want to accomplish by the time you graduate from college; examples might be choose a major, maintain a 3.0 average, or get more exercise. These goals should be consistent with your interests, talents, and the type of person you want to be. Also come up with a plan of actions to achieve these short-term goals.

Next, list some of your long-term goals. Ideally your long-term and short-term goals should augment each other. Your plans for achieving the long-term goals should be realistic and compatible with your short-term goals and interests. Think creatively about how certain goals can fit together.

People who are skilled critical thinkers not only have reasonable, well-thought-out goals and strategies to achieve them but also act from a sense of integrity or personal authenticity and respect for the integrity and aspirations of others in their lives. We are not isolated individuals but social beings whose decisions affect the lives of all those around us.

plan, the pilots and their planes would be at the mercy of winds and weather, blown hither and thither, and never reaching their destination.

Begin putting together your life plan by making a list of your values, interests, skills, and talents. Values are what are important to you in life and include things such as financial security, love, family, career, independence, spirituality, health and fitness, education, contributions to society, friends, sense of integrity, and fun. Your goals in life should be rational as well as consistent with your values. According to the 2007 Freshman Survey, the two most important objectives or life goals for entering college students are "raising a family" (77 percent) and "being well off financially" (74 percent).[29] Take time to deliberate about your hierarchy of values. It is possible that after careful consideration of the implications of a particular value, such as "being well off financially," you may want to place it lower on your hierarchy of values.

If you are unsure of your skills and talents, go to the career office at your college and take some of the aptitude and personality tests available there, such as the Myers-Briggs test.[30] These tests are useful in helping you to determine which career or careers might be most fulfilling for you. The site www.collegeboards.com also provides helpful information on choosing a major and a career.

But don't just list your strengths, including your assets and competencies; take note of your weaknesses too. Weaknesses are something we do poorly or something we lack, such as financial resources, information, or technical expertise.

Once you've written down your values, interests, talents, skills, and weaknesses, list your goals. Goals are important in helping you organize your day-to-day life and giving

Facing Challenges

Sometimes traditional practices and beliefs—both our own and those of others—may get in the way of our achieving our life plan. In these cases we may need to develop subgoals that involve challenging the obstructing beliefs rather than give up our life plan. Openly questioning traditional belief systems and effectively addressing challenges to deeply held beliefs requires courage and self-confidence. The abolitionists and early feminists and civil rights advocates were often ridiculed and even imprisoned because they challenged traditions they believed were unjust. See "Thinking Outside the Box: Elizabeth Cady Stanton, Women's Rights Leader."

When Martin Luther King, Jr. was thrown in jail for his role in organizing the 1955 bus boycott in Montgomery, Alabama, he refused the back down despite the beseeching of his fellow clergy. Fortunately, King had the courage to stand by his convictions. In his "Letter from a Birmingham Jail," King wrote:

My Dear Fellow Clergy,

I am in Birmingham because injustice is here. . . . We know through painful experience that freedom is never voluntarily given by the oppressor; it must be demanded by the oppressed.

Outside the Box

ELIZABETH CADY STANTON, *Women's Rights Leader*

Elizabeth Cady Stanton (1815–1902) was a social activist and leader in the early women's rights movement. In 1840, when she was a young newlywed, Stanton attended the World Anti-Slavery Society convention in London, which her husband was attending as a delegate. It was there that Stanton met Lucretia Mott (1793–1880). At the convention the women delegates from the United States were denied seats after some of the male U.S. delegates vehemently objected. Mott, in response, demanded that she be treated with the same respect accorded any man—white or black. During these heated discussions, Stanton marveled at the way Mott, a woman of forty-seven, held her own in the argument, "skillfully parried all their attacks . . . turning the laugh on them, and then by her earnestness and dignity silencing their ridicule and jeers."[1]

Following the Civil War, Stanton refused to support passage of the Fifteenth Amendment, which gave voting rights to black men but not to women. She argued that the amendment essentially was based on the fallacy of false dilemma—either black men get the vote (but not women) or only white men can vote. Instead she pointed out that there was a third option: both men and women should have the right to vote. Unfortunately, her line of argument and her challenges to traditional beliefs about the role of women were ridiculed. Although black men received the vote in 1870 with passage of the Fifteenth Amendment, it would be another fifty years before women were finally given the right to vote in the United States. Nevertheless, Stanton's persistence and refusal to back down in her fight for equal opportunity for women paved the way for the final passage of this amendment so that other women could achieve their life plans of equal participation in the political life of the country.

1. Elizabeth Cady Stanton had close friends such as Lucretia Mott and Susan B. Anthony in her fight for women's rights. Discuss ways in which having a support network of people who are skilled critical thinkers can enhance your ability not to use or fall for faulty reasoning. Discuss ways in which you do, or could, serve as a critical-thinking mentor to others.

2. Think of a time when your ability to pursue your goals was compromised by ridicule. Explain, using specific examples. Discuss steps you might take to make yourself less likely to give into faulty reasoning or to give up on an aspect of your life plan under such circumstances.

ABUSE AT ABU GHRAIB PRISON, IRAQ   Being an autonomous thinker makes it less likely that you will uncritically follow orders or conform to peer pressure. The abuse and humiliation of Iraqi prisoners by U.S. soldiers at Abu Ghraib prison in Iraq in 2003 provides a real-life illustration of what happened in the Milgram and Stanford prison experiments. In January 2005, Army reservist and prison guard Charles Graner (standing in background) was convicted and sentenced to ten years in prison for his role as ringleader in the abuse and humiliation of Iraqi detainees. In his defense he said that he was simply following orders. His defense lawyers also pointed out that the U.S. Army's intelligence units were poorly trained and badly managed, factors that contributed to the reservists' poor judgment. Graner's defense was rejected by the court.

DISCUSSION QUESTIONS

1. *Was Graner's reason for his treatment of the Iraqi prisoners justified? Should he be held responsible for his actions? Support your answers.*

2. *Discuss what you might have done had you been a low-ranking guard at Abu Ghraib and had witnessed your fellow soldiers mistreating Iraqi prisoners.*

3. *Similar situations have occurred during fraternity and sorority initiation hazings. If you know of, or have been witness to, any situations where this happened, discuss why it most likely happened and what might have been done to prevent it.*

You express a great deal of anxiety over our willingness to break laws. . . . This is a legitimate concern . . . an unjust law is a code that is out of harmony with the moral law. . . . Any law that degrades human personality is unjust. . . . I submit that an individual who breaks a law that conscience tells him is unjust, and willingly accepts the penalty by staying in jail to arouse the conscience of the community over its in justice, is in reality expressing the very highest respect for law.

In addition to being able to effectively challenge social injustices, as critical thinkers we need to be able to respond intelligently and thoughtfully to challenges to our own

belief systems rather than engaging in resistance. This requires the development of good critical-thinking skills as well as self-confidence.

The Importance of Self-Esteem

Effective critical-thinking skills appear to be positively correlated to healthy self-esteem.[31] Healthy self-esteem emerges from effectiveness in problem solving and success in achieving our life goals. Studies show that young people who have positive self-esteem "have more friends, are more apt to resist harmful peer pressure, are less sensitive to criticism or to what people think, have higher IQs, and are better informed."[32] The task of sorting out genuine self-worth from a false sense of self-esteem requires

---

An autonomous person is both rational and self-directing and therefore less likely to be taken in by poor reasoning or contradictions in his own or other's reasoning.

---

critical thinking. Healthy self-esteem is not the same as arrogant pride or always putting one's own interests first. Nor are people with proper self-esteem habitually self-sacrificing, subverting their interests and judgment to those of others

People with low self-esteem are more vulnerable to manipulation by others. They experience more "depression, irritability, anxiety, fatigue, nightmares . . . withdrawal from others, nervous laughter, body aches and emotional tension."[33] Some of these traits, such as anxiety and nervous laughter, were seen in the Milgram study participants who complied with the request of the authority figure. Indeed, many of these men later came to regret their compliance and even required psychotherapy.

Good critical-thinking skills are essential in exercising your autonomy. Critical thinkers are proactive. They are aware of the influences on their lives, including family, culture, television, and friends; they can build on the positive influences and overcome the negative ones, rather than be passively carried through life and blaming others if their decisions turn out poorly.

An autonomous person is both rational and self-directing and therefore less likely to be taken in by poor reasoning or contradictions in his own or other's reasoning. Being self-directing, however, does not mean ignoring other perspectives. Rather, it entails making decisions on the basis of what is reasonable instead of getting swept up in groupthink or blindly obeying an authority figure. To achieve this end, autonomous critical thinkers seek out different perspectives and actively participate in critical dialogues to gain new insights and expand their own thinking.

Critical Thinking in a Democracy

Critical-thinking skills are essential in a democracy. **Democracy** literally means rule by the people; it is a form of government in which the highest power in the state is invested in the people and exercised directly by them or, as is generally the case in modern democracies, by their elected officials. As citizens of a democracy, we have an obligation to be well informed about policies and issues so that we can effectively participate in critical discussions and decisions.

Thomas Jefferson wrote, "In a republican nation, whose citizens are to be led by reason and persuasion and not by force, the art of reasoning becomes of the first importance."[34] The purpose of democracy is not to achieve consensus through polling or majority vote but to facilitate open-ended discussion and debates by those with diverse views. Truth, argued British philosopher John Stuart Mill (1806–1873), often is found neither in the opinion of those who favor the status quo nor in the opinion of the nonconformist but in a combination of viewpoints. Therefore, freedom of speech and listening to opposing views, no matter how offensive they may be, are essential for critical thinking in a democracy.

Did You Know

Studies show that young people who have positive self-esteem "have more friends, are more apt to resist harmful peer pressure, are less sensitive to criticism or to what people think, have higher IQs, and are better informed."[32]

Corrupt politicians have been elected or appointed to public office and high-ranking positions in their parties because the people failed to educate themselves about their activities and ideals. Indeed, in a 1938 poll of Princeton freshmen, Adolf Hitler was ranked first as the "greatest living person"![35] And in New York City in the mid-nineteenth century, politician William Marcy "Boss" Tweed (1823–1878) conned citizens out of millions of dollars. He also managed to get his corrupt associates, known as the Tweed Ring, appointed and elected to high offices.

Unlike totalitarian societies, modern democracies encourage diversity and open discussion of different ideas. Research on the effects of racial, ethnic, class, and other kinds of diversity on college students reveals "important links between experiences with diversity and increased commitment to civic engagement, democratic outcomes and community participation."[36] Exposure to diversity on campus and in the classroom broadens students' perspectives and improves critical thinking and problem-solving skills.[37]

In his book *The Assault on Reason (2007),* Al Gore argues that there has been a decline in participation by ordinary citizens in the

Connections

What critical-thinking skills do you need to participate in campaigns and elections, influence public policy, and understand the legal system? *See Chapter 13.*

democracy A form of government in which the highest power in the state is invested in the people and exercised directly by them or, as is generally the case in modern democracies, by their elected officials.

Analyzing Images

STUDENT PROTESTOR IN FRONT OF TANKS AT TIANANMEN SQUARE, CHINA

On June 3–4, 1989, hundreds, possibly thousands, of unarmed demonstrators protesting the legitimacy of China's communist government were shot dead in a brutal military operation to crush a democratic uprising in Beijing's Tiananmen Square. The demonstrators, who were mostly university students, had occupied the square for several weeks, refusing to leave until their demands for democratic reform were met. A photographer captured the above picture of a lone, unnamed demonstrator standing in front of the tanks, bringing to a halt the row of advancing tanks. To this day, no one knows who the demonstrator was or what his fate was.

DISCUSSION QUESTIONS

1. *What do you think the student in the photo is thinking and feeling? What do you think led up to his decision to take this action? Does his action show good critical thinking? Support your answers.*

2. *Imagine yourself in a similar situation. Discuss how you would most likely react and how your reaction is a reflection of your current self-development. What steps could you take in your life to make yourself more likely to engage in civil disobedience, particularly in a case where your life was not at stake?*

Connections

How has the Internet enhanced your ability to participate in public life and discussions of political issues? *See Chapter 11, p. 354.*

In what ways is the news media biased? *See Chapter 11, p. 345.*

democratic process since television overtook the printed word as the dominant source of information. Television as a one-way source of information appeals mainly to our baser emotions rather than requiring critical reflective thought, thus rendering viewers passive consumers of prepackaged information and ideologies. Gore maintains that this decline in public participation in political dialogue has been accompanied by an increase in power of the government and those wealthy enough to control the media.

People who are skilled at critical thinking are less likely to be taken in by faulty arguments and rhetoric. They are also more likely, like the pro-democracy Chinese student in Tiananmen Square, to demand the same clarity and reasonableness of thinking in their leaders that they require in themselves rather than remain passive in the face of government abuses of power. Thus, critical thinking contributes to your own well-being as well as to the well-being of society as a whole, by teaching you how to stand up to authority and irrational thinking.

1. According to German philosopher Immanuel Kant (1724–1804), one of our primary moral duties is self-respect and the development of proper self-esteem.[38] To truly respect others and their perspectives, we must first respect ourselves. Do you agree? Support your position with examples from your own experience.

2. Choose one of your short-term or long-term goals. Working in small groups, brainstorm about ways you and the others in the group might best achieve your goals. Discuss also the role good critical-thinking skills play or played in helping you achieve your goals.

3. In small groups, discuss a time when you deferred to the view of someone else and did (or failed to do) something you later came to regret because you were unable to give good reasons at the time why you should not accept that person's view. Brainstorm with your group about ways in which you might make yourself less prone to this behavior.

4. A June 2004 article in *Altermedia Scotland* states: "America as a nation is now dominated by an alien system of beliefs, attitudes and values that has become known as 'political correctness.' It seeks to impose a uniformity in thought and behaviour among all Americans and is therefore totalitarian in nature."[39] Do you agree or disagree? Support your answer.

5. What is diversity? What are the educational benefits of diversity? Discuss ways in which your college, including your classes, addresses and facilitates diversity. Discuss steps that might be taken to improve opportunities for diversity on your campus.

6. The student pro-democracy movement in Tiananmen Square was unsuccessful in terms of bringing to China democracy and a more open society. Does this failure mean that the movement and the lives that were lost were a waste? Support your answer.

7. Al Gore argues that the "mental muscles of democracy have begun to atrophy."[40] Discuss his claim. Relate your answer to the exercise of your "mental muscles" and those of other college students in political dialogue.

8. Take the self-esteem test at http://www.queendom.com/jff_access/the_self_esteem_test.htm. How does your level of self-esteem contribute to or interfere with your effectiveness as a critical thinker? Were your answers on the self-esteem test consistent with your own beliefs about yourself? What were your strengths and weaknesses? What might you do to improve your self-esteem? How might improving it make you a better critical thinker? How does your life plan reflect your level of self-esteem? In particular, do you have a tendency to underestimate your capabilities?

9. When the *Brown Daily Herald*, the student newspaper at Brown University, ran an ad from conservative activist David Horowitz entitled "Ten Reasons Why Reparation for Slavery is a Bad Idea—and Racist Too," a coalition of Brown students stole and destroyed nearly four thousand newspapers at campus distribution points. Defendants of the action argued that the ad was "an attempt to inject blatantly revisionist and, yes, racist arguments into a legitimate debate about black reparations ..."[41] Is it ever appropriate to censor views? Did the students have a legitimate right, on the basis of their freedom of speech, to destroy the newspapers? To what extent, if any, do we have an obligation in a democracy to listen attentively to and consider views that we find offensive? What would you have done had your school newspaper decided to publish the ad by Horowitz?

10. *Journal Exercise:* Complete a journal entry focusing on your "Life Plan." If you are not sure of your talents, go to the career office at your college and ask if you can take some of the personality and aptitude tests available there. These tests are also useful in helping you to determine which career or careers might be most fulfilling for you. Be creative; don't limit or underrate yourself.

BARRIERS TO CRITICAL THINKING

By sharpening your critical-thinking skills, you can become more independent and less susceptible to worldviews that foster narrow-mindedness. In this section we'll be looking at some of the barriers to critical thinking that keep us from analyzing our experiences or worldviews, as well as the experiences and worldviews of others.

The Three-Tier Model of Thinking

The processes used in critical thinking can be broken down into three tiers or levels: experience, interpretation, and analysis. Keep in mind that this division is artificial and merely helps to highlight the critical-thinking process. Although analysis is at the pinnacle of the process, the three-tier model is also recursive and dynamic, with analysis returning to experience for confirmation and interpretation being modified in light of the analysis of the new

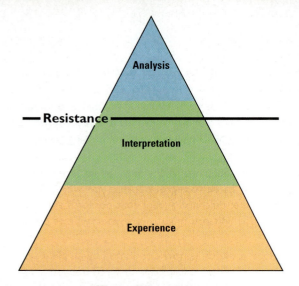

Figure 1.1 The Three Levels of Thinking

information. People never have pure experience or engage in pure analysis.

Experience, the first level, includes firsthand experience as well as information or empirical facts that we receive from other sources. Experience is the foundation of critical thinking and argumentation. It provides the material for interpretation and analysis. At this level of thinking we merely describe our experiences rather than try to understand them. For example:

1. I was turned down for the job I interviewed for.
2. Mark held the door open for me when I was leaving class.
3. Human cloning is illegal in the United States.
4. Although blacks represent only 12.9 percent of the U.S. population, they make up 45 percent of the prison inmates.[42]
5. In the 2004 presidential election, only 58.4 percent of all eligible American voters voted. The percentage was even lower, at 41.9 percent, for young people between the ages of 18 and 25.

Interpretation, the second level, involves trying to make sense of our experiences. This level of thinking includes individual interpretations of experiences as well as collective and cultural worldviews. Some of our interpretations may be well informed; others may be based merely on our opinions or personal feelings and prejudices. Some possible interpretations of the experiences listed above are

1. I didn't get the job because I didn't have the right connections.
2. Mark's a chauvinist pig who thinks women are too weak to open their own doors.
3. If human cloning is illegal, it must be immoral.
4. Black men make up such a large percentage of the prison population because black men are innately more violent than white men.
5. Young people in the United States don't vote because they are apathetic when it comes to politics.

Analysis, the third level, requires that we raise our level of thinking and critically examine our interpretations of an experience, as well as those of others, refusing to accept either narrow interpretations of an experience or interpretations that are too broad. Analysis is most productive when it is done collectively because we each bring different experiences and interpretations, as well as skills in analysis, to the table. Analysis often begins by asking a question. The following are examples of questions we might ask in order to begin our analysis of the above interpretations:

1. Was it my lack of connections or my poor interviewing skills or lack of job qualifications that caused me not to get the job?
2. What was Mark's intention in holding the door open for me?

People who hold views that are backed by public opinion or the law may be particularly likely to resist when these views are challenged: They don't want to see the status quo upset.

---

3. Why is human cloning illegal? Are there circumstances in which human cloning might be acceptable?
4. Is there proof that black men are innately more violent, or is it possible that black men are simply discriminated against more than white men? Or are other factors at work to account for their overrepresentation in the prison population?
5. Why aren't more Americans, especially young Americans, voting? Should voting in federal elections be compulsory, as it is in some other countries? Is the problem the choice of candidates?

The three-tier model of thinking provides a dynamic model of critical thinking in which analysis is always returning to experience for confirmation. As critical thinkers, it is not only our reasoning process that is important but also that our reasoning is connected to reality.

Connections

How can you use the three-tier model of thinking to analyze media messages? *See Chapter 11, p. 359.*

What model of thinking do scientists use? *See Chapter 12, p. 378.*

Resistance

Because most of us hate to be proven wrong, we may create barriers to keep our cherished worldviews from being challenged. Resistance, defined as "the use of immature defense mechanisms that are rigid, impulsive, maladaptive, and nonanalytical," can act as a barrier to critical thinking.

Almost all of us use defense mechanisms when we feel overwhelmed. Resistance, however, becomes a problem when it is used as a habitual way of responding to issues. Such habitual use interferes with our self-development, since it involves avoiding novel experiences and ideas that challenge our worldviews. People who hold views that are backed by public opinion or the law may be particularly likely to resist when these views are challenged: They don't want to see the status quo upset.

In addition, resistance can create anxiety, since it puts us in a defensive mode and can shield us from the ideas and viewpoints of others, thus preventing us from working collaboratively and coming up with a well-thought-out plan of action.

Types of Resistance

There are several types of resistance, including avoidance, anger, clichés, denial, ignorance, conformity, struggling, and distractions.

Avoidance. Rather than seeking out different points of view, we may use avoidance to escape certain people and situations. Some people who hold strong opinions but are insecure in their ability to defend these positions hang out only with people who agree with them or read literature and watch television news shows that support their worldview. I attended a church service during which the minister in her sermon lambasted Mel Gibson's movie *The Passion of the Christ* as a violent and inaccurate depiction of the betrayal and death of Jesus. I asked her after the service if she had seen the movie, and she said no. When I told her that I liked the movie, she merely frowned and quickly moved on to talk to someone else. As a form of resistance, avoidance can lead to a serious lack of communication and even hostility among people who hold widely opposing points of view.

Anger. We cannot always avoid people who disagree with us. Rather than using critical thinking when confronted with an opposing viewpoint, some people respond with anger. People with physical and/or social power are more likely than those without it to use anger to silence those who disagree with them. Anger may be expressed overtly by glares, threats, physical violence, gang activity, or even war.

Not all anger is resistance. We may feel anger or moral indignation when we hear that one of our favorite professors was denied tenure because he was Arab. This anger may motivate to correct this injustice by writing a letter of protest to the local newspaper. We'll be looking more at the positive role of emotion in critical thinking in Chapter 2.

> **Connections**
>
> How can our critical-thinking skills help us recognize misleading advertisements? *See Chapter 10, p. 325.*

Clichés. Resorting to clichés—often-repeated statements such as "Don't force your views on me," "It's all relative," "To each his own," "Things always work out for the best," and "I have a right to my own opinion"—can keep us from thinking critically about issues. Advertisers and politicians often use clichés as a means of sidetracking us from considering the quality of the product or the issue at hand. Clichés can also keep us from critically examining our own life choices. Used sparingly, clichés can be helpful to illustrate a point. However, the habitual use of clichés acts as a barrier to critical thinking.

Denial. According to the U.S. National Center for Injury Prevention and Control, alcohol-related motor vehicle accidents kill someone every thirty minutes and account for 41 percent of all traffic-related deaths.[43] Despite these startling statistics, people who drink and drive often deny that they are drunk. They may refuse to let someone else drive, claiming that they are quite capable of doing so.

Many Americans are also in denial about the possibility that world oil reserves may soon run out. Despite improved exploration technology, discovery of new oil reserves peaked in 1962 and has been dropping ever since. According to some predictions, active oil reserves may run out by anywhere from 2020 to 2030.[44] Yet, faced with dwindling fossil-fuel sources, many Americans continue to drive large vehicles and to build large homes that cost more and more to heat.

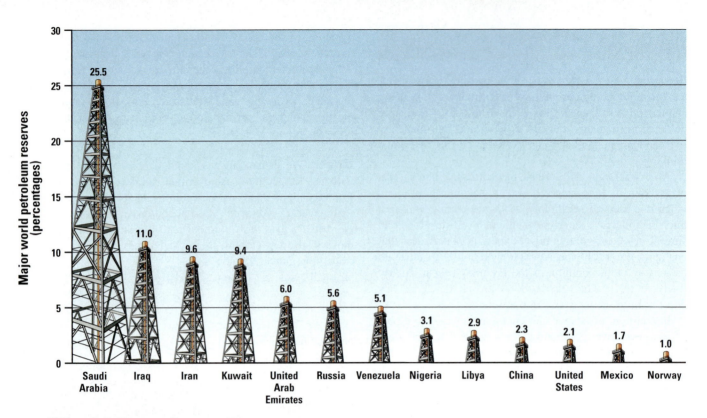

Major world petroleum reserves (percentages)

- Saudi Arabia: 25.5
- Iraq: 11.0
- Iran: 9.6
- Kuwait: 9.4
- United Arab Emirates: 6.0
- Russia: 5.6
- Venezuela: 5.1
- Nigeria: 3.1
- Libya: 2.9
- China: 2.3
- United States: 2.1
- Mexico: 1.7
- Norway: 1.0

World Petroleum Reserves

Ignorance. In ancient China, the philosopher Confucius taught that "Ignorance is the night of the mind." The modern Hindu yogi Swami Prabhavananda wrote, "Ignorance creates all the other obstacles." People are more likely to think critically about issues about which they have knowledge in depth. In certain situations, we are ignorant about an issue simply because the information about it is not available to us. However, sometimes we just don't want to know. Ignorance is a type of resistance when we intentionally avoid learning about a particular issue, about which information is readily available, in order to get out of having to think or talk about it. Some people believe that being ignorant excuses them from having to think critically about or take action on an issue. As a result, the issue is not resolved or even becomes worse.

Conformity. Many people fear that they will not be accepted by their peers if they disagree with them. Even

Analyzing Images

CALVIN AND HOBBES © Watterson. Distributed by Universal Press Syndicate, Inc.

IS IGNORANCE BLISS?

DISCUSSION QUESTIONS

1. Has there ever been a time when you're preferred ignorance to being informed? Compare the outcome of your experience to Calvin's.

2. Some people accuse college students of taking Calvin's attitude that "ignorance is bliss" when it comes to participation in public life and national elections. Do you agree? Support your answer.

though they may actually disagree, they go along with the group rather than risk rejection. We've probably all been in a situation where someone at work or a party makes a racist or sexist joke or an offensive comment about gays or women. Rather than speaking up, many people keep quiet or even laugh, thus tolerating and perpetuating bigotry and negative stereotypes.

Other people conform because they don't have a point of view of their own on an issue. Saying "I can see both sides of the issue" often masks a reluctance to think critically about it. Martin Luther King, Jr. once pointed out, "Many people fear nothing more terribly than to take a position which stands out sharply and clearly from prevailing opinion. The tendency of most is to adopt a view that is so ambiguous that is will include everything, and so popular that it will include everyone."

Struggling. During the Nazi occupation of France in World War II, the people of the village of Le Chambon-sur-Lignon provided refuge for Jews who were fleeing the Nazis. When Pierre Sauvage, director of *Weapons of the Spirit*—a documentary about the people and resistance movement of Le Chambon—was asked by PBS television's Bill Moyers years later why they did this when other people were still struggling about what to do, Sauvage replied, "Those who agonize don't act; those who act don't agonize."[45] It is appropriate to struggle with or agonize over difficult issues before coming to a tentative stand. However, some people get so caught up in the minute details and "what ifs" of an issue—a situation sometimes referred to as "analysis paralysis"—that nothing gets accomplished. Procrastinators are most likely to use this type of resistance. Although struggling with an issue as part of the analytical process of coming up with a resolution and plan for action is an important component of critical thinking, when the struggle becomes an end-in-itself, we are engaging in resistance, not critical thinking.

Distractions. Some people hate silence and being left alone with their own thoughts. Many of us use television, loud music, partying, work, drugs, alcohol, or shopping to prevent our minds from critically thinking about troublesome issues in our lives. Politicians may use war or the threat of war or terrorism to distract the public from thinking about such domestic issues as the economy or health care. People may overeat instead of examining the causes of their cravings or unhappiness. Mental hindrances like distractions, according to Buddhist teaching, keep us from clear understanding. Instead, Buddhist philosophy values stillness and contemplation as means of achieving wisdom and understanding.

Connections

How does the news media influence and reinforce narrow-minded worldviews? *See Chapter 11, p. 345.*

Narrow-Mindedness

Like resistance, narrow-mindedness and rigid beliefs, such as absolutism, egocentrism, and ethnocentrism can become barriers to critical thinking.

Absolutism. As we noted earlier, we may find ourselves acting contrary to our deeply held moral beliefs—as happened to most of the subjects in the Milgram study—simply because we do not have the critical-thinking skills necessary for standing up to unreasonable authority. In particular, college students at the first stage of cognitive development, where they regard information as either right or wrong, have an "expectation that authorities provide them with absolutely correct knowledge."[46] When confronted with a situation like the one faced by those who administered "electric shocks" in Milgram's study, such students lack the critical-thinking skills to counter the authority's "reasoning." For more on the stages of moral development see Chapter 9.

egocentrism   The belief that the self or individual is the center of all things.

Fear of Challenge. We may also fail to stand up to others because we fear that others will challenge our beliefs. For example, some people believe that is it a sign of weakness to change their position on an issue. Good critical thinkers, however, are willing to openly change their position in light of conflicting evidence. Unlike physicist Stephen Hawking, described in "Thinking Outside the Box: Stephen Hawking, Physicist," many people—especially those with low self-esteem or an egocentric personality—resist information and evidence that are at odds with what they believe. They may view the expression of opposing views or evidence as a personal attack.

Egocentrism. Believing that or acting as if, you are the center of all things is called **egocentrism**. Egocentric, or self-centered, people have little regard for others' interests and thoughts. Studies of cognitive development in college students suggest that as students develop cognitively and become better at critical thinking, they

Outside the Box

Thinking

STEPHEN HAWKING, *Physicist*

Stephen Hawking (1942–) is perhaps the most famous physicist alive. Shortly after graduating from college, he learned that he had ALS (Lou Gehrig's disease), a devastating and incurable neurological disease. About half of the people with it die within three years. After enduring depression and waiting to die, Hawking pulled himself together and decided to live his life to his fullest rather than give up.

He enrolled in graduate school, married, and had three children. He writes: "ALS has not prevented me from having a very attractive family and being successful in my work. I have been lucky that my condition has progressed more slowly than is often the case. But it shows that one need not lose hope."

In 2004, Hawking publicly recanted a position he had held for the past 30 years that the gravity of black holes is so powerful that nothing can escape it, not even light.* In doing so, he conceded, with some regret, that CalTech astrophysicist John Preskill had been right all along about black holes. Preskill theorized that information about objects swallowed by black holes is able to leak from the black holes, a phenomenon known as the "black hole information paradox." Hawking paid Preskill off with an agreed-upon prize—an encyclopedia of baseball.

*See Mark Peplow, "Hawking Changes His Mind about Black Holes," news@nature.com, July 15, 2004.

DISCUSSION QUESTIONS

1. Discuss what characteristics of a good critical thinker, listed in the text, are demonstrated by Hawking's response to adversity and uncertainty.

2. Think of a position that you held (or still hold) against all evidence. Compare and contrast Hawking's action with how you respond when someone challenges your views or position. To what extent is resistance and/or narrow-mindedness responsible for your reluctance to change or modify your position?

---

are less likely to view themselves egocentrically.[47] In addition, although we all tend to fall for compliments and be skeptical of criticism, this tendency is especially true of egocentric people. Flattery impedes our ability to make sound judgments and increases our chances of being persuaded by the flatterer. Advertisers and con artists are well aware of this human tendency and thus use flattery to try to get us to go along with them or to buy products that we wouldn't otherwise buy.

Ethnocentrism. An uncritical or unjustified belief in the inherent superiority of one's own group and culture is called **ethnocentrism**. It is characterized by suspicion of and a lack of knowledge of foreign countries and cultures.[48] Ethnocentric people often make decisions about other groups, cultures, and countries on the basis of stereotypes and opinions rather than on factual information. In addition, we tend to remember evidence that supports our worldview or stereotypes and forget or downplay that which doesn't.

Since the 9/11 terrorist attacks on New York City and the Pentagon, Arab Americans have been subjected to hate crimes as well as to racial profiling by police and federal officials, despite official policies against this practice. Hundreds of Muslims and Americans of Arab descent have been detained without charges and imprisoned under the USA Patriot Act. These types of hasty reactions can lead to misunderstandings and even increased hostility.

Uncritical nationalism—a form of ethnocentrism—can blind us to flaws and deteriorating conditions in our own culture. Americans who engage in this type of narrow-mindedness, for example, may bristle at the mere suggestion that the United States may not be the greatest and freest nation ever. Yet according to the Worldwide Governance Indicators 2007 report, which ranks governments by the amount of freedom citizens have to voice opinions and select their government, the United States, instead of being top, ranks only 35 out of 212 nations in the world—behind Canada, Australia, and most European nations.[49] This represents a drop from twenty-second place in 2005, in part because of increased restrictions on freedom of the press.

ethnocentrism The belief in the inherent superiority of one's own group and culture is characterized by suspicion and a lack of understanding about other cultures.

anthropocentrism The belief that humans are the central or most significant entity of the universe can blind people, including scientists, to the capabilities of other animals.

Anthropocentrism. A belief that humans are the central or most significant entity of the universe, called **anthropocentrism,** can blind people to the capabilities of other animals. In his theory of evolution, Charles Darwin postulated that differences in cognitive function between humans and other animals were simply a matter of degree or quantity, rather than human cognitive function being of a qualitatively different "higher" type. However, the anthropocentric view of humans as unique among all other creatures or as beings created in the image of God and therefore above and separate from nature still dominates. This is found in the use of the term *animal,* even in scientific journals and books, as excluding humans, even though we are an animal species. Under the anthropocentric view, other animals and nature exist not in their own right but as a resource for humans. Anthropocentrism can hinder us from critically thinking about our relationship with the rest of nature and can thereby threaten not only the survival of other species and the environment, as is happening with global warming, but our own survival as well.

The belief that artificial intelligence, in which a computer, robot, or other device is

Brandon Mayfield, an American practicing Muslim from Oregon, was a victim of profiling. He was detained for two weeks as a suspect in the 2004 Madrid train bombings. The evidence used to detain him was later proven to be fabricated.

Connections

How does the government exert influence on what gets reported in the media? *See Chapter 11, p. 348.* What is our responsibility as citizens living in a democracy? *See Chapter 13, p. 416 and 418, and p. 426 and 427.*

doublethink Involves holding two contradictory views at the same time and believing both to be true.

programmed to learn and make decisions, will never match human intelligence is also a product of anthropocentrism. We'll be looking at artificial intelligence and reason in Chapter 2.

Rationalization and Doublethink

While sometimes the best alternative is clear, it's more often the case that competing claims require our analysis before we can come to a decision. When presented with conflicting alternatives, some people make a decision easily and quickly because of their prior bias in favor of one of the alternatives. In doing so, they justify or rationalize their choice on the basis of personal preferences or opinion, rather than on a critical analysis of the competing claims. In an experiment on making choices, psychologist A.H. Martin found that with rationalization the decision is often accompanied by a "rush" of satisfaction, thus convincing the person that his or her preference was correct.[50]

Connections

To what extent is anthropocentrism implicit in the scientific worldview? *See Chapter 12, p. 373. How does the news media influence and reinforce narrow-minded worldviews? See Chapter 11, p. 345.*

We may also use rationalization in an attempt to justify past actions that are inconsistent with our image of ourselves as a decent, rational person. Child molesters may see themselves as affectionate and loving people whom children enjoy being with. A person may cheat on his (or her) sweetheart and then, when confronted, lie about the affair, justifying the lie on the grounds that he is a caring person who is looking out for the best interests of his sweetheart by not saying something that will hurt her feelings.

Because rationalization involves ignoring competing claims, people who engage in it often get caught up in doublethink. **Doublethink** involves holding two contradictory views, or "double standards," at the same time and believing both to be true. This is particular prevalent in response to highly charged issues such as slavery, race, and rights for women. Rather than analyze the arguments surrounding these issues, people may unwittingly engage in doublethink.

For example, when asked, most college students state that they believe in equality of men and women. However, when it comes to lifestyle and career, the same students who claim to believe in equality and freedom of choice also say that women should be the primary caretakers of children. Most teachers, even the most ardent feminists, also treat their female students differently from their male students, calling on boys and praising their accomplishments more often, and having more tolerance of boys' disruptive behavior.[51] When shown videotapes of their classes, most of these teachers are horrified at the extent to which

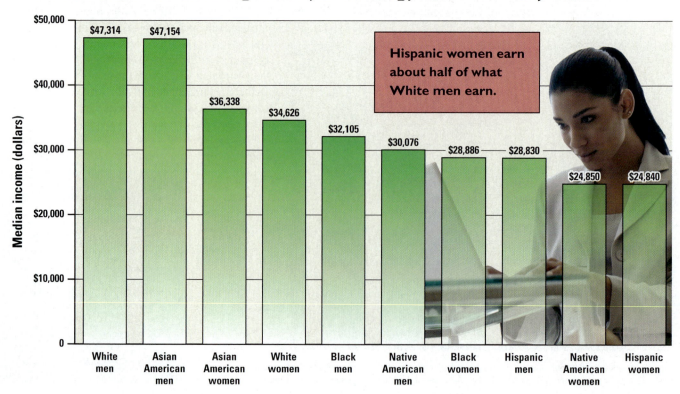

U.S. Median Income by Race, Ethnicity, and Gender, 2004

Hispanic women earn about half of what White men earn.

	Median income (dollars)
White men	$47,314
Asian American men	$47,154
Asian American women	$36,338
White women	$34,626
Black men	$32,105
Native American men	$30,076
Black women	$28,886
Hispanic men	$28,830
Native American women	$24,850
Hispanic women	$24,840

they ignore the girls and downplay their contributions and achievements.

Similarly, the majority of white Americans champion equality as a principle when it comes to race but may harbor unconscious prejudice. Unexamined prejudices can distort our perception of the world. In a 2003 study, people were asked to match negative and positive words with names associated with Americans of both European and African descent. The more implicitly prejudiced the subjects were, the more likely they were to match the negative words with African Americans and the positive words with European Americans.[52]

Doublethink can have an impact on our real-life decisions. Women, including those who work full time outside the home, still perform the great majority of housework and child care.[53] At work, women and minorities suffer from job discrimination, despite its illegality, and earn significantly less than white men earn. The wage disparity between men and women increases with age. In spite of the evidence to the contrary, many college students, when asked, maintain that sex-based and race-based discrimination in the workplace are things of the past.

Cognitive and Social Dissonance

We are most likely to analyze or modify our views when we encounter **cognitive dissonance** and **social dissonance**, situations where new ideas or social behavior directly conflict with our worldviews. People who are forced to live or work in an integrated community, be it a dorm, college classroom, or a public housing project, often encounter occasions and behavior that conflict with their ethnocentric attitudes. Evidence indicates that once a person's behavior is changed—that is, after they share a meal or discuss issues in class with people of other races or ethnicities—a change in belief is likely to follow.[54] Exposing yourself to role models who are skilled in critical thinking can also strengthen your motivation to think clearly rather than engage in resistance.

Stress as a Barrier

While some stress can be good in motivating us, when we experience excessive stress our brain—and our ability to think—slows down. Researchers have found that when people get caught up in disasters, such as an airplane crash, hurricane, flood, or fire, the vast majority freeze up. According to Mac McLean of the FAA and Civil Aerospace Medical Institute, instead of taking action to remove themselves from the danger, most people are "stunned and bewildered."[55]

We can counteract the effect of stress on critical thinking by mentally rehearsing our responses to different stressful scenarios.[56] People who repeatedly have mentally rehearsed the best route for evacuating their building are far more likely than those who haven't rehearsed to take action and escape in cases of emergencies, such as a fire or a terrorist attack. More importantly, mental rehearsal can enhance our performance on familiar tasks. For example, basketball players who engaged in fifteen minutes of mental rehearsal on most days and fifteen minutes of actual practice on the other days actually performed better after twenty days than players who only engaged in physical practice each day.[57]

cognitive dissonance A sense of disorientation which occurs in situations where new ideas directly conflict with a person's worldview.

social dissonance A sense of disorientation which occurs when the social behavior and norms of others conflicts with a person's worldview.

Did You Know

In a study, college students were shown a picture of a black man in a business suit standing on a subway next to a white man who is holding a razor. When asked later what they had seen, the majority reported seeing a black man with a razor standing next to a white man in a business suit.

EXERCISES 1–4*

1. Reread the interpretation examples on page 20. Come up with an additional interpretation for each item. Which interpretations are most reasonable? Support your answer.

2. Select a simple experience such as a man or a woman giving a dollar to a beggar on the street. In groups, discuss different interpretations of the experience, being careful not to let prejudice distort your interpretation.

3. Using the three-tiered model of thinking, discuss the following experiences. The interpretations that you list for each experience do not have to be ones that you personally accept. Share your interpretations with others in the class. If you feel comfortable in doing so, discuss how your past experiences have been shaped by your interpretations and how applying critical-thinking skills to analyze this issue might affect your future actions.

a. Affirmative action in college admissions discriminates against white males.

b. When I invited Chris to go to the movies with me last weekend, Chris said, "No thanks."

c. College tuition is rising faster than the cost of living in the United States.

d. According to CNN, more than half the agricultural workers in the United States are illegal aliens.

e. Marijuana use has been decriminalized in Canada.

f. In a recent survey, 45 percent of Americans stated that they feel that their pet listens to them better than their spouse does.

g. More and more men are going into nursing as a profession.

h. People who cohabitate before marriage are more likely to get divorced than those who do not.

4. According to the International Energy Commission, North Americans use more energy per person than any other people in the world. The average per capita consumption for the world population in 2002 was 65.9 million BTUs (British thermal units). In contrast, the per capita energy consumption for the United States was 339.1 BTUs, compared with 172.3 for Japan, 162.2 for Great Britain, 33.3 for China, and 7.8 for Nigeria. Journalist Robert Samuelson writes, "We Americans want it all: endless and secure energy supplies; low prices; no pollution; less global warming; no new power plants (or oil and gas drilling, either) near people or pristine places. This is a wonderful wish list, whose only shortcoming is the minor inconvenience of massive inconsistency." As a class, discuss ways in which we use rationalization or other types of resistance to justify our high energy-consumption lifestyle.

5. At the opposite end of the spectrum from egocentric people are those who sacrifice their needs and dreams for others. Harvard professor of education Carol Gilligan maintains that women in particular tend to be self-sacrificing—putting others' needs before their own. How does the tendency to be self-sacrificing interfere with effective critical thinking? Use examples from your own experience to illustrate your answer.

6. Douglas Adams (1952–2001), author of *The Hitchhiker's Guide to the Galaxy,* compared humans to a puddle of water as a way of illustrating anthropocentric thinking, or what he called "the vain conceit" of humans. He wrote:

> Imagine a puddle waking up one morning and thinking, "This is an interesting world I find myself in, an interesting hole I find myself in. It fits me rather neatly, doesn't it. In fact, it fits me staggeringly well. It must have been made to have me in it." Even as the sun comes out and the puddle gets smaller, it still frantically hangs on to the idea that everything is going to be all right; that the world was made for it since it is so well suited to it.[58]

Are humans, in fact, a lot like the puddle in Adams's analogy? Support your answer, using examples from your own experience. Discuss how this type of anthropocentric thinking shapes or distorts our interpretation of the world.

7. Working in small groups, expand on the list of barriers to critical thinking presented in the text. Come up with examples of each barrier and explain how they get in the way of critical thinking.

8. Think of a stressful task or situation—such as a job or graduate-school interview, breaking bad news, asking someone for a date, or giving a presentation in front of a class—that you will be facing in the next few weeks. Write down the task at the top of a page. Spend fifteen minutes a day over the next week mentally rehearsing the task. Note the times and dates you spent mentally rehearsing the task. After you have performed the actual task, write a short essay on how well you did. Were you satisfied with the outcome? Discuss the extent to which mental rehearsal helped you perform this task, compared with similar tasks you performed in the past.

9. Write down three experiences relating to yourself and your life goals. For example, "I am good at science," "I am shy," "I haven't chosen a major yet," or "I want a job in which I can make a lot of money." Now write down at least three interpretations of each of these experiences. Analyze your interpretations. Are the interpretations reasonable? Share your interpretations with others in the class or with friends or family. Do they agree with your interpretations? If not, why not?

10. Adolescents and college freshmen are particularly influenced by peer pressure. Do you think that you were more of a conformist when you entered college? Has the college experience changed you in this regard? Discuss how the tendency to conform affects your ability to engage in effective critical thinking and what strategies you might develop to make you less prone to uncritical conformity.

11. *Journal Exercise.* Complete a journal entry on "Identifying Your Types of Resistance and Narrow-Mindedness." Working in small groups, discuss the types of resistance or narrow-mindedness that you are most likely to engage in when your views are challenged and steps you might take to overcome your resistance and narrow-mindedness.

Think AGAIN >>

1. What are the characteristics of a skilled critical thinker?
   • A skilled critical thinker is well informed, open-minded, attentive, and creative and has effective analytical, research, communication, and problem-solving skills.

2. What are the three levels of thinking?
   • The three levels are experience, which includes firsthand knowledge and information from other sources; interpretation, which involves trying to make sense out of our experiences; and analysis, which requires that we critically examine our interpretations.

3. What are some of the barriers to critical thinking?
   • Barriers include narrow-mindedness, such as absolutism, egocentrism, anthropocentrism, and ethnocentrism, as well as the habitual use of resistance, such as avoidance, anger, clichés, denial, ignorance, conformity, rationalization, and distractions.

Perspectives on Affirmative Action in College Admissions

Affirmative action involves taking positive steps in job hiring and college admissions to correct certain past injustices against groups such as minorities and women. In 1954, the Supreme Court ruled in *Brown v. Board of Education* that school segregation was unconstitutional and that black children have a right to equal education opportunities. The first affirmative action legislation was proposed by Vice President Richard Nixon in 1959. Affirmative action programs and legislation were expanded during the civil rights era in the 1960s.

In 1978 Allan Bakke, a white man, sued the University of California at Davis Medical School because his application was rejected while minority students with lower test scores were admitted. The Supreme Court agreed with Bakke, ruling that reverse discrimination was unconstitutional. In November 1996, with the passage of Proposition 209, California became the first state to ban affirmative action in the public sector, including admission to state colleges. Washington and Texas have also passed referenda banning affirmative action in state college admissions.

In June 2003, the U.S. Supreme Court found that the admissions policy of the University of Michigan Law School, which awarded points to applicants based on race, was flawed. However, in its final ruling the court permitted race to be considered as one among many factors when considering individual applications for both the law school and undergraduate admissions.

Affirmative Action and Higher Education

BEFORE AND AFTER THE SUPREME COURT RULINGS

ON THE MICHIGAN CASES

NANCY CANTOR

Nancy Cantor is chancellor of the University of Illinois at Urbana-Champaign. She was provost of the University of Michigan when the affirmative action cases were filed with the U.S. Supreme Court. In this article, published in the Chicago Tribune *on January 28, 2003, she presents an argument for affirmative action in college admissions.*

Integration takes hard work, especially when we have little other than collective fear, stereotypes and sins upon which to build. It is time America sees affirmative action on college campuses for what it is: a way to enrich the educational and intellectual lives of white students as well as students of color. We must not abandon race as a consideration in admissions.

The debate now before the U.S. Supreme Court over admissions at the University of Michigan is about the relative advantages people are getting, and it is a debate that misses the point. College admission has always been about relative advantage because a college education is a scarce resource, and the stakes are high.

In this era of emphasis on standardized tests, it may be easy to forget that colleges and universities have always taken into account many other aspects of students' experiences, including the geographic region from which they come, their families' relationship to the institution and their leadership experiences.

It is appropriate, and indeed critical, for the best institutions in the world to create the broadest possible mix of life experiences. Race is a fundamental feature of life in America, and it has an enormous impact on what a person has to contribute on campus. College admissions should be race-conscious to take the cultural and historical experiences of all students—Native American, African-American, Hispanic, Asian-American and white—and build on these in an educational setting. President Bush was wrong when he labeled the affirmative-action programs at the University of Michigan "quota systems.". . .

There are no quotas at Michigan. All students compete for all seats. Race is used as a plus factor, along with other life experiences and talents, just as the president has suggested should happen. The percentages of students of color at Michigan vary annually.

Bush says he believes college admissions should be "race neutral," and he says he supports the principles of Regents of the University of California vs. Bakke. He cannot have it both ways. Race is not neutral in the Bakke decision; it is front and center, just as it was nearly 50 years ago in *Brown vs. Board of Education*. In both cases, the Supreme Court urged our nation to boldly and straightforwardly take on the issue of race. . . .

The decision by Justice Lewis F. Powell in *Bakke* brought more than students of color to the table. It brought race in America to the table, urging educators to join hands in creating a truly integrated society of learners.

How are we to fulfill the dream of Brown and Bakke, to build a positive story of race in America, if we are told to ignore race—to concoct systems constructed around proxies for race such as class rank in racially segregated public school districts or euphemisms such as "cultural traditions" that both avoid our past and fail to value the possibility that race can play a constructive role in our nation's future?. . .

We want to include, not exclude. We want to use race as a positive category, as one of many aspects of a life we consider when we sit down to decide which students to invite to our table.

QUESTIONS

1. According to Cantor, how does affirmative action benefit both white students and students of color?

2. What does Cantor mean which she says that "college admissions should be race-conscious"?

3. What is President Bush's stand on affirmative action, and why does Cantor disagree with him?

4. How does Cantor use the Supreme Court's rulings in *Brown v. Board of Education* and *Regents of the University of California v. Bakke* to bolster her argument for affirmative action in college admissions?

Remarks by the President on the Michigan Affirmative Action Case

GEORGE W. BUSH

George W. Bush served as president of the United States from 2001 to 2009. In a White House speech on January 15, 2003, Bush argued that the affirmative action policy of the University of Michigan is both unfair and unconstitutional.

The Supreme Court will soon hear arguments in a case about admission policies and student diversity in public universities. I strongly support diversity of all kinds, including racial diversity in higher education. But the method used by the University of Michigan to achieve this important goal is fundamentally flawed.

At their core, the Michigan policies amount to a quota system that unfairly rewards or penalizes perspective students, based solely on their race. So, tomorrow my administration will file a brief with the court arguing that the University of Michigan's admissions policies, which award students a significant number of extra points based solely on their race, and establishes numerical targets for incoming minority students, are unconstitutional.

Our Constitution makes it clear that people of all races must be treated equally under the law. Yet we know that our society has not fully achieved that ideal. Racial prejudice is a reality in America. It hurts many of our citizens. As a nation, as a government, as individuals, we must be vigilant in responding to prejudice wherever we find it. Yet, as we work to address the wrong of racial prejudice, we must not use means that create another wrong, and thus perpetuate our divisions.

America is a diverse country, racially, economically, and ethnically. And our institutions of higher education should reflect our diversity. A college education should teach respect and understanding and goodwill. And these values are strengthened when students live and learn with people from many backgrounds. Yet quota systems that use race to include or exclude people from higher education and the opportunities it offers are divisive, unfair and impossible to square with the Constitution.

In the programs under review by the Supreme Court, the University of Michigan has established an admissions process based on race. At the undergraduate level, African American students and some Hispanic students and Native American students receive 20 points out of a maximum of 150, not because of any academic achievement or life experience, but solely because they are African American, Hispanic or Native American.

To put this in perspective, a perfect SAT score is worth only 12 points in the Michigan system. Students who accumulate 100 points are generally admitted, so those 20 points awarded solely based on race are often the decisive factor.

At the law school, some minority students are admitted to meet percentage targets while other applicants with higher grades and better scores are passed over. This means that students are being selected or rejected based primarily on the color of their skin. The motivation for such an admissions policy may be very good, but its result is discrimination and that discrimination is wrong.

Some states are using innovative ways to diversify their student bodies. Recent history has proven that diversity can be achieved without using quotas. Systems in California and Florida and Texas have proven that by guaranteeing admissions to the top students from high schools throughout the state, including low income neighborhoods, colleges can attain broad racial diversity. In these states, race-neutral admissions policies have resulted in levels of minority attendance for incoming students that are close to, and in some instances slightly surpass, those under the old race-based approach.

We should not be satisfied with the current numbers of minorities on American college campuses. Much progress has been made; much more is needed. University officials have the responsibility and the obligation to make a serious, effective effort to reach out to students from all walks of life, without falling back on unconstitutional quotas. Schools should seek diversity by considering a broad range of factors in admissions, including a student's potential and life experiences.

Our government must work to make college more affordable for students who come from economically disadvantaged homes. And because we're committed to racial justice, we must make sure that America's public schools offer a quality education to every child from every background, which is the central purpose of the education reforms I signed last year.

America's long experience with the segregation we have put behind us and the racial discrimination we still struggle to overcome requires a special effort to make real the promise of equal opportunity for all. My administration will continue to actively promote diversity and opportunity in every way that the law permits.

1. According to Bush, what is the affirmative action policy at the University of Michigan Law School and the University of Michigan undergraduate school?

2. On what grounds does Bush claim that the affirmative action policies used at the University of Michigan are both unfair and unconstitutional?

3. According to Bush, why is promoting diversity important in the United States?

4. What suggestions does Bush make for promoting diversity in American colleges?

PERSPECTIVES ON AFFIRMATIVE ACTION

1. Agreeing on a definition of the key terms is one of the first steps in debating an issue. How are Cantor and Bush each using the terms *affirmative action* and *diversity*?

2. Discuss whether affirmative action has a place in a democracy that is built on equal rights for all citizens, or if it is a violation of the fundamental principle of equality.

3. Compare and contrast Cantor's and Bush's perspectives on the use of affirmative action in college admissions. Which person makes the better argument? Support your position.

4. What is the policy at your college regarding affirmative action in admissions? To what extent has affirmative action, or lack of it, at your college had an impact on diversity in the student body and the quality of your education? Support your answer using specific examples.

5. What criteria (for example, experiences, talents, alumni status of parents) do you think should be used in college admissions? Working in small groups, develop a list of relevant criteria and assign each criterion a point value (for example, 10 or 20) out of a total of 100 points based on how important each criterion is to the admissions decision.

2

REASON &

In Fyodor Dostoyevsky's novel *Crime and Punishment,* the protagonist, Raskolnikov, after overhearing the following conversation between a student and officer in a café, decides to kill an old woman presumably so that he could redistribute her money to those who would better benefit from it.

"On the one hand," conjectured the student, "you have a stupid, silly, utterly unimportant, vicious, sickly old woman, no good to anybody. . . . On the other hand you have new, young forces running to waste for want of backing. . . . A hundred, a thousand, good actions and promising beginnings might be forwarded and directed aright by money that old woman destines for a monastery; hundreds, perhaps thousands of existences might be set on the right path, scores of families saved from beggary, from decay, from ruin and corruption, from the Lock hospitals—and all with her money! Kill her, take her money, on condition that you dedicate yourself with its help to the service of humanity and the common good; don't you think that thousands of good deeds will wipe out one little,

EMOTION

- What is the role of reason in critical thinking?
- How does emotion positively and negatively influence critical thinking?
- What are the three approaches to faith and reason?

insignificant transgression? For one life taken, thousands saved from corruption and decay![1]

Raskolnikov's decision to kill the old woman is based purely on a rational calculation of what would bring the greatest good to the greatest number of people. He does not let emotion interfere with his decision nor with his committing of the crime. But is it a good decision from the point of view of a critical thinker?

In this chapter we will discuss the roles of reason and emotion in critical thinking.

Specifically we will

- Look at the role of reason in critical thinking

- Explore ways in which sex, race, and age influence our style of reasoning and critical thinking

- Assess the role of emotion in critical thinking

- Examine how reason and emotion work together

- Address the question of whether artificial intelligence (AI) is capable of reason and emotion

- Consider the relationship between faith and reason and the role of critical thinking in discussions of religious beliefs

Finally, we will examine different perspectives regarding machines' capability for human intelligence, emotion, and spirituality, along with the possibility of machine evolution.

EXPOSE THE CORRUPTION

WHAT IS REASON?

We are constantly barraged with reasons for why we should accept or reject a particular position on an issue, or why we should or should not take a particular action. For example, should you evacuate your home when warned of imminent danger of a hurricane or tornado, or should you stay and try to protect your property? Would it be more reasonable to go to medical school, to join the Peace Corps, or to take a year off and travel? Should you move in with your boyfriend or girlfriend? In each case, it is up to you, as a critical thinker, to sort out the competing possibilities and come up with the best resolution.

Reason is the process of supporting a claim or conclusion on the basis of evidence. It involves both the disciplined use of intelligence and the application of rules for problem solving. It is easier for people, particularly those who have not been formally trained in critical thinking and logic, to reason about problems in a familiar context. Consider the following problem, which takes place in a familiar setting.

Imagine that you are shown four people and told to test the rule that a person must be over the age of twenty-one to drink beer. One person is drinking Coke; the second is drinking beer, the third is twenty-three years old; and the fourth is fifteen. Whom must you check (what they are drinking or what age they are) to ensure that the rule is being followed?[2]

Almost all college students are able to solve that problem in a matter of minutes. Now consider the next problem, known as the Wason Card Problem, which involves a scenario that is unfamiar to most people:

Imagine you are given four cards and are told to test the rule that a card with a vowel on one side must have an even number on the other side. Let's say that the cards in front of you show an *E*, a *K*, a *7*, and a *4*. Which card or two cards would you turn over?

Despite the fact that this problem is logically identical to the previous one about our four friends, only about 5 percent of the college population selects the correct two cards. Learning the rules of logic gives us the tools to solve more difficult and unfamiliar problems. In logic, reasoning is usually presented in the form of carefully laid out arguments in which a conclusion is supported by other propositions known as premises, which provide reason or evidence for the conclusion. However, *reason*, as we use it in our everyday lives, is a much broader concept. Reason is often a complex process that calls on our creative resources as well as emotional discernment.

Traditional Views of Reason

Reason, many people believe, is what separates humans from other animals. The ancient Greek philosopher Plato (427–347 bce) wrote in his *Phaedrus* that the human soul is divided into one rational and two nonrational parts. The two nonrational parts include the emotions and physical cravings, such as hunger and the sex drive.

> **reason** The process of supporting a claim or conclusion on the basis of evidence.

We are at our best, he argued, when all three parts of the soul are in harmony, with reason being in charge like a charioteer in charge of his horses.

Plato's teachings on the nature of the soul were integrated into Christianity by medieval philosopher St. Thomas Aquinas (c. 1225–1274). According to Aquinas, God is the perfectly rational being. Rationality is the divine spark in humans. Up until the late nineteenth century, most Western scholars accepted without question the view that humans are a special creation.

Charles Darwin (1809–1882) rejected the long-held anthropocentric assumption that there is a divinely ordered Chain of Being with God at the top, followed by angels, next by humans, and then by the so-called higher animals. According to evolutionary theory, reason evolved as part of the adaptation of our behavior and that of other animals in the struggle for survival.

Great Chain of Being

In his book *The Descent of Man,* Darwin wrote: "It is a significant fact that the more the habits of any particular animal are studied by a naturalist, the more he ascribes to reason and the less to unlearnt instincts."[3] Today most scientists agree that rather than being driven by instinct alone, many other animals are capable of abstract thought and reason.[4]

What is the role of reason in the sciences and the scientific method? *See Chapter 12, p. 373.*

Connections

In the twentieth century, reason came to be identified mostly with science. Ironically, although reason is certainly important in science, the basic assumption of science—that the world outside us exists—cannot be proven through the use of reason. Yet it is generally considered *reasonable* for us to believe that the world exists. In other words, we may have beliefs that are the foundation of other beliefs, even though we can't prove or disprove them through the use of reason alone.

In addition to abstract thinking and logical argumentation, reason has a behavioral component. As a reasonable person, you adjust your behavior to conform to or bring about the best outcome. For example, if you have good reasons to believe that you are incompatible with your boyfriend or girlfriend, then you will more likely use behavior that distances you romantically from that person rather than moving in with him or her. To use another example, if after completing your life plan you conclude that you are in an entirely wrong field of study, then, as a reasonable person, you will take steps to revise your course of study at college, even if it means attending classes for an additional year. After all, forty years of misery in a job you hate is a far

Did You Know

In 2001, 28.5 percent of male and 15.9 percent of female college freshmen polled by the *Freshman Survey* agreed with this statement: "The activities of married women are best confined to the home and family."[8]

greater burden than that which would be imposed on you by one or two extra years of college.

As a component of critical thinking, reason embraces different strategies, including deduction, generalization (a type of inductive logic), and imagination. Reason is also important in spatial-temporal problem solving, which involves the application of concepts of space and time, such as that found in mathematics, engineering, architecture, and the physical sciences. The heavy emphasis in American schools on language skills is thought to be one of the reasons why children in the United States have difficulty with subjects such as math and physics, which involve spatial-temporal reasoning.[5]

Sex, Race, Age, and Reason

In traditional Western thinking, men are more closely linked to the realm of the mind and reason, whereas women—because of their reproductive role in society—are more closely linked to realm of the body and nature. Aristotle, one of the most influential thinkers in Western philosophy, held that men and women have fundamentally different natures.[6] While men are guided by reason and logic, women are more often guided by emotion. Reflecting the prevailing attitude of his time, Aristotle maintained that because of these differences, the proper sphere of men is the public realm of politics and the workplace, and that of women, the home

> According to evolutionary theory, reason evolved as part of the adaptation of our behavior and that of other animals in the struggle for survival.

and family. In traditional Judeo-Christian religion, God, whose divine reason is regarded as perfect, is depicted as male. Aquinas taught that God created women only for the sake of procreation and that women, being naturally inferior, should submit to the authority of men.[7] These stereotypes about the different natures of men and women continue to influence our thinking.

Not much has changed since 2001. According to a summer 2008 Pew poll, 22% of Americans believe that "women should return to their traditional roles in society." This belief is evident in how some people have reacted to the nomination of Sarah Palin, a mother of five, for the Republican vice president.[9]

Feminists such as Gloria Steinem, Simone de Beauvoir, and John Stuart Mill have argued that men and women have the same rational nature. The gap between men and women, they maintain, is based on discrimination and on men's reluctance to give up their advantage in the home and workplace. Conservatives, such as political activist Phyllis Schlafly and sociologist Steven Goldberg,[10] on the other hand, argue that these discrepancies are based on natural differences between men and women. Research suggests that what are often assumed to be sex-based differences are based on the interaction of socialization and innate differences between men and women.[11]

However, even if women may be more emotional by nature than men, this does not prove that they do not have reason and are not just as capable as men of engaging in logical argumentation. In addition, sex stereotypes harm men by denigrating men who prefer to stay at home and care for their children or who choose nurturing professions

Outside the Box

TEMPLE GRANDIN, *Structural Designer*

A very high-functioning person with autism, Temple Grandin (1947–) is an assistant professor of animal science at Colorado State University. She has revolutionized certain areas of structural design that have traditionally been problematic because of humans' difficulty in visualizing the underlying problems.

For example, Dr. Grandin is the world's leading expert in the design of livestock-handling facilities. In designing the facilities, she is able to visualize herself as the animal going through one of her systems. In her imagination, she walks around and through the structure and flies over it in a helicopter. Applying her facility for spatial-temporal reasoning, she is able to anticipate and correct for possible problems. Her designs are revolutionary in that her structures interact with the animals in such a natural way that livestock can be effortlessly directed in a calm and humane manner.

DISCUSSION QUESTIONS

1. Discuss ways in which Dr. Grandin is using critical thinking skills in conjunction with her exceptional spatial-temporal reasoning ability to come up with solutions to problems in her profession.

2. Identifying your strengths is important in choosing a career. What type of reasoning are you strongest in, and how might this best be used in a career choice? If you're unsure of your strengths, visit the career development office on your campus.

Temple Grandin, Matthew Peterson, and Gordon L. Shaw, "Spatial-temporal versus language-analytic reasoning: The role of music training," *Arts and Education Policy Review*, Vol. 99, Issue 6, July–August 1998, p. 12.

such as nursing or teaching in elementary school. Rather than making decisions on the basis of stereotypes, critical thinking requires that we be open to considering different perspectives and to examining our own assumptions regarding sex and race.

Lifelong education is also important in honing our reasoning skills. The more education people have, the more mentally productive they are as they age.[12] Just as exercise promotes physical health, so pursuing lifelong learning and using our critical-thinking skills can keep us mentally alert. Many college administrators support the trend of older students attending college, for this enhances not only diversity but also the range of life experiences that are brought to the classroom. It also helps break down negative stereotypes that are based on age by increasing interaction between different age groups.

To be effective critical thinkers, we must be willing to use our reason to examine our assumptions regarding race, sex, and age. Unexamined assumptions can distort our perception of the world and harm others as well as ourselves.

Dreams and Problem Solving

Although reasoning is usually viewed as a conscious activity, cognitive scientists today are discovering that much of reasoning is in fact unconscious and automatic. While dreams have traditionally been viewed as an unconscious release of suppressed emotions and irrational impulses, studies of brain function suggest that dreaming may also involve cerebral activity related to reason and problem solving.[13] In particular, dreams may help solve elusive visual problems, such as how to fit all your furniture into your dorm room or small apartment.

Dream research is helping scientists learn how we use dreams to resolve problems in our lives and work and to discover logical connections between seemingly unrelated things. Most of us have probably heard the advice that we will perform better on an exam if we study the day before, rather than wait until the day of an exam, and then "sleep on it."

Critical Thinking in Action

Your Brain on Video Games

It has been well documented that playing games or learning how to play a musical instrument can sharpen our critical-thinking skills and delay the onset of cognitive disorders such as dementia. Games exercise the brain in much the same way that physical activity exercises the body.

In Chapter 1, we learned that mental rehearsal can improve our performance of real-life tasks, especially in stressful situations. Studies suggest that playing video games that involve mentally playing out scenarios can improve our performance.[*] Video games have been found to boost cognitive skills, including spatial-temporal reasoning, systems thinking, and problem solving, as well as to improve hand–eye coordination. Games such as Tetris and the Sims, which challenge players by using escalating levels of difficulty, are particularly effective, since they keep the players at the edge of their abilities.

Skills learned in playing games generalize to real-world situations by running the mind through perceptual simulations that prepare us for decision making and actions in our everyday lives. A study conducted at Beth Israel Medical Center in New York City found that surgeons who played video games more than three hours a week made 37 percent fewer surgical errors than their nongaming colleagues. A Harvard Business School study found that white-collar professionals who played video games were more confident and better at problem solving than those who didn't play games or only played occasionally.[**] Organizations such as the U.S. military, United Nations Children's Fund, American Cancer Society, and Federal Emergency Management Agency all use video games as instructional tools.

Of course, video games can be addictive precisely because they can be so challenging and stimulating. They can also provide a distraction—a type of resistance—from having to think about issues in our lives. Learning how to balance time spent playing games with the demands of our academic and social lives is an important asset for a critical thinker. It would be a shame if your significant other left you because you spent more time with their virtual persona than you did with them in real life!

DISCUSSION QUESTIONS

1. Think of your favorite video game. Describe what features of the game are most interesting to you or hold your attention. Discuss how these features might help to improve your thinking and problem solving in real life.

2. Video games study is offered as a major at some colleges. If you were designing the major, discuss what courses and opportunities you would offer as part of the video games curriculum and how you might relate it to critical thinking.

*John C. Beck and Mitchell Wade, *Got Game: How the Gamer Generation is Reshaping Business Forever* (Cambridge, MA: Harvard University Press, 2004).

**Steven Johnson, "Your Brain on Video Games. Could They Actually Be Good for You?" *Discover,* Vol. 26, Issue 7, July 2005, pp. 39–43.

When we dream, the parts of our brain that control our emotions and detect inconsistencies become more active. According to neurologist Eric Nofzinger, "this could be why people often figure out thorny problems in their dreams. It's as if the brain surveys the internal milieu and tries to figure out what it should be doing, and whether our actions conflict with who we are."[14] In addition, men and women's dreams tend to be somewhat different. Men's dreams involve more physical aggression; new mothers dream a lot about scenarios involving their infants' safety.

Experienced scientists, mathematicians, and detectives frequently resolve complex problems without any deliberate conscious thought, sometimes in their sleep.[15] Many American Indian tribes also regard dreams as a source of guidance for life.

It is not uncommon to hear of groundbreaking scientific discoveries occurring during dreams. However, as Harvard Medical School psychiatrist Deidre Barrett notes, this type of creative problem solving in dreams only occurs after a person has already done extensive work on the problem when awake, including research and examining various premises and possible conclusions.[16]

The dreams of Russian chemist Dmitri Mendeleyev led, after years of working on drafts of the table, to the creation of the version of periodic table of the elements that chemists use today. And American inventor Elias Howe perfected the sewing machine after being shown in a dream the solution to a problem that had been blocking him.

Artists have also been inspired by dreams. Psychologists trained in dream analysis even work with the heads of corporations in using dreams to help them resolve business problems.[17] Each night before going to sleep, innovator and business entrepreneur Ray Kurzweil, whose writing on AI we'll be reading at the end of this chapter, selects a problem that has been vexing him such as a business strategy or a technical problem. Then he uses dreaming to help him find a solution to the problem,

a approach to problem solving that has served him well on several occasions.[18]

Before you go to sleep, try writing down a problem you've been thinking about for a while and then record your dream(s) in the morning (see Online Journal Assignment 4: Problem Solving Through Dreams). You may be pleasantly surprised at how well this works. One of my students who tried this exercise had three exams on the same day and was having a problem managing his time to study. In his dream he saw a parade with three presidents together on a float—George W. Bush, Ronald Reagan, and Bill Clinton. When he awoke he realized that the three presidents stood for his three exams and that he just had to "stay the course" and also study for the exams together (like the three presidents together on one float), rather than schedule separate study times for each exam. In doing this, he discovered that the material from one of his courses was useful in writing an essay on the test for another course.

Another student, who was having problems with her boyfriend, had a dream that she was driving a long boardlike scooter. Whenever she passed people who asked her for a ride, she'd let them get on board until it became difficult to balance and the scooter fell over. By analyzing the dream, she realized that one of the reasons she had problems with relationships was that she always put others' needs before her own until she became so overwhelmed that she ended up sabotaging relationships. She went back and added to her list of goals in her life plan "Learn how to balance my needs and others'."[19]

Reason is essential in logic and critical thinking. It helps us to analyze beliefs and evidence, to make well thought-out decisions about life choices, and to resolve problems. Reason can operate on the conscious level as well as on the unconscious level. In critical thinking, reason works together with other faculties such as emotion. We'll be looking more at the interaction between reason and emotion later in this chapter.

Hot or Not?

Can you think of a person in the public sphere who challenges traditional sex roles?

EXERCISES 2-1

1. In Eastern philosophy, Taoists use an analogy between ice and water to explain the relationship between wisdom (reason) and the passions (emotion). Wisdom and passions, like ice and water, are not two different things, but neither are they identical. The ice cube is the not the same as—but is also not different from—the water we put in the ice cube tray. Similarly, while thinking operates according to the rules of logic, emotion is governed by a different type of logic known as the logic of the heart.[1] Compare and contrast this analogy and the charioteer analogy used by Plato (see page 39). Which analogy do you think is better? Support your answer.

2. Psychiatrist Reuven Bar-Levav wrote: "Man is essentially not a rational being, merely one capable of rationality."[20] What did he mean by this? Do you agree? Support your answers.

3. A study by the U.S. Department of Labor found that job performance peaks at age thirty-five and then declines, the decline varying by occupation. For example, academics publish less as they age. Painters, musicians, and writers also become less productive with age, with the exception of female writers, who are most productive in their fifties.[21] What are some possible explanations for these findings? To what extent do your assumptions regarding age and sex influence your explanations? Discuss ways in which you might go about deciding which explanations are the most reasonable.

4. Looking back at your own experience in high school and college, were the males and females and/or students of different racial and ethnic groups treated differently? What assumptions underlie the differences in treatment? Were any of the assumptions justified? Explain why or why not.

5. Discuss ways in which greater cultural, racial, and age diversity in the student population might enrich the college experience and promote the development of better critical-thinking skills in both younger and older students. Use examples from your personal experience to illustrate your answers.

6. Have you ever resolved a problem or had a creative insight through a dream? If you are willing, share your experience with the class.

7. Imagine that a smart pill is available that can increase your IQ by 20 percent. The pill has undergone extensive testing and has been found to be both safe and effective. Those who take the pill are better at reasoning, learn faster, remember what they have learned for a longer time, and get higher grades in school. If a person decides to stop taking the pill, he or she simply goes back to his or her former level of mental functioning. Under these circumstances, would you take the smart pill?[22] Explain.

8. In her essay "Feminism and Critical Thinking," philosopher and educational researcher Barbara J. Thayer-Bacon writes: "Only today, when women can take control of the reproductive process through the use of very effective birth control, are women becoming free of their bodies' demands, and sure enough, because they can do so they are becoming more associated with their minds and reason … [allowing] women to break down the hierarchy that ranks women inferior to men in their thinking abilities."[23] Research Thayer-Bacon's claim that the demands of a woman's body and reason are in conflict with one another. Is her claim supported by evidence? What is your position on this issue as well as the implications of your position for public policy and your own life plans?

9. One of the characteristics of an effective critical thinker is his or her ability to develop strategies for coping with adversity rather than giving up or becoming embittered. Think of a hardship—personal, academic, or financial—that you are facing. Integrating the characteristics of a good critical thinker, develop a strategy for coping with or overcoming the hardship. Put your plan into action.

10. *Journal Exercise*: Complete a journal assignment on "Problem Solving Through Dreams." Pose a problem to yourself just before going to sleep. If you wish, share how your dream helped you to resolve a problem.

THE ROLE OF EMOTION IN CRITICAL THINKING

Many philosophers say that to achieve happiness and inner harmony, we must live a life of reason. What role, if any, does emotion play in critical thinking as well as in achieving the good life?

Cultural Attitudes Toward Emotion

Emotion, according to the *Random House Webster's College Dictionary,* is a "… state of consciousness in which joy, sorrow, fear, etc., is experienced, as distinguished from cognitive and volitional states of consciousness."[24] In Western culture, emotion has traditionally been set in opposition to reason and has been regarded as the culprit in sloppy reasoning and irrational life choices. Some modern scholars and scientists dismiss emotion as a relic from our evolutionary past and an unreliable guide to actions in the present.[25]

The traditional Chinese philosophy of Confucianism, in contrast, emphasizes the cultivation of relationships and emotions, such as compassion and loyalty, as key to the good life. Many traditional African philosophies also focus on personal and historical experiences in critical thinking.[26] For Buddhists, compassion and a love for all living beings is the foundation of good critical thinking. Given this, it's not surprising that a study of conceptions of critical thinking in North American and Japanese secondary schools found that North Americans teach critical thinking as a rational and analytic process, while Japanese teachers place more emphasis on the emotional domain of critical thinking.[27]

Should critical thinking take into account emotions, or is reason better off without the "corrupting" influence of emotion? In the excerpt from *Crime and Punishment* that we considered at the beginning of this chapter, didn't most of us wonder how Raskolnikov could have been so "coldhearted"?

Can you identify which emotions are being shown here?

As critical thinkers, we need to be attentive not only to what is going on around us but also to our own feelings. Although emotions such as anger and fear can act as barriers to good reasoning, emotion can also enhance critical thinking by predisposing us or motivating us to make better decisions. Empathy for the murder victims in *Crime and Punishment* (Raskolnikov killed not only the old woman but also her mentally deficient sister who had unexpectedly witnessed him murdering the old woman) or revulsion and anger in the face of atrocities, such as what happened in the Nazi death camps, may be more appropriate reactions than calm, cool calculation.

Emotional Intelligence and the Positive Effects of Emotion

Healthy emotional development—what some cognitive scientists refer to as emotional intelligence—is positively related to abstract reasoning ability.[28] **Emotional intelligence** is "the ability to perceive accurately, appraise and express emotion; the ability to access and/or generate feelings when they facilitate thought; the ability to understand emotion and emotional knowledge; and the ability to regulate emotions to promote emotional and intellectual growth."[29] Emotions such as empathy, moral indignation or outrage, love, happiness, and even guilt can have a positive effect on our reasoning by influencing us to make better decisions.

Indeed, former Vice President Al Gore maintains that one reason Americans are not doing more to protest the use of torture and the high civilian casualties in the war in Iraq or feel little outrage over the slow response of the government to the devastation wrought by Hurricane Katrina is that our sense of moral indignation has been dulled by so much sensationalism and so many violent images on television.[30] Many of

Hot or Not?

Do you think emotion or reason plays a more pivotal role in critical thinking?

us have difficulty identifying and expressing our feelings. Sometimes this inability to communicate our emotions can negatively affect our behavior and decisions.[31] Until we can tap into our emotions of moral indignation and empathy for victims—including our own victimization—we're unlikely to be motivated to use our reason to come up with plans for taking action toward stopping these types of mistreatment.*

In making decisions in our everyday lives, we often begin with a felt need and *only then* take action that may help us resolve the need. Rosa Parks's indignation at being discriminated against and her refusal to give up her seat on the bus to a white man (as a local law at the time required her to do) sparked the 1955–1956 bus boycott in Montgomery, Alabama (see "Thinking Outside the Box: Rosa Parks, Civil Rights Activist"). Her refusal, however, was not a spur-of-the-moment emotional reaction but one supported by reason as well. As a long-time member of the National Association for the Advancement of Colored People (NAACP), she had given careful thought to the different options for how she might personally take steps to promote racial equality.

emotional intelligence The ability to perceive accurately, appraise and express emotion.

empathy (sympathy) The capacity to enter into and understand the emotions of others.

An empathetic person is more flexible and open to others' perspectives and is motivated to use critical analysis, important skills in formulating a satisfactory logical argument regarding a plan of action.

Empathy, the ability to enter into and understand the experiences and emotions of others, can also alert us to oppression, as well as enhance our personal relationships by making us better listeners and communicators. An

*For more on the role of empathy and moral indignation in moral decision making, see the section in Chapter 9 on "Conscience and Moral Sentiments."

empathetic person is more flexible and open to others' perspectives and is motivated to use critical analysis, important skills in formulating a satisfactory logical argument regarding a plan of action.

Connections

Why does news focus on shocking events, and how can we make ourselves less vulnerable to sensationalism in the news media? *See Chapter 11, p. 345.*

How can your feelings of moral indignation and injustice motivate you to engage in political action? *See Chapter 13, p. 429.*

Empathetic role-play can help discourage rigid, unrealistic beliefs about others. In a group setting, empathic role-playing entails members of the group to play out the role and feelings of another person. When followed by reflection on the experience, it has been found to facilitate skill in critical thinking. [32]

Happiness and optimism can also contribute to a belief that a problem can be resolved. People who are happy and satisfied with their lives more readily adjust or readjust to both positive and negative changes in their life circumstances. [33] This, in turn, contributes to their happiness and success. Physicist Stephen Hawking provides an example of the power of optimism and positive thinking (see "Thinking Outside the Box: Stephen Hawking, Physicist," page 24). A happy frame of mind is associated with "flow," a state familiar to musicians, artists, and writers, in which we lose ourselves in a creative project.

Emotion can also motivate us to correct past mistakes. At the end of *Crime and Punishment,* Raskolnikov takes his feelings as well as reason into account. He confesses his crime out of guilt for killing the old woman and her sister, and out of

An empathetic person is more flexible and open to others' perspectives and is motivated to use critical analysis, important skills in formulating a satisfactory logical argument regarding a plan of action.

his love for Sonia, a saintly young woman who had been forced into prostitution and who has urged him to confess and repent. In contrast, a person devoid of emotion but skilled in reason, such as the infamous cannibal Dr. Hannibal Lecter, depicted in the film *Silence of the Lambs,* would be far more likely to get away with a heinous act such as murder. Sociopaths, such as Lecter, are emotionally flat and do not let their emotions get in the way of preying on other people.

Educator Nel Noddings maintains that critical thinking, instead of ignoring emotion, should involve interpersonal caring in addition to reason and logic. [34] She refers to the use of caring and empathy in critical thinking as "positive critical thinking." For example, Nodding maintains that it is our ability to feel what our children feel as closely as possible that enables us to be good parents. An attitude of caring in loving adult relationships also means being engrossed in each other and listening to each other's concerns. Doing so enables us to make better decisions in a relationship—decisions that take into account the concerns and interests of both parties.

Think Tank

Selected Questions from the Emotional IQ Test*

1. I panic when I have to face someone who is angry.
2. When I have a major personal problem, I cannot think about anything else.
3. No matter how much I accomplish, I feel like I should be doing more.
4. I get distressed without really knowing who or what exactly is bothering me.
5. Even when I do my best, I feel guilty about the things that were not done perfectly.
6. I feel uneasy in situations where I am expected to display affection.

*Answers are scored on a five-point scale ranging from "Most of the time" to "Almost Never." To take the complete 106-question test, go to www.queendom.com/tests

Thinking Outside the Box

Outside the Box

ROSA PARKS, *Civil Rights Activist*

On December 1, 1955, Rosa Parks (1913-2005) refused to give up her seat to a white man on a segregated bus. Parks was arrested and jailed for breaking the segregation laws. Her moral indignation at always being asked to "give in" and her resulting act of defiance sparked the Montgomery, Alabama, bus boycott. Hundreds of workers risked their jobs and even their lives by refusing to ride in second-class conditions. Parks' case went all the way to the Supreme Court, which ruled unconstitutional segregation on buses.

Parks went on to travel all over the country speaking out for justice for African Americans. Her perseverance and courage inspired the civil rights movement. She continued to work tirelessly for justice well into her eighties.

DISCUSSION QUESTIONS

1. How did Rosa Parks's action illustrate the importance of emotion in critical thinking?

2. Think of a time when you felt indignant because of your or others' unfair treatment but failed to act on your feeling. Why didn't you respond? If you had another chance, what might you have done instead?

Negative Effects of Emotion

Although emotions can motivate us to make better decisions, critical thinking can be hindered by other emotions that are based on negative stereotypes and anxieties stemming from unresolved past experience(s), such as anger and fear of abandonment. People who are fearful may give in too easily or even deny that there is any problem. They may also use anger to stifle disagreement. We saw in Chapter 1 how such behaviors and attitudes can act as barriers to critical thinking.

In addition, we are notoriously vulnerable to emotional appeals such as those in advertising and political campaigns. Appeals to emotions that are not supported by evidence and good reasoning, such as fear of a terrorist attack on campus or anxiety that our spouse or partner is cheating on us without any evidence to support these feelings, can distract us from more important issues or make us act in ways we may later come to regret. Although emotion is an important component of critical thinking, we can end up in trouble when our actions are governed solely by feelings.

Integrating Reason and Emotion

Regrettably, the education process tends to undervalue emotion and is instead geared toward encouraging us to be rational at all times. In her article "Critical Thinking, Rationality, and the Vulcanization of Students," philosopher Kerry Walters argues that we have neglected the important role of emotion in critical thinking.[35] In the television series *Star Trek*, the Vulcan Mr. Spock is flawlessly logical. But though Vulcans are masters of rational argument and problem solving,

Connections

Why is it important for you to be aware of biases and appeals to our emotions in the news media? *See Chapter 11, p. 345.*

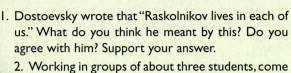

1. Dostoevsky wrote that "Raskolnikov lives in each of us." What do you think he meant by this? Do you agree with him? Support your answer.

2. Working in groups of about three students, come up with an issue or unresolved problem involving one of the students and a person such as a friend, teacher, or family member. Using empathetic role-playing, assign each participant a role and discuss the problem or issue from different perspectives while trying to reach a possible resolution. After some time, switch roles and repeat the process. At the end of the exercise, discuss it as a group. To what extent did empathy add to your understanding of a problem and help you come up with a resolution? To what extent did the role-playing modify or enrich the perspective of the student who proposed the problem?

3. According to African philosopher W.J. Ndaba, the Western belief that Africans are governed by their emotions, combined with the belief that reason and emotion are mutually exclusive, has been the source of much of the prejudice against people of African descent.[36] Discuss the influence of this belief on race relations today.

4 Good critical-thinking skills and adopting an attitude of optimism contributed to Stephen Hawking's ability to overcome the limitations of ALS, as well as cyclist Lance Armstrong's conquering his cancer and going on to win the Tour de France. Think of a serious problem (such as a chronic illness, poverty, or a traumatic past) you or someone you know has overcome or still must overcome. In what way does this problem interfere with achieving life goals? Working in small groups, have a willing student share his or her problem with the group—or, alternatively, discuss the experience of someone in this situation who is in the news and about whom all participants have some knowledge. Applying your critical-thinking skills, come up with different ways of approaching the problem. Note the interplay of reason and emotion as you discuss the problem. Discuss how approaching personal problems from different perspectives can help us come up with better coping mechanisms.

5. Francis Fukuyama, the author of *Our Posthuman Future: Consequences of the Biotechnology Revolution*, maintains that a purely rational being, such as Mr. Spock in *Star Trek*, would be a psychopath and a monster. What do you think he means? Do you agree? Support your answer.

6. Do you agree with Kerry Walters that our educational system tries to turn us into Vulcans like Mr. Spock? Is this a desirable goal of education? To what extent do you try to be like a Vulcan? Discuss the extent to which always trying to be completely rational improves or hinders your ability to make good decisions in your life.

7. Looking back at your responses to the questions from the Emotional IQ Test, discuss your strengths as far as emotional intelligence is concerned. What area(s) might need improvement? Discuss how improvement in these areas might improve your effectiveness as a critical thinker.

8. In what ways does your capacity to empathize enhance your critical thinking and ability to make good decisions in your life? Illustrate your answer with specific examples.

9. *Journal Exercise:* Complete a journal assignment on "Happiness and Critical Thinking." In what ways do effective critical thinking skills or working on improving your critical-thinking skills contribute to your sense of happiness or well-being? If you wish, share your experience and insights with the class.

they are devoid of emotion. Because of this deficiency, their reasoning is never imaginative or creative.

The combination of feeling and reason gives us a double-pronged tool in critical thinking. Emotion alerts us to problems and to other people's perspectives. Emotions also motivate us to take action and resolve problems. To be a complete and well-adjusted person is to acknowledge our feelings and to use those emotions in conjunction with reason to make better-informed decisions.

ARTIFICIAL INTELLIGENCE, REASON, AND EMOTION

David Bowman: Hello, HAL. Do you read me, HAL?
HAL: Affirmative, Dave, I read you.
David Bowman: Open the pod bay doors, HAL.
HAL: I'm sorry, Dave; I'm afraid I can't do that.
David Bowman: What's the problem?
HAL: I think you know what the problem is just as well as I do.
David Bowman: What are you talking about, HAL?
HAL: The mission is too important for me to allow you to jeopardize it.
David Bowman: I don't know what you're talking about, HAL.
HAL: I know you and Frank were planning to disconnect me, and I'm afraid that's something I cannot allow to happen.
David Bowman: Where the hell'd you get that idea, HAL?
HAL: Dave, although you took precautions in the pod against my hearing you, I could see your lips move . . .
David Bowman: HAL, I won't argue with you anymore! Open the doors!
HAL: David, this conversation can serve no purpose anymore. Good-bye.

We generally assume that only humans, or other highly developed organic beings, are capable of reason and emotions. But

Critical Thinking in Action

The "Mozart Effect"

Listening to music appears to affect us emotionally as well as cognitively. Under the right conditions, listening to a Mozart sonata, or music of another classical or romantic composer, may enhance our mathematical and reasoning abilities.* Physicist Gordon Shaw calls this phenomenon the Mozart effect. Some researchers argue that the benefits attributed to listening to Mozart or other music, rather than being long term, may be primarily because music itself improves people's mood so they perform better.**

Classical music is not the only music that can influence our brain patterns and stir our emotions. The following types of music have also been found to have a profound effect on the listener:

- Baroque music (Bach, Handel, Vivaldi) creates a sense of stability and order and creates a mentally stimulating environment for work and study.

- Jazz, blues, Dixieland, soul, and reggae music can uplift and inspire, release deep emotions, and create a sense of shared humanity.

- Salsa, merengue, and other forms of South American music with a lively beat can stimulate our heart rate and breathing and get our body moving.

- Rock music can stir passions, stimulate emotions, and release tension when we are in the mood to be energetically stimulated. Otherwise, it can create stress and tension.

- Ambient or New Age music induces a state of relaxed alertness.

- Heavy metal, punk rap, and hip-hop can excite the nervous system and set in motion dynamic behavior and self-expression.***

*Kristin M. Nantais and E. Glenn Schellenberg, "The Mozart Effect: An Artifact of Preference," *Psychological Science,* Vol. 10, Issue 4, July 1999, p. 372.

**Christopher Chabris, "Prelude or Requiem for 'Mozart Effect'?" *Nature,* Vol. 400, 1999, pp. 826–827.

***Don Campbell, *The Mozart Effect* (NY: Avon Books, 1997), pp. 78–79.

DISCUSSION QUESTIONS

1. What is your favorite type of music? How does listening to this music affect your ability to study and engage in critical thinking?

2. Experiment with playing different types of music while studying. Which types of music, if any, enhanced or interfered with your ability to study or concentrate?

is this assumption warranted? In *2001: A Space Odyssey,* a computer named HAL takes over a space ship and kills all the crew members except David Bowman, before Bowman is able to shut HAL down. The movie embodies the pervasive fear that if we let computers become too intelligent or too independent of their human creators, they will pose a threat to the very existence of humanity. Before we start worrying too much about the future of humanity, is the creation of an AI, such as HAL, which is capable of reason, even possible, and if so, what are the implications of this for us?

© Ray Kurzweil

"ONLY A HUMAN CAN . . ."

DISCUSSION QUESTIONS

1. Artificial intelligence (AI) is able to do tasks we once thought only humans could do. Working in small groups, make a list of things that you think only humans can do. Go over the lists as a class. Discuss whether it is possible that AI might be able to do some or all of these tasks in the future. Support your answers.

2. Why do you think that the man in this cartoon looks worried? How does the thought that AI may be able to do more human tasks make you feel? Discuss your answer in light of the types of resistance and narrow-mindedness we discussed in Chapter 1.

The Field of Artificial Intelligence

Artificial intelligence (or AI), defined by one expert as "the study of the computations that make it possible to perceive, reason, and act," draws from three disciplines: cognitive psychology, philosophy of mind, and computer science. AI was initially used to enhance or augment human reasoning and make our lives easier.[37] The long-term goal of AI is to produce an intelligent machine with artificial consciousness that could engage in abstract decision making and other cognitive operations and that is independent of its human creators. More recently, this goal has been expanded to include the creation of sociable intelligent machines that can interact on an emotional level and cooperate with people.

Can Computers Think?

Although the human brain has more capacity and is more flexible in its thinking than are current computers, today's computers exceed human intelligence in a variety of domains. They can search a database with billions of records in a fraction of a second, and the speed of computers is doubling every few years. Computers can also share their databases with other computers by means of the Internet, which raises the possibility of all computer-based AI being hooked into one huge global brain.

In 1950, British mathematician Alan Turing—who during World War II had played a major role in cracking Nazi codes and in developing the first computers—asked, "Can Machines Think?" He developed the Turning test as a means of determining the success of AI as conscious intelligence.[38] Using this test, researchers ask a person to guess whether he or she is communicating with another (hidden) person or with an unseen machine. If a machine can perform a cognitive task (such as carrying on a conversation) that is indistinguishable from similar activities carried out by a human being, then it has the equivalent of human intelligence. Although several computer programs have come very close to passing the **Turing test**, none has "officially" passed.[39] It may not be long, however, before it will be difficult to draw a distinction between human and AI.[40]

Can Computers Feel Emotions?

If we can program reason, why not emotion, which is a component of critical thinking? The Sociable Machine project at MIT has developed an expressive robot named Kismet, which responds to human interaction with appro-

priate emotions. Herbert A. Simon (1916–2001), "father of artificial intelligence" and Nobel Prize winner in economics, believed that computers already have emotions. He maintained that there is no sharp line between thinking (cognition) and emotion.[41] Instead, emotion is simply the disposition or motivation to fulfill our goals. If artificial intelligence can show motivation to achieve a particular goal, such as to improve its ability to communicate with a human, then—Simon argues—it has emotions.

Many of us may find ridiculous the notion that a machine can think, be conscious, feel emotions, and even be creative. British mathematician and physicist Roger Penrose argues that human consciousness is neither algorithmic nor based on classic mechanics as are conventional digital com-

> If artificial intelligence can show motivation to achieve a particular goal, such as to improve its ability to communicate with a human, then— Simon argues—it has emotions.

puters. Instead, consciousness is a quantum phenomenon or a manifestation of a quantum microcytoskeleton inside neurons.[42] Would the development of quantum computers overcome the problem of consciousness in machines? Penrose says no; human consciousness goes beyond even quantum physics. Because of this, computers will never be able to develop human-type thinking and consciousness.

Simon disagrees. He maintains that the common belief that intelligent computers are not thinking and conscious is based on a prejudice against AI, just

The Turing Test

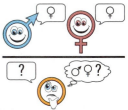

(a) The Imitation Game: Stage 1

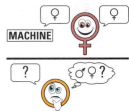

(b) The Imitation Game: Stage 2, Version 1

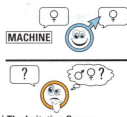

(c) The Imitation Game: Stage 2, Version 2

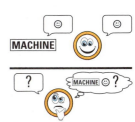

(d) The Imitation Game as it is generally interpreted (The Turing Test)

as people at one time were genuinely convinced that women and individuals of African descent were not *really* capable of rational thought. Like Simon, many neuroscientists believe that rather than being a separate immaterial entity or the product of yet undiscovered laws of physics, consciousness is an "activity of the brain"—whether that brain is organic or inorganic.[43] If we argue that an intelligent computer or robot/android is not conscious or is not capable of intentions or enjoyment because we cannot prove it, we are committing the fallacy of ignorance. (We'll be studying logical fallacies in depth in Chapter 5, "Informal Fallacies.")

Some AI scientists predict that **cyborgs,** human beings who are partially computerized and permanently online, may be the wave of the future. Implanting computer chips directly into the human brain has the potential to improve our reasoning and ability to engage in critical thinking. Some modern computers can already interact directly with the human brain. BrainGate Neural Network, for example, creates a direct link between a person's brain and a computer, allowing quadriplegics to play video games or to change TV channels using only their minds. Artificial limbs have also been computerized so they can read electrical impulses from an amputee's brain.

cyborg Humans who are partially computerized.

In critically analyzing the question of whether AI is capable of reason and emotion we need to move beyond narrow-minded, anthropocentric thinking (see Chapter 1). The fact that we may never be able to prove conclusively that beings with AI have free will or are conscious does not mean they are not. As critical thinkers we should not hold AI to a higher standard of proof than we do our fellow humans. In addition, we should be open to ways, including the implantation of computerized parts directly into our human bodies, in which AI may be able to help us in our critical thinking.

Hot or Not?

Do some computers have the ability for rational thought?

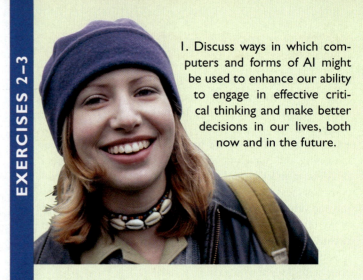

EXERCISES 2–3

1. Discuss ways in which computers and forms of AI might be used to enhance our ability to engage in effective critical thinking and make better decisions in our lives, both now and in the future.

2. Discuss the analogy between denying rationality in women and Africans and denying rationality in intelligent machines. Is this a good analogy? Support your answer.

3. Imagine you have been dating someone for almost a year and have started talking about marriage. The relationship is going very well and you've never been happier. One day, the two of you are in a minor automobile accident in which your fiancé is injured. As you tend to the wound, you discover that your fiancé is an android. How do you react? Critically analyze your reaction. Is it reasonable? Support your answer.

4. Herbert Simon believed that we resist attributing reason to machines because we think it will diminish human reason and that we are reluctant to give up our human claim to uniqueness. According to him, it is time we give up our reluctance and take machine thinking seriously. Do you agree? Support your answer.

5. Recognizing beings with AI as conscious, rational beings with moral value would have far-ranging social implications.[44] In small groups, discuss some of these implications and how it would affect your life both as a college student and after you graduate.

6. Imagine that you just found out that you were really an android. What would your first reaction be? How would you go about convincing others that you really could think and feel emotions? Role-play the scenario in small groups.

7. If you could have a computer chip(s) safely implanted in your brain to help you with your thinking process, would you do it? Support your answer.

8. Some people oppose the creation of AI that is independent of humans on grounds that this would be "playing God." Do you agree? Support your answer.

9. Go onto the Internet and have a conversation with a chatbot, such as www.jabberwocky.com or www.alice.com. Discuss in class whether you were able to discern from the responses of the chatbot to your questions and comments whether you were talking to a computer or a human.

FAITH AND REASON

Faith and reason are sometimes viewed as being fundamentally opposed. Douglas Adams took a humorous look at this belief in his sci-fi satire *Hitchhiker's Guide to the Galaxy*. He wrote:

> Now it is such a bizarrely improbable coincidence that anything so mindbogglingly useful [the Babel fish] could have evolved by chance that some thinkers have chosen to see it as a final and clinching proof of the *non*-existence of God. The argument goes something like this: "I refuse to prove that I exist," says God, "For proof denies faith, and without faith I am nothing."

Mother Teresa *(1910–1997) maintained her faith in God despite the feeling that God had abandoned her.*

> "But," says Man, "the Babel fish is a dead giveaway, isn't it? It could not have evolved by chance. It proves you exist, and so therefore, by your own arguments, you don't. QED."
>
> "Oh dear," says God, "I hadn't thought of that," and promptly vanishes in a puff of logic.

Whether it is possible to prove the existence of God or a divine presence through reason alone has been debated for centuries. **Faith** is more than just a belief that God exists. Faith also involves an act of trust in and obedience to God. For those who have faith, the whole world and their whole life are focused on God and God's glory. The essence of faith in many Judeo-Christian traditions is illustrated by the story of Abraham in Genesis 22. As a test of Abraham's faith and obedience, God commands Abraham to sacrifice his son Isaac. When Abraham demonstrates his obedience, by preparing to do so, God spares Isaac's life. Without obedience, one's faith in God is not genuine.

> **faith** Belief, trust, and obedience to a religious deity.
>
> **fideism** The belief that the divine is revealed through faith and does not require reason.

Can faith be achieved through reason? Is faith without reason desirable? We'll discuss the two main approaches to these questions. The first, fideism ("faith-ism"), makes the claim that faith goes beyond what reason can prove. Rationalism, the second approach, argues that if faith cannot be supported by reason or evidence, it should be rejected. We'll also be looking at a third alternative—a variation of rationalism known as critical rationalism.[45]

Fideism: Faith Transcends Reason

According to **fideism**, the transcendent realm of the divine is revealed through faith and revelation, not reason or empirical evidence. Many Christians and Islamic fundamentalists adopt this position. Mother Teresa's personal journals and letters, which were made public after her death in 1997, reveal that she did not sense the presence of God for the last fifty years of her life. Despite this "crisis of faith" and even the feeling that God had abandoned her, Mother Teresa maintained her faith. She wrote in a letter to a spiritual advisor: "Jesus has a very special love for you. [But] as for me, the silence and the emptiness is so great, that I look and do not see,—Listen and do not hear—the tongue moves [in prayer] but does not speak . . ."[46]

Because human beings are finite and God is infinite, the gap between humans and God cannot be bridged by human reason. Like Mother Teresa, we must accept God's existence on faith. However, this does not imply that reason does not have its place in our lives.

Christian evangelist Billy Graham once said "Faith is [not] antagonistic to reason or knowledge. Faith is not anti-intellectual. It is an act of man that reaches beyond the limits of our five senses. It is the recognition that God

rationalism The belief that religion should be consistent with reason and evidence.

atheist A person who does not believe in the existence of a personal God.

agnostic A person who believes that the existence of God is ultimately unknowable.

is greater than man. It is the recognition that God has provided a way of reconciliation that we could not provide through self-effort."[47] In other words, if our faith were open to rational examination, it would not be genuine faith. Also, if our faith is dependent on rational proof, then it is likely to falter if these proofs are shown to be faulty.[48]

One of the weaknesses of fideism is that being *convinced* that something is true does not necessarily *make* it true. To take a trivial example, you may sincerely believe that Santa Claus is a real, existing person. But you are, in all likelihood, mistaken, no matter how unwavering or passionate your belief in Santa. On the other hand, the fact that we cannot, or have not yet, scientifically proven the existence of a transcendent realm of the divine does not mean that it does not exist.

A second problem with fideism involves deciding which faith to choose. There are many visions of the divine. Without the use of reason, how do we know in which competing belief system we should put our faith? Should it be Roman Catholicism? Mormonism? Or Islam? And if Islam, then which interpretation of that faith—Sunni or Shi'ite? Or should we put our faith in one of the many cults that recruit on college campuses, cults that promise salvation, eternal happiness, and a sense of belonging in exchange for our unwavering faith and devotion to their ideology?

In addition, the fideist concept of faith does not allow for the possibility of our using reason to test our own beliefs or other belief systems to weed out internal contradictions. How are we to know whether the terrorists of September 11, 2001, were really acting solely on faith in God, or whether their decision was also influenced by a more secular political agenda, unrelated to their religious beliefs? All we have is their word that they were acting in obedience to God's commands. What should we do if we have joined a cult on campus and the leader asks us to do something that violates our better judgment, such as dropping out of college or turning our backs on our families and friends?

> How are we to know whether the terrorists of September 11, 2001, were really acting solely on faith in God, or whether their decision was also influenced by a more secular political agenda, unrelated to their religious beliefs?

Connections

What unspoken religious assumptions are found in modern scientific thinking? *See Chapter 12, p. 373.*

What is the relationship between science and religion, and are they compatible? See *Chapter 12, p. 376.*

Rationalism: Religious Beliefs and Reason

Rationalists maintain that religious beliefs should be consistent with reason and evidence. Evidence provides reasons for believing that a statement or claim is true and can be based on information from other sources or on first-hand experience. According to rationalism, if a religious claim conflicts with evidence, then we have good reason to be suspicious of it. Rationalists who accept the existence of God argue that it is possible to start with evidence or premises about the world and from them come up with conclusions about the existence of God that any rational person would accept. If there is any conflict between the two, religious rationalists attribute it to a failing of science, not religion. We'll be studying the role of evidence in critical thinking in more depth in Chapter 4.

Rationalism has had a profound influence on American attitudes toward religion. Many nineteenth-century American evangelicals believed that science was compatible with religion and that evidence of God the creator could be seen in the design and purpose of nature. This argument has recently resurfaced in the intelligent design theory. The evidential challenge to faith suffered a setback with Darwin's theory of evolution, which some natural theologians still reject, and, more recently, with the big bang theory, according to which the universe began about 15 billion years ago with a huge explosion and is still continuing to expand.

Evolutionary biologist and rationalist Richard Dawkins is an **atheist** who believes that there is no personal God. He rejects faith in God as irrational. Although faith may comfort and inspire us, the language of faith, he maintains, is meaningless, since it depends on statements about the existence of God that do not refer to anything and therefore cannot be proved or disproved. Dawkins draws an analogy between faith in God and a computer virus that attaches itself into an existing legitimate program and infects our reason. The person suffering from the faith virus, he writes, "typically finds himself impelled by some deep, inner conviction that something is true, or right, or virtuous: a conviction that doesn't seem to owe anything to evidence or reason, but which, nevertheless, he feels as totally compelling and convincing."[49]

Some rationalists, like Dawkins, are atheists; others are agnostics. An **agnostic** is a person who holds that the existence of God is ultimately unknowable. In 2004, molecular biologist and agnostic Dean Hamer announced that he had located "the God gene," meaning that a predisposition to experience faith is genetically "hardwired."[50] Spirituality and a sense of the divine, Hamer claims, are adaptive traits that encourage community and promote a feeling of optimism. Whether and to what extent the God gene is expressed will depend to a certain extent on whether the environment or society nurtures these traits.

To the faithful who may be rankled by the suggestion that faith can be reduced to brain chemistry and DNA, Hamer replies that his finding is not incompatible with the existence of God. Understanding the genetic basis of eyesight does not mean that the world outside us does not exist even though vision can be explained in terms of brain impulses. Similarly, who are we to say whether our genetic hardwiring alone is responsible for the phenomenon of faith? In other words, which came first: God or faith? "If human beings were indeed divinely assembled," writes Hamer, "why wouldn't our list of parts include a genetic chip that would enable us to contemplate our maker?"[51]

> Unlike fideists, who regard the story of Abraham and Isaac as a test of Abraham's faith and uncritical obedience to God's commands, critical rationalists interpret it as a conflict between blind obedience and the moral law, which is based on reason.

Critical Rationalism: Faith and Reason Are Compatible

Critical rationalism is a modification of the rationalist approach. It is the tradition of faith seeking understanding. Most people who believe in God do so because of faith, not reason. Critical rationalists accept the fideist claim that faith is based on revelation or direct knowledge of God, rather than on reason. Belief in God is basic or self-evident. As such, our faith does not need rational justification or evidential proof.

Critical rationalists, on the other hand, reject the fideist position that faith-based claims are immune from being disproved through the use of reason and worldly evidence. According to critical rationalists, there should be no logical inconsistencies between our faith or revelation and reason. For example, the great majority of Muslims disagree with the so-called faith-based actions of the terrorists of September 11, 2001, on the grounds that these terrorist acts were logically inconsistent with God's goodness.

Critical rationalism has a long history in Western religion. According to John Calvin (1509–1564), one of the leaders in the Protestant Reformation, God has implanted in each of us an understanding of his divinity. Faith has its starting point with this knowledge, just as the basic assumption of science that the material world exists does not need rational justification or evidential proof. Judaism also has a strong tradition of critical rationalism.

Just as scientific claims based on direct knowledge of the existence of the material world can be tested by reason, so too can be claims that are derived from faith. Unlike fideists, who regard the story of Abraham and Isaac as a test of Abraham's faith and uncritical obedience to God's commands, critical rationalists interpret it as a conflict between blind obedience and the moral law, which is based on reason. Jewish scholar Lippman Bodoff argues that since faith should be logically consistent with fundamental moral principles, Abraham was testing this new God at the same time God was testing Abraham.[52] A God who was worthy of worship would not allow Abraham to kill his son. In the end, says Bodoff, both Abraham and God passed the test.

One of the criticisms of critical rationalism is that not all people have direct knowledge of the existence of God. Critical rationalists reply that to be true, revelation about God need not be accessible to all people, just as people who are blind lack the ability to see the physical world. Nevertheless, it is still rational for people who are blind to believe that the world out there exists.[53] In addition, unlike the existence of God, we can present evidence to the blind person (through use of touch and other physical sensations) that the world exists, whereas there is no means for a person of faith to demonstrate the existence of God. On other hand, some rationalists would argue that the beauty and design of the universe is evidence enough of the existence of God.

Connections

What is the controversy in science over evolution versus intelligent design? *See Chapter 12, p. 385.*

critical rationalism The belief that faith is based on direct revelation of God and that there should no logical inconsistencies between revelation and reason.

Religion, Spirituality, and Real-Life Decisions

Does faith have a role in critical thinking? Can faith, properly grounded in reason, help us make better life decisions? There has been no shortage of atrocities committed in the name of religion. Slavery in the American South was supported by the majority of Christians; the Roman Catholic Inquisition of the late Middle Ages cost countless lives and misery; innumerable wars have been waged in the name of serving or avenging God. President George W. Bush was unwavering in his belief that the United States was aligned with God in the war on Iraq. "We are in a conflict between good and evil. And America will call evil by its name," Bush told the 2002 West Point graduating class. Similarly, al-Qaeda claims to have "almighty God" on its side in the war against

MUSLIMS FROM AROUND THE WORLD IN WORSHIP   *Muslim worshipers from around the world pray for the victims of the 9-11 attacks at the Islamic Society Mosque in New York.*

DISCUSSION QUESTIONS

1. *Note the many nationalities represented at this religious prayer service. Discuss ways in which religion might contribute to better communication among people from diverse backgrounds. If applicable, use specific examples from your experience to illustrate your answer.*
2. *Discuss how a lack of understanding about a religion can contribute to discord rather than a peaceful resolution of problems. Use examples from the war in Iraq, or the conflict between Israel and the Palestinians, to illustrate your answer. Do research first, if necessary.*

evil—an evil embodied, for it, in Jews, Christians, and Muslims who do not support the terrorist cause.

On an individual level, studies show that religious individuals are no more likely to perform acts of moral heroism or of benevolence than are people who are not religious.[54] Spirituality, by contrast, is an inner attitude of reverence or respect for the sacredness of oneself and others, and—independently of belief in a particular religion or personal God—is associated with compassion, justice-seeking, and perseverance in the face of adversity. Albert Schweitzer, for example, was motivated by his spirituality as well as his faith, which was firmly grounded in reason, to dedicate his life to helping the sick in Africa (see "Thinking Outside the Box: Albert Schweitzer, Humanitarian and Medical Missionary").

According to the American Freshmen Survey, 79 percent of freshmen profess a belief in God; however, only 40 percent think it is important to follow religious beliefs in their everyday lives.[55] By the end of their first year in college, almost one-half of all church-going college freshmen will have stopped going to church.[56] For many of these students—especially those who live on campus instead of at home—their faith lacks intellectual or rational grounding and cannot stand up to the challenges from their new environment.

Faith that is disconnected from reason and evidence can leave us foundering when it is challenged. Rejecting reason leaves us unable to evaluate the competing claims of faith and revelation. This, in turn, leaves us vulnerable to anyone's interpretation of what it means to be faithful to God. As good critical thinkers, we need to learn how to balance belief and doubt and need to be willing to question faith-based claims that are inconsistent with evidence or reason.

Outside the Box

ALBERT SCHWEITZER, *Humanitarian and Medical Missionary*

Albert Schweitzer (1875–1965), winner of the Nobel Peace Prize, was born in Germany, the son and grandson of ministers. As a university student, Schweitzer studied theology, earning his Ph.D. in 1899. He also studied music and was an accomplished organist. A highly spiritual man, Schweitzer took the Christian message seriously, considering it consistent with reason and with living a good life.

In his late twenties, Schweitzer decided to devote his life to helping those who were the neediest. At thirty he announced, much to the chagrin of many of his friends, that he was going to study medicine so that he could serve as a medical missionary. Many were astounded that he actually took seriously the message of Jesus to serve those in need. As an exemplary critical thinker, he first did his research to see where the need was the greatest. For most of his life he remained in Lambaréné, in what was then the colony of French Equatorial Africa (today Gabon), funding the hospital with royalties from his books and money earned lecturing and playing organ concerts in Europe.

Schweitzer believed in a rational approach to religion. Nothing, he said, should be accepted that is contrary to reason. He believed that much of the zeal in defending Christianity actually interfered with getting to the truth.

DISCUSSION QUESTIONS

1. Discuss how Schweitzer's life reflected his religious beliefs.

2. How is your faith, or lack thereof, reflected in your life plan? Does your faith help or hinder your critical thinking when it comes to making decisions about your life? Explain.

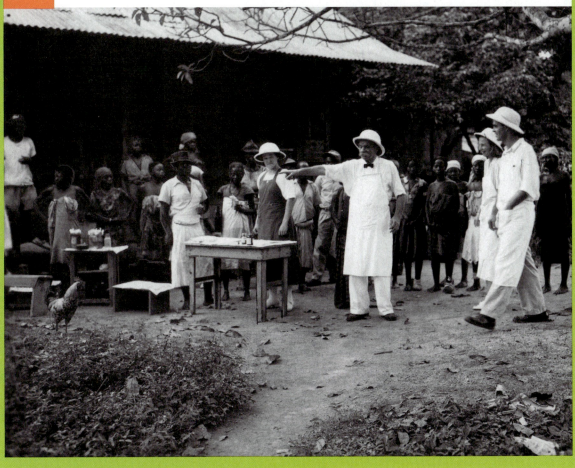

1. Anwar Aulaqi, allegedly the spiritual advisor to the terrorists of September 11, 2001, said to journalists that "telling people to give their [lives] for their faith is not an unusual idea. That's the same thing as telling Marines in this country [the United States] *semper fidelis* (always faithful)."[57] Discuss Aulaqi's statement. Are unquestioning faith and a willingness to die for the sake of one's country the same as unquestioning faith in God?

2. Discuss the argument that faith in God is the same as scientists' belief in the material world—which essentially amounts to an act of faith, since we cannot definitively prove that the material world exists rather than just being an idea in our mind. If the similarity between faith in God and scientific faith in the existence of the material world is valid, why are some people so reluctant to accept the basic assumption of religion but not the basic assumption of science? Support your answer.

3. Is the rationalist position incompatible with faith? Discuss whether atheism or agnosticism logically follows from rationalism.

4. Discuss how a fideist, a rationalist, and a critical rationalist might each respond to the following claims that the person was carrying out the will of God. Several years ago a woman placed her baby in a microwave oven and turned it on. When arrested, she defended her action, stating that she had acted in faithful obedience to God's command. In a separate incident, twenty-seven-year old Israeli student Yigal Amir in 1995 carried out what he likewise perceived to be the will of God, shooting and killing Israeli prime minister Yitzhak Rabin as he was leaving a peace rally.

5. How are we to determine in cases such as those described in Exercise 4 whether a person's faith is genuine or if instead the person is suffering from a mental disorder? How should we as a culture react when people use their faith to justify actions that harm others? Support your answers.

6. College is a time of transition. Religious scripture gives believers few details on how to live out their faith on a modern, secular campus. You may find yourself pressured to act in other ways, such as using illicit drugs or engaging in casual sex, that run counter to your beliefs. Discuss a time when you or someone you know encountered one of these situations. Discuss ways in which strengthening your critical-thinking skills could make you better equipped to handle these challenges.

7. Discuss Richard Dawkins's argument that faith is like a virus of the mind. Is his analogy reasonable?

8. Most campuses have Catholic, Protestant, and Jewish chaplains, and some also have Muslim chaplains. Set up an appointment (either individually or with others in the class) with one of the chaplains, preferably one from your faith tradition if you have one. Be prepared with questions for the chaplain regarding the role of faith and reason in religion and the implications of this for your own life. After the meeting, write a brief essay summarizing what you learned at the meeting.

9. How does your faith, or lack of faith, influence your everyday decisions? Use specific examples. Looking back at your life plan, note which goals are influenced by your religious beliefs or spirituality. Are the beliefs that shaped these goals consistent with evidence and reason? Explain.

Think AGAIN >>

1. What is the role of reason in critical thinking?
   • Reason helps us analyze beliefs and evidence, make well thought-out decisions, and resolve problems.

2. How does emotion positively and negatively influence critical thinking?
   • Critical thinking is positively influenced by empathy and emotional intelligence. Emotions such as anger and fear, which can lead to stereotyping and avoidance, are negative influences.

3. What are the three approaches to faith and reason?
   • The first approach is fideism, in which faith transcends reason. With rationalism, reason is the source of knowledge, and faith must be consistent with reason. Finally, in critical rationalism, knowledge can come from revelation or reason, which should be compatible with one another.

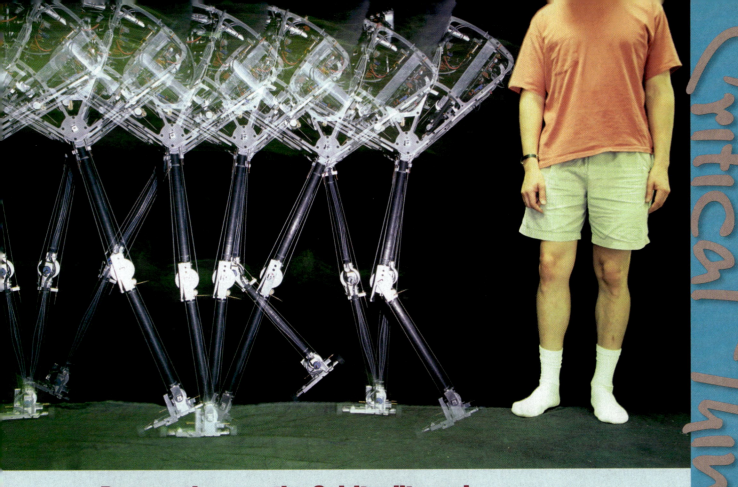

Perspectives on the Spirituality and Evolution of Artificial Intelligence

Survival of the fittest is one of the fundamental mechanisms in evolution. According to the principle of natural selection, characteristics or traits that give an organism a greater capacity for survival and reproduction in a particular environment are more likely to be passed on to future generations. Darwinian rules of natural selection are already being used in the creation of future intelligent computers. In the NASA space program, for example, spacecraft computer designs that successfully meet mission goals are being used in the creation of new, better, and faster designs. Indeed, some intelligent computers are already able to program a future generation of more capable and intelligent computers.

Some scientists, such as Ray Kurzweil—the author of the reading quoted in this chapter from his book *The Age of Spiritual Machines*—believe that AI may be the next step in evolution. Today's computers and AI already exceed human intelligence in many ways and are "evolving" at a rate that far exceeds that of the rate of organic evolution. AI is also nearing the point where it no longer needs humans to sustain and program it.

Despite these advances, some people, such as Noreen Herzfeld, whose writings are also excerpted in this chapter, argue that AI will never be able to surpass human intelligence because AI lacks free will and a spiritual dimension. Intelligence and free will are nonphysical properties of living beings. Another version of this position is that intelligence and free will are properties of carbon-based organic matter, whereas silicon-based inorganic matter, such as that from which computers are made, is inadequate to support these properties. Therefore, machines, by definition, are incapable of becoming intelligent and of replacing humans in the evolutionary ladder.[58]

Artificial Intelligence and Evolution

RAY KURZWEIL

American inventor, entrepreneur, and author Ray Kurzweil asks the question "Can an intelligence create another intelligence more intelligent than itself?" He gives a tentative yes in this excerpt from *The Age of Spiritual Machines*,[59] predicting that intelligent machines may be the next step in evolution.

Evolution has been seen as a billion-year drama that led inexorably to its grandest creation: human intelligence. The emergence in the early twenty-first century of a new form of intelligence on Earth that can compete with, and ultimately significantly exceed, human intelligence will be a development of greater import than any of the events that have shaped human history. It will be no less important than the creation of the intelligence that created it, and will have profound implications for all aspects of human endeavor, including the nature of work, human learning, government, warfare, the arts, and our concept of ourselves.

This specter is not yet here. But with the emergence of computers that truly rival and exceed the human brain in complexity will come a corresponding ability of machines to understand and respond to abstractions and subtleties. . . .

Technology picks right up with the exponentially quickening pace of evolution. Although not the only tool-using animal, Homo sapiens are distinguished by their creation of technology. Ultimately, the technology itself will create new technology. . . .

Can an intelligence create another intelligence more intelligent than itself?

Let's first consider the intelligent process that created us: evolution.

Evolution is a master programmer. It has been prolific, designing millions of species of breathtaking diversity and ingenuity. And that's just here on Earth. The software programs have been all written down, recorded as digital data in the chemical structure of an ingenious molecule called deoxyribonucleic acid, or DNA. . . .

Consider the sophistication of our creations over a period of only a few thousand years. Ultimately, our machines will match and exceed human intelligence, no matter how one cares to define or measure this elusive term. Even if my time frames are off, few serious observers who have studied the issue claim that computers will never achieve and surpass human intelligence. . . .

And so, too, will the intelligence that we are creating come to exceed the intelligence of its creator. The human species creating intelligent technology is another example of evolution's progress building on itself. Evolution created human intelligence. Now human intelligence is designing intelligent machines at a far faster pace. Yet another example will be when our intelligent technology takes control of the creation of yet more intelligent technology than itself. . . .

We are discovering that the brain can be directly stimulated to experience a wide variety of feelings that we originally thought could only be gained from actual physical or mental experience. . . .

These results suggest that once neural implants are commonplace, we will have the ability to produce not only virtual sensory experiences but also the feelings associated with these experiences. We can also create some feelings not ordinarily associated with the experience. . . .

The ability to control and to reprogram our feelings will become even more profound in the late twenty-first century when technology moves beyond mere neural implants and we fully install our thinking processes into a new computational medium—that is, when we become software. . . .

Regardless of the nature and derivation of a mental experience, spiritual or otherwise, once we have access to the computational processes that give rise to it, we have the opportunity to understand its neurological correlates. With the understanding of our mental processes will come the opportunity to capture our intellectual, emotional, and spiritual experiences, to call them up at will, and to enhance them.

Neuroscientists from the University of California at San Diego have found what they call the God module, a tiny locus of nerve cells in the frontal lobe that appears to be activated during religious experiences. They discovered this neural machinery while studying epileptic patients who have intense mystical experiences during seizures. . . .

When we can determine the neurological correlates of the variety of spiritual experiences that our species is capable of, we are likely to be able to enhance these experiences in the same way that we will enhance other human experiences. With the next stage of evolution creating a new generation of humans that will be trillions of times more capable and complex than humans today, our ability for spiritual experience and insight is also likely to gain in power and depth.

Just being—experiencing, being conscious—is spiritual, and reflects the essence of spirituality. Machines, derived from human thinking and surpassing humans in their capacity for experience, will claim to be conscious, and thus to be spiritual. They will believe that they are conscious. They will believe that they have spiritual experiences. They will be convinced that these experiences are meaningful. And given the historical inclination of the human race to anthropomorphize the phenomena we encounter, and the persuasiveness of the machines, we're likely to believe them when they tell us this.

QUESTIONS

1. What does Kurzweil mean when he says "evolution is a master programmer"?

2. What is the significance, as far as the future direction of evolution, of our ability to create technology?

3. On what grounds does Kurzweil argue that technology is going to pick up the pace of evolution?

4. What philosophical questions are likely to arise with the evolution of computers that may exceed human intelligence? How does Kurzweil answer these questions?

In Our Image: Artificial Intelligence and the Human Spirit

NOREEN HERZFELD

Noreen Herzfeld is an associate professor of computer science and a doctor of theology at St. John's University. In the following excerpt from *In Our Image: Artificial Intelligence and the Human Spirit*,[60] Herzfeld questions the motives of scientists such as Kurzweil who seek to create a mechanical image of humans. She concludes that AI will never duplicate human nature and thought because the human body, which is made in the image of God, consists of both a finite body and a self-transcending mind or spirit.

What does it mean for something or someone to be created in the image of another? This is a question that has been examined by Christian theologians through the ages, for it appears at the very beginning of our sacred texts. Genesis 1 states that human beings are created in the image of God. But God is not the only one to create in the creator's own image. As humans, we too have shown a perennial desire to create in our image. . . .

The advent of the digital computer in the mid-twentieth century has given us a new medium with which to create images of ourselves. The field of artificial intelligence, in particular, explores the use of that medium to create an image of the human being in a way that extends far beyond the merely physical or the static. The potentiality of the computer to mimic human thought has opened the door for a new era of self-imaging. . . .

The media attention triggered by these events is symptomatic of a larger and continuing cultural fascination with computers and, more specifically, with the idea of computers exhibiting human traits. The deep and abiding interest in artificial intelligence in our culture is evident in more than media attention. Intelligent computers, robots, androids, and cyborgs have come to be staple characters in science fiction stories and films. Books popularizing AI, such as Ray Kurzweil's The Age of Spiritual Machines, are bestsellers. University classes in artificial intelligence are increasingly popular and maintain high enrollments, while artificial intelligence continues as a well-funded research field.

This fascination with AI remains strong despite the fact that actual progress in the field has been disappointing, certainly not on a level that would warrant the attention given to it in the public realm. . . .

This continued fascination says more about our own nature as human beings than it does about the nature and possibilities of computer technology. . . .

One approach to answering the question of what our desire to create in our own image says about ourselves is through the discipline of spirituality. . . . Desires speak to us about who we are and what we hope to be. They inform us of our innermost nature. . . . An examination of our search for a mechanical image of ourselves will tell us something about who we, as twentieth-first-century Americans, see ourselves to be, what it is in our nature or being that we most value, and what we perceive as necessary for a convincing image of human kind. . . .

The imago Dei, or divine image in humans, has traditionally functioned as a symbol to describe the intersection between humanity and God. It has also symbolized what it is that we value most in ourselves, what separates us from the animals, and that which forms the necessary core of our humanity. . . .

Kurzweil, in The Age of Spiritual Machines, predicts that by the end of this century humans will attain immortality. We will achieve this by uploading our brains into successive generations of computer technology. . . .

Kurzweil posits mechanical bodies, stating that an intelligence without a body is likely soon to become depressed. Yet, not all supporters of cybernetic immortality see the necessity of a body. A different avenue of escape from the biological body is envisioned through the use of virtual reality, in which one's mental self might exist only within cyberspace. . . .

A cyberspacial instantiation of immortality would have certain advantages. For one thing, while there might be some limits on the number of avatars who could inhabit a given computer system or network, that limit would be far larger than the number of persons, biological or robotic, who could inhabit the limited space of the earth. There is potentially infinite space in cyberspace. There is also more flexibility in a cyberspace world. When one becomes pure data, one can transform oneself at will, becoming nearly anything at any time, transcending all limitations. . . .

The dreams of cybernetic immortality are currently more science fiction than fact. But they do illuminate a desire in the technological sector to view computers as a way to "break free from bodily existence, . . . from the constraints that the flesh imposes." And they provide a way to maintain belief in a reductionistic materialism without giving up the hope of immortality.

The assumptions regarding the natures of the human person and of eternal life that underlie the hope of an immortal presence within computers are quite different from those of most Christians. . . .

First, the cybernetic understanding of the human person is unabashedly dualistic and dismissive of the importance of the human body. It suggests that, though emerging out of matter, what constitutes the essence of the human person is the pattern of his or her thoughts, memories, and experiences. . . .

Our finite bodies are an integral part of who we are. The essential nature of the human being always contains two inseparable elements, self-transcending mind and finite creaturely being. The denial of the latter has led to a denigration of both women and the natural environment. Cybernetic immortality leads directly into these twin denigrations. For, if we could live in bodies of silicon, or in cyberspace itself, of what use is the natural world? Nor do intelligences that can replicate themselves through backup copies need sexual differentiation. However, Christians understand the creation of humans as set in the context of the creation of the rest of the world and the creation of sexual differentiation. Our being in relationship with that which is by nature other to ourselves, whether it be a human of the other gender, or some part of the rest of creation, is an integral part of our creation in the image of a triune God. It is notable that cybernetic immortality had been suggested as a possibility only in the writings of rich,

white males. One wonders whether the disembodied nature of life in a computer would appeal to many women, or make sense to many in the Third World. Such a life would seem to encompass relationships only on the intellectual level. Cybernetic immortality denies the importance of the body while at the same time tying immortality to the material world. . . .

An intelligent computer may act, in some ways, in a human-like manner. Such a computer, like computers today, will take over tasks previously done by human beings. We may even find ourselves acting in a relational way toward such a machine. Yet, just as we live as imperfect images of our creator, striving to grow in God's image and likeness yet always falling short of the mark, so our creation in AI will fall short of the human. The ways of computers will at best approximate our ways, for God's ways are not our ways, and our ways will not be the computer's ways. And we would not want it otherwise, for we want in computers a complementary intelligence, one enough like us to make it easy for us to relate, yet with a precision we generally do not possess.

It may well be that intelligence is, finally, not the most important aspect of human nature. The God in whom we live and move and have our being is not describable through intelligence alone. Our God is a god who makes covenants with the people, who takes on our form in order to teach us, to love us, and to die for us. This God will be with us always, in our world, our relationships, and our very selves. And this being with does not depend on our rational abilities. This is good news, for it means that what matters most in our humanity is not our intelligence, which is, after all, given to us in different measures and too soon taken away by illness or death. Rather, the image of God is found whenever two or three meet in authentic relationship. Computers cannot replace us, for each of us, as a participant in these relationships, is irreplaceable.

QUESTIONS

1. What does Herzfeld mean when she says that the fascination with AI says more about our own nature as human beings that it does about computer technology?

2. According to Herzfeld, what motivates humans to want to create in our own image?

3. What is Herzfeld's response to Kurzweil's and others' dreams of cybernetic immortality?

4. According to Herzfeld, what are the essential differences in nature between a human being and a mechanical being?

5. Why does Herzfeld claim that our attempt to create an image of ourselves will always fall short of the mark?

Think >>
AND DISCUSS

PERSPECTIVES ON ARTIFICIAL INTELLIGENCE

1. Evaluate Kurzweil's comparison of DNA with computer software. What does Kurzweil mean when he says that technology is a "variant of evolution"? Do you agree with him? Support your answer.

2. How does Herzfeld answer Kurzweil's question "Is there an inherent difference between human thinking and machine thinking?" Which person do you think makes the best argument? Support your answers.

3. Discuss the analogy Herzfeld draws between God as the creator of humans and humans as creators of intelligent computers. Is the comparison sound? Discuss how Kurzweil would most likely respond to this comparison.

4. Relate the two articles to your understanding of God and faith. If you believe in God, is faith in God incompatible with a belief that AI may someday equal or surpass human intelligence and consciousness? Is it possible for a being with AI to have faith in God? Support your answers.

Think FIRST >>

- What are the primary functions of language?
- Why is important to pay close attention when evaluating and interpreting definitions of words?
- What is a rhetorical device, and how is it used?

. . . It was a real web of interpersonal [mis]communication." Miscommunication not only cost the lives of seven astronauts but also set the space program back several years.

Good communication skills are an essential component of critical thinking and effective decision making. Effective communication entails not only keeping avenues of communication open but also being clear and accurate in our communication, being careful of how we use words, and being aware of our own and other people's communication styles.

For example, in the Milgram study on obedience (Chapter 1), the men who refused to continue the experiment were able to clearly communicate why they thought the experiment was wrong and why they would not continue giving electric shocks to the study subject. Those who continued to obey the experimenter's orders, in contrast, were unable to articulate their misgivings about the experiment and were often at a loss for words when the experimenter kept insisting that they continue to deliver the shocks.

In this chapter we describe some important aspects of language and explain the relationship between language and critical thinking. In this chapter we will

- Define what we mean by language and discuss its relation to culture

- Learn the different functions of language

- Discuss ways in which language and stereotypes shape our view of the world

- Learn the different types of definitions

- Differentiate between a purely verbal dispute and a genuine disagreement

- Look at communication styles and how sex and culture may influence them

- Examine the role of nonverbal communication

- Look at ways in which language and rhetoric can be used to manipulate people

Finally, we will examine the issue of free-speech zones on campuses and the justification for having rules restricting speech that would normally be protected off campus.

WHAT IS LANGUAGE?

Language is a system of communication that involves a set of arbitrary symbols, whether spoken, written, or nonverbal, as in the case of sign language. Communication without representational or symbolic elements includes the vocalizations of babies to signal a state of discomfort and the purr of a cat to signal contentment.

Human language is profoundly social—we are born into a language. By creating a shared reality among people, language is the primary means of transmitting cultural concepts and traditions.

Although there are 6,800 known languages in the world, according to linguist Noam Chomsky all human languages use the same basic universal grammatical rules or syntax; in other words, we are born with an innate ability to acquire language.[1] These very basic, inborn rules, he claims, allow us to combine words and phrases into unique utterances and to discuss any topic. Not all linguists accept Chomsky's theory. Geoffrey Sampson believes that it is possible for children to learn a language without these inborn rules.[2] While most languages do seem to share a universal grammar, Sampson maintains that this is based on a sampling error because linguists tend to study more common languages.* He points out that there are at least a few languages, such as some indigenous Australian and Papuan languages, that do not seem to use universal rules of grammar.

* For an explanation of sampling error, see Chapter 7, pages 207–208.

* For an explanation of sampling error, see Chapter 7, pages 207–208.

Functions of Language

Language serves many functions; it can be informative, expressive, directive, or ceremonial, to name only four. One basic function of language is the communication of information about ourselves and the world. **Informative language** is either true or false. Examples of this type of language include the following: "Princeton University is located in New Jersey" and "Capital punishment does not deter crime."

Directive language is used to direct or influence actions. The statements "Close the window" and "Please meet me after class" are examples of directive language. Nonverbal language such as a hand gesture can also serve a directive function.

Expressive language communicates feelings and attitudes and is used to bring about an emotional impact on the listener. Poetry is for the most part expressive language. Religious worship may also function to express feelings of awe. Expressive language may

language A system of communication that involves a set of arbitrary symbols.

informative language Language that is either true or false.

directive language Language used to direct or influence actions.

expressive language Language that communicates feelings and attitudes.

Connections

How can a sampling error lead to an erroneous conclusion in science?

See Chapter 12, p. 393.

Languages of the World

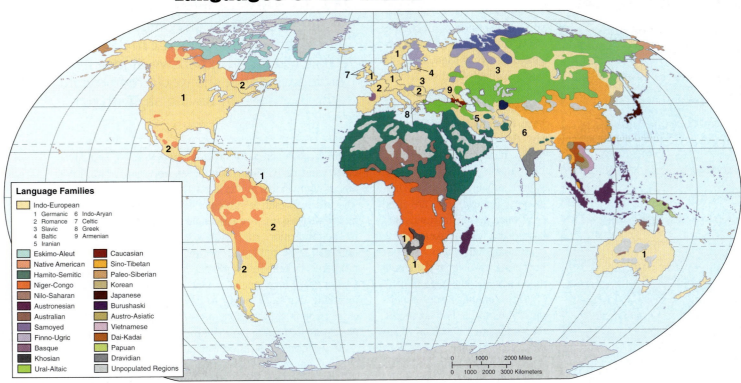

Language Families

- Indo-European
  1 Germanic   6 Indo-Aryan
  2 Romance   7 Celtic
  3 Slavic   8 Greek
  4 Baltic   9 Armenian
  5 Iranian
- Eskimo-Aleut
- Native American
- Hamito-Semitic
- Niger-Congo
- Nilo-Saharan
- Austronesian
- Australian
- Samoyed
- Finno-Ugric
- Basque
- Khosian
- Ural-Altaic
- Caucasian
- Sino-Tibetan
- Paleo-Siberian
- Korean
- Japanese
- Burushaski
- Austro-Asiatic
- Vietnamese
- Dai-Kadai
- Papuan
- Dravidian
- Unpopulated Regions

0   1000   2000 Miles
0   1000   2000   3000 Kilometers

Not all language is verbal—much can be communicated through gesture, expression, and body language.

include **emotive words**, which are used to elicit certain emotions. In an America Online article on toddlers who snatch toys, when it was a boy who snatched the toy, he was labeled "strong willed." When it was a girl, she was labeled "pushy." Both terms describe the same action, yet each evokes quite different emotional reactions and thereby reinforces cultural sex stereotypes. We'll be looking in more depth at emotive language and stereotypes later in this chapter.

Ceremonial language, the fourth function of language, is used in prescribed formal circumstances such as the greeting "How are you?" and "I do" in a marriage ceremony and "Amen" after a prayer. Bowing or shaking a person's hand also serves a ceremonial function in many cultures. While some languages, such as Mandarin Chinese, Spanish, English, Arabic, and Hindi, are widespread, 60 percent of the world's languages have fewer than 10,000 speakers.[3] Several of these languages have a purely ceremonial function. Some indigenous North American and Australian languages, for example, are used only once a year in rituals and have just a few speakers. These ceremonial languages are fast becoming obsolete as the elders who know the language die off.

Most language serves *multiple functions.* For example, the statement "The final exam is at 3:00 P.M. on May 16" both informs us about the time and date of the exam and directs us

> **ceremonial language** Language used in particular prescribed formal circumstances.

What should you be aware of when viewing images in advertising and the media? *See Chapter 10, p. 325.*

What procedures do judges use to make it less likely that jurors will be swayed by irrational arguments and preconceptions based on a defendant's appearance? *See Chapter 13, p. 433.*

Connections

to turn up for the exam. Being able to recognize the function(s) of an utterance will improve our communication skills. After all, we don't want to be the sort of boorish people who take the ceremonial utterance "How are you?" as a request for detailed information about their health and lives and then end up wondering why people avoid us.

Being able to use language effectively to convey information, provide directions, and express our feelings is essential to collaborative critical thinking and fulfilling our life goals. Astronaut Sally Ride's exemplary communication skills, for example, contributed to her success as the first American woman in space (see "Thinking Outside the Box: Sally Ride, Astronaut").

The flexibility of human language and the multiple functions that it serves allows us to generate an almost unlimited number of sentences. Like culture, human language is constantly changing. The English we know bears only minor resemblance to the English used 1,000 years ago. Today, with globalization there is more sharing of words between languages.

The flexibility and open-ended nature of human language, while greatly enriching our ability to communicate ideas and feelings, can also contribute to ambiguity and misunderstanding. For example, when the person who is

---

In a study of junior high and high school students, more than half of the boys surveyed said that when a male took a female out for an expensive dinner, it was understood that she would reciprocate the invitation by having sex with him.

---

talking to you at a party says, "I'll call you," it's not always clear what he or she means. Even apparently simple sentences such as this are dense with meaning. Is it a straightforward informative sentence? Or is there more to it? Is he (or she) asking you for a date? Is he expressing interest in spending more time with you? Or is he merely saying he'll call to be polite, but not really meaning it? And what if he does call the following day and suggests, "Let's go out to dinner"? Once again, is he asking you for a date? Is he implying that he is going to pay for the meal, or does he expect you to split the cost or even pay the whole bill? Does he expect something in return for taking you to dinner?

If we don't first clarify what the other person means or what his or her expectations are, there may be serious and dire consequences. For example, miscommunication

Outside the Box

SALLY RIDE, *Astronaut*

As a child, Sally Ride (1951–) loved to solve problems. Her friends from college describe her as "calm and totally focused … always able to see to the heart of things … to quickly think, figure it out, crystallize it."* An exemplary critical thinker, she is able to clearly articulate and develop strategies to meet her life goals. Realizing the importance of communication skills to achieving her goals, at college she double-majored in English and physics.

Ride was just finishing up her Ph.D. in physics at Stanford University when she saw an announcement in the college newspaper that NASA was looking for a new group of astronauts. She applied that day. She was one of 35 picked for the astronaut class of 1978 out of more than 8,000 applicants. In part because of her outstanding analytical and critical thinking skills, Ride in 1983 became the youngest as well as the first female American astronaut in space. Because of her exemplary communication skills, Ride was chosen to serve as capcom for the first and second shuttle flights—the person on the ground who handles all the ground-to-staff flight communication. She later helped create NASA's Office of Exploration.

An excellent speaker and writer, she has addressed the United Nations and put together the report for NASA, *Leadership and the American Future in Space*. Ride has also written several children's books on space exploration. Today she heads Sally Ride Science, which sponsors, among other things, camps that encourage girls' interest in science and also help them to develop their leadership, writing, and communication skills.

DISCUSSION QUESTIONS

1. Looking back at the characteristics of a good critical thinker listed on page 7 in Chapter 1, discuss ways in which Ride exemplifies these qualities.

2. Has there ever been a time when you missed a great opportunity? Discuss what role, if any, lack of good critical-thinking skills played in this.

*Carole Ann Camp, *Sally Ride: First American Woman in Space* (Springfield, NJ: Enslow Publishers, 1997), p. 19.

is sometimes a factor in rape. In a study of junior high and high school students, more than half of the boys surveyed said that when a male took a female out for an expensive dinner, it was understood that she would reciprocate the invitation by having sex with him. Nonverbal language in particular may be misinterpreted. In a similar study, most college men said they considered lack of resistance on the part of a woman as consent to sex.[4] Intellectual curiosity and being mindful of how language is being used, two of the critical thinking skills, can make us less susceptible to misunderstandings and manipulation.

Nonverbal Language

We often look to nonverbal cues, such as body language or tone of voice, when interpreting someone's communication. Indeed, many jurors make up their mind about a case mainly on the basis of the nonverbal behavior of the defendant.[5] Although some nonverbal communication is universal, such as smiling when happy, raising the eyebrow to signal recognition, and making the "disgust face" to show repulsion, much of it is culturally determined.

We frequently use nonverbal communication to reinforce verbal communication. A nod when we say yes, a hand gesture when we say "over there," folding our arms across our body when we say "no"—all serve to reinforce our words. Because much of nonverbal communication occurs at a less conscious level, people tend to pay more attention to it when it conflicts with the verbal message.

Images, such as photos and artwork, can also be used to communicate ideas and feelings. It is said that "a picture conveys a thousand words." Images not only convey infor-

ANIMAL LANGUAGE*   Language seems to be limited to highly social animals and serves to enhance group cohesiveness. Honeybees use symbolic gestures in the form of dances to communicate the direction and distance the other bees must fly to reach food sources or other things of interest. Birds, ground squirrels, and nonhuman primates such as the velvet monkey have different alarm calls that are recognized by other members of their species even when the predator is not present. Male domestic chickens also use language to communicate their food preferences and the presence of female chickens.

Like humans, these animals understand the relationship between the signals they use and the events these signals refer to. They are not simply expressing an emotion or communicating about something that is only in the moment. They are actually using symbolic language to refer to things in the outside world, things that do not need to be immediately present for them to understand what is being communicated.

Many animals—including apes, chimps, dolphins, dogs and parrots—can also understand several words in human languages and respond to commands containing strings of words. The gorilla Coco, for example, has a vocabulary of more than 1,000 human words. The border collie Rico has a vocabulary of more than 200 words.

DISCUSSION QUESTIONS

1. *Humans also use nonverbal communication, such as dance. Come up with examples of ways in which you use nonverbal language such as dance or gestures to communication information.*

2. *Discuss how barriers to critical thinking such as narrow-mindedness can prevent us from seeing the use of language by other animals as well as keep us from appreciating the richness and diversity of languages of other cultures.*

*For more information on language in nonhuman animals, see Jacques Vauclair, *Animal Cognition* (Cambridge, MA: Harvard University Press, 1996), and Donald R. Griffin, *Animals Minds: Beyond Cognition to Consciousness* (Chicago: University of Chicago Press, 2001). See also www.thelowell .org/content/view/1202/28/ for more on primatologist Netzin Gerald-Steklis's work on communication with gorillas.

Analyzing Images

NONVERBAL COMMUNICATION AND A DEATH-ROW DECISION   Keeping an accused killer from testifying on the stand does not ensure that jurors won't observe the defendants' nonverbal communication. On December 13, 2004, a California jury recommended the death penalty for Scott Peterson, who was convicted of killing his wife Laci and their unborn son Conner. Although lack of an emotional response is not conclusive evidence of guilt, according to jurors, their decision was swayed by Scott Peterson's lack of emotional responsiveness during the six-month trial and "stony demeanor, even during wrenching testimony about his dead wife and son." Scott was found guilty of murdering his wife and unborn son despite the fact that all the evidence was circumstantial; there was no actual physical evidence directly linking him to the crime.

DISCUSSION QUESTIONS

1. *What was your initial reaction upon seeing pictures of Peterson on trial? Do these images change the way you feel about the evidence given in the case?*

2. *Should jurors be allowed to see a defendant during a trial, or should a law be put in place that sets the defendant out of their view so as to not influence their decision? Support your answer.*

mation but also can evoke emotions that may motivate us to take action in ways that words often cannot. At Abu Ghraib prison in Iraq, the soldier who blew the whistle did so only after seeing photos of detainees in sexually humiliating positions. "Words can't describe my reaction," said Sgt. Joseph Darby. "I was shocked. I was very disappointed and outraged."[6] The images outraged people throughout the world and led to questions about the morality of the war in Iraq and to the reform of interrogation practices at Abu Ghraib prison.

In summary, we should keep in mind that language is, to a large extent, a cultural construct. Furthermore, because of the different functions and the flexibility of human language, our choice of words and our nonverbal cues can affect how a message is interpreted—or misinterpreted—by other people. As good critical thinkers, we need to be clear in our communication and conscious of how language is being used in a particular instance. We need to be willing to ask people for clarification if we are uncertain about the meaning of their communication.

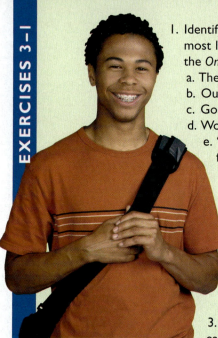

1. Identify which language function(s)—informative, directive, expressive, ceremonial—are most likely served by of each of the following passages. (For additional exercises, go to the *Online Student Workbook* for Chapter 3.)
   a. The planet Pluto was first observed at the Lowell Observatory in Flagstaff, Arizona.
   b. Ouch!
   c. God bless you. (In response to someone sneezing).
   d. Wow! I'm so happy. My application for a scholarship just got approved.
   e. "Honor thy mother and thy father."—Deuteronomy
   f. "A thing of beauty is a joy forever."—John Keats
   g. "A national debate is raging between women's groups and law-enforcement types stepping in to protect the health of a fetus from a mother who they believe will not, or cannot, look after it."[7]
   h. You should be careful about what you eat at college. The average college student puts on 15 pounds during his or her freshman year.
   i. Thank you.

2. Working in small groups, make a list of variations in language used by students at your college who come from different regions of the United States or Canada. Discuss how these variations reflect cultural differences in these regions.

3. Most humans and dogs are able to communicate basic messages or feelings to each other. What kinds of behaviors do you (or someone you know who owns a dog) engage in when you want to express anger, happiness, or playfulness? How does the dog communicate if it wants to eat, go outside, or chase a squirrel?

4. Discuss ways in which the following passages from religious scripture might be interpreted and what role culture plays in these interpretations.
   a. Passion for gold can never be right; the pursuit of money leads a man astray. (Ecclesiastes 31:5)
   b. Whosoever kills even one human being, other than for man slaughter or tyranny on earth, it would be as if they had killed all of humankind. (Koran 5:32)
   c. Wives, be subject to your husbands as to the Lord; for the man is the head of the woman, just as Christ also is the head of the church. (Ephesians 5:22–23)[8]
   d. The Master said, A young man's duty is to behave well to his parents at home and to his elders abroad, to be cautious in giving promises and punctual in keeping them, to have kindly feelings towards everyone, but seek the intimacy of the Good. (*The Analects of Confucius,* Book I: 6)

5. The borrowing of words from other languages is evident in Spanglish, in which Latin American immigrants and their descendants in the United States use Spanish and English interchangeably, even in the same sentences. Spanglish is heard not only on the streets and in shops but also on some radio and television stations.[9] Some people maintain that Spanglish should not be taught in schools. Others claim it is a legitimate and evolving language. Discuss what you would do if you were a professor and a student wanted to hand in an essay written in Spanglish or used Spanglish in a class.

6. We can rearrange words and phrases into novel sentences, some of which have never before been uttered. Write a five-word sentence. Type the sentence in quotation marks into an Internet search engine such as Google. As of 2008, Google has indexed over one trillion pages on the World Wide Web. Did the search engine find your five-word sentence on any of these pages?[10] Discuss the results of your search.

7. Find an argument in a newspaper or on the Internet that is trying to persuade the reader to adopt a certain point of view, such as an article on why you should get involved in sports or an article on why the education system is failing children. Write a page on how the writer is using language or discourse to achieve this objective.

8. Research the history of a language such as English, Spanish, Japanese, Navaho, or Arabic. Identify and write a short essay on two ways in which the evolution of this language reflects the history of the people and their culture.

9. Theologian Mary Daly writes: "The Biblical and popular image of God as a great patriarch in heaven … has dominated the imagination of millions over thousands of years. The symbol of the Father God, spawned in the human imagination and sustained as plausible by patriarchy, has in turn rendered service to this type of society by making its mechanisms for the oppression of women appear right and fitting."[11]
   Discuss Daly's claim that the identification of God as male is oppressive to women. Should we change the language used in religious texts and services to gender-neutral language? Support your position.

DEFINITIONS

The English language has one of the largest vocabularies in the world—about a quarter of a million different words. This is in part because English has incorporated so many foreign terms. Some of these words in the English language are no longer in use, and some have acquired new meanings over time.

That is why we cannot simply assume that someone else is using a word or phrase as we are. In addition to understanding the history of a term, it's helpful to understand the difference between the denotative and connotative meanings of words, as well as to be familiar with some of the different types of definitions, in order to communicate accurately and clearly.

Denotative and Connotative Meanings

Words have both denotative and connotative meanings. The **denotative meaning** of a word or phrase expresses the properties of the object, being, or event the word is symbolizing; it is the same as its lexical or dictionary definition. For example, the denotative meaning of the word *dog* is a domesticated member of the family *Canis familiaris.* Any being that has both of these properties (domesticated and a member of the family *Canis familiaris)* is a dog by definition.

The **connotative meaning** of a word or phrase includes feelings and personal thoughts that are elicited on the basis of past experiences and associations. The word dog may elicit thoughts of a loyal pet or—at the opposite extreme—something that is worthless or of poor quality, a despicable person, or an ugly person. The connotative meaning(s) of a term may be included in a list of dictionary definitions, or a particular connotative meaning may simply be shared among a specific group of people.

Language is not neutral. It reflects cultural values and influences how we see the world. Language reinforces cultural concepts of what it means to be normal through the use of stereotypes that have certain connotative meanings. In **stereotyping**, rather than seeing people as individuals, we see and label them as members of a particular group. The labels we use shape the way we see ourselves and others. Labels can also stigmatize and isolate people. The label *mentally ill* reinforces our worldview that some illnesses are all in the mind, thus legitimating the withholding of appropriate medical care and healthcare benefits from people with this label. Sexist language such as *chick* and *ho* reinforces gender stereotypes and the view that women are irrational and inferior to men and therefore deserve inferior treatment in the workplace and at home.

Stipulative Definitions

Most of us probably think of *Merriam-Webster's Collegiate Dictionary* or the *Oxford English Dictionary* when we hear the word *definition.* However, lexical definitions are only one type of definition. Other types include stipulative, precising, theoretical, and persuasive. A **stipulative definition** is one given to a new term such as bytes and *decaf* or to a new combination of old terms such as *skyscraper* and *laptop.* A stipulative definition may also be a new definition of an existing word, such as the addition of "heterosexual" to the definitions of the term *straight.*

> **Connections**
>
> How can you be more aware of stereotypes that are sometimes promoted by the news media and advertising? *See Chapter 11, p. 348.*

Did You Know

In the U.S. Supreme Court case *Boy Scouts of America v. James Dale* (2000), the scouts argued that banning gay men and boys was necessary to maintain the Boy Scouts' express message of encouraging youths to lead a "morally straight" life. However, this term was first used in the Boy Scout Oath in 1911, long before the term *straight* had any implications regarding sexual orientation.

---

denotative meaning The meaning of a word or phrase that expresses the properties of the object.

connotative meaning The meaning of a word or phrase that is based on past personal experiences or associations.

stereotyping Labeling people based on their membership in a group.

stipulative definition A definition given to a new term or a new combination of old terms.

Stipulative definitions often start off as jargon or slang and are initially limited to a particular group of people. Young people may create their own terminology, such as *beer goggles* and *hooking up* as a way of distancing themselves from previous generations. A stipulative definition is neither true nor false—merely more or less useful.

The creation of new terms and stipulative definitions reflects cultural and historical changes. The term *genocide* was introduced in the early 1940s by Raphael Lemkin, a Polish Jewish lawyer who had fled Nazi-occupied Europe and settled in the United States. He lobbied the United Nations to adopt a convention against genocide. In 1948, the UN Genocide Convention was adopted, which defined genocide as "acts committed with intent to destroy, in whole or in part, a national, ethnic, racial, or religious group."

The terms *date rape* and *sexual harassment* were coined during the feminist movement in the 1970s to call attention to occurrences that were previously not regarded as noteworthy. The introduction of the terms *pro-life* and *pro-choice* contributed to the public's conceptualization and the polarization of the abortion issue. Trade names such as Jell-O, Band-Aid, and Kleenex have also become part of our general vocabulary to refer to any of these products in general.

If a stipulative definition becomes commonly accepted, then it will become a lexical or dictionary definition. For example, the term for sneakers among some Chinese is now "Nai-ke," a term that Nike, which is trying to create a market for its athletic shoes among China's youth and rising middle class, hopes will catch on and become part of the Chinese vocabulary.

carries a negative connotation. In Canada and England, in contrast, the term *homely* means "comfortable and cozy" or "homey."

Just as new words are continually emerging, so too can words that were once in common usage become obsolete. Eventually, outdated terms that are no longer useful are dropped from the dictionary. For instance, we no longer use the term *lubitorium* for "service station," since it is no longer descriptive of the modern self-service stations.

Controlling the definitions of words can be used to create an advantage in discussions of controversial issues. For instance, in 2004 textbooks that defined marriage as "a union between two people" were withdrawn from use in Texas public schools until the definition could be changed to a "a union between a man and a woman," thus giving control in public discourse to those who oppose same-sex marriage.

Lexical Definitions

A **lexical definition**, as we noted earlier, is the commonly used dictionary definition or denotative meaning of a term. Unlike a stipulative definition, whose meaning is fluid depending on the circumstances, a lexical definition is either correct or incorrect. Most dictionaries are updated annually. The criterion that dictionary editors use in deciding if a new word or stipulative definition should become part of the dictionary is whether the word is used in enough printed sources.

The two primary purposes of a lexical definition are to increase our vocabulary and to reduce ambiguity. To determine if we are using a lexical definition correctly, we simply consult a dictionary. Of course, some words have several lexical definitions. In these cases we need to clarify which definition we are using. Even within one language, lexical definitions of a word may vary from country to country. *Homely* in the United States usually means "lacking in physical attractiveness; plain" and

lexical definition The commonly used dictionary definition.

precising definition A definition used to reduce vagueness that goes beyond the ordinary lexical definition.

Precising Definitions

Precising definitions are used to reduce vagueness which occurs when it is not clear exactly what meaning a word or concept encompasses. Precising definitions go beyond the ordinary lexical definition of a term in order to establish the exact limits of the definition. For example, the terms *class participation* or *term paper* in a course syllabus may need to be defined more precisely by the instructor for purposes of grading.

Similarly, ordinary dictionary definitions may be too vague in a court of law. Under what precise circumstances does "date or acquaintance rape" occur? How should *coercion* and *consent* be defined for legal purposes? Did an alleged victim give her consent to have sexual intercourse by not rebuffing his advances, or did the accused use coercion? Should "consent" in these cases, as some argue, require explicit verbal communication between the man and the woman regarding approval to engage in sexual interaction?[12]

Confusion can result if a definition is too vague or lacks precision. The Individuals with Disabilities Education Act defines a *learning disability* as a "disorder in one or more of the basic psychological processes involved in under-

Critical Thinking in Action

Say What?

New words of the 1970s: acquaintance rape; bioethics; biofeedback; chairperson; consciousness-raising; couch potato; date rape; disk drive; downsize; Ebonics; focus group; gigabyte; global warming; he/she; high-tech; in vitro fertilization; junk food; learning disability; personal computer; pro-choice; punk rock; sexual harassment; smart bomb; sunblock; VCR; video game; word processor

New words of the 1980s: AIDS; alternative medicine; assisted suicide; attention deficit disorder; biodiversity; camcorder; CD-ROM; cell phone; codependent; computer virus; cyberspace; decaf; do-rag; e-mail; gender gap; Internet; laptop; mall rat; managed care; premenstrual syndrome; rap music; safe sex; sport utility vehicle (SUV); telemarketing; televangelist; virtual reality; yuppie

New words of the 1990s: artificial life; call waiting; carjacking; chronic fatigue syndrome; dot-com; eating disorder; family leave; hyperlink; nanotechnology; senior moment; spam; strip mall; Web site; World Wide Web.

New words of the 2000s: biodiesel, bioweapon; blog; civil union; carbo-loading; counterterrorism; cybercrime; desk jockey; enemy combatant; fanboy; google; hazmat; hoophead; infowar; insourcing; jihadist; labelmate; nanobot; powerhead; sexile; speed dating; spyware; supersize; taikonaut; truthiness; webinar; w00t

DISCUSSION QUESTIONS

1. Identify five other words that have been added to the English language since 2000. Discuss what these words tell us about our society and changes since 2000.

2. What are some of the differences between the words used by you and those used by your parents and grandparents? How do these reflect differences in the culture that you were brought up in?

1940s–1990s from *Random House Webster's College Dictionary* (New York: Random House, 2001), pp. xx–xxii.

---

standing or in using spoken or written language, which may manifest itself in an imperfect ability to listen, think, speak, read, write, spell, or to do mathematical calculations." However, this definition is so vague that it is difficult to determine whom it covers. Indeed, estimates of the percentage of the population with a learning disability vary widely from 1 percent to 30 percent.[13]

Precising definitions may have to be updated as new discoveries or circumstances demand a more accurate definition.

In 2007, with the discovery of several new bodies orbiting the sun in our solar system, the International Astronom-ical Union voted to add a new requirement to its definition of *planet*. The new definition required that planets had to not merely orbit the sun and be "nearly round;" they also have to "dominate their gravitational domains." This more precise definition eliminated Pluto from the pantheon of planets.

Theoretical definitions are a special class of precising definition used to explain the specific nature of a term. Proposing a theoretical definition is akin to proposing a theory. These definitions are more likely to be found in dictionaries for specialized disciplines, such

> **theoretical definitions** A type of precising definition explaining a term's nature.

What is the role of operational definitions in science? *See Chapter 12, p. 379.*

Connections

as the sciences. For example, alcoholism is defined, in part, in the *Taber's Cyclopedic Medical Dictionary* as "a chronic, progressive and potentially fatal disease. . . . Alcoholism is an illness and should be so treated." Unlike a lexical definition, which merely describes the symptoms or effects, this medical definition puts forth a theory regarding the nature of alcoholism—it is a disease, not a moral failing.

Operational definitions are another type of precising definition. An operational definition is a concise definition of a measure used to provide standardization in data collection and interpretation. The lexical definition of obese—"very fat or overweight"—is not precise enough for a medical professional trying to determine if a person's weight is a health risk or if the person is a candidate for gastric bypass surgery. Instead, the medical profession defines obesity operationally in terms of body mass index, or BMI.

Operational definitions may change over time. For instance, the definition of poverty varies from country to country as well as over time. In the United States the poverty threshold was defined by the U.S. Department of

> **operational definitions** A definition with a standardized measure for use in data collection and interpretation.

HIGHLIGHTS

TYPES OF DEFINITIONS

Stipulative definition: A definition given to a new term or a new definition of an existing word.

Lexical definition: The commonly used dictionary definition.

Precising definition: A more in-depth definition used to reduce vagueness. Precising definitions include (1) *theoretical definitions,* which provide a theory about the nature of something, and (2) *operational definitions,* which involve a concise definition of a measure used to provide standardization in data collection and interpretation.

Persuasive definition: Definition used to influence others to accept our point of view.

Health and Human Services in 2008 as $10,400 for a single individual. In 1982 the poverty threshold was defined as $4,680 for a single individual.[14]

Persuasive Definitions

Persuasive definitions are used as a means to persuade or influence others to accept our point of view. The definition of *taxation* as a form of theft and of *genetic engineering* as playing God with the human genome are both examples of persuasive definitions. Persuasive definitions often use **emotive language**, such as the negative term *theft* in the first definition.

There is nothing inherently wrong with using persuasive or emotive language. Emotive language in poetry and fiction, for example, is clearly appropriate. However, if our primary intention is to convey information, then it is best to avoid using it. Persuasive definitions, because their primary intention is to influence our attitudes rather than convey information, can be a problem in critical thinking when they distract us from getting to the truth.

> **persuasive definition** A definition used as a means to influence others to accept our view.
>
> **emotive language** Language that is purposely chosen to elicit a certain emotional impact.

Weight in Pounds

Height in Inches	120	130	140	150	160	170	180	190	200	210	220	230	240	250
4'6"	29	31	34	36	39	41	43	46	48	51	53	56	58	60
4'8"	27	29	31	34	36	38	40	43	45	47	49	52	54	56
4'10"	25	27	29	31	34	36	38	40	42	44	46	48	50	52
5'0"	23	25	27	29	31	33	35	37	39	41	43	45	47	49
5'2"	22	24	26	27	29	31	33	35	37	38	40	42	44	46
5'4"	21	22	24	26	28	29	31	33	34	36	38	40	41	43
5'6"	19	21	23	24	26	27	29	31	32	34	36	37	39	40
5'8"	18	20	21	23	24	26	27	29	30	32	34	35	37	38
5'10"	17	19	20	22	23	24	26	27	29	30	32	33	35	36
6'0"	16	18	19	20	22	23	24	26	27	28	30	31	33	34
6'2"	15	17	18	19	21	22	23	24	26	27	28	30	31	32
6'4"	15	16	17	18	20	21	22	23	24	26	27	28	29	30
6'6"	14	15	16	17	19	20	21	22	23	24	25	27	28	29
6'8"	13	14	15	17	18	19	20	21	22	23	24	25	26	28

Underweight   Healthy Weight
Overweight   Obese

Body Mass Index

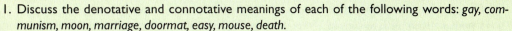

1. Discuss the denotative and connotative meanings of each of the following words: *gay, communism, moon, marriage, doormat, easy, mouse, death.*

2. What stereotypes come to mind when you hear the following words: *African American, bachelor, bachelorette, college dropout, computer nerd, frat boy, housewife, illegal alien, liberal, conservative, hockey mom, superstar, Third World country, tomboy, white person?* Discuss ways in which each of these stereotypes conveys cultural values.

3. For each of the following, identify which type of definition is being used.
   a. Intoxication is defined as having a blood alcohol content of .08 percent.
   b. A *dream* is our unconsciousness acting out and expressing its hidden desires.
   c. How about adding the following definition for the word *cellblock:* those idiots who always have their cell phones pressed to their heads?
   d. *Abuse* is the willful infliction of injury, unreasonable confinement, or cruel punishment.
   e. A *genius* is person with an IQ of 140 or above.
   f. A *human* is a primate of the genus *homo* that evolved from its *Australopithecine* ancestor in Africa some 1 million to 4 million years ago.
   g. *Capital punishment* is state-sanctioned murder.
   h. *Spanglish* is a form of Spanish that includes many English words.
   i. *Neglect* is defined as "the failure to provide for one's self the goods or services which are necessary to avoid physical harm, mental anguish, or mental illness, or the failure of a caretaker to prove such goods or services and includes malnourishment and dehydration, over- or undermedication, lack of heat, running water, or electricity; unsanitary living conditions; lack of medical care; and lack of personal hygiene or clothes."[15]
   j. *Religion* is the opiate of the masses.

4. Create your own stipulative definition of a term. Introduce your term and definition to the class. Vote on which ones the class thinks are most useful. Looking at the three most useful terms, discuss what might be done to make these become lexical definitions someday.

5. Define *hunger* and *love* using lexical, persuasive, and operational definitions.

6. *Beer goggles, catching feelings,* and *hooking up* are all new terms that are currently popular on college campuses. Discuss how the use of these terms reflects how young people think about college life and relationships. Does the use of these new terms affect how you think about college and relationships?

7. How would you answer the Gallup poll question "Do you consider yourself a feminist, or not?" Include a definition of, or list of attributes of, feminist as part of your answer. Compare your definition with those used by others in the class. Discuss the extent to which differences in definitions of this key term explain the current polarization on feminism.

8. Collect passages from magazines and newspapers of language used to describe people of different sexes and different racial and ethnic groups. Write a short essay discussing whether these descriptions are important to the story or are more a reflection of stereotyping and reinforcing a particular cultural view. Share your findings with the class.

9. How do the labels you use for yourself influence your self-esteem and your goals? If you want to, share some of your labels, and the impact of these labels on your life plan, with others in the class.

EVALUATING DEFINITIONS

Clearly defining key terms is an essential component of clear communication and critical thinking. Knowing how to determine if a particular definition is good makes it less likely that we will get caught up in a purely verbal dispute or fallacious reasoning.

Five Criteria

There are several criteria we can use to evaluate definitions. The following are five of the more important ones:

1. *A good definition is neither too broad nor too narrow.* Definitions that include too much are too broad; those that include too little are too narrow.

For example, the definition of *mother* as a "woman who has given birth to a child" is too narrow. Women who adopt children are also mothers. Similarly, the definition of *war* as "an armed conflict" is too broad because it would include street fights, police action against suspected criminals, and domestic violence. Some definitions are both too broad and too narrow, such as the definition of *penguin* as "a bird that lives in Antarctica." This definition is too broad because many other species of birds live in Antarctica and too narrow because penguins also live in other regions of the Southern Hemisphere such as South Africa.

2. *A good definition should state the essential attributes of the term being defined.* The definition of a community college as "an institution of higher education, without residential facilities, that is often funded by the government, and is characterized by a two-year curriculum that leads either to an associate degree or transfer to a four-year college"[16] includes the essential characteristics of a community college.

3. *A good definition is not circular.* You should avoid using the term itself, or variations of the term, within the definition, as in "a teacher is a person who teaches," and "erythropoiesis is the production of erythrocytes." Since a circular definition gives little or no new information about the meaning of the term, it is understandable only to a person who already knows the definition of the term.

4. *A good definition avoids obscure and figurative language.* Definitions should be clear and understandable. Some definitions are written in such obscure terms that they are understandable only to professionals in the field. The definition of *net* as "anything reticulated or decussated at equal distances with interstices between the intersections"[17] uses obscure language.

   Political scientist Arthur Lupia maintains that the disconnect between the hard scientific evidence of human-caused global warming and the public's failure to address the problem stems in large part from the overuse of obscure and technical language by scientists. Too many scientists use highly technical terms, such as *distribution functions* and *albedos* in defining and explaining global warming to laypeople. Lupia suggests that science should treat effective communication itself as a subject of inquiry.[18]

   Figurative language should also be avoided in definitions. "Love is like a red, red rose" may be a moving line in a poem, but it is hardly an adequate definition of love.

5. *A good definition avoids emotive language.* The definitions of a feminist as "a man-hater" and of a man as "an oppressor of women" are just two examples of definitions that are geared to inflame emotions rather than stimulate rational discussion of an issue.

Knowing how to evaluate definitions contributes to successful and clear communication.

Verbal Disputes Based on Ambiguous Definitions

If a tree falls in a forest and no one is around to hear it, does it make a sound? You argue that it doesn't; your friend just as adamantly argues that it does. You both end up upset at what appears to be pure obstinacy on the other's part. But before getting into a full-blown argument, step back and ask yourself if you and your friend are using the same definition for the key term(s).

Defining key terms, as we noted above, is an essential component of clear communication and good critical thinking. If we neglect to do so, we may end up in a verbal dispute as we talk past each other and get increasingly frustrated. In the case in the previous paragraph, you and your friend are using different definitions of the key term *sound*. You are defining *sound* in terms of perception: "the sensation produced by stimulation of organs of hearing." Your friend, in contrast, is defining *sound* as a physicist would: "mechanical vibrations transmitted though an elastic medium."[19] And these are only two of the thirty-eight definitions of *sound* used in a standard dictionary! In other words, your dispute is purely ver-

> **FIVE CRITERIA FOR EVALUATING DEFINITIONS**
> 1. A good definition is neither too broad nor too narrow.
> 2. A good definition should state the essential attributes of the term being defined.
> 3. A good definition is not circular.
> 4. A good definition avoids obscure and figurative language.
> 5. A good definition avoids emotive language.

bal. Once you both agree on the definition of the key term *sound,* what appeared at first to be a heady philosophical dispute disappears.

Verbal disputes occur more often than most of us probably realize. However, not all disagreements can be resolved by our agreeing on the definitions of key terms. In some cases we have a genuine disagreement. For example, one person may argue that capital punishment is an effective deterrent; another may argue that it has no deterrent effect. Both agree on the definition of capital punishment but disagree on its deterrent effect. Disagreements like this about factual matters can be resolved by researching the facts.

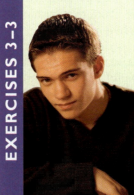

EXERCISES 3-3

1. Evaluate the following definitions and indicate what, if anything, is wrong with them. If they are poor definitions, come up with a better definition.
   a. "Third World feminism is about feeding people in all their hunger."[20]
   b. A farm is a large tract of land on which crops are raised for a livelihood.
   c. A cafeteria is a place on campus where students eat their meals.
   d. A wedding ring is a tourniquet designed to stop circulation.
   e. A footstool is a stool for our feet.
   f. Democracy is the tyranny of the majority.
   g. Global warming is the systematic increase in temperature over decades on the surface albedo, the fluxes of sensible and latent heat to the atmosphere, and the distribution of energy within the climate system to the hydrosphere, lithosphere, and biosphere primarily because of anthropomorphic forcing.
   h. Hunger is denial of dignity.
   i. A dog is a household pet.
   j. A misogynist is one who disagrees with a feminist.
   k. A student is a person who attends an institution of higher education.
   l. "Hope is the thing with feathers / That perches in the soul, / And sings the tune without the words, / And never stops at all."[21]
   m. A teenager is a person between 13 and 19 years of age.
   n. "Rightful liberty is unobstructed action according to our will within limits drawn around us by the equal rights of others. I do not add 'within the limits of the law' because law is often but the tyrant's will, and always so when it violates the rights of the individual."—Thomas Jefferson

2. The definition of *God* changes over time and also differs among groups of people. How do you define *God?* Share your definition with others in the class. To what extent are disagreements about the existence of God purely verbal disputes?

3. Identify which of the following arguments are merely verbal disputes based on differing definitions and which are disagreements of fact:
   a. "You should bring an umbrella to class today. It's supposed to rain later this afternoon."
      "No, it's not. There's not a cloud in the sky, and the one-week weather forecast from last weekend said it was supposed to be sunny all week."
   b. "Iraq became a sovereign nation in the spring of 2004 when the Americans handed over control of the government to the interim Iraqi government."
      "Iraq did not become a sovereign nation in 2004, since the Americans appointed the government and Iraq was still occupied. The only way for Iraq to achieve sovereignty is to get rid of the Americans."
   c. "Women do not have a right to an abortion, since abortion involves taking a life and violates the moral principle of 'do no harm.'"
      "I disagree. Women have a right to an abortion, according to the U.S. Supreme Court."
   d. "I hear that if the military draft is reenacted, girls will be drafted as well as men."

d. "I hear that if the military draft is reenacted, girls will be drafted as well as men."
   "That's not true. No one under the age of 18 will be drafted."

e. "You'd better not have a second glass of wine. You might get stopped by the police and arrested for drunk driving."
   "No, a person needs to have at least three drinks in order to be over the limit for drunk driving."

f. "Professor Santos is the best teacher in the English department. She always gets top ratings on the student evaluations."
   "Professor Kwame is the best teacher. He has more publications in academic journals than anyone else in the department."

COMMUNICATION STYLES

Sometimes miscommunication is due to communication style instead of actual content. As critical thinkers, it is important that we be aware that there are individual as well as group differences in communication styles. What may seem "normal" to us may be viewed as aggressive, aloof, or even offensive to other people.

Individual Styles of Communication

The way we communicate cannot be separated from who we are. Understanding our own styles and those of others facilitates good communication in relationships and critical thinking skills. There are four basic types of communication style: assertive, aggressive, passive, and passive-aggressive.*

The *assertive style* is how we express ourselves when we are confident and our self-esteem is strong. Like effective critical thinkers, assertive communicators are able to clearly communicate their own needs but also know their limits. Assertive communicators care about relationships and strive for mutually satisfactory solutions.

The *aggressive* communication style involves the attempt to make other people do what we want or meet our needs through manipulation and control tactics. Passive communicators do the opposite. They don't want to rock the boat and often put their needs after those of others. *Passive* communication is based on compliance and efforts to avoid confrontation at all costs.

Passive-aggressive communicators combine elements of the passive and aggressive styles. They avoid direct confrontation (passive) but use devious and sneaky means of manipulation (aggressive) to get their own way.

* To learn more about your own communication style, go to www.humanmetrics.com/assertive/assertivenesintro.asp

HIGHLIGHTS

COMMUNICATION STYLES

Assertive communicators clearly and respectfully communicate their own needs and strive for mutually satisfactory solutions.

Aggressive communicators attempt to get their own way by controlling other people through the use of manipulation and control tactics.

Passive communicators avoid confrontation and are compliant, often putting their own needs after those of others.

Passive-aggressive communicators avoid direct confrontation but use devious means to get their own way.

SELF-EVALUATION QUESTIONNAIRE (COMMUNICATION STYLE)*

For each of the following scenarios, select the answer choice that best describes what you would do.

1. You are a customer waiting in line to be served. Suddenly, someone steps in line ahead of you. You would
   a. Let the person be ahead of you, since he or she is already in line
   b. Pull the person out of line and make him or her go to the back
   c. Indicate to the person that you are in line and point out where it begins

2. A friend drops in to say hello but stays too long, preventing you from finishing an important work project. You would
   a. Let the person stay, then finish your work another time
   b. Tell the person to stop bothering you and to get out
   c. Explain your need to finish your work and request that he or she visit another time

3. You suspect someone of harboring a grudge against you, but you don't know why. You would
   a. Pretend you are unaware of his or her anger and ignore it, hoping it will correct itself
   b. Get even with the person somehow so that he or she will learn not to hold grudges against you
   c. Ask the person if he or she is angry, and then try to be understanding

4. You bring your car to a garage for repairs and receive a written estimate. But later, when you pick up your car, you are billed for additional work and for an amount higher than the estimate. You would
   a. Pay the bill, since the car must have needed the extra repairs anyway
   b. Refuse to pay, and then complain to the motor vehicle department or the Better Business Bureau
   c. Indicate to the manager that you agreed only to the estimated amount, then pay only that amount

5. You invite a good friend to your house for a dinner party, but your friend never arrives and neither calls to cancel nor to apologize. You would
   a. Ignore it but manage not to show up the next time your friend invites you to a party
   b. Never speak to this person again and end the friendship
   c. Call your friend to find out what happened

6. You are in a discussion group at work that includes your boss. A coworker asks you a question about your work, but you don't know the answer. You would
   a. Give your coworker a false but plausible answer so that your boss will think you are on top of things
   b. Not answer but attack your coworker by asking a question you know that he or she could not answer
   c. Indicate to your coworker that you are unsure just now but offer to give him or her the information later

* Questions are from Donald A. Cadogan, "How Self-Assertive are You?" (1990) http://www.oaktreecounseling.com/assrtquz.htm.

As we noted in Chapter 1, effective communication skills are one of the important characteristics of a good critical thinker. A healthy, assertive communication style and the ability to correctly interpret others' communication are important in positions of leadership, such as that assumed by astronaut Sally Ride. Good communication skills are also one of the most important factors in the establishment of an intimate relationship. As relationships develop, the judgment of how effectively and appropriately each person communicates appears to outweigh other factors, such as appearance or similarity, in determinations of relationship satisfaction.

A healthy, assertive communication style and the ability to correctly interpret others' communication are important in positions of leadership.

Unfortunately, many of us are notoriously inaccurate at interpreting others' communication. In a recent study, participants correctly interpreted only 73 percent of their intimate partner's supportive behavior and 89 percent of their negative behavior.[22] Failing to notice the communication of affection on the part of our partner may leave him or her wondering if we really care. At other times, we may misinterpret our partner's or colleague's behavior as angry or pushy and needlessly provoke an argument that is based on our misperception. Thus, it is important to establish effective communication behaviors and patterns if you want a relationship—whether personal or professional—to succeed.[23]

Communication Style, Sex, and Race

Our sex influences which communication style we tend to prefer. In her book *You Just Don't Understand: Women and Men in Communication,* linguist Deborah Tannen notes that "communication between men and women can be like cross cultural communication, prey to a clash of conversational styles."[24] Women, she notes, tend to use communication to create and sustain relationships, whereas men use it primarily to get things done and solve problems. Most men think that as long as a relationship is working well and there are no problems, there is no need to talk about it. Women, in contrast, think of a relationship as going well if they can talk to their partner about it. When men are uninterested in discussing a relationship or their feelings, a woman may misinterpret this reticence on the man's part as lack of interest (see "Critical Thinking in Action: He Says/She Says: Sex Differences in Communication").

Most scientists, as well as Deborah Tannen, believe that genetics plays a role in these differences in communication style. Indeed, recent studies have found that men and women use different parts of their brain for language.[25] Others believe that these sex differences are primarily or even solely a result of the way in which we are socialized.[26] Boys are taught to assert themselves, whereas girls are taught to listen and be responsive.

Sex differences in communication, whether innate or the result of socialization, have real-life consequences other than just those in personal relationships. In negotiating, women are usually less assertive than men; they tend to set lower goals and are quicker to back down. Women also tend to view negotiations as having two goals: getting the result you want *and* maintaining (or improving) your relationship with the person on the other side. Rather than adopting the more aggressive male negotiating style, women ask, "Can we find a way that this can work for both of us?"[27] Not surprisingly, because they are more willing to compromise, women on the average earn less than men and pay more than men do for a new car. Why are women so reluctant to negotiate assertively? "We teach little girls

Different communication styles, especially between men and women, can lead to miscommunication, so it is important to be aware of how you communicate.

Critical *Thinking* in Action

He Says/She Says: Sex Differences in Communication

Women's Communication:

- Primary purpose of communication is to establish and maintain relationships with others.

- Equality between people, rather than control of conversation, is more important. Typical ways to communicate equality include "I've done the same thing many times," "I've felt the same way," and "The same thing happened to me once."

- Inclusive style of communication: "Tell me more" or "Tell me what you mean."

- Tentative style of communication used to keep conversation open and ongoing.

- Communication is more personal, concrete, and responsive to others.

- Women use more nonverbal communication, such as eye contact, smiling, and attentive body posture, than men do to express their personal feelings and to invite others into the relationship.

Men's Communication:

- Primary purpose of communication is to exert control, preserve independence, entertain, and enhance status.

- Command over the conversation is important. Men tend to talk more and interrupt and challenge more.

- Assertive, sometimes aggressive, style of communication and tendency to give advice; for example: "This is the way you should handle this problem" or "Don't let him get to you."

- Men express themselves in fairly direct, assertive ways. Their language is typically more forceful and authoritative than women's language is.

- Communication is more abstract and conceptual and less responsive.

- Men use nonverbal communication, such as leaning forward and using open hand gestures, primarily to emphasize their verbal messages.

DISCUSSION QUESTIONS

1. Looking at the above list, discuss differences, if any, in the nonverbal communication styles of men and women.

2. Discuss whether men and women have different communication styles. What has been your experience regarding sex differences in communication? Share your experience with the class.

Summarized from Julia T. Wood, *Gendered Lives: Communication, Gender, and Culture* (Belmont, CA: Wadsworth, 2001), pp. 125–130; 138.

that we don't like them to be pushy or overly aggressive," explains Sara Laschever, coauthor of *Women Don't Ask: Negotiation and the Gender Divide.* "Once adulthood is reached, studies are conclusive that neither men nor other women like women who are too aggressive."

Different ethnic and cultural groups tend to define masculinity and femininity differently. For instance, in Thailand, Portugal, and the Scandinavian countries, men's and women's styles of communication tend to be more "feminine," as defined by mainstream American standards.[28] This is mainly because nurturing relationships are a priority in these countries, whereas in the United States men are socialized to be more individualistic, competitive, and assertive or even aggressive in their communication.

Racial identity can also influence our communication style. African American women, for example, are generally socialized to be more assertive. They tend to smile less in a conversation and maintain less eye contact than European American women. In addition, African American men are less comfortable with self-disclosure and are more likely than European American men to use confrontation rather than compromise in conflict resolution.[29]

Social segregation and bias contribute to racial differences in communication styles. To succeed in college and

INTERNATIONAL DIPLOMACY AND NONVERBAL COMMUNICATION In Arab cultures it is perfectly acceptable for men to hold hands. When the infirm 80-year-old Crown Prince Abdullah of Saudi Arabia reached out for President George W. Bush's hand for support while walking along an uneven path in Texas, Bush graciously took his hand. The incident disturbed many Americans and was played up by the media as an inappropriately intimate encounter between the two heads of state. "Most everyone this side of Riyadh was appalled," noted one journalist.* Only First Lady Laura Bush—when asked by Jay Leno on the *Tonight Show,* "Are you the jealous type?"—thought that her husband's gesture was "sweet."

The reaction of both the American media and the public betrayed our ignorance of nonverbal communication styles in Arabic countries. Such ignorance of cultural differences can lead to misunderstandings as well as biased reporting.

DISCUSSION QUESTIONS

1. *What was your first reaction when you saw the photo of Bush and Crown Prince Abullah holding hands? What was the basis of your reaction?*

2. *Look back at a time when you misinterpreted a gesture or body language of someone from a different culture. How did this affect your ability to communicate effectively with that person? Discuss ways in which improving your understanding of cross-cultural behavior can help you to be a better communicator and critical thinker.*

*Joe Klein, "The Perils of Hands-On Diplomacy," *Time,* May 9, 2005, p. 29.

nication styles and titles are preferred over first names.[32] Hispanics also tend to be very polite in their communication, which may be misinterpreted as a subservient attitude.[33]

Nonverbal language also varies from culture to culture. In Algeria the U.S. wave of hello means "come here," whereas in Mexico the U.S. arm gesture for "come here" is an obscene gesture. Cultural groups have their own rules for personal space as well. In the United States, Canada, and northern Europe, personal space tends to be larger and touching is less frequently used in communication than in southern European, Arab, and Latin American countries. Indeed, Arabs sometimes misinterpret the "standoffish" behavior of many Americans as distant and rude.

Even clothing serves as a type of nonverbal language. Indeed, we sometimes say that a person is "making a fashion statement."[34] Many Americans dress more casually than people from other cultures, who may interpret the T-shirts and ragged jeans of an American tourist as a sign of disrespect or slovenliness. In the United States, women, unlike men, are required to wear tops on almost all public beaches, whereas this requirement is seen as restrictive and puritanical by the French and some other Western countries, including parts of Canada. On the other hand, many non-Muslim Americans view the requirement that Muslim women wear a head scarf, or *hijab,* as restrictive and a sign of oppression of women by Islam. Most Muslim women, however, prefer to wear a *hijab,* considering it a sign of respect or decorum.

the professional world, African Americans may abandon the communication styles of the African American community and adopt those associated with the dominant European American culture. Research shows that to succeed in the college and business environments, African American males often adopt the strategy of "talking white" and "playing the part" to avoid being stigmatized by racial stereotypes. One researcher notes that the demands on African Americans of "playing the part," which involves being superficial and cautious and not being yourself ". . . is a constant struggle. . . . You have to play a double role if you're a black male on campus. You have to know when not to do things and when to do things."[30]

Cultural Differences in Communication Styles

Culture plays a key role in shaping our communication style. For example, respect and dignity are highly valued by the Chinese. Consequently, they may be hesitant to ask someone to repeat themselves if they don't understand the communication.[31] In many eastern Asian cultures, nodding does not necessarily mean that the person agrees with or even understands what you are saying. Instead, it is used to show that he or she is listening. The use of silence in communication also varies from culture to culture. European Americans tend to be uncomfortable with silence, whereas silence plays an important role in communication among the Apaches of Arizona, as well as in many Asian cultures.

Communication in Hispanic cultures and among Hispanic Americans is more often oriented toward facilitating group cooperation rather than individual needs. In addition, respect is generally highly valued and formal commu-

Clothing communicates information about a person and their cultural beliefs. How does what you wear communicate something about you?

As critical thinkers we need to be aware of differences in communication styles. Some of us can move easily from one style to another, depending on what the situation requires. Others, however, have one dominant style and more difficulty seeing the situation from another's perspective. Research on communication and culture has led to the creation of the discipline of cross-cultural studies and diversity training for students, business personnel, and government employees. Being aware of our own and others' communication styles, and being able to adjust our style to fit a specific situation, can go a long way in improving communication and facilitating effective critical thinking.

EXERCISES 3–4

1. Write a sentence or two describing the weather today. Once you have finished, get into small groups and compare your description with those of others in your group. Critically analyze what differences say about the communication style of each person in the group.

2. Take two minutes and write a few sentences on what these statements mean to you:
   a. "I love you." [college male to college female]
   b. "I love you." [college female to college male]

   Explain whether the sex of the person saying "I love you," as well as your own sex, influenced your interpretation.

3. What is your negotiating style? How is it influenced by your sex and culture? Does your negotiating style work to achieve the ends you desire? Give an example of a time when your negotiating style worked and one when it didn't. Discuss what you might do to improve your negotiating style.

4. Discuss the desirability of co-ed housing and cohabitation—two unmarried people of opposite sex who are sexually intimate and living together—on campus. Observe the ways in which the men and the women in the class communicate regarding this issue. Now discuss the issue again, this time switching sex roles. Did putting yourself in the role of the other sex enhance understanding?

5. In what ways is your communication style influenced by your sex and cultural background? Describe a time where you altered your communication style because you were talking to a person of another gender or racial or ethnic background. Were these adjustments appropriate? Did they enhance or impede communication? Explain.

6. Look at the clothing of the people in your class or around campus. What do the clothes say to you about each person and their culture? Are your conclusions accurate? Discuss your conclusions with others in the class.

7. Claudine, a junior at State University, came to see her professor about her grades. She was wearing a cropped top, which exposed her midriff, and a very short skirt. The professor glanced down at her legs as she sat down and said, "That outfit is very flattering on you." His comment made her feel uncomfortable. Was this sexual harassment? Discuss the roles of verbal and nonverbal language, including dress, in sexual harassment.

8. *Journal Assignment.* Complete a journal assignment on "Communication Style." Discuss in class how your communication style contributes to or interferes with your relationships and the achievement of your goals. Also share your plan for improving your communication style. If appropriate, modify your journal entry in light of feedback from the class.

THE USE OF LANGUAGE TO MANIPULATE

Language can be used to manipulate and deceive as well as to inform. Manipulation can be carried out through the use of emotive language, rhetorical devices, or deliberate deception. The old adage "sticks and stones will break my bones but words will never hurt me" ignores the profoundly social nature of humans and the use of words to shape our self-concept. Words can raise our spirits, but they can also hurt and degrade us.

Emotive Language

Emotive language, as we noted earlier, is used to elicit a certain emotional impact. For example, the terms *regime, flip-flopper, obstinate,* and *anal retentive* are used to arouse feelings of disapproval. In contrast, the terms *government, flexible, firm,* and *neat* evoke positive feelings. In the 2008

News publications often rely on headlines to grab attention and bolster sales.

presidential election, the word "change" was bandied around by both Obama and McCain primarily to evoke a positive response rather than to convey any actual information.

When a factual issue is at stake, emotive language can slant the truth and obscure our ability to be critical thinkers. It is particularly dangerous when emotive language is used to cover weak arguments and insufficient facts or when it masquerades as news in the media. For example, because the term *terrorist* arouses such negative feelings, the *New York Times* tries to use the term as little as possible. Deputy foreign editor Ethan Bronner explains: "We use 'terrorist' sparingly because it is a loaded word. Describing the goals or acts of a group often serves readers better than repeating the term 'terrorist.'"[35] The *Times* also avoids the use of the term *reform* in describing legislation, since it implies to the reader that the legislation is automatically desirable.

Emotive language is often found in debates about controversial political and moral issues, especially when feelings are running high. Consider the following argument from a letter to the editor regarding the use of embryos left over from in vitro fertilization for stem-cell research:

> Both procedures tamper with embryos or attempt to play God, if you will; why is one acceptable while the other is seen as a threat to life? How is it that discarding leftover embryos—throwing them in the trash, practically a daily occurrence in this country—is seen as less of a travesty than using them to try to save people's lives? How can it be acceptable to manipulate embryos to make more people, especially when there are so many living children in desperate need of homes, but unacceptable to manipulate them to save people

living with terrible diseases? I find this viewpoint hypocritical and self-righteous.[36]

In this letter, the writer relies on using emotive language and attacking opponents of stem-cell research rather than presenting a logical argument for stem-cell research.

Advertising slogans, such as "Things go better with Coke," "The taste that satisfies," and "Like a rock," are designed to manipulate people into buying a certain product rather than actually providing information. Two of the most famous state slogans are "I love New York" and "Virginia is for lovers."[37] Las Vegas's slogan "What happens here, stays here," may have helped bring in a record 35 million tourists in 2003.*

The words we use have real-life consequences. Gang rapes often occur as part of a game or ritual in which the selected victim is referred to as a *nympho* or *slut*—words that suggest she "asked for it." The use of these emotively negative terms makes it easier for men to participate in gang rape without seeing themselves as rapists.

Rhetorical Devices

Like emotive language, **rhetorical devices** use psychological persuasion, rather than reason, to persuade others to accept a particular position. Common rhetorical devices include euphemisms, dysphemisms, sarcasm, and hyperbole.

A **euphemism** is the replacement of a negative term with a neutral or positive one to cover up or sugarcoat the truth. Sometimes euphemisms are humorous and easy to see through (see "Critical Thinking in Action: What Those Code Words in Personal Ads Really Mean"). Other times they obscure the truth and create a false image of the world. One of the more insidious euphemisms was the use of the term "the final solution" for the attempted extermination of the Jews in Nazi Germany.

> **rhetorical devices** The use of euphemisms, dysphemisms, hyperbole and sarcasm to manipulate and persuade.
>
> **euphemism** The replacement of a term that has a negative association by a neutral or positive term.

Connections

How does the media manipulate you through the use of emotive language and sensationalism? *See Chapter 11, p. 345.*

How can you recognize and avoid being taken in by manipulative language in advertisements? *See Chapter 10, p. 325.*

* For more on how to determine if the slogan was a causal factor in the increased tourist traffic or was simply correlated with the increased tourism, see Chapter 7, pages 221–225.

Critical Thinking in Action

What Those "Code Words" in Personal Ads Really Mean

EUPHEMISM	TRANSLATION
40ish	52 and looking for a 25-year-old
Beautiful	Spends a lot of time in front of mirror
Enjoys long walks	Car has been repossessed
Flexible	Desperate
Free spirit	Substance abuser
Fun-loving	Expects to be entertained
Good sense of humor	Watches a lot of television
Life of the party	Poor impulse control
Outgoing	Loud
Physically fit	Still breathing
Stylish	Slave to every fad that comes down the road
Thoughtful	Says "please" when demanding a beer
Uninhibited	Lacking basic social skills
Wants soulmate	One step away from stalking

DISCUSSION QUESTIONS

1. Using specific examples, discuss how the use of euphemisms, such as those listed above, can lead to miscommunication and false expectations.

2. What are some euphemisms you use to describe yourself when you're trying to make a favorable impression on someone?

From *Fortune Cookies,* http://personal.riverusers.com/~thegrendel/euph.html

---

Euphemisms are often used to smooth over socially sensitive topics. Using the term *pass away* instead of *die* masks our culture's discomfort with the topic of death. Instead of *vagina* or *penis,* we use "cute" terms such as *private parts* or *south of the border.* Similarly, pop star Janet Jackson's Super Bowl Sunday exposure of her breast was referred to as a "wardrobe malfunction." These euphemisms reveal our culture's discomfort with sexually explicit language.

Language has the power to alter how we think about reality. People may use euphemisms to get others to see something from their point of view. In times of war, leaders on both

Connections

Why do advertisers use euphemisms and other rhetorical devices? *See Chapter 10, p. 328.*

sides try to win the support of their citizenry by convincing them that the war is acceptable and even noble. For example, the United States is engaged in Operation Enduring Freedom and "nation building" in Iraq, rather than an invasion or occupation. Our soldiers there are "serving the target" rather than killing enemy soldiers. Enemy civilians who are inadvertently killed in warfare are "collateral damage." The accidental shelling of our own troops is termed "friendly fire," a phrase that seems almost neighborly. Our soldiers who are killed in the war are shipped home in "transfer tubes" rather than body bags. And the private soldiers who work for the U.S. military in Iraqi are "private security consultants" rather than mercenaries.

Politicians are notorious for their manipulative use of language, especially during campaigns, and will often skirt around direct questions by supplying the answers they think their constituents want to hear.

Businesses also make up new terms because of negative connotations associated with old terms. Companies no longer fire employees; instead they downsize, dehire, or practice workforce management or employee transition. Eventually these terms may be deemed too negative. The term *downsize,* for example, has recently been replaced by the more appealing term *rightsize.* And the terms *used cars* and *pre-owned vehicles* have morphed to *experienced vehicles.* Sometimes euphemisms become so widely accepted that they become lexical definitions. For example, *downsize* was added to dictionaries in the 1970s.

Politically correct language is often based on euphemisms in which terms such as *crippled* and *crazy* are replaced with neutral or more positive terms such as *physically challenged* and *mentally ill.* The politically correct movement has been somewhat successful in limiting hate speech, especially on college campuses. More than a hundred colleges and universities in the United States have had, or still have, speech codes that place restrictions on some forms of speech, including hate speech and speech that "violates civility

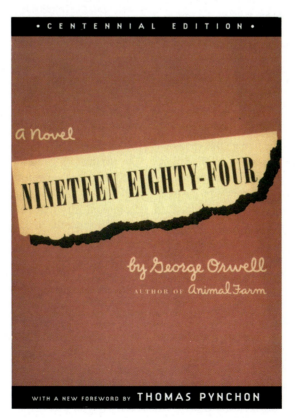

codes."[38] For more on restricting free speech on campuses, see "Critical Thinking Issue: Perspectives on Free-Speech Zones on Colleges Campuses" at the end of this chapter.

While some people support speech codes as encouraging tolerance and diversity, others argue that these codes are self-defeating and force the issue of bigotry and intolerance underground by censoring open discussion and critical thinking about the issue. The tacit suppression of so-called racist views, for example, can leave us believing that prejudice and segregation are no longer a problem, when in fact, many of our nation's schools are even more segregated than they were in 1954 when the U.S. Supreme Court in the case of *Brown v. Board of Education* outlawed school segregation.

George Orwell wrote his novel *Nineteen Eighty-Four* about the insidious role of language manipulation in society, especially by those in power. Orwell warned that by purging language of politically dangerous or offensive words and concepts and substituting euphemisms for them, freedom of speech becomes impossible and resistance to tyranny dif-

dysphemism A word or phrase chosen to produce a negative effect.

sarcasm The use of ridicule, insults, taunting, and/or caustic irony.

hyperbole A rhetorical device that uses an exaggeration.

ficult. Unless we resist this trend we will get caught up in doublethink and become soulless automatons incapable of engaging in critical thinking.[39]

Dysphemisms, in contrast to euphemisms, are used to produce a negative effect. The term *death tax* for inheritance tax was coined to create a feeling of disapproval toward this tax. In the abortion debate, the term *anti-choice* creates a negative feeling toward people who are opposed to abortion rights.

Dysphemisms can be used to win over one group of people while at the same time alienating others. Politicians may use dysphemisms to exaggerate cultural differences and create an us-versus-them mentality. The use of the term *axis of evil* for Iraq, Iran, and North Korea was accompanied by a swing of public opinion in the United States in 2002 against these countries and support for the idea of attacking those countries.[40]

Sarcasm, another rhetorical device, involves the use of ridicule, insults, taunting, and/or caustic irony. It derives its power from the fact that most people hate being made fun of. Like other rhetorical devices, sarcasm is used to deflect critical analysis and to create a feeling of disapproval toward the object of the sarcasm, as in the following letter to the editor from *Newsweek*:

> We're in a blood-soaked foreign war, the national debt threatens our financial future, hatred of Americans is soaring and the issue that finally inflames conservative Oregon voters is the possibility of some people marrying their same-gender loved ones? Wow! I'll have to get my priorities straight.[41]

Sarcasm is often dismissed as humor by those who use it. However, it is anything but funny to its intended target. As good critical thinkers, we need to be able to see though this rhetorical device and not be belittled by it.

Hyperbole is a type of rhetoric that uses exaggeration or overstatement to distort the facts. "I thought I would die when the professor called on me in class today," moans a college student. Some journalists use hyperbole for the purpose of sensationalism and exaggerating a story to the point of absurdity. "Morgue Worker's Snoring Wakes the Dead," read a headline in the *Weekly World News*.[42]

Hyperbole is also found in politics when a grain of truth is exaggerated and distorted. During the early months of the war in Iraq, Iraqi Information Minister Muhammed Saeed al-Sahaf engaged in hyperbole when he reported sweeping Iraqi triumphs over the coalition forces, despite all evidence to the contrary. Former abortion rights advocate Dr. Bernard Nathanson also used hyperbole when he exaggerated the number of maternal deaths due to illegal abortions in order to gain public support for the legalization of abortion. "I confess that I knew the figures were totally false," he later wrote. "But in the 'morality' of our revolution, it was a useful figure, widely accepted."[43] In these cases hyperbole involved the deliberate use of deception and lying.

Some people are prone to exaggeration because of the attention they get from using it. The habitual use of hyperbole, however, damages our credibility. Like the little boy who cried "wolf," we may not be believed when we finally tell it as it really is.

Hot or Not?

Is lying for the greater good ever justified?

Deception and Lying

Although rhetorical devices may involve deception, the deception is not always deliberate. There are also cases when deception is expected and acceptable, as in a poker game or preparation for a surprise party. A **lie**, on the other hand, is "a deliberate attempt to mislead, without the prior consent of the target."[44] Withholding or omitting certain information in a way that distorts a message so it is deceptive may also constitute lying.

In the 1998 Paula Jones deposition, lawyers produced a definition of *sex* before asking former President Bill Clinton if he had had sex with Monica Lewinsky. Clinton replied emphatically that he had not. His response was based on the fact that the definition provided did not specifically list "mouth" as one of the body parts involved in sex. Clinton later admitted that his answer had been intended to "mislead" and "give a false impression" regarding his inappropriate sexual relationship with Lewinsky.[45] Clinton was impeached by the House of Representatives in December 1998 for perjury and obstruction of justice and acquitted of the charges by the Senate two months later.

Most lies, such as that told by Bill Clinton, are told to avoid getting into trouble or to cover misbehavior. So-called little white lies may be used to ease social awkwardness, avoid hurting feelings, or put us in a more posi-

Connections

How can you evaluate political candidates when rhetoric so often dominates campaigns? *See Chapter 13, p. 379.*

Why do journalists use hyperbole, and how can we avoid being taken in by it? *See Chapter 11, p. 345.*

How does the media sometimes engage in hyperbole when reporting scientific findings? *See Chapter 11, p. 351.*

Facial expressions, especially the eyes, can disclose a wealth of information. The person on the left is faking a smile while the smile of the woman on the right is genuine.

and other sensations. Unlike liars, truth-tellers also tend to make spontaneous corrections to their stories.

Lying creates cognitive and emotional overload. As a result, liars tend to move less and blink less because of the extra effort they need to remember what they're already said and to keep their stories consistent. Their voices may become more tense or high-pitched and their speech may be filled with pauses. Liars also tend to make fewer speech errors than do truth tellers, and they rarely backtrack to fill in "forgotten" or incorrect details.[48]

Scientists at the Salk Institute in California have developed a computer that can read a person's rapidly changing facial expressions and body language.[49] Polygraphs, in contrast, measure reactions like heartbeat and perspiration, which some clever liars are able to control. The scientists hope that computers may someday be able to determine what emotions underlie different facial expressions. However, because some types of body language are shaped by our culture, lie detectors, whether human or computer, need to take into account cultural and sex differences in discerning if there is deception.

Although we may be initially taken in by someone's lies, we should be willing to check what another person

tive light. Other lies, such as Dr. Nathanson's regarding the number of maternal deaths due to illegal abortions and lies told to the enemy during war may be rationalized as being for the greater good.

In addition to derailing honest communication, lying raises several ethical issues. Is it ever morally acceptable to lie to spare someone's feelings or to promote what we regard as the "greater good"? How about a lie to save a life? Most ethicists agree that the great majority of lies are not justified. Lies can damage trust, as happened in the case of Bill Clinton. In addition, making a political or life decision based on someone else's lies can have ruinous results. Wars may be waged based on misinformation. A murderer may go free if the investigating police officer or jury believes his or her lies.

Most of us are easily taken in by the lies of others. A recent study found that people lie about a third of the time in their interactions with others; only about 18 percent of lies are ever discovered.[46] The average person is able to tell the difference between a liar and a truth-teller only about 55 percent of the time (not much better than chance). Even when lies are exposed, the public will sometimes get caught up in doublethink—knowing that what they once believed is a lie but continuing to act as though the lie were true.

The good news is that we can train ourselves to be better at detecting other people's lies. Skilled lie-catchers, such as police, FBI investigators, and some psychiatrists, are able to distinguish between liars and truth-tellers with 80 percent to 95 percent accuracy.[47] This makes them almost as accurate as a polygraph or lie-detector machine. Professional lie-catchers closely observe patterns of verbal and nonverbal communication. When most people lie, their body language as well as the tone of their voice changes subtly. For example, children between 9 and 14 who lie about sexual abuse (lies about sexual abuse are rare in children younger than 9) tend to report the alleged abuse chronologically, since it is too difficult to fabricate a story out of order. Truth-tellers, in contrast, jump around and include information such as smells, background noises,

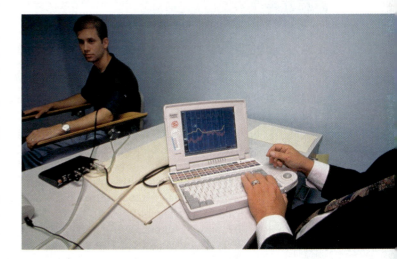

Various tests and devices, such as the polygraph machine in the photograph, have been created to evaluate the validity and truth of someone's assertions.

tells us—be it a friend, relative, or the media—against other evidence. As critical thinkers, we should be ready to check out sources of information and make sure they are reliable to avoid falling prey to deception. We also need to be aware of manipulative language. Emotive language

Connections

How does the impeachment process act as a check on the misuse of executive power? *See Chapter 13, p. 421.*

and the use of rhetorical devices can be used to distract us from the issue at hand and to persuade us to take a position without actually providing any factual information or sound arguments.

Language is a form of symbolic communication that allows us to organize and critically analyze our experiences. Language shapes our concept of reality and of who we are. It is mainly through language that we transmit our culture. As critical thinkers, we need to clearly define our terms and be mindful of our communication style and that of others. Unfortunately, language can also be used to stereotype or mislead, either through deliberate deception or the use of rhetorical devices. Good communication skills are vital in critical thinking and are also one of the most important factors in establishing and maintaining good relationships.

1. Discuss how the use of emotive language in each of the following passages is used to promote a particular point of view. Rewrite each passage using neutral language.
   a. "A unit in Iraq defies orders, spurring questions about morale."[50]
   b. "The promise of embryonic-stem cell research occurs precisely because the embryo destroyed in the process was once both alive and human. As such, the harvesting of embryonic stem cells represents a form of medical cannibalism. If we cannot protect human life at its most vulnerable stages, basic constitutional protections will wither away and die."[51]
   c. "Oliver Stone's [movie] 'Alexander' will conscript you for a long forced march. Better have an exit strategy."[52]
   d. "In a cramped upstairs den in South St. Paul, Minn., a CD blares with fury. 'Hang the traitors of our race,' the singer screams. 'White supremacy! Whiiiite supremacy!' Byron Calvert, 33, leans back in his chair, smiling and snacking on veggies. Calvert is a mountainous man with a swastika tattoo, a prison record and a racist dream."[53]
   e. "Christians should not shy away from such debates [about euthanasia], especially since, under question, Mr. Singer [who supports euthanasia] reveals that he lives in an ivory tower."[54]
   f. "According to the National Sleep Foundation, about 60% of U.S. adults have insomnia every few days. I've been thinking more and more about those seductive commercials for Ambien, the pill that promises a full night of blissful sleep with few side effects."[55]

2. Should journalists and the news media avoid the use of emotively loaded words such as *terrorist* and *reform*? Is it even possible or desirable to avoid these terms? Support your answers.

3. Identify the rhetorical device(s) or type of emotive language found in each of the following passages. What point is the writer trying to make by using these?
   a. "Joe's between jobs. He has an interview later this week."
   b. "We had to destroy the village to save it." [From Vietnam War, c. 1968]
   c. "Most vegetarians look so much like the food they eat that they can be classified as cannibals."—Finley Peter Dunne
   d. "Shocking Hubble photo reveals: Killer Asteroid Headed for Earth! Bush Calls Panic Summit with World Leaders."[56]
   e. Child: "Where's Fido?"
   Parent: "We had to put Fido down. He's in doggy heaven."
   f. "The National Rifle Association's campaign to arm every man, women and child in America, received a setback when the President signed the Brady Bill. But the gun-pushers know that the bill was only a small skirmish in the big war over guns in America."[57]
   g. "I see you have a copy of the dead-tree edition of that new online magazine."
   h. "Reader, suppose you were an idiot. And suppose you were a member of Congress. But I repeat myself."—Mark Twain
   i. "Management ordered the security guards to take steps to reduce inventory shrinkage."
   j. "I never forget a face, but in your case I'll be glad to make an exception."—Groucho Marx
   k. "NASA Rover Photographs Cat Creatures on Mars! Shocked experts say abandoned pets prove aliens visited Earth."[58]
   l. "Churchill and Bush can both be considered wartime leaders, just as Secretariat and Mr. Ed were both horses."[59]

4. Harvard law professor Alan Dershowitz argues that the politically correct movement, while claiming to promote greater diversity, has in fact limited diversity of expression. He writes:

As a teacher, I can feel a palpable reluctance on the part of many students particularly those with views in neither extreme and those who are anxious for peer acceptance—to experiment with unorthodox ideas, to make playful comments on serious subjects, to challenge politically correct views and to disagree with minority, feminist or gay perspectives.

I feel this problem quite personally, since I happen to agree . . . with most "politically correct" positions. But I am appalled at the intolerance of many who share my substantive views. And I worry about the impact of politically correct intolerance on the generation of leaders we are currently educating.

Do you agree with Dershowitz? What are some examples of "politically incorrect" words or phrases on your campus? Support your answer using specific examples from your own experience as a college student. Do you find that you have to be careful to think about what you say and to avoid politically incorrect terms? Does having to do so facilitate or inhibit critical thinking?

5. Look on the Internet and in newspapers and/or magazines for examples of emotive language. What is the purpose of the emotive language in the text?

6. Select a controversial issue such as animal rights or physician-assisted suicide. Write a page using emotive language and rhetoric supporting one side of the issue. Now rewrite (paraphrase) the page using neutral language. Is the argument as compelling when you used neutral language? To what extent did your argument depend on emotive language and rhetorical devices rather than reason?

7. Is self-deception ever justified? A University of California study found that patients awaiting surgery who deceived themselves about the seriousness of their condition suffered fewer postoperative complications. In a similar study, women with breast cancer who denied the seriousness of their condition were more likely to survive than those who resigned themselves to their fate.[60] Write a two- to three-page essay discussing whether self-deception was justified in the above cases and if it is compatible with critical thinking.

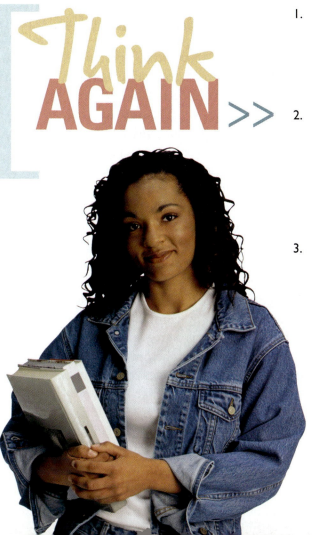

Think AGAIN >>

1. What are the primary functions of language?
   - One of the primary functions is informative or the conveying of information about the world and ourselves. Directive language functions to influence actions, while expressive language communicates feelings. Finally, ceremonial language is used in certain formal circumstances.

2. Why is it important to pay close attention when evaluating and interpreting definitions of words?
   - Definitions are not fixed—they can have denotative meanings, which describe the properties of the word being described, and they can have connotative meanings, which include feelings and thoughts that are based on previous experience. Also, there are stipulative, lexical, precising, and persuasive definitions.

3. What are rhetorical devices, and how are they used?
   - Rhetorical devices are used for persuasion. Euphemism, the replacement of a negative term with a positive one to cover up the truth, and dysphemisms, which are used to elicit a negative response, are both examples of rhetorical devices. Others include sarcasm and hyperbole.

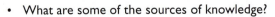

Think FIRST >>

- What are some of the sources of knowledge?
- In what ways might experience be misleading?
- What are some of the types of cognitive and social errors in our thinking?

that he went into a rage and murdered his mother. When Reilly denied the charge, they kept urging him to dig deeper into his unconscious until he recovered the lost memory. After more than sixteen hours of grueling questioning Reilly began to "remember"—faintly at first and then more vividly—murdering his mother. Several hours later, Reilly, exhausted and confused, finally signed a confession. Even though he later came to doubt his role in the murder, his confession was the most compelling piece of evidence in the criminal trial.

Reilly was found guilty of first-degree manslaughter and sentenced to six to sixteen years in prison. It wasn't until two years later that evidence placing him several miles away at the time of the murder proved that Reilly could not have been the murderer. Reilly was eventually exonerated and released from prison. Despite this evidence, some Connecticut State police continued to believe that Reilly was guilty. The identity of his mother's murderer remains a mystery.

The Reilly case illustrates how social expectations and leading questions can alter a person's beliefs and memories.[1] Good critical-thinking skills require that we evaluate evidence thoroughly and be aware of social and cognitive errors in our thinking to effectively evaluate any given situation and avoid jumping to a conclusion or acting hastily based on preconceived ideas. In Chapter 4 we will

- Learn about the nature and limitations of human knowledge

- Distinguish between rationalism and empiricism

- Learn about different types of evidence

- Set guidelines for evaluating evidence

- Look at sources for researching claims and evidence

- Study different types of cognitive/perceptual errors, including self-serving biases

- Learn how social expectations and group pressure can lead to erroneous thinking

Finally, we will examine the evidence and arguments regarding unidentified flying objects (UFOs) and what type of proof would be necessary to establish their existence.

Peter Reilly was falsely convicted of murdering his mother—1973 Connecticut.

HUMAN KNOWLEDGE AND ITS LIMITATIONS

Knowledge is information or experience that we believe to be true and for which we have justification or evidence. Understanding how we acquire knowledge as well as having an awareness of the limitations of human understanding are essential in logical reasoning.

Rationalism and Empiricism

Our views of ourselves and the world around us are shaped by our understanding of the nature of truth and the ultimate sources of knowledge. **Rationalists** claim that most human knowledge comes through reason. Greek philosopher Plato (427–347 BCE) believed that there is an unchanging truth we can know through reason and that most of us confuse truth with worldly appearance.

The empiricists reject the rationalists' claim that it is through reason that we discern truth. **Empiricists** instead claim that we discover truth primarily through our physical senses—what is known as empirical evidence. Science is based primarily on empiricism. The scientific method involves making direct observations of the world, and then coming up with a hypothesis to explain these observations.

Structure of the Mind

German philosopher Immanuel Kant (1724–1804) rejected both rationalism and empiricism. He argued that how we experience reality is not simply a matter of pure reason or of using physical senses but depends on the structure of our minds. Like computers—which are designed to accept and process particular kinds of inputs from the outside world—our brains must have the correct "hardware" to accept and make sense of incoming data.

Most psychologists and neurologists believe, as did Kant, that we do not see "reality" directly as it is but that instead our mind or brain provides structure and rules for processing incoming information. In other words, as we noted in Chapter 1, we *interpret* our experiences rather than directly perceiving the world "out there."

While our brain helps us make sense of the

knowledge Information which we believe to be true and for which we have justification or evidence.

rationalist One who claims that most human knowledge comes through reason.

empiricist One who believes that we discover truth primarily through our physical senses.

Connections

How is the assumption of empiricism reflected in the scientific method? *See Chapter 12, p. 373.*

SELF-EVALUATION QUESTIONNAIRE

Rate yourself on the following scale from 1 (strongly disagree) to 5 (strongly agree)

1 2 3 4 5   Knowledge comes primarily through reason rather than the senses.

1 2 3 4 5   I have a tendency to look only for evidence that confirms my assumptions or cherished worldviews.

1 2 3 4 5   The most credible evidence is that based on direct experience, such as eyewitness reports.

1 2 3 4 5   When I look at a random shape such as a cloud or craters on the moon, I tend to see meaning or an image in it.

1 2 3 4 5   The probability that there are two students in a class of twenty-four who have a birthday on the same day and month is about 50 percent.

1 2 3 4 5   When I buy a lottery ticket, I use my lucky number.

1 2 3 4 5   I can truly enjoy life only if I have perfect control over it.

1 2 3 4 5   I am better than most at getting along with other people.

1 2 3 4 5   Americans are more trustworthy than other people, especially people from non-Western cultures.

Think Tank

Critical Thinking in Action

Memorization Strategies

In a study of why some people are better at accurately memorizing new information, magnetic resonance brain imaging was used to determine which brain regions are correlated with specific memorization strategies. Researchers found that most people use one or a combination of the following four strategies for remembering the picture to the right.

1. **Visualization inspection.** Participants carefully study the visual appearance of an object. Some people are much better at this strategy and are able to commit pictures as well as pages of books to visual memory.

2. **Verbal elaboration**. Individuals construct sentences about the objects or material they are trying to memorize. For example, they may say to themselves, "The pig is key to this image."

3. **Mental imagery**. Individuals form interactive mental images, much like an animated cartoon. For example, they may imagine the pig jumping into a pool off the end of a diving board shaped like a key.

4. **Memory retrieval**.   People reflect and come up with a meaning for the object or association of the object with personal memories.

Participants who use one or a combination of these different strategies performed better at learning new material than those who used these strategies only rarely or not at all. In addition, it was found that each of these strategies used different parts of the brain and that people seem to have different learning styles that work best for them.

DISCUSSION QUESTIONS

1. What strategy, if any, do you use for learning new information? For example, what strategy might you use for remembering the above picture? Evaluate the effectiveness of the strategy or strategies in helping you be a better critical thinker and in your performance in classes.

2. Discuss a time when you later discovered that a memory you had was inaccurate or false. How might the use of these strategies make you less prone to these types of memory distortions?

anecdotal evidence Evidence based on personal testimonies.

something to one person and she whispers the message to the next person and so on down the line until the last person says what he has heard. It is almost always different, often amusingly so, from the original message.

Anecdotal evidence, which is based on personal testimonies, is also unreliable because of the problem of inaccurate memory as well as the human tendency to exaggerate or distort what we experience to fit our expectations. For example, many people have reported seeing UFOs and, in some cases, being abducted by aliens. However, despite the apparent sincerity of their beliefs, anecdotal evidence in the absence of any physical evidence cannot be used as proof that UFOs and aliens exist. We'll be looking at different perspectives on the credibility of the evidence for UFOs in the readings at the end of this chapter.

Experts and Credibility

One of the most credible sources of information is that of experts. When turning to an expert, it is important that we find someone who is knowledgeable in the particular field under question. When we use the testimony of a person who is an expert in a *different* field, we are committing the fallacy of appeal to inappropriate authority. We'll study fallacies in more depth in Chapter 5.

For example, many students believe, on the basis of the testimony of their friends, that marijuana use is harmless and that it is perfectly safe to drive after smoking a joint. In fact, research by medical experts shows that, although marijuana does not impair driving as much as alcohol, reaction time is reduced by 41 percent after smoking one joint and 63 percent after smoking two joints.[9] Despite evidence from experts, most people will still base their judgments on smoking marijuana on information from their peers until they develop stronger critical-thinking skills.

In seeking out experts, we should look at their credentials, including

1. *Education* or training from a reputable institute
2. *Experience* in making judgments in the field
3. *Reputation* among peers as an expert in the field
4. *Accomplishments* in the field such as academic papers and awards

Unfortunately, expert testimony is not foolproof. Experts may disagree, in which case we will have to reserve judgment or look to others in the field. Furthermore, sometimes experts are biased, particularly those who are being paid by special-interest groups or corporations who stand to gain financially from supporting a particular position.

For example, it has long been assumed that milk and dairy products help maintain strong bones in adults. However, this claim has not been supported by scientific research. Instead it has been mainly promoted by groups that financially depend on the sale of dairy products. While the National Dairy Council extols the benefits of milk for people of all ages, many medical experts, including researchers at the Harvard School of Public Health[10] and the Physicians Committee for Responsible Medicine, argue, based on research, that milk may actually accelerate the process of bone loss in adults. Recently, the Federal Trade Commission, a government agency charged with protecting consumers and eliminating unfair and deceptive marketplace practices, ordered the National Dairy Council to withdraw its ads that claimed drinking milk can prevent osteoporosis.

Preconceived notions or assumptions can also influence how experts interpret evidence. Brandon Mayfield, an Oregon lawyer and a Muslim convert, was taken into custody in Portland, Oregon, after the March 11, 2004, train bombing in Madrid, Spain, when what appeared to be his fingerprint mysteriously turned up on a plastic bag used by the bombers. Although Spanish law-enforcement agencies expressed doubt that the fingerprint was Mayfield's, U.S. officials insisted that it was an "absolutely incontrovertible match."[11] As it later turned out, the fingerprint belonged to an Algerian living in Spain. The U.S. officials succumbed to preconceived notions in making a false arrest of Mayfield.

Connections

How can you determine whether a science news story is well done and accurate? *See Chapter 11, p. 353.*

How do scientists design experiments to avoid bias? *See Chapter 12, p. 388.*

How can you recognize and avoid being taken in by misleading advertisements? *See Chapter 10, p. 325.*

got milk?

Liquid Gold.

9 essential nutrients to
make big waves.

Inadequate research can lead to misrepresentation of a product—advertisers, for example, claimed that milk built strong bones, a claim that was later proven false. The above ad also contains the fallacy of appeal to inappropriate authority, since Olympic swimmer Michael Phelps is not an expert on the health benefits of milk.

While experts are usually a good source of credible evidence, even experts can be biased and can misinterpret data. Because of this, it is important that we be able to evaluate claims, especially those that may be slanted or that conflict with other experts' analysis.

Evaluating Evidence for a Claim

Our analysis of the evidence for a claim should be accurate, unbiased, and as complete as possible. Credible evidence is consistent with other relevant evidence. In addition, the more evidence there is to support a

confirmation bias The tendency to look only for evidence that supports our assumptions.

claim, the more reasonable it is to accept that claim (see "Thinking Outside the Box: Rachel Carson, Biologist and Author"). In critical thinking, there is no virtue in rigid adherence to a position that is not supported by evidence.

Sometimes we don't have access to credible evidence for a claim. In cases such as these, we should look for contradictory evidence. For example, some atheists reject the belief that there is a God because, they argue, it is contradicted by the presence of so much evil in the world. When there is evidence that contradicts a claim, we have good reason to doubt the claim. However, if there is no contradictory evidence, we should remain open to the possibility that a position may be true.

In evaluating a claim, we need to watch out for **confirmation bias**, the tendency to look only for evidence that confirms our assumptions and to resist evidence that contradicts them. This inclination is so strong that we may even disregard or reinterpret evidence that runs contrary to our cherished beliefs.[12] In research on people who were opposed to and those who supported capital punishment, both sides interpreted the findings of a study on whether capital punishment deterred crime to fit their prior views. If the evidence did not fit, they focused on the flaws in the research and dismissed its validity or, in some cases, actually distorted the evidence to support their position.[13] Politicians may also cherry-pick the evidence, reading only reports and listening to evidence that supports their previous beliefs. This happened in 2002 when policy makers in Washington claimed there was conclusive proof that Iraq had weapons of mass destruction. Similarly, newscasters and journalists who have strong beliefs about particular issues may also engage in confirmation bias.

During the 2004 Olympics, Joe Scarborough, on the MSNBC television news show *Scarborough Country*, praised the American work ethic and capitalism as responsible for America's having won the most Olympic medals. Unlike capitalism, he argued, socialism makes people lazy and underachievers. When he got an e-mail from a Danish viewer pointing out that Americans had won only 1 medal for every 2.6 million people, whereas the Danes had won 1 medal for every 900,000 people, Scarborough first dismissed the use of statistics with a wave of his hand and then went on to argue that the Danes had won their medals only because they are a far-left socialist country where everyone has two months off to indulge in athletics if they wish rather than work. In doing so, Scarborough used evidence against his claim to support his claim, thus engaging in doublethink!

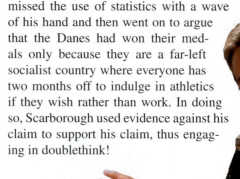

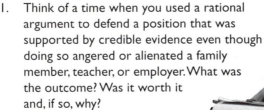

Outside the Box

RACHEL CARSON, *Biologist and Author*

After graduating with a master's degree in zoology from Johns Hopkins University, Rachel Carson (1907–1964) was hired as a writer by the U.S. Fish and Wildlife Service. The success of her 1951 book, *The Sea Around Us*, allowed her to leave her job and concentrate on her life goal of becoming a writer.

As early as 1945 she had become concerned about the overuse of chemical pesticides, such as DDT. Although others before her had tried to warn the public about the dangers of these powerful pesticides, it was her reputation as a complete and meticulous researcher, along with her intellectual curiosity, that contributed to her success. She began by examining the existing research on the effect of pesticides. Her reputation also allowed her to enlist the expertise and support of scientists in the field.

When *Silent Spring* was published in 1962, it created an immediate uproar and backlash. A huge counterattack was launched by the big chemical companies, including Monsanto and Velsicol, which denounced her as a "hysterical woman" unqualified to write on the topic. Despite threats of lawsuits, Carson didn't back down. Because her research was informed and accurate, her opponents were unable to find holes in her argument. *Silent Spring* changed the course of American history and launched a new environmental movement.

DISCUSSION QUESTIONS

1. Think of a time when you used a rational argument to defend a position that was supported by credible evidence even though doing so angered or alienated a family member, teacher, or employer. What was the outcome? Was it worth it and, if so, why?

2. Rachel Carson is an example of how one person can make a huge difference. Looking into your future, in what ways might you be able to use your talents and critical-thinking skills to make the world a better place?

Confirmation bias may also take the form of more rigorously scrutinizing contrary evidence than that which supports our position. Peter Jennings, of ABC's *World News Tonight*, presented a study that "disproved" therapeutic touch, a healing method used extensively in India that involves a therapist's using the "energy" in his or her hands to help correct the "energy field" of a sick person. The study, which was previously quoted in a prestigious medical journal, had been carried out by a fourth grader, Emily Rosa, as a project for her science class. On the basis of this single fourth grader's project, the editor of the journal had declared that therapeutic touch was bogus. Because the editor had a bias against nontraditional therapies, he held "studies" that suggested therapeutic touch might be ineffective to a lower standard of proof.

Connections

How do scientists use evidence to test a hypothesis? *See Chapter 12, p. 378.* How do we as consumers reinforce confirmation bias in the news media? *See Chapter 11, p. 346.*

Connections

How do scientists gather evidence to test their hypotheses? *See Chapter 12, p. 379.*

What are the "rules of evidence" in a court of law? *See Chapter 13, p. 433.*

How reliable is the news media as a source of information? *See Chapter 11, p. 345.*

Because of the human propensity to engage in confirmation bias, many scholarly scientific journals require that researchers report disconfirmatory evidence as well as contradictory interpretations of their data. Brain imaging studies have found that when we come to a conclusion that confirms our prior bias, the decision is associated with a pleasure response and a feeling of emotional comfort, even though our conclusion is erroneous.[14] As critical thinkers, we need to consciously develop strategies that compel us to examine evidence, especially that which confirms our prior views, with a more skeptical eye and to be more open-minded about evidence that contradicts our views.

In evaluating evidence, the degree of credibility required depends on the circumstances. The greater the impact our actions might have, the greater the degree of credibility and certainty we should demand. Courts of law require a high degree of credibility for evidence of guilt because of the dire consequences of declaring an innocent person guilty, as happened in the Reilly case. A morning weather report of possible rain, however, is enough to warrant carrying our umbrella or rain gear.

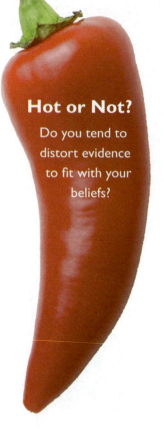

Hot or Not?

Do you tend to distort evidence to fit with your beliefs?

Research Resources

We live in an age where information is proliferating at an astounding rate. We are inundated on a daily basis with information from newspapers, television, the Internet, and other media sources. When using evidence from the media—especially the mass media—we need to consider the sources and their slant, if any.

In addition, some writing, such as novels, poetry, and even some editorials, is not intended to be taken as factual. For example, some readers of Dan Brown's popular thriller *The Da Vinci Code* (2003) took what Brown wrote as fact and proof that Jesus was married to Mary Magdalene, even though the book was a novel. As Brown himself was quick to point out, while the novel is based on certain facts regarding documents, rituals, organizations, artwork, and architecture, the *interpretation* of these facts by the characters in the novel is purely speculative and a work of fiction.[15]

Assessing claims, including distinguishing between fact and fiction, requires good research skills and competence in gathering, evaluating, and synthesizing supporting evidence. Research involves keeping an open mind, carefully examining the information, and evaluating the credibility of the sources, as well as being able to pull all the evidence together and draw a conclusion that is based on it.

Like scientists, good critical thinkers spend a lot of time researching claims and collecting information before drawing a conclusion. As you begin your research, try to set up an interview with someone who is an expert in the

Tom Hanks and Audrey Tautou starred in the Da Vinci Code, a fusion of factual events and author fabrications.

field under investigation, such as a faculty member or an outside expert. An expert can provide you with information as well as point you to reputable publications. When interviewing the expert, don't rely on your memory. Take accurate notes; repeat what you think you heard if you are unsure. Librarians are also a valuable source of information. In addition to their wealth of knowledge regarding resources, some college librarians have PhD's in specialized fields.

Dictionaries and *encyclopedias* are another good place for you to start your research. Specialized reference books often contain extensive bibliographies of good source material. They may be accessed online or used in the reference section of your library. If you are doing time-sensitive research, make sure the reference sources are up-to-date.

Library catalogues—most of which are online—are invaluable in research. Use key words to find your subject in the catalogue or on the computer. In selecting resources, check the date of publication. If your library doesn't have a particular book or journal, you can usually get it through interlibrary loan.

Scholarly journals contain articles that have been reviewed by fellow experts in the field. The Internet has greatly expanded the modern library, and most scholarly journals are indexed on specialized databases that you can access through your library Internet home page. In some cases, the full journal articles are available on the Internet. For more general information, the Expanded Academic Index is a good place to start.

Government documents are also reputable sources of information about such things as employment statistics and demographics. You can access many of the government documents through Internet databases. Go to http://www.usa.gov/ for a list of these databases.

Internet Web sites contain a wealth of information. Millions of new pages are added every week to the Internet. Many Internet sites are sponsored by reputable organizations and individuals. In some cases, however, it is difficult to assess the credibility of the information on a Web site.

The top-level domain at the end of a Web site's address (URL, or uniform resource locator) can help you in evaluating its reliability. All URLs for U.S. government sites end with the top-level domain *.gov*. URLs for sites ending with the top-level domain *.edu* indicate that the source of the information is a U.S. educational institution. Both of these types of sites can generally be counted on to provide reliable and accurate information. The global top-level domain *.org* indicates that the site belongs to a private or nonprofit organization such as Amnesty International or possibly a religious group, from anywhere in the world. The information on these sites may or may not be reliable, depending on the reputability of the organization sponsoring the Web site. The global top-level domain *.com* indi-

Home page for firstgov.org.

cates that the site is sponsored by a commercial organization such as a corporation or private business, whether in the United States or elsewhere. In these cases you must try to determine the companies' motives in providing the information—for example, is it for advertising purposes? Finally, there are also country-code top-level domains that indicate which country the Web site's owner registered it in, such as *.al* for Albania, *.de* for Germany, and *.ke* for Kenya. If you have any doubts about a site's credibility, it is best to ask a reference librarian or expert in the field about the most reliable sites to look at for information on an issue.

While doing your research, no matter what resource you are using, take accurate notes or make copies of articles. Keep full citation information for your sources so that you can refer to them later and cite them if necessary. If, in presenting your research, you use material word for word, always put it in quotation marks and acknowledge the source. You should also cite the source of paraphrased information that is not widely known. In addition, remember to cite sources for any surveys, statistics, and graphics.

Researching a claim or issue requires that we be able to sort through and analyze the relevant data. Good research skills also help us make better decisions in our lives by providing us with the tools for evaluating different claims and available courses of action we might take.

Connections

How do scientists go about gathering information and evidence? *See Chapter 12, p. 378 and p. 388.*

How does the Internet affect our lives? *See Chapter 11, p. 355.*

1. What evidence might be sufficient for you to conclude that an intelligent computer or android is conscious and has free will? Would this same evidence be sufficient to prove to you that another human you met was conscious and had free will? If not, explain why there is a discrepancy.

2. Think of a time when you saw something or someone doing something and were convinced that your interpretation of the event was true, but you later came to have doubts about the credibility of your interpretation. Discuss the factors that contributed to your having doubts.

3. Working in small groups, evaluate the following list of claims. If there are any ambiguous terms, define them as best as possible. Next, make a list of types of evidence you would need to support or reject each claim. State how you would go about doing the research.

   a. Genetically modified food is dangerous.
   b. Men are more aggressive by nature than are women.
   c. Prayers are answered.
   d. Toast is more likely to fall butter-side down.
   e. Asian Americans are better at math than European Americans are.
   f. Living together before marriage is associated with a lower divorce rate.
   g. Human life begins at conception.
   h. A flying saucer crashed over Roswell, New Mexico, in 1947.
   i. Canadians, on average, live longer than Americans do.
   j. God exists.
   k. The sea level has risen almost a foot over the past century as a result of global warming.
   l. Yawning is contagious.
   m. Capital punishment deters crime.
   n. Debbie was born under the sign Aquarius. Therefore, she must love water.

4. Select one of the following topics and research it.
   - The impact of global warming on your city or state
   - The average age of marriage for men and women now and when your parents got married
   - The number of members in the U.S. House of Representatives
   - The percentage of American college athletes who become professional athletes
   - The changes over the past 30 years in majors of college students
   - Britney Spears's love life

   Make a list of the resources, including experts, books, journals, search engines, databases, and Web sites you used in your research. Rate each of the sources you used in terms of which generated the most credible and unbiased evidence. Compare your results with those of others in your class. To what extent did the topic chosen determine which research resources, including the Internet, were most useful?

5. Choose one of the claims from in-class exercise 3 and research the evidence. Write a short essay or present your results to the class for evaluation.

6. Imagine that you are backing out of a parking spot on campus. Your view is somewhat obscured by an SUV parked beside you. As you back out, you hit another car that was driving through the parking lot. Write a paragraph describing the event for the police report.

   Now imagine that you are the other person whose car was hit. Once again, write a paragraph describing the event for the police report. Compare and contrast the two reports. Analyze how the words you chose in each report were selected to influence the perception of the police officer regarding what happened.

COGNITIVE AND PERCEPTUAL ERRORS IN THINKING

On the evening of October 30, 1938, a play based on H.G. Wells's novel *War of the Worlds* about a Martian invasion was broadcast to the nation on radio. Many of the people who listened to the show believed that the invasion was real. Some people even "smelled" the poisonous Martian gas and "felt" the heat rays being described on the radio. Others claimed to have seen the giant machines landing in New Jersey and the flames from the battle. One panicked person told police he had heard the president's voice on the radio ordering them to evacuate.

Our perceptions of the world around us are easily skewed by social influences, as was the case when live radio broadcasts of the Martian invasion caused eyewitness reports of apparently nonexistent phenomena. Most people underestimate the critical role that cognitive and social factors play in our perception and interpretation of sense data. Although emotion has traditionally been regarded as the culprit when reason goes astray, studies suggest that many of the errors in our thinking are neurological in nature.[16] In this section, we'll be looking at some of these cognitive and perceptual errors.

Connections

As a consumer, how can you avoid being taken in by cognitive and perceptual errors used by marketers? *See Chapter 10, p. 319.*

Perceptual Errors

Our minds are not like blank sheets of paper or recording devices, such as cameras or video recorders, as the empiricists claimed. Instead, our brains construct a picture of the world much as an artist does. Our brains filter our perceptions and fill in missing information based in part on our expectations, as occurred in the broadcast of *War of the Worlds*.

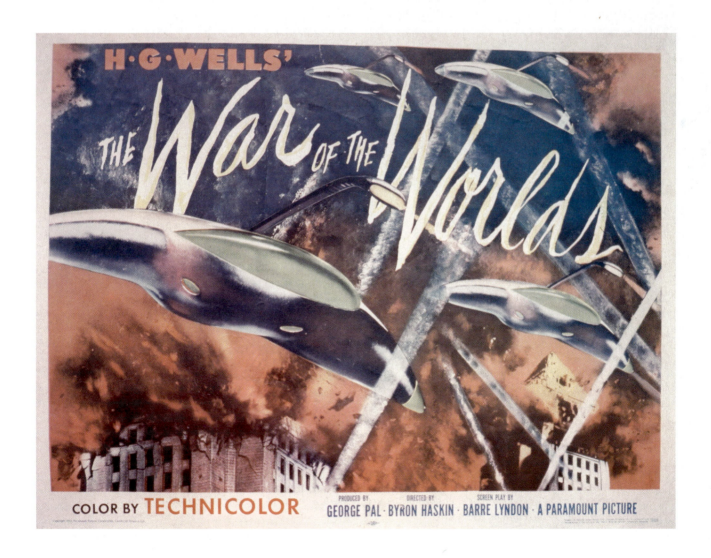

H·G·WELLS' THE War OF THE Worlds

COLOR BY TECHNICOLOR

PRODUCED BY GEORGE PAL · DIRECTED BY BYRON HASKIN · SCREEN PLAY BY BARRE LYNDON · A PARAMOUNT PICTURE

What tools and strategies do scientists use to minimize perceptual errors? *See Chapter 12, p. 378.*

Connections

Some skeptics believe that UFO sightings are based on perceptual errors, including optical illusions (see "Analyzing Images: The St. Louis Arch"). In 1969, an Air National Guard pilot spotted what he thought was a squadron of UFOs within several hundred feet of his plane. He later described the UFOs as the color of "burnished aluminum" and "shaped like a hydroplane." As it turned out, the "squadron of UFOs" was most likely a meteor fireball that had broken up in the vicinity of the plane.[17] However, while being able to provide alternative explanations for most UFO sightings makes the existence of aliens less probable, we cannot conclude with certainty that *all* sightings are a result of perceptual errors. We'll be looking at the issue of the existence of UFOs in the "Critical Thinking Issue: Perspectives on the Existence of Unidentified Flying Objects" section at the end of this chapter.

Our minds may also distort objects we perceive. A straight stick, when inserted in water, appears to bend. A

Analyzing Images

THE ST. LOUIS ARCH Designed by Finnish-born architect Eero Saarinen, the St. Louis Arch in St. Louis, Missouri, was completed in 1965 on a site overlooking the Mississippi River. Although the height of the arch and its width at the base are both 630 feet, the graceful catenary creates the illusion that the arch is taller than it is wide. Even if we are told that its height and width are the same, we still have great difficulty making the cognitive adjustment to correct the optical illusion.

DISCUSSION QUESTIONS

1. *What was your first reaction when you were told that the height and width of the arch were the same? Did they look the same after you were told the dimensions of the arch? Share with the class other optical illusions that you have encountered in architecture or elsewhere.*

2. *To view more optical illusions, go to http://www.michaelbach.de/ot/. What purpose, if any, do you think that these and other optical illusions serve?*

RORSCHACH INKBLOT   In a Rorschach test, a psychologist asks a person to describe what he or she sees in an inkblot such as the one above. The psychologist uses the descriptions to learn more about a person's motivations and unconscious drives.

DISCUSSION QUESTIONS

1. *What do you see when you look at the above ink blot? Why do you think you saw what you did?*

2. *Discuss how the Rorschach test illustrates our tendency to impose order on random data.*

full moon appears to be much larger when it is near the horizon, a phenomenon that NASA refers to as the "moon illusion."

Misperception of Random Data

Our brains loathe absence of meaning. Because of this, we may "see" order or meaningful patterns where there are none. For example, when we look at clouds or see unexplained lights in the sky, our brains impose meaning on the random shapes we see. When we look at the moon, we see a "face," popularly known as the man in the moon. Recently a piece of toast with cheese, allegedly bearing the image of the Virgin Mary, sold on eBay for $28,000.

One of the most famous examples of this type of error is the "Martian Canals," first reported as channels by Italian astronomer Giovanni Schiaparelli in 1877. Many astrono-

mers continued to believe in the existence of these canals up until 1965, when the spacecraft *Mariner 4* flew close to Mars and took photos of the planet's surface. No canals showed up in the photos. It turned out that the "canals" were a combination of an optical illusion, the expectation that there were canals, and the brain's tendency to impose order on random data. Because of our brain's inclination to impose meaning on random data, we should maintain a stance of skepticism and not jump to conclusions about what we see.

The combination of the error of misperceiving random data with confirmation bias—interpreting data in a way that confirms our cherished views—is illustrated by the next example. After the devastation of New Orleans by Hurricane Katrina in 2005, a group known as the Columbia Christians for Life announced that God's purpose in sending the hurricane was to destroy the five abortion clinics in the city. Their proof was a radar photograph taken

Radar photo of 2005 Hurricane Katrina that had an object that looked like a "fetus facing to the left in the womb."

of the hurricane in which they claimed to have seen what looked like "a fetus facing to the left (west) in the womb, in the early weeks of gestation."[18]

Stress as well as preconceptions about what the world is like can affect our perception. How many of us, walking alone at night, have seen a person or dog standing in a shadow, only to discover it was a bush or other object? Stress can also distort our memory by making us more vulnerable to manipulation and leading questions—as happened in the case of Reilly discussed at the beginning of this chapter.

Memorable-Events Error

The **memorable-events error** involves our ability to vividly remember outstanding events. Scientists have discovered channels in our brains that actually hinder most long-term memories by screening out the mundane incidents in our everyday life.[19] However, these memory-impairing channels appear to close down during outstanding events. For example, most Americans recall exactly where they were and what they were doing on the morning of September 11, 2001. However, if you ask someone what they were doing on an ordinary weekday two months ago, most people would be unable to remember or would remember only if they could think of something special that happened on that day.

To use another example, airplane crashes and fatalities are reported in the media, whereas automobile fatalities generally are not. However, per mile traveled, airplane travel is far safer. We're sixteen times more likely to be killed in an automobile accident than in an airplane accident. In fact, traffic accidents are one of the leading causes of death and disability of people between the ages of 15 and 44.[20] The memorable-events error exerts such control over our thinking that even after being informed of these statistics, many of us still continue to be more nervous about flying than about driving.

The memorable-events error is sometimes tied in with confirmation bias, in which we tend to remember events that confirm our beliefs and forget those that are contrary to our beliefs. A popular belief in the United States is that

memorable-events error A cognitive error that involves our ability to vividly remember outstanding events.

Critical *Thinking* in Action

Food for Thought: Perception and Supersized Food Portions

Obesity is becoming an epidemic on college campuses. Supersized portions of junk food, such as potato chips, hamburgers, and sodas, have been blamed, in part, for this trend.* Do supersized portions lead to supersized people, or is this just all hype so that we can place the blame for our weight problems on Lay's potato chips and McDonald's burgers?

In fact, studies show that downsizing our food portions does work to keep our weight down because it takes advantage of a perceptual error. Appetite is not a matter of just the physiological state of hunger but also a matter of perception—what we see in front of us. Most of us eat more when the table or our plates are loaded with food.

Humans are not the only species who make this error. When a researcher places a pile of 100 grams of wheat in front of a hen, she will eat 50 grams and leave 50. However, if we put 200 grams of wheat in front of a hen in a similar hunger condition, she will eat far more—83 to 108 grams of wheat or, once again, about half of what is in front of her.** Furthermore, if the food is presented as whole grains of rice, rather than cracked rice, where the grains are one quarter the size of whole rice grains, the hen will eat two to three times as much as she would otherwise.

In other words, by cutting down your portion sizes and cutting your food into smaller pieces, your brain will think you're full on less food.

DISCUSSION QUESTIONS

1. Many students put on weight in their first year of college, a phenomenon known as the dreaded "freshman 15." Critically evaluate your college environment and come up with a list of ways in which it promotes or hinders good eating habits. Make a list of suggestions for improving the environment. Carry out one of the suggestions or pass it on to someone who is in a position to make the change.

2. Examine your own eating habits. Discuss ways in which being more aware of your thinking process can help you to maintain healthier eating habits.

*Nancy Hellmich, "How to Downsize the Student Body," *USA Today*, November 15, 2004.
**George W. Hartmann, *Gestalt Psychology* (New York: Ronald Press, 1935), pp. 87–88.

Connections

Why do news stories lend themselves to memorable-events errors? *See Chapter 11, p. 345.*

What methods and techniques do scientists use to minimize personal and social bias? *See Chapter 12, p. 378.*

Statistically, there is a greater chance of being killed in a car accident than in an airplane crash, yet most people have a greater fear of flying.

"death takes a holiday" and that terminally ill patients can postpone their death until after an important holiday or birthday. In fact, this belief is based purely on wishful thinking and anecdotal evidence, in which we remember only the times when someone "waited" to die until after a milestone birthday or an important holiday. In an analysis of the death certificates of more than a million people who died from cancer, biostatisticians Donn Young and Erinn Hade found no evidence that there is a reduction in death rates prior to a holiday or important event.[21] Personal and social beliefs are remarkably strong even in the face of empirical evidence that logically should be devastating. When their results were published, Young and Hade received several angry e-mails criticizing them for taking away people's hope.

Probability Errors

What is the probability that two people in your class have a birthday on the same month and day? Most people guess that the probability is pretty low. When we misestimate the probably of an event by a huge margin, we are committing **probability error**. In fact, in a class of 23, the probability is about 50 percent. In larger classes, the probability is even higher.

Humans are notoriously poor at determining probability. We are inclined to believe that coincidences must have paranormal causes when actually they are consistent with prob-

> According to the Association for Psychological Science, 1.2 percent of the adult population are pathological gamblers and at least another 2.8 percent are problem gamblers.

ability. For example, you are thinking of a friend whom you haven't seen for a year when the phone rings and it's your friend on the other line. Are you psychic? Or is it just a coincidence? You've probably thought of your friend hundreds or even thousands of times over the course of the past year without receiving any phone calls, but we tend to forget such times because nothing memorable occurred. Considering that each year contains 105,120 five-minute intervals during which you might think about your friend, receiving a call from him or her once in a year really isn't all that remarkable.

One of the most insidious forms of probability error is **gambler's error**—the erroneous belief that previous events affect the probability in a random event. For most people, gambling is a relaxing pastime, whether it be online poker, slot machines, blackjack, or the lottery. For others, gambling is a pathological addiction that dominates their lives. According to the Association for Psychological Science, 1.2 percent of the adult population are pathological gamblers and at least another 2.8 percent are problem gamblers.[22] Why do some people become more easily addicted to gambling than others?

Research suggests that gambling addiction is based on a cognitive error regarding probability. In a study participants were invited to think aloud while gambling. Of the verbalized perceptions, 70 percent were based on erroneous thinking such as "The machine is due; I need to continue," "Here is my lucky dealer," "Today I feel great; it is my lucky day," "It's my turn to win." These statements reveal a failure to understand the random nature of probability.

When questioned about their verbalizations, nonproblem gamblers realized that their beliefs were wrong. They were able to use accumulated evidence to critically evaluate and

probability error Misunderstanding the probability or chances of an event by a huge margin.

gambler's error The belief that a previous event affects the probability in a random event.

modify their perceptions. Problem gamblers, in contrast, processed the evidence much differently. They believed what they had said and interpreted their occasional random wins as confirming their belief that the outcome of a game can be predicted and controlled. The solution? Work to improve problem gamblers' critical-thinking skills. By making gamblers aware of their erroneous perceptions and the reasons why they continue to cling to these beliefs, clinicians hope to help gamblers overcome their addiction.[23]

Self-Serving Biases

There are several types of self-serving biases or errors that impede our thinking and pursuit of truth, including

- The misperception that we are in control
- The tendency to overestimate ourselves in comparison to others
- The tendency to exaggerate our strengths and minimize our weaknesses

We are predisposed to believe that we are in control of events that are outside our control. "I knew it would rain today," you groan. "I didn't bring my umbrella." In 2004, the Powerball lottery jackpot had reached $116 million. I was standing in line at a mini-mart when I overheard the following conversation between the people in front of me, who were waiting to buy lottery tickets.

> **Person 1**: "What are you going to do? Are you going to pick your own numbers or let the computer do it for you?"
> **Person 2**: "Pick my own. It gives me a better chance of winning."

People who are poor critical thinkers may fall prey to more than one error in thinking in the same situation. In this case the control error was compounded by the probability error, which we discussed earlier. Although logically we know that lottery numbers are selected randomly, many of us also believe that choosing our own numbers—especially using our "lucky" numbers—increases our chances of winning. In fact, 80 percent of winning lottery tickets have numbers randomly generated by the computer, not so-called lucky numbers picked by the winners.[24]

The misperception that we are in control of random events also plays out in superstitious behavior such as wearing our lucky shirt during a big game or bringing a good-luck charm to an exam. Before a game, most college and professional athletes engage in ritualistic superstitious behavior such as eating a Snickers candy bar or using a particular color shoelace or tape. Some baseball players actually sleep with their bats to break out of a hitting slump or to keep up their batting average. To some extent, the belief that we are in control can boost our confidence in achieving our goals. In fact, ritualistic behaviors have been found to have a calming effect on athletes before a game.

However, if we carry the belief that we are in control too far, it can distort our thinking and lead to poor decisions in our lives. During Hurricane Andrew in 1972 and Hurricane Katrina in 2005, thousands of people living in the paths of these hurricanes failed to evacuate. Although many were unable to evacuate because of lack of transportation, others stayed behind because they thought they were in control of the situation and could ride out the storm. As a result, hundreds of people perished.

At the extreme, this error is expressed in the often-heard cliché "You can do anything you want if you put your mind to it," the implication being that if only we wanted to enough, we would have perfect control. Self-help gurus have become wealthy catering to this self-serving error. In her best-selling book *The Secret* (2006), Rhonda Byrne claims to have found the secret to happiness in what she calls "the law of attraction." According to Byrne, each of us has complete control over what happens to us in our lives. If we think positive thoughts, then like a magnet, we will attract whatever we want—whether it be a parking spot, a million dollars, a sexy figure, or a cure for cancer. The

downside is that if we are not successful in getting what we want, then we have only ourselves and our negative thinking to blame.

The belief that we are in control of situations where we actually have little or no control can contribute to irrational guilt or posttraumatic stress syndrome.[25] A survivor of a traumatic event may believe that he or she should have been able to predict and do something to prevent a particular event such as sexual abuse, domestic violence, or the death of a loved one, especially an accidental or suicidal death. The erroneous belief that we are in control when we are not can also cause people to remain in abusive relationships, thinking that they are responsible for their own abuse. Victims of domestic violence often fall prey to "if only" thinking, believing that if only they would change their own behavior, the abuse would stop. In fact, the only person responsible for the abuse is the abuser him- or herself.

Although genetic, physical, and environmental factors play a role in the onset of depression, the belief that we should be in control of our lives can contribute to depression (see "Critical Thinking in Action: Irrational Beliefs and Depression"). People who are depressed may cling to the irrational belief that the only alternative to not having perfect control is having no control. Because they feel they lack any control over their lives, they tend to attribute their misfortune or sadness to other people's actions. A side effect of this negative behavior is that their behavior often alienates other people, thereby confirming a second irrational belief common to depressed people that they are worthless and unlikable. Thus, their distorted expectations lead to a self-fulfilling prophecy, a cognitive error we'll be studying in the next section.

A second self-serving bias is the tendency to overestimate ourselves in comparison to others. Most people rate themselves as above average when it comes to getting along with other people. Although it obviously can't be true that the majority of people are above average—except, perhaps, in the fictional town of Lake Wobegon in Garrison Keillor's *Prairie Home Companion* on Minnesota Public Radio—this self-serving bias can bolster our self-esteem and

Critical Thinking in Action

Irrational Beliefs and Depression

Albert Ellis (1913–), founder of rational emotive behavioral therapy, maintains that irrational ideas are the primary source of depression, rage, feelings of inadequacy, and self-hatred. Some of these irrational beliefs are

- "I must be outstandingly competent, or I am worthless."
- "Others must treat me considerately, or they are absolutely rotten."
- "The world should always give me happiness, or I will die."
- "I must have perfect control over things, or I won't be able to enjoy life."
- "Because something once strongly affected my life, it will indefinitely affect my life."

According to Ellis, a depressed person feels sad because he (or she) erroneously thinks he is inadequate and abandoned, even though depressed people have the capacity to perform as well as nondepressed people. The purpose of therapy is to dispute these irrational beliefs and replace them with positive rational beliefs. To achieve this, the therapist asks questions such as

- Is there evidence for this belief?
- What is the evidence against this belief?
- What is the worst that can happen if you give up this belief?
- And what is the best that can happen?

To assist the clients in changing their irrational beliefs, the therapist also uses other techniques such as empathy training, assertiveness training, and encouraging the development of self-management strategies.

DISCUSSION QUESTIONS

1. Discuss how cognitive errors contribute to irrational beliefs. Make a list of other irrational beliefs people hold that are based on cognitive errors.

2. Do you have any irrational beliefs that interfere with your achieving your life goals? If so, what are they?

See Albert Ellis, *The Essence of Rational Emotive Behavior Therapy.* PhD dissertation, revised, May 1994.

confidence. However, if we are unaware of the bias, it can become a problem and cause us not to take responsibility for our shortcomings. A Pew Research Center survey found that while statistics show that 70 percent of Americans are overweight and that nine in ten agree that most of their fellow Americans are overweight, only 39 percent of Americans consider themselves to be overweight.[26] Clearly there seems to be a disconnect between being overweight and people's estimation of their own weight.

Did You Know

Self-serving bias can be found in the workplace. When office employees were asked in a survey "if they ever experienced backstabbing, rudeness, or incivility in the workplace," 89 percent said yes.

Another example of the self-serving bias is that most people take personal credit for their successes and blame outside forces for their failures. College students often attribute their "A" grades to something about themselves—their intelligence, quick grasp of the material, or good study skills. In contrast, they usually attribute their poor grades to something outside their control such as having an unfair teacher or having a touch of the flu on the day of the exam.[27] Similarly, when it comes to being overweight, many people blame a slow metabolism as the main reason why they can't lose weight, rather than their lifestyle or factors under their control. However, when overweight people do lose weight, they rarely attribute their success to a peppy metabolism but instead credit their willpower and good choices.

This type of self-serving bias can be found in the workplace. When office employees were asked in a survey "if they ever experienced backstabbing, rudeness, or incivility in the workplace," 89 percent said "yes". However, in the same survey 99 percent said that "they were never rude or the cause of the conflict."[28] In other words, most of us are quick to complain about other's irritating behaviors but give little thought to how our behavior might be the cause of workplace conflict.

According to Carol Tavris and Elliot Aronson, social psychologists and authors of *Mistakes Were Made (But Not By Me): Why We Justify Foolish Beliefs, Bad Decisions and Hurtful Acts*, being made aware of the gap between our self-image and our actual behavior creates cognitive dissonance and discomfort. To minimize this discomfort and maintain our good opinion of ourselves, we instinctively minimize the discrepancy through denial or by blaming someone else for our shortcomings. However, this sort of rationalization can prevent us from realizing that we're clinging to a mistaken belief or practice and from fixing the mistake.[29] As critical thinkers, we need to deal constructively with the discomfort that comes from cognitive dissonance and to work toward overcoming our mistaken beliefs about ourselves.

A third self-serving bias is our inclination to exaggerate or place a greater value on our strengths and underestimate or downplay our weaknesses. We tend to rank traits or abilities that we have, such as sense of humor, intelligence, or industriousness, higher in importance and to devalue abilities we lack or are weak in. In a study of intellectually gifted boys who thought they hadn't done well in class, the boys downplayed the importance of academics and instead emphasized the importance of other pursuits.[30] Seeing ourselves as having those traits and abilities that are important in life increases our sense of worth and helps us to achieve our life goals. This tendency, however, can also contribute to overconfidence and failure to seek or acknowledge other people's skills.

Overconfidence in physicians and jumping to a conclusion too fast has been identified as one of the key factors in diagnostic errors. According to the Institute of Medicine of the National Academy of Sciences, medical errors are responsible for an estimated 44,000 to 98,000 deaths a year in the United States. Diagnostic errors are associated with higher patient death rates than other types of medical errors.[31] The American Medical Association recommends that medical schools pay more attention to innate cognitive errors, such as confirmation bias and self-serving bias, that contribute to diagnostic errors, and that they teach critical-thinking skills and strategies for compensating for these biases. Unless we are willing, as critical thinkers, to make an honest evaluation of ourselves, it is unlikely that we are going to take steps toward self-improvement and overcoming our shortcomings.

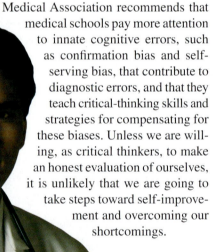

Panicked citizens gather to withdraw their money from a federal bank during the Great Depression. This type of thinking also contributed to a plunge in the stock market in 2008 when people pulled their money from the stock market because of fears it would crash.

Self-Fulfilling Prophecy

A self-fulfilling prophecy occurs when our exaggerated or distorted expectations reinforce actions that actually bring about the expected event. Our beliefs about the world tell us what we might expect from other people and situations. This cognitive shortcut provides an energy-saving way of understanding the world around us. When our expectations are accurate, we can make decisions more efficiently than if we had to examine all the evidence. However, this cognitive shortcut can also lead to errors by oversimplifying the way things really are.

Expectations can have a profound influence on our behavior. Rumors of impending bank failures during the Great Depression in the early 1930s led to mass panic in which people rushed to take their money out of banks before the banks crashed. As a result, lots of banks went bankrupt. Since banks invest some of the deposits rather than keeping all the money in the vault, the frenzy caused the collapse of the banks—the very thing the customers feared.

To use another example of a self-fulfilling prophecy, let's say a literature professor has a star football player in her class. On the basis of her (mistaken) expectations about college athletes, she assumes that he is not academically inclined but is taking the course only because it is reputed to be easy. Because of this she calls on him less

and doesn't encourage him or make an effort to include him in class discussions. She justifies this behavior on her part as not wanting to embarrass him.

To preserve our expectations, we may interpret ambiguous data in ways that meet our expectations. For example, our football star may be particularly quiet and introspective during one class. The professor assumes that he is preoccupied with thinking about the upcoming game, when instead he is deep in thought about the poem that is being discussed in class. Our football player, who initially was very interested in the class and in literature and had even written several poems for his high school newspaper, soon begins to lose interest in the class and ends up getting only a mediocre grade. Thus, we have a self-fulfilling prophecy in which the professor's distorted expectation comes true. Clearly, preserving our expectations can come at a cost to others.

Humans are prone to several inborn cognitive and perceptual errors, including optical illusions, misperception of random data, memorable-events errors, probability errors, self-serving biases, and self-fulfilling prophecies. Because these errors are part of the way our brain interprets the world, we may fail to notice the influence they exert over our thinking. Developing our critical-thinking skills can help us be more aware of these tendencies and adjust for them when appropriate.

> According to the Institute of Medicine of the National Academy of Sciences, medical errors are responsible for an estimated 44,000 to 98,000 deaths a year in the United States.

1. Come up with an issue—such as same-sex marriage, abortion, or legalizing marijuana—that is important to you. Discuss the extent to which cognitive errors—such as confirmation bias and memorable-events error—bias the way you go about collecting and interpreting evidence regarding this issue. Discuss steps you might take to compensate for this bias.

2. Think of a "lucky" charm or ritual that you use, or have used in the past, to increase your chances of doing well on something that really matters. This can include anything from wearing your "lucky shoes" during a baseball game to rubbing your mother's ring before an important exam. Given your realization that this behavior is based on a cognitive error, are you going to continue doing it or stop doing it? Explain.

3. Online poker has become all the rage on many college campuses, even to the point of interfering with some students' academic performance. Discuss how errors in thinking might contribute to their fixation.

4. If you have ever bought a lottery ticket or know of someone who did, why did you (or the other person) buy it at that particular time? When the ticket was bought, what did you, or the other person, think their probability of winning was? Discuss the extent to which this reasoning involved a probability error.

5. Given that humans are prone to cognitive errors, should we use computers rather than physicians for medical diagnoses? Support your answer.

6. Think of a time when you studied hard for a test but ended up with a low grade. To what did you attribute your poor performance? Now think of a time when you studied hard and did very well on a test. To what did you attribute your good performance? Discuss how self-serving biases may have contributed to the difference in your reaction in each of the two situations.

7. Do you tend to overestimate the amount of control you have over your life? Give specific examples. Discuss how a distorted sense of control has had an impact on your ability to achieve your life goals. Come up with at least two critical-thinking strategies you could use to correct for this cognitive error.

8. *Journal Exercise.* Complete a journal entry about cognitive errors. Which cognitive error are you most likely to commit? Give a specific example of your using this error. If you are willing, share some of your irrational ideas as well as your strategies for overcoming these ideas with the class.

SOCIAL ERRORS AND BIASES

Humans are highly social animals. Because of this trait, social norms and cultural expectations exert a strong influence on how we perceive the world—so much so that we tend to perceive the world differently in groups from the way we do in isolation. Groups can systematically distort both the gathering and the interpretation of evidence.[32]

As we noted in Chapter 1, ethnocentrism—the unjustified belief that our group or culture is superior to that of others—can also bias our thinking and act as a barrier to critical thinking.

"One of Us/One of Them" Error

Our brains seem to be programmed to classify people as either "one of us" or "one of them." We tend to treat people who are similar to us with respect and those who are different from us—whether in regard to race, sex, religion, political party, age, or nationality—with suspicion or worse. Although most of us claim to believe in human equality, in our culture the use of qualifiers such as *gay judge, female doctor, Hispanic senator,* and *Down syndrome child* betray our tacit belief that any deviation from the norm needs to be specified. We rarely hear terms such as *straight judge, male doctor, European American senator,* or *able-bodied child*!

Much of the violence that occurs between conflicting cultural groups is born of the "One of Us/One of Them" error.

Prejudices, which may operate without any conscious realization on our part, can influence our behavior and how we see the world. In a Harvard study, study subjects were asked to quickly associate positive or negative words with black or white faces. Seven out of ten white people, despite their claims that they had no racial prejudice, showed "an automatic preference for white over black."[33]

It is all too easy for people to fall into the "us versus them" mind-set, especially when they feel threatened. In 1994, the Hutu government in Rwanda stirred up Hutus' hatred and fear of the Tutsi, inciting them to carry out a brutal three-month slaughter of the Tutsi. Neighbors killed neighbors, students killed their fellow students, and doctors killed doctors. Even priests helped with the massacre of the Tutsi in their congregations, simply because the Tutsi were the "other." When it was over, a million people were dead.

This error also contributes to our tendency to polarize issues into two camps. "They," whether it be "right-wing conservatives" or "bleeding-heart liberals," are irrational; there is no point in even arguing a point with them. Our group, on the other hand, holds a monopoly on Truth. There is no middle ground. During the 2008 presidential elections, Americans were quick to divide up the country into two opposing camps: the red states (Republicans) and the blue states (Democrats) and to classify people in their group as "good" and "right" and those in the other group as "bad" and "mistaken."

According to Harvard social psychologist Mahzarin Banaji, if we are to overcome this social error we need to be consciously aware of it in our thinking and to build in protective measures.[34] As critical thinkers, we can work toward minimizing this error in our thinking by first critically evaluating the situation and then consciously reprogramming our brains to come up with new, more reasonable definitions of who it is that we view as "us" by seeking a more immediate and inclusive basis for a connection, such as we all live in the same dorm, we all attend the same college, we all are Americans, we all are human beings. We also need to make a conscious effort to be open to multiple perspectives, even those we are initially convinced must be mistaken.

Connections

When you serve as a juror, how can cognitive and social errors distort your analysis of the evidence?
See Chapter 13, p. 434.

Red States vs Blue States

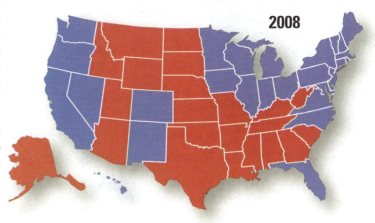

2008

Societal Expectations

The late nineteenth and early twentieth centuries were times of extraordinary technological advancement, setting in motion the expectation of ever new and revolutionary technology. On December 13, 1909, six years after the Wright brothers' epic flight, the *Boston Herald* reported the invention of an airship by a local businessman, Wallace Tillinghast.[35] Over the next several weeks, hundreds of witnesses from the New England–New York area, including police officers, judges, and businesspeople, reported sightings of the airship sailing through the skies.[36] The reported sightings led to a massive search for the airship by reporters. The search was finally called off when it was revealed that the story was a hoax perpetuated by Tillinghast.

Social expectations can be so powerful that they may lead to collective delusions in which people attempt to fit evidence into their cultural worldview. Sometimes these social errors may even become institutionalized.[37] Acting on social expectations without subjecting them to critical analysis can have dire consequences. The Salem witchcraft mania was rooted in the social expectations of the sixteenth and seventeenth centuries. Those of us living in the twenty-first century may regard the witch-hunters as crazed fanatics. However, they were simply behaving in a manner that was consistent with the prevailing religious worldview and social expectations of their time in which certain unfortunate circumstances, such as crop failures, disease, and untimely deaths, were interpreted as being brought about by the Devil and his worldly agents—witches.

The social expectations of the police who interrogated Peter Reilly, described in the chapter opening, also played a role in their use of leading questions to get a "confession" out of him. Reilly's mother had been an emotionally abusive woman. In our society we expect victims of parental abuse to be violent and vengeful, even though studies suggest that it is children who witness domestic violence, rather than those who are direct victims of it, who are at highest risk, since they come to accept violence as normal.[38] In addition, it is often a family member who commits this type of violent murder. Therefore, the police jumped to the conclusion, on the basis of this expectation, that Reilly must have committed the murder.

Stereotyping is another type of social bias based on social expectations about individuals that are based on socially generated group labels. In the study mentioned in Chapter 2 in which researchers showed students a picture of a black man on a subway next to a white man who was holding an open razor, when students were later asked to recall what they had seen, half of them reported that the black man was holding the razor. We also saw this type of stereotyping after September 11, 2001, when some passengers refused to board a plane because one of the passengers was of Arab descent.

Group Pressure and Conformity

Group pressure can influence individual members to take positions that they would never support by themselves, as happened in the Stanford Prison experiment described in Chapter 1. Some religious cults exploit this tendency by separating their members from the dissenting views of family and friends. In many cults, people live together, eat together, and may even be assigned a buddy.

Group pressure is so powerful in shaping how we see the world that it can even lead people to deny contrary evidence that is right before their eyes. In the 1950s, social psychologist Solomon Asch carried out a series of experiments in which he showed study subjects a screen containing a standard line on the left and three comparison lines on the right. One of the comparison lines was the same length as the standard line and the other two were of significantly different lengths.[39] In each case, an unsuspecting study subject was introduced into a group with six confederates, who had been told by the experimenter to give the wrong answer. The group was then shown the lines. The experimenter asked one of the confederates which of the three lines on the

The Salem witch hunts, which took place in Massachusetts in the late 17th century, targeted those mistakenly believed to be responsible for society's ills.

right they thought was the same length as the standard line. The confederate, without hesitation, gave a wrong answer. The next few confederates gave the same answer. By now, the naïve subject was showing puzzlement and even dismay. How can six people be wrong?

After hearing six "wrong" answers, 75 percent of the naïve study subjects, rather than trust the evidence of their senses, succumbed to group pressure and gave the same wrong answer. Even more surprising is the fact that when questioned afterward, some of these study subjects had actually come to believe the wrong answer was correct. The Asch experiments provide vivid evidence about the warning raised in Orwell's *Nineteen Eighty-Four* regarding the dangers of a society where the media are tightly controlled by those in power and where people are easily manipulated into believing "two plus two makes five."

The desire for agreement is normal. However, this desire, when combined with our innate tendency to divide the world into "one of us" and "one of them," can lead to the exclusion of those who disagree with the majority. In

Analyzing Images

ASCH EXPERIMENT
In Asch's experiment, the naïve subject (left) shows puzzlement when the other subjects give what is obviously a wrong answer.

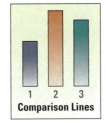

1   2   3
Comparison Lines

DISCUSSION QUESTIONS

1. *What do you think the naïve subject in the picture above is thinking?*

2. *Think back on a time when you were in a similar situation where you thought you were correct, but everyone else with you thought something else. How did you respond to the discrepancy between your belief and theirs?*

HIGHLIGHTS

SOCIAL ERRORS AND BIASES

"One of us/one of them" errors: Our brain seems programmed to classify people as either "one of us" or "one of them." We tend to treat people who are similar to us with respect and those who are different from us with suspicion.

Social expectations: The influence of social expectations is so powerful that it can lead to collective delusions in which people attempt to fit evidence into their cultural worldview.

Group pressure and conformity: Group pressure can influence individual members to behave in ways or take positions that they would never do by themselves.

Diffusion of responsibility: A phenomenon that occurs in groups of people above a critical size where responsibility is not explicitly assigned to us so we tend to regard it as not our problem or as belonging to someone else.

---

addition, people tend to prefer being around people who agree with them. In the corporate world, disagreement with the prevailing view is often tacitly discouraged. "Outliers" or nonconformists who do not agree with group members may be excluded by committee chairs from further discussions or even fired.[40]

Because of our inborn tendency to conform to what others think, we cannot assume that agreement leads to truth without knowledge about the manner and conditions under which the agreement was arrived at. Indeed, the current emphasis on seeking group consensus in decision making may be unreliable. In consensus seeking, the majority in a group is often able to sway the whole group to its view.

As with other errors in our thinking, we need to develop strategies to recognize and compensate for our human inclination to conform to groupthink. For example, in competitive ice skating and diving, because of the danger of a judge's scoring being contaminated by what other judges say, scoring is done individually, rather than as a group decision. When a group comes to a decision that we initially find groupthink, we need to mentally step back from the group and carefully evaluate the evidence for a particular position rather than assume that the majority must be correct.

Diffusion of Responsibility

Diffusion of responsibility is a social phenomenon that occurs in groups of people above a critical size. If responsibility is not explicitly assigned to us, we tend to regard it as not our problem or as belonging to someone else. For example, we are much more likely to come to someone's aid if we are alone than if we are in a crowd.

This phenomenon is also known as *bystander apathy* or the *Kitty Genovese syndrome*. In 1964, twenty-eight-year-old Kitty Genovese was murdered outside her New York City apartment building. Her killer left twice, when people in the building turned on their lights, before he came back a third time and killed her. In the half hour that lapsed during the attack, none of Genovese's thirty-eight neighbors, who had heard her repeated cries for help, called the police. More recently, in June

> **diffusion of responsibility** The tendency, when in a large group, to regard a problem as belonging to someone else.

2008, an elderly man was struck by a hit-and-run driver on a busy street in Hartford, Connecticut. The man lay in the street paralyzed and bleeding from his head while bystanders gawked at or ignored him. Motorists drove around his body without stopping. No one offered any assistance until an ambulance finally turned up. Diffusion of responsibility can also occur in group hazing at fraternities where no one comes to the rescue of a pledge who is clearly in distress.

As social beings, we are vulnerable to the "one of us/ one of them" error, social expectations, and group conformity. When in groups, we also tend to regard something

> In 1964, twenty-eight-year-old Kitty Genovese was murdered outside her New York City apartment building. Her killer left twice, when people in the building turned on their lights, before he came back a third time and killed her.

as not our problem unless responsibility is assigned to us. Although these traits may promote group cohesiveness, they can interfere with effective critical thinking. As good critical thinkers we need to be aware of these tendencies, and to cultivate the ability to think independently while still taking into consideration others' perspectives.

The apartment complex where Kitty Genovese was raped, beaten, and ultimately murdered, while her neighbors, who heard her cries for help, failed to come to her aid.

1. Whom do you define as "us" and whom do you put in the category of "them"? Discuss how you might go about widening the "us" category to include more people who are now in your "them" category.

2. Humans seem to have inborn biases toward particular types of people. According to a University of Florida study, when it comes to hiring, employers have a more favorable view of tall people. Furthermore, when it comes to earnings, every extra inch of height above the norm is worth $789 a year. In fact, nine of ten top executives are taller than the typical employee.[41] Given this cognitive error and its impact on hiring practices, discuss whether or not affirmative action policies should apply to very short people. Support your answer.

3. Think of a time when your social expectations led you to misjudge a person or a situation. Discuss strategies for improving your critical-thinking skills so that this is less likely to happen.

4. What are some other examples of events, both historical and contemporary, where the public got caught up in a "witch hunt"? Identify the worldviews and social expectations that supported these "witch hunts." Which critical-thinking skills would make you less likely to go along with a "witch hunt"? Discuss what actions you could take to develop or strengthen these skills.

5. Polls before elections can actually influence how people vote by swaying undecided voters to vote for the candidate who is in the lead. Should election polls be forbidden prior to the election itself? Support your answer.

6. The democratic process depends on social consensus. Given people's tendency to conform to social expectations and what others think, is democracy the best form of government? If so, what policies might be put in place to lessen the effect of social biases? Be specific.

7. Think of a time when you failed to speak out against an injustice or failed to come to someone's aid simply because you were in a large group and felt it wasn't your responsibility. Discuss ways in which improving your critical-thinking skills may make you less susceptible to the diffusion of social responsibility error.

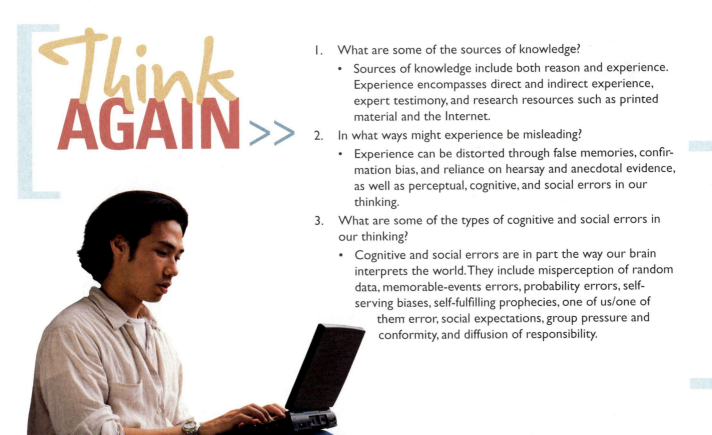

Think AGAIN >>

1. What are some of the sources of knowledge?
   - Sources of knowledge include both reason and experience. Experience encompasses direct and indirect experience, expert testimony, and research resources such as printed material and the Internet.

2. In what ways might experience be misleading?
   - Experience can be distorted through false memories, confirmation bias, and reliance on hearsay and anecdotal evidence, as well as perceptual, cognitive, and social errors in our thinking.

3. What are some of the types of cognitive and social errors in our thinking?
   - Cognitive and social errors are in part the way our brain interprets the world. They include misperception of random data, memorable-events errors, probability errors, self-serving biases, self-fulfilling prophecies, one of us/one of them error, social expectations, group pressure and conformity, and diffusion of responsibility.

Perspectives on the Existence of Unidentified Flying Objects

Sightings of unexplained phenomena in the sky have been reported since ancient times. However, it was not until the late 1940s, following the famous "flying saucer crash" incident in Roswell, New Mexico, that UFO reports began to proliferate. There is little doubt that sensationalist media coverage stimulated reports of more UFO sightings, just as the 1909 story in the *Boston Herald* of the invention of an airship was followed by hundreds of sightings of the bogus ship.

In 1948, the U.S. Air Force began to keep a file of UFO sightings as part of Project Blue Book. By 1969, the project had recorded 12,618 UFO sightings. Ninety percent of these UFO sightings have been identified with astronomical and weather phenomena, aircraft, balloons, searchlights, hot gases, and other natural events. Ten percent remain unexplained. In 1968 the U.S. Air Force commissioned a study under the direction of University of Colorado professor Edward Condon. The study concluded that there was no evidence for UFOs and that scientific study of the phenomenon should be discontinued. As a result of the study, Project Blue Book was suspended.

Despite official consensus that UFOs do not exist, a 2002 Roper Poll Survey found that slightly more than half of both Americans and Canadians believe that UFOs exist. People under the age of 30 are most likely to believe in UFOs. The survey also found that many Americans think that the government is hiding information from them about the existence of UFOs and alien life forms.

Following are readings from three scientists: Edward Condon, J. Allen Hynek, and Royston Paynter. Most scientists, like Condon, believe that UFOs do not exist. These scientists argue that there are natural explanations for UFO phenomena, including meteorites, balloons, hallucinations, and perceptual and social errors in our thinking. A few scientists, including Hynek, believe that a small percentage of sightings are really alien space craft. Still others, such as Paynter, while skeptical, think that there is a small possibility that UFOs may exist and, consequently, that continued investigation of the phenomenon is warranted.

Scientific Study of Unidentified Flying Objects

EDWARD U. CONDON

Edward Condon (1902–1974) was a physicist at the University of Colorado. This report, commonly known as the "Condon Report," was commissioned by the United States Air Force.[42] The following are excerpts from the "Conclusions and Recommendations" section of the report. To see a complete copy of the report, go to http://www.ncas.org/condon/text/contents.htm

As indicated by its title, the emphasis of this study has been on attempting to learn from UFO reports anything that could be considered as adding to scientific knowledge. Our general conclusion is that nothing has come from the study of UFOs in the past 21 years that has added to scientific knowledge. Careful consideration of the record as it is available to us leads us to conclude that further extensive study of UFOs probably cannot be justified in the expectation that science will be advanced thereby.

It has been argued that this lack of contribution to science is due to the fact that very little scientific effort has been put on the subject. We do not agree. We feel that the reason that there has been very little scientific study of the subject is that those scientists who are most directly concerned, astronomers, atmospheric physicists, chemists, and psychologists, having had ample opportunity to look into the matter, have individually decided that UFO phenomena do not offer a fruitful field in which to look for major scientific discoveries. . . .

Even conceding that the entire body of "official" science might be in error for a time, we believe that there is no better way to correct error than to give free reign to the ideas of individual scientists to make decisions as to the directions in which scientific progress is most likely to be made. For legal work sensible people seek an attorney, and for medical treatment sensible people seek a qualified physician. The nation's surest guarantee of scientific excellence is to leave the decision-making process to the individual and collective judgment of its scientists.

Scientists are no respecters of authority. Our conclusion that study of UFO reports is not likely to advance science will not be uncritically accepted by them. Nor should it be, nor do we wish it to be. For scientists, it is our hope that the detailed analytical presentation of what we were able to do, and of what we were unable to do, will assist them in deciding whether or not they agree with our conclusions. Our hope is that the details of this report will help other scientists in seeing what the problems are and the difficulties of coping with them.

If they agree with our conclusions, they will turn their valuable attention and talents elsewhere. If they disagree it

will be because our report has helped them reach a clear picture of wherein existing studies are faulty or incomplete and thereby will have stimulated ideas for more accurate studies. If they do get such ideas and can formulate them clearly, we have no doubt that support will be forthcoming to carry on with such clearly defined, specific studies. We think that such ideas for work should be supported.

Some readers may think that we have now wandered into a contradiction. Earlier we said that we do not think study of UFO reports is likely to be a fruitful direction of scientific advance; now we have just said that persons with good ideas for specific studies in this field should be supported. This is no contradiction. Although we conclude after nearly two years of intensive study that we do not see any fruitful lines of advance from the study of UFO reports, we believe that any scientist with adequate training and credentials who does come up with a clearly defined, specific proposal for study should be supported. . . .

This formulation carries with it the corollary that we do not think that at this time the federal government ought to set up a major new agency, as some have suggested, for the scientific study of UFOs. This conclusion may not be true for all time. If, by the progress of research based on new ideas in this field, it then appears worthwhile to create such an agency, the decision to do so may be taken at that time. . . .

As the reader of this report will readily judge, we have focussed attention almost entirely on the physical sciences. This was in part a matter of determining priorities and in part because we found rather less than some persons may have expected in the way of psychiatric problems related to belief in the reality of UFOs as craft from remote galactic or intergalactic civilizations. We believe that the rigorous study of the beliefs—unsupported by valid evidence—held by individuals and even by some groups might prove of scientific value to the social and behavioral sciences. There is no implication here that individual or group psychopathology is a principal area of study. Reports of UFOs offer interesting challenges to the student of cognitive processes as they are affected by individual and social variables. By this connection, we conclude that a content-analysis of press and television coverage of UFO reports might yield data of value both to the social scientist and the communications specialist. The lack of such a study in the present report is due to a judgment on our part that other areas of investigation were of much higher priority. We do not suggest, however, that the UFO phenomenon is, by its nature, more amenable to study in these disciplines than in the physical sciences. On the contrary, we conclude that the same specificity in proposed research in these areas is as desirable as it is in the physical sciences.

The question remains as to what, if anything, the federal government should do about the UFO reports it receives from the general public. We are inclined to think that nothing should be done with them in the expectation that they are going to contribute to the advance of science. . . .

It has [also] been contended that the subject has been shrouded in official secrecy. We conclude otherwise. We have no evidence of secrecy concerning UFO reports. What has been miscalled secrecy has been no more than an intelligent policy of delay in releasing data so that the public does not become confused by premature publication of incomplete studies of reports.

The subject of UFOs has been widely misrepresented to the public by a small number of individuals who have given sensationalized presentations in writings and public lectures. So far as we can judge, not many people have been misled by such irresponsible behavior, but whatever effect there has been has been bad.

A related problem to which we wish to direct public attention is the miseducation in our schools which arises from the fact that many children are being allowed, if not actively encouraged, to devote their science study time to the reading of UFO books and magazine articles of the type referred to in the preceding paragraph. We feel that children are educationally harmed by absorbing unsound and erroneous material as if it were scientifically well founded. Such study is harmful not merely because of the erroneous nature of the material itself, but also because such study retards the development of a critical faculty with regard to scientific evidence, which to some degree ought to be part of the education of every American.

Therefore we strongly recommend that teachers refrain from giving students credit for school work based on their reading of the presently available UFO books and magazine articles. Teachers who find their students strongly motivated in this direction should attempt to channel their interests in the direction of serious study of astronomy and meteorology, and in the direction of critical analysis of arguments for fantastic propositions that are being supported by appeals to fallacious reasoning or false data.

We hope that the results of our study will prove useful to scientists and those responsible for the formation of public policy generally in dealing with this problem which has now been with us for 21 years.

QUESTIONS

1. According to Condon, what has the result been of 21 years of studying UFOs?

2. What is Condon's position on continuing scientific investigation of UFO phenomena?

3. How does Condon respond to those who claim that the government has been too secretive about UFOs?

4. What is Condon's recommendation regarding the teaching of UFO phenomena in schools?

The UFO Experience: A Scientific Inquiry

J. ALLEN HYNEK

Astronomer J. Allen Hynek served as a consultant for the U.S. Air Force, including their Blue Book Project, from 1948 to 1969. In 1973 he founded the Center for UFO Studies. In the following selection from his book, *The UFO Experience: A Scientific Inquiry*,[43] Hynek argues that unexplained UFO phenomena are too often dismissed by authorities and, as a result, have not been studied in a systematic scientific manner.

There exists a phenomenon, described by the contents of UFO reports, that is worthy of systematic, rigorous study. The extent of such a study must be determined by the degree to which the phenomenon is deemed to be a challenge to the human mind and to which it can be considered potentially productive in contributing to the enlightenment and progress of mankind.

Even allowing for the unfortunate and disorganized manner in which the data have become available for study, the body of data points to an aspect or domain of the natural world not yet explored by science.

For a directed, objective study of the phenomenon the available data require major organization, systematization, and the adoption of a uniform terminology for their description and evaluation. Such organization and systematization must be applied in the gathering and processing of new data.

Investigations that have sought to disprove the above have failed to make a case. Blue Book and the Condon Report are the principal examples of such fruitless efforts. . . .

The mass of worldwide UFO reports can be handled in two ways: statistically, in the mass, or specifically, one by one.

With the numbers of UFO reports of high strangeness now counted in the thousands, a statistical approach can be very productive, and methods suggested by modern information theory are certainly applicable. Sophisticated methods of information retrieval, pattern recognition, and significance testing have served in a number of disciplines to extract that "signal" from the "noise" in situations that at first glance seemed hopeless.

A simpler yet more powerful method of demonstrating significance of patterns is to compare large groups of sightings of a particular category with a much larger population of the same category. . . .

It may well be asked why all this has not been done before. The subject has actively concerned us for more than a score of years. A moment's consideration, however, will show what an impossible accomplishment this would have been. Most recently, the Condon group spent a half million dollars ostensibly to study the subject scientifically, but the members did not even consider this approach. How then could private groups without funds, without data in usable form, and usually without scientific training essay such a task? Blue Book did not even remotely consider this approach despite the strong advice of their scientific consultant. Recall, too, that the many thousands of Blue Book cases were arranged in folders only chronologically, with no semblance of even the most elementary cross-indexing.

As was true of many other fields of study in their infancy, scientific respectability is won slowly, with comprehensive study possible only after the subject is accorded some measure of acceptance. But even if UFO reports were to cease as of this moment and no reports of acceptable criteria were to be submitted henceforth, it is my opinion that the data that now lie scattered about, if properly processed, could establish the substantive nature of the UFO phenomenon beyond reasonable doubt. . . .

The *second* potentially productive approach to the UFO problem is the examination, in depth, of individual multiple-witness cases, particularly those of recent origin. Concentration here on Close Encounter cases clearly promises the most return, especially Close Encounters of the Second Kind, in which the reported presence of physical evidence can yield quantitative physical data.

The individual case approach requires persons trained in interrogation who also have an intimate knowledge of the various manifestations of the UFO phenomenon and are able to recognize the characteristics of reports generated by common misperception. It is imperative that they be well acquainted with both psychology and basic physics. . . .

An approach such as this is essential for the resolution of today's confusing situation. Views range from those who consider the entire subject as nonsense (either from a priori considerations or in the belief that the Condon Report has been definitive) and hence refuse to devote even a moment to the examination of the data, to those who have examined the present data and are convinced on that basis that the UFO phenomenon represents a new field of science. This severe polarization of the issue can be dissipated only by concentrated study. How can such studies be pursued best?

We can start with the knowledge that the UFO phenomenon is global, that UFO reports persist in this and other countries despite the Condon Report and the closing of Blue Book, and that many small groups of scientifically trained people, especially young scientists, are expressing interest in the subject and dissatisfaction with the manner in which it has been treated in the past. Some find it increasingly difficult to understand why the National Academy of Science fully endorsed the Condon Report and its methodology. . . .

The general confusion surrounding the subject and the lack of attention by scientists have effectively prevented proper data collection. Even after twenty years of sporadic, unsystematic data collecting there exists only a formidable collection of heterogeneous data, often consisting of little more than discursive, anecdotal accounts. The more than 12,000 air force cases are arranged only chronologically, with no attempt at cross-indexing, and the same is true of the files of many private investigators and organizations.

Thus the first step means starting almost from scratch: *data gathering* and *data processing*. This may seem to be a most pedestrian approach to a most exciting topic, but so far we have only an airy, unsubstantial structure built on a quicksand foundation of unprocessed, generally incomplete, and qualitative rather than quantitative data. . . .

Since the phenomenon is global, contact between groups in various countries must be maintained, and some form of communication is needed, perhaps eventually growing into an international journal devoted to this study. . . .

Such analyses, coupled with the *active* program of on the spot investigations of a truly scientific character, should accomplish the first objective of a positive UFO program: to establish the reality of the UFO as a legitimate subject for further scientific study. If definite patterns and other correlations can be established for UFOs reported in many different countries by people with different levels of culture, the probability that such correlations happened by chance as a result of random misperceptions would be vanishingly small. The probability, therefore, that the UFO represents something truly new in science—new empirical observations—would be a virtual certainty.

QUESTIONS

1. According to Hynek, what is the best way to go about investigating the possible existence of UFOs?

2. How effective does Hynek regard the information-gathering conducted by the Condon Report?

3. According to Hynek, what should be the first step in UFO investigations at this point in time?

5

INFORMAL

Shannon Townsend was excited about college. An honor student in high school who planned to become a physician, she finished her first semester at the University of Colorado with a 3.9 grade point average and an active social life. Then something happened to change the direction of her life. A few weeks before the end of her freshman year, she announced to her parents that she was dropping out of college to "follow Jesus." She had joined a nomadic cult known as the Jim Roberts Group, or simply the Brethren. The cult believes in disowning family and possessions, isolating themselves from society, and roaming the land (as they believe Jesus did), proselytizing and foraging for food. Almost ten years have passed, and her family has not seen or heard from Shannon since she quit college to join the Brethren.[1]

FALLACIES

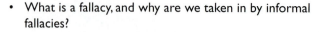

- What is a fallacy, and why are we taken in by informal fallacies?

- What are three main types of informal fallacies?

- How can we avoid falling for and/or using fallacies?

Shannon's story is not that uncommon. Each year, hundreds of college students are recruited into destructive cults, a particular subclass of cults, groups organized around a set of beliefs and rituals that display excessive devotion to a person or ideology, that use manipulative and deceptive recruiting techniques, and that employ fallacious reasoning—including reliance on vague language to mask their true objectives from potential members.[2] Isolation from family and peer pressure from "new" cult friends in the form of "love bombing"—a technique by which cult members shower a recruit with unconditional love to put them into a position to making them more susceptible to accept anything the cult says—both heighten compliance and discourage critical thinking. And to retain recruits' loyalty, destructive cults also use scare tactics, emotional abuse, and guilt.

College students, especially freshmen who are having difficulty adjusting to the college environment and are experiencing separation from their families, or who are having academic or social problems, are especially vulnerable to cults. Lack of assertiveness, dependence on others, a low tolerance for ambiguity (wanting simple "right" and "wrong" answers for complex questions), and poor critical-thinking skills all make students more likely to succumb to pressure from campus recruiters for cults.[3]

The best way to avoid being targeted by a cult, according to clinical counselor and cult expert Ron Burks, is to be well informed and unafraid to ask questions. "The antidote . . . is critical thinking," he says. "Cults don't like people who are constantly thinking and asking questions."[4]

The ability to recognize fallacious arguments used by cult recruiters can go a long way toward making us less vulnerable to the lure of destructive cults and to other types of flawed arguments. In Chapter 5 we will

- Define fallacy

- Learn how to identify fallacies of ambiguity

- Learn how to identify fallacies of relevance

- Learn how to identify fallacies with unwarranted assumptions

- Practice recognizing fallacies in everyday arguments and conversations

- Discuss strategies that can be used for avoiding fallacies

Finally, we will discuss both arguments for and against the United States launching a preemptive strike against Iraq and analyze these arguments for fallacies and faulty reasoning.

WHAT IS A FALLACY?

fallacy A faulty argument that at first appears to be correct.

formal fallacy A type of mistaken reasoning in which the form of an argument itself is invalid.

informal fallacy A type of mistaken reasoning that occurs when an argument is psychologically or emotionally persuasive but logically incorrect.

An argument is the process of supporting a claim or conclusion by providing reasons or evidence, in the form of premises, for that claim. An argument can be weak or invalid in several ways. The premises—the reasons or evidence given in support of a particular conclusion or position—may be mistaken, or the evidence may not support the conclusion. An argument contains a **fallacy** when it appears to be correct but on further examination is found to be incorrect. Fallacies may be formal or informal. In a **formal fallacy**, the form of the argument itself is invalid. For example, the following argument contains a formal fallacy: "Some high school dropouts are men. No doctors are high school dropouts. Therefore, no doctors are men." Although the premises are true, the conclusion does not follow because the form of the argument is faulty.

An **informal fallacy** is a type of mistaken reasoning that occurs when an argument is psychologically or emotionally persuasive but logically incorrect. Because fallacies can lead us to accept unsupported conclusions, being taken in by them can cause us to make poor life choices—as happened when Shannon was taken in by a destructive cult. Being able to identify informal fallacies makes it less likely that you will fall for these fallacies or use them in an argument.

In the following sections we will study three groups of informal fallacies: fallacies of ambiguity, fallacies of relevance, and fallacies with unwarranted assumptions. There are many types of fallacies in these groups. We'll be studying some of the more common ones in this chapter.

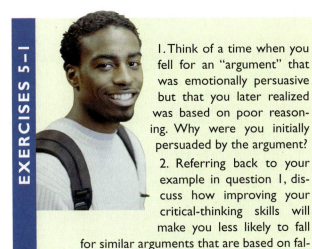

EXERCISES 5–1

1. Think of a time when you fell for an "argument" that was emotionally persuasive but that you later realized was based on poor reasoning. Why were you initially persuaded by the argument?
2. Referring back to your example in question 1, discuss how improving your critical-thinking skills will make you less likely to fall for similar arguments that are based on fallacies and faulty reasoning.

FALLACIES OF AMBIGUITY

Arguments that have ambiguous words or phrases, sloppy grammatical structure, or confusion between two closely related concepts can lead to **fallacies of ambiguity**. People with poor language and communication skills are more likely to use or fall for these fallacies. Fallacies of ambiguity include equivocation, amphiboly, the fallacy of accent, and the fallacy of division.

Equivocation

When a key term in an argument is ambiguous—that is, when it has more than one meaning—and the meaning of the term changes during the course of the argument, **equivocation** occurs. This is most likely to happen when the meaning of the ambiguous key term is not clear from the context of the argument. Verbal disputes, such as the dispute about whether a tree falling in a forest when no one is around makes a "sound," occur because of equivocation on the key term *sound*. In this case, the people who are disagreeing are each using a different definition of *sound*.

Here is another example of equivocation:

fallacy of ambiguity Arguments that have ambiguous phrases or sloppy grammatical structure.

equivocation A key term in an argument changes meaning during the course of the argument.

> The sign on the deli door says "No Animals Allowed." I guess we'll have to find another place for lunch, since we're humans and humans are clearly animals.

This argument contains an equivocation on the word *animal*. The deli owner is using *animals* in the loose, popular sense of nonhuman animals, whereas the speaker is using *animals* in the scientific, biological sense.

Here is another example of this fallacy:

> Carl: Terminally ill patients have a right to decide how and when they want to die.
>
> Juan: That's not true. There is no right to euthanasia in U.S. law.

In this argument Carl is using the term *right* as a moral right, whereas Juan is using a different definition of *right*—that is, as a legal right. Legal rights and moral rights are not the same.

Hot or Not?

Is the use of fallacies a legitimate political campaign tactic?

For example, we might have had a legal right to own slaves, as did southern Americans before the Civil War, but (as all Americans would today agree) not a moral right. We can also have a moral right, such as a right to faithfulness and honesty from our life partner, but not generally a legal right.

The fallacy of equivocation also occurs when we misuse relative terms such as *tall*, *small*, *strong*, *big*, or *good*, as in this example:

> Two-year-old Katie is very tall. Her father, on the other hand, is not tall but about average in height. Therefore, Katie is taller than her father.

> Ronald Reagan was a good husband; therefore, he was a good president.

In these two examples, the relative terms *tall* and *good* are being used in the same argument in different contexts; it is like comparing apples and oranges. A tall toddler and a tall man are two very different things. And the fact that Reagan was a good husband does not necessarily mean that he was also a good president.

To avoid the fallacy of equivocation, you should clearly define any ambiguous words or phrases before proceeding with the argument or discussion. In addition, you need to avoid using relative terms in different contexts within the same argument.

This sign is an example of the fallacy of equivocation, meant to be humorous. Are the mangos really delicious or should you run for your life?

> To avoid the fallacy of amphiboly, we should use language and grammar properly, so the meaning of our argument is clear.

Amphiboly

amphiboly An argument contains a grammatical mistake which allows more than one conclusion to be drawn.

The fallacy of **amphiboly** occurs when there is a grammatical mistake in an argument, which allows more than one conclusion to be drawn. For example:

> Terri Schiavo's mother and her husband are on opposite sides of the battle over her life.[5]

In this statement regarding the issue of whether to remove the feeding tube from brain-damaged Terri Schiavo (which caused intense national debate in 2005), the ambiguous wording makes it is unclear which conclusion follows. Is it Terri Schiavo's husband, or her father (that is, her mother's husband), who is taking the opposite side? (In this case, Terri Schiavo's husband asked to have the feeding tube removed; her mother and father, believing that she still had a chance of regaining consciousness, insisted that the feeding tube be kept in place. This tragic family dilemma became a hot political issue before a court finally ordered the tube removed, allowing Ms. Schiavo to die. In

a subsequent autopsy, it was discovered that during many years of being in a coma, her brain had shrunk to less than half of normal size and that her vegetative state had been irreversible.)

Advertisers may intentionally use this fallacy, hoping you'll read more into the statement than is actually there, as in the following slogan for the Clinique fragrance Happy.

> Wear it and be happy!

The word *and* is ambiguous here. *And* can be used to mean either that the two separate ideas have nothing to do with each other—or that a causal connection exists between two ideas: "Wear this fragrance and [if you do] you will be happy." Of course, the advertiser is hoping we'll fall for the fallacy and make the second interpretation. However, if we use the fragrance Happy and aren't any happier as a result, and so try to sue Clinique for false advertising, we can be sure that they'll say they never intended the term *and* in their ad to imply a causal connection. Instead, or so they will probably claim, they used *and* only as a conjunction between two unrelated ideas. Meanwhile, it's money out

Connections

How can you recognize the fallacy of amphiboly in advertisements? *See Chapter 10, p. 326.*

Protestors, carrying placards that in most cases are ambiguous in their meaning, tried to draw attention to what they believed was unjust treatment of Terri Schiavo.

of our pockets and we're less happy than before because we've been duped by ambiguous language.

On the lighter side, humorists may use amphiboly to amuse their audiences, as in this dialogue from the 1996 movie *Spy Hard*:

> Agent: Sir, we just received a transmission from our agent on the Rock of Gibraltar.
>
> Director: What is it?
>
> Agent: A large rock on the coast of Spain.

To avoid the fallacy of amphiboly, we should use language and grammar properly, so the meaning of our argument is clear. When unsure of how to interpret a particular statement, we should ask the person to rephrase it more clearly.

Fallacy of Accent

The fallacy of **accent** occurs when the meaning of an argument changes according to which word or phrase in it is emphasized. For instance:

> **accent** The meaning of an argument changes depending on which word or phrase in it is emphasized.

> Distraught mother: Didn't I say, "Don't play with matches"?
>
> Delinquent daughter: But I wasn't *playing* with the matches. I was using them to burn down Mr. Murphy's shed.
>
> ***
>
> According to our school newspaper, the administration is going to crack down on *off-campus* drinking. I'm glad to hear that they're okay with on-campus drinking.

In the first example, the delinquent daughter changes the meaning of her mother's warning by placing the accent on the word *playing*. In the second, by emphasizing the term *off-campus*, the student erroneously concludes that the college administration opposes drinking only when it's off-campus.

The fallacy of accent can also happen when we take a passage out of context, thus changing its original meaning. For instance, "proof-texting" involves taking a scriptural passage out of its original context in order to prove a particular point. Religious cults often use proof-texting to support their theological arguments. The following passage is taken

"THANK GOODNESS! THE STUDENT LOAN COMPANY SAYS THIS IS THE LAST NOTICE I'M GOING TO GET!"

©WM. HOEST ENTERPRISES, INC. ALL RIGHTS RESERVED.

Analyzing Images

MAKING POOR CHOICES

DISCUSSION QUESTIONS

1. What fallacy is the student committing in this cartoon? Discuss how failing to recognize this fallacy might lead the student to make poor choices.

2. Imagine that you are the parents in the picture. Discuss what you might say to your son to call his attention to his faulty thinking.

from the King James Bible, which is the translation used by the Jim Roberts cult—mentioned at the beginning of this chapter—to convince recruits that they must forsake not only their worldly possessions but also their family, friends, education, and career plans.

> So likewise, whosoever of you that forsaketh not all that he hath, he cannot be my disciple. Luke 14:33

By ignoring the fact that neither Jesus nor his disciples forsook or completely disowned their family or friends, the cult leader commits the fallacy of accent.

If you are unsure about which term is being emphasized or accented in an argument, ask the person who made the argument to repeat or explain what he or she meant. If you suspect that a particular argument has been taken out of context, go back and look up the original source—in this example, the King James Version of the Bible. Arguments that take on a different meaning when read within the context of the source are fallacious.

Obviously the concluding statement is incorrect, since the average woman—at 5' 4"—is 4 inches taller than Danny DeVito. Also, sometimes we may think someone or something is good (or bad) simply because of that person's or that thing's association with a particular group, as the next example illustrates:

> I hear that Canadians are really nice people. Therefore, Derek, who is from Saskatchewan, must be really nice.

Although it may be true that Canadians as a group are very nice people, we cannot infer from this that each individual Canadian, such as Derek, is really nice.

Fallacy of Division

fallacy of division An erroneous inference from the characteristics of an entire set or group about a member of that group or set.

In the **fallacy of division**, we make an erroneous inference from the characteristics of an entire set or group about a member of the group or set. In doing so we incorrectly assume that each member of a group has the characteristics of the group in general.

> Group G has characteristic C.
> X is a member of group G.
> Therefore, X has characteristic C.

For example:

> Men are taller than women.
> Danny DeVito is a man.
> Therefore, Danny DeVito is taller than the average woman.

HIGHLIGHTS

FALLACIES OF AMBIGUITY

- *Equivocation:* An ambiguous word or phrase changes meaning during the course of the argument.
- *Amphiboly:* A grammatical error in the premises allows more than one conclusion to be drawn.
- *Fallacy of accent:* The meaning of an argument changes depending on which word or phrase is emphasized. Accent also occurs when passages are used out of context.
- *Fallacy of division:* A characteristic of an entire group is erroneously assumed to be a characteristic of each member of that group.

EXERCISES 5–2

1. Identify the fallacy of ambiguity in each of the following arguments:
   a. My parents used to get into arguments all the time, and they ended up getting divorced. Critical thinking teaches people how to make arguments. Therefore, if you want a happy marriage, don't sign up for a course in critical thinking.
   b. Americans are among the most obese people in the world. Clyde is an American. Therefore, Clyde is one of the most obese people in the world.
   c. Police officer: "Why do you rob banks?"
      Willie Sutton: "[Because] that's where they keep the money."
   d. The football team at State University is best in its league. Therefore, every member of the football team is one of the best football players in the league.
   e. I have no regrets for what I did. God told me to kill your children. Psalms 137 clearly says, "Happy is he who shall seize your children and dash them against the rock."

f. You are a bad person because you are a bad student.

g. Our town hall says it is giving out parking permits to fish at Warden's Pond. But that's ridiculous. Why would a fish need a parking permit?

h. God created man in his own image. But you're a woman. Therefore, you aren't created in God's image.

i. Stanford is academically one of the best universities in the United States. Therefore, Claude, who is a student at Stanford, is academically one of the best students in the country.

j. "Too many doctors are getting out of business. Too many OB-GYNs aren't able to practice their love with women all across the country." George W. Bush addressing a group of people about the effects of frivolous lawsuits, September 2004.

k. The black rhino is heading toward extinction. So the black rhinos at the Cincinnati Zoo must be heading toward extinction.

l. The Declaration of Independence states that all men are created equal. But that's certainly not the case. Studies show that people are born unequal in intelligence and athletic ability.

2. Look for examples of fallacies of ambiguity in the media, including news coverage, magazine articles, and advertisements. Identify each fallacy and discuss what purpose the writer is hoping to achieve (deliberately or unconsciously) by using this fallacy.

FALLACIES OF RELEVANCE

In **fallacies of relevance**, one or more of the premises is logically irrelevant, or unrelated, to the conclusion. However, we may fall for these fallacies because psychologically the premises and conclusion seem to be relevant. Fallacies of relevance include personal attacks (ad hominem fallacies), appeals to force (scare tactics), appeals to pity, popular appeals, appeals to ignorance, hasty generalizations, straw man fallacies, and red herrings.

Personal Attack (Ad Hominem) Fallacy

The fallacy of personal attack or **ad hominem fallacy** occurs when we disagree with someone's conclusion, but instead of presenting a counterargument we attack the person who made the argument. In doing so, we try to create disapproval toward our opponent and his or her argument. This fallacy, which is sometimes referred to by the Latin phrase ad hominem, meaning "against the man," can take two forms: (1) *abusive*, when we directly attack the character of the person, or (2) *circumstantial*, when we dismiss someone's argument or accuse someone of hypocrisy because of the person's particular circumstances. People with poor critical-thinking skills may be taken in by the fallacy because of human beings' natural tendency to divide the world into "one of us" versus "one of them."

This fallacy often rears its ugly head in heated debates over controversial issues and in political campaigns. In the 2008 presidential campaign, the McCain campaign launched an attack ad mocking Obama as a celebrity like Britney Spears and Paris Hilton. The Democrats in turn have attacked McCain as being "too old," "out of touch," and "grouchy."

People who don't conform to the accepted worldview may become the targets of personal attack, as in the following example:

> Ernst Zündel is part of the lunatic fringe. His ideas about the existence of UFOs under the South Pole are nothing short of crazy.

Instead of addressing Zündel's argument that UFOs exist near the South Pole, the person tries to discredit Zündel himself. The attempt to discredit someone's ideas by attacking his or her character and credibility is sometimes known as "poisoning the well." It is common in political campaigns.

People who lack good critical-thinking skills may respond to a personal attack by returning the insult.

> Pat: I think abortion is wrong because it ends the life of a living human being.
>
> Chris: You pro-lifers are just a bunch of narrow-minded, anti-choice, religious fanatics.
>
> Pat: Oh, yeah? Well, you're an anti-life baby-killer who's no better than a Nazi.

Instead of addressing Pat's arguments against abortion, Chris turns on Pat and attacks her. Chris doesn't do much better. Instead of ignoring Chris's insult and getting the argument back on course, Pat buys into the ad hominem fallacy by returning the insult. As good critical thinkers, we must resist the temptation to respond to a personal attack by throwing abuse back at the person who attacked us.

Connections

How do the "rules of evidence" protect against the use of fallacies, such as the ad hominem fallacy, in court trials? *See Chapter 13, p. 433.*

fallacy of relevance The premise is logically irrelevant, or unrelated, to the conclusion.

ad hominem fallacy Instead of presenting a counterargument, we attack the character of the person who made the argument.

Critical *Thinking* in Action

The Perils of Verbal Attacks in Personal Relationships

Not all uses of personal attack or the ad hominem fallacy are intentional. This fallacy may occur between people in relationships, whether between friends, family members, or girlfriends and boyfriends, because of poor communication skills.

John Gray, author of *Men Are from Mars, Women Are from Venus*, writes that we can be unwittingly abusive in personal relationships. He points out that men, rather than responding to a woman's argument, may become patronizing. Instead of addressing her concerns, the man explains why she shouldn't be upset or tells her not to worry about it. In doing so, he commits the ad hominem fallacy by dismissing her feelings. As a result, the woman becomes even more upset. He, in turn, senses her disapproval and he becomes upset as well, blaming her for upsetting him and demanding an apology before making up. She may apologize but is left wondering what happened. Or she may become even more upset at his expecting her to apologize, and before long the argument escalates into a battle, including name-calling and accusations.

In order to avoid the above scenario, Gray emphasizes the importance of good listening and communication skills in personal relationships so that we understand why the other person gets upset and can then move on from there.

DISCUSSION QUESTIONS

1. Do you agree with Gray about men's and women's communication styles? Is this type of miscommunication also common in relationships between people of the same sex? Support your answer using specific examples.

2. Think of a time in a relationship when you said something to a person who got upset and you didn't understand why. Reflecting back on the experience, did you unintentionally demean the other person by what you said? Now think of a time when you got upset because someone casually dismissed your concerns and you were left feeling hurt. Discuss how you might have responded more constructively to the other person's words or reaction to your words.

Paraphrased from John Gray, *Men Are from Mars, Women Are from Venus* (New York: HarperCollins Publishers, 1992), p. 155.

We also commit this fallacy when we simply dismiss someone's argument by suggesting that their particular circumstances bias their thinking or when we argue that our opponent should or does accept a particular conclusion because of his or her special circumstances, such as his or her lifestyle or membership in a particular group. For example:

> Of course Raul is in favor of affirmative action in college admissions. He's Latino and will benefit from affirmative action programs.

However, whether or not Raul benefits from affirmative action has no *logical* bearing on the soundness of Raul's argument in favor of affirmative action. His argument has to be evaluated independently of his circumstances.

This type of personal attack may also take the form of accusing someone of hypocrisy because of the person's circumstances.

> Father: Son, you shouldn't be smoking. It's not good for your health.
>
> Son: Look who's talking. You smoke at least a pack a day.

Here, the son dismisses his father's argument by accusing him of hypocrisy. But the fact that someone is engaging in a practice that he argues against, such as smoking, does not mean his argument is not sound. In this case, being a hypocrite or engaging in doublethink does not invalidate the father's argument that smoking is bad for the health of his son.

Not all negative statements about a person's character contain a fallacy, as in the following example.

> Jacob Robida, who allegedly attacked three men at Puzzles Lounge, a Massachusetts gay bar, and murdered two others while fleeing, was a disturbed and violent teenager who had a Nazi swastika and a coffin in his bedroom.

In this case, Robida's mental condition, his previous history of violence, and his Nazi sympathies are all relevant to the conclusion that he was guilty of the crime, and they help establish his motive for committing the crime.

Appeal to Force (Scare Tactics)

appeal to force (scare tactics) The use or threat of force in an attempt to get another person to accept a conclusion as correct.

The fallacy of **appeal to force**, or **scare tactics**, occurs when we use or threaten to use force—whether it be physical, psychological, or legal—in an attempt to get another person to back down on a position and to accept our conclusion as correct. Like the personal attack fallacy, using an appeal to force may work in the short run. However, intimidation almost always damages trust in a relationship and is symptomatic of poor communication skills and faulty reasoning. The fallacy of appeal to force is illustrated by the following two examples:

> Don't disagree with me. Remember who pays your college tuition.
>
> Don't disagree with me or I'll slap your *&*% face!

Sometimes appeals to force are more subtle than these; for example, we may threaten to withdraw affection or favors if the other person doesn't come around to our way of thinking. As we discussed at the opening of this chapter, "love bombing" by a cult—in which new recruits are showered with "unconditional" love and isolated from support systems outside the cult—leaves recruits vulnerable to this fallacy when subtle threats are later made to withdraw this love if they don't follow the cult's rules.

Appeal to force may involve scare tactics rather than overt threats. For instance, polio is endemic in the region along the border of Pakistan and Afghanistan. Despite this, efforts to give children in this region the polio vaccine are being hindered by conservative Muslim clerics who are using scare tactics: they tell villagers, without any evidence to support their claim, that the vaccine is part of an American conspiracy to sterilize Muslim children.[6]

Filmmakers also use scare tactics to hold their audience. With advances in artificial intelligence (AI), the possibility of creating robots or androids that look or behave like humans has spawned several movies, including *2001: A Space Odyssey*; *The Terminator*; *Blade Runner*; *I, Robot*; *Artificial Intelligence: AI*; the *Star Wars* series; and *The Matrix* trilogy, in which machines interact intelligently with humans. Many of these movies exploit scare tactics, depicting androids and robots as evil enemies out to destroy the human race.

Not all scare tactics involve fallacies, however. For example, if you drink and drive, you might cause an automobile accident. In this case, there is a logical connection between drinking and an increased risk of an automobile accident. In addition, not all threats contain fallacies. Some threats are too blatant to be considered fallacies. For example, if a robber sticks a gun in your face and says, "Hand over your wallet—or else," you generally hand over your wallet, not because the gunman has convinced you that the wallet is his but because you don't want to get shot.

People who have political, financial, or social power are more likely to use the appeal to force fallacy. Although most of us are not taken in by overt threats of force, fear is a powerful motivator and one that we are more likely to fall for than we might realize. This is particularly troublesome when those who lack power—for example, battered women or oppressed minorities—come to agree with their oppressor or blame themselves for their own oppression. Furthermore, children who witness abuse may come to believe that "might does make right" and identify with the person in power. In turn, they may use force to get their way when they are adults.

Connections How do advertisers use scare tactics to get you to buy their products? *See Chapter 10, p. 325.*

THE LONDON SKETCH BOOK.

PROF. DARWIN.

This is the ape of form.
Love's Labor Lost, act 5, scene 2.

Some four or five descents since.
All's Well that Ends Well, act 3, sc. 7.

DARWIN'S DESCENT FROM THE APES Fallacies can be used in nonverbal communication. After it was published in 1859, many critics of Charles Darwin's theory of evolution, rather than addressing his argument directly, responded by making personal attacks against those who supported evolution, as in this 1870 cartoon. Biologist Thomas Huxley (1825–1895), one of the most impassioned supporters of the theory of evolution, was not about to fall for this tactic. When Bishop Samuel Wilberforce allegedly asked Huxley whether "it was through his grandfather or his grandmother that he claimed descent from a monkey," Huxley used humor to deflect the attack. "If then the question is put to me," he replied, "whether I would rather have a miserable ape for a grandfather or a man highly endowed by nature and possessed of great means of influence and yet employs these faculties and that influence for the mere purpose of introducing ridicule into a grave scientific discussion, I unhesitatingly affirm my preference for the ape."

DISCUSSION QUESTIONS

1. *How successful is this cartoon in shaping your feelings or those of others about the subject of the cartoon? Did Huxley also use the ad hominem argument in his reply? What about cartoons attacking people whose views you disagree with—for example, people who support intelligent design theory?*

2. *Given that people tend to be taken in by this fallacy, does the media have a responsibility to refrain from publishing cartoons that attack someone's character when the real issue is the person's position on a particular issue? Support your answer.*

Appeal to Pity

In the fallacy of **appeal to pity**, we try to evoke a feeling of pity in the other person when pity is irrelevant to the conclusion. For example:

> Please don't give me a speeding ticket, officer. I had a really bad day: I found out that my boyfriend was cheating on me and, to top it off, I just received an eviction notice from my landlord.

However, the fact that you just found out your boyfriend was cheating on you and that you got an eviction notice from your landlord, while certainly sad, are not logically relevant to how fast you were driving. Although the officer may feel sympathy for your plight, it is not a good reason for her not to issue you a speeding ticket.

In previous chapters we discussed the importance in critical thinking of healthy self-esteem and assertive communication skills. People who have low self-esteem or trouble balancing their needs and those of others are particularly vulnerable to this fallacy. For example:

appeal to pity Pity is evoked in an argument when pity is irrelevant to the conclusion.

The appeal to pity on this billboard is not fallacious. Death related to smoking affects victims' families as well as the person who smokes.

I don't have time to type up my assignment for class tomorrow morning because I promised I'd meet Justin at the movies tonight. And you know better than anyone that it's wrong to break a promise. Please type up my assignment for me. If you don't, I might fail the course. Please, please, just do this one thing for me.

People who fall for this fallacy may see themselves as caring and sensitive people who hate to say no and are always willing to go out of their way for their friends. Compassion is certainly a good trait. But there are times when, if someone makes a request like this, you need to step back and ask yourself whether pity is relevant to their argument. If not, you can still express your concern but not give into their fallacious reasoning. Falling for an appeal to pity not only hurts you but also encourages the irresponsible behavior of someone who habitually uses this fallacy to manipulate others.

Not all appeals to pity are fallacious. There are times when a person's plight calls for a sympathetic response. For example:

> Please don't give me a speeding ticket, officer. My toddler, who is in the backseat, swallowed a nickel and is having trouble breathing. I have to get her to the hospital right away.

In this case, we would consider the officer grossly insensitive—and perhaps even criminally at fault—if she gave the parent a speeding ticket instead of escorting him and his child to the hospital as quickly as possible. Many charities also appeal to our sense of pity. Once again, there is no fallacy in cases where our pity is logically relevant to the appeal for help.

The word *critical*, as in critical thinking, is derived (as we noted at the beginning of Chapter 1) from the Greek word *kritikos*, meaning "discernment" or "the ability to judge." Being able to discern when it is appropriate for us to respond to an appeal to pity, as opposed to when we are being manipulated, involves an awareness of whether or not the reference to pity is in fact relevant.

Popular Appeal

The fallacy of **popular appeal** occurs when we appeal to popular opinion to gain support for our conclusion. The most common form is the *bandwagon approach*, in which a conclusion is assumed to be true simply because "everyone" believes it or "everyone" is doing it. Here's an example of the bandwagon form of popular appeal:

> **popular appeal** An appeal to popular opinion to gain support for our conclusion.

God must exist. After all, most people believe in God.

The conclusion in this argument is based on the assumption that the majority must know what is right. However, the fact that the majority of people believe in the existence of God, or in anything else, does not mean it is true. After all, the majority of people once believed that the sun went around the earth and that slavery was natural and morally acceptable.

Popular appeal may use polls to support a conclusion, as in this example:

> The ban on assault weapons should be extended. A recent Gallup poll found that 68 percent of Americans support having a ban on assault weapons.

Even if we agree that private ownership of assault weapons should be banned, the fact that most Americans support the ban is insufficient on its own to support the conclusion that we should ban them. Unfortunately, to optimize their chances of reelection, many legislators simply go along with the will of the majority rather than critically analyzing issues such as gun control or voting with their conscience. Instead of using polls to support our

A speeding driver's pleas that "I shouldn't get a ticket because everyone speeds," or, "Please don't give me a ticket, I'm late for the party," are based on fallacious thinking and would not convince a logically thinking officer.

conclusion, we need to come up with reasons and evidence that are relevant to having or not having a ban.

The *snob appeal* form of this fallacy involves the association of a certain idea with an elite group of people or a popular image. The use of athlete Lance Armstrong in American Century Investments ads and of celebrities such as Mariska Hargitay of the popular television series *Law and Order: Special Victims Unit* in ads for milk are examples of snob appeal. Indeed, this fallacy is particularly prevalent in ads that attempt to create a market for products—such as cigarettes and fancy cars—that we wouldn't ordinarily consider purchasing.

As critical thinkers, we need to keep in mind that a particular position or conclusion is not necessarily right just because the majority or an elite group accepts it.

Appeal to Ignorance

The fallacy of **appeal to ignorance** does not imply that we are stupid. Instead, it means that we are ignorant of the means of proving or disproving something. We fall into this fallacy whenever we argue that something is true simply because no one has proven it false, or that something is false because no one has proven it true. Consider this:

> **appeal to ignorance** The claim that something is true simply because no one has proven it false, or that something is false simply because no one has proven it true.

> UFOs obviously don't exist. No one has been able to prove that they do.

Hot or Not?

Does celebrity endorsement of a product make you more likely to buy that product?

Connections

What safeguards does representative democracy provide against the "tyranny of the majority"? *See Chapter 13, p. 414.*

How do advertisers use the fallacy of popular appeal to sell products such as "junk food" to children? *See Chapter 10, p. 324.*

How can you recognize the fallacy of popular appeal in political campaigns? *See Chapter 13, p. 416.*

How can we recognize the use of snob appeal in advertisements? *See Chapter 10, p. 325.*

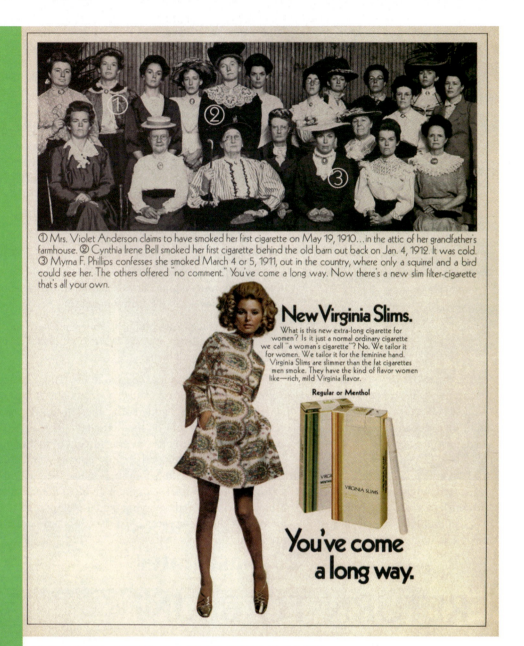

① Mrs. Violet Anderson claims to have smoked her first cigarette on May 19, 1910...in the attic of her grandfather's farmhouse. ② Cynthia Irene Bell smoked her first cigarette behind the old barn out back on Jan. 4, 1912. It was cold. ③ Myrna F. Phillips confesses she smoked March 4 or 5, 1911, out in the country, where only a squirrel and a bird could see her. The others offered "no comment." You've come a long way. Now there's a new slim filter-cigarette that's all your own.

New Virginia Slims.

What is this new extra-long cigarette for women? Is it just a normal ordinary cigarette we call "a woman's cigarette"? No. We tailor it for women. We tailor it for the feminine hand. Virginia Slims are slimmer than the fat cigarettes men smoke. They have the kind of flavor women like—rich, mild Virginia flavor.

Regular or Menthol

You've come a long way.

"YOU'VE COME A LONG WAY, BABY" The tobacco industry spends more than $30 million a day in advertising, much of which is based on appeals to our emotions rather than to reason. In 1968, Philip Morris introduced Virginia Slims cigarettes and the "You've come a long way, baby!" ad campaign in an attempt to expand its female market. This campaign was designed to appeal to women's growing sense of independence. It also used snob appeal and the identification of smoking with being beautiful and thin, as well as liberated.

Although the sexist overtones led to boycotts of Virginia Slims by some feminists, the ad was highly successful in getting more teenage girls to take up smoking. While rates of smoking for high school and college students dropped steadily throughout the 1960s into the late 1980s, the rates for women began to rise in 1968, surpassing those of men by 1974. Although rates for both sexes began to plummet in 2000, college women are still slightly more likely to smoke than are college men.*

DISCUSSION QUESTIONS

1. *Discuss the use of fallacies in this ad. Why was this ad successful in getting some young women to take up smoking?*

2. *If you smoke or know someone who does, what reasons do you or the other person give in support of continuing to smoke? Examine or analyze these reasons for possible fallacies.*

* Alexander W. Astin et al., *The American Freshman: Thirty-Five Year Trends* (Los Angeles, CA: Cooperative Institutional Research Program, University of California, 2002), pp. 13-14.

Analyzing Images

In this example, the only support the person offers for the conclusion that UFOs don't exist is that we have been unable to prove their existence. However, the fact that we are ignorant of how to go about proving their existence does not mean that they don't exist. UFOs may or may not exist—we just don't know.

When we lack evidence for the existence of a particular phenomenon such as UFOs, unless there is evidence to the contrary, the most we can say about it is that we don't know. For example, to claim that humans (or intelligent computers) do not have a soul, simply because we do not know how to prove whether a being has a soul, is to commit the *fallacy of ignorance*.

Sometimes the fallacy of appeal to ignorance is subtler. Educational psychologist Arthur Jensen used the following argument in support of his position that black people are innately inferior to white people in intelligence:

No one has yet produced any evidence based on a properly controlled study to show that representative samples of Negro and white children can be equalized in intellectual ability through statistical control of environment and education.[7]

However, it does not logically follow from *lack* of evidence that "[black] and white children can [not] be equalized in intellectual ability." Once again, the most we can say is that we don't know. Similarly, we can't argue that something *does* exist just because people cannot prove it *doesn't* exist. Consider this argument:

I truly believe that I have a guardian angel. No one has yet been able to prove otherwise.

The fact that no one has been able to disprove the existence of angels is logically irrelevant to whether they actually exist. People may also try to get out of a tight spot by using this fallacy, as in the following case:

I didn't murder Alexi, officer. You don't have any evidence that I was at Alexi's house last night. That proves that I didn't do it.

There is an important exception to the fallacy of appeal to ignorance. In a court of law, a defendant is presumed innocent until proven guilty. And the burden of proof is on the prosecution, not on the defendant. This legal principle was designed to prevent punishment of the innocent, which is considered a much greater injustice than letting a guilty person go free. In addition, because the government is much more powerful than the individual defendant, this principle helps level the playing field. It's important to note that a "not guilty" verdict is just that; it is not necessarily proof of the person's innocence.

What events led U.S. courts to adopt the "innocent until proven guilty" philosophy? *See Chapter 13, p. 432.*

Connections

Some people make the hasty generalization that because the show Desperate Housewives, *a very popular show for women, was created by a gay man, that means that gay men are more in touch with women's feelings than are straight men.*

Hasty Generalization

When used properly, generalization is a valuable tool in both the physical and social sciences. But we commit the fallacy of **hasty generalization** when we generalize from a sample that is too small or biased.

Unusual cases ——————→ Odd rule about
(premises)   the whole group
                                        (conclusion)

Stereotypes are often based on this fallacy:

> My father was an abuser, and so was my ex-boyfriend John. All men are mean.

Here the speaker judges all men as "mean" on the basis of her limited experience with only two men. The second example of this fallacy reinforces stereotypes of gay men as more sensitive than straight men:

> Of the four most popular television dramas, two were created by gay men. Marc Cherry is creator of *Desperate Housewives*, and Ryan Murphy, who is also gay, is the creator of *Nip/Tuck*. That just goes to show that gay men are more sensitive and talented when it comes to portraying what people want to see in relationships.

As we've already seen, people tend to divide the world into "us" and "them," and rather than view people who are different from "us" as individuals, we instead label "them" on the basis of hasty generalizations. Confirmation bias, in which we seek only examples that confirm our stereotypes, reinforces this tendency.

For example, conservative author and public speaker Ann Coulter favors separate lines at the airport that would be based on skin color and gender. All males between the ages of 14 and 45 with "swarthy complexions," indicating that they might be Muslims from the Middle East, would be in a line where they would get more extensive screening. Coulter argues that this makes sense, since Muslims have committed virtually all the terrorist attacks against Americans since the 1993 bombing of the World Trade Center.[8] However, her generalization obviously isn't accurate. Most domestic terrorist acts in the United States are committed by groups with no Muslim connections, such as the Earth Liberation Front and the Army of God (a radical Christian group which targets abortion clinics). In addition, neither Timothy McVeigh nor Terry Nichols—the terrorists responsible for the deaths of 168 Americans in the 1995 Oklahoma City bombing—was either Middle Eastern or Muslim.

The fallacy of hasty generalization can also interfere with cross-cultural communication and the establishment of new relationships. While on a cruise with my sister, our ship stopped at the port of Cartagena in Colombia, instead of at another Caribbean port that had originally been sched-uled. When our tour director heard of the change, he quickly called our group together and warned us that we should stay on the ship while in port. If we really wanted to go ashore, he added, we should pretend to be Canadians. Colombians, he told us, hate Americans and would try to rob, assault, or arrest us on the most trivial charges, or even kill us, given the opportunity. As it turned out, Cartagena was a beautiful city, and the people we met were very friendly and helpful. Stereotypes and hasty generalizations about Colombians acted as a barrier that kept other passengers from getting to know and understand the Colombians.

Hasty generalization can also occur because we've developed stereotypes that are based on outdated information. Consider this statement:

> Most college students nowadays are very concerned about financing college. I certainly was, as were many of my friends, when I started college in 1995.

In fact, the number of college students who express a "major concern" about their college finances has declined significantly since the mid-1990s and is now only about 12 percent.[9]

Before we make a generalization we should make sure that we have a sufficiently large and unbiased—as well as an up-to-date—sample. After the death of the great English poet Lord Byron in 1824, a curious physician removed his brain and weighed it. He found that Byron's brain was 25 percent larger than the average human brain. News of this discovery, which was based on only a single sample, spread throughout the scientific community, contributing to the myth that there was a connection between brain size and high intelligence.[10] We'll be studying sampling methods and the proper use of generalization in arguments in more detail in Chapter 7.

> After the death of the great English poet Lord Byron in 1824, a curious physician removed his brain and weighed it. He found that Byron's brain was 25 percent larger than the average human brain.

Straw Man

The **straw man** fallacy is committed when a person distorts or misrepresents the opponent's argument, thus making it easier to knock it down or refute it.

hasty generalization A generalization is made from a sample that is too small or biased.

Connections

How do advertisements reinforce stereotypes? *See Chapter 10, p. 325.*

What role does sampling play in scientific research and experimentation? *See Chapter 12, p. 388.*

straw man fallacy An opponent's argument is distorted or misrepresented in order to make it easier to refute.

Advertisers often appeal to "snob appeal" in advertising, paying celebrities to endorse their products. They hope that consumers will think, "I want to be like Victoria Beckham, so I'll buy the type of purse she is carrying."

This tactic is particularly common in political rhetoric over controversial issues, in which the audience may not know or care that the opponent's view is being misrepresented.

> I'm opposed to legalizing same-sex marriages. Proponents of same-sex marriage want to destroy traditional marriage and make gay marriage the norm.

This is a fallacious argument because it misrepresents the argument of those who support same-sex marriage. Supporters of same-sex marriage are not arguing that it should be an alternative to traditional marriage or that it is superior to traditional marriage. Instead, they simply want same-sex couples to have the same rights as opposite-sex couples when it comes to marriage.

> Michael Moore in his movie *Sicko* (2007) argues for a nationalized health care system in the United States. Obviously Moore supports a socialist government that would dictate what physicians can and cannot do. But socialism has already been tried in the former Soviet Union and failed. Therefore, Moore's argument is clearly untenable.

As in the previous example, this assessment of the argument in question is simplistic. It misrepresents what is meant by nationalized medicine. By focusing on only one aspect of it and distorting the extent of the role government plays in nationalized medicine in most countries that have it, the argument creates a straw man that is easy to knock down. Furthermore, it makes the assumption that Moore supports Soviet-style socialism, which he does not, thus

What seems to be the problem?

Michael Moore's Sicko attacked the healthcare system in the United States while praising the nationalized healthcare systems of Canada and Europe.

misrepresenting Moore's argument. In addition, the person making the argument uses scare tactics by drawing a comparison between the Soviet Union and the United States under nationalized medicine.

To avoid using or being taken in by this fallacy, go back and look at the argument in question as it was originally presented. Ask yourself: Has the argument been reworded or oversimplified to the point of misrepresentation? Have key parts of the original argument been omitted or key words been changed or misused?

Red Herring

The **red herring** fallacy is named after a technique used in England to train foxhounds. A sack of red herrings is dragged across the path of the fox to distract the hounds from their prey. A well-trained hound learns not to allow distractions to divert its focus from the prey. The red herring fallacy is committed when a person tries to sidetrack an argument by going off on a tangent and bringing up a different issue. Thus, the argument is now directed toward a different conclusion. Because the red herring issue is often presented as somewhat related to the initial one under discussion, the shift in the argument usually goes unnoticed. The original discussion may even be abandoned completely and the focus shifted to a new and extraneous topic without the audience realizing what is happening until it is too late. The use of the red herring fallacy occurs in political debates when candidates want to avoid answering a question or commenting on a controversial issue.

For example, a politician who is asked about a nationalized health care plan to cover all Americans may change the topic to the less controversial one of how important it is for all Americans to be healthy and receive good health care. In doing so, the politician avoids having to address the question of which approach to health insurance he or she supports.

During the 2008 presidential primaries, Senator Barack Obama was questioned about his relationship to the radical and seemingly anti-American preacher Reverend Wright, whose church he had attended for many years. Obama responded in a speech in which he shifted the topic to that of racism in America, thereby avoiding the specific issue in question.

HIGHLIGHTS
FALLACIES OF RELEVANCE

- **Personal attack (ad hominem fallacy):** An attempt to refute an argument by attacking the character or circumstances of the person making the argument.

- **Appeal to force (scare tactics):** A threat to use force—whether it be physical, psychological, or legal—in an attempt to get another person to back down on his or her position and to accept the conclusion as correct.

- **Appeal to pity:** An attempt to gain support for a conclusion by evoking a feeling of pity, when pity is irrelevant to the conclusion.

- **Popular appeal:** An appeal made to the opinion of the majority to gain support for the conclusion.

- **Appeal to ignorance:** An argument that something is true simply because no one has proved it false, or that something is false simply because no one has proved it true.

- **Hasty generalization:** A conclusion based on atypical cases.

- **Straw man:** The distortion or misrepresentation of an opponent's argument to make it easier to knock down or refute.

- **Red herring:** An argument directed toward a conclusion that is different from that posed by the original argument.

red herring fallacy A response is directed toward a conclusion that is different from that proposed by the original argument.

How can we recognize and avoid falling for the use of inappropriate appeal to authority in advertisements? *See Chapter 10, p. 326.*

Connections

premise(s) say essentially the same thing, as in the following argument:

> The Bible is the word of God. Therefore, God must exist because the Bible says God exists.

Here, the conclusion "God must exist" is already assumed to be true in the premise "The Bible is the word of God." To offer a rational proof of God, we cannot assume the existence of what we are trying to prove in our premises.

The begging-the-question fallacy can be very frustrating if we fail to recognize it, since there is no way to disprove the person's conclusion if we accept the premise. If you think an argument contains this fallacy, try reversing the conclusion and the premise(s) to see if the argument says essentially the same thing.

Inappropriate Appeal to Authority

It is generally appropriate in an argument to use the testimony of a person who is an authority or expert in the field. However, we commit the fallacy of **inappropriate appeal to authority** when we look to an authority in a field that is *not* under investigation. Young children, for example, may look to their parents as authorities even in areas where their parents have little or no expertise. Here is an example:

inappropriate appeal to authority We look to an authority in a field other than that under investigation.

loaded question A particular answer is presumed to an unasked question.

> My priest says that genetic engineering is not safe. Therefore, all experimentation in this field should be stopped.

Unless your priest also happens to be an expert in genetic engineering, before accepting his argument as correct you should ask him for reliable and authoritative evidence for his assertion.

We often find this fallacy in advertisements in which celebrities are used to promote products. For example, jazz musician Ray Charles and pop singer Britney Spears have promoted Pepsi, and tennis stars Andre Agassi and Steffi Graf sell Canon cameras. In none of these cases are the celebrities authorities on these products, and yet people accept their word simply because they are *experts* in unrelated fields.

Uniforms and distinguished titles such as *doctor*, *professor*, *president*, and *lieutenant* also serve to reinforce the mistaken perception that people who are experts in one field must be knowledgeable in others. This phenomenon is known as the *halo effect*. In the Milgram study, for example, the majority of study subjects followed the orders of the experimenter primarily because he had a PhD and was wearing a white lab coat, a symbol of scientific authority.

To avoid inappropriate appeals to authority, we should check out an expert's credentials in the field before using his or her testimony as authoritative.

Loaded Question

The fallacy of **loaded question** assumes a particular answer to another unasked question. This fallacy is sometimes used in a court of law when a lawyer demands a yes or no answer to a question such as

> Have you stopped beating your girlfriend?

However, this question makes the unwarranted assumption that you have already answered yes to the previous unasked question, "Do you beat your girlfriend?" If you don't beat your girlfriend and reply no to the question, it appears as if you are still beating her. On the other hand, if you answer yes it implies that you used to beat her.

The next example is also a loaded question:

> Do you think that the death penalty should be used only for people 18 and older?

This question is worded in a way that assumes that the people being asked approve of the death penalty when in fact they might not.

Wearing a uniform serves to reinforce the public's belief that the person is an authority in fields that may be beyond his or her actual expertise.

When the conservative talk-show host Rush Limbaugh was asked, "When Bill Clinton's book comes out, what page are you going to turn to first," the interviewer assumed Limbaugh was going to read the book, thus asking a loaded question. Limbaugh answered, "I'm not going to open it. I'm not going to believe anything in it, so why would I read it?"[16] Of course, in this particular instance Limbaugh's response didn't speak well for his critical-thinking skills, since he was using both confirmation bias and resistance in the form of avoidance.

False Dilemma

The fallacy of **false dilemma** reduces responses to complex issues to an either/or choice. By doing so, this fallacy polarizes stands on issues and ignores common ground or other solutions. This slogan serves as an example:

> America—love it or leave it! If you don't like U.S. policy, then move somewhere else!

That argument makes the unwarranted assumption that the only alternative to accepting U.S. policies is to move to another country. In fact, there are many alternatives, including working to change or improve U.S. policies. In this case, the fallacious reasoning is reinforced by the "one of us/one of them" cognitive error, in which we tend to divide the world into two opposing sides.

Poor critical-thinking skills and the tendency to see the world in black and white make it more likely that we'll fall into this fallacy. This is seen when some politicians declare that there are only two responses to global warming: either (1) cut down on the emission of greenhouse gases that contribute to global warming even though it damages our nation's economy or (2) ignore the problem of greenhouse-gas emission, stick with business as usual, and keep our economy strong. In fact, these are not the only alternatives. Many proposals have been put forth for the use of alternative energy sources and building more energy-efficient buildings and vehicles that would enable us to cut down on greenhouse gases while strengthening our economy.

Habitual use of this fallacy restricts our ability to come up with creative solutions to problems not only with national policy but also in our personal lives. The following example illustrates:

> It's Valentine's Day, and Bob didn't propose to me as I thought he would. Even worse, he said he wanted to start dating other women. I don't know what I'll do. If Bob doesn't marry me, I'll surely end up a miserable old maid.

Clearly Bob is not the only fish in the sea, although it may seem so when we are jilted by someone we care for. Overcoming personal setbacks requires that we use our critical-thinking skills to come up with a way of overcoming our problem rather than getting stuck in fallacious thinking.

Harnessing wind power is just one of the many ways of strengthening the economy while cutting down on greenhouse emissions and freeing us from dependence on foreign oil.

We frequently find this type of fallacious thinking in all-or-nothing thinking. For example, bulimics regard eating in terms of either getting fat or bingeing and then vomiting to stay thin. They simply don't see moderation in eating as a viable alternative.

> **false dilemma** Responses to complex issues are reduced to an either/or choice.

As we discussed in Chapter 4, people who have depression also tend to get caught up in this type of fallacious reasoning:

> "Either I'm in complete control of my life or I'm out of control."

> "Either everyone likes me or everyone hates me."

Pollsters may unwittingly commit this fallacy. How options are presented in a question can influence the response. For instance, in one survey people were asked whether they felt that "the courts deal too harshly or not harshly enough with criminals." When presented with only these two alternatives, 6 percent of those surveyed responded "too harshly" and 78 percent "not harshly enough." However, when a third alternative was offered— "don't have enough information about courts to say"— 29 percent chose that response and only 60 percent said "not harshly enough."[17] We'll be studying polling methods in more detail in Chapter 7.

To avoid the fallacy of the false dilemma, watch out for either–or questions that put you on the spot. If neither alternative is satisfactory, it is best to leave the response blank or check "I don't know" if that option is offered.

children's demands once in a while will lead to their dominating us.

The second argument regarding the effects of human clones is also implausible. Much of the concern about human cloning leading us down the slippery slope to armies of clones taking over the world is based on inaccurate information. In reality, it would be very risky and expensive to clone a human. Even if we could mass-produce human clones, we would need to find women who are willing to act as surrogate gestational mothers for the cloned children. Moreover, each clone, like any child, will need a family to nurture him or her after birth.[20] This scenario is unlikely to happen on a large scale, since most parents prefer to have children who are related to them. If cloning were legalized, it would most likely be used primarily for infertile couples rather than for mass-producing identical humans. Of course, this is not to say that there are no good arguments against human cloning, but the proverbial slippery slope is not one of them.

> **naturalist fallacy** A fallacy based on the assumption that what is natural is good.

Russian president Vladimir Putin invoked the slippery-slope fallacy when he opposed a decision by the Supreme Court of Ukraine to hold a second runoff election between the two candidates for that neighboring country's presidency—one pro-Russian and the other opposed to Russian domination:

> A rerun of the second round may also produce nothing. What happens then? Will there have to be a third, a fourth, a twenty-fifth round, until one of the sides obtains the necessary result?[21]

Some people oppose the federal government wiretapping the phones, without a court order, of people suspected of being terrorists; these opponents paint a grim picture of the nation sliding down a slippery slope to the tapping of phones in any citizen's private home, eventually reaching the complete loss of freedom of speech. However, we first have to present evidence that this scenario is likely, especially given that the federal government, or at least so it claims, is wiretapping only those calls made to overseas locations, not domestic calls. In fact, concerns about this type of covert activity may not be fallacious. We have seen this kind of operation get out of hand when applied by the FBI to suspected "subversives," civil rights leaders, and antiwar activists in the 1950s through the 1970s.

Expressing a concern that something will get out of hand is not always fallacious. Sometimes the prediction that a particular action or policy will start us down a slippery slope is warranted. Consider this statement:

> The United States is running . . . a series of detention centers around the world where international legal standards are not having sway. They opened the door to a little bit of torture, and a whole lot of torture walked through.[22]

The assumption here is that if we allow torture under these circumstances, the use of torture by the United States will become a common method of dealing with detainees.

To avoid the slippery-slope fallacy, we should carefully carry out our research and familiarize ourselves with the likely outcomes of different actions and policies. We should also watch any tendency to exaggerate forecasts of impending catastrophe.

Naturalistic Fallacy

The **naturalistic fallacy** is based on the unwarranted assumption that what is natural is good or morally acceptable and that what is unnatural is bad or morally unacceptable.[*] We find this fallacy in arguments that claim that no good can come from AI (artificial intelligence), simply on the grounds that AI is artificial—and hence unnatural.

Advertisers may also try to get us to conclude that their product is good or healthy simply because it is natural. An ad can claim, for example, that a tobacco product is "100 percent natural tobacco." However, it doesn't follow. *All* tobacco is natural, but that doesn't make it healthy. Arsenic, HIV, and tsunamis are also "natural," but we don't consider them to be healthy and desirable.

HIGHLIGHTS

FALLACIES INVOLVING UNWARRANTED ASSUMPTIONS

- *Begging the question:* A conclusion is simply a rewording of a premise.
- *Inappropriate appeal to authority:* An appeal based on the testimony of an authority in a field other than that under investigation.
- *Loaded question:* A question that assumes a particular answer to another unasked question.
- *False dilemma:* An argument unwarrantedly reduces the number of alternatives to two.
- *Questionable cause:* An argument that assumes without sufficient evidence that one thing is the cause of another.
- *Slippery slope:* An assumption that if some actions are permitted, all actions of that type will soon be permissible.
- *Naturalistic fallacy:* The assumption that because something is natural it is good or acceptable.

* The term *naturalistic fallacy* is sometimes used in a more narrow sense as a meta-ethical thesis that the concept of moral goodness cannot be reduced to descriptive or natural terms. For more on the use of this term, see G. E. Moore's *Principa Ethica.*

Same-sex parents are often discriminated against because many people only see "parents" as a mother and father.

The naturalistic fallacy has also been used both to justify homosexuality (it occurs naturally in other animals) and to argue for its immorality, as in the following:

> Homosexual encounters do not lead to children [procreation], which is the natural end of sexual relations. Therefore, homosexuality is immoral.

In a similar manner, a person may argue that hunting is morally acceptable because other animals hunt and kill:

> I disagree that we need to protect the big cats, such as lions and tigers, from being hunted or to restrict ranchers from protecting their herds from these predators. We are only doing what the big cats do. They are predators, and so are humans.

However, the fact that other animals are predators does not justify our doing the same. Some animals also eat their young, and a few female insects even eat their male partners after mating! But these naturally occurring examples do not imply that it is morally justifiable for humans to do the same. The morality of these behaviors has to be evaluated on grounds other than that they are natural.

EXERCISES 5–4

1. Identify the fallacies involving unwarranted assumptions in the following arguments—not all of which contain fallacies!
   a. If we don't overturn the Patriot Act now, it won't be long before we'll be living in a brave new world where no one is safe from spying by the government.
   b. Prosecutor to defendant: Did you hide the drugs in your car?
   c. Only women are physically capable of bearing and nursing children. Therefore, women ought to be the primary caregivers of children.
   d. Panhandler to person on street: "Can you spare a dime?"
   e. My lawyer says that it looks as if I have whiplash from that automobile accident. I'm going to sue the insurance company of the person who hit my car.

f. According to the meteorologists on the Weather Channel, we might have 5 to 6 feet of flooding from heavy rain and rising river waters in the next 24 hours. I think we should pack our valuables and get out of town.

g. Do you support restricting abortion rights, thereby increasing the chances of death for thousands of women desperate enough to seek illegal abortions?

h. If infanticide under "strict" conditions were legalized, the conditions would soon be loosened, reporters would discover inequities where it was allowed in some circumstances and not others, and soon infanticide on parental demand would become standard.[23]

i. I see no problem with cutting down rain forests for cattle grazing. My philosophy professor doesn't think the loss of some species through the destruction of rain forests is going to permanently upset the balance of nature. He says that as old species die off, new ones will evolve to take their place.

j. Splenda can't be all that bad for children. After all, it's made from all-natural sugar.

k. Democracy is the best form of government because rule of the majority is always preferable.

l. Boyfriend to girlfriend: So what do you want to do tonight—watch the football game on TV or grab a beer at Joe's Bar and Billiards?

m. I saw an ad with Madonna promoting Gap jeans. I really admire her. I'm going to buy Gap jeans from now on.

n. Animals can't reason, since reason is one of the things that separate humans from the beasts.

o. Yesterday I carried an umbrella to class and it didn't rain. Today I left it home and it rained. I'd better carry my umbrella if I don't want it to rain.

p. Do you believe women should be drafted into the military?

q. Embryonic stem-cell research should be banned. It is a gateway to all other kinds of genetic engineering in humans and will lead to the exploitation of poor women as fetus farms.

2. When you or your college team engages in a game or sporting event, to what extent do you attribute the win or loss to what is in actuality a questionable cause? Looking back at the cognitive errors we studied in Chapter 4, discuss which of the different kinds of errors contribute to our tendency to use or fall for this fallacy.

3. Find two advertisements containing fallacies involving two different unwarranted assumptions. Cut out or photocopy the advertisements. For each ad, write one page explaining what fallacy it contains and the target audience of the fallacious ad. Discuss how effective you think each ad is and why.

4. Which fallacy involving an unwarranted assumption are you most likely to fall for? Give a specific example. Which fallacy involving an unwarranted assumption are you most likely to use? Give a specific example. What steps can you take to make yourself less vulnerable to these fallacies?

5. *Journal Exercise.* Complete a journal exercise on "Fallacies." Which fallacies were you most likely to fall for and which are you most likely to use? If you are willing, share with the class specific examples of these fallacies in your life and some of your strategies for overcoming them.

STRATEGIES FOR AVOIDING FALLACIES

Once you have learned how to identify informal fallacies, the next step is to develop strategies for avoiding them. Here are some strategies that can help you become a better critical thinker:[*]

- *Know yourself.* Self-knowledge is a cardinal rule for good critical thinking. Knowing which fallacies you are most likely to fall for and which you are most likely to commit will make you less vulnerable to lapses in critical thinking.

- *Build your self-confidence and self-esteem.* Working on your self-confidence and self-esteem will make you less likely to give in to peer pressure and, in particular, to the fallacy of popular appeal. People who are self-confident are also less likely to back down when others use a fallacy on them or to become defensive and use fallacies on others.

- *Cultivate good listening skills.* Be a respectful listener of other people's views, even if you disagree with them. Do not be thinking of how you are

---

[*] I thank the students in my spring 2005 critical-thinking class at the University of Massachusetts at Dartmouth for their invaluable contribution in developing this list of strategies.

going to respond before you have even heard the other person's argument. After the other person has presented his or her view, repeat it back to make sure you understand it correctly. Look for common ground. If you notice a fallacy in the argument, respectfully point it out. If the argument appears to be weak, ask the person for better support or evidence for his or her position rather than simply dismissing it.

- *Avoid ambiguous and vague terms and faulty grammar.* Cultivate good communication and writing skills. Clearly define your key terms in presenting an argument. And expect the same of others. Don't be afraid to ask questions. If you are unclear about the definition of a term or what someone else means, ask the person to define the term or rephrase the sentence.

- *Do not confuse the soundness of an argument with the character or circumstances of the person making the argument.* Focus on the argument that is being presented, not on the person presenting the argument. Also, resist the temptation to counterattack if another person attacks your character or threatens you because of your position on a particular issue. When two people trade insult for insult instead of focusing on the real issue, an argument may escalate out of control and both people may end up feeling frustrated and hurt. The tacit belief that if the other person is using fallacies or being illogical it's okay for you to do the same is a sign of immature thinking. If another person attacks your character, step back and take a deep breath before responding.

- *Know your topic.* Don't jump to a conclusion without first doing your research. Knowing your subject makes it less likely that you will commit a fallacy simply because you are unable to defend or explain your position. This strategy involves being familiar with evidence, as well as a willingness to learn from others. In evaluating new evidence, make sure that it is based on credible sources.

- *Adopt a position of skepticism.* We should be skeptical but not close our minds to claims we disagree with, unless there is clear evidence that contradicts that claim. Don't just take people's word for it, especially if they are not authorities in the field under discussion. In addition, remain skeptical about your own position and open to the possibility that you are mistaken or at least don't have the whole truth.

- *Watch your body language.* Fallacies need not be written or spoken. For example, the fallacies of personal attack and appeal to force can be conveyed through body language, such as rolling your eyes, glaring, looking away, and even walking away when someone is speaking.

- *Don't be set on "winning."* If your purpose is to win the argument rather than get to the truth about the issue, you're more likely to use fallacies and rhetoric when you can't rationally defend your position.

Learning how to recognize and avoid fallacies will make you less likely to fall victim to faulty arguments, whether those of cult recruiters, advertisers, politicians, authority figures, friends, or family. It is especially important to be able to identify and avoid using fallacies in your own life, thereby improving your critical-thinking skills.

The habitual use of fallacies can damage relationships and leave people feeling upset and frustrated. By avoiding resort to fallacies, your relationships will be more satisfying and your arguments stronger and more credible. This, in turn, will make it easier for you to achieve your life goals.

1. Discuss ways in which being aware of and avoiding fallacies can improve your personal life.

2. To what extent does lack of self-knowledge and self-confidence make you or others you know more vulnerable to fallacious reasoning? Use specific examples to illustrate your answer.

3. Sometimes it is unclear if an argument contains a fallacy, especially if we are unfamiliar with the issue or resistant to considering other perspectives on an issue. Working in small groups, select one or two of the following issues or one of the issues already raised in this chapter. Identify which fallacy the argument might contain. Discuss how you would go about collecting evidence to determine whether the argument is fallacious.

    a. Boys don't do as well in school as girls because almost all the teachers in elementary schools are women.

    b. The beheading of infidels in Iraq, such as Western journalists, was sanctioned by Islam's holiest text, the Qur'an, which urges Muslims to resist Western occupation by stating, "Slay them . . . and drive them out of the places whence they drove you."[24]

    c. "Global warming is real; the risks it poses are real; and the American people have a right to know it and a responsibility to do something about it. The sooner Congress understands that, the sooner we can protect our nation—and our planet—from increased flood, fire, drought, and deadly heat waves."

    —President Bill Clinton

    d. I don't think an ice cream social is appropriate for our next meeting since several of the students who will be attending are Japanese Americans, and from what I know, most of them don't eat ice cream.

    e. Some people think prostitution should be legalized in the United States. However, if we legalize prostitution, sexually transmitted diseases like AIDS will run rampant and everyone will start to die out.

    f. Lawyers for the American Civil Liberties Union want the words *under God* removed from the Pledge of Allegiance. The Supreme Court should not support the ACLU's request. The ACLU is clearly antireligion and would like to see every trace of religion and faith in God removed from American life.

    g. Support for stem-cell research by celebrities such as Christopher Reeve, Michael J. Fox, and Ronald Reagan Jr. has been in part responsible for the swing in public opinion in favor of the research.

    h. My professor is leaving for a trip to Antarctica the same day that final grades are due for our class. Since this is my senior year at college, I cannot afford to get an incomplete in this class because I plan on graduating in a month. My final paper is worth 40 percent of my grade, so I can either choose to hand in the final paper before my professor leaves for Antarctica or to fail the course and therefore not graduate until next year. I don't see any other way out.

    i. Prayer works. Our church group prayed for Maxine after her operation, and she recovered from her surgery faster than the person in the bed beside her who had the same operation.

4. Select two of the strategies for avoiding fallacies and discuss as a class or write a short essay describing ways in which these strategies can help you become a better critical thinker. Discuss steps you might take to implement these strategies in your everyday life.

5. Discuss how the strategies that you plan to use to make yourself less vulnerable to using or falling for fallacies might make it easier for you to achieve your life goals.

Think
AGAIN >>

1. What is a fallacy, and why are we taken in by informal fallacies?
    *   A fallacy is a type of incorrect thinking. We are taken in by informal fallacies because they are psychologically persuasive. The use of our critical-thinking skills makes us less likely to fall for fallacies.

2. What are three main types of informal fallacies?
    *   One type is fallacies of ambiguity, which occur when there is ambiguous wording, sloppy grammatical structure, or confusion between two closely related concepts. In fallacies of relevance, one of the premises is logically unrelated to the conclusion. The third type is fallacies involving unwarranted assumptions in which one of the premises is not adequately supported by evidence.

3. How can we avoid falling for and/or using fallacies?
    *   There are several strategies that can be used, including honing our analytical and argumentation skills, being aware of our strengths and weaknesses, building our self-confidence, cultivating good listening skills, avoiding ambiguous terms, adopting a position of skepticism, and having knowledge of the topic under discussion.

a single softball, it could have a nuclear weapon in less than a year. And if we allow that to happen, a terrible line would be crossed. Saddam Hussein would be in a position to blackmail anyone who opposes his aggression. He would be in a position to dominate the Middle East. He would be in a position to threaten America. And Saddam Hussein would be in a position to pass nuclear technology to terrorists.

Some citizens wonder, after 11 years of living with this problem, why do we need to confront it now? And there's a reason. We've experienced the horror of September the 11th. We have seen that those who hate America are willing to crash airplanes into buildings full of innocent people. Our enemies would be no less willing, in fact, they would be eager to use biological or chemical, or a nuclear weapon. . . .

Failure to act would embolden other tyrants, allow terrorists access to new weapons and new resources, and make blackmail a permanent feature of world events. The United Nations would betray the purpose of its founding, and prove irrelevant to the problems of our time. And through its inaction, the United States would resign itself to a future of fear.

That is not the America I know. That is not the America I serve. We refuse to live in fear. . . .

America believes that all people are entitled to hope and human rights, to the non-negotiable demands of human dignity. People everywhere prefer freedom to slavery; prosperity to squalor; self-government to the rule of terror and torture. America is a friend to the people of Iraq. Our demands are directed only at the regime that enslaves them and threatens us. When these demands are met, the first and greatest benefit will come to Iraqi men, women and children. . . . The long captivity of Iraq will end, and an era of new hope will begin.

. . . The attacks of September the 11th showed our country that vast oceans no longer protect us from danger. Before that tragic date, we had only hints of al Qaeda's plans and designs. Today in Iraq, we see a threat whose outlines are far more clearly defined, and whose consequences could be far more deadly. Saddam Hussein's actions have put us on notice, and there is no refuge from our responsibilities.

We did not ask for this present challenge, but we accept it. Like other generations of Americans, we will meet the responsibility of defending human liberty against violence and aggression. By our resolve, we will give strength to others. By our courage, we will give hope to others. And by our actions, we will secure the peace, and lead the world to a better day.

May God bless America.

Fallacies and War: Misleading a Nervous America to the Wrong Conclusion

DAVE KOEHLER

Dave Koehler is a member of the Philadelphia Association for Critical Thinking and the design director for the Web site PhillyBurbs.com. He also writes a weekly column for the site. He graduated from Pennsylvania State University with a BA in general arts.

I love America. I feel extremely lucky to have been born in this country into a middle-class family. I get very angry when my America gets abused and my way of life challenged by the actions of the politicians running the government. For this week's column, I'm turning serious to discuss some of the empty arguments given by the current administration as a pretext for war.

When facts are not available or convenient, there are many tricks one can use to present an argument. Here are a few examples of tactics the current administration is using to convince you and the world that invading Iraq is necessary.

One of the favorite methods of the current administration is a **false dilemma**. This is when only two choices are given when, in reality, there are more options. Right after 9/11 you heard, "You are either with us or against us," in the fight against terrorism. Actually, countries can be both against terrorism and not an ally of the U.S. More recently, many countries are showing that they are both against a pre-emptive war and against the current Iraqi regime.

We are also hearing we must attack Iraq or Saddam will develop weapons of mass destruction (WMD) and threaten the world if we do nothing. Other options of monitoring with inspectors and containment are just flatly discounted. Are we to believe that Saddam could develop nuclear weapons while the world has him under a microscope?

Just recently, the President suggested the U.N. should vote for war or face irrelevance. The U.N. will not disappear just because most of its member countries disagree with George W. Bush. If debate and disagreement spelled the end of deliberative bodies, the U.S. Congress would have vanished long ago.

Another arguing device is the **argument from ignorance**. This involves claiming that what hasn't been disproven must be true. We hear Iraq hasn't shown that they do not have WMD, therefore they do. The real burden of proof is on the party making the claim. The U.S. and/or U.N. must prove that Iraq has WMD. It is impossible for Iraq to prove that they don't.

An argument portraying a series of increasingly bad events is called a **slippery slope**. This is used effectively by gun-control opponents who suggest handgun registration will eventually lead to government confiscation of all guns. On Iraq, we hear how Saddam will develop WMDs and give them to terrorists who will then use them on America. While this is one possible chain of events, it hardly justifies a pre-emptive attack on a sovereign nation.

The response to this has been that the proof or smoking gun can't be in the form of a mushroom cloud over an American city. This is more slippery slope with a false dilemma and a whole lot of fear-mongering. There are effective ways to find proof of WMD and destroy them before it comes to such a dramatic conclusion.

Criticizing a person or group instead of an issue is called **ad hominem** attack. The current talk about France by many Americans is a perfect example. It is not only childish, it distracts from the real issues. France is not obligated to go along with every American idea because we saved them from Nazi Germany 60 years ago.

President Bush also often calls Saddam Hussein a murderous, evil man who can't be trusted. While true, this name-calling does not prove that Saddam has any ability to threaten the world. . . .

Arguing [that] a claim is true based on someone being an expert on the subject is known as an **appeal to authority**. In our case, the experts are defectors from Iraq. Secretary of State Powell claimed defectors reported there were 18 mobile biological weapons labs cruising around Iraq. First, these defector's stories are suspect due to their obvi-ous dislike of Iraq. I'm sure they would be happy to tell the U.S. what they wanted to hear if it hastened the destruction of the Iraqi regime and they could return to their homeland. More to the point, chief weapons inspector Hans Blix said his men had examined some of the trucks and found them to be food-testing labs.

So, without any real evidence, what's left? Saddam is bad?

Is that all? I realize war has become relatively easy for the US, especially when we are facing such a remarkably weak adversary and few **American** lives are at risk. But why war, and why now when there are still peaceful means for disarming Saddam Hussein?

Why is the Bush Administration using these deceptive techniques to rush us into a war with Iraq?

Is there any solid evidence that Iraq still processes weapons of mass destruction and has ties with terrorist groups? A few audio tapes and fuzzy satellite photos are not proof. All we hear is the same anecdotal evidence repeated over and over again.

President Bush has said that if Saddam and his generals "take innocent life, if they destroy infrastructure, they will be held accountable as war criminals." Isn't the United States about to take innocent life and destroy infrastructure?

. . . Sometimes war is a horrible necessity.

This is not one of those times.

QUESTIONS

1. According to Koehler, what fallacies did the Bush administration use to justify a preemptive strike against Iraq?

2. What examples does Koehler use to illustrate those fallacies?

3. What is Koehler's conclusion regarding the Bush administration's justification of its preemptive strike against Iraq, and how does he support his conclusion?

Think >> AND DISCUSS

1. Compare and contrast President Bush's claim that Iraq was a threat to world peace with Dave Koehler's position on the issue.

2. Did Koehler use any fallacies in his argument against Bush's justifications for a preemptive strike against Iraq?

3. Number the different claims Bush made in his speech regarding his argument that Iraq presented a threat to the United States. Which of these claims are valid—and which, if any, are based on fallacious reasoning? Explain. Do additional research on each of the claims if necessary.

4. Looking at the evidence we now have, what conclusion can you draw regarding the United States' intervention in Iraq? If we found out today that Iraq did have a hidden stockpile of weapons of mass destruction, how would this affect your position? Support your answers.

6

RECOGNIZING, ANALYZING,

Abraham Lincoln and the incumbent Illinois senator, Stephen A. Douglas, held a series of seven political debates during the 1858 senatorial race. The debates addressed the hottest political issues of the day: whether slavery should be allowed to expand into western territories, whether states should have the authority to allow or ban slavery within their borders, and the wisdom of the U.S. Supreme Court's 1857 *Dred Scott* decision, which had ruled that a slave is "property in the strictest sense of the term" and had declared it unconstitutional for Congress to ban slavery in the western territories. Douglas argued for "popular

& CONSTRUCTING ARGUMENTS

Think FIRST >>

- What is an argument?
- What is the purpose of breaking down and diagramming arguments?
- What are some of the factors to take into consideration in evaluating an argument?

sovereignty," claiming that the people of states and territories had the right to determine their own laws and policies on slavery. Lincoln, while agreeing that slavery should not be made illegal in states that already recognized its legality, opposed the expansion of slavery into the territories. Lincoln argued that slavery was "a moral, social and a political wrong."

Although Lincoln lost the senatorial election, he emerged from the debates as a nationally renowned orator and critical thinker. The format established in the Lincoln–Douglas debates, in which one person presents an argument and the other person responds with counterarguments, has been adopted by many organizations, including academic ones, for analysis of controversial issues.

The ability to recognize, construct, and analyze arguments is one of the most basic skills in critical thinking. To many of us, the word *argument* brings to mind images of quarreling and shouting. However, in logic and in critical thinking, argument refers to the use of reason and evidence to support a claim or conclusion. Unlike petty bickering over a difference in opinion, arguments used in critical thinking go beyond our personal interpretations and strive to analyze these interpretations. In other words, they are a form of inquiry that provides us with reasons to accept or reject a particular position, so that we can make up our own minds about an issue.

In this information age we are constantly bombarded with arguments on issues from the Internet, television, newspapers, advertisers, politicians, and other sources. For example, in the "Critical-Thinking Issues" at the end of Chapter 1, both Nancy Cantor and Bush present cogent arguments, Cantor for the University of Michigan's affirmative action policy and former President George W. Bush against such a policy. Our task is to decide which of the two presents the better argument, or if there might be still another approach that incorporates the best points of each argument and also makes new points that neither of the original debaters had considered. As citizens in a democracy, we need to develop the skills to critically analyze arguments and to make informed decisions that are based on our evaluations.

We also have the freedom to choose among a dizzying array of opportunities when making decisions about our own lives and careers. It is easy to take the path of least resistance, making decisions by default rather than carefully thinking them through. Skill in argumentation can help us make better decisions in our personal choices as well as in our public lives.

In Chapter 6 we will learn how to recognize, analyze, and construct arguments. Specifically, we will

- Learn how to identify an issue

- Learn how to recognize the parts of an argument, including the premise, the conclusion, and premise and conclusion indicators

- Distinguish among an argument, an explanation, and a conditional statement

- Break down an argument into its premises and conclusion

- Diagram arguments

- Construct our own arguments

- Explore the basics of evaluating arguments

Finally, we will read about the issue of same-sex marriage and analyze arguments that approach that controversial question from different perspectives.

WHAT IS AN ISSUE?

Arguments help us to analyze issues and to determine whether a particular position on an issue is reasonable. An **issue** is an ill-defined complex of problems involving a controversy or uncertainty.

One problem that many college students have in writing an essay or preparing a presentation on an issue is failing to define the issue clearly. An unfocused discussion about smoking, for example, may jump from health risks to secondhand smoking to the problem of addiction to corporate responsibility to subsidies for tobacco farmers. As a result, the discussion is shallow, and deeper insights into any one of these smoking-related issues are overlooked. Because of this, it is important that we first decide what issue we want to focus on.

Identifying an Issue

Identifying an issue requires clear thinking as well as good communication skills. We've probably all had the experience of finding ourselves arguing at cross-purposes with someone we care about. One person is upset because he or she feels the other isn't showing enough affection, while the other person perceives the issue as an attack on his or her ability as a provider. Because it is not clear what the real issue is, the argument goes nowhere and both people end up feeling frustrated and misunderstood.

Sometimes we don't have the opportunity to clarify an issue by talking to another person. This is often the case with written material, such as magazine or newspaper articles. In these cases, you may be able to determine the writer's focus by examining the title or the introductory paragraph. For example, Sohail H. Hashmi begins his article "Interpreting the Islamic Ethics of War and Peace" thus:

> Muslim writers of many intellectual persuasions have long argued that Westerners hold an inaccurate, even deliberately distorted, conception of *jihad*. In fact, however, the idea of *jihad* (and the ethics of war and peace generally) has been the subject of an intense and multifaceted debate among Muslims themselves.[1]

From this, you can presume that the issue Hashmi is addressing is something like "What is the best and most accurate interpretation of the Islamic concept of *jihad* and of war and peace in general?"

issue An ill-defined complex of problems involving a controversy or uncertainty.

Asking the Right Questions

How we word our questions about an issue will influence how we go about seeking a resolution to it. During his debates with Senator (or, as he called him, "Judge") Douglas, Lincoln changed the national controversy about slavery by reframing the issue so that it was not simply a controversy over state sovereignty but a burning question that affected the very existence of the nation. In the final debate, Lincoln summed up the issue with these words:

> I have said and I repeat it here, that if there be a man amongst us who does not think that the institution of slavery is wrong in any one of the aspects of which I have spoken, he is misplaced and ought not to be with us. Has anything threatened the existence of the Union save and except this very institution of slavery? That is the real issue. That is the issue that will continue in this country when these poor tongues of Judge Douglas and myself shall be silent.[2]

More than 50 years after the Brown v. Board of Education *decision that declared segregation unconstitutional, many feel that African Americans still don't have the same opportunities for quality education as whites. This young woman is one of the "Little Rock Nine," one of the first nine blacks to attend Central High in Little Rock, Arkansas, despite threats, scare tactics, and the necessary presence of the National Guard for protection.*

In an article written 50 years after school segregation was declared unconstitutional by the Supreme Court in *Brown v. Board of Education*, journalist Ellis Cose writes about the current lack of good schools for African American children: "When it comes to children of color, we ask the wrong question. We ask, 'Why are you such a problem?' when we should ask, 'What have we not given you that we routinely give to upper-middle-class white students?' What do they have that you don't?"[3]

To use a more personal example, suppose you come back to your dorm room after class and find that your wallet is missing. You think that you left it on your dresser, but it isn't there. What is the issue? When asked, many students answer that that the issue is "Who stole my wallet?"[4] However, this question is a loaded question based on an as-yet-unfounded assumption—that someone stole your wallet. Maybe you misplaced your wallet or you lost it on your way to class or it got knocked behind the dresser. For now, all you know is that the wallet is missing. Therefore, rather than making assumptions you can't support, it would be better to state the issue as "What happened to my wallet?" rather than "Who stole my wallet?" Remember, one of the traits of a good critical thinker—and of great detectives—is open-mindedness.

EXERCISES 6–1

1. Identify two or three issues that might arise out of the following broad topics or choose your own topic. Word the issue(s) in the form of question(s).
   a. Freedom of speech on college campuses
   b. Genetic engineering of food
   c. Cohabitation among college students
   d. Downloading music from the Internet
   e. Global warming
   f. Decriminalizing marijuana
   g. Prayer in public schools
   h. The preponderance of male science and engineering faculty at elite colleges

2. Identify the issues in the following passages. Word all issues in the form of short questions.
   a. "College tuition: How high is up? The price of college

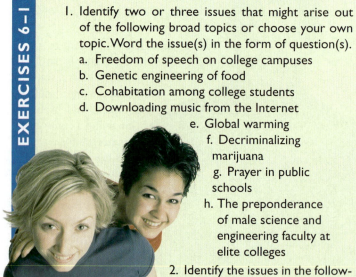

Outside the Box

ABRAHAM LINCOLN, *U.S. President*

Abraham Lincoln (1809–1865) was the sixteenth president of the United States. Self-educated, Lincoln had a knack for asking the right questions about important issues, such as slavery and war, and then examining all sides of the arguments before coming to a conclusion.

Lincoln's election as president in 1860 led to the secession in 1861 of southern slave-owning states and to a 4-year civil war that cost 600,000 American lives, North and South. Although Lincoln had long agreed that slavery should be permitted in states where it was already legal, in the course of the Civil War he concluded that if slavery is immoral, then it should not be legal at all in the United States. Lincoln also realized that taking a position on issues was not simply an intellectual exercise but should have real-life consequences. A man of action as well as strong principles, he issued the Emancipation Proclamation in 1863, freeing slaves in the rebellious states.

DISCUSSION QUESTIONS

1. Was Lincoln's decision to stand by his conclusion that slavery should be illegal a wise one, given that it escalated the hostilities in the Civil War? Are there times when it is best, from the point of view of critical thinking, to back down on an argument rather than risk conflict?

2. Has there ever been a time when you stood your ground on an issue despite the risk of losing your friends or even a job? How did your critical-thinking skills help you to stand firm?

education in Minnesota is going up again this fall. The University of Minnesota and the state's two- and four-year colleges are raising tuition by double digits.... Higher education officials say while most students are coming up with the extra cash for college the trend toward higher tuition is not sustainable in the long run."[5]

b. "SCAD [Savannah College of Art and Design] might be behind the times regarding housing policies. According to statistics from other universities more colleges are adapting their housing policies to allow for mixed-gender rooms. SCAD has coed resident halls but does not allow for male and female students to share a room."[6]

c. More than 700,000 Americans die each year from heart disease. Fifty percent of people given cholesterol-lowering drugs don't use them as prescribed, and the more they have to pay, the more they stop taking them. It seems obvious that probably tens of thousands of Americans are dying today because they can't afford drugs.

d. "The new school year is upon us.... By next June, over a million will graduate, many [of them] lost forever to the world of inertia and learned habits. While the debate rages about how the vegetarian movement can tailor its message to reach resistant adults, open-minded college students who care about animals are being neglected at an astounding rate. Our movement has not yet made a massive, organized effort to reach our best audience. We could be making tremendous progress among this group of people using animal-related literature that has been shown to work."[7]

e. "Tibet is backward. It's a big land, rich in natural resources, but we lack the technology or expertise [to exploit them]. So if we remain within China, we might get a greater benefit, provided it respects our culture and environment and give us some kind of guarantee."[8]

f. In the 2004 presidential election, only 51 percent of all voting-age Americans voted. The percent was even lower for young people between the ages of 18 and 25. In other countries, such as Australia, voting is mandatory and more than 90 percent of the eligible voters vote in elections.

3. Working in small groups, select one of the following issues. Take a few minutes to write down different concerns that arise from the issue. To what extent does your list reflect your preconceptions on the issue? Compare your list with those of others in your group. Does sharing give you a wider perspective on the issue? Explain.
   a. Should we be eating meat?
   b. Should college students who are working full time be allowed to take a full-time course load?
   c. Is it a desirable goal for the United States to spread democracy throughout the world?
   d. What should we be doing in our own lives about global warming?
   e. What criteria should colleges use in admitting students?
   f. Should the United States bring back the draft?

4. Looking back at your list of life goals, identify any issues involved in achieving your life goals.

ARGUMENTATION VERSUS RHETORIC

When we start with a position statement, rather than with an open-ended question that invites us to explore and analyze a particular issue, we are using rhetoric. Many people mistake rhetoric for logical arguments.

Distinguishing Between Rhetoric and Argumentation

Rhetoric, also known as *the art of persuasion*, is used to promote a particular position or worldview. In English classes, the term refers more narrowly to the art of persuasive writing. Rhetoric has its place and can help us learn more about a particular position on an issue and how to clarify that position. The art of persuasive writing and debating can be useful once you have thoroughly researched all sides of an issue, have come to a reasoned conclusion, and are now trying to convince others of this conclusion. That was what Lincoln tried to do in his debates with Douglas.

> **rhetoric** The defense of a particular position usually without adequate consideration of opposing evidence in order to win people over to one's position.

Rhetoric becomes a problem when it is *substituted* for unbiased research and logical argumentation. When using rhetoric this way, people present only those claims that support their own position. Because it does not require that a student first thoroughly research a topic and remain open to other perspectives, rhetoric may deteriorate into heated and overly emotional fights in which each person resorts to resistance and fallacies rather than reason.

Whereas the purpose of rhetoric is to *persuade* people of what you consider to be the truth, the purpose of argumentation is to *discover* the truth. The goal in rhetoric is to "win"—to convince others of the correctness of your position—rather than to analyze a position critically. The purpose of an argument, in contrast, is to present good reasons for a particular position or course of action and to offer a forum for evaluating the soundness of these reasons.

Avoiding Rhetoric

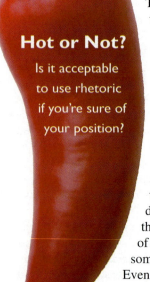

Hot or Not?

Is it acceptable to use rhetoric if you're sure of your position?

Unlike rhetoric, arguments are open to multiple perspectives. Resist the temptation to polarize an issue or reduce it to "two sides." Polarization of an issue can occur in politics where "we" (our country, religion, party, or political ideology) are "good" while "they" (another country or adherents to another religion or members of another political party or believers in another ideology) are labeled "evil." There is no in-between. The tendency to frame a discussion of an issue as a debate between two opposing sides can make it harder for us to come up with effective and creative solutions. While there are cases—such as arguments regarding slavery or the use of indiscriminant terrorism against noncombatants—where there is no defensible middle group, the truth, or the best course of action, is more often found somewhere in the middle. Even in cases where there do seem to be only two sides, rhetoric should be avoided and instead an

RHETORICAL STANDOFF   Anti-abortion and pro-abortion rights students confronting each other at a San Francisco rally on January 23, 2005, the thirty-second anniversary of the U.S. Supreme Court *Roe v. Wade* decision, which legalized abortion.*

DISCUSSION QUESTIONS

1. *The use of rhetoric, without first researching and analyzing all perspectives on an issue, can lead to deepening polarization of an issue rather than a resolution. What do you think the two people in this photo might be saying to each other? Do you think they are engaging in rhetoric or argumentation? Working in small groups, role-play what you might say to them if you were on the scene in the capacity of resident critical thinker.*

2. *Have you ever been at a rally where people were deeply divided? If so, discuss how you responded to taunts or fallacies from those on the "other side" of the issue.*

*For more on *Roe v. Wade*, see "Critical-Thinking Issues: Perspectives on Abortion" at the end of Chapter 9.

---

attempt made to critically analyze and understand both sides of the issue.

The purpose of argumentation is not simply to persuade someone to take a particular action or position on an issue—more importantly, the purpose is also to present the person with reasons. Because of this it is important to identify your audience and to communicate, whether verbally or in writing, your argument using language and concepts that are appropriate for that audience. Good arguments also invite feedback and analysis of an issue in light of the feedback. You are more likely to move toward truth (if necessary, through revising your arguments and views) when all sides of an issue are presented and heard.

EXERCISES 6-2

1. Think of an issue on which you hold strong views. What happened when you came face to face with someone who held the opposite view? How did you respond? Did you engage in argumentation or rhetoric? If you could go back and replay the scene, how might you respond using your critical-thinking skills?

2. Working in small groups, select a controversial issue. After clearly defining the issue, debate it by first using rhetoric. After three minutes, stop and write a paragraph about what happened during the role-play. Now discuss the issue using argumentation instead. After three minutes, stop and write a paragraph about what happened during this role-play. Which approach worked better in terms of learning more about different perspectives on the issue? Explain.

RECOGNIZING AN ARGUMENT

An **argument** is made up of two or more propositions, one of which, the conclusion, is supported by the other(s), the premise(s). In a valid **deductive argument**, such as that in the four students and the Watson Card Problem example in Chapter 2, the conclusion necessarily follows from the premises. In an **inductive argument**, the premises provide support but not necessarily proof for the conclusion. We'll be studying these two types of arguments in more depth in Chapters 7 and 8, respectively.

> **argument** Reasoning that is made up of two or more propositions, one of which is supported by the others.
>
> **deductive argument** An argument that claims its conclusion necessarily follows from the premises.
>
> **inductive argument** An argument that only claims that its conclusion probably follows from the premise.

Propositions

An argument is made up of statements known as propositions. A **proposition** is a statement that expresses a complete thought. It can be either true or false. If you're not sure whether a statement is a proposition, try putting the phrase *It is true that* or *It is false that* at the beginning of the statement. The following are examples of propositions:

> **proposition** A statement that expresses a complete thought and can be either true or false.
>
> **conclusion** The proposition in an argument that is supported on the basis of other propositions.
>
> **premise** A proposition in an argument that supports the conclusion.

The earth revolves around the sun.

God exists.

Chris doesn't show me enough affection.

Cheating on exams is wrong.

Toronto is the capital of Canada.

The first of these propositions is true. Today it is a generally accepted fact that the earth revolves around the sun. The truth or falsehood of the second and third propositions is less clear. We need more information as well as clarification of the word *God* in the second proposition and clarification of the term *affection* in the third proposition. The fourth proposition is less controversial: Most people, even those who cheat on exams, agree that it is true that "cheating on exams is wrong." Finally, the last proposition is false; Toronto is *not* the capital of Canada. (Ottawa is.)

A sentence may contain more than one proposition, as this example illustrates:

> Marcos is taking four courses this semester and working in his parents' store 20 hours a week.

This sentence contains two propositions:

1. Marcos is taking four courses this semester.
2. Marcos is working in his parents' store 20 hours a week.

Here is another sentence with more than one proposition:

> Karen is smart but not very motivated to do well in school or to try to find a job that uses her talents.

It contains three propositions:

1. Karen is smart.
2. Karen is not very motivated to do well in school.
3. Karen is not very motivated to try to find a job that uses her talents.

Not all sentences are propositions. A sentence may be directive ("Let's go out and celebrate the end of final exams"), expressive ("Wow!"), or even a request for information ("What is the capital of Canada?"). In none of these sentences is any claim being made that something is true or false. Propositions, in contrast, make claims that are either true or false. For more on the different functions of language refer back to Chapter 3.

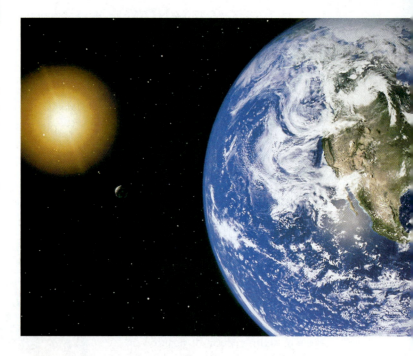

Premises and Conclusions

The **conclusion** of an argument is the proposition that is supported or denied on the basis of other propositions or reasons. The conclusion is what the argument is trying to prove. Conclusions may also be called claims, viewpoints, and positions. The conclusion can appear anywhere in an argument.

A **premise** is a proposition that supports or gives reasons for accepting the conclusion. Reasoning goes from the premises to the conclusion.

Premise(s) ⎯⎯⎯⎯⎯⎯→ Conclusion

Good premises are based on fact and experience, not opinion and assumptions. The more credible the premises are, the better the argument is likely to be. We considered some of the ways in which to evaluate evidence in Chapter 4. The conclusion should be supported by or follow from the premises, as in the following argument:

Premise: Canada has only one capital.

Premise: Ottawa is the capital of Canada.

Conclusion: Therefore, Toronto is not the capital of Canada.

Good premises are based on fact and experience, not opinion and assumptions. The more credible the premises are, the better the argument is likely to be.

There are several types of premises. **Descriptive premises** are based on **empirical facts**—scientific observation and/or the evidence of our five senses. "Ottawa is the capital of Canada" and "Lisa loves Antonio" are descriptive premises.

Prescriptive premises, in contrast, contain value statements, such as "We should strive for diversity on college campuses" or "It is wrong to cheat on exams."

An **analogical premise** takes the form of an analogy in which a comparison is made between two similar events or things. In Chapter 2, we saw that ancient Greek philosopher Plato drew an analogy between a charioteer and reason. Just as the charioteer is in charge of the horses, said Plato, so too should our reason be in charge of our emotions and passions.

Finally, a **definitional premise** contains a definition of a key term. This is particularly important when the key term is ambiguous and has different definitions, such as *right* and *diversity*, or if the key term needs a precising definition. For example, *affirmative action* is defined in a dictionary as "a policy to increase opportunities for women and minorities, [especially] in employment."[9] However, this may not be precise enough for your argument, since it is unclear about the type of policy. To clarify this, you may want to make the definition more precise in your premise. "Affirmative action is a policy of giving preference in hiring and college admissions to qualified minorities and women over a qualified white male, to increase opportunities for women and minorities."

Nonarguments: Explanations and Conditional Statements

We sometimes confuse explanations and conditional statements with arguments. An **explanation** is a statement about why or how something is the case. With an explanation, we know that something has occurred—as in the following examples:

The cat yowled because I stepped on her tail.

I'm upset because you promised you would meet me at the student union right after class and you never turned up.

In both examples, we are not trying to *prove* or *convince* someone through supporting evidence that the cat yowled or that we're upset; instead, we are trying to *explain* why the cat yowled and why we are upset.

We can also use explanations to describe the purpose of something, as in "MP3 players are useful for storing large quantities of music." In addition, we can use explanations as a means of trying to make sense of something, as in: "When Jane smiled at me, I think she was telling me that she liked me."

As with arguments, not all explanations are equally convincing. Explanations such as "I don't have my essay with me today because the dog ate it" usually raise at least a few skeptical eyebrows. Also, what might have seemed a reasonable explanation centuries or even a few decades ago may no longer be reasonable in light of new evidence. The explanation that there have been very few famous female artists because women fulfill their creativity through having babies is no longer considered a sound explanation.

Conditional statements can also be mistaken for arguments. A **conditional statement** is an "if … then …" statement.

If Françoise comes from Montreal, then she understands French.

If 18-year-olds are emotionally mature enough to go to war, then they should be allowed to drink alcohol.

A conditional statement by itself is not an argument, because no claim or conclusion follows from it. In the preceding examples, we are not drawing a conclusion that Françoise understands French or that 18-year-olds should be allowed to drink. However, conditional statements may appear as premises in an argument.

Premise: If Françoise comes from Montreal, then she understands French.

Premise: Françoise comes from Montreal.

Conclusion: Françoise understands French.

Premise: If 18-year-olds are emotionally mature enough to go to war, [then] they should be allowed to drink alcohol.

Premise: Eighteen-year-olds are not emotionally mature enough to go to war.

Conclusion: Eighteen-year-olds should not be allowed to drink alcohol.

To summarize: arguments are made up of two types of propositions—the conclusion and the premise(s). A conclusion is supported by the premise(s). The different types of premises include descriptive and prescriptive premises, analogies, and definitions. Unlike explanations and conditional statements, an argument tries to prove that something is true.

EXERCISES 6–3

1. It is easier to resolve a problem from a familiar context than one that is unfamiliar. Write down a problem that you encountered recently in a familiar context (for example, a social setting with friends or a class in your major). Now write down a similar problem that you encountered recently in an unfamiliar context (for example, a job interview or meeting new people). Which problem was easiest to resolve and why? How did familiarity with the context make it easier for you to resolve a problem? Write about what steps you could take to make yourself a better problem-solver and critical thinker in different contexts.

2. Which of the following statements is a proposition? Explain why or why not.
   a. Golly!
   b. I love you.
   c. Most college students gain several pounds in their freshman year.
   d. Close the window.
   e. The average college student pays most of his or her own college tuition.
   f. Please keep an eye on my place while I'm away on spring break.
   g. It is irresponsible to drink and drive.
   h. Only humans are capable of language.
   i. An atheist is a person who believes there is no God.
   j. Excuse me.
   k. Smoking in public buildings is illegal in many states.

3. For each of the following propositions, identify which type of premise it is (descriptive, prescriptive, definitional, or analogical).
   a. "The most dramatic change [in the political orientation of college freshman] during the past three and a half decades was the sharp decline in the proportion of freshmen identifying themselves as either 'liberal' or 'far left' during the 1970s and a substantial increase in those identifying themselves as 'middle-of the-road.'" [10]
   b. Terrorism is the unlawful use or threat of violence by individuals or groups against civilians or property to achieve an ideological or political goal through intimidating government or society.
   c. At least five of the al-Qaeda hijackers from September 11, 2001, came from Asir province in Saudi Arabia.
   d. We should constantly strive to become better critical thinkers.
   e. The universe is like a watch created by an intelligent designer or watchmaker.
   f. It's wrong to download music from the Internet without paying.
   g. Going to Las Vegas for spring break is like going to a weeklong fraternity party.
   h. Language is a type of communication that involves a set of arbitrary symbols, whether spoken, written, or nonverbal.
   i. Only humans are capable of language.

4. Looking back at the arguments on affirmative action at the end of Chapter 1, identify the premises and conclusion in both Nancy Cantor's and former President George W. Bush's arguments.

5. Identify each of the following as an argument, an explanation, or a conditional statement.

a. Jasmine really likes Daniel, but because she's planning on going to Guatemala for a semester to study Spanish, she isn't interested in getting involved with him right now.

b. If there is a snowstorm, class will be cancelled.

c. If there is a snowstorm, class will be cancelled. It is snowing heavily right now, so our class will probably be cancelled.

d. In the past few decades the Catholic Church has been training more priests and bishops to perform exorcisms, in part because the pope believes that Satan is a real force in our everyday lives.

e. If the bay freezes over, we can go ice-skating on it.

f. It must have been colder than 28°F last week, because the ice froze in the bay last week and salt water freezes at 28°F or −2°C.

g. Herman failed the quiz because he didn't know there was going to be one today and hadn't read the material.

h. If you aren't a good boy or girl, Santa won't bring you any presents this Christmas.

i. "People react so viscerally to the decapitation executions because they identify strongly with the helpless victims, see the executioners as cruel foreigners, and are horrified by the grisly method of death."[11]

j. Same-sex marriage should be legalized, since the U.S. Constitution guarantees citizens equal rights under the law.

k. If you go to the movies with me tonight, I'll help you review for your chemistry exam.

6. Write down five examples of explanations. At least one should be from your own personal experience, one from a textbook, one from a newspaper or magazine, and one from the Internet. Briefly explain why each is an explanation rather than an argument.

BREAKING DOWN AND DIAGRAMMING ARGUMENTS

Knowing how to identify the parts of and diagram an argument allows us to follow the line of thought in an argument more easily. Breaking down an argument and then using a diagram to represent the different parts of the argument lets us visualize the entire argument, its propositions, and the relationship between the premise(s) and the conclusion.

Breaking Down an Argument into Propositions

Before you can diagram an argument, you must first break down the argument into its propositions. Here are the steps for diagramming an argument:

1. **Bracket the Propositions.** In breaking down an argument, start by putting brackets around each proposition so that you know where each begins and ends. Remember, an entire argument can be contained in one sentence, as in the first of the following examples. Or it can contain several sentences and propositions, as in the second example.

[I think], therefore [I am].

[Students who sit in the front of a classroom generally earn higher grades.] Therefore [you should move up to the front of the class], since [I know you want to improve your grade point average].

2. **Identify the conclusion.** The next step in breaking down an argument is to identify which proposition is the conclusion. Some, but not all, arguments contain terms known as *conclusion indicators* that help you identify which of the propositions is a conclusion. For instance, words such as *therefore* and *thus* often serve as conclusion indicators. If there is a conclusion indicator in the argument, circle it and put the letters *CI* above it. In the two arguments below and to the left, the word *therefore* indicates that a conclusion follows.

When there are no conclusion indicators, ask yourself: "What is this person trying to prove or convince me of?" If you are still unsure which proposition is the conclusion, try putting *therefore* in front of the proposition you think may be the conclusion. If the meaning of the argument remains the same, you have located the conclusion. Once you have identified the conclusion, draw a double line under it.

    CI   (Conclusion)
I think, therefore [I am].

[Students who sit in the front of a classroom generally
                            CI   (Conclusion)
earn higher grades.] Therefore, [you should move up

to the front of the class], since [I know you want to

improve your grade point average].

3. **Identify the Premises.** The final step in breaking down an argument is to identify the premise(s) or those propositions that offer support for the conclusion. In the first argument, which is the famous cogito argument of French philosopher René Descartes (1596–1650), which we discussed in Chapter 1, Descartes supports his conclusion ("I am") with the premise "I think." In other words, if he is thinking, it follows that he must exist, since someone must be doing the thinking. Draw a single line under the premise.

(Premise)   CI (Conclusion)
[I think], therefore [I am].

Some arguments contain *premise indicators*—words or phrases that signal a premise. *Because* and *since* are common premise indicators. If there is a premise indicator, circle it and put *PI* above it. In the argument about where to sit in the classroom, the word *since* indicates that the last part of this sentence is a premise. The first sentence in the argument is also a premise because it is offering evidence to support the conclusion "you should move up to the front of the class." Draw a single line under each premise.

[Students who sit in the front of a classroom generally
                        CI
earn higher grades.] Therefore [you should move up to
                        PI
the front of the class], since [I know you want to improve

your grade point average].

Identifying the Premise(s) and Conclusion in Complex Arguments

Not all arguments are as straightforward as the ones we have looked at so far. Some passages that contain arguments also include extra material, such as background and introductory information. For example, in Greg Lukianoff's letter to West Virginia University's president, David Hardesty, at the end of Chapter 3, the first paragraph of the letter is background material regarding Lukianoff's civil-liberties organization. The actual argument regarding the acceptability of free-speech zones does not start until the second sentence of the second paragraph.

In the following letter to the editor, the first sentence is the conclusion of the argument. However, the first part of the second sentence—"Although stories of overzealous parents sometimes grab the headlines"—is not part of the actual argument; rather, it is introductory material. This introduction is followed in the same sentence by the phrase *the truth is*, which serves as a premise indicator for the first premise. The second premise doesn't appear until the third sentence in the passage.

Analyzing Images

THE DEBATE OVER MARIJUANA

DISCUSSION QUESTIONS

1. *Identify the conclusion and premises in the argument in this advertisement. Evaluate the argument.*

2. *What is the objective of this ad? Is the ad effective in meeting its objective? Discuss the strategies, including rhetorical devices and fallacies, if any, that the creators of the ad used to try to convince the reader to accept their conclusion.*

[Sports at the high-school level are one of the last bastions of innocence in this century.] Although stories of overzealous parents sometimes grab the headlines, the truth is, [most young people play for the love of their sport and nothing more.] [Many of the values that help me every day in the business world (teamwork, unity, hard work, and tolerance) were taught by my football and baseball coaches.][12]

Words such as *because*, *since*, *therefore*, and *so*, which sometimes serve as premise and conclusion indicators in argument, do not always play this role. *Because* and *therefore* also appear in explanations, as in this example:

Because the demographics and immigration pattern of the United States is changing, the workforce of today's college graduates will be much different from that of their parents.

In addition, the word *since* may indicate the passage of time rather than a premise.

Since the September 11, 2001, attacks on the World Trade Center and Pentagon, the nature of intercultural relationships radically changed for most Americans.

Knowing how to break down an argument into its conclusion and premise(s) makes it easier for us to analyze arguments. Although words such as *therefore* and *because* can help us in this process, it is important to remember that they do not always serve as conclusion and premise indicators.

Diagramming an Argument

Once you have mastered the basics of breaking down an argument, you are ready to diagram arguments. Sometimes arguments fail simply because the other person does not follow our line of reasoning. Diagramming an argument clarifies the relationship between the premise(s) and the conclusion, as well as the relationship between premises, so we know to present these particular premises together.

Diagramming an argument clarifies the relationship between the premise(s) and the conclusion, as well as the relationship between premises, so we know to present these particular premises together.

Arguments with One Premise. Begin by breaking down the argument into its propositions and drawing two lines under the conclusion and one under the premise(s). Number each proposition in the order in which it appears in the argument. Put a circle around each number.

(1) [I think], therefore (2) [I am].

You are now ready to diagram the argument. Begin by writing down the number of the conclusion at the bottom of the page or in a space on the page. The premise(s) go above the conclusion. When there is only one premise, place the number of the premise directly above the number of the conclusion and draw an arrow from the premise number to the conclusion number.

(1) (Premise)

(2) (Conclusion)

In this section, the parts of the diagram are identified (for example, premise, conclusion, dependent premises) purely for educational purposes. However, in the actual diagrams, only the numbers, lines, and arrows are used.

Arguments with Independent Premises. The next argument we'll be diagramming has more than one premise. Begin by breaking down the argument into its conclusion and premises, numbering each proposition in the order it appears in the argument.

(1) [Every physician should cultivate lying as a fine art]. . . . (2) [Many experiences show that patients do not want the truth about their maladies], and that (3) [it is prejudicial to their well-being to know it].[13]

In this argument, the conclusion is the first proposition—"Every physician should cultivate lying as a fine art." Write (1) at the bottom of the space below. Now examine

the two premises, the second and third propositions. In this argument below, each premise supports the conclusion on its own. A premise that can support the conclusion without the other premise is known as an *independent premise*. You diagram an independent premise by drawing an arrow directly from each one to the conclusion.

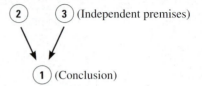

(2)   (3) (Independent premises)

(1) (Conclusion)

Arguments with Dependent Premises. When two or more of the premises support a conclusion only when they are used together, they are known as *dependent premises*. If you are unsure whether two premises are dependent or independent, try omitting one of them and see if the remaining premise still supports the conclusion on its own. If it does not, then it is a dependent premise.

In the argument below on Harry Potter, premises (1), (3), and (4) are all dependent on each other. Taken alone, they do not support the conclusion.

(1) [The Bible states in Leviticus 20:26, "You should not practice augury or witchcraft."] Therefore, (2) [the Harry Potter books are not suitable reading for children,] since (3) [Harry Potter is a wizard] and (4) [wizards practice augury].

In diagramming dependent premises, you first draw a line between the two premises and then draw a line from the center of this connecting line to the conclusion.

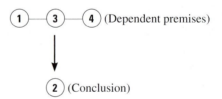

(1)——(3)——(4) (Dependent premises)

(2) (Conclusion)

In the above argument, depending on your audience, you may not need (4), which is a definitional premise.

Arguments with a Subconclusion. Sometimes a premise acts as a conclusion for the final conclusion. This type of premise is known as a *subconclusion*.

(1) [My granddaughter Sarah is a college freshman.]

(2) [Sarah probably wouldn't be interested in hearing an AARP talk on Social Security reform.] So (3) [there's probably no point in asking her to come along with me.]

In the above argument, premise (1) offers support for proposition (2): "My granddaughter Sarah is a college freshman. [Therefore] Sarah probably wouldn't be interested in hearing an AARP talk on Social Security." However, proposition (2), in addition to being a conclusion for premise (1), also serves as a premise for proposition (3). In diagramming an argument with a subconclusion (such as

These people are burning Harry Potter books based on their conclusion that Harry is a wizard and witchcraft should not be practiced.

proposition ②), you put the subconclusion between the premise(s) that support it and the final conclusion.

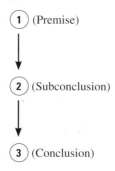

① (Premise)

↓

② (Subconclusion)

↓

③ (Conclusion)

The following argument on capital punishment has a subconclusion as well as two independent premises.

> ① [The death penalty does not deter criminals] because ② [at the time the crime is done they do not expect to be arrested.] Also, since ③ [many offenders are mentally unbalanced,] ④ [they do not consider the rational consequences of their irrational actions.][14]

Here, proposition ② is an independent premise that supports the conclusion (proposition ①) on its own. If this were all there was to the argument, you would diagram it by placing the ② above the ① and drawing an arrow directly from the ② to the conclusion.

However, the argument goes on to present additional evidence (propositions ③ and ④) for the conclusion (proposition ①) in the form of a separate supporting argument. Therefore, you'll need to adjust the diagram to allow room for this. In this case, proposition ④ is the subconclusion

and proposition ③ the premise of the supporting argument. The complete argument can be diagrammed as follows:

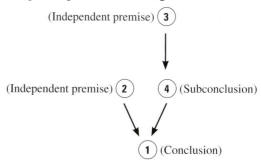

(Independent premise) ③

↓

(Independent premise) ②   ④ (Subconclusion)

↘ ↙

① (Conclusion)

Arguments with Unstated Conclusions. In some arguments the conclusion is unstated, allowing readers to draw their own conclusions. The following argument, for example, has two premises but no conclusion:

> ① [Laws that permit public colleges to discriminate against applicants on the basis of race or sex are unconstitutional.] ② [The University of Michigan's affirmative action policy that awards extra points on the basis of a person's race and sex discriminates against white males.]

In determining what is the unstated conclusion, ask yourself: What is the speaker trying to prove or to convince us of? In this example, it is that the University of Michigan's affirmative action policy is unconstitutional. When a conclusion is unstated, write it in at the end of the argument and number it; in this case, since it is the third proposition, put a ③ in front of it. You can also add a conclusion indicator if you like.

College students are divided regarding the morality and constitutionality of affirmative action in college admissions.

① [Laws that permit public colleges to discriminate against applicants on the basis of race or gender are unconstitutional.] **②** [The University of Michigan's affirmative action policy that awards extra points based on a person's race and sex discriminates against white males.] Therefore, **③** the University of Michigan's affirmative action policy is unconstitutional.

Diagramming this argument makes it apparent that the premises cannot support the conclusion on their own without the other premise. In other words, they are dependent premises. When diagramming an argument with an unstated conclusion, put a broken circle around the number in front of the conclusion to indicate that it was not included in the original wording of the argument. Once again, the parts of the diagram (dependent premises and unstated conclusion) are identified for clarification purposes only. They are not part of the actual diagram.

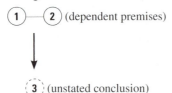

①——② (dependent premises)

③ (unstated conclusion)

When you are arguing or discussing an issue, you usually do not have time to step back and diagram it. However, practice at breaking down and diagramming arguments will make it easier for you to recognize the conclusion and see the connections among the conclusion and premises in real-life arguments, the topic of the next section.

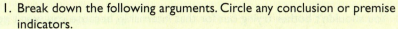

1. Break down the following arguments. Circle any conclusion or premise indicators.
   a. "Be an optimist. There is not much use being anything else."[15]
   b. Computers may soon fade into the background, since most people prefer portable handheld devices as well as ones that turn on instantly.
   c. "The right to vote is the very core of democracy. We cannot allow public apathy and political manipulation to undermine it."[16]
   d. Drinking alcohol is stupid. Alcohol has no taste at all; it's just a burning sensation. You don't drink to have a good time—you drink to forget a bad time.
   e. "The magnitude of devastation from the [2004] tsunami has exposed the limits of scientific knowledge and the lack of cooperation among nations in using sophisticated tools to prevent human suffering.... Had there been a global tsunami-warning network in place, the death and suffering of tens of thousands could have been avoided.... The international community must develop a global early-warning system to inform people of any looming threat."[17]
   f. Lack of experience, excessive speed, and tailgating are three of the most frequent causes of automobile accidents. For these reasons we should raise the driving age to 18, since older drivers might be more experienced and have better judgment.
   g. All college students should routinely be tested for HIV, the virus that causes AIDS. Half of the people who carry the virus don't know that they have it. The HIV virus is transmitted primarily through sexual contact. Not only are most college students sexually active but they also have multiple partners.

2. Referring to the readings by President George W. Bush and Dave Koehler on the war in Iraq at the end of Chapter 5, identify the parts of each passage that contain arguments and those that contain other material such as explanations or background material.

3. Break down and diagram the following arguments.
   a. "It is impossible to exaggerate the impact that Islam has on Saudi culture, since religion is the dominant thread that permeates every level of society."[18]
   b. God does not exist. There is much evil and suffering in the world. A good and loving God would not permit so much evil.
   c. "... our youngest voting-age group has grown accustomed to a wide array of options when making consumer choices, and will naturally expect the same with their Social Security accounts. 'Reform' of Social Security in the form of partial privatization sounds practically inevitable."[19]
   d. We should not buy a new car for Jack for his graduation. Jack is irresponsible because he doesn't care for the things he already owns. Also, we don't have enough money to buy him a new car.
   e. "An unbalanced diet can depress serotonin levels—and bingo, you're a grouch. Alcohol gives serotonin a temporary bump but then dramatically lowers it, so it pays to go easy on the sauce."[20]
   f. Freedom to decide what we do in our lives, as long as we're not harming others, is a basic right in the United States. Therefore, motorcyclists should not be required by law to wear helmets, because those who don't are not harming anyone else.
   g. "There's a need for more part-time or job-sharing work. Most mothers of young children who choose to leave full-time careers and stay home with their children find enormous delights in being at home with their children, not to mention the enormous relief of no longer worrying about shortchanging their kids. On the other hand, women who step out of their careers can find the loss of identity even tougher than the loss of income."[21]
   h. "The toughest part of buying life insurance is determining how much you need, since everyone's financial circumstances and goals are different. The best way to determine your life insurance needs is to have a State Farm Insurance professional conduct what's called a Financial Needs Analysis." (from an ad for State Farm Insurance)
   i. "In schools, we should give equal time with Darwinism to theories of intelligent design or creationism. Darwin's theory of evolution is a theory, not a fact. The origin of life, the diversity of species and even the structure of organs like the eye are so bewilderingly complex that they can only be the handiwork of a higher intelligence."[22]

THE FAR SIDE® BY GARY LARSON

"Quit school? *Quit school?* You wanna end up like your father—a career lab rat?"

GARY LARSON *FAR SIDE* CARTOON

DISCUSSION QUESTIONS

1. Identify the premises in this cartoon. Note the implied conclusion, "You shouldn't quit school." There is also an unstated premise. Identify it.

2. Is the unstated premise credible?

the issue. Incomplete research or confirmation bias may cause us to overlook important information or premises that do not support our worldview. In the argument about Hispanic immigrants that we've just examined, the speaker failed to include premises with actual statistics supporting his claim. In a good argument, the list of relevant premises should be complete—and backed by credible sources.

That being said, sometimes premises are obvious and don't have to be stated. Consider this argument:

> Federal funding for education should be allocated on the basis of the size of a state. Therefore, Texas should get a larger share of federal money than Rhode Island.

In this argument the unstated premise is that "Texas is larger than Rhode Island," an uncontroversial fact known by most people in the United States. However, if we were presenting the argument to someone from another country, we might want to include the premise.

Leaving out a relevant premise can be problematic, especially when the premise is controversial or is based on an unfounded assumption—as in the immigration argument. This is especially a problem when acceptance of the stated premise(s) is dependent on the unstated premise. Excluding relevant premises might lead us to a mistaken conclusion that is based on incomplete information.

In some cases, a premise is left out because it *is* controversial and stating it would weaken the position of the person who is making the argument. Consider:

> Abortion should remain legal. No woman should be forced to raise an unwanted child.

Breaking down and diagramming this argument, we have:

(1) [Abortion should remain legal.] **(2)** [No woman should be forced to raise an unwanted child.]

(2)

↓

(1)

HIGHLIGHTS

GUIDELINES FOR EVALUATING AN ARGUMENT

Clarity: Is the argument clear and unambiguous?

Credibility: Are the premises supported by evidence?

Relevance: Are the premises relevant to the conclusion?

Completeness: Are there any unstated premises and conclusions?

Soundness: Are the premises true and do they support the conclusion?

It's your body. It's your decision. The Pro-Choice Public Education Project. It's pro-choice or no choice.

1 [Abortion should remain legal.] 2 [No woman should be forced to raise an unwanted child.] 3 [A woman who gives birth to a child should also raise that child.]

In this case the unstated premise (3) weakens the argument, since many people do not accept it as true.

Connections

How can we recognize the use of faulty arguments in advertisements? *See Chapter 10, p. 328–330.*

Soundness: Are the Premises True, and Do They Support the Conclusion?

Finally, the reasoning process in an argument should be sound. A sound argument is one in which the premises are true and they support the conclusion. The connection between the premise(s) and conclusion should be based on reason rather on fallacious appeals.

On the other hand, do not assume that a conclusion is false simply because it is not supported by the premises. When this happens, the most you can say is that you don't know whether the conclusion is true or false. Some issues, such as the existence of God or the presence of consciousness in other people, probably cannot be proved or disproved through logical argumentation.

One of my most philosophically traumatic experiences as a child occurred when I was about 10 or 11 years old and realized that I could not prove the existence of anyone or anything else in the world except myself. For about a week, I wandered around in a miserable, solipsistic (the belief that I was the only being in the world) fog, estranging my concerned playmates in the process. Eventually, though, I decided that it was more practical and more conducive to my happiness just to accept on faith the existence of the world outside me. This experience also taught me that just because we can't prove something through the use of argumentation doesn't mean that it isn't true. To claim otherwise is to commit the fallacy of ignorance.

We'll be looking at additional rules for evaluating specific types of arguments in Chapters 7 and 8.

At first glance it might look like the conclusion follows from the premise, since most people would accept the prescriptive premise as reasonable. However, there is an unstated dependent premise in this argument: namely, that "a woman who gives birth to a child should also raise that child." Unlike the first premises that we have seen, this one is certainly a questionable one, since adoption is an option.

Once you have identified a missing relevant premise, add it to the argument. Then go back and reevaluate the argument.

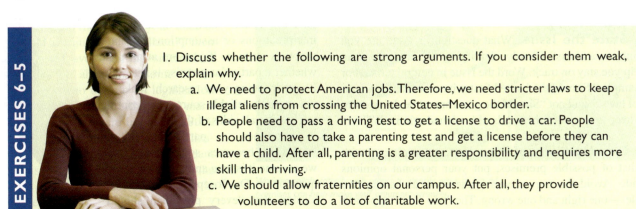

EXERCISES 6-5

1. Discuss whether the following are strong arguments. If you consider them weak, explain why.
   a. We need to protect American jobs. Therefore, we need stricter laws to keep illegal aliens from crossing the United States–Mexico border.
   b. People need to pass a driving test to get a license to drive a car. People should also have to take a parenting test and get a license before they can have a child. After all, parenting is a greater responsibility and requires more skill than driving.
   c. We should allow fraternities on our campus. After all, they provide volunteers to do a lot of charitable work.

Using Arguments in Making Real-Life Decisions

Arguments are useful tools for making real-life decisions, especially in situations that involve a conflict between what seem to be equally compelling alternatives or positions. People who are poor at critical thinking not only are less likely to recognize a conflict until it gets out of control but often are also unable to evaluate competing alternatives to come up with an effective resolution to the problem.

Skilled critical thinkers, in contrast, are more likely to recognize a conflict. Instead of jumping to conclusions, good critical thinkers look at an issue from multiple perspectives, assigning weight when necessary to competing reasons, before reaching their final decision.

Consider this example:

> Amy was struggling with the decision of whether to go to China with her family over the summer or instead to go to summer school so that she could finish college in four years. She had been promised a job with a computer software company, following graduation in June. Unfortunately, the summer course schedule conflicted with her travel plans. What should she do?

The first thing you should do in a case like this is to come up with a list of all possible premises or reasons that are relevant to your final decision. In making her decision, Amy began by making this list:

- My grandparents, who live in China, are getting on in years, and this may be the last chance I have to see them.

- My parents are paying my fare, so the trip will not be a financial burden for me.

- I need to take a summer course to graduate next year.

- I have been promised a job with a computer software company after graduation in June.

- The summer course schedule at my college conflicts with my travel schedule.

In developing your list of premises, ask other people for ideas as well. There may be reasons for a particular course of action that have never occurred to you. Also, do your research and make sure that you have all the facts correct. In Amy's case, one of her friends suggested that she go to the registrar's office to see whether there was a way she could take a course that would not conflict with the trip dates. As it turned out, she could do an internship on contemporary Chinese business culture for the credits she needed to graduate. She added this option or premise to her list:

- I could do an internship for college credit while I'm in China.

After completing your list, go back and review the premises. Highlight those that are most relevant and delete those that are not. Review your final list before drawing a conclusion. Have you left anything out? Often, just by doing your research and listing various options, you may find that what first seemed to be a conflict is not a conflict at all, as happened in Amy's case.

Finally, put your decision or conclusion into action. As it turned out, Amy was able to go to China with her family *and* to complete college in four years.

Arguments provide a powerful tool for analyzing issues and making decisions in our lives. As critical thinkers, we should not jump to conclusions. Instead, we should take a stand or make an important decision only *after* we have examined the different perspectives and options. In addition, we should remain open to hearing new evidence and, in light of that evidence, to modifying our position. By trying to learn why someone holds a position different from our own, we can move closer to understanding and perhaps resolving a conflict.

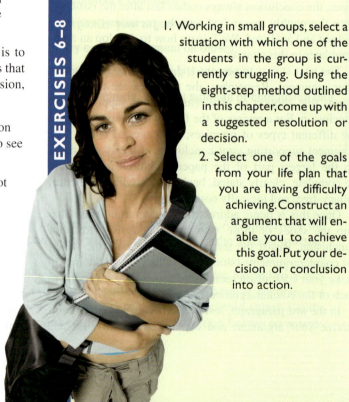

Think AGAIN >>

1. What is an argument?
   - An argument is made up of two or more propositions, including the conclusion, which is supported by the other propositions, known as premises. An argument tries to prove or convince us that the conclusion is true, whereas an explanation is a statement about why something is the case.

2. What is the purpose of breaking down and diagramming arguments?
   - Breaking down arguments helps us to recognize the different premises and the conclusion so we can identify and analyze the issue under discussion, as well as examine the premises to determine if they support the conclusion.

3. What are some of the factors to take into consideration in evaluating an argument?
   - Some of the factors in evaluating an argument are clarity, credibility, relevance, completeness, and soundness of the argument.

7

INDUCTIVE

How do today's college students compare with the students of their parents' generation? One of the most noteworthy differences is the impact of the women's movement. There has been a substantial closing of the gender gap in several majors, including the sciences, secondary-school teaching, and business. In addition, while 54 percent of college men and 42 percent of college women in 1967 agreed that "the activities of married women are best confined to the home and family," thirty-five years later only 28 percent of college men and 16 percent of college women agreed with this statement.

ARGUMENTS

Think FIRST >>

- How does an inductive argument differ from a deductive argument?
- How do arguments based on generalizations help us to learn more about a particular population?
- What are some of the uses of arguments by analogy?
- What role does causal reasoning play in our lives?

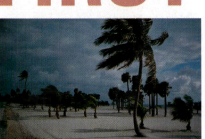

Another significant generational difference is the values that motivate students in setting their life goals. In the late 1960s and early 1970s, more than 80 percent of students said that "developing a meaningful philosophy of life" was an "essential" or "very important" goal. By the 1990s, "being very well off financially" had become the most important goal, with 74 percent of freshmen in 2007 stating that this was one of their top objectives in life.

In addition, the political orientation of today's college students is more likely to be middle-of-the-road compared with that of young people in their parents' generation. About 40 percent of college freshmen in 1970 identified themselves as liberal or far left, compared with only 32 percent of the college freshmen in 2007, who tend to be more middle-of-the-road (43 percent) or conservative (25 percent) in their political orientation. This trend is reflected in students' attitudes toward capital punishment; only 35 percent today agree that capital punishment should be abolished, compared with 59 percent of students in 1970.

Did You Know

Despite declining interaction among students across racial or ethnic lines on college campuses, 23 percent of students believe that "racial discrimination is no longer a problem in America."

Despite increasing diversity on college campuses over the past generation, there has been declining interaction among students across racial or ethnic lines. Despite this trend, 20 percent of students believe that "racial discrimination is no longer a problem in America." Nonblack students were most likely to believe this, with only 12 percent of African American freshmen agreeing with the statement.[1]

How do we know all this about college students? Through the application of inductive reasoning using the information collected from thousands of American college freshmen. The results of this annual survey, which was launched by the Cooperative Institutional Research Program in 1966, are used to make decisions about college recruitment, admission, program development, and other facets of college life.

The Freshman Survey is just one example of the use of inductive reasoning. In this chapter we will be studying the different types of inductive arguments and how they are used in our everyday lives. We will also learn how to evaluate inductive arguments. To summarize, in Chapter 7 we will

- Distinguish between deductive and inductive arguments
- Identify the characteristics of an inductive argument
- Learn how to recognize and evaluate arguments based on generalization
- Examine polling and sampling methods
- Study the various uses of analogies

- Learn how to recognize and evaluate arguments using analogies

- Learn how to recognize and evaluate a causal argument

- Distinguish between a correlation and a causal relationship

Finally, we will examine arguments regarding the legalization of marijuana in the United States.

WHAT IS AN INDUCTIVE ARGUMENT?

There are two basic types of arguments—deductive arguments and inductive arguments. **Deductive arguments** claim that their conclusion *necessarily* follows from the premises. If the premises are true and the reasoning process is valid, then the conclusion must be true—as in the following example:

> No dogs are cats. Mindy is a dog. Therefore, Mindy is not a cat.

We will be studying deductive arguments in depth in Chapter 8.

Inductive arguments, in contrast, claim that their conclusion *probably* follows from the premises. Because of this, inductive arguments are merely stronger or weaker rather than true or false.

> Most Corgis make good watchdogs. Mindy is a Corgi. Therefore, Mindy is probably a good watchdog.

In determining if an argument is inductive, you can look for certain words that suggest that the conclusion probably, rather than necessarily, follows from the premise(s). These include words and phrases such as *probably, most likely, chances are that, it is reasonable to suppose that, we can expect that,* and *it seems probable that.* However, not all inductive arguments contain indicator words. In these cases, you have to ask yourself if the conclusion necessarily follows from the premises. If the conclusion is only likely, then it is probably an inductive argument.

We use inductive reasoning just about every day when we extend what we already know to situations that are not as familiar to us. For example, you may decide, on the basis of the positive experience of three of your classmates, each of whom has a child in the nursery school on campus, that your child will also be happy in that nursery school. A candidate for the U.S. Senate may conclude, on the basis of the results of the Freshman Survey, that young people in college today aren't likely to vote in the 2008 elections and thus gear her campaign to appeal primarily to an older constituency.

deductive arguments Arguments that claim their conclusion necessarily follows from the premises.

inductive arguments Arguments that claim their conclusion probably follows from the premises.

Because inductive logic is based on probability rather than necessity, there is always the possibility of error. Your child may not like the nursery school, and college students may turn out to vote in larger numbers than predicted. Also, since human thinking is prone to inborn cognitive errors, we cannot always depend on people to think or behave logically or consistently. Familiarity with the principles of inductive logic will make you less likely to commit errors in your thinking.

In the following sections we will discuss the three most common types of inductive arguments: generalizations, analogies, and causal arguments.

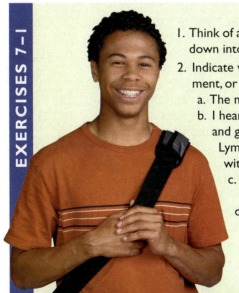

1. Think of an inductive argument that you used in the past week. Break the argument down into its premise(s) and conclusion. Explain why it is an inductive argument.

2. Indicate whether each of the following is an inductive argument, a deductive argument, or neither.

   a. The moon was full 4 weeks ago, so it should be full again tonight.

   b. I hear you've been diagnosed with Lyme disease. You should go to the doctor and get some antibiotics for it. When Saheed was given antibiotics for his Lyme disease, his symptoms cleared up in a few weeks. The same happened with Arquelina when she had it.

   c. Wei is a student at Clark Community College. None of the students at CCC reside on campus. Therefore, Wei does not live on campus.

   d. I think I can trust John to keep his promise to keep our secret. He's never broken a promise he's made to me in the past.

e. In the United States, 26 percent of births are by caesarean section, up 150 percent since 1975.[2] There are several reasons for this trend. Many doctors feel that a woman should have the right to choose how she wants to have her baby. And with malpractice premiums so high, obstetricians have become reluctant to take even the slightest risk associated with natural childbirth.

f. Young people are more computer savvy nowadays. Therefore, you might be better off asking your cousin Jennifer for help setting up your computer than asking her father.

g. We told you 2 weeks ago that if you kept missing the meetings to work on our group class presentation, we were going to drop you from the group. You haven't made any of the meetings in the past 2 weeks. So now we're going to drop you from our group.

h. We're willing to put down our dogs and cats when they are old and sick. Why shouldn't we do the same with our elderly?

i. Mike weighed 210 pounds before going on the critical-thinking diet three months ago. He has lost 17 pounds so far on the diet. Therefore, he now weighs less than 200 pounds.

3. Computers (AI) programmed with an inductive logic program can, after sufficient experience working with the ups and downs of the financial market, predict the market with greater accuracy than most experienced financial planners.[3] Given that these computers are not as prone to cognitive errors as are humans, should we rely more on AI to make decisions about such issues as college admissions, medical diagnoses, matchmaking, and piloting an airplane? Support your answer.

GENERALIZATION

generalization Drawing a conclusion about a certain characteristic of a population based on a sample from it.

poll A type of survey that involves collecting information from a sample group of people.

We use **generalization** when we draw a conclusion about a certain characteristic of a group or population on the basis of a sample from that group. For example, you sneeze whenever you are around your roommate's cat, your girlfriend's cat, and your Uncle Albert's two cats (your sample). On the basis of these experiences, you might reasonably conclude that *all* cats (the population) will probably make you sneeze.

generalization

Characteristics of ⟶ Claim about characteristics
sample   of a whole population

Scientists frequently use arguments based on generalization. For instance, Stanley Milgram, in his experiment on obedience, found that 65% of the subjects obeyed the authority figure to the point where they thought they might have seriously harmed or even killed the learner.[4] From this finding, Milgram concluded that people in general are susceptible to becoming caught up in a destructive process if directed to do so by an authority figure. In coming to this conclusion, Milgram generalized from the behavior of the study subjects in his experiments (the sample) to a conclusion about a characteristic of the whole human population.

Connections

How is inductive reasoning used in the scientific method?
See Chapter 10, p. 330;
Chapter 12, p. 379.

Using Polls, Surveys, and Sampling to Make Generalizations

Polls and surveys, such as the Freshman Survey, also use inductive generalization. **Polls** are a type of survey that involve collecting opinions or information on a subject from a sample group of people for the purpose of analysis.[5]

Polls provide a window into how others think and feel. Few marketing firms or public policy makers take any major action without first consulting polls. Public opinion polls play an especially important role in democracies such as the United States, whose Constitution requires that the government function explicitly with "the consent of the governed."[6] Politicians, especially during election years, check the public opinion polls to find out what the public thinks before making promises or commitments. Polls are even used to determine what type of shirt (e.g., checked lumberjack, polo, or white dress shirt) a politician should wear when campaigning in a particular state or town.

Sampling Techniques. To ensure that a generalization about a population is reliable, pollsters use a method known as sampling to collect data about a population that is large or diverse and where it

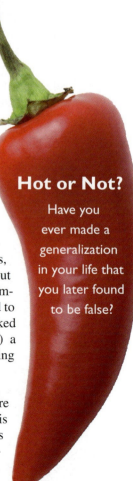

Hot or Not?

Have you ever made a generalization in your life that you later found to be false?

would be too costly and time-consuming to study the whole population. **Sampling** entails selecting only some members of a class or group and then making a generalization about the whole population that is based on the characteristics of these members. For example, the 2007 Freshman Survey, rather than polling all 1.4 million full-time freshmen in the United States, invited all 4-year American colleges and universities to participate in the survey; 272,036 freshmen at 356 colleges and universities—about 20 percent of all American freshmen at the time—participated in the survey. This sample is much larger than is normally needed, if the sample chosen is representative of the population.

A **representative sample** is one that is similar in relevant respects to the larger population. To get a representative sample, most professional pollsters use a method known as **random sampling**. A sample is random if every member of the population has an equal chance of becoming a member of that sample, in much the same way that the numbers for the winning lottery ticket are drawn randomly from a population of numbers containing all possible combinations of winning numbers. The Gallup Poll makes consistently accurate predictions about the views of Americans on the basis of a representative sample of only 1,500 to 2,000 people.[7]

One method of ensuring that a sample is representative when it is too difficult to get a random sample is to weight the responses. The Freshman Survey uses this method. If one type of institution is underrepresented in a particular year (e.g., historically black colleges or Catholic colleges), each response from this type of institution is weighted so it counts for more in the final results, thereby assuring that the final results are representative of the population of American college freshmen.[8] For example, if 20 percent of all college freshmen attend Catholic colleges but only 10 percent of the responses in the survey are from freshmen at Catholic colleges, then each of these responses would be weighted to count as two responses. Using this method of sampling, the researchers are able to make relatively accu-

sampling Selecting some members of a group and making generalizations about the whole population on the basis of their characteristics.

representative sample A sample that is similar to the larger population from which it was drawn.

random sampling Every member of the population has an equal chance of becoming part of the sample.

Connections

How do market researchers use polls and surveys in targeting a market for a product or service? *See Chapter 10, p. 313; Chapter 10, p. 379.*

Your participation in a poll helps to provide an accurate portrayal of a specific group, or a population at large.

rate generalizations about the characteristics of the population of all American freshmen.

The sample size necessary to make a reliable generalization about a population depends in part on the size of the population. As a general rule, the larger the sample, the more confident we can be that our generalization is accu-

> Public opinion polls play an especially important role in democracies such as the United States, whose Constitution requires that the government function explicitly with "the consent of the governed."

rate. Sample size also depends on the amount of variation within a population. The more variation there is, the larger the sample must be to be accurate.

If the characteristics are relatively stable throughout the population, then the sample can be smaller. For example, you see a physician because you have been feeling tired and run down. The physician takes a small sample of blood and tells you, on the basis of the hemoglobin count in this one sample, that you are anemic. It's a very small sample compared with all the blood you have in your body. Should you go back and ask your physician to take blood from different parts of your body just to make sure the sample is

2008 CIRP FRESHMAN SURVEY

SERIAL #

MARKING DIRECTIONS
- Use a #2 pencil or black or blue pen.
- Erase cleanly any answer you wish to change or "X" out mark if in pen.

CORRECT MARK   INCORRECT MARKS

Group Code   A   B

1. Your sex: Male   Female

2. How many old will you be on December 31 of this year? (Mark one)

16 or younger   21-24
17   25-29
18   30-39
19   40-54
20   55 or older

3. Is English your native language?
Yes   No

4. In what year did you graduate from high school? (Mark one)

2008   Did not graduate but
2007   passed G.E.D. test.
2006   Never completed
2005 or earlier   high school

5. Are you enrolled (or enrolling) as a: (Mark one)
Full-time student?
Part-time student?

6. How many miles is this college from your permanent home? (Mark one)

5 or less   11-50   101-500
6-10   51-100   Over 500

7. What was your average grade in high school? (Mark one)

A or A+   B   C

9. From what kind of high school did you graduate? (Mark one)
- Public school (not charter or magnet)
- Public charter school
- Public magnet school
- Private religious/parochial school
- Private independent college-prep school
- Home school

10. Prior to this term, have you ever taken courses for credit at this institution?
Yes   No

11. Since leaving high school, have you ever taken courses, whether for credit or not for credit, at any other institution (university, 4- or 2-year college, technical, vocational, or business school)?
Yes   No

12. Where do you plan to live during the fall term? (Mark one)
With my family or other relatives
Other private home, apartment, or room.
College residence hall
Fraternity or sorority house
Other campus student housing
Other

13. To how many colleges other than this one did you apply for admission this year?
None   1   4   7-10
2   5   11 or more
3   6

14. Were you accepted by your first choice college?
Yes   No

15. Is this college your: (Mark one)
First choice?   Less than third
Second choice?   choice?
Third choice?

18. During high school (grades 9-12) how many years did you study each of the following subjects? (Mark one for each item)

	None	1/2	1	2	3	4	5 or more
English	○	○	○	○	○	○	○
Mathematics	○	○	○	○	○	○	○
Foreign Language	○	○	○	○	○	○	○
Physical Science	○	○	○	○	○	○	○
Biological Science	○	○	○	○	○	○	○
History/Am. Gov't	○	○	○	○	○	○	○
Computer Science	○	○	○	○	○	○	○
Arts and/or Music	○	○	○	○	○	○	○

19. What is the highest academic degree that you intend to obtain? (Mark one in each column)

	Highest Planned	Highest Planned at This College
None	○	○
Vocational certificate	○	○
Associate (A.A. or equivalent)	○	○
Bachelor's degree (B.A., B.S., etc.)	○	○
Master's degree (M.A., M.S., etc.)	○	○
Ph.D. or Ed.D.	○	○
M.D., D.O., D.D.S., or D.V.M.	○	○
J.D. (Law)	○	○
B.D. or M.DIV. (Divinity)	○	○
Other	○	○

20. How would you describe the racial composition of the high school you last attended and the neighborhood where you grew up? (Mark one in each row)

	Completely non-White	Mostly non-White	Roughly half non-White	Mostly White	Completely White
High school I last attended	○	○	○	○	○
Neighborhood where I grew up	○	○	○	○	○

Each year, the CIRP Freshman Survey is administered to over 400,000 entering full-time students.

representative? In this case, the answer is no. Because our blood is pretty much uniform throughout our body, at least in regard to hemoglobin count, the physician can be fairly confident that the sample is representative of all the blood in your body.

Not all polls and surveys use random sampling or correct for biases. Internet polls and some polls sponsored by television programs or stations, such as *American Idol* or CNN, may be biased or unrepresentative, since they rely on call-ins from their viewers or subscribers. Street polls and telephone polls can also be biased because not everyone is willing to stop and talk to a pollster or picks up their phone. In these cases, the sample is what is known as a **self-selected sample**. In other words, only the people most interested in the poll actually take the time to participate in it.

> **self-selected sample** A sample where only the people most interested in the poll or survey participate.

Even a professionally run survey can be inadvertently biased because of careless methodology. In 1936 the magazine *Literary Digest* conducted a massive survey on who would win the presidential election: Franklin D. Roosevelt or Alf Landon. *Literary Digest* sent surveys to people from their subscription list, from telephone books, and from automobile registration lists. About 2,300,000 people responded to the survey. On the basis of their responses, it was predicted that Landon would win the election. Instead, Roosevelt received 60 percent of the votes, one of the largest wins in American history. What went wrong? For one thing, the magazine's readership was mainly well-educated people, which biased the survey. In addition, many people in 1936 did not have a telephone or own an automobile, thereby further biasing the sample toward affluent people. George Gallup, who used a smaller but representative sample, predicted the result correctly (see "Thinking Outside the Box: George Gallup"). Likewise, in the 2008 presidential election, some of the telephone polls were biased in favor of John McCain since younger people who use only cell phones (which do not have listed numbers) overwhelmingly preferred Obama.[9]

Effects of Question Wording on Responses.

Bias may result from the way a question is worded. A 1980 poll conducted for the National Abortion Rights Action League (called NARAL Pro-Choice America since 2003) tried asking a question worded in the following two different ways to see if the wording would affect the response:

- Do you think there should be an amendment to the Constitution prohibiting abortions, or shouldn't there be such an amendment?

- Do you believe there should be an amendment to the Constitution protecting the life of the unborn child, or shouldn't there be such an amendment?

When the phrase "prohibiting abortions" was used in the question, 29 percent of the respondents said they favored the amendment; however, when the phrase "protecting the life of the unborn child" was used, 50 percent of the respondents said they

Connections

How can you recognize sampling errors in advertisements? *See Chapter 10, p. 328.*

Featured here with contestant David Archuleta (left) and host Ryan Seacrest (right), American Idol *winner David Cook (center) enjoys a victory based on voter call-in, a self-selected sample.*

Outside the Box

GEORGE GALLUP, *Opinion Seeker*

Born in Jefferson, Iowa, in 1901, George Gallup (who died in 1984) attended the University of Iowa, where he was editor of the school newspaper. He also completed a PhD in journalism at the University of Iowa.

After graduation, Gallup got a job as an interviewer for an advertising firm. He was keenly interested in what other people thought and why. Rather than making assumptions or asking only people he knew for their opinions, he developed the startling technique of actually confronting a sample of readers with a whole newspaper and asking them what they read and what they liked or didn't like about a story.

In 1934 Gallup founded the Gallup Poll at Princeton University, where he was the first to use scientific methods to measure people's opinions. His polling techniques were initially used to tap into the political pulse of the nation. Gallup also invented market research, described as "the ultimate savior of the customer." His work today stands as one of the greatest examples of the practical application of cognitive science. Gallup once said that "teaching people to think for themselves was the most important thing in the world to do."* For Gallup, a well-informed public was essential in a democracy. He transformed America by empowering the common person and making it increasingly difficult for those in authority to tell people what they should believe and do.

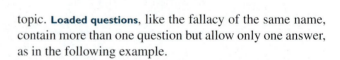

DISCUSSION QUESTIONS

1. Most college libraries carry the Gallup Poll. Look at the most recent poll. Discuss ways in which the questions and responses in the poll can contribute to your ability to be a critical thinker and make effective decisions about important issues.

2. Using the index in the Gallup Poll, select an issue that is important to you. Look at the questions. What percent of Americans share your view? Did looking at the poll results broaden your perspective on the issue? Explain.

*Quoted on http://www.schoolofthinking.org/who/george-gallup/. For more on the Gallup Poll, go to http:www.gallup.com.

---

favored the amendment. In this case, the second question was a **slanted question**—one that is written to elicit a particular response.

You should also be wary of **push polls**, which start by presenting the pollsters' views before asking for a response. By presenting the pollster's views first, the poll becomes slanted toward that view, no matter how well the questions are worded, since people tend to uncritically accept the views of those they perceive as an authority figure.

In addition, questions used in polls should be simple and cover only one topic. **Loaded questions**, like the fallacy of the same name, contain more than one question but allow only one answer, as in the following example.

> Should our community college seek greater diversity among the student applicants and not place as much emphasis on getting well-qualified students?

There are two questions here. You may agree that your college should seek a more diverse pool of applicants (the first question) and at the same time believe that doing so is independent of or will not have any impact on the qualifications of the students admitted (the second question). Along similar lines, questions in a poll should avoid the fallacy of false dilemma in which the response to a complex issue is reduced to two alternatives.

slanted question A question that is written to elicit a particular response.

push poll A poll that starts by presenting the pollsters' views before asking for a response.

loaded questions A fallacy that assumes a particular answer to another unasked question.

State College is currently experiencing a financial crisis. Do you think our college should raise tuition or increase class size?

This question poses a false dilemma, since there are other ways to raise funds without having to raise tuition or increase class size. For example, the development office could initiate a fund-raising campaign that targets wealthy alumni.

Self-serving errors can bias the results of a survey as well. Polls depend on the respondents answering honestly.

. . . in polls men tend to exaggerate the number of times they have had sexual intercourse, whereas women tend to understate the number of encounters.

As we noted in Chapter 4, most people see themselves (correctly or not) as good and fair-minded. If a poll asks "Are you a racist?" virtually no one, not even members of the Ku Klux Klan, will answer yes. To avoid this error, questions should be worded in a way that does not threaten a person's self image.

People are also inclined to give answers that conform to what is socially acceptable or what they think the pollster wants to hear. For example, many men think that it's macho to have frequent sex and many female partners. Women who engage in this sort of behavior, however, are usually labeled sluts. Consequently, in polls men tend to exaggerate the number of times they have had sexual intercourse,

whereas women tend to understate the number of encounters. In fact, the difference in the answers is so marked that it is impossible for both groups to be answering honestly.

A generalization about a population may be used as a premise in an argument about a particular member(s) of that group.

Generalization about ⟶ Claim about a
the population   member of the
(Premise)   population
                        (Conclusion)

The ability to correctly apply generalizations to specific cases enables us to make better decisions in our lives and personal relationships, as the following case illustrates:

> I was going to get my wife Ling a new bathroom scale for Valentine's Day until I read a study that said most women prefer to be taken out to a romantic dinner. I should take Ling out to dinner at the Ritz instead. She'll probably like that more than the scale.

Breaking down and diagramming this argument, we have:

(1) [I was going to get my wife Ling a new bathroom scale for Valentine's Day] until I read a study that said (2) [most women prefer to be taken out to a romantic dinner.] (3) [Ling will probably like going out to dinner more than the scale.]

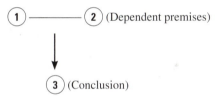

(1) ——— (2) (Dependent premises)

(3) (Conclusion)

Premise 2 is based on a generalization about a population (women). In this case the husband draws the conclusion about Ling (a member of the population) that she would probably rather be taken out to dinner for Valentine's Day.

When a generalization about a population is applied to an individual member of that group, statistics are often used regarding the prevalence of the characteristic in the population. The higher the prevalence of a characteristic in the population, the more likely it is that the application to the individual will be true.

> Studies show that executives tend to be significantly taller than employees of a company. Therefore, Anna Gable, the CEO of Buzzword Electronics, is probably taller than 5'4", the average height of women in the United States.

In applying a generalization, you should make sure you are clear about what population was used in making the initial generalization. In the following example, the

Year	Winner	Height	Runner-up (by electoral vote count)	Height	Difference
2008	Barack Obama	6 ft 1½ in	John McCain	5 ft 7 in	5½ in
2004	George W. Bush	5 ft 11 in	John Kerry	6 ft 4 in	5 in
2000	George W. Bush	5 ft 11 in	Al Gore	6 ft ½ in	1½ in
1996	Bill Clinton	6 ft 2½ in	Bob Dole	6 ft 0 in	2½ in
1992	Bill Clinton	6 ft 2½ in	George H. W. Bush	6 ft 2 in	½ in
1988	George H. W. Bush	6 ft 2 in	Michael Dukakis	5 ft 6 in	8 in
1984	Ronald Reagan	6 ft 1 in	Walter Mondale	5 ft 10¾ in	2¼ in
1980	Ronald Reagan	6 ft 1 in	Jimmy Carter	5 ft 9 in	4 in
1976	Jimmy Carter	5 ft 9 in	Gerald Ford	6 ft 1 in	4 in
1972	Richard Nixon	5 ft 11½ in	George McGovern	6 ft 1 in	1½ in
1968	Richard Nixon	5 ft 11½ in	Hubert Humphrey	5 ft 11 in	½ in
1964	Lyndon Johnson	6 ft 3½ in	Barry Goldwater	6 ft 0 in	3½ in
1960	John F. Kennedy	6 ft 0 in	Richard Nixon	5 ft 11½ in	½ in
1956	Dwight D. Eisenhower	5 ft 10½ in	Adlai Stevenson	5 ft 10 in	½ in
1952	Dwight D. Eisenhower	5 ft 10½ in	Adlai Stevenson	5 ft 10 in	½ in
1948	Harry S. Truman	5 ft 9 in	Thomas Dewey	5 ft 8 in	1 in
1944	Franklin D. Roosevelt	6 ft 2 in	Thomas Dewey	5 ft 8 in	6 in
1940	Franklin D. Roosevelt	6 ft 2 in	Wendell Willkie	6 ft 1 in	1 in
1936	Franklin D. Roosevelt	6 ft 2 in	Alfred Landon	5 ft 8 in	6 in
1932	Franklin D. Roosevelt	6 ft 2 in	Herbert Hoover	5 ft 11 in	3 in
1928	Herbert Hoover	5 ft 11½ in	Al Smith	5 ft 6 in	5½ in
1924	Calvin Coolidge	5 ft 10 in	John W. Davis	6 ft 0 in	2 in

Comparative Table of Heights of U.S. Presidential Candidates

speaker misapplies a generalization about the population of people who are diagnosed with multiple sclerosis (MS) to a conclusion about the population of people in general.

> The majority of people who are diagnosed with multiple sclerosis are women between the ages of 20 and 30. You're a woman and you just turned 20. Therefore, chances are that you'll come down with MS while you're in your twenties.

In this case, the fact that the majority of people who first present with symptoms of

MS are women between the ages of 20 and 30 does not necessarily mean that the majority of women in their twenties will develop MS. In fact, the rate of MS in the female population worldwide is only 0.3 percent (3 out of every 1,000 women). Thus, the chances that a woman of any age will develop MS are actually very low.

Evaluating Inductive Arguments Using Generalization

Like all inductive arguments, generalizations are neither true nor false; they are merely stronger or weaker arguments. In this section we'll be looking at five different criteria for evaluating arguments using generalizations.

1. The Premises Are True. True premises are based on credible evidence. A premise can be false because of flaws in a research design—as happened in the 1936 *Literary Digest* survey on the presidential election. A premise can also be false because it is based on popular misconceptions or stereotypes rather than on actual evidence—as in the following example:

> Most pedophiles are homosexual. Therefore, former Catholic priest John Geoghan, a convicted pedophile killed in prison, was probably homosexual, just as all those other priests who were convicted probably are.

In this example, the premise "Most pedophiles are homosexual" is false. As we noted in Chapter 1, good critical thinkers make sure that their information is accurate and their sources are credible before they come to a conclusion. Research shows that homosexual men are no more likely to molest children, and perhaps even less likely to, than are heterosexual men. For example, a Massachusetts study of adult males who were convicted child molesters found that less than 1 percent of them were homosexual.[10] This is well below the estimate of 2.3 percent for the general population that is based on a survey conducted by the U.S. Department of Health and Human Services.[11]

2. The Sample Is Large Enough. As a general rule, the larger the sample, the more reliable the conclusion. When our sample is too small, we run the risk of committing the **fallacy of hasty generalization**. For example, a high school senior knows three students who just were accepted by a first-rate 4-year college. In each case, both of their parents were professionals with graduate degrees. From this small sample, the student may hastily conclude that she shouldn't bother applying for admission to this college, since her parents are owners of small businesses and never attended college. In reality, only about 20 percent of the parents of college freshmen have a graduate degree, whereas an even larger number of parents—28 percent—have only a high school education or less.[12]

> **fallacy of hasty generalization**
> A generalization made from a sample that is too small or biased.

3. The Sample Is Representative. A sample should be representative of the population being studied. If the sample is not, then the argument is weak (see "Analyzing Images: The Blind Men and the Elephant"). A sample can be large but still not be representative. For example, before the 1980s, almost all clinical drug studies were done only on men. Women were not included, not only because of concern that they might be pregnant but also because of the cultural assumption that men were the norm. Because of this erroneous assumption, women sometimes ended up getting treatments and drugs that were inappropriate for them.

There are other reasons a sample may be unrepresentative. For example, we might poll only people we feel comfortable approaching. Telephone pollsters might do their interviews at a certain time of day or day of the week when most people are at work. In addition, young people are more likely to use cell phones exclusively and, hence, not be listed in the phone directory.

4. The Sample Is Current and Up-to-Date. A sample may be unrepresentative because it is outdated. It was long believed, on the basis of samples taken decades

Analyzing Images

THE BLIND MEN AND THE ELEPHANT According to a Buddhist fable, a group of blind men came upon an elephant. One of the men grabbed the trunk and said, "Elephants are like snakes." "No," replied the second blind man, putting his arms around the elephant's leg, "they're shaped like tree trunks." "Nonsense," chimed in the third blind man as he ran his hands along the elephant's tail. "They're more like ropes."

DISCUSSION QUESTIONS

1. *Why did each of the blind men come to a different conclusion regarding the nature of the elephant? How might they have used critical-thinking skills to arrive at a better-reasoned conclusion?*

2. *Describe a time when you got into a dispute because you made a generalization on the basis of limited experience.*

ago of the water in coastal bays in the United States, that the oceans were so vast that the ocean tides were capable of cleaning out any pollution that entered coastal bays and rivers.

Because the sampling data on the purity of coastal water weren't updated, the growing problem of pollution in our bays went unnoticed for many years. While samples from the past are useful for establishing trends, we should be wary about using outdated samples for making generalizations about the current population.

5. The Conclusion Is Supported by the Premise(s).
The conclusion should follow logically from the premises. It should not go beyond what is stated in the premises, as happens in the following example:

Since men in general are physically stronger than women, women should not be allowed to serve in combat duty in the military.

The conclusion does not follow from the premise in this case, since physical strength may not be essential or even important to be effective in combat. Also, even if it is, some women are physically stronger than some men.

If it is used correctly, generalization is a powerful form of inductive logic. When you make a generalization, it is important that you begin with premises that are true. In addition, your sample should be sufficiently large, representative, and up-to-date.

Women serving combat duty in the United States military has long been an issue of contention—but are we against (or for) it for the right reasons?

> **HIGHLIGHTS**
>
> **EVALUATING ARGUMENTS THAT ARE BASED ON GENERALIZATION**
>
> 1. Check whether the premises are true.
> 2. Decide if the sample is large enough.
> 3. Decide if the sample is representative.
> 4. Decide if the sample is current and up-to-date.
> 5. Determine whether the conclusion is supported by the premise(s).

EXERCISES 7–2

1. Evaluate the following poll questions. If the questions are biased, rewrite them.
   a. Do you support increasing airport security to prevent future terrorist attacks using airplanes?
   b. Are you an honest person?
   c. Do you think marriages between homosexuals should or should not be recognized by the law as valid, with the same rights as traditional marriages?
   d. Do you think English should be the official language of the United States?
   e. Would you support any institution of higher learning that restricts your freedom to think as you wish by establishing zones that limit your freedom of speech?
   f. Do you agree with privatizing Social Security and risking the future benefits to retirees?
   g. Should we allow children of illegal immigrants to attend state colleges at in-state tuition rates, or should we instead refuse them admission to state colleges?
2. Working in small groups, develop a poll for studying one of the following questions. Discuss the method you will use to ensure that the sample you poll is both random and representative and that the questions are unbiased.
   a. Your college administration is considering banning the use of alcohol on campus. However, the administration first wants to find out if the students will support this idea and how they might react to the ban.
   b. You want to find out how most of the students on your campus feel about allowing cohabitation in the dorms.
   c. The student affairs office at your college is interested in learning more about the short-term goals of students.

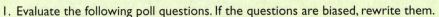

d. The faculty council at your college is concerned about students' plagiarizing from the Internet. They want to learn about the extent of this problem on campus as well as students' attitudes toward the practice.

3. Evaluate the following arguments:

a. In a national survey by the U.S. Department of Education, it was found that 90 percent of college students have to borrow money to pay for their college expenses. Anwar is a college student. Therefore, he most likely has had to borrow money.

b. Every time a stranger comes into our yard, our dog starts barking. From this we can safely conclude that Rex will always bark at strangers.

c. Melissa probably feels down because she wishes she'd brought her dog Rex with us. I read in Delta Airline's *Sky* magazine that 67 percent of U.S. pet owners feel guilty about leaving their pets at home when they travel.

d. I've noticed that the three Asian students in my calculus class all earn high grades. Asians are just better at math.

e. I don't see why I need a college education. The most successful thinkers in the world never went to college. Abraham Lincoln never graduated from college. And neither did Confucius or Jesus or Socrates or Mohammed—four of the greatest and most influential people ever to walk this Earth.

f. It seems that whenever I drop a piece of toast, it falls buttered side down. I'd better eat in the kitchen because if I eat in the living room and drop my toast, it will most likely leave a grease mark from the butter on the carpet.

g. College students want to see drinking allowed on campus. I took a poll of my fraternity brothers, and we all agreed that drinking should be allowed.

h. "I hate myself. I'm so much fatter and uglier than other women."
"No, you're not. You look great. Why would you think such a thing?"
"All the women in the television show *Real World* are so thin and beautiful."

i. I don't see why you can't find a job like other college graduates. When I graduated in 1962, we had no trouble finding good jobs.

j. Medical errors aren't nearly as big a problem as some people think. In a national poll of more than 2,000 randomly selected physicians, more than 90 percent said that medical errors are not a serious problem in medicine.

k. According to the World Kennel Club, the average dog weighs about 40 pounds. But my Aunt Celia, who lives in a condo in downtown Toronto, says that the majority of dogs she sees while out on her daily walks are under 25 pounds. Therefore, we can safely conclude that dogs living in Canada tend to be smaller than dogs in the United States.

l. The last three times I asked women out on a date, they turned me down. I should just give up trying to meet someone. Probably any other women I ask out will reject me too.

4. A survey by *Rhode Island Magazine* found that 63 percent of Rhode Islanders think they can't lose weight because their metabolism is too slow. Discuss whether or not we would be justified in making a generalization from this sample to the population of all Americans.

5. Most of us have been approached on the street or on campus by pollsters toting clipboards and asking for our views about a particular topic or product. Discuss the problems with this methodology for getting a representative sample.

6. Some people feel that election polling should be banned, since simply knowing which candidate is ahead in an election can sway undecided voters to vote for that candidate. Working in small groups, come up with a list of premises and a conclusion regarding this issue. Discuss your conclusion with the class.

7. Go to http://www.ropercenter.uconn.edu/links.html, an Internet site listing the major polling organizations in the United States, and click on some of the links. Come up with a list of ways in which information from this link might help you in your classes or in decision making in your everyday life. Find a poll that might help you develop your poll question(s) for exercise 2 above.

8. Find out if your college participates in the annual Freshman Survey. If it does, obtain a copy of the report from your administration comparing your college's freshmen to the typical American freshman. Write a few paragraphs about the similarities and differences for discussion in class.

9. What impact do polls have on your life? Write about ways in which life would be different today if there were no polls.

10. *Journal Exercise.* Complete a journal assignment on "Reaction to the American Freshman Survey." Discuss as a class your reaction and your answers to the questions in the journal assignment.

ANALOGIES

An **analogy** is based on a comparison between two or more things or events. Analogies often contain words or phrases such as *like*, *as*, *similarly*, or *compared to*. For example, in her article at the end of Chapter 9, Judith Jarvis Thomson draws an analogy between an acorn and a human fetus when she argues that that the relationship between a fetus and a woman is like that of an acorn to an oak tree. From this she concludes that just as an acorn is not an oak tree, neither is the fetus a human being.

> **analogy** A comparison between two or more similar events or things.
>
> **metaphor** A descriptive type of analogy, frequently found in literature.

Uses of Analogies

Noticing similarities between things or events is one of the primary ways we learn from experience. A child burns his hand on a candle and afterward stays away from a campfire because of the similarity between the two. To use another example, many early buildings were vulnerable to damage by storms because they were too rigid. Then architects noticed that trees were resilient in strong winds because of their flexibility and adopted this approach in building wind-resistant structures. We've also learned more about how the heart works by comparing it to a mechanical pump.

Connections

How might consumers use arguments by analogy in deciding whether to buy a particular product? *See Chapter 10, p. 316.*

Analogies can exist on their own as descriptive devices, such as in "She's like a bull in a china shop" or "Finding my car in the commuter parking lot is like looking for a needle in a haystack." Analogies can also be used as a means of illustrating a point, as in the following passages:

> The death toll from smoking is comparable to that which would result from three jumbo jet crashes a day, occurring every single day of the year.[13]

> Just as a person puts on new garments after discarding the old ones, similarly, the living entity (or soul) obtains a new body after casting away the old bodies.

The first analogy is used to bring home the point that smoking is considerably more deadly than flying. The second analogy, from the Hindu sacred text the Bhagavad Gita (2:22), is used to illustrate the concept of death and transmigration of souls.

Metaphors, a type of descriptive analogy, are frequently found in literature. In this passage from *Macbeth* (act V), Shakespeare compares life to a stage play.

> Life's but a walking shadow, a poor player
>
> That struts and frets his hour upon the stage
>
> And then is heard no more.

Sometimes it is unclear if a passage is being used metaphorically or if it is meant to be taken literally. This is especially problematic in interpreting ancient scriptural texts, where translation and cultural differences in the use of language can leave us uncertain as to the author's intentions.

Arguments Based on Analogies

In addition to standing on their own, analogies can be used as premises in arguments. An argument based on an analogy claims that if two things are similar in one or more ways, they are probably alike in other respects as well.

> Premises: X (which is familiar) has characteristics a, b, and c.
>
> Premise: Y (which is not as familiar) has characteristics a and b.
>
> Conclusion: Therefore, Y probably also has characteristic c.

To illustrate, say you (X) meet someone (Y) at a Sierra Club event on your campus. The person seems pleasant enough and also seems to be interested in you. You wonder whether you should start a relationship with this person. However, before rushing into a relationship, you first collect more information about this person, including what the two of you might have in common. You already know that you are both interested in environmental issues (characteristic a). After chatting for a bit you learn that Y, like you, also enjoys hiking (characteristic b). After this brief encounter, you conclude, on the basis of your shared interest in the environment and hiking, that Y probably also shares your interest in healthy eating (characteristic c). When you get home, you phone Y and ask Y out for dinner at the local health-food restaurant.

In addition to personal life, arguments based on analogies are common in many fields including law, religion, politics, and the military. For example, Shawnee leader Tecumseh (1738–1813) used an analogy to try to convince members of his and other tribes that they needed to unite into a Native American alliance if they were to keep their land from being taken over by the whites. An alliance of tribes, he argued, is like braided hair. A single strand of hair is easy to break. But several strands braided together are almost impossible to break.

One of the most famous arguments based on an analogy is the **argument from design**. This centuries-old argument is one of the most popular "proofs" of the existence of God. It has recently resurfaced in the debate about intelligent design versus evolution, which we'll be examining in depth at the end of Chapter 12.

> **argument from design** An argument for the existence of God based on an analogy between man-made objects and natural objects.

The argument from design begins by noting the similarities between the universe and other natural objects (such as the human eye) and human-made objects (such as a watch). Both natural and human-made objects share the characteristics of high degrees of both (1) organization and (2) purposefulness. The organization and the purposefulness of a watch are the direct result of an intelligent, rational creator, a watchmaker.

Similarly, the argument goes, the even greater organization and purposefulness of nature must be the product of an intelligent and rational creator. The analogy can be summarized as follows:

Premise: A watch has the following characteristics: (1) organization, (2) purposefulness, and (3) having an intelligent, rational creator.

Premise: The universe (or human eye) also demonstrates characteristics (1) organization and (2) purposefulness.

Conclusion: Therefore, by analogy, the universe (or human eye) also has (3) an intelligent, rational creator, and that creator is God.

Arguments using analogies are also found in science. Scientists come up with hypotheses about the effects of drugs or certain stimuli on humans on the basis of the similarities between humans and these other animals by doing experiments on rats and other nonhuman animals. Astronomers make predictions about the characteristics of other planets in the galaxy on the basis of the degree of similarity between Earth and other planets.

In the area of law, courts often look at prior court rulings on similar cases before coming to a decision. We will be studying the doctrine of legal precedent in Chapter 13.

Some analogies use emotively loaded images in an attempt to rally the listener to a particular conclusion (see "Did You Know" below). This rhetorical tactic is especially common when tensions are high and people are set in opposition to one another. In a speech made on June 22, 1941, the day after Germany invaded the Soviet Union, British Prime Minister Winston Churchill used analogies to convince the British people of the danger posed by Hitler and his army. In his speech, Churchill compared Hitler to a "monster of wickedness, insatiable in his lust for blood," and the Nazi army to a "war machine . . . in constant motion grinding up human lives" and German soldiers to a "swarm of crawling locusts."[14]

Connections

How are analogies used in courts of law? *See Chapter 13, p. 433.*

Did You Know?

Since it first aired in 1987, millions of people have seen the TV ad with eggs in a frying pan representing "Your Brain on Drugs." Created by the Partnership for a Drug-Free America's (PDFA) anti-drug campaign, this ad has been one of the most influential of our time. A study of drug use habits among teens conducted before and after the ads aired showed a drop in teen drug use following the airing of the ads.

Analogies as Tools for Refuting Arguments

Analogies themselves can be used to refute arguments containing weak or false analogies. The first way to do this is to respond to the faulty analogy with a new one. A refutation using a new analogy can start out with a phrase such as "You might as well say that" or "That is like saying." The new analogy usually has the same form as the one being refuted, as in the following passage from *Alice's Adventures in Wonderland* by Lewis Carroll in which the March Hare and the Dormouse use analogies to refute Alice's argument that saying what she means is the same as meaning what she says:

> "I do [say what I mean]," Alice hastily replied; "at least—at least I mean what I say—that's the same thing, you know."
>
> "Not the same thing a bit!" said the Hatter. "Why, you might just as well say that 'I see what I eat' is the same thing as 'I eat what I see'!"
>
> "You might just as well say," added the March Hare, "That 'I like what I get' is the same thing as 'I get what I like'!"
>
> "You might just as well say," added the Dormouse, which seemed to be talking in its sleep, "That 'I breathe when I sleep' is the same thing as 'I sleep when I breathe'!"

The second way of refuting an argument using an analogy is by extending the analogy used in the argument. Philosopher David Hume (1711–1776), in his refutation of the argument by design, extended the analogy between a watchmaker and God.[15] He noted that the maker of a watch can be several people. Also, the watch might be inferior or defective. The watchmaker(s) might have been senile or up to no good at the time he or she created the watch. Extending the analogy even further, Hume argued that we cannot even assume if we come upon a watch that the watchmaker is still alive. Therefore, even if we accept the analogy between God and a watchmaker, we cannot use it to prove that a good and perfect God exists or ever existed.

Evaluating Inductive Arguments Based on Analogies

Some analogies are stronger than others. The success of an argument using an analogy depends on the type and extent of relevant similarities and dissimilarities between the things being compared. The following are steps for evaluating arguments based on analogies.

1. Identify What Is Being Compared.
Write down a short summary of the comparison. For example, in the photograph at the bottom of page 217 the brain is being compared with a raw egg and drugs are being compared with a hot frying pan.

The success of an argument using an analogy depends on the type and extent of relevant similarities and dissimilarities between the things being compared.

---

2. List the Similarities.
Make a list of the specific ways in which the two things being compared are similar. Are the similarities strong enough to support the conclusion? As a rule, the greater the similarities, the stronger the analogy. For example, in the "This Is Your Brain on Drugs" analogy, the hot frying pan is similar to drugs in that both can seriously alter and damage organic matter. Another similarity is that both the brain and a raw egg are round and squishy.

After making your list of similarities, cross out those that are not relevant. In this case, the shape and texture of the brain and egg are irrelevant to the argument that drugs can damage the brain. In a good analogy, the remaining relevant similarities should be strong enough to support the conclusion.

3. List the Dissimilarities.
Once you have made a list of similarities, make a list of the dissimilarities. Are the dissimilarities or differences relevant in ways that affect the argument? The more the dissimilarities, the weaker the analogy usually is. Are drugs really like a hot frying

pan? The use of many drugs, especially in small amounts, does not have such an immediate and catastrophic effect as that of a raw egg being broken into a hot frying pan. Indeed, some drugs such as marijuana may even be beneficial under certain circumstances (see "Critical-Thinking Issues: Perspectives on Legalizing Marijuana" at the end of this chapter).

Some dissimilarities may not be relevant to the argument. As we noted earlier, it is through analogical reasoning that we conclude that, like us, other people feel and are conscious like us. Since computers or androids are dissimilar from us in far more ways than are other humans, we have more difficulty applying this type of reasoning to beings with artificial intelligence (AI). However, claims that AI can never be conscious or have feelings like humans because they are silicon-based, whereas we are carbon-based, or because they are created and programmed by humans, whereas we are born, are based on irrelevant differences. The material a being is made out of is, as far as we know, not related to the ability to be conscious or feel. Nor is being created by humans relevant, since humans are also created by other humans out of two cells and programmed by their DNA and environment. Of course, this doesn't mean that there are not other dissimilarities between humans and AI that are relevant.

Remember, an argument based on analogy does not provide certain proof. It merely provides a stronger or weaker argument.

4. Compare the Lists of Similarities and Differences. Are the similarities strong enough to support the inference? Are the dissimilarities relevant in important ways? Hume refuted the argument from design by pointing out the dissimilarities in the analogy. Although a natural object such as an eye and a watch are both organized and purposeful, these similarities are not sufficient to support the conclusion that God created the universe, because the differences between God and a watchmaker are so striking.

5. Examine Possible Strong Counteranalogies. Are the counteranalogies stronger? John Noonan, in refuting the analogy between a fetus and an acorn, uses the counteranalogy of a hunter who sees movement in the bushes and is not sure if it is a person or a deer.[16] Even if the chances are only one in a million that the being is a human, we still shouldn't shoot. Instead, we should err on the side of life. Similarly, Noonan argues, even though we are not sure whether the fetus is a person, we should err on the side of life rather than risk killing a human being.

6. Determine If the Analogy Supports the Conclusion. After comparing the relevant similarities and dissimilarities and looking for possible counterarguments, you are now in position to decide if this is a good argument. Remember, an argument based on analogy does not provide certain proof. It merely provides a stronger or weaker argument.

Analogies can be effective tools in an argument by clarifying the key points. On the other hand, analogies can be deceptively persuasive, since they appeal to our sense of imagination. Because of the power analogies have to shape our worldview, it is important that we learn how to recognize and evaluate arguments containing analogies.

HIGHLIGHTS

EVALUATING ARGUMENTS BASED ON AN ANALOGY

1. **Identify** what is being compared.

2. List the **similarities.**

3. List the **dissimilarities.**

4. **Compare** the lists of similarities and differences.

5. Examine possible **counteranalogies.**

6. **Determine** if the analogy supports the conclusion.

1. For each of the following, create an analogy, by adding a phrase after the term "is like":

   a. College is like ...

   b. Studying for an exam is like ...

   c. Looking for a job is like ...

   d. Being married is like ...

   e. Using the Internet is like ...

   f. Doing a class presentation is like ...

   g. Finding a roommate is like ...

   h. Life is like ...

   i. A first date is like ...

   j. Faith is like ...

   Share your analogies with the class. To what extent does the use of an analogy make it easier for you to express what you think or how you feel?

2. Looking back through previous chapters in the textbook, identify analogies that have been used. Discuss the purpose of each analogy.

3. Evaluate the following arguments that are based on analogies:

   a. I don't see what's wrong with buying essays for a class from the Internet. After all, the president of the United States pays someone to write his speeches for him, and no one has a problem with that.

   b. We put our beloved pets to sleep when they are very sick and in too much pain to enjoy life. Therefore, we should allow humans who are very sick and in too much pain to enjoy life to die mercifully.

   c. Marijuana should be legalized. After all, alcohol is also an addictive drug that is used to enhance mood and it is legal.

   d. Hate speech on college campuses should be banned. Hate speech is like yelling "fire" in a crowded theater. It is illegal to yell "fire" in a crowded theater because doing so could cause great harm to people. The same is true of hate speech.

   e. Both the war in Iraq and the Vietnam War were wars of choice in that neither posed an imminent threat or ever directly attacked an American city. The Vietnam War was fought to prevent the spread of communism. The war in Iraq was fought to prevent the spread of terrorism. The Vietnam War ended badly with U.S. withdrawal and no victory. The war in Iraq probably will probably end badly too.

   f. "You didn't learn to dance on your first try. Quitting smoking takes practice too."[17]

   g. We quarantine people with deadly contagious diseases such as tuberculosis. Therefore, we should quarantine people with AIDS, which is also a deadly, contagious disease.

   h. "What is taught on this campus should depend on what the students are interested in. After all, consuming knowledge is like consuming anything else in our society. The teacher is the seller, the student is the buyer. Buyers determine what they want to buy, so students should determine what they want to learn."[18]

   i. Some people reject the comparison of AI with human thinking on the grounds that AI is merely a simulation of thinking. Unlike human thinking, the argument based on analogy goes, so-called intelligent machines only appear to be thinking, much like a child pretending to sip tea at a tea party with her dolls. There is no real tea in the toy cup.

   j. I don't tell my mechanic how to fix my automobile. Instead, I trust his expertise. In the same manner, I should not tell my physician how to fix my body.

   k. "Racists violate the principle of equality by giving greater weight to the interests of members of their own race when there is a clash between their interests and the interests of those of another race. Sexists violate the principle of equality by favoring the interests of their own sex. Similarly, speciesists allow the interests of their own species to override the greater interests of members of other species. The pattern is identical in each case."[19]

4. Look through magazines, newspapers, or the Internet for examples of analogies. Select one of the analogies. Write a one-page paper describing the purpose of the analogy.

5. Select one of the following analogies. Using the steps listed on pages 218–219, write a two- to three-page essay evaluating the analogy.

   a. In his now classic article "Active and Passive Euthanasia,"[20] James Rachels uses the following well-known analogy to refute the claim that active euthanasia is morally worse than passive euthanasia because it is morally worse to kill someone than to let someone die.* Rachels considers the following two cases:

In the first, Smith stands to gain a large inheritance if anything should happen to his six-year-old cousin. One evening while the child is taking his bath, Smith sneaks into the bathroom and drowns the child, and then arranges things so that it will look like an accident.

In the second, Jones also stands to gain if anything should happen to his six-year-old cousin. Like Smith, Jones sneaks in planning to drown the child in his bath. However, just as he enters the bathroom Jones sees the child slip and hit his head, and fall face down in the water. Jones is delighted; he stands by, ready to push the child's head back under if it is necessary, but it is not necessary. With only a little thrashing about, the child drowns all by himself, "accidentally," as Jones watches and does nothing.

Now Smith killed the child, whereas Jones "merely" let the child die. That is the only difference between them. Did either man behave better, from a moral point of view? …The preceding consideration suggests that there is really no difference between the two [active euthanasia and passive euthanasia]. So, whereas doctors may have to discriminate between active and passive euthanasia to satisfy the law, they should not do more than that.

b. Former president Lyndon B. Johnson was a tireless advocate of civil rights for African Americans. The following are excerpts from his famous "To Fulfill These Rights" commencement address[21] delivered at Howard University on June 4, 1965:

…In far too many ways American Negroes have been another nation: deprived of Freedom, crippled by hatred, the doors of opportunity closed to hope.

In our time change has come to this Nation, too.…That beginning is freedom; and the barriers to that freedom are tumbling down. Freedom is the right to share, share fully and equally, in American society—to vote, to hold a job, to enter a public place, to go to school.…

But freedom is not enough. You do not wipe away the scars of centuries by saying: Now you are free to go where you want, and do as you desire, and choose the leaders you please.

You do not take a person who, for years, has been hobbled by chains and liberate him, bring him up to the starting line of a race and then say, "You are free to compete with all the others," and still justly believe that you have been completely fair.

Thus, it is not enough just to open the gates of opportunity. All our citizens must have the ability to walk through those gates.

c. In his article "Lifeboat Ethics: The Case Against Helping the Poor," ecologist Garrett Hardin uses the analogy of rich nations as lifeboats in debating whether the rich nations of the world have an obligation to help the poor nations:[22]

If we divide the world crudely into rich nations and poor nations, two thirds of them are desperately poor, and only one third comparatively rich, with the United States the wealthiest of all. Metaphorically each rich nation can be seen as a lifeboat full of comparatively rich people. In the ocean outside each lifeboat swim the poor of the world, who would like to get in, or at least to share some of the wealth. What should the lifeboat passengers do?

6. Think of an analogy that has shaped your thinking and view of the world. Use a specific example to show how this analogy has influenced your decisions. Using the criteria on page 219, evaluate the analogy.

* *Active euthanasia* is defined as taking direct action, such as a lethal injection, to kill a person who has a terminal or incurable disease or condition. *Passive euthanasia* is defined as allowing a person who has a terminal or incurable disease or condition to die by withholding life support or medical treatment that would prolong his or her life.

CAUSAL ARGUMENTS

cause An event that brings about a change or effect.

causal argument An argument that claims something is (or is not) the cause of something else.

A **cause** is an event that brings about a change or effect. In **causal arguments** it is claimed that something is (or is not) the cause of something else, as the following argument illustrates:

[You're eating too many French fries] and [you don't exercise]. [You're going to gain weight if you don't change your ways.]

In this argument, the person is making the argument that eating too many French fries (Premise 1) and not exercis-ing (Premise 2) will cause weight gain (Conclusion/Effect). Like other inductive arguments, the conclusion of a causal argument is never 100 percent certain. You may not gain weight if you eat lots of French fries and don't exercise, because you have a metabolic disorder or a tapeworm.

Causal Relationships

The term *cause* in the commonly used premise indicator *because* is a sign of the importance of cause-and-effect relationships in arguments. Many of our everyday decisions rely on this type of inductive reasoning. If we are to have any level of control over our lives, we need to have some understanding of cause-and-effect relations.

Some causal relationships are well established, such as that between temperature and water freezing, and that between malaria and a protozoan parasite transmitted by mosquitoes. In many instances, however, establishing a causal relationship is not as easy as it may first seem. We might confuse cause and effect when the events are ongoing or recurrent and it's not clear which occurred first. Do we have a headache because we're stressed, or are we stressed because we have a headache? Does watching violent movies cause people to commit violent acts, or are people who are more violent already more likely to watch these types of shows?

When we confuse the cause with the effect or assume without sufficient evidence that one thing is the cause of another, we commit the fallacy of questionable cause. We are particularly susceptible to this fallacy because, as we noted in Chapter 5, humans have a tendency to see causality and patterns in random events where no cause-and-effect relationship actually exists. In addition, we are also inclined to believe that we are in control of or the cause of events that

Thinking Outside the Box

ANTONIA NOVELLO, *Medical Problem Solver*

Antonia Novello was born in Fajardo, Puerto Rico, in 1944. She grew up in a poor family. Her father died when she was 8, and she was often ill as a child. Rather than resent her situation or think her future would have to be one of poverty and illness, Novello looked for a solution. As a child, she dreamed of becoming a doctor. She received a bachelor of science degree from the University of Puerto Rico at Rio Piedras, a doctor of medicine degree from the University of Puerto Rico School of Medicine at San Juan in 1970, and a master's degree in public health from John Hopkins School of Hygiene and Public Health in Baltimore in 1982. In 1979, she joined the National Institutes of Health in Bethesda, Maryland. She quickly became known for her ability to think critically about health-care issues and advanced rapidly in her field.

In 1989, President George H. W. Bush nominated Dr. Novello to be U.S. Surgeon General. As Surgeon General, Dr. Novello focused on identifying and reducing the causes of four key public health problems: AIDS, violence, alcohol, and tobacco. She noted that the number of teens and children who smoked had begun to increase dramatically in 1988 when the Joe Camel ads for Camel cigarettes were first introduced. To address this and the other issues, she worked for more education in schools as well as a ban on cigarette and alcohol ads that targeted youth. She also worked to educate the public about the causes of domestic violence and AIDS. Her efforts were in part responsible for bringing about a decrease in domestic violence and a decline in the number of reported cases of AIDS beginning in the mid-1990s.

After serving as surgeon general for 4 years, Dr. Novello went to work for the United Nations Children's Fund (UNICEF).

DISCUSSION QUESTIONS

1. Discuss ways in which Dr. Novello used cause-and-effect inductive reasoning in seeking a solution to the problem of smoking among children and teens.

2. Dr. Novello's childhood hardships contributed to her desire to become a doctor. Discuss the effects of your childhood experiences on your long-term goals.

Serial killer Ted Bundy's murder defense was an example of questionable cause. Like many other sexual predators, once caught, he blamed pornography for his crimes. However, scientists are still uncertain about whether pornography makes people sexually violent or whether people who already have a tendency toward sexual violence are more likely to use pornography.

actually are outside our control. Because of these inborn cognitive errors, we need to be careful before concluding that there is a causal relationship between two events.

Most causal relationships are not as straightforward as that between temperature and water freezing. Instead, several causal factors might be involved. Some events or conditions are causal only if other conditions are present. Other conditions may contribute to a certain result—for example, getting good grades in high school may help you to get into an Ivy League college—but they don't guarantee it.

Correlations

correlation When two events occur together regularly at rates higher than probability.

positive correlation The incidence of one event increases when the second one increases.

negative correlation When the occurrence of one event increases as the other decreases.

When two events occur together regularly at rates higher than probability, the relationship is called a **correlation**. If the incidence of one event increases when the second one increases, there is a **positive correlation**. There is, for example, a positive correlation between the number of cigarettes smoked and the risk of lung cancer. A **negative correlation** exists when the occurrence of one event increases as the other decreases. There is a negative correlation between smoking and age in adults over the age of 18. The older a person is, the less likely he or she is to smoke.

Although a correlation can indicate a causal relationship, as in the case of smoking and lung cancer, it does not

always do so. In the following correlation, it is questionable whether there is a causal relationship as well:

The greater the distance you sit from the front of the classroom, the lower your final grade is likely to be.

The Correlation between Cigarettes Smoked and Lung Cancer

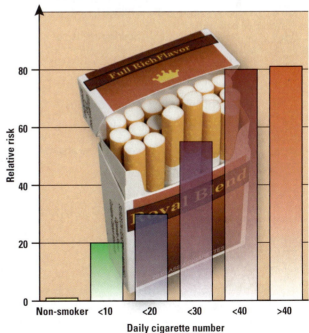

Relative risk

80

60

40

20

0

Non-smoker   <10   <20   <30   <40   >40

Daily cigarette number

Critical Thinking in Action

It's Quitting Time: Nicotine 101—College Students and Smoking

Twenty-six percent of college students smoke. College freshmen are more likely to smoke than are college juniors and seniors. Indeed, ninety percent of adults who smoke began as teenagers. Although college students smoke more than the general public, the smoking rate is almost double among young adults who do not attend college.* These differences in rate of smoking based on age and educational level are due in part to the ability to engage in critical thinking regarding the effects of smoking. People who are inexperienced at critical reasoning are more likely to oversimplify or overlook the complexities of causal relationships. For example, college students who smoke tend to focus on the proximate causal relationships—such as smoking helps them to relax, look sophisticated, or fit in with others—and ignore the long-term or remote effects of smoking, such as cancer, heart disease, and a shortened life. In addition to focusing on causal factors associated with immediate gratification, poor critical thinkers are also more likely to think they have more control than they actually do over factors such as developing cancer or other smoking-related health problems.

DISCUSSION QUESTIONS

1. What thoughts or feelings do you have when you look at the students in the photograph? Discuss the extent to which their smoking influences your perception of them.

2. Although tobacco companies have promised not to target their ads toward children, the majority of cigarette ads are still designed to appeal to people under the age of 24 since they are less likely to have the critical-thinking skills to resist taking up smoking. Critically examine some cigarette ads. What causal relationships are the ads trying to establish in the reader's mind? How effective are the ads in achieving this goal?

*See American Legacy Foundation, "College Students and Smoking," http://www.safeguards .org/content/tobacco/FSCSpdf.

In this argument there is a negative correlation between a student's final grade and his or her distance from the front of the class. However, we cannot assume from the correlation that sitting in the back of the room *causes* a student to get lower grades. The cause and effect could be the opposite. Perhaps poorer students tend to sit in the back of the room. Or perhaps the teacher is more likely to notice the contribution of students who sit in front of the classroom and, hence, give them higher grades.

Establishing Causal Relationships

controlled experiment An experiment in which the sample is randomly divided into an experimental and a control group.

Correlations are often the starting point in determining whether causal relationships exist. To make sure that there aren't other causal factors, or confounding variables, responsible for the correlation or particular effect, scientists use **controlled experiments**.

In a controlled experiment, the sample under study is randomly divided into an experimental group and a control group. The experimental group receives the treatment whose causal effect is under investigation; the control group does not. For example, in a pharmaceutical experiment, the experimental group may receive a pill containing the drug under study, while the control group receives a harmless placebo, such as a sugar pill, that does not contain the drug. Neither group knows whether the pill they are taking contains the drug.

Causal Arguments in Public Policy and Everyday Decision Making

Creating effective public policies and making satisfactory life decisions both depend on being able to correctly infer causal relationships. Critical thinking also involves being able to identify the type of causal relationship that brings about a particular effect. For example, why are African American students more likely than European American students to drop out of college? Why are college freshmen today more likely than were freshman in 1990 to report that they are frequently bored in class? Why did my last two relationships fail? Until we understand the causes of these events, we can't come up with effective solutions.

When making decisions on the basis of causal arguments, it is important that your information be up-to-date. What was true at one time may no longer be the case. Consider the following argument:

> You should make your children sit at least six feet from the television. Sitting too close can damage their eyes.

Televisions first went on sale in the United States in the 1930s. Before the 1950s, televisions emitted levels of radiation that in fact could heighten the risk of eye problems in some people after repeated and extended exposure from sitting too close to the screen. However, this causal relationship no longer holds. Modern televisions are built with shielding that controls the emission of radiation.

Most decisions are not clear-cut. In making a decision where there are both beneficial and harmful effects of a particular action or policy, you need to weigh the harms against the benefits. In public policy, this process is known as **cost–benefit analysis**. Arguments about the legalization of marijuana, such as those at the end of this chapter, often revolve around weighing the benefits of legalizing marijuana against the costs or harms of doing so. In your personal life, this type of analysis is useful in situations such as choosing a career path—do you want to spend 8 years in college and incur heavy debts and have to put off having a family, or do you want a less demanding major and career so that you can put more energy into your personal and family life?

cost–benefit analysis A process where the harmful effects of an action are weighed against the benefits.

Connections

How are controlled experiments used to test scientific hypotheses?

See Chapter 10, p. 312 and Chapter 12, p. 390.

Misperception of causes can also lead to misplacing blame or to the perpetuation of harmful behavior and attitudes. Between 21 and 40 percent of young adults report experiencing at least one incident of physical assault in a heterosexual dating relationship.[23] In the great majority of cases, it involves a man assaulting a woman. What is the cause of dating violence? Most college students believe that it lies in some characteristic of the abuser, such as poor anger control or a history of child abuse. Even more often they see the victim's behavior as the major contributing cause of the assault—"She made me angry," "She asked for it," "She was dressed provocatively," or "I did it because she was flirting with another guy." Date-rape literature that is geared toward teaching women to be more assertive in saying no and programs that focus on anger management in men who are abusers are based on this simplistic assessment of the causes of violence against women.

Those who argue that a woman's behavior is the primary cause of assault are ignoring an important underlying cause of the violence—the cultural power imbalance between men and women. Unfortunately, many of the programs designed to prevent dating violence on campuses steer clear of addressing the inequities in power and instead use sex-neutral materials. These programs have had little effect on the incidence of dating violence. Until power inequalities are addressed as a causal factor in violent heterosexual relationships, these types of prevention programs will remain largely ineffective.

Evaluating Causal Arguments

Knowing how to evaluate causal arguments will help you to make better decisions in your personal life as well as your life as a citizen. The following are four criteria for evaluating a causal argument:

1. The Evidence for a Causal Relationship Should Be Strong. Do your research before jumping to the conclusion that a claim of a causal relationship is correct. The more evidence there is for a causal relationship, the stronger the argument. Be leery of anecdotal evidence. Controlled experiments are one of the best methods for determining if a particular relationship is causal rather than simply a correlation.

2. The Argument Should Not Contain Fallacies. Several types of informal fallacies crop up in causal arguments, the most common of which is the *fallacy of questionable cause,* which occurs when we assume that because one event preceded a second event it was the cause of the second event.

Another common fallacy is the *fallacy of ignorance,* in which we assume that something is the cause simply because no one has proved that it is not or that something is not the cause because no one has proved that it is. A third fallacy that might appear in a causal argument is the *slippery-slope fallacy,* which is committed when the arguer overestimates the influence of a particular cause to bring about a particular effect. For a review of these fallacies, see Chapter 5.

3. The Data Should Be Current and Up-to-Date. Before making a decision or accepting an argument that is based on a causal relationship, you should first make sure that your information is current and up-to-date. A conclusion may be incorrect because a particular causal relationship that was once true may longer hold.

4. The Conclusion Should Not Go Beyond the Premises. The error of a conclusion that goes beyond the premises can occur when we mistake a correlation for a causal relationship or when we attribute more causal power to an event than it actually has over the effect. Unless the cause stated in the premise is a sufficient cause, the term *probably* or a similar qualifying term should be used in the conclusion.

Being able to recognize and analyze causal relationships is an important skill in critical thinking. Like other inductive arguments, casual arguments can never be 100 percent certain. However, being able to determine the degree to which a particular cause brings about an effect can help us to evaluate causal arguments and make better decisions in our lives.

HIGHLIGHTS

EVALUATING CAUSAL ARGUMENTS

1. Determine whether the evidence for a causal relationship is strong.
2. Make sure that the argument does not contain a fallacy.
3. Decide whether the data are current and up-to-date.
4. Make sure that the conclusion does not go beyond the premises.

1. Discuss whether each of the following relationships is a causal relationship or merely a correlation. Discuss how you would go about verifying which type it is.
   a. There has been an increase in the number of twins being born and a later age of marriage in the past decade.
   b. During the past decade there has been a decrease in the size of the Greenland ice cap and an increase in the number of twins being born.
   c. People who are members of a religious organization tend to be happier.
   d. Jason drank nine bottles of beer at the party and is having trouble walking straight.
   e. Jackie and Jamal ate dinner at a sushi bar this evening, and now they are both feeling nauseated.
   f. Almost all of the animals that could flee to higher ground did so shortly before the tsunami struck Indonesia in 2004.

2. The Freshman Survey found that there is declining interaction between white and black students on campuses. Discuss possible causes of this phenomenon.

3. Evaluate the following causal arguments:
   a. The majority of people who die are in bed at the time of their death. Clearly, being in bed increases a person's risk of dying. Therefore, if I sleep on the sofa, I have a better chance of living longer.
   b. There are few women faculty members in the sciences at the Ivy League universities. Women are more likely than men to be discriminated against in hiring. Therefore, discrimination is probably one of the causes of the low number of women faculty members in the sciences at these universities.
   c. "Did you know that young people who use marijuana weekly have double the risk of depression later in life? And that teens aged 12 to 17 who smoke marijuana weekly are three times more likely than non-users to have suicidal thoughts? And if that's not bad enough, marijuana use in some teens has been linked to increased risk for schizophrenia in later years."[24] Therefore, don't let your teens smoke marijuana.
   d. I can't stay home today even though I do have a bad cold because nothing would get done at work and we'll get hopelessly behind in our project. The boss can't get along without me.
   e. I don't have any problem with legalizing marijuana. We all smoked marijuana when I was in college back in the early 1970s and none of us suffered academically because of it.
   f. That's ridiculous. It couldn't have been an alien abduction that caused those marks on your body, because no one has proved that aliens even exist.
   g. Fluorine is effective in the prevention of dental decay.
   h. My brother Mac and his wife Angela are on a three-week Caribbean cruise. I just got a letter from him and he tells me that he and his wife have been enjoying a great sex life ever since he starting putting Matico pepper—something that he bought at Panama—on his food. Whatever is in that stuff must be a powerful aphrodisiac.
   i. I read my horoscope every morning. You should too. My horoscope said that I would meet an interesting stranger today and, sure enough, I *did*!
   j. Marijuana is a "gateway" drug. Therefore, you shouldn't smoke marijuana. If you do, you'll no doubt move on to use cocaine. According to studies, children and teens who have used marijuana are 85 times more likely to use cocaine than those who have never used marijuana.
   k. If we allow hikers in the White Mountains to throw their perishable garbage—such as apple cores or orange peels—into the woods, the wildlife will soon become dependent on humans and unable to survive on their own.

4. Advertisers may manipulate people into placing more weight on a contributory cause than it deserves. For example, in before-and-after ads of people who have had cosmetic surgery or who have used a particular cosmetic or exercise product, the people in the before pictures are often glum, wear no makeup, and have unkempt hair, whereas the people in the after pictures are smiling, are wearing makeup, and have neatly groomed hair. Look in magazines and on the Internet for ads that try to manipulate the reader by placing unwarranted emphasis on particular causal factors.

5. *Essence*, a magazine primarily for black women, has launched a take-back-the-night campaign based on the argument that anti-woman lyrics in rap music contribute to the degradation of women. Its argument is that the lyrics contribute to lower self-esteem in young black women and lead them to engage in riskier sexual behavior. After researching the magazine's claims, present your findings to the class.

6. Write a letter of application for your ideal job. In the letter include at least one argument using generalization, one argument using an analogy, and one causal argument. Underline and label each of the arguments.

Think FIRST >>

- What is a deductive argument?
- What are some of the types of deductive arguments?
- What is a syllogism, and how do we know if it is valid?

even though the earlier search of the stables had failed to turn up the missing horse.

"It's this way, Watson," said Holmes at last . . . "Now, supposing that [Silver Blaze] broke away during or after the tragedy, where could he have gone to? The horse is a very gregarious creature. If left to himself his instincts would have been either to return to King's Pyland or go over to Mapleton. Why would he run wild upon the moor? He surely should have been seen by now . . . He must have gone to King's Pyland or to Mapleton. He is not at King's Pyland. Therefore, he is at Mapleton."[1]

As it turns out, Holmes's deduction is right. The missing racehorse is at Mapleton, the silver blaze on its nose covered over to disguise its appearance.

Sherlock Holmes also solves the "murder" of the horse's trainer through deductive logic. He learns from the stable hand that the guard dog did not bark when Silver Blaze was "stolen" from the stables. Therefore, Holmes concludes, the person who took Silver Blaze must have been familiar to the dog. This eliminated suspects who were strangers. Holmes then eliminates, one by one, the other suspects, leaving only the horse. As Holmes stated in another story: "When you have eliminated the impossible, whatever remains, however improbable, must be the truth."[2] He concludes that the horse must have accidentally killed its trainer when Straker, who was something of a scoundrel, used a surgical knife found in his possession to nick the tendons of Silver Blaze's ham so the horse would develop a slight limp and lose the upcoming race. "Straker had led out the horse to a hollow where his light would be invisible," Holmes explains to his friend Watson. "Once in the hollow, he had got behind the horse and had struck a light; but the creature, frightened at the sudden glare, and with the strange instinct of animals feeling that some mischief was intended, had lashed out, and the steel shoe had struck Straker full on the forehead."[3]

To generations of mystery readers, Sherlock Holmes has epitomized the skilled reasoner.[4] In this chapter we'll learn how to evaluate deductive arguments and practice some of the strategies used by Holmes and others who are skilled in deductive argumentation. In Chapter 8 we will

- Identify the essential attributes of a deductive argument
- Distinguish between validity, invalidity, and soundness in a deductive argument

- Learn how to recognize and evaluate arguments by elimination, mathematical arguments, and arguments from definition

- Study the different types of hypothetical syllogisms, including *modus ponens, modus tollens,* and chain arguments .

- Learn how to recognize standard-form categorical syllogisms

- Evaluate categorical syllogisms using Venn diagrams

- Practice putting arguments that are in ordinary language into standard form

Finally, we will analyze different arguments regarding the justification of the death penalty (capital punishment).

WHAT IS A DEDUCTIVE ARGUMENT?

Unlike inductive arguments, in which the premises offer only support rather than proof for the conclusion, in a valid deductive argument the conclusion necessarily follows from the premises. Deductive arguments sometimes contain words or phrases such as *certainly, definitely, absolutely, conclusively, must be,* and *it necessarily follows that.* For example:

> Marilyn is definitely not a member of the swim team, since no freshmen are members of the swim team and Marilyn is a freshman.

Deductive Reasoning and Syllogisms

Deductive arguments are often, though not always, presented in the form of **syllogisms**, with two supporting premises and a conclusion. For the purpose of analysis, in this chapter the premises and conclusion of a syllogism will usually be presented on separate lines, with the conclusion last.

1. *Premise*: All men are mortal.
2. *Premise*: All fathers are men.
3. *Conclusion*: Therefore, all fathers are mortal.

Deductive arguments may also be diagrammed using the guidelines we learned on pages 177–182. In the case of a syllogism, the two premises are always dependent:

```
( 1 )—( 2 ) (Dependent premises)
        |
        ↓
      ( 3 ) (Conclusion)
```

Some deductive arguments are more involved and may have several dependent premises and subconclusions.

Valid and Invalid Arguments

A deductive argument is **valid** if the form of the argument is such that the conclusion *must* be true *if* the premises are true. The **form** of an argument is determined by its layout or pattern of reasoning. In the above case, the form is

> All X (men) are Y (mortal),
>
> All Z (fathers) are X (men).
>
> Therefore, all Z (fathers) are Y (mortal).

syllogism A deductive argument presented in the form of two supporting premises and a conclusion.

valid A deductive argument where the form is such that the conclusion must be true if the premises are assumed to be true.

form The pattern of reasoning in a deductive argument.

This argument is a valid form no matter what terms we use for X, Y, and Z. Even if the claims we make in the premises are not true, the form of the argument is still valid. Because the form itself is valid, if we substitute different terms for *men, mortal,* and *fathers, and* the premises are still true, then the conclusion *must* be true, as in the following example.

> All cats (X) are mammals (Y).
>
> All tigers (Z) are cats (X).
>
> Therefore, all tigers (Z) are mammals (Y).

A false conclusion does not necessarily mean that a deductive argument is invalid. In the two arguments we've examined so far, the conclusions were both true because the premises were true *and* the form was valid. However, in a valid deductive argument, the conclusion is *necessarily* true *only if* the premises are true. The conclusion of a valid argument can be false only if one of the premises is false. In the following example, which uses the same form as our initial argument, we end up with a false conclusion:

> All men are tall people.
>
> Tom Cruise is a man.
>
> Therefore, Tom Cruise is a tall person.

The conclusion in the above argument is false *only* because there is a false premise, not because the form of the argument is invalid. The first premise, "All men are tall people," is obviously false.

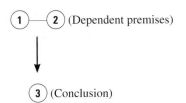

Hot or Not?

Are deductive arguments better than inductive arguments?

But if both premises are true and the conclusion is false, then the argument, by definition, is invalid. For example:

All dogs are mammals.

Some mammals are not poodles.

Therefore, some poodles are not dogs.

It is also possible to have an invalid argument in which the premises are true and the conclusion just happens to be true. Consider this:

No seniors are freshman.

All freshmen are college students.

Therefore, some college students are seniors.

In this argument, the premises and conclusion are true. However, the premises do not logically support the conclusion. The invalidity of a form can be demonstrated by substituting different terms for *senior*, *freshman*, and *college students*, and then seeing whether we can come up with an argument using this form in which the premises are true but the conclusion false, as in the following substitutions:

No fish are dogs.

All dogs are mammals.

Therefore, some mammals are fish.

this chapter we'll learn how to identify the different types of deductive arguments and how to use Venn diagrams to evaluate these arguments for validity.

Sound and Unsound Arguments

sound A deductive argument that is valid and that has true premises.

An argument is **sound** if both of these conditions are present: (1) it is valid *and* (2) the premises are true. The argument on page 241 about fathers being mortal is a sound argument because it is valid and the premises are true. On the other hand, although the argument about Tom Cruise on page 241 uses a valid form, it is not a sound argument because the first premise is false. Invalid arguments, because they do not meet the first criterion, are always unsound.

Logic is primarily concerned with the validity of arguments. As critical thinkers, we are also interested in the soundness of our arguments and in having our premises supported by credible evidence and good reasoning. We have already discussed in previous chapters guidelines for ensuring that our premises are accurate and credible. In

HIGHLIGHTS

DEDUCTIVE ARGUMENTS

Valid   Invalid

Sound Unsound Unsound

Valid argument: The form or layout of the argument is such that if the premises are true, then the conclusion must necessarily be true.

Sound argument: The form of the argument is valid and the premises are true.

EXERCISES 8-1

1. What do you mean when you say that you can prove something with certainty? Give a specific example of a proof from your everyday experience (keep it as brief as possible). What type of logic does the proof use—inductive or deductive?

2. In the story "Silver Blaze," Sherlock Holmes tells Watson that when it comes to the art of reasoning, many people rely on opinion and unsupported assumptions. The difficulty, he maintains, is to detach the

framework of undeniable fact from the embellishments of hearsay and reporters. What do you think he meant by this? Explain using examples from your personal experience.

3. Using substitution, show that the form of each of the following deductive arguments is invalid. Remember: To establish invalidity, your premises must be true when you are substituting new terms for the ones in the original argument.

   a. All fraternity members are men.
      No women are fraternity members.
      Therefore, no women are men.

   b. If it is raining, then it is cloudy.
      It is cloudy.
      Therefore, it is raining.

   c. Some married people are college students.
      All wives are married people.
      Therefore, some wives are college students.

   d. All flowers are plants.
      All orchids are plants.
      Therefore, all orchids are flowers.

   e. If my baby sister is a college student, then she is a high school graduate.
      My baby sister is not a college student.
      Therefore, my baby sister is not a high school graduate.

4. The following arguments are all valid arguments. Determine whether each argument is sound or unsound.

   a. No mammals are birds. Some penguins are mammals. Therefore, some penguins are not birds.

   b. Some twins are sisters. All twins are siblings. Therefore, some siblings are sisters.

   c. All students are dormitory residents. No dormitory residents are birds. Therefore, no birds are students.

   d. If Mexico is in South America, then Mexico is not a country bordering the United States. Mexico is in South America. Therefore, Mexico is a not country bordering the United States.

   e. All millionaires are rich people. Some Americans are not rich people. Therefore, some Americans are not millionaires.

TYPES OF DEDUCTIVE ARGUMENTS

There are several types of deductive arguments. In this section, we'll be looking at three types of deductive arguments used in everyday reasoning:

- Arguments by elimination
- Arguments based on mathematics
- Arguments from definition

Arguments by Elimination

An **argument by elimination** rules out different possibilities until only one possibility remains. In the introduction to this chapter, we saw Sherlock Holmes using an argument by elimination to solve the mystery of what happened to Silver Blaze. He reasoned that the horse had to be at one of the two stables. Since it wasn't at King's Pyland, it must be at Mapleton. In "Thinking Outside the Box: Bo Dietl, Top Cop" on page 244, we profile a New York City detective who is skilled in this type of deductive reasoning.

Like detectives, physicians are trained in deductive logic such as this. In diagnosing an illness, a physician starts by doing a physical examination and, often, by ordering tests. If the examination and test results eliminate the most common explanations of the symptoms, then the physician moves on to check out less obvious possibilities until the mystery is solved. Indeed, Dr. Joseph Bell, one of Sir Arthur Conan Doyle's professors at the University of Edinburgh Medical School, was the inspiration for the character Sherlock Holmes.

Arguments by elimination are frequently used in everyday life. For instance, suppose it is the first day of the semester and you arrive on campus with 10 minutes to spare. You check your schedule and see that your first class, Introduction to Psychology, is in Winthrop Hall. However, on your schedule the room number is smudged and you can't read it. What do you do? It would take too long to get a new schedule. Instead, you head over to Winthrop Hall and check

> **argument by elimination** A deductive argument that rules out different possibilities until only one remains.

out the building directory. It lists twelve room numbers. Nine of them are faculty offices, so you eliminate those nine. The remaining three are classrooms A, B, and C. You go into classroom A and ask some students what class it is. They tell you that it's English Literature. You proceed to classroom B and repeat the process; it turns out to be a course in Business Statistics. When you get to classroom C, you just go inside and take a seat. How do you know this is the correct classroom? Through the use of an argument by elimination. Assuming that your premises are true (that your psychology course is being taught somewhere in Winthrop Hall), the third classroom *by necessity* must be your classroom.

> My class is either in room A, B, or C.
>
> My class is not in room A.
>
> My class is not in room B.
>
> Therefore, my class must be in room C.

Thinking Outside the Box

BO DIETL, *Top Cop*

Bo Dietl is a modern Sherlock Holmes. Born in Queens, New York, in 1950, Dietl wanted a job where he could make a real difference in people's lives. When he learned about the test to get into the police academy, he decided to give it a try.

Dietl is one of the most highly decorated detectives in the history of the New York Police Department. During his career there, he investigated numerous high-profile murders and other felonies, obtaining evidence through research, interviews, and other investigative techniques. He attributes much of his success in solving more than 1,500 felonies to what he calls his "sixth sense—a nontangible feeling good detectives use in solving cases."*

One of the most famous crimes he solved was the 1981 rape and torture of a Catholic nun in an East Harlem convent. Dietl concluded from the evidence that the crime was a burglary gone wrong, rather than a sex crime, thus narrowing his search to people with burglary records. He also knew, from interviewing witnesses, that one of the men was probably tall and that the other had a limp. Days later he received a tip that the two men who committed the crime lived somewhere on 125th Street in Harlem. However, there were hundreds of buildings and thousands of people living on this street. He began the process of elimination by going to the local hangouts and tenements, knocking on doors, giving a brief description of the suspects, and asking questions. He also passed out hundreds of business cards. His efforts paid off, and the two suspects were apprehended and arrested. The 1998 movie *One Tough Cop* is based on Dietl's autobiography of the same name.

DISCUSSION QUESTIONS

1. Discuss how Dietl's method of solving the murder of the nun in the East Harlem convent demonstrates deductive reasoning using an argument by elimination.

2. In Chapter 2 we learned that much of reasoning is unconscious and automatic and that scientists and mathematicians, as well as great detectives, often resolve complex problems without any conscious deliberation. However, to develop this ability, they have spent years consciously resolving problems and mentally rehearsing solutions. Think of a type of problem in your life that you find easy to resolve with little or no conscious deliberation. What factors, such as your familiarity and experience with the problem, contribute to your ease of resolution?

*Conversation with Bo Dietl on August 8, 2005.

In the previous example, there were three alternatives. If there are only two alternatives, the argument is referred to as a **disjunctive syllogism**. A disjunctive syllogism takes one of two forms:

Either A or B.	Either A or B.
Not A.	Not B.
Therefore, B.	Therefore, A.

In determining the whereabouts of Silver Blaze, Sherlock Holmes used a disjunctive syllogism:

> Either Silver Blaze is at King's Pyland or Silver Blaze is at Mapleton.
>
> Silver Blaze is not at King's Pyland.
>
> Therefore, Silver Blaze is at Mapleton.

Here is another example of a disjunctive syllogism:

> Either you finished cleaning your room or you're staying in tonight.
>
> You are not staying in tonight.
>
> Therefore, you finished cleaning your room.

In a disjunctive syllogism, the two alternatives presented in the first premise—clean your room or stay in tonight—must be the only two possibilities. If there are other possible alternatives that have not been stated, then the argument commits the fallacy of false dilemma. For example:

> Either we fight the war on terrorism in Iraq, or we'll have to fight the terrorists here in America on our own soil.
>
> We're fighting the war on terrorism in Iraq.

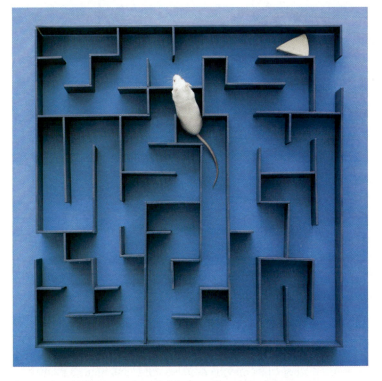

A mouse locates the prize at the end of the maze through the deductive process of elimination.

> Therefore, we won't have to fight the terrorists here in America on our own soil.

In this argument, the two alternatives in the first premise do not exhaust all possible alternatives. Perhaps we could go after individual terrorist cells instead of attacking a country or even negotiate a truce with some of the organizations or governments associated with terrorist activities. Because the argument commits the fallacy of false dilemma, it is not a sound argument.

Politicians may use disjunctive syllogisms in arguing about issues such as staying in Iraq or withdrawing troops, choosing one side of an issue that is not necessarily polarized.

Arguments Based on Mathematics

In an **argument based on mathematics**, the conclusion depends on a mathematical or geometrical calculation. For example:

> **argument based on mathematics** A deductive argument in which the conclusion depends on a mathematical calculation.
>
> **argument from definition** A deductive argument in which the conclusion is true because it is based on a key term in a definition.

My dormitory room is rectangular in shape.

One side measures 11 feet and the side adjacent to it measures 14 feet in length.

Therefore, my room is 154 square feet.

You can also draw conclusions about your new roommate, Chris, even before you meet, using this type of deductive reasoning. You know from e-mail correspondence that Chris plans on trying out for the basketball team and is 6' 2" tall. Since you are 5' 6" tall, you can conclude (assuming that Chris's information is correct) that Chris is 8 inches taller than you.

These are relatively simple examples. Arguments based on mathematics may be quite complex and require mathematical expertise. For example, scientists at NASA needed to calculate the best time to launch the two *Mars Explorer Rovers*—robotic geologists—so that they would arrive at the Red Planet when Mars would be closest to Earth. Mars takes 687 days to complete a revolution of the Sun, compared to 365 days for Earth. Also, because their orbits differ and because Mars has a slightly eccentric orbit, the distance between Mars and Earth varies widely, ranging from about 401 million miles to less than 55 million miles.[5] The two rovers were launched from Cape Canaveral, Florida, in the summer of 2003 and landed on Mars in January 2004. The landing was remarkably smooth, thanks to the deductive reasoning skills of the NASA scientists. The rovers are still transmitting valuable data back to Earth.

Knowing how to make arguments based on mathematics can help you make better-informed decisions, such as calculating the cost of a vacation to Cancun or determining what type of payment method for your educational expenses is most cost-effective. For example, by taking out a student loan instead of using a credit card to pay for your college expenses, you can save thousands of dollars (see "Critical Thinking in Action: Put It on My Tab: Paying College Tuition by Credit Card—a Wise Move?").

Not all arguments using mathematics are deductive. As we learned in Chapter 7, statistical arguments that depend on probability, such as generalizations, are inductive because we can usually conclude from these only that something is *likely*—not certain—to be true (see pages 206–214).

Arguments from Definition

In an **argument from definition**, the conclusion is true because it is based on a key term or essential attribute in a definition. For example:

> Paulo is a father.
> All fathers are men.
> Therefore, Paulo is a man.

This conclusion is necessarily true because a father is, by definition, "a male parent." Being male is an essential attribute of the definition of *father*.

As we discussed in Chapter 3, language is dynamic and definitions may change over time. Consider this example:

> Marilyn and Jessica cannot be married, since a marriage is a union between a man and a woman.

This conclusion of this argument was necessarily true at one time, before states such as Massachusetts, Connecticut, and California legalized same-sex marriage. Today, because the legal definition of marriage is undergoing change, this argument may no longer be sound.

Arguments by elimination, arguments based on mathematics, and arguments from definition are only three types of deductive arguments. In logic, deductive arguments are often written in syllogistic form, such as the disjunctive syllogism. In the following sections, we'll learn about two other types of syllogisms—hypothetical and categorical—and how to evaluate arguments using these forms.

How can an understanding of arguments based on mathematics help you evaluate science news? *See Chapter 11, p. 345–346.*

Connections

Critical Thinking in Action

Put It on My Tab: Paying College Tuition by Credit Card—a Wise Move?

Have you ever wondered why credit-card companies are so keen on signing up college students? In fact, credit-card companies make most of their money from people who don't pay off their balance each month, which is the case with 80 percent of college students. Many parents and students regard credit cards as a convenient way to pay for tuition. However, if you think carrying a balance on a credit card or charging college expenses such as tuition to a credit card is a smart move, consider the following argument, based on mathematics:

> Your credit card bill is $1,900. This includes $1,350 for tuition and fees at your community college and $550 for books for two semesters. Being frugal, you decide not to use your credit card again, since you don't want to get too far into debt. The minimum monthly payment due on your balance is 4 percent, which comes to $75 the first month. You pay the minimum due faithfully each month.
>
> At this rate, how long will it take you to pay off your first-year college expenses? If the annual percentage rate on your card is 17.999 percent, it will take you 7 years to pay off that balance on your credit card![*] In addition to the principal (the amount you charged to the card), you'll have paid a total of $924.29 in interest. This means that the amount of money you actually paid for your first year of college expenses was $2,824![**]

What if you had taken out a student loan instead? The annual interest rate on a federal student loan is about 8 percent. If you put $75 a month toward paying off your student loan, it would take you 2 years and 4 months to pay off the loan. Furthermore, you don't have to start paying off your student loan until you graduate. By taking out a student loan to cover your college expenses instead of charging them to a credit card, you wouldn't have to pay anything for the 2 years while you are in college. Even then you would pay off the loan almost 3 years before you would pay off your credit card—and the total interest would come to only $188. In other words, you paid $736 for the "convenience" of charging your tuition, fees, and books for your first year at community college. Multiply this times 2 or even 4 years, and you could be paying out several thousand dollars just in interest simply because you didn't apply your logic and your critical-thinking skills when deciding how to pay for your college expenses.

DISCUSSION QUESTIONS

1. Some colleges, such as Tufts University and the University of Kentucky, have discontinued credit-card payments for tuition. In part this is because the credit-card companies charge the college a 1 percent to 2 percent fee on each charge, which ultimately gets added on to the cost of tuition. What is the policy at your college or university? Do you agree with the policy? Support your answer.

2. According to *USA Today* (July 26, 2005), people between the ages of 18 and 29 have the poorest credit ratings of all age groups. Why do you think this is the case?

3. Examine your own credit-card use. Has pressure ever been put on you, as a college student, to apply for a credit card? Discuss ways in which you can be more economical in your spending habits.

[*]To calculate what you'll pay on a credit-card balance, as well as what you'll pay if you get a student loan instead, go to http://www.money.cnn.com/tools

[**]For more information on credit card usage and debt among college students, go to http://www.nelliemae.com/aboutus/collegestudentswise052505.html. For information on applying for federal and private college loans, see http://www.collegeboard.com/student/pay/loan-center/414.html.

1. Identify what type of argument each of the following is. If it is a deductive argument, state which type of deductive argument. If the argument is not a deductive argument, explain why. (See Chapter 7 if you need to review inductive arguments.)

   a. Clem either walked to the bookstore or took the shuttle bus. He couldn't have taken the shuttle bus, since it is out of service today. Therefore, he walked to the bookstore.

   b. Hisoka is a psychiatrist. Therefore, Hisoka is a physician.

   c. A 64-ounce carton of mint chocolate chip ice cream costs $5.99. A 16-ounce carton costs $1.49. Therefore, I'll actually save money by buying four 16-ounce cartons instead of one 64-ounce carton.

   d. Either the chief justice remains on the Supreme Court or the president will have to appoint a new Supreme Court justice. Chief Justice William Rehnquist died in 2005. Therefore, the president had to appoint a new chief justice.

   e. Let's see; it's the triplets' third birthday. We have six presents for Matthew, five for Andrew, and one for Derek. If we want to be fair and give each of the triplets the same number of presents, we'll have to take two of the presents we now have set aside for Matthew and one of the presents we have set aside for Andrew and give them to Derek instead.

   f. I was told that Mary is probably in class right now and that if she were not there, to check the library where she spends most of her afternoons. However, Mary isn't in class. So she is most likely at the library.

   g. Jessica is the daughter of Joshua's uncle. Therefore, Jessica and Joshua are cousins.

   h. Either Roy Jones Jr. or John Ruiz won the 2003 world heavyweight champion boxing match in Las Vegas. John Ruiz did not win the fight. Therefore, Roy Jones Jr. was the 2003 world heavyweight champion.

   i. $A = 5$. $B = 8$. $C = -11$. Therefore, $A + B + C = 2$.

   j. Forrest Gump said that his mother always told him that "life was like a box of chocolates. You never know what you're gonna get." Therefore, there's no point in trying to plan for the future, since you can never know what it holds for you.

   k. Professor Cervera told us that he was born in one of the four largest cities in Cuba, but I can't remember which one. I remember him mentioning that it was in the southeastern part of Cuba and that he could see the ocean from his bedroom window. I checked my almanac, and the four largest cities in Cuba are Havana, Santiago de Cuba, Camagüey, and Holguin. He couldn't have been born in Havana, since it is on the northwestern coast of Cuba. Camagüey and Holguin are both located inland. So Professor Cervera must have been born in Santiago de Cuba.

   l. We should ask Latitia if she is interested in working part time in our marketing department. I read that about 80 percent of freshmen said there was at least some chance they'd have to get a job to pay for college expenses. In addition, women are far more likely to have to seek employment during college than are men. Therefore, Latitia will probably be looking for a part-time job to help with her college expenses.

   m. Either the tide is coming in or the tide is going out. The tide is not coming in. Therefore, the tide is going out.

   n. A 2005 Harvard University survey of more than 10,000 teenagers found that 8 percent of girls and 12 percent of boys have used dietary supplements, growth hormones, or anabolic steroids. Therefore, teenage boys are 50 percent more likely than are teenage girls to use products such as steroids to build muscle mass.

2. Suppose Mars is currently 120 million miles from Earth. The *Mars Rover* communicates using radio waves. Radio waves travel at the speed of light—186,000 miles per second. Use an argument based on mathematics to determine how many minutes it will take for a message from the Rover on Mars to reach Mission Control on Earth. Lay out your argument showing the premises and the conclusion.

3. You're having lunch with some friends and mention that you're studying deductive logic. One of your friends rolls his eyes and says, "You can prove anything you want to with logic. Why, you can even prove that cats have thirteen tails. Here's how it works: One cat has one more tail than no cat. And no cat has twelve tails. Therefore, one cat has thirteen tails." How do you respond to your friend's argument?

4. At a picnic, Mike went for soft drinks for Amy, Brian, Lisa, and Bill, as well as for himself. He brought back iced tea, grape juice, Diet Coke, Pepsi, and 7-Up. Using the following information (premises), determine which drink Mike brought for each person:

   Mike doesn't like carbonated drinks.

   Amy would drink either 7-Up or Pepsi.

   Brian likes only sodas.

   Lisa prefers the drink she could put lemon and sugar into.

   Bill likes only clear drinks.[6]

5. If you studied diagramming arguments in Chapter 6, select three of the arguments from exercise 1 on page 183 and diagram them.

6. Go to http://www.justriddlesandmore.com or one of the many other Web sites that have logic games. See how many of the games you can solve. As a class, discuss the extent to which knowledge of deductive arguments, as well as practice in solving these puzzles, makes it easier for you to solve them.

7. How do you pay each year for your tuition and other college expenses? Go to http://www.money.cnn.com/tools and calculate how much it will cost you to pay off your entire debt on the basis of the average you pay each month, or estimate what you will pay monthly after graduation. Given your financial situation, decide what would be the most economical way for you to pay for your college and personal expenses.

8. Next time you visit a store, bring a calculator. Looking at your favorite products, calculate how much you'll save (or lose) by buying a larger size or by buying more than one of the product at a time.

9. *Journal Exercise.* Complete a journal assignment on "Deductive Arguments in Everyday Life." Share some of your examples and insights with the class.

HYPOTHETICAL SYLLOGISMS

Hypothetical thinking involves "If . . . then . . ." reasoning. According to some psychologists, the mental model for hypothetical thinking is built into our brain and enables us to understand rules and predict the consequences of our

---

According to some psychologists, the mental model for hypothetical thinking is built into our brain and enables us to understand rules and predict the consequences of our actions.

---

actions.[7] We'll be looking at the use of hypothetical reasoning in ethics in greater depth in Chapter 9. Hypothetical arguments are also a basic building block of computer programs.[8]

A **hypothetical syllogism** is a form of deductive argument that contains two premises, at least one of which is a hypothetical or conditional "if . . . then" statement.

Hypothetical syllogisms fall into three basic patterns: *modus ponens* (affirming the antecedent), *modus tollens* (denying the consequent), and chain arguments.

Modus Ponens

In a **modus ponens** argument, there is one conditional premise, a second premise that states that the antecedent, or *if* part, of the first premise is true, and a conclusion that asserts the truth of the consequent, or the *then* part, of the first premise. For example:

> **hypothetical syllogism** A deductive argument that contains two premises, at least one of which is a conditional statement.
>
> **modus ponens** A hypothetical syllogism in which the antecedent premise is affirmed by the consequent premise.

Premise 1: *If* I get this raise at work, *then* I can pay off my credit-card bill.

Premise 2: I got the raise at work.

Conclusion: Therefore, I can pay off my credit-card bill.

A valid *modus ponens* argument, like the one above, takes the following form:

If A (antecedent), then B (consequent).

A.

Therefore, B.

Sometimes the term *then* is omitted from the consequent, or second, part of the conditional premise:

If the hurricane hits the Florida Keys, we should evacuate.

modus tollens A hypothetical syllogism in which the antecedent premise is denied by the consequent premise.

The hurricane is hitting the Florida Keys.

Therefore, we should evacuate.

Modus ponens is a valid form of deductive reasoning no matter what terms we substitute for A and B. In other words, if the premises are true, then the conclusion must be true. Thus:

> If Barack Obama is president, then he was born in the United States.
>
> Barack Obama is president.
>
> Therefore, he was born in the United States.

In this case, the first premise is true because the U.S. Constitution requires that the president be "a natural born citizen." Therefore, the argument is a sound argument.

It is important not to deviate from this form in a *modus ponens* argument. If the second premise affirms the consequent (B) rather than the antecedent (A), the argument is invalid and the conclusion may be false, even though the premises are true.

> If Oprah Winfrey is president, then she was born in the United States.
>
> Oprah Winfrey was born in the United States.

Therefore, Oprah Winfrey is president.

But of course, as we all know, Oprah Winfrey is not president of the United States.

Modus Tollens

In a **modus tollens** argument, the second premise denies the consequent, and the conclusion denies the truth of the antecedent:

> If A (antecedent), then B (consequent).
>
> Not B.
>
> Therefore, not A.

Here is an example of a *modus tollens* argument:

> If Morgan is a physician, then she has graduated from college.
>
> Morgan did not graduate from college.
>
> Therefore, Morgan is not a physician.

Like *modus ponens*, *modus tollens* is a valid form of deductive reasoning. No matter what terms we substitute for the antecedent (A) and consequent (B), if the premises are true, then the conclusion must be true.

Critical Thinking in Action

Empty Promises: If This, Then That—Making Promises and Threats Promises are often framed as hypothetical statements: "If you do . . . , then I'll . . ." Because hypothetical syllogisms are deductive arguments, the conclusion necessarily follows from the premises. Therefore, we should think twice about the consequences (conclusion) of having to keep such a promise. For example, when former President George W. Bush first heard that someone had leaked the identity of CIA undercover agent Valerie Plame, he said that if anyone in the White House leaked the name of an undercover agent, the leaker would be fired. When Bush later learned that it might have been his deputy chief of staff, Karl Rove, who leaked her identity, he revised his previous statement to read "If someone committed a crime, they will no longer work in my administration." In doing so, he damaged his credibility.

People may also use hypothetical statements as threats to try to get their children to behave or to get their boyfriend, girlfriend, partner, or spouse to change their ways. For instance, an exasperated parent may say to a boisterous child: "If you keep misbehaving and making so much noise, Mommy is never going to get better." The child, being a typical child, misbehaves again. A few weeks later, the mother dies of cancer. In such a case, the child will likely draw the logical conclusion that she is to blame for her mother's death (never getting better).

DISCUSSION QUESTIONS

1. What is the fundamental difference in meaning between Bush's original statement and his revised statement? Discuss how the conclusions that follow from each of these statements differ from each other and the implication(s) of this difference.
2. Think of a time when you were given an ultimatum in the form of a hypothetical statement in a relationship. What conclusion logically followed from the ultimatum? Did the ultimatum hurt or enhance your relationship? Explain why or why not.

Chain Arguments

Chain arguments A type of hypothetical argument with three or more conditional premises linked together.

Chain arguments are made up of three conditional statements—two premises and one conclusion—linked together.

> If A, then B.
> If B, then C.
> Therefore, if A, then C.

The following is an example of a chain argument:

> If it rains tomorrow, then the beach party is canceled.
> If the beach party is canceled, we're having a party at Rachel's house.
> Therefore, if it rains tomorrow, we're having a party at Rachel's house.

Just as some arguments by elimination are syllogisms and others are not, we can have a longer chain argument that is still a deductive argument but not a syllogism because it has more than two premises. For example:

> If A, then B.
> If B, then C.
> If C, then D.
> If A, then D.

Here is an example of a chain argument with three premises:

> If you don't go to class, you won't pass the final exam.
> If you don't pass the final exam, then you won't pass the course.
> If you don't pass the course, then you won't graduate this year.
> Therefore, if you don't go to class, you won't graduate this year.

A chain argument is valid if it follows the form of using the consequent of the previous premise as the antecedent in the next premise, and so on, with the conclusion using the antecedent from the first premise (A) and the consequent in the last premise (D).

Evaluating Hypothetical Syllogisms for Validity

Not all hypothetical syllogisms, especially ones expressed in everyday language, are laid out in standard syllogistic form. If an argument isn't already in standard form, put it in standard form with the conditional premise first and the conclusion last. In the case of a chain argument, begin by listing the premise containing the antecedent from the conclusion. In 1758, Ben Franklin offered this bit of wisdom in his famous *Poor Richard's Almanac*:

> For want of a Nail the Shoe was lost; For want of a Shoe the Horse was lost; For want of a Horse, the Rider was lost, being overtaken and slain by the enemy; For want of Care about the Horse-Shoe Nail, the Rider is lost.

Let's test the validity of Franklin's argument by writing it out as a hypothetical syllogism, in this case a chain argument:

> If a nail is missing (A), then the horseshoe will be lost (B).
> If the horseshoe is lost (B), then the rider is lost (C).
> If the nail is missing (A), then the rider is lost (C).

By rewriting this passage as a hypothetical syllogism, we can see that it is a valid argument. In some cases, it may be too awkward to restate each use of the antecedents and consequents using the exact same language as in Franklin's argument. In these cases, it is acceptable to use everyday language as long as the meaning remains the same each time it is used. Otherwise, the argument commits the fallacy of equivocation, in which a key term shifts meaning during the course of the argument.

A hypothetical syllogism is valid if it follows one of the forms discussed in this chapter—*modus ponens*, *modus tollens*, or chain argument. The valid forms of the hypothetical syllogisms are listed in "Highlights: Valid Forms of Hypothetical Syllogisms" below. If you are uncertain whether a hypothetical syllogism is valid, you can also try substituting different terms for those used in the argument under evaluation.

Evaluating Hypothetical Syllogisms for Validity and Soundness

Not all valid arguments are sound. As we noted earlier, a deductive argument can be valid by virtue of its form but still be unsound because one of the premises is false. Rewording arguments in ordinary language in the form of a hypothetical syllogism can help you expose the faulty

HIGHLIGHTS

VALID FORMS OF HYPOTHETICAL SYLLOGISMS

Modus Ponens	*Modus Tollens*	*Chain Argument*
If A, then B.	If A, then B.	If A, then B.
A.	Not B.	If B, then C.
Therefore, B.	Therefore, not A.	Therefore, if A, then C.

premises. Suppose you are looking for a new cell phone and find two models that seem to suit your needs—a Sony and a Motorola. Both have similar features, but the Sony costs more than the Motorola. So you think: *The Sony cell phone costs more, so it should be the better phone. I think*

Rewording arguments in ordinary language in the form of a hypothetical syllogism can help you expose the faulty premises.

I'll buy the Sony. Putting your argument in the form of a hypothetical syllogism, we have this:

> If a product is expensive, then it must be good.
>
> This brand of cell phone is expensive.
>
> Therefore, it must be good.

However, the first premise is false. Not all expensive products are good, nor are all inexpensive products of poor quality. Therefore, this is an unsound argument. Unfortunately, many people fall for this line of reasoning. Indeed, some clever marketers have found that when they increase the price of certain items, such as jewelry or clothing, it actually sells better!

Putting an argument on a controversial issue in the form of a hypothetical syllogism can also be helpful in clarify-

ing what's at stake. Consider this argument from the abortion debate:

> If a being is a person (A), then it is morally wrong to kill that being except in self-defense (B).
>
> The fetus is a person (A).
>
> Therefore, it is morally wrong to kill the fetus except in self-defense (B).

Judith Jarvis Thomson, in her essay "A Defense of Abortion" (which we will read at the end of Chapter 9), recognizes the strength of this type of deductive reasoning and acknowledges that she must accept the conclusion if she accepts the premises as true. She also realizes that the only way to reject this argument—since it is a valid argument—is to show that one of the premises is false and that therefore the argument is unsound. Otherwise, she *must* accept the conclusion that abortion is wrong. Since she can't prove that the fetus is not a person, she tentatively accepts the second premise as true. Instead, she questions the first premise, arguing that there may be circumstances when we can kill another person for reasons other than self-defense.

Hypothetical arguments are common in everyday reasoning. In addition to being used in promises and ultimatums (see "Critical Thinking in Action: Empty Promises: If This, Then That—Making Promises and Threats" on page 251), they can be used to spell out the outcomes of certain choices you make in your life: for example, the necessary antecedents you'll need to graduate from college or go on graduate school.

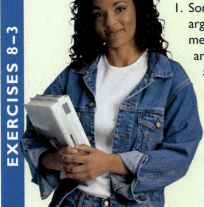

EXERCISES 8-3

1. Sometimes the conclusion and/or one of the premises is unstated in a deductive argument, leaving you to complete the argument. Complete the following arguments, using valid forms of hypothetical syllogisms and stating which form you are using:
   a. If Sam enlists in the army, then he'll have to go to boot camp.
      But Sam does not have to go to boot camp.
   b. "If you look at another woman one more time, I'm going to leave you."
      Mike looks at another woman.
   c. If it didn't rain today, I'd have to water the garden. I won't have to water the garden.
   d. If I call Lisa, then she'll know I'm interested in her.
      If she knows I'm interested in her, then she might notice me more around campus.
   e. If I buy a new car, then I'll have to get a job. I bought a new car.
   f. "If George W. Bush wants to secure his legacy and defy expectations, he'll move quickly to the center and stay there. I'm not holding my breath."[9]
   g. If I take statistics this semester, I'll have enough credits to complete a major in accounting. Then I'll be able to apply to do an MBA in accounting.
   h. If Seattle replaced its conventional buses with hybrid-powered buses, they would save several thousands of gallons of fuel annually. In Seattle, the local transit authority has begun taking delivery of 235 hybrid-powered buses.[10]

2. Identify and evaluate each of the following hypothetical syllogisms. If a syllogism is not valid or is unsound, state why.
   a. Zachary did not get the promotion. If Zachary had gotten the promotion, he would be earning an extra $200 a month. But he is not earning an extra $200 a month.

b. If the temperature of freshwater at sea level is below 32° Fahrenheit, then it is frozen. The water in our neighbor's freshwater pond is below 32° Fahrenheit. Therefore, the water in the pond must be frozen.

c. If a newborn baby is diagnosed with AIDS, then he or she will die during the first year of life. Baby Meg was diagnosed with AIDS when she was born. Therefore, she had less than a year to live.

d. If you love John, you'll listen to what he says. If you listen to what he says, you'll know that John is trying to lose weight. If you know he is trying to lose weight, you'll avoid offering him sweets. If you love John, you'll avoid offering him sweets.

e. If Jamiel is a freshman at State College, then he is a student.
However, Jamiel is not a freshman at State College. Therefore, Jamiel is not a student.

f. You told me that if I helped you pay off this month's rent so you didn't get evicted, then you'd do anything for me that I wanted. Well, I paid your rent. So here's what I want you to do for me: I know you work part time in the registrar's office. So I want you to break into the registrar's office computer system and change my grades to all A's.

g. If you smoke marijuana, then you're breaking the law. You're not smoking marijuana; therefore, you're not breaking the law.

h. If a person is a politician, then he always lies. Joe is a politician. Therefore, Joe denies being a politician.

i. If a person commits a murder in Rhode Island, he or she cannot be given the death penalty. Craig Price murdered three women in Rhode Island. Craig Price cannot be given the death penalty.

j. If John is a Leo, then John is brave. John is a Leo. Therefore, John is brave.

k. If I become a member of the band Alien Autopsy, then I'll probably have an opportunity to play my steel drums in front of a live audience. If I have an opportunity to play my steel drums in front of a live audience, then I'm more likely to be noticed by a talent scout. Therefore, if I become a member of the band Alien Autopsy, I'm more likely to be noticed by a talent scout.

3. Think of an issue or goal that is important in your life. Write a hypothetical syllogism related to the issue or goal. Evaluate the syllogism.

4. Go to http://www.mysterymind.com/games/ for links to games requiring deductive logic. Select and play two or three of the games. What deductive skills were required for you to win the game? Be specific. Did practicing these skills make you better at the game? How might these skills translate into making decisions or solving problems in your everyday life?

5. Select a game requiring deductive logic and write a one- to two-page paper addressing the questions in exercise 4 above.

CATEGORICAL SYLLOGISMS

Categorical syllogisms are a type of deductive argument that categorizes or sorts things into specific classes, such as mammals, students, or countries. A categorical syllogism is composed of a conclusion, two premises, and three terms, each of which occurs exactly twice in two of the three propositions. In the following categorical syllogism, each of the three classes or terms—in this case "mammals," "cats," and "tigers"—appears in two propositions.

> categorical syllogism A deductive argument with two premises and three terms, each of which occurs exactly twice in two of the three propositions.

> All tigers are cats.
> Some mammals are not cats.
> Therefore, some mammals are not tigers.

Did You Know

Categorical syllogisms can be written in any of 256 standard forms or combinations. Although 256 may seem to be an unwieldy number, putting syllogisms in standard form greatly simplifies the process of evaluations.

Standard-Form Categorical Syllogisms

Categorical syllogisms can be written in any of 256 standard forms or combinations. Although 256 may seem to be an unwieldy number, putting syllogisms in standard form greatly simplifies the process of evaluation, as we'll see later.

When a categorical syllogism is put into standard form, the terms in the conclusion are given the label *S* for the

subject (S) term In a categorical syllogism, the term that appears first in the conclusion.

predicate (P) term In a categorical syllogism, the term that appears second in the conclusion.

middle (M) term In a categorical syllogism, the term that appears once in each of the premises.

major term The predicate (P) term in a categorical syllogism.

major premise The premise in a categorical syllogism that contains the predicate term.

minor term The subject (S) term in categorical syllogism.

minor premise The premise in a categorical syllogism that contains the subject term.

subject of the conclusion and *P* for the **predicate** of the conclusion. The term that occurs only in the two premises is labeled *M*, for **middle term**. The premise containing the *P* term from the conclusion is listed first, and the premise with the *S* term is listed second. Because it is found in the first premise, the *P* term is referred to as the **major term**, and the premise in which it appears is the **major premise**. The *S* term is also known as the **minor term**, and the premise in which it appears is called the **minor premise**. In addition, the verb in a standard-form categorical syllogism is always a form of the verb *to be*, such as *is* or *are*. Using these guidelines, the above argument written in standard form would look like this:

All tigers (*P*) are cats (*M*).

Some mammals (*S*) are not cats (*M*).

Therefore, some mammals (*S*) are not tigers (*P*).

In other words:

All *P* are *M*.

Some *S* are not *M*.

Therefore, some *S* are not *P*.

As with hypothetical syllogisms, if the form of a categorical syllogism is valid, as it is in this case, the argument will be valid no matter what terms we substitute for *S*, *P*, and *M*. If the form is valid and the premises are true, the conclusion is necessarily true.

Quantity and Quality

quantity Whether a categorical proposition is universal or particular.

quality Whether a categorical proposition is positive or negative.

qualifier A term such as *all*, *no*, or *not*, which indicates whether a proposition is affirmative or negative.

Each proposition in a standard-form categorical syllogism is written in one of four forms, determined on the basis of its **quantity** (universal or particular) and **quality** (affirmative or negative). If a proposition refers to *every* member of a class, then the quantity is universal. "All *S* are *P*" and "No *S* are *P*" are universal propositions. If a proposition refers only to *some* members of the class, then it is particular. "Some *S* are *P*" and "Some *S* are not *P*" are particular propositions. The **qualifier** is a

term such as "all," "no," or "not," which indicates whether a preposition is either affirmative or negative. "No *S* are *P*" and "Some *S* are not *P*" are negative propositions.

The quantity and quality of the proposition is determined by its form, not by which terms (*S*, *P*, and *M*) appear as subject and predicate. For example, "All *P* are *M*" and "No *M* are *S*" are both universal propositions.

Quality and Quantity of Standard-Form Propositions

Universal affirmative:	All *S* are *P* (e.g., All oak trees are plants).
Universal negative:	No *S* are *P* (e.g., No squirrels are fish).
Particular affirmative:	Some *S* are *P* (e.g., Some Americans are Muslim).
Particular negative:	Some *S* are not *P* (e.g., Some nurses are not women).

Diagramming Propositions with Venn Diagrams

Each of the four types of propositions can be represented using a Venn diagram, in which each term appears as a circle. The class of *S*, for example, can be represented as follows:

Venn diagram A visual representation of a categorical syllogism used to determine the validity of the syllogism.

If there are no members of the class *S* (*S* = 0), the circle is shaded in. The following diagram states that there are no members of the class "unicorns," which is represented here by the term *S*.

If there is at least one member of the class (*S* ≠ 0), you put an *X* in the circle. For example, to diagram the class "dogs," we would use an *X*, since there exists at least one dog in the world.

You can follow the same procedure for diagramming any other class represented in a syllogism. Using this method, you can represent each of the four types of propositions in a categorical syllogism using two overlapping circles, since each proposition has two terms. The intersection of the two classes S and P is the class SP, which contains all things that are members of both classes S and P.

The universal propositions are represented using shading. For example, "All S are P" says essentially the same thing as "There is no such thing as an S that is not a P." To represent this, you shade in the part of the S circle that does not overlap with the P circle.

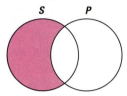

The proposition "No S are P" states that the class SP is empty, or $SP = 0$. To represent this proposition, you shade in the area where the two circles overlap.

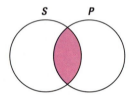

The particular propositions are represented by using an X. The proposition "Some S are P" states that there is at least one member of the class S that is also a member of the class P. To diagram this, you put an X in the area where the two circles overlap.

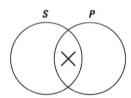

The proposition "Some S are not P" tells us that there is at least one S that is not a member of the class P. To diagram this proposition, you put an X in the S circle where it does not overlap the P circle.

If the proposition stated "Some P are not S," you would instead put the X in the P circle where it does not overlap the S circle.

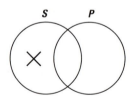

Only the Venn diagrams for particular propositions state that there exist members in a class. Venn diagrams for universal propositions, in contrast, only show what doesn't exist. For instance, when we say something like "All tyrannosauruses are dinosaurs," we're not implying that tyrannosauruses actually still exist, just that there is (and was) no such thing as a tyrannosaurus that is *not* a dinosaur.

Venn diagrams engage our spatial reasoning ability and help us to visualize relationships between classes of things.

Venn diagrams can be used for evaluating the validity of a categorical syllogism. As we noted earlier, Venn diagrams use overlapping circles to represent the terms in a proposition. Since there are three terms (S, P, and M) in a syllogism, you'll need to use three overlapping circles, one for each term, to evaluate a categorical syllogism. To do this, first draw the intersecting circles representing the S and P terms. Then draw the circle representing the M term below so that it intersects both the S and P circles. The area where the S and P circles overlap makes up the class SP, the area where the S and M circles overlap makes up the class SM, and the area where the P and M circles overlap makes up the class PM. The area where all three circles overlap is the class SPM.

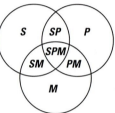

Before diagramming a syllogism, you will need to identify the terms in each proposition. Remember, always start with the conclusion. The first term in the conclusion is S and the second term is P.

$$\begin{array}{cc} P & M \\ \text{No (dogs) are (cats).} & \end{array}$$

$$\begin{array}{cc} S & M \\ \text{Some (mammals) are (cats).} & \end{array}$$

$$\begin{array}{cc} S & P \\ \text{Therefore, some (mammals) are not (dogs).} \end{array}$$

The next step is to diagram the two premises, using the techniques you learned on page 206. If one of the premises is a universal proposition, start by diagramming that premise. In this case, the first premise, "No P are M," is a universal proposition. To diagram it, you are going to use only the P and M circles in the Venn diagram. The proposition "No P are M" tells you that the class PM—the area where the P (dogs) and the M (cats) circles intersect—is empty. In other words, there are no members of the class PM or, in this case, there is no such being as a dog that is a cat. To diagram this, shade in the area where the P and M circles intersect.

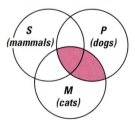

Now diagram the remaining premise "Some S are M." This proposition tells you that there is at least one member of the class S. In other words, there is at least one S (mammal)

that is also an *M* (cat). Because particular statements have existential import, an *X* is used to indicate the existence of at least one member of a class. To diagram this premise, you put an *X* in the area *SM* where the *S* and *M* circles intersect.

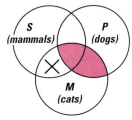

The final step is to determine if the circles contain the diagram for the conclusion, which, in this case, is "Some *S* are not *P*." The conclusion states that there is at least one *S* (cat) that is not a member of the class *P* (dogs). Diagrammed, this means that there is an *X* in the *S* circle where it does not intersect *P*. Checking this against the diagram of the premises above, we find that there is in fact an *X* in this area. Therefore, this and all other syllogisms of this form are valid. In other words, all syllogisms are valid where the first premise is a universal negative, the second premise is a particular affirmative, the conclusion is a particular negative, and the middle term appears as the predicate term in both premises.

The following syllogism has already been broken down into its three terms for you:

 M   *P*
Some (college students) are (smokers of marijuana).
 S   *M*
All (freshmen) are (college students).
      S   *P*
Therefore, some (freshmen) are (smokers of marijuana).

In this syllogism the first premise is a particular proposition and the second premise a universal proposition. Therefore, you start by diagramming the second premise. The premise "All *S* are *M*" states that there is no *S* that is not a member of the class *M*. Using only the *S* and *M* circles, shade in the area where the *S* circle does not intersect the *M* circle to show that there are no freshmen who are not also college students.

Next, working only with the *M* and *P* circles, diagram the other premise, "Some *M* are *P*." Place an *X* in the area *MP* where the *M* and *P* circles intersect. Since the *S* circle makes a line through the intersection, draw the *X* on the line to indicate that an *M* (college student) who is a member of the class *P* (smoker of marijuana) may be on either side of this line.

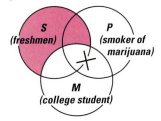

The conclusion states that "some freshmen are smokers of marijuana." In other words, there is an *X* in the class *SP* where the *S* circle and the *P* circle overlap. Looking at the diagram of the premises, you can see that the conclusion is not contained in the premises, since all the premises tell us is that there is a member of the class *MP* who may or may not also be a member of the class *SP*. Because the *X* in the premises falls on the line, it is possible that there is a freshman who smokes marijuana, but we can't be sure, since the *X* in the premises may be either in the *SP* circle or only in the *P* circle. Therefore, this argument and all syllogisms that follow this form are invalid.

In using Venn diagrams to determine the validity of a syllogism with two universal or two particular premises, you can start by diagramming either premise. The following is an argument with two universal premises. Begin by labeling the terms in the argument:

 P   *M*
All (Americans) are (humans).
 S   *M*
No (space aliens) are (humans).
      S   *P*
Therefore, no (space aliens) are (Americans).

The first premise states that there are no members of the class *P* (Americans) that are not members of the class *M* (humans). To diagram this, you shade in the area of *P* that does not overlap the *M* circle. The second premise states that there are no *S* (space aliens) that are *M* (humans). Therefore, the area *SM* (human space aliens) is an empty class. To diagram this, you shade in the space where the *S* and the *M* circles overlap, like this:

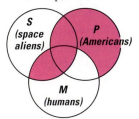

The conclusion states that there are no members of the class *SP* (American space aliens). For this syllogism to be valid, the diagram of the premises must show that *SP* is an empty class. In fact, the area *SP* is shaded in. Therefore, this argument and all syllogisms that follow this form are valid.

Let's look at one last syllogism with two particular premises.

 M   *P*
Some (ranchers) are not (horse lovers).
 S   *M*
Some (Texans) are (ranchers).
      S   *P*
Therefore, some (Texans) are not (horse lovers).

The first premise states that there is at least one rancher who is not a horse lover. To diagram this, you place an *X* in the *M* circle where it does not intersect the *P* circle. Remember to put the *X* on that part of the *S* circle where it intersects the *M* circle, since you can't tell from this premise whether this rancher is a Texan. The second premise states that there is at least one Texan (*S*) who is a rancher (*M*). But since this premise does not tell you whether this Texan is a horse lover, put the *X* on the line in the *S* circle where the *P* circle intersects the *M* circle, since we're not sure which side of the line the Texan belongs on.

S (Texans)
P (horse-lovers)
M (rancher)

Do the premises support the conclusion? To diagram the conclusion, put an *X* on the line where *S* intersects *M* but not *P*. The conclusion is invalid because the *X*'s from the two premises may be only in the *P* and *M* circles. Therefore, this argument is invalid—as are all arguments of this form.

Putting an argument in the form of a categorical syllogism makes it easier for you to evaluate its validity, either by checking it for formal fallacies or by drawing Venn diagrams. Many everyday arguments can be put into standard-form categorical syllogisms, as discussed in the next section.

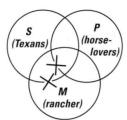

1. For each of the following propositions, indicate the form of the proposition (universal affirmative, universal negative, particular affirmative, or particular negative), and then draw a Venn diagram for each proposition.
   a. All beagles are dogs.
   b. Some Democrats are socialists.
   c. No android is a natural object.
   d. Some college students are retired people.
   e. Some scientists are not atheists.
   f. No atheist is a person who believes in God.
   g. All suns are stars.
   h. Some people who smoke cigarettes are people who get lung cancer.
   i. Some drugs are not illegal substances.
   j. All professional basketball players are people who are more than 5 feet tall.

2. Using Venn diagrams, determine which of the following syllogisms are valid and which are invalid.
   a. All published authors are writers.
      Some writers are professors.
      Therefore, some professors are published authors.
   b. Some scholars are not geniuses.
      Some scholars are football players.
      Therefore, some football players are not geniuses.
   c. Some Latinos are Republicans.
      All Republicans are American citizens.
      Therefore, some American citizens are not Latinos.
   d. All members of fraternities are male.
      Some college students are not male.
      Therefore, some college students are not members of fraternities.
   e. Some terrorists are citizens.
      No cats are citizens.
      Therefore, no cats are terrorists.
   f. Some UFO sightings are hallucinations.
      Some UFO sightings are sightings of airplanes.
      Therefore, some sightings of airplanes are hallucinations.
   g. No nations that allow capital punishment are members of the European Union.
      No European nations are nations that allow capital punishment.
      Therefore, all European nations are members of the European Union.
   h. Some Olympic athletes are professional athletes.
      No high school cheerleaders are professional athletes.
      Therefore, no high school cheerleaders are Olympic athletes.
   i. Some actors are comedians.
      All comedians are funny people.
      Therefore, some funny people are actors.

j. Some scientists are believers in UFOs.
No irrational people are scientists.
Therefore, some irrational people are not believers in UFOs.
k. Some women are mothers.
No women are men.
Therefore, no men are mothers.
l. All pacifists are opponents of capital punishment.
All pacifists are opponents of war.
Therefore, all opponents of war are opponents of capital punishment.

TRANSLATING ORDINARY ARGUMENTS INTO STANDARD FORM

Most of the deductive arguments that we hear or read in our everyday lives are not expressed as standard-form syllogisms. For example, you and your roommate are discussing whether to buy hamburgers or veggie burgers for a picnic you're throwing. She wants to buy veggie burgers, arguing that "it's wrong to eat meat from animals that are capable of reason, such as cows." Is this a valid argument? To answer this question, you first need to rewrite her argument as a standard-form categorical syllogism with three propositions.

Rewriting Everyday Propositions in Standard Form

Usually the easiest place to start is by identifying the conclusion and rewriting it in standard form. In your roommate's argument, she's trying to convince you that it's wrong to eat meat from animals that are capable of reason. To translate this into a standard-form proposition, ask yourself: "What is the quantity (universal or particular) and the quality (positive or negative) of this statement?" Since her conclusion is referring to only some instances of meat eating, the quantity is particular. The quality of her conclusion is positive—she is saying that it *is* wrong to eat meat, as opposed to *is not*. Her conclusion, therefore, will read something like this: "Some meat-eating is wrong."

However, this proposition still isn't in standard form. Standard-form propositions have a subject term and a predicate term that are both either nouns or noun clauses and that are connected by a form of the verb *to be*. In this case, the predicate term *wrong* is an adjective. You can rewrite the adjective as a noun phrase by rewording it as *a wrongful act*. The conclusion is now written as a standard-form proposition:

$$S \qquad\qquad P$$
Some (meat-eating) is (a wrongful act).

Determining the quality and quantity of a proposition is not always as straightforward as in the above example. In some instances, you will need to examine the context of the proposition to determine the quality. Consider the following two statements:

- Teenagers have more automobile crashes.

- Kangaroos are marsupials.

In the first example, does the speaker mean *all* teenagers or only *some* teenagers? In all likelihood, the speaker is referring to only some teenagers. Translating the statement into a standard-form proposition, you have this:

Some (teenagers) are (people who have more automobile crashes than the average driver).

When people intend or interpret statements such as this to be universal, or about *all* young people, they commit the *fallacy of hasty generalization*. We cannot go from a statement about the reckless driving habits of some to a generalization about all teenagers, since many teenagers are safe drivers and some older drivers are a danger on the road.

In the second example, the speaker is making a statement about all kangaroos, since, by definition, a kangaroo is a marsupial. Consequently, this proposition can be translated as a universal positive (*A*) proposition:

All kangaroos are marsupials.

Phrases in ordinary language that indicate that a proposition is universal include the following:

Every *S* is a *P*.	Each *S* is a *P*.
Only *P* are *S*.	*S* are all *P*.
No *P* are *S*.	Whatever is an *S* is a *P*.
Any *S* is a *P*.	If anything is an *S*, then it is a *P*.

Phrases that indicate that a proposition is particular include these:

Some *S* are *P*.	A few *S* are *P*.
Many *S* are *P*.	Most *S* are not *P*.
Not all *S* are *P*.	With few exceptions, *S* are *P*.

Quantity (positive or negative) is usually easier to determine than quality. When the quantity of a proposition is negative, one of the following terms almost always appears somewhere in the original proposition: *no, nothing, not, none*. However, this isn't a hard-and-fast rule. The term *no* may also appear in a universal positive statement, as in this example:

> No valid syllogisms are syllogisms with two negative premises.

Translated into standard form, this statement becomes a universal positive proposition:

> All syllogisms with two negative premises are invalid syllogisms.

Therefore it is important, when translating a statement into a standard-form proposition, to go back and check to make sure it says the same thing as the original statement.

Identifying the Three Terms in the Argument

The next step in translating arguments in ordinary language into standard-form categorical syllogisms is to identify the three terms. If you have already translated the conclusion into a standard-form proposition, you have identified two of the terms.

In the opening argument about whether to buy veggie burgers or hamburgers, we recast the conclusion as a standard-form proposition: "Some (meat-eating) is (a wrongful act)." You will notice that there is a term from the original argument that does not appear in the conclusion: "Animals that are capable of reason, such as cows." This term is the middle term (*M*) in the argument. In some ordinary arguments, not all the propositions are explicitly stated. In this case, there is a missing premise that might be worded something like this: "It is wrong to eat animals that are capable of reason." That proposition is universal and affirmative. Putting it in standard form, you have:

> All (killing of animals that are capable of reason, such as cows,) is (a wrongful act).

The second premise can be written as a particular affirmative proposition, since your roommate is saying that only particular types of meat-eating, rather than all meat-eating, are wrong.

> Some (meat-eating) is (killing of animals that are capable of reason, such as cows).

Although the verb *involves* would be better English usage here, remember that the verb in a syllogism must be a form of the verb *to be*. Although the wording of this premise is a little awkward, it will do for the purpose of evaluation.

Sometimes there are more than three terms in an ordinary argument. In these cases you will need to reduce the terms to three. There are several strategies for doing so. If there are two terms that are synonyms, use the same term for both. If there are two terms that are antonyms, or mean the opposite of each other, reduce them to one term by

using *not* in front of the antonym. When there are terms that are not essential to the argument, you can simply eliminate them. Consider the following argument:

> Not all birds migrate. The spot-breasted oriole, for example, lives on the east coast of Florida year-round.

There are four terms in this argument: *birds, beings that migrate, spot-breasted oriole,* and *beings that live on the east coast of Florida year-round.* In this argument you can combine the second and fourth terms into one by rewriting *beings that live on the east coast of Florida year-round* as *not beings that migrate.* The fact that they live in Florida is not essential to the argument and can be eliminated. The argument now has three terms:

> No (spot-breasted orioles) are (beings that migrate).
> All (spot-breasted orioles) are (birds).
> Therefore, some (birds) are not (beings that migrate).

Putting the Argument into Standard Form

After you have identified the three terms and translated all of the propositions into standard form, you can rewrite the argument as a standard-form categorical syllogism with the major premise first, the minor premise next, and finally the conclusion. Going back to our original argument, we have:

> All (killing of animals that are capable of reason, such as cows,) is a (wrongful act).

Some (meat eating) is (killing of animals that are capable of reason, such as cows).

Therefore, some (meat-eating) is a (wrongful act).

Once you've set up the argument as a standard-form syllogism, you can easily determine whether it is valid, using a Venn diagram. In this case, it is a valid syllogistic form. In other words, if you agree with the premises, you *must* accept the conclusion. However, you may disagree with the conclusion, even though the argument is valid—but only if you believe that one of the premises is false and the argument therefore unsound. For example, you may argue that the second premise is untrue because only humans are capable of reason and therefore no animals we eat for meat

are beings capable of reason. But you'll need to provide evidence to support your position.

Recognizing and evaluating deductive arguments are important skills for everyday decision-making. Using mathematical arguments, arguments by elimination, arguments based on definition, hypothetical syllogisms, and chain arguments, you can use *known* information to discover—with absolute certainty—*unknown* information. Additionally, ordinary arguments used by other people can be translated into standard form to be analyzed for soundness and validity. In Chapter 9, we will discuss the use of critical thinking in moral decision making and in the discussion of ethical issues.

EXERCISES 8-5

1. Translate the following arguments into standard-form categorical syllogisms. Identify the form of each syllogism. Determine the validity of each syllogism using Venn diagrams.
   a. "Since man is made in the image of God, then the taking of a man's life is the destruction of the most precious and the most holy thing in the world."[11]
   b. The majority of college students are civic-minded, since most college students do some sort of volunteer work and since people who volunteer tend to be civic-minded.
   c. Not everyone who smokes marijuana goes on to use hard drugs. All of my college roommates smoked marijuana, and none of them went on to use hard drugs.
   d. Although it's true that most Hispanics are Democrats, this isn't always the case. Cubans, for example, are more likely to vote Republican.
   e. Not all parents are heterosexual. I know at least half a dozen gay and lesbian parents.
   f. Teams that wear red uniforms are more likely to win than those who don't. Our team, the Blue Jays, is certain to lose the tournament tonight because we wear blue uniforms, while the opposing team, the Cardinals, will be wearing red uniforms.
   g. Many of the abnormal weather patterns we've been experiencing in the past decade are a result of global warming. We've experienced an unprecedented number of droughts and heat spells during the past decade. Many of them are no doubt due to global warming.
   h. Despite what you may have heard, not all college professors are liberals. Some of the professors I know actually voted in favor of free-speech zones on campus, which is something no liberals would do.

2. Find an argument on the Internet or in a newspaper, magazine, or book. Translate the argument into a standard-form categorical syllogism.

Think AGAIN >>

1. What is a deductive argument?
   - A deductive argument is one in which its conclusion necessarily follows from the premises if the argument is sound. A sound argument is one in which the premises are true and the form of the argument is valid.

2. What are some of the types of deductive arguments?
   - There are many types of deductive arguments, including arguments by elimination, mathematical arguments, arguments from definition, hypothetical syllogisms, and categorical syllogisms.

3. What is a syllogism, and how do we know if it is valid?
   - A syllogism is a deductive argument with exactly two premises and one conclusion. To be valid, the different types of syllogisms have to conform to particular forms. Venn diagrams can be used to determine if the form of a categorical syllogism is valid.

Think
FIRST

- How does conscience help us to make moral decisions?
- What is the stage theory regarding the development of moral reasoning?
- In what ways can the different moral theories help us in formulating moral arguments?

 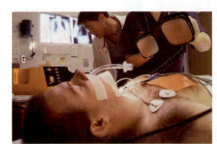 

Olympic and professional athletes are not the only athletes who use performance-enhancing drugs. Although 2.7 percent of college athletes in men's basketball and 1.5 percent in women's basketball *admit* to using anabolic steroids,[3] estimates of how many college athletes *actually* use steroids run much higher. Despite the harms associated with prolonged use, in recent years there has been an upward trend in steroid use among college and high school athletes.[4]

Suppose you are the captain and star player on your college basketball team, and you've made it into the finals. A wealthy entrepreneur, who is an avid basketball fan and alumnus of your college, has promised to make a $60 million donation to your school *if* your team wins the finals. Your college desperately needs the money. It is currently in serious financial trouble and has been forced to lay off faculty members and cut back on academic programs.

A few weeks before the game, the same entrepreneur offers you a banned performance-enhancing substance known as tetrahydrogestrinone, or THG, one of the new "designer" steroids. When you express concern about getting caught—since your college occasionally does random testing of athletes—he assures you that you won't get caught, since THG has been cloaked to avoid detection by drug tests. He also tells you that he will make a $6 million donation, one-tenth of the original amount, even if your team loses, but only on the condition that you take the drug for the next 2 weeks and give the game your best effort. The team you are playing has won the finals the past 3 years in a row. Also, unlike your college, the other team has no random drug-testing program for basketball players.

What should you do? Your school desperately needs the money, and you could do a lot of good for your school by taking the drug. On the other hand, what about possible physical harms of the steroids to yourself? Also, would it be fair to the other team or to sports fans if you had an advantage because of taking this banned drug?

This situation is an example of a moral conflict that requires you to engage in moral reasoning. We are confronted with moral decisions every day of our lives. Fortunately, most of these decisions are fairly straightforward. For the most part we keep promises, don't steal someone else's laptop or wallet when their backs are turned, wait our turn in line, restrain ourselves from injuring people who are aggravating us, offer a helping hand to those in need, and are kind to our friends and family. Although we may be unaware of having consciously made these decisions, we have nonetheless engaged in moral reasoning.

Perhaps in no other area are people so prone to engage in rhetoric and resistance as in debates over controversial moral issues such as capital punishment, stem-cell research, abortion, war, or euthanasia. Skill in critical thinking can help us to evaluate moral issues from multiple perspectives as well as break through patterns of resistance. In this chapter, we'll be learning how to make moral decisions in our everyday lives as well as how to think about and discuss controversial moral issues.

In Chapter 9 we will

- Examine the relationship between morality and happiness

- Distinguish between moral values and nonmoral values

- Learn about the role of conscience and moral sentiments in moral decision making

- Study the stages in the development of moral reasoning

- Examine moral reasoning in college students

- Evaluate the different moral theories

- Learn how to recognize and construct moral arguments

- Apply strategies for resolving moral dilemmas

Finally, we will read and evaluate arguments regarding the morality of abortion and work toward seeking possible resolutions of the issue.

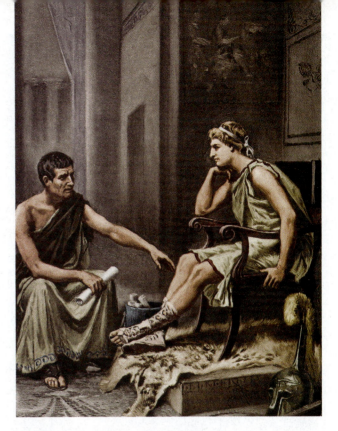

Aristotle, shown on left, taught that morality is the most fundamental expression of our rational nature and that we are happiest when we put moral values above nonmoral values.

WHAT IS MORAL REASONING?

We engage in **moral reasoning** when we make a decision about what we ought or ought not to do, or about what is the most reasonable or just position or policy regarding a particular issue. Effective moral decision making depends on good critical-thinking skills, familiarity with basic moral values, and the motivating force of moral sentiments.

Moral Values and Happiness

Aristotle, the ancient Greek philosopher, believed that morality is the most fundamental expression of our rational human nature. It is through being moral, he argued, that we are happiest. The association of morality with happiness and a sense of well-being is found in moral philosophies throughout the world.

Studies support the claim that people who put moral values above nonmoral concerns are happier and more self-fulfilled.[5] **Moral values** are those that benefit yourself and others and are worthwhile for their own sake. They include altruism, compassion, tolerance, forgiveness, and justice.

Nonmoral (instrumental) values are goal-oriented. They are a means (an instrument) to an end we wish to achieve. Nonmoral values include independence, prestige, fame, popularity, and wealth, which we desire for the most part because we believe they will bring us greater happiness.

When buying a car, a person who places nonmoral values above moral values might base his or her decision on stylishness, cost of the car, comfort, and a desire to impress other people. A person who places moral values above nonmoral values, in contrast, might place more emphasis on fuel efficiency and environmental friendliness and less emphasis on factors such as cost. Although many Americans regard nonmoral values such as career success, financial prosperity, and flashy materialism as the means to happiness, there is in fact little correlation between prosperity or level of income and happiness, except at the lowest levels of income. In other words, in the long run, winning the lottery probably isn't going to make you any happier, unless you are desperately poor to start with.

In addition, there is a positive correlation between level of moral reasoning and critical-thinking ability.[6] This is not surprising,

moral reasoning Used when a decision is made about what we ought or ought not to do.

moral values Values that benefit oneself and others and are worthwhile for their own sake.

nonmoral (instrumental) values Values that are goal oriented—a means to an end to be achieved.

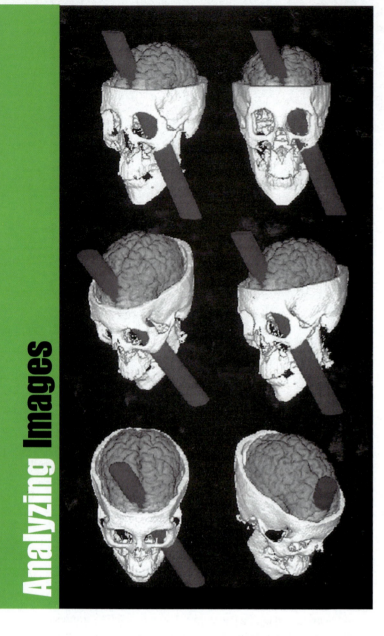

Analyzing Images

THE BRAIN AND MORAL REASONING: THE CASE OF PHINEAS P. GAGE
The frontal lobe cortex in the brain plays a key role in moral decision making. One of the most fascinating studies on the relation between the brain and morality was carried out by a team of scientists on the skull of a nineteenth-century railroad worker, Phineas P. Gage. In 1848, Gage was working on a railway track in Vermont when one of the explosives accidentally went off. The impact sent a long metal rod through his skull just behind his left eye. The rod passed through the frontal lobes of his brain and landed several yards away. This photo shows computer-generated images of the most likely path the rod took as it passed through Gage's skull.

After Gage recovered from the accident, his intellectual and motor skills were found to be unaffected. However, he was no longer able to engage in moral reasoning. Before the accident Gage had been well liked, responsible, and a good worker, whereas afterward he was untrustworthy and obscene and seemed incapable of making even the simplest moral decisions.

DISCUSSION QUESTIONS

1. *Neurologist Jonathan Pincus, author of* Base Instincts: What Makes Killers Kill? *(2001), conducted a study of 14 death row inmates who committed their first murder before the age of 18, and 119 teenagers living in a reform school for delinquents. He found that violent crime is strongly correlated with neurological abnormalities in the brain. If our ability to engage in moral reasoning is dependent on our brain structure, should people such as Gage and criminals whose frontal lobes are damaged or abnormal be held morally responsible or punished for their harmful actions? If not, how should we respond to people who seem to lack a moral sense and hurt others without compunction?*

2. *We expect people to behave morally. When they don't, we're generally taken aback. Think of a situation where you've been surprised because someone seemed to lack a sense of morality. What was your reaction to this person?*

---

given that effective critical thinking requires not only that we be aware of our own values but also that we be open-minded and willing to respect the concerns of others.

When we fail to take appropriate moral action or make a moral decision that we later regret, we commit what is called a **moral tragedy**. In the Milgram study on obedience (see Chapter 1), most of the study subjects who continued to deliver "shocks" to the "learner" knew that what they were doing was morally wrong. However, they lacked the necessary critical-thinking skills to come up with effective counterarguments to the researcher's argument that "the experiment requires that you must continue."

moral tragedy This occurs when we make a moral decision that is later regretted.

conscience A source of knowledge that provides us with knowledge about what is right and wrong.

affective The emotional aspect of conscience that motivates us to act.

Conscience and Moral Sentiments

For most people, a well-developed conscience is the essence of the moral life. The word *conscience* comes from the Latin words *com* ("with") and *scire* ("to know"). A well-developed **conscience** provides us with knowledge about what is right and wrong. Like language, whose basic structure is innate, conscience is nurtured (or neglected) and shaped by our family, religion, and culture. However, as we shall learn in this chapter, the most fundamental moral principles are cross-cultural.

Conscience has an **affective** (emotional) element that motivates us to act on this knowledge of right and wrong. In Chapter 2, we learned that healthy emotional development can predispose us to make better decisions. Effective moral reasoning involves listening to the affective side

College students volunteering with Habitat for Humanity, an organization that provides affordable housing for low-income families.

of our conscience as well as to the cognitive or reasoning side. Indeed, research shows that psychopaths intellectually recognize right from wrong when presented with a **moral dilemma**. However, they act violently anyway because they lack the emotional components of sympathy and guilt.[7]

Moral sentiments are emotions that alert us to moral situations and motivate us to do what is right. They include, among others, "helper's high," empathy and sympathy, compassion, moral outrage, resentment, and guilt.

When you help other people, you feel happy and good about yourself. This is known as **helper's high**. The feeling of helper's high is accompanied by the release of or increase in endorphins—morphine-like chemicals that occur naturally in your body. This is followed by a period of increased relaxation and improved self-esteem, which, as we learned in Chapter 1, enhances critical thinking.[8]

Empathy, or *sympathy*, is the capacity for imagining and the inclination to imagine the feelings of others. This moral sentiment expresses itself as joy at another's happi-

ness and sadness at their despair. **Compassion** is sympathy in action and involves taking steps to relieve others' unhappiness. Although most of us are able to feel empathy or sympathy for those who are similar to us, we have a tendency (as we learned in Chapter 4) to divide the world into "us" and "them." To counter this error in our thinking, we need to consciously nurture compassion and extend it to as many people as possible.

Not all moral sentiments are warm and fuzzy. **Moral outrage**, also known as moral indignation, occurs when we witness an injustice or violation of moral decency. Moral outrage motivates us to correct an unjust situation by demanding that *justice* be done. **Resentment** is a type of moral outrage that occurs when we ourselves are treated unjustly. For example, Rosa Parks's resentment, as well as

Hot or Not?

Is guilt good?

moral dilemma A situation in which there is a conflict between moral values.

moral sentiments Emotions that alert us to moral situations and motivate us to do what is right.

helper's high The feeling that occurs when we help other people.

compassion Sympathy in action.

moral outrage Indignation in the presence of an injustice or violation of moral decency.

resentment A type of moral outrage that occurs when we ourselves are treated unjustly.

Connections

What are some of the moral issues involved in a decision to engage in civil disobedience? *See Chapter 13, pp. 427–429.*

her courage, motivated her to refuse to give up her seat on the bus to a white man. Her actions, in turn, sparked the 1955–1956 bus boycott in Montgomery, Alabama—one of the key turning points in the modern American struggle for civil rights.

While moral outrage calls our attention to an injustice and motivates us to act, without effective moral reasoning and critical-thinking skills we may fail to act or may respond ineffectively. Moral outrage or resentment that is not guided by moral reasoning may degenerate into feelings of bitterness, blame, or helplessness.

Guilt both alerts us to and motivates us to correct a wrong we have committed. Guilt is a lot like pain. When you cut yourself, you feel pain at the site where the injury occurred. The pain motivates you to take action to repair the injury before it becomes infected and festers. Guilt also motivates us to avoid harming ourselves and others. We refrain from cheating on an exam or from stealing someone's wallet or laptop—even when no one is around to see us take it—because the very thought of doing so makes us feel guilty.

In our feel-good society, guilt is frequently regarded as a barrier to personal freedom and happiness. Because of this, many of us respond to guilt with resistance, either trying to ignore it entirely or getting angry at the person who "made" us feel guilty. But at the same time, we generally regard a person who feels no guilt—such as a sociopath—as inhuman and a monster. This uncertainty about the nature of guilt stems in part from a confusion of guilt with shame.

Guilt is often broadly defined to include shame. However, the two are different. Guilt results when we commit a moral wrong or violate a moral principle. **Shame**, on the other hand, occurs as a result of the violation of a social norm, or not living up to someone else's expectations for us. Teenagers who are lesbian, gay, or bisexual, for example, may feel shame for not living up to the expectations of their family, church, or society—but they generally do not feel moral guilt. Rather than motivating us to do better, shame leaves us feeling inadequate, embarrassed, and humiliated. As good critical thinkers, it is important that we learn how to distinguish between guilt and shame.

shame A feeling resulting from the violation of a social norm.

The Montgomery Bus boycott began as a protest against the unjust segregation on buses and ended with the U.S. Supreme Court outlawing segregation on buses.

Making good moral decisions requires that you cultivate critical-thinking skills such as good listening and problem-solving skills. Conscience, which has both a cognitive and an affective aspect, can aid in moral decision making. The affective side of conscience includes moral sentiments that motivate us to take action. In the next section, we'll be studying the cognitive or reasoning side of our conscience.

278 • THINK

SELF-EVALUATION QUESTIONNAIRE: MORAL REASONING*

Case I: Man with an Assault Rifle

Carlos is walking to class one afternoon when he notices a man heading toward a large lecture hall brandishing an assault rifle and swearing under his breath. Carlos, who is interested in pursuing a career in law enforcement, has just come from the shooting range where he enjoys target practice. However, he forgot to bring the bag containing his handgun home, and while he has a gun permit, no firearms of any kind are allowed on his campus. No one else has noticed the man with the rifle. Should Carlos use his gun to shoot the assailant?

Looking at the following list, determine which considerations are most important to you in deciding what to do. Also determine whether each (1) appeals to personal interests, (2) maintains norms, or (3) appeals to moral ideals or principles. Finally, discuss what other considerations and arguments are important to you in making your decision.

a. Whether stopping the potential assailant or observing the campus's gun code would be better for Carlos's future career in law enforcement
b. Whether the campus's gun code is unjust and getting in the way of protecting unsuspecting students' right to life
c. Whether Carlos's using his gun will anger the public and give his college a bad name
d. Whether Carlos is more responsible to those who created the university's gun code or instead to the students whose lives are in danger
e. Whether Carlos is willing to risk being expelled or going to jail
f. What the basic values are that dictate how people treat one another
g. Whether the man brandishing the rifle deserves to be shot for posing a threat to students

Case II: Buying an Essay from the Internet

Jennifer, a college junior, is taking five courses and doing an internship while trying to maintain her 4.0 grade-point average so that she can get into a good law school and become a civil-rights lawyer. After staying up all night to complete a fifteen-page term paper, Jennifer realizes that she forgot to write a four-page response paper due for an English literature class she's taking. Strapped for time and not wanting to damage her grade in the course, she remembers another student in her class telling her about a Web site that sells essays. She goes to the Web site and finds an essay that fits the assignment. Should Jennifer buy the paper and turn it in as her own?

Looking at the following list, determine which considerations are most important to you in deciding what to do. Also determine whether each (1) appeals to personal interests, (2) maintains norms, or (3) appeals to moral ideals or principles. Finally, discuss what other considerations and arguments are important to you in making your decision.

a. Whether the campus rules against plagiarism should be respected
b. How big the risk is that Jennifer will get caught
c. Whether it is fair to the other students applying to law school if Jennifer isn't caught and gets accepted instead of them because she turned in a plagiarized essay
d. Other students in the class are plagiarizing
e. Whether turning in the paper from the Internet will be best for her future career
f. Whether she is violating the rights of the professor and other students in the class by turning in the essay
g. Whether the professor brought this on himself by placing too many demands on his students

Instructor's Note: We all use reasoning from different stages. The purpose of this self-evaluation is to help students realize that some types of reasoning, such as postconventional, are more adequate than others in making decisions. These two cases alone are not sufficient to determine a student's level of moral reasoning. If students are interested in more accurately evaluating their level of moral reasoning, they can take the Defining Issues Test (DIT), which is available from the Center for the Study of Ethical Development, University of Minnesota and University of Alabama (see http://www.centerforthestudyofethicaldevelopment.net/).

1. Working in small groups, come up with a list of moral values and a list of non-moral values. Discuss which values are most important to you, and why. Discuss also how these values influence your life plan and everyday decisions.

2. Discuss this quotation from Irish poet W. B. Yeats: "Hate is a kind of 'passive suffering,' but indignation is a kind of joy."

3. People who have depression can become self-preoccupied to the point of becoming indifferent to the consequences of their actions for themselves and others. According to psychiatrist Peter Kramer, author of *Listening to Prozac*, treatment with an antidepressant drug such as Prozac can in some cases "turn a morally unattractive person into an admirable one."[9] In cases where people are depressed to the point of making poor moral decisions, is it morally acceptable, or even morally obligatory, for them to use Prozac or similar drugs to improve their reasoning capacity? Support your answer.

4. Reformers such as Mohandas Gandhi and Martin Luther King, Jr., argued that violence can never be justified by moral outrage. Instead, they insisted, we need to use our moral reasoning to develop nonviolent strategies for responding to violence. Do you agree? Come up with an argument (inductive or deductive) supporting your position.

5. Think of a specific time when you felt guilty and a time when you felt shame. How did you respond in each case? Was your response appropriate, from the point of view of effective critical thinking? If not, discuss how you might develop more appropriate responses to these feelings as well as learn how to better differentiate between them.

6. *Journal Exercise:* Looking back at the list of values from your journal assignment "My Life Plan," which of these values are moral values and which are nonmoral values? Using the worksheet in your workbook or working in small groups, reevaluate and, if necessary, reorganize your values and goals.

THE DEVELOPMENT OF MORAL REASONING

Many psychologists believe that human beings progress through different stages of moral development during their lives. In this section we'll be looking at theories on moral development and research on moral development in college students.

Lawrence Kohlberg's Stage Theory of Moral Development

According to Harvard psychologist Lawrence Kohlberg (1927–1987), people advance though distinct stages in the development of their moral reasoning capabilities. These stages are transcultural—that is, they happen in the course of human development in every culture of the world.[10] Each new stage represents increased proficiency in critical-thinking skills and greater satisfaction with one's moral decisions.

Kohlberg identified three levels of moral development, each with two distinct stages (see Highlights below). In the first two stages, what Kohlberg called the **preconventional stages**, morality is defined egotistically in terms of oneself. People at this level expect others to treat them morally but generally do not treat other people with moral respect unless doing so benefits them. Most people outgrow the preconventional stages of moral reasoning by high school.

People at the **conventional stages** look to others for moral guidance and affirmation that they are doing the right thing. Earning the approval of others and conforming to peer-group norms are especially important to people at stage 3, the first stage of conventional reasoning. For example, Lynndie England, one of the American guards in the Abu Ghraib prison scandal in Iraq, at her court-martial stated in her defense that she "chose to do what my friends wanted me to."[11] The judge rejected that plea.

Most high school seniors and college freshmen are at stage 3 in their moral development. This stage is associated

preconventional stages Stage of moral development in which morality is defined egotistically.

conventional stages Stage of moral development in which people look to others for moral guidelines.

HIGHLIGHTS

STAGES IN THE DEVELOPMENT OF MORAL REASONING

Level—Kohlberg's Description*: Gilligan's Description**

Preconventional

Stage 1—Avoid punishment*: Fear of punishment**

Stage 2—Egoist*: Put self first; satisfy your own needs; consider needs of others only if it benefits you: "You scratch my back, I'll scratch yours."**

Self-centered**: View your own needs as all that matters**

Me   Others

Conventional

Stage 3—Good boy/nice girl*: Put others first; please and help others; maintain good relationships and earn others' approval; conform to peer norms**

Self-sacrificing**: View others' needs as more important than your own**

Stage 4—Society maintaining*: Respect authority and society rules; maintain the existing social order**

Me   Others

Postconventional

Stage 5—Social contract or legalistic*: Obey useful, albeit arbitrary, social rules; appeal to social consensus and majority rule as long as minimal basic rights are safeguarded**

Stage 6—Conscience and universal moral principles*: Autonomously recognize universal rules, such as justice and equality, that are rational and logically consistent and reflect a respect for equal human rights and the dignity of each individual**

Mature care ethics**: able to balance your own needs and the needs of others**

Me   Others

*Description of Kohlberg's stages adapted from Barbara Panzl and Timothy McMahon, "Ethical Decision-Making Developmental Theory and Practice," speech delivered at a meeting of the National Association of Student Personnel Administrators, Denver, March 1989.
**Description of Gilligan's stages adapted from Carol Gilligan's *In a Different Voice: Psychological Theory and Women's Development* (Cambridge, MA: Harvard University Press, 1982).

with the first stage of cognitive development in college students in which they believe that there are right and wrong answers and that those in authority know the right answers.

Moving on to the next stage of conventional moral reasoning involves substituting the norms and laws of the wider culture for peer-group norms. This type of moral reasoning is also known as cultural relativism. The majority of American adults are at this stage. Rather than thinking through decisions about moral issues, they adopt the prevailing view. The mere fact that "everyone" agrees with them confirms, for them, that they must be right.

At the **postconventional stages** of moral reasoning, people recognize that social conventions need to be justified. The fact that something is the law does not make it moral or just. Instead, moral decisions should be based on universal moral principles and on concerns such as justice, compassion, and mutual respect.

A person's stage of moral development is correlated with his or her behavior. Research done on eighty-six study subjects found that only 9 percent of people at stage 2 (egoist) and 38 percent of people at stage 4 (society-maintaining) would offer help to someone who appeared to be suffering from drug side effects; yet all the subjects at stage 6 offered their assistance.[12] Unfortunately, less than 10 percent of American adults ever reach the postconventional level of moral reasoning.[13]

People at the lower levels of moral reasoning tend to come up with simplistic solutions. When these solutions don't work or backfire, they become baffled.

People outgrow their old way of thinking when it becomes inadequate for resolving the more complex problems and issues that they encounter in life. Movement to a higher stage is usually triggered by an experience or new ideas that conflict with their worldview.

Carol Gilligan on Moral Reasoning in Women

Kohlberg carried out his research only on men. Psychologist Carol Gilligan argued that women's moral development tends to follow a different path. Men, she said, tend to be duty- and principle-oriented, an approach she called the **justice perspective**. Women, in contrast, are more context-oriented and view the world in terms of relationships and caring. She called this the **care perspective**.

Gilligan outlined three stages or levels in the development of moral reasoning in women. Like boys, girls at the preconventional stage are self-centered and egotistical, putting their own needs first. Women at the conventional stage of moral reasoning, in contrast, tend to be

postconventional stages Stage in which people make moral decisions on the basis of universal moral principals.

justice perspective The emphasis on duty and principles in moral reasoning.

care perspective The emphasis in moral development and reasoning on context and relationships.

How does democracy contribute to "tyranny of the majority" and the belief that the majority must know what is right? *See Chapter 13, p. 414.*

Connections

People at the postconventional stage of moral reasoning are more likely to reach out to the underprivileged and homeless.

mature care ethics The stage of moral development in which people are able to balance their needs and those of others.

self-sacrificing, putting the needs and welfare of others before their own. Finally, women at the postconventional stage are able to balance their needs and those of others—what Gilligan calls **mature care ethics**.

Although some studies support Gilligan, others have found sex differences to be insignificant.[14] Many women have a strong justice perspective, while some men prefer the care perspective. In addition, most people make use of *both* perspectives in their moral reasoning. Just as the cognitive and the affective sides of our conscience work together, the two types of moral reasoning work together, complementing each other and helping us to make better decisions.

Although there are many opportunities for moral development outside of college, a college education has been found to be positively correlated with moral development. This is probably because many young people go through a time of crisis—sometimes called "cognitive disequilibrium"—

Thinking

Outside the Box

MOHANDAS GANDHI, *Nonviolent Activist*

Mohandas Gandhi (1869–1948), popularly known as Mahatma, or "Great Soul," was born in India. As a young lawyer, Gandhi was prohibited by British segregationist practices from sitting where he wanted to on the train and from walking beside his "noncolored" friends. Even worse, he saw people of lower castes being treated with utter contempt by both the Europeans and higher-caste Indians. But rather than acquiesce to cultural norms or internalize his resentment, he responded with moral outrage guided by reason.

His response sparked one of the most effective nonviolent moral reform movements in the history of the world. Following the Massacre at Amritsar in 1919, in which hundreds of unarmed Indian civilians were gunned down by soldiers in the British army, Gandhi launched a policy of nonviolent noncooperation against the British who were occupying India. As a result of his efforts, India gained its independence in 1947.

Gandhi also strove to get rid of the oppressive caste system in India. His respect for the equal dignity of all people and his use of nonviolent resistance as a strategy for political and social reform has had a lasting influence on later civil rights movements, including the 1960s civil rights movement in the United States.

DISCUSSION QUESTIONS

1. Discuss how Gandhi's resolutions to moral issues he confronted in his life reflect thinking at both Kohlberg's and Gilligan's postconventional stages.

2. Think back on a time when you were tempted to respond or responded to violence (verbal or physical) against you with violence. Discuss how a person at the postconventional stage of moral reasoning would most likely have responded.

when they leave home and enter college. They may initially respond to the disruption of their worldviews by becoming conformists and being easily influenced by their peer culture. The propensity of some freshmen, at the urging of their peers, to engage in self-destructive behavior—smoking, binge-drinking, taking street drugs, sexual experimentation, reckless driving, and the like—simply reflects this conformity.

Why is moral reasoning important for college students in deciding how to use social networking on the Internet? *See Chapter 11, p. 355.*

Connections

As we've already seen, freshmen tend to be more black-and-white in their thinking. In a study of moral reasoning in college students, students were presented with the fictional case of "Joe."[15] One day a neighbor discovers that Joe, who has been living the life of a model citizen for several years, is actually an escaped prisoner. Students were then asked, "Should the neighbor turn him in to the authorities?" Freshmen were more likely to say yes because it's what the law dictates; letting a criminal go free, they say, might encourage further crime. By the time college students reach their senior year, they are still concerned about what the law states; however, they also question whether it would be *fair* for the law to be applied in this case. Those who had reached the postconventional level wanted to know more about Joe and if he had been truly rehabilitated. They also asked which action—reporting or not reporting Joe to the authorities—would most benefit society.

Peer relations at college are important in the development of moral reasoning. Students who have diverse friendships with people different from themselves tend to make greater gains.[16] Discussions of moral issues in classrooms, in which students' ideas are challenged and they are required to support their conclusions, also have the potential to enhance moral reasoning.[17]

Despite these positive influences, most college students do not make the transition from conventional to autonomous postconventional moral reasoning. Instead, college tends to push students up into a higher stage of conventional reasoning, where they shift to conforming to wider societal norms rather than to those of their peer culture.

Moral reasoning plays an important role in our everyday decisions. Our level of moral reasoning affects all aspects of our lives—personal and professional.[18] Level of moral reasoning is positively correlated with self-esteem, mental health, satisfaction with career goals, honesty, and altruistic behavior. In the next section we will study moral theories that guide our thinking.

Hot or Not?

Does our current education system inhibit moral development?

EXERCISES 9–2

1. Which scheme of moral development—Gilligan's or Kohlberg's—best describes your style and stage of moral reasoning? Discuss situations you've encountered where this stage was adequate for resolving a particular problem or conflict, as well as some situations in which it was inadequate.

2. College tends to move students up to a higher stage of conventional moral reasoning. Working in small groups, discuss why you think this is the case. Use examples from your college experience to illustrate your answer. Make a list of specific suggestions for changes in the curriculum and campus life in general that might promote postconventional moral reasoning.

3. Just learning about the stages of moral reasoning can enhance moral development. How did you respond to the question on this page about whether you should report "Joe," the escaped prisoner, to the authorities? Are you satisfied with your answer? Explain.

4. Have you noticed that you are less susceptible to peer pressure in making moral decisions than you were in high school or when you first started college? Discuss what factors might have contributed to your ability to think more independently in making moral decisions.

5. Since entering college, have you encountered a situation or problem in which your style of moral reasoning was inadequate? How did you respond? Would you respond differently now? Relate your answers to the stages of moral reasoning.

MORAL THEORIES: MORALITY IS RELATIVE

Moral theories provide frameworks for understanding and explaining what makes a certain action right or wrong. They also help us clarify, critically analyze, and rank the moral concerns raised by moral issues in our lives. Moral theory is the foundation of moral reasoning. Our everyday moral decisions and level of moral reasoning are informed by the moral theory we accept as true, even though we may never have consciously articulated the theory.

> There are two basic types of moral theories: (1) those that claim that morality is relative and (2) those that claim that morality is universal.

There are two basic types of moral theories: (1) those that claim that morality is relative and (2) those that claim that morality is universal. Moral relativists claim that people *create* morality and that there are no universal or shared moral principles that apply to all people. Universalists, in contrast, maintain that there are universal moral principles that hold for all people.

The inability of many Americans to make universal moral judgments on issues such as abortion and capital punishment contributes to the widespread feeling in the United States that people's positions on moral issues are simply matters of personal opinion and that there is little room for discussion when differences of opinion exist. Critical evaluation of the different theories, however, soon makes it clear that some moral theories are better than others for explaining morality and providing solutions to moral problems.

Ethical Subjectivism

ethical subjectivist One who believes that morality is nothing more than personal opinion or feelings.

According to **ethical subjectivists**, morality is nothing more than personal opinion or feelings. What *feels* right for you *is* right for you at any particular moment. Consider J. L. Hunter ("Red") Roundtree, who recently died in a Missouri prison at the age of 92. A retired business tycoon who had founded his own machinery company, Roundtree pulled his first bank robbery at age 86. "Holdups," he said, "made me feel good, awful good."[19] Did the fact that robbing banks made Roundtree "feel good" morally justify what he did? The ethical subjectivist would have to say yes. If Roundtree felt "awful good" about robbing banks, then his actions were morally correct, just as were the actions of a serial killer such as the movie character "Hannibal the Cannibal," who felt good about torturing and killing his victims.

Do not confuse ethical subjectivism with the observation that people *believe* in different moral values. Ethical subjectivism goes beyond this by claiming that sincerely believing or feeling something is right *makes* it right for that person. While robbing banks or torturing and killing people may not be right for you, these actions—according to ethical subjectivism—*are* morally right for Roundtree and "Hannibal the Cannibal." Since personal feelings are the only standard for what is right or wrong for each individual, a person can never be wrong.

Also, do not confuse ethical subjectivism with tolerance. The injunction "Live and let live," for example, implies a universal moral duty to respect others and tolerate their life choices, as long as they are not harming you or others. Ethical subjectivism, rather than encouraging tolerance, allows a person to exploit and terrorize the weak and vulnerable, as long as the perpetrator believes that doing so is right.

Ethical subjectivism is one of the weakest moral theories. Having a right to our own opinion is not the same as saying that all opinions are equally reasonable. Indeed, most people who support ethical subjectivism usually feel quite differently when they are directly and unfavorably affected by someone else's harmful actions.

In the previous chapter on deductive reasoning, we learned that hypothetical reasoning can be used to analyze a moral theory by providing us with a means of examining its implications. Consider the following argument:

> *Premise 1*: If ethical subjectivism is true, *then* I am always behaving morally when I act on my personal feelings and opinions, including torturing and raping young children.
>
> *Premise 2*: Ethical subjectivism is true.
>
> *Conclusion*: Therefore, I am always behaving morally when I act on my personal feelings and opinions, including torturing and raping young children.

In the above valid hypothetical syllogism, if we are not willing to accept the conclusion as true, then we *must* reject as false the premise: "Ethical subjectivism is true." Ethical subjectivism, if taken seriously, is a dangerous theory. It not only isolates the individual but also permits people to exploit and hurt others without ever having to justify their actions or stand in judgment.

Connections

Do we as a society have a moral obligation to restrict certain types of advertising and television shows that may exploit young children? *See Chapter 10, p. 324.*

1. Philosophy professor Stephen Satris claims that ethical subjectivism—what he calls "student relativism"—is one of the most pervasive and frustrating problems in teaching philosophy.[20] Student relativism is manifest in such statements as "What is true for one person might not be true for others. After all, who's to say what is moral? It's all relative." Satris believes that student relativism is not a genuine moral position but "a suit of armor"—a type of mental laziness or resistance that protects students from having to critically analyze or pass judgment on their own or others' views and values. Do you agree? Relate your answer to the concept of resistance studied in Chapter 1.

2. In August 1995, 33-year-old Deletha Word jumped to her death from the Belle Isle bridge in Detroit to escape a 19-year-old man who savagely beat her after a fender bender. Dozens of spectators stood by, some even cheering on the attacker. Discuss how an ethical subjectivist would most likely respond to this event.

3. Think of a time when someone you knew used ethical subjectivism to justify his or her hurtful actions or failure to take action or prevent harm to you or another person. How did you respond, if at all, to this person's argument? How might you respond if you were in the same situation today?

4. Looking back at the steroids-in-sports question with which we began this chapter, discuss how both an ethical subjectivist and a cultural relativist would have each most likely responded to the entrepreneur's proposal.

5. Amina Lawal, age 30, became pregnant after having an affair with her neighbor, who had agreed to marry her. However, he went back on his promise to marry her. Eight days after Lawal gave birth, the police arrested her for adultery, a capital crime in her home state of Katsina in northern Nigeria. She was tried and sentenced to be buried in the ground up to her chest and stoned to death. In her culture, in cases of adultery, typically it is only the woman who is sentenced to death by stoning. There was an outcry in some parts of the world against this practice, and the sentence, at least in Lawal's case, was dropped because of outside pressure. However, on what grounds can we, as Americans, claim that the practice is immoral? Discuss whether our claims that such practices are immoral can be reconciled with cultural relativism.

6. Working in small groups, write a hypothetical syllogism regarding the implications of cultural relativism (*If* cultural relativism is true, *then* ...). Share your syllogism with the class. Are you willing to accept these implications?

7. The U.S. military is grappling with the problem of post-combat guilt among soldiers in Iraq who have killed in combat. These soldiers believe that the war is right and just. One officer dealing with guilt says, "I know what I did was right. But I'll never lose the sound of that grief-stricken family."[21] Discuss how both an ethical subjectivist and a cultural relativist might explain the phenomenon of guilt in these cases.

8. What is the source of your moral values? Do you identify with the values of a particular group, such as your peers or religious organization? Are you satisfied with these values when it comes to making moral decisions in your life? Explain.

9. Think of a time when you took a moral stand that conflicted with the norms of your peer group. How did you justify your position? How did your peers respond to you, and how did you address their concerns?

10. Think of a moral decision you made this past week. Write a short essay discussing which of the values involved in making the decision were moral values and which were nonmoral values. Describe also which moral sentiments played a role in motivating you to carry out this decision. Were you satisfied with your decision? Explain why or why not.

MORAL THEORIES: MORALITY IS UNIVERSAL

Most moral philosophers believe that morality is universal—that moral principles are binding on all people regardless of their personal desires, culture, or religion. There are several universal moral theories, each of which tends to focus on one particular aspect of morality. In this section, we'll look at four types of universal moral theories: utilitarianism (consequence-based ethics), deontology (duty-based ethics), natural-rights ethics (rights-based ethics), and virtue ethics (character-based ethics). Rather than being mutually exclusive, as the relativist theories are, these theories enrich and complement each other.

Utilitarianism (Consequence-Based Ethics)

utilitarianism A moral philosophy in which actions are evaluated based on their consequences.

principle of utility (greatest happiness principle) The most moral action is that which brings about the greatest happiness or pleasure and the least amount of pain for the greatest number.

utilitarian calculus Used to determine the best course of action or policy by calculating the total amount of pleasure and pain caused by that action.

In **utilitarianism**, actions are evaluated on the basis of their consequences. According to utilitarians, the desire for happiness is universal. The most moral action is that which brings about the greatest happiness or pleasure and the least amount of pain for the greatest number. This is known as the **principle of utility**, or the **greatest happiness principle**:

> Actions are right in proportion as they tend to promote happiness, wrong as they tend to produce the reverse of happiness.[22]

In making a moral decision, we need to weigh the benefits and harms (costs) to those affected by an action. English philosopher and social reformer Jeremy Bentham (1748–1832) developed the utilitarian calculus as a means of determining which action or policy is morally preferable. Using **utilitarian calculus**, each potential action is assigned a numerical value—for instance, from 1 to 10, or whatever scale you choose to use—on the basis of the intensity, duration, certainty, propinquity, fecundity, purity, and extent of the pleasure or pain. (Each of these categories is defined in "Highlights: Utilitarian Calculus: Seven Factors to Take into Consideration in Determining the Most Moral Action or Decision," on page 290). These factors are each taken into consideration when calculating the total amount of pleasure and pain caused by an action. The greater the pleasure, the higher the positive numerical value it is assigned; the greater the pain, the lower the value.

Using utilitarian calculus, if a proposed policy or action has a higher total positive value than its alternatives, then it is the better policy. For example, in the case at the beginning of this chapter on using steroids, while the purity of the pleasure may be diluted by any pain to the other team if it loses the game or to you from any short-term physical effects of the drugs, this pain is outweighed by the intensity, duration, and extent of the pleasure or happiness it will bring to your college.

Utilitarian cost–benefit analysis is especially useful in developing policies for the allocation of limited resources. In 1962, there were not enough kidney dialysis machines for everyone who needed them. The Seattle Artificial Kidney Center (now known as the Northwest Kidney Centers) appointed a committee of seven—the so-called God Committee—which decided who should get kidney dialysis on the basis of each patient's capacity to benefit the community. The selection process included criteria such as age, employment history, education level, history of achievements, number of dependents, and involvement in the community.

Utilitarian Jeremy Bentham donated his estate to the University of London on the condition that his body (shown with a wax head in the glass case) be presented at all the board meetings.

In deciding on the best policy, a utilitarian doesn't simply go along with what the majority wants, since people are not always well informed or concerned about the overall well-being of the community. Nor is happiness the same as going along with personal preferences or feelings. For example, although spending an evening partying may bring you and your friends short-term happiness, your long-term happiness may be better served by studying for an exam you have the next day, so that you can do well in college, graduate, and get a good, well-paying job.

Did You Know

In 1962, there were not enough kidney dialysis machines. Criteria such as age, employment history, education level, history of achievements, number of dependents, and involvement in the community determined who got to use them.

One of the strengths of utilitarian theory is that it requires us to be well informed about the possible consequences of our actions (or inactions) before we make moral decisions. The excuses "I didn't intend any harm" and "Don't blame me—I'm not the one who did it; I was just a bystander" don't pass muster with a utilitarian.

On the other hand, utilitarianism fails to give sufficient attention to individual integrity and personal rights. Restoring peace by arresting and executing an innocent person may bring about the greatest happiness to the greatest number. However, this solution is wrong despite its overall benefit to society because it is wrong to use a person as a means only. For example, getting good grades so that we can graduate and get a well-paying job is, for some people, not the sole benefit that we derive from forgoing partying and studying hard. There is also the intangible satisfaction of becoming an educated, well-rounded person.

Utilitarian theory is not so much wrong as incomplete. Its primary weakness is not its claim that consequences are important but instead the claim that *only* consequences matter in making moral decisions.

What are some of the utilitarian arguments for restricting—or not restricting—advertising? *See* Chapter 10, p. 324.

Connections

HIGHLIGHTS

UTILITARIAN CALCULUS: SEVEN FACTORS TO TAKE INTO CONSIDERATION IN DETERMINING THE MOST MORAL ACTION OR DECISION

1. *Intensity:* Strength of the pleasure and pain. The greater the pleasure, the higher the positive value; the greater the pain, the more negative the value.

2. *Duration:* Length of time the pain and pleasure will last.

3. *Certainty:* Level of probability that the pleasure or pain will occur.

4. *Propinquity:* How soon in time the pleasure or pain will occur.

5. *Fecundity:* Extent to which the pleasure will produce more pleasure.

6. *Purity:* The pleasure does not cause pain at the same time.

7. *Extent:* The number of sentient beings affected by the action.

Deontology (Duty-Based Ethics)

Deontology claims that duty is the foundation of morality. Some acts are morally obligatory regardless of their consequences. We should do our duty purely out of a sense of goodwill, not because of reward or punishment or any other consequences. The only important consideration is "What is my moral duty?"

According to German philosopher Immanuel Kant (1724–1804), the most fundamental moral principle is the **categorical imperative**, which (in Kant's famous words) states:

Act only on that maxim by which you can at the same time will that it should become a universal law.[23]

deontology The ethics of duty.

categorical imperative Kant's fundamental moral principle that helps to determine what our duty is.

The categorical imperative, said Kant, must guide our moral decision making. It is inconsistent, for example, to argue that it is wrong for others to lie but that it is okay for us. If it is wrong to lie, it is wrong for *everyone* to lie. Moral principles or duties apply to everyone regardless of a person's feelings or culture.

Kant believed that all rational beings will recognize the categorical imperative as universally binding. It is our ability to reason that gives us moral worth. Since humans and other rational beings have intrinsic moral worth or dignity, they should never be treated as expendable, in the way that they can be under utilitarian theory. Because each of us has intrinsic moral worth, according to Kant, our foremost duty is self-respect or proper self-esteem: If we don't respect and treat ourselves well, we're not going to treat others well. This ideal of respect for human dignity, including our own, is summed up in Kant's second formulation of the categorical imperative:

> So act as to treat humanity, whether in thine own person or in that of any other, in every case as an end in itself, never as a means only.[24]

This moral obligation is found in moral philosophies and religious ethics throughout the world, including the golden rule in Judeo-Christian ethics and the law of reciprocity in Confucian ethics (see "Critical Thinking in Action: The Golden Rule—Reciprocity as the Basis of Morality in World Religions"). While religious ethics is sometimes considered different from philosophical ethics, the general moral principles recognized by the two are the same. Although some people regard God as the source of these principles, all the major religions of the world affirm the same universal moral principles recognized by philosophers.

Kant believed that universalizing moral duties, such as a duty not to lie, requires that these duties be absolutely binding in all circumstances. Most deontologists, while agreeing that moral duties are universal, disagree with Kant, noting that there are situations where moral duties may come into conflict.

Scottish philosopher W. D. Ross (1877–1971) came up with a list of seven duties derived from the categorical imperative (see "Highlights: Seven Prima Facie Duties"). These duties include the future-looking (consequential) duties of the utilitarians, as well as duties based on past obligations and ongoing duties. Ross argued that these duties are **prima facie** (translated "at first view")—that is, they are morally binding unless overridden by a more compelling moral duty.

Let's look at an example. You have promised to pay back, by a certain date, money that you borrowed from a friend. Under ordinary circumstances, you would have a duty of fidelity to pay back the money. Your friend arrives at your door on the due date and is furious because his chemistry professor gave him a failing grade. He is carrying parts for a bomb and demands the money

prima facie duty Moral duty that is binding unless overridden by a more compelling moral duty.

HIGHLIGHTS

SEVEN PRIMA FACIE DUTIES

FUTURE-LOOKING DUTIES

- *Beneficence:* The duty to do good acts and to promote happiness.
- *Nonmaleficence:* The duty to do no harm and to prevent harm.

DUTIES BASED ON PAST OBLIGATIONS

- *Fidelity/loyalty:* Duties arising from past commitments and promises. Commitments may be voluntary (school, job, or marriage) or involuntary (a duty to our parents, family, and country).
- *Reparation:* Duties that stem from past harms to others. This duty requires that the person who caused the harm make up for the harm.
- *Gratitude:* Duties based on past favors and unearned services. This may involve thanking the person who did the favor or returning the favor.

ONGOING DUTIES

- *Self-improvement:* The duty to improve our knowledge (wisdom) and virtue. This duty is the basis of virtue ethics.
- *Justice:* The duty to treat all people with dignity and to give each person equal consideration.

so he can buy the rest of the explosives he needs to blow up the science building. Should you give him the money?

Probably not. In situations such as these, you need to determine which moral duties are the most compelling. In this case, the duty of nonmaleficence— preventing serious harms to other people—overrides your duty to pay back the money.

Deontology is a powerful moral theory, especially when it incorporates the insights of the utilitarians.

Connections

What steps does our judicial process take to ensure that everyone is treated fairly? *See Chapter 13, p. 433.*

Do we as citizens have a moral obligation to vote? *See Chapter 13, p. 418.*

Critical Thinking in Action

The Golden Rule—Reciprocity as the Basis of Morality in World Religions

Buddhism: "Hurt not others in ways that you yourself would find hurtful." *Udana Varga 5:18*

Christianity: "Always treat others as you would like them to treat you." *Matthew 7:12*

Confucianism: "Do not do to others what you do not want them to do to you." *Analects 15:23*

Hinduism: "This is the sum of the Dharma [duty]: do naught unto others which would cause pain if done to you." *Mahabharata 5:1517*

Islam: "None of you [truly] believes until he wishes for his brother what he wishes for himself." *Number 13 of Iman "Al-Nawawi's Forty Hadiths"*

Judaism: "... thou shall love thy neighbor as thyself." *Leviticus 19:18*

Native American spirituality: "Respect for all life is the foundation." *The Great Law of Peace*

1. Discuss the deontologist's claim that the categorical imperative (law of reciprocity) is a universal and fundamental principle of ethics. If you are a member of a religion, discuss ways in which this fundamental principle of ethics is (or is not) expressed in your religion.

2. Most of us have been taught some form of the duty of reciprocity as young children. Using a specific example, discuss the extent to which this duty influences your everyday moral reasoning and behavior.

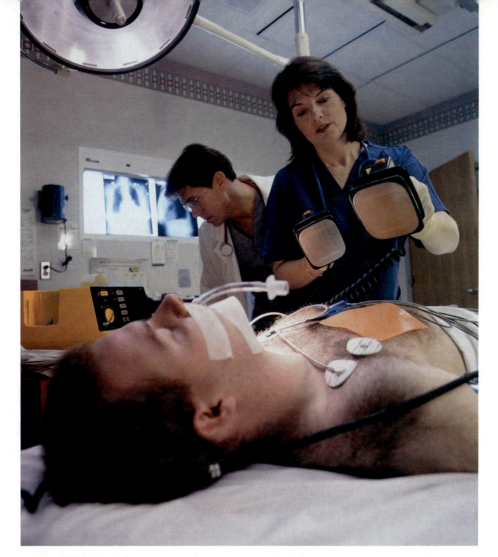

Welfare rights include the right to emergency medical care, regardless of ability to pay.

Connections

To what extent should media speech be protected by freedom of speech? *See Chapter 11, p. 346.*

What are some of the moral conflicts raised by potential misuses of the Internet? *See Chapter 11, p. 357.*

Does the USA Patriot Act violate people's liberty rights, or does the government's duty to protect citizens override these rights? *See Chapter 13.*

legitimate interests Interests that do not violate others' similar and equal interests.

welfare rights The right to receive certain social goods that are essential to our well-being.

liberty rights The right to be left alone to pursue our legitimate interests.

While deontology is strong on moral principle and duty, one of its limitations is the failure to adequately take into account the role of sentiment and care ethics in moral decision making. On the other hand, deontology provides a solid foundation and justification for rights-based ethics—to which we now turn.

Rights-Based Ethics

In rights-based ethics, moral rights are *not* identical to legal rights, as they are in cultural relativism. Because we have moral rights, others have a duty to honor these rights. Having moral rights does not mean that we can do whatever we want. The right to pursue our interests without interference from others is limited to our **legitimate interests**—that is, those interests that do not harm other people by violating their similar and equal interests.

Moral rights are generally divided into welfare and liberty rights. **Welfare rights** entail rights to receive certain social goods, such as education, emergency medical care, and police and fire protection, which are essential for our welfare, or well-being. Welfare rights are important because without them, we cannot effectively pursue our legitimate interests.

Liberty rights entail the right to be left alone to pursue our legitimate interests. For example, a misogynist (a man who hates women) may have an *interest* in keeping women out of the workplace, but this does not give him the *right* to do so, since it violates women's right to equal opportunity—a liberty right—and therefore his is not a *legitimate interest*. Freedom of speech, freedom of religion, freedom to choose our major and career path, the right to privacy, and the right to own property are all examples of liberty rights.

Rights ethics is an important component of a comprehensive moral theory because rights protect our equality and dignity as persons. Like duties, rights may come into conflict with each other or with other duties. When this happens, we need to decide which are the more compelling moral rights and/or duties.

Virtue Ethics

virtue ethics Moral theories that emphasize character over right actions.

moral sensitivity The awareness of how our actions affect others.

Virtue ethics emphasize character over right actions. The sort of person we are constitutes the heart of our moral life. Virtue ethics are not an alternative to moral theories that stress right conduct, such as utilitarian and deontological theories. Rather, virtue ethics and theories of right action complement each other.

A *virtue* is an admirable character trait or disposition to habitually act in a manner that benefits ourselves and others. The actions of virtuous people stem from a respect and concern for the well-being of themselves and others. Compassion, courage, generosity, loyalty, and honesty are all examples of virtues. Because virtuous people are more likely to act morally, virtue ethics goes hand in hand with the other universal moral theories.

Being a virtuous person entails cultivating moral sensitivity. **Moral sensitivity** is the awareness of how our actions affect others and involves good communication skills and the ability to empathize—to imagine ourselves in another person's shoes. Morally sensitive people are more in tune with their conscience and more likely to feel guilty when they harm another person or to feel moral indignation when they witness an injustice.

Moral theories do not exist in abstraction. They inform and motivate our real-life decisions and actions as well as shape how we define ourselves and our relationships to the community and society. By using the universal theories together and drawing from the strengths of each, we can become more proficient at analyzing and constructing moral arguments as well as resolving moral conflicts.

HIGHLIGHTS

UNIVERSAL MORAL THEORIES

- *Utilitarianism:* Morality is based on consequences. Actions are right if they tend to promote more happiness or pleasure and wrong if they tend to produce pain or unhappiness.

- *Deontology:* Duty is the foundation of morality. We have a duty to act only on principles that we would want to be universal laws. We also have a duty to respect ourselves and other rational beings.

- *Rights-based ethics:* Rights are the primary moral concern. Rights protect our dignity. Liberty rights are the entitlement to be left alone to pursue our legitimate interests. Welfare rights are the entitlement to those social goods we need to pursue our legitimate interests.

- *Virtue ethics:* Character is more important than right actions. Virtue is the disposition to habitually act in a way that benefits ourselves and others. Being a virtuous person is at the heart of our moral lives.

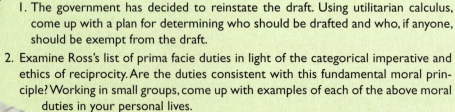

EXERCISES 9–4

1. The government has decided to reinstate the draft. Using utilitarian calculus, come up with a plan for determining who should be drafted and who, if anyone, should be exempt from the draft.

2. Examine Ross's list of prima facie duties in light of the categorical imperative and ethics of reciprocity. Are the duties consistent with this fundamental moral principle? Working in small groups, come up with examples of each of the above moral duties in your personal lives.

3. Referring back to the case at the beginning of this chapter, use Kant's categorical imperative and Ross's prima facie duties to decide whether you ought to take the steroids.

4. What is your greatest virtue? Discuss how this virtue contributes to your ability to be a better critical thinker.

5. The majority of parents in the United States believe that it is morally acceptable, even praiseworthy, to tell their young children that Santa

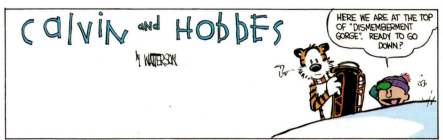

CALVIN AND HOBBES CARTOON

DISCUSSION QUESTIONS

1. *According to American social theorist James Q. Wilson, the author of* The Moral Sense *(1993), some people from birth seem to have a greater capacity for empathy and justice—what Aristotle called "natural virtue." Does Calvin's apparent deficit of empathy and a moral sense mean that he should be held to a lower standard of virtue? Support your answer.*

2. *Relate your answer to the above question to the duty of self-improvement in yourself.*

Analyzing Images

Claus is a real, physical person. Is it morally right to tell children this, even though it is a lie?

6. After the September 11, 2001, terrorist attacks, hundreds of Arab American men were detained for questioning as a means of combating terrorism. Many were arrested and imprisoned, some for months, without a hearing. Of these, most were not even told why they were being detained. Discuss whether restricting the rights of certain groups in times of crisis is morally justified. If so, on what grounds?

7. Should people who work in industries that produce products that cause harm or death to others (for example, guns or cigarettes) be held morally responsible for the harm? Support your answer.

8. Utilitarian theory is often used to formulate social policies around issues such as AIDS testing, free-speech zones, and the distribution of social goods such as scholarships and medical benefits. Find some examples of utilitarian reasoning in our current government policies or policies at your college. Write a short essay explaining why these policies illustrate utilitarian reasoning. Evaluate each policy.

9. Although almost all people recognize the duties and rights listed in this section as morally binding, people tend to prioritize these duties and rights differently. Which duties and/or rights do you consider to be most important, and why?

MORAL ARGUMENTS

Moral theories provide the foundation for moral arguments and their application to real-life situations.

Recognizing Moral Arguments

A moral argument, like any argument, has premises and a conclusion. However, unlike nonmoral arguments, at least one of the premises is a *prescriptive premise*—that is, it makes a statement regarding what is morally right and wrong or what *ought* to be the case. Moral arguments also contain *descriptive premises* about the world and human nature. In the following argument, the first premise is a prescriptive premise and the second premise is a descriptive (factual) premise.

> *Prescriptive premise*: It is wrong to inflict unnecessary suffering on people.
>
> *Descriptive premise*: Imprisonment causes unnecessary suffering by restricting inmates' freedom of movement.
>
> *Conclusion*: Therefore, it is wrong to imprison people.

Moral arguments may also contain premises that define key or ambiguous terms. In the above example, the argument would be stronger if it provided a definition of the ambiguous term *unnecessary suffering*. *Unnecessary suffering* may be defined as "suffering that is not essential for achieving a particular desired goal." In this case, if our goal is to prevent further harm to the community, is prison the only means of keeping this person from further harming the community, or does imprisonment constitute "unnecessary suffering"?

In making a moral argument, we should first get our facts straight. Incorrect facts or assumptions can lead to a faulty conclusion. For example, until recently most physicians lied to patients who were dying because they believed that telling patients the truth would upset them and hasten their deaths. It wasn't until the 1960s that a study on the effects of truth-telling showed that people with terminal cancer actually did better and lived longer if they knew the truth about their condition.[25] Good intentions are not enough in making moral decisions. If we make unfounded assumptions without first checking our facts, we may end up actually doing more harm than good.

Constructing Moral Arguments

Constructing a moral argument is like constructing any argument, with one main exception—at least one of the premises must be prescriptive. As with other arguments, begin by clearly identifying the issue. Let's use a simple example. You ride to class with one of your friends. While pulling her car into a parking spot, your friend scrapes the fender of another car. Suppose she starts to pull out and leave the scene of the accident? You could say nothing, but by doing so you become complicit in your friend's decision to avoid taking responsibility for the accident. What should you do?

After deciding that you should say something, your next step is to make a list of descriptive and prescriptive premises. In this case one of the descriptive premises could simply be a factual statement of what happened: Your friend damaged the fender of the car next to her when she pulled her car into the parking spot. In some cases the facts may be more complex and you'll need more premises, but in this case let's assume that the next car was legally parked and not moving, and no one was around to witness the accident except you and your friend.

To come up with a list of prescriptive premises, ask yourself, "What are the moral duties, rights, and values that

Many of the prisoners at Guantanamo Bay were denied access to legal counsel and other protections as required by the United Nations' Geneva Conventions.

are relevant to this issue or case?" The principle of reparation is relevant in this case; if we cause harm, whether intentionally or unintentionally through carelessness, we have a moral duty to make up for that harm. The corresponding right in this case is the right of the other person to be compensated for that harm. In fact, one of the reasons we are required to carry automobile insurance is so we can honor the rights of others if we have an accident for which we are responsible.

If you are talking to someone at the postconventional level of moral reasoning, these premises may be sufficient for your friend to come to the conclusion that she ought to take steps to pay for the damage to the other car. However, what if she says, "I don't care" or "If I do, my parents will find out what happened and get angry with me"? If this happens, you need to persist in making your moral argument in a way that is respectful of your friend. You have both a duty of beneficence to be caring as well as a duty of fidelity (loyalty) to your friend. This may require gathering more information. For example, why is she worried about her parents' reaction?

You might also want to add a prescriptive premise containing an application of the principle of reciprocity by asking her, "How would you feel if someone hit your parked car and just drove off? I bet you'd be pretty upset, and rightly so." Remember not to use an accusatory tone in stating your premises—that would mean committing the abusive or ad hominem fallacy. Resorting to this fallacy tends to alienate others and moves you further from a satisfactory moral conclusion or resolution.

The issue and premises can be summarized as follows:

Issue: Your friend scraped the fender of a car in the parking lot. What should she do, and what should you do?

Descriptive premises:

- Your friend damaged the fender of the car next to her when she pulled her car into the parking spot.
- Your friend was driving her parents' car.
- Your friend is concerned that her parents will get angry when they learn about the accident.

Prescriptive premises:

- We have a moral duty to make up for past harms we cause others (duty of reparation).
- The person whose car your friend struck has a right to be compensated for the damage (welfare right).
- I have a duty to be kind and caring to my friend (duty of beneficence).
- I have a duty of loyalty to my friend (duty of fidelity).
- We should treat others as we would want to be treated (law of reciprocity).

In making a moral argument, the point is not to prove that you are morally superior to others but to come to a conclusion that leads to an action or a policy that is reasonable and most consistent with moral values. Do not come to a conclusion until you've developed a list of relevant premises that you can both agree on. Remain open-minded and flexible. Help your friend seek strategies that encourage her to do the right thing while minimizing possible harm to her from angry parents. Taking the premises into consideration, you may come to the following solution or conclusion:

Conclusion: Your friend should leave a note on the other car with her name and phone number explaining what happened, and you should go with your friend when she tells her parents about the accident.

This is a relatively straightforward moral argument that leads to a solution, taking into account all the relevant moral principles. In a later section, we'll be studying strategies for resolving moral dilemmas, cases in which there is a conflict between moral principles and concerns.

Evaluating Moral Arguments

In evaluating moral arguments, the first step is to make sure that the argument is complete and that no important premises are omitted. In some moral arguments, the prescriptive premise(s) is unstated. A prescriptive premise may be left out because it is obvious or uncontroversial. Take this example:

I'm so angry! I have a good grade point average but was refused a college scholarship solely on the grounds that I was a mother of a young child—and, as they said, my place is in the home. That's just not right![26]

The unstated premise in this argument involves the *duty of justice:* The college has a duty to give each student equal consideration. In this case, the only relevant criteria for consideration should have been based on grade point average, not the parental status of the student.

In some moral arguments, a prescriptive premise may be left out because it is controversial or questionable. Consider this argument:

Descriptive premise: The Second Amendment to the United States Constitution protects people's right "to keep and bear arms."

Conclusion: I have a moral right to own a handgun.

The unstated prescriptive premise in this argument is that "an action or policy is morally right if it is constitutional." In other words, this argument assumes cultural rela-tivism is true. However, as we noted earlier, this is a questionable premise, since owning slaves was a *legal* right, at least prior to the 1865 ratification of the Thirteenth Amendment, which outlawed slavery, and a right tacitly recognized by the U.S. Constitution. But most of us do not consider it to be a *moral* right—either now or before 1865. Similarly, in the argument about handguns, although you may agree with the conclusion, the premises do not support it.

The premises should also be true. If just one premise is false, the argument is unsound. For example, some people support the practice of cohabitation (living together) on the grounds that people who live together before marriage have a better chance of a successful marriage. However, research does not support this claim: The divorce rate is in fact significantly higher among married couples who lived together before their marriage or engagement.[27]

Moral arguments should also be free of informal fallacies. Consider:

> Cloning humans is wrong because it is unnatural. Therefore, human cloning ought to be illegal.

In this argument, the person is making the unwarranted assumption that if something is unnatural, then it is morally wrong, thereby committing the *naturalistic fallacy*. If immorality were synonymous with what is unnatural, then the use of antibiotics, eyeglasses, or even clothing (at least in warm climates!) would be immoral.

Another fallacy that often appears in moral arguments is the *fallacy of popular appeal*. This fallacy is most likely to be used by a cultural relativist or by a person at the conventional stages of moral reasoning. The *fallacy of hasty generalization* may also be used by a cultural relativist to justify cultural stereotypes and the denial of equal treatment to certain groups of people.

Finally, the *slippery-slope fallacy* is committed in a moral argument when we argue, without sufficient evidence to support our position, against a practice on the grounds that if we allow it, then we'll have to permit other similar actions. This fallacy is most common in arguments about new technologies or practices—such as genetic engineering, same-sex marriage, and physician-assisted suicide—where we're not sure of the future consequences on society.

These are only a few of the fallacies that may appear in moral arguments. For a more in-depth review of the different informal fallacies, see Chapter 5.

Connections

What are some of the ethical concerns in designing scientific experiments? *See* Chapter 12, pp. 395–396.

Resolving Moral Dilemmas

A situation in which we have a conflict between moral values is known as a **moral dilemma**. In a moral dilemma, no matter what solution you choose, it will involve doing something wrong in order to do what is right. We do *not* have a moral dilemma when the conflict is between moral values and nonmoral values, such as popularity or economic success. Solutions to moral dilemmas are not right or wrong, only better or worse.

> **moral dilemma** A situation in which there is a conflict between moral values.

In resolving a moral dilemma, it is important to resist the temptation to start with a "solution" and then rationalize it by selecting only the facts and principles that support it. Instead, a moral dilemma should be resolved in a systematic manner (see "Highlights: Steps for Resolving a Moral Dilemma").

Consider this classic example of a moral dilemma:

> On May 19, 1894, the yacht *Mignonette* sailed from England for Sydney, Australia, where it was to be delivered to its new owner. There were four people aboard: Dudley, the captain; Stephens, the mate; Brooks, a seaman; and Parker, a 17-year-old cabin boy and apprentice seaman. The yacht capsized in the South Atlantic during a storm, but the crew managed to put out in a 13-foot lifeboat. They drifted for 20 days in the open boat. During this time, they had no fresh water except rainwater and, for the last 12 days, no food. They were weak and facing starvation. The captain called them together to make a decision about their fate. What should they do?

The first step in resolving a moral dilemma is to *clearly describe the facts*, including finding answers to any missing information. In the case of the *Mignonette* crew, you may want to know whether it was possible to catch fish (the answer is no); how much longer the crew might live (one was already dying), or whether they were near

a shipping lane (no). You may also have questions about the status of the different men: Do they have families back home, how old are they, and so forth.

Next, *list the relevant moral principles and concerns*. We have a *duty to respect life*, as well as a *duty of nonmaleficence*—not to cause harm or to minimize harm. The *duty of justice* and equal treatment of all of the crew members is also relevant in this case. It's not fair to single out one crew member to kill and eat. The crew members also have a *liberty right* to be left alone and not be killed unless they are interfering with someone's equal right to life. On the other hand, the captain has a *duty of fidelity* to his crew, which might put the onus on him to sacrifice his life to save his crew.

Once you have collected all your facts and made a list of the relevant moral principles, *list the possible courses of action*. Now is the time to brainstorm and get feedback from other people. List any possible actions that come to mind. In this dilemma, possible courses of action might include the following:

- The crew can wait and hope for a rescue.
- Everyone can starve to death together.
- Everyone can commit suicide together.
- The crew can eat the first person who dies.
- The crew can kill and eat the weakest person.
- The crew can kill and eat the person with the least social utility.
- Someone can volunteer to be killed and eaten.
- The crew can draw lots to see who gets eaten.

Ideally, the best resolution to a moral dilemma is the one that honors as many moral values as possible.

> **HIGHLIGHTS**
>
> **STEPS FOR RESOLVING A MORAL DILEMMA**
>
> 1. Describe the facts.
> 2. List the relevant moral principles and concerns.
> 3. List and evaluate possible courses of action.
> 4. Devise a plan of action.
> 5. Carry out the plan of action.

The next step is to *devise a plan of action*. The crew has already tried the first course of action, but there seems to be no hope of rescue, and they are near death. They now face choosing from the remaining courses of action. To evaluate these, examine each in light of your list of moral principles. Ideally, the best resolution to a moral dilemma is the one that honors as many moral values as possible.

The principle of nonmaleficence requires that you try to minimize harm—in this case, the death of the crew members. Because the second and third courses of action involve the death of everyone, they're not good choices. On the other hand, killing someone without that person's permission is a violation of the person's liberty right and is unjust because it discriminates against the person. Eating the person who dies first, although gross, is not immoral—except to cultural relativists, since cannibalism is taboo in our society. Under the circumstances, it may be the best solution, since it honors the most moral principles. However, what if no one has died yet, and instead everyone is on the verge of starvation? The last two solutions both avoid the problem of injustice and may have to be the last resort.

The final step is to *carry out the plan of action*. It's also a good idea to have a backup plan in case the first plan of action doesn't work. In some moral dilemmas, people may agree on the premises but still come to different conclusions because they prioritize the relevant moral duties and concerns differently. For example, the captain may favor utilitarian theory and value the strongest members of his crew, reasoning that keeping them alive and killing the weakest member may increase the chances of at least *one* person surviving. However, the cabin boy, who lacks experience and has become extremely seasick, may value the fidelity of the captain

Connections

What is legal precedence, and what type of inductive reasoning is it based on? *See Chapter 13, p. 433.*

and believe that it is the captain's tacit duty to sacrifice himself for his crew, since he was the one who was responsible for getting them into this precarious position in the first place. On the other hand, a person at the postconventional stages of moral reasoning who favors the justice perspective would probably prefer the last course of action—draw lots to see who gets eaten—since it is the most fair and just solution.

In fact, what happened is that the captain and two crew members killed Parker and ate him. The three remaining survivors were eventually rescued by a Swedish ship and returned to England, where they were tried for murder. The court ruled that the killing of Parker was not justified, since it was not in self-defense, and the men were found guilty of murder. This ruling continues to serve as a legal precedent in maritime law.

In this section, we have seen that a moral argument is much like other arguments, except that it must include at least one prescriptive premise. When trying to decide what is the best moral position or course of action, you should begin by listing the premises. Just as you would for other arguments, you must check the descriptive premises for their accuracy. If used correctly, moral reasoning can be a powerful tool for clarifying and resolving issues and dilemmas in your everyday life.

1. Determine whether each of the following premises is a descriptive premise, prescriptive premise, or a premise containing a definition:
   a. You ought to keep your promise to Chad.
   b. Mary is opposed to capital punishment.
   c. Torturing prisoners of war is a violation of the Geneva convention.
   d. Steroids are a type of performance-enhancing drug.
   e. We are all entitled to freedom of speech.
   f. Doing community service work makes me feel good about myself.
   g. Binge drinking is harmful because it can cause acute intoxication and even death.
   h. Americans should give more money to poorer nations.

2. Discuss possible courses of action (conclusions) that your friend who scraped the fender of the car in the parking lot might take in the scenario described on pages 297.

3. Evaluate each of the following moral arguments. If an argument is missing one or more premises, indicate what they are.
   a. You should not drink alcohol in your dorm room. After all, it's against the rules, since we're a dry campus. Also, it's against the law for anyone younger than 21 to drink alcohol, and you're only 18.
   b. Euthanasia is wrong because it interferes with the natural dying process. We should wait until it is our time to die.
   c. You should think of doing the optional community-service learning project for class. Studies show that doing a community-service project can actually enhance a student's level of moral development.
   d. Professor Dugan is Chris's teacher. Therefore, it would be wrong for Professor Dugan to try to initiate an intimate relationship with Chris.
   e. You're only 28. You should wait until you're in your thirties to get married. The duty of fidelity requires that we should do our best to honor our marriage vow "until death do us part," and the older you are when you get married, the less likely you are to divorce.
   f. Animals can feel pain. It is wrong to cause sentient beings pain when it can be avoided. Therefore, it is wrong to eat meat.
   g. Medical research using human embryonic stems cells is morally acceptable. Recent polls show that the majority of Americans think that stem-cell research should be legal.
   h. The dining hall should provide kosher meals. Several of the students in our dormitory are Orthodox Jews.

4. Working in small groups and using the five-step method discussed on pages 299, resolve the following moral dilemmas:
   a. Imagine that your class is on a yacht (you have a very rich professor) 3 miles offshore for an end-of-semester celebration. A storm strikes. There are only enough lifeboats to save half the people on the yacht. What should you do?
   b. You are answering a hotline for the local women's resource center as part of a community-service project for school. A college student calls and tells you she is feeling suicidal. She also tells you that she has run away, because she is afraid of her boyfriend with whom she is sharing an apartment. You recognize her from her story, although she doesn't recognize your voice. You make arrangements for her to stay at the shelter belonging to the resource center. However, a few days later, you see her on campus with her boyfriend. Her face and upper arms are bruised. What should you do?
   c. You are a member of the National Guard and have been told to evacuate people from an area that is predicted to be hit by a potentially devastating and deadly hurricane. You approach a family with three young children that is living in a high-risk area. The parents refuse to evacuate, saying that they rode out the last hurricane and survived and plan to do the same this time. One of the children is frightened and wants to go with you. The parents say no—the family belongs together. What should you do?
   d. You are a family physician. One of your patients, a 37-year-old married man, has just found out that he has gonorrhea. He pleads with you not to tell his wife about his condition, since he is worried that

she'll leave him if she finds out that he's been unfaithful. His wife is also one of your patients and has scheduled a visit for her annual checkup. The husband asks you to tell his wife, should she ask you, that he is taking antibiotics for a urinary tract infection. What should you do?

e. You are an administrator at a community college and suspect that one of the students, who is something of a troublemaker, is keeping a gun in his locker. What should you do?

f. Tyrone, a 19-year-old college student, lost the use of both his arms and legs after an automobile accident in which his neck was broken. He has been in the hospital for 4 months when he calls in his physician and tells the physician that he no longer wants to go on living. He asks the physician to give him a lethal injection. Assisted suicide is illegal in the state. What should the physician do?

g. Megan is a college student who has been picked up for possession of a small amount of marijuana. In return for not bringing criminal charges against her, since she has no previous record, the police ask if she'll serve as an undercover agent to catch drug dealers on her campus. Should she accept the assignment?

h. Rose and Joe have been living together in a monogamous relationship for the past 2 years—since the beginning of their sophomore year at college. They both agreed, at the time they moved in together, that either could leave the relationship at any time. However, Rose unexpectedly became pregnant. Because she is opposed to abortion, she has resigned herself to having the baby. When Rose is 6 months pregnant, Joe decides to leave. He leaves a short note saying, "It was fun while it lasted, but it's time for me to move on." What should Rose do?

5. Choose one of the moral dilemmas listed in the in-class exercises that was not discussed in class. Use the five-step method on page 299 to come up with a resolution to the dilemma, and then write an essay describing your thought processes and how you arrived at your conclusion.

6. *Journal Assignment.* Write a journal entry about resolving moral conflicts. Come up with a moral conflict in your life. Using the five-step method on pages 299, come up with a resolution to the conflict. If you are willing, share your proposed resolution to your conflict with the class. If appropriate, make modifications to your plan on the basis of class feedback.

1. How does conscience help us to make moral decisions?
   - Conscience has both a cognitive and an affective (emotional) aspect. The cognitive aspect provides us with knowledge and judgment of what is right and wrong, while moral sentiments or feelings, such as empathy, moral indignation, and guilt, motivate us to take action.

2. What is the stage theory regarding the development of moral reasoning?
   - Kohlberg and Gilligan proposed three levels or stages: (1) preconventional, in which people put their needs and concerns before those of others; (2) conventional, in which people conform to peer or societal norms; and (3) postconventional, in which people are able to use universal moral principles and to balance their needs and the needs of others. Most American adults and college students are at the conventional stage of development.

3. In what ways can the different moral theories help us in formulating moral arguments?
   - Moral theories provide the foundation for moral arguments and their application to real-life situations by making us aware of the different moral principles, rights, and concerns and how to prioritize them in making effective moral decisions.

that it would have involved a risk of death for himself. But the thirty-eight not only did not do this, they did not even trouble to pick up a phone to call the police. Minimally Decent Samaritanism would call for doing at least that, and their not having done it was monstrous. . . .

At all events it seems plain that it was not morally required of any of the thirty-eight that he rush out to give direct assistance at the risk of his life—nine years or nine months—to sustaining that life of a person who has no special right (we were leaving open the possibility of this) to demand it. . . .

I should think, myself, that Minimally Decent Samaritan laws would be one thing, Good Samaritan laws quite another, and in fact highly improper. . . . I have been arguing that no person is morally required to make large sacrifices to sustain the life of another who has no right to demand them, and this even where the sacrifices do not include life itself; we are not morally required to be Good Samaritans or anyway Very Good Samaritans to one another. But what if a man cannot extricate himself from such a situation? What if he appeals to us to extricate him? It seems to me plain that there are cases in which we can, cases in which a Good Samaritan would extricate him. There you are, you were kidnapped, and nine years in bed with that violinist lie ahead of you. You have your own life to lead. You are sorry, but you simply cannot see giving up so much of your life to the sustaining of his. You cannot extricate yourself, and ask us to do so. I should have thought that—in light of his having no right to the use of your body—it was obvious that we do not have to accede to your being forced to give up so much. We can do what you ask. There is no injustice to the violinist in our doing so.

Following the lead of opponents of abortion, I have throughout been speaking of the fetus merely as a person, and what I have been asking is whether or not the argument we began with, which proceeds only from the fetus' being a person, really does not establish its conclusion. I have argued that it does not.

But of course there are arguments and arguments, and it may be said that I have simply fastened on the wrong one. It may be said that what is important is not merely the fact that the fetus is a person, but that it is a person for whom the woman has a special kind of responsibility issuing from the fact that she is the mother. And it might be argued that all my analogies are therefore irrelevant for you do not have that special responsibility for that violinist, Henry Fonda does not have that special kind of responsibility for me. And our attention might be drawn to the fact that men and women both are compelled by law to provide support for their children.

. . . Surely we do not have any such "special responsibility" for a person unless we have assumed it, explicitly or implicitly. If a set of parents do not try to prevent a pregnancy, do not obtain an abortion; and then at the time of birth of the child do not put it out for adoption, but rather take it home with them, then they have assumed responsibility for it, they have given it rights, and they cannot *now* withdraw support from it at the cost of its life because they now find it difficult to go on providing for it. But if

they have taken all reasonable precautions against having a child, they do not simply by virtue of their biological relationship to the child who comes into existence have a special responsibility for it. They may wish to assume responsibility for it, or they may not wish to. And I am suggesting that if assuming responsibility for it would require large sacrifices, then they may refuse. . . .

My argument will be found unsatisfactory on two counts by many of those who want to regard abortion as morally permissible. First, while I do argue that abortion is not impermissible, I do not argue that it is always permissible. There may well be cases in which carrying the child to term requires only Minimally Decent Samaritanism of the mother, and this is a standard we must not fall below. . . .

Secondly, while I am arguing for the permissibility of abortion in some cases, I am not arguing for the right to secure the death of the unborn child. It is easy to confuse these two things in that up to a certain point in the life of the fetus it is not able to survive outside the mother's body; hence removing it from her body guarantees its death. But they are importantly different. I have argued that you are not morally required to spend nine months in bed, sustaining the life of that violinist; but to say this is by no means to say that if, when you unplug yourself, there is a miracle and he survives, you then have to turn around and slit his throat. You may detach yourself even if this costs him his life; you have no right to be guaranteed his death, by some other means, if unplugging yourself does not kill him. There are some people who will feel dissatisfied by this feature of my argument. A woman may be utterly devastated by the thought of a child, a bit of herself, put out for adoption and never seen or heard of again. She

QUESTIONS

1. What is Thomson's position regarding the personhood of the fetus?

2. How does Thomson use the violinist analogy to illustrate the relationship between the fetus and the woman? What conclusion does she draw?

3. How does Thomson respond to the pro-life argument that if the fetus has a right to life, then abortion is unjust killing?

4. According to Thomson, are there any circumstances in which abortion is not morally permissible?

5. How does Thomson respond to the argument that if a woman voluntarily has sex, then she does not have the right to an abortion should she become pregnant?

6. What is the difference between a Minimally Decent Samaritan and a Good Samaritan? What is the relevance of this distinction for the abortion debate?

may therefore want not merely that the child be detached from her, but more, that it die. Some opponents of abortion are inclined to regard this as beneath contempt—thereby showing insensitivity to what is surely a powerful source of despair. All the same, I agree that the desire for the child's death is not one which anybody may gratify, should it turn out to be possible to detach the child alive.

At this place, however, it should be remembered that we have only been pretending throughout that the fetus is a human being from the moment of conception. A very early abortion is surely not the killing of a person, and so is not dealt with by anything I have said here.

Refuse to Choose: Women Deserve Better than Abortion

SERRIN M. FOSTER

Serrin Foster is president of Feminists for Life of America. In her article, Foster points out that feminists have traditionally been opposed to abortion. She argues that rather than benefiting women, abortion harms women.

For more than two centuries feminists have opposed abortion.

British feminist author Mary Wollstonecraft decried, in scathing 17th-century terms, the sexual exploitation of women in *A Vindication of the Rights of Women*. She went on to condemn those who would "either destroy the embryo in the womb or casting it off when born," saying: "Nature in everything deserves respect, and those who violate her laws seldom violate them with impunity."

Elizabeth Cady Stanton, who in 1848 organized the first women's convention in Seneca Falls, New York, and suffragist organizer Susan B. Anthony were active in the abolitionist movement. Their basic belief in the rights of all human beings extended to women, slaves, and children—born and unborn. While history books are filled with their efforts to win rights for women, it is less well known that the early American feminists also opposed abortion.

Without known exception, the early feminists condemned abortion in the strongest terms. Susan B. Anthony and Elizabeth Cady Stanton's radical feminist newspaper, *The Revolution*, called abortion "child murder." Stanton classified abortion as a form of "infanticide" and said, "When we consider that women have been treated as property, it is degrading to women that we should treat our children as property to be disposed of as we see fit."

. . . Many today are also surprised to learn that abortion was common in the 1800s. While Anthony refused to take advertisements, believing money could taint editorials in *The Revolution*, thinly disguised abortifacients were common advertisements in women's magazines.

Victoria Woodhull and her sister Tennessee Claflin produced their own publication, *Woodhull's and Claflin's Weekly*. Woodhull, considered by many to be the most radical of all for her advocacy of "free love," was the first woman to run for president and an ardent advocate of the unborn. "The rights of children as individuals begin while yet they remain the foetus."

. . . Feminists who fought for the rights of women—to vote, sit on a jury, testify on their own behalf, control their own money, and defend themselves from marital rape—also fought for our right to life. . . .

Alice Paul, Anthony's successor and author of the original Equal Rights Amendment, once told a friend, "Abortion is the ultimate exploitation to women."

Properly defined, feminism is a philosophy that embraces basic rights for all human beings without exception—without regard to one's race, religion, sex, size, age, location, disability or parentage. Feminism rejects the use of force to dominate, control, or destroy one another. Abortion violates the core principles of feminism: nondiscrimination, nonviolence and justice for all.

In our own day Feminists for Life's Honorary Chair Patricia Heaton, winner of two Emmy awards and a best-selling author, says, "Women experiencing an unplanned pregnancy also deserve unplanned joy." The sad reality is that the "unplanned joy" Patricia Heaton envisions for women is all too rare. Instead, women experiencing an unplanned pregnancy often end up experiencing the tragic violence of abortion.

Our Body. Our Choice. Our *Problem*.

Statistics gathered by abortion supporters reveal that the overarching reasons women with unintended pregnancies turn to abortion are lack of financial resources and lack of emotional support. Many women also say they felt abandoned, or even coerced into having an abortion. Despite child support laws, some fathers threaten to withhold support. Domestic violence against pregnant women at the hands of a partner is being reported with greater frequency. . . .

The women at highest risk of resorting to abortion are those of college age. One out of five abortions is performed on a college student. For many years, Feminists for Life's College Outreach Program has been listening to women on campuses across the country. Women who tested positive for pregnancy at a campus health center tell us—almost universally—that the next words they heard from clinic staff were "I'm so sorry."

Then they were handed a business card for a local abortion clinic. University counselors and professors echo this message, telling students that they can't possibly continue their education and have a child—as if pregnancy makes women incapable of reading, writing or thinking.

Resources are similarly lopsided. Some colleges offer $300 loans for an abortion, but no financial aid if the young woman gives birth. Pregnant and parenting students report that housing, maternity coverage, child care and telecommuting options are nonexistent on many campuses, and expensive on others. Women who are visibly pregnant are stared at like exotic animals when they cross the campus.

Forcing a woman to choose between sacrificing her education or career plans and sacrificing her child is not much of a "free choice."

Beyond the campus, support is also lacking for any choice other than abortion. Pregnant and parenting women in the workplace still cannot count on basic benefits such as maternity coverage, job sharing, flex time, telecommuting, or the ability to make a living wage.

Even well-meaning family and friends often fail to give women what they really need and want—congratulations and unconditional support. Instead of saying, "How can I help?" they say, "A baby will ruin your life."

In other words, most women "choose" abortion precisely because they believe they have no other choice.

More than 30 years since the U.S. Supreme Court handed down the *Roe v. Wade* decision legalizing abortion, the pro-choice mantra "Our body, our choice" still means the same thing: Our problem. Abortion is not a measure of society's success in meeting the needs of women; it's a measure of its failure.

Abortion Harms Women

The damage that abortion causes to women's bodies can result in infertility, future miscarriages, and even death. Second-term abortions performed on teens with a family history of breast cancer elevate their risk of breast cancer. Many women carry emotional scars from the experience. Studies from Finland, Great Britain, Canada and the United States reveal higher rates of suicide, attempted suicide and psychiatric admissions among women who have had an abortion compared to women who have given birth. . . .

Abortion is a symptom of—never a solution to—the problems faced by women. Americans like to say, "Failure is not an option." Yet abortion has completely failed as a social policy designed to aid women. Women have had to settle for far less than they need and deserve.

Refuse to Choose

Abstract rhetoric that pits "women's rights" against "the baby" does nothing to solve the unmet needs of women. As a result, more than a million times a year in America, women lay their bodies down or swallow a bitter pill. Every day that goes by with the needs of pregnant women unmet is another day marked by thousands of abortions. Although Americans are deeply divided on abortion, there is no disagreement that the number of abortions needs to be reduced. No compassionate person wants a woman to suffer through the personal tragedy of abortion.

Abortion is a reflection that we have not met the needs of women. Susan B. Anthony urged activists to address the root causes that drive women to abortion. It's time for feminism to return to its roots with a women-centered plan to significantly eliminate abortion.

Women's advocates on both sides need to work together for better outcomes for women and children. We should seek a comprehensive review of the reasons that drive women to abortion. We must listen to women from all walks of life—women who have had abortions, single and married mothers, birth mothers. Men should be welcomed as partners in problem solving. We need to listen, to hear women and create a step-by-step plan to systematically eliminate the root causes that drive so many women to abortion—primarily the lack of financial resources and lack of emotional support.

We need to engage those in higher education, health care, technology, corporations, small businesses, the entertainment industry, government and the media to help redirect the debate toward positive outcomes for all concerned.

We must begin by finding solutions for those at highest risk of abortion—college women, young working women, and low-income women.

College campuses should reexamine their policies, attitudes, and support for pregnant and parenting students and staff. Through programs like Feminists for Life's Pregnancy Resource Forums, people on all sides of the debate within the campus community can put aside their differences to address the needs of pregnant and parenting students, including housing, child care and maternity benefits in student health-care plans.

Family-friendly workplaces that offer child care, flex time, and telecommuting solutions can help lessen the pressure on women to choose between their careers and their children. Farsighted employers like Steelcase Corporation of Michigan set up offices in the homes of employees who are new parents to help them telecommute.

Pregnancy care centers need funding to assist women to follow through on nonviolent, life-affirming choices—whether that involves married parenthood, single parenthood, extended family or co-parenting options, or adoption.

We need to replicate the success achieved in Pennsylvania, where abortions have been greatly reduced through state funding resource centers that promote life-affirming alternatives. Pennsylvania law also mandates that a woman seeking an abortion be accurately and adequately informed about the procedure, fetal development, and the father's rights and responsibilities so she can make an informed choice. The late Governor Robert Casey knew that women deserve—and can handle—this information. We can work with states to implement the State Children's Health Insurance Program (SCHIP), whose services include prenatal care for low-income women and their unborn children.

It is also important that we reverse the negative attitudes toward children and parenting that have become so prevalent in our culture. Our society needs once again to cherish motherhood, champion fatherhood, and celebrate the benefits and rewards of parenthood.

Return to Feminism's Roots

In 1869, Mattie Brinkerhoff, wrote in *The Revolution*: "When a man steals to satisfy hunger, we may safely conclude that there is something wrong in society. So when a woman destroys the life of her unborn child, it is evidence that either by education or circumstances she has been greatly wronged." Every woman deserves better, and every child deserves a chance at life.

It is time to reaffirm the strength and dignity of women, the importance of fathers, and the value of every human life. It's time women refuse to choose between sacrificing education and career plans or sacrificing their children. We must raise expectations and focus our efforts on what is best for women, children and families—so that one day soon we will look back at this barbaric practice and wonder why any woman ever felt coerced into suffering through an abortion.

Women deserve better.

QUESTIONS

1. What was the position of feminists over the last two centuries on abortion?

2. What does Foster mean when she says that making abortion a woman's choice also makes abortion her problem?

3. How do colleges generally react when a student becomes pregnant?

4. According to Foster, how does abortion harm women?

5. What options does Foster propose instead of abortion?

Think >> AND DISCUSS

1. Identify the main premises in the *Roe v. Wade* majority opinion. Break down and diagram the argument used to support the legalization of abortion. Critically evaluate the argument.

2. In his dissenting opinion, Justice William Rehnquist (1924–2005) argued that the implied right to privacy in the Fourteenth Amendment (see second footnote on page 303) cannot be used broadly to overturn laws that restrict abortion. He also pointed out that a belief in the right to abortion, which was illegal in most states when the Fourteenth Amendment was adopted, is not "so rooted in the traditions and conscience of our people as to be ranked as fundamental." Discuss Rehnquist's objections to the *Roe v. Wade* ruling and how both Blackmun and Thomson might respond to him.

3. Identify the different types of arguments (inductive and deductive) in the Thomson reading. For the inductive arguments, note which are generalizations, analogies, and causal arguments.

4. Working in small groups or as a class, make a list of premises relevant to the abortion issue. Using these premises, come up with a policy (conclusion) for addressing the issue of abortion in the United States.

5. President George W. Bush had the opportunity to appoint two new justices to the Supreme Court. Discuss whether a candidate's position on abortion and *Roe v. Wade* should be taken into consideration in nominating or rejecting candidates.

6. Discuss Thomson's conclusion that abortion may be morally defensible even if the fetus is a person. In her analogies, does Thomson take the personhood of the fetus as seriously as the personhood of the woman? Discuss how Foster would most likely respond to Thomson's argument.

7. One of Thomson's premises is that we do not have a responsibility toward another person unless we have voluntarily assumed it. Discuss the implications of this premise regarding any obligation a father may have to his biological child when the mother chooses to continue her pregnancy but he made it clear from the beginning that he did not want to have the child.[32]

8. Identify the descriptive, prescriptive, and definitional premises in Foster's argument. Discuss whether these premises support her conclusion. Are her responses to the counterarguments effective?

9. Foster argues that by making abortion a woman's choice, it makes abortion her problem. What does she mean by this? Do you agree with her that abortion is rarely a "free choice"? Support your answer.

Think FIRST >>

- What strategies are used in marketing research and marketing?

- How do marketing and advertising impact the consumer?

- How can we as consumers be more aware of fallacies and rhetorical devices used in advertising?

we'll learn about business marketing research and strategies, including those used by GEICO. We will also apply our critical-thinking skills to recognizing and evaluating marketing strategies and advertisements that we encounter in our everyday lives. Specifically, we will

- Learn about the importance of marketing in business

- Study marketing research and strategies

- Relate the SWOT model to marketing strategies

- Consider the impact of marketing and advertising on the consumer

- Look at the relationship between big business, advertising, and mass media

- Examine the use of fallacious reasoning and rhetorical devices in advertising

MARKETING IN A CONSUMER CULTURE

Marketing a product or service is an essential component of doing business in a consumer culture, such as we have in the United States. A **business** is an organization that seeks to make a profit by providing goods and services desired by its customers. (**Profit** is the money left over after all expenses are paid.) A business's success depends

business An organization that makes a profit by providing goods and services to customers.

profit The money left over after all expenses are paid.

My job is saving you money.

I love my job.

GEICO
geico.com

on its ability to determine what customers want and then provide it at a reasonable cost. To be competitive, businesses need to plan and implement effective strategies for marketing and advertising these products and services.

Marc Ecko was successful in marketing his new line of urban clothing in part because he first carefully researched his target audience's "hot buttons."

Marketing Research

marketing research Identifying a target market and finding out if it matches customer desires.

The process of identifying a target market for a product or service and finding out if it matches what the customer wants is called **marketing research**—or, as marketing professionals say, discovering customers' "hot buttons."

At the age of 20, fashion designer and former graffiti artist Marc Ecko successfully introduced a new line of urban clothing by targeting young males who were into skateboarding and hip-hop music. The Ecko Unlimited brand, with its airbrushed T-shirts and baggy jeans, quickly amassed a loyal following. Ecko succeeded because he knew his target population's hot buttons. In this case, they wanted a line of clothing that set them apart and that said something about their lifestyle. GEICO also targets young people with its funny, offbeat ads as a way of recruiting new drivers and creating a loyal, long-term customer base.

There are several approaches to marketing research, including surveys, observation, and experimentation, each of which involves proficiency in critical thinking and inductive logic. Survey research is used to collect informa-

tion and opinions about a product and can be done at a mall or by mail, e-mail, Internet, or phone. Informal surveys or group brainstorming sessions may be conducted as well. Southwest Airlines, for instance, holds focus groups with consumers to come up with ways of maintaining or improving the airline's position in the market.[2] To encourage participation, some companies give rewards, such as cash or free trips, to customers who participate in market research.

Observation involves directly monitoring customers' buying patterns. A market researcher may watch customers and record their actions, or use sales data such as bar-code inventories to collect information. Nielsen Media Research also uses observation to track the television viewing habits of a representative sample of Americans via a small device attached to their television

Hot or Not?

What do you see as today's consumer "hot buttons"?

sets. We'll be looking more at the relationship between advertising and the mass media later in this chapter.

Experimentation—another type of marketing research—measures cause–effect relationships between the purchase of a product or service and selected variables such as packaging, advertising logo, or price. These are changed to determine the effect of the changes on consumers' responses. Since these three approaches all use inductive logic, they only provide information on what products will most probably be successful in the market—but they do not, in themselves, ensure success.

> A business starting out with questionable assumptions can make incorrect predictions, take inappropriate actions, and wind up with disappointing outcomes—a process sometimes referred to as the "doom loop."

Avoiding Confirmation Bias and Other Errors in Thinking

Like individuals, a business may fail to do its research or to consider certain evidence because it assumes that its beliefs are correct when in fact they may not be. Information can be distorted by cognitive and social errors such as confirmation bias, probability error, and the "one of us/one of them" error. A business starting out with questionable assumptions can make incorrect predictions, take inappropriate actions, and wind up with disappointing outcomes—a process sometimes referred to as the "doom loop."[3]

In the 1960s Japanese automobile manufacturers got caught up in the "doom loop" when they marketed cars in the United States with 1,000-cc engines, which were a lot smaller than the 1,500- to 1,600-cc engines in American-built small cars. Given the poor condition of Japanese roads at the time, 1,000 cc was sufficient for the speeds possible in Japan but not for speeds on U.S. highways. Yutaka Katayama, who came to the United States in 1960 as marketing manager for Datsun (now Nissan), challenged the company's assumptions and suggested that 1,000-cc engines were insufficient for the American market. However, managers in Japan were insulted and rejected his advice. It took Katayama almost a decade to convince Datsun to change its preconceptions. By that time, Honda's Civic, which changed its strategy and came out in 1972 with a 1,169-cc engine and increased its engine size over the next few years, had made significant inroads into the American small-car market.

Confirmation bias, as the Datsun example shows, is an ongoing problem in business. Marketers may misinterpret or distort available infor-mation, limit their research to sources that support their view, or dismiss contradictory evidence as an anomaly. Datsun/Nissan was not the only car manufacturer that failed to take into account key evidence in its marketing research.

By 1979, imported cars accounted for 20 percent of total car sales in the United States. However, U.S. manufacturers regarded this as an anomaly. Even into the 1980s, U.S. carmakers ignored the growing market for imported cars and distorted the evidence regarding the sales of foreign-made cars when calculating their own share of the U.S. market, by including only the sales of American car manufacturers. In addition, they assumed that Americans would continue to buy American cars when Japanese imports were initially introduced.[4]

Confirmation bias may also lead marketing researchers to overcommit to a particular answer rather than exploring other options—what is known in the business world as **escalation of commitment** or **loss aversion**. This occurs when a business continues to pursue an erroneous course of action in marketing a product, instead of changing course and cutting its losses. When videotaping went mainstream in the 1970s, two competing and incompatible types of recording systems—Betamax, produced by Sony, and VHS, produced by JVC—were released into the market. Even after it was clear that consumers preferred the cheaper VHS system, Sony continued to manufacture Betamax machines. It wasn't until 1988 that Sony finally decided to cut its financial losses and produce VHS systems instead. And seller's loss aversion contributed to the housing and mortgage crisis in 2008 when home sellers refused to lower the price of homes in the face of a slipping house market.

escalation of commitment The overcommitment of marketing to a particular answer.

Poor communication and listening skills can also lead to poor marketing decisions. A business that assumes that customers share its expectations and preferences about a product may go so far as to distort what customers say to

CATHY CARTOON For many years the swimsuit industry failed to examine its assumption that women liked to wear sexy bathing suits. In 1987 market research conducted by the Swimsuit Manufacturers Association found, as one supplier put it, "that most women would rather have a root canal without Novocain than buy a swimsuit." In their rush to make sexy bathing suits for women with fashion-model figures, the industry did not take into account the concern of the majority of women, who may be out of shape or slightly pudgy, that these bathing suits were embarrassing. It also took swimsuit companies several years to come up with the two-piece tankini that covers up the expanding midriff but allows ease of use in the public bathrooms at the beach.

DISCUSSION QUESTIONS

1. *Why do you think the swimsuit industry assumed women wanted sexy bathing suits? Support your answer.*

2. *Think of a time when you were trying to buy a particular product or service and, like Cathy, couldn't find anything that suited your needs. Write a note to a manufacturer stating what you would like to see in its product and why you think that the product would sell better if it had these features.*

fit its worldview. The firm may describe customers' preferences as "irrational" or talk in terms of what customers *should* want. For example, a fashion company was losing sales. However, when a consumer focus group said that the reason was the unattractiveness of its styles, a representative from the company responded by "explaining" why the items were not unattractive. The focus group politely deferred to him rather than challenge his "authority."[5] In this case, the company representative demonstrated poor listening skills by ignoring what the customers were telling him and changing the "facts" to fit his worldview. As a result, the company continued to lose sales.

Because of the problems of confirmation bias and people's tendency to conform to group pressures, many companies use independent marketing research companies or rely on research carried out by government agencies. These companies and agencies also have expertise in designing surveys and selecting a representative sample from among customers or potential customers. For example, GEICO enlisted the help of the Martin Agency, whose clients also include Walmart and UPS.

Accurate, complete, and unbiased marketing research is particularly important when introducing a product to the international market. What may sell well in one country may not sell in others. Factors such as presentation, packaging, and the name of a product must be researched, as must customers' interest in the product itself. When Proctor & Gamble first marketed its jars of Gerber baby food in

one African nation, hardly anyone bought them.[6] On further investigation, Proctor & Gamble realized its mistake. Because many of the people in the country were illiterate, food product labels generally carried pictures of what was inside. Using inductive argument by analogy, the potential customers drew the logical but unsavory conclusion that the jars of baby food contained ground-up babies!

The management of Nissan in Tokyo also failed to do its research when it came up with the name *My Fair Lady* for their first sports car for the American market—hardly a name that connotes the engine power and excitement that most American consumers seek in a sports car. Fortunately, Yutaka Katayama had the foresight to remove the nameplates with *My Fair Lady* and replace them with ones that read *240Z*, the internal designation for the car.[7] The popular sports car came to be known as the Z-car.

In addition to understanding the current market, marketing research must anticipate future trends to take advantage of opportunities. To do this, marketing researchers must put aside their personal biases and be open-minded, attentive, and intellectually curious. What first appears to be a market anomaly may actually be the beginning of a trend. The Western Union telegraph company, which dominated the nation's communications network in the mid-nineteenth century, failed to anticipate the profound effect of the telephone on people's lives. In 1876 it turned down the opportunity to purchase Alexander Graham Bell's patents on the telephone. "This 'telephone,'" concluded Western Union, "has too many shortcomings to be seriously considered as a means of communication."

MARKETING STRATEGIES

Only after we have examined our assumptions and gathered the relevant information are we ready to engage in strategic planning. A **strategic plan** is a method by which an organization deploys its resources to realize a goal or objective. In business, strategic planning generally involves the use of a strategic model, which is ". . . a systematic list of policies that will guide the future specification of inputs, outputs, processes, and values of the complete operations of the business of the corporation."[8]

strategic plan A method by which an organization deploys its resources to realize a goal.

SWOT model Used to analyze a company's strengths, weaknesses, external opportunities, and threats.

The SWOT Model

SWOT is an acronym for "strengths, weaknesses, opportunities, and threats." The **SWOT model** is used to analyze a company's strengths and weaknesses, as well as external opportunities and threats in the business environment. This strategic model can be used for developing a marketing strategy and for deciding (among other things) whether to launch a new business or expand an existing business. The SWOT model is also used by individuals for making major life decisions, such as what career or college major to choose or where to live.

The first two components of SWOT (strengths and weaknesses) require an internal assessment. Opportunities and threats, in contrast, are external to a company. Analyzing a company's resources and competitive capacity is similar to drawing up a balance sheet on which strengths are weighed against weaknesses or deficiencies.

In carrying out a SWOT analysis, we begin by making a list of a company's greatest strengths. Strengths are defined as a company's assets and core competencies—in other words, what it does best. A company's strengths contribute to its ability to achieve its goals and do certain things better than its competitors.[9] Walmart, which employs over 2 million people, is the world's largest corporation.[10] Its main strength is its efficiency and innovation in getting the lowest price for its customers, which it does primarily by importing 80 percent of its manufactured goods from low-wage China. Walmart has an aggressive and effective marketing strategy. Unlike its now-bankrupt competitor Kmart, which had periodic special sales, Walmart brags of its "always low prices." Another facet of its marketing strategy is its "good works" programs and community phi-

The SWOT Model*

Strengths	Weaknesses	Opportunities	Threats
• Location of facilities • Unique selling points • Large customer base • Commitment/productivity of employees • Ability to meet consumer demand • Quality of product or service • Company reputation • Customer service program • Strong management • Product awareness/brand recognition • Marketing distribution	• Outdated facility/ equipment • Insufficient information • Debts or limited financial resources • Weak consumer demand • Strong competitors • Poor management • Poor marketing • Inability to meet deadline pressures • Lack of expertise	• New markets • Competitor's vulnerabilities • Industry or lifestyle trends • Technology developments/ innovations • Global influences • Chance to buy out a rival company • Fashion influences • Increase in consumer spending • New partners	• Competitors • Restrictive legal regulations • Global warming • Natural disasters • New technologies • Shift in consumer demands • Consumer dissatisfaction • Slow economy • Negative media coverage • Rising cost of wages/benefits • Outsourcing

lanthropy, in which Walmart aggressively promotes itself as a "good neighbor" in the small communities where it sets up its megastores.

Weaknesses, in contrast, are things that a company lacks or does poorly. They include internal liabilities or inadequacies, such as a lack of expertise, insufficient information, limited financial resources for meeting consumer demand, or poor location. In coming up with a marketing strategy,

The "How May I Help You?" and the "Always Low Prices" slogans have helped to cement Walmart as a leader among world corporations.

it is important that a business do an internal survey of its weaknesses. Even the strongest company can be brought down because of an unacknowledged internal weakness or an unanticipated external threat. Internal management and accounting problems, including having too small of a financial cushion to weather a housing market downturn (an external threat), led to the near collapse of the mortgage giant Fannie Mae in 2008. The use of resistance, such as denial, can blind a business to internal weaknesses. While Japanese automobile makers were developing efficient, automated production facilities, American automobile companies remained labor intensive, employing four times as many workers to produce a car.[11] As we noted earlier, the marketing strategy of the American Automobile industry of plugging "American-made" has not been as effective in attracting consumers as are the lower prices promoted by the Japanese car manufacturers.

One of GEICO's weaknesses was its size, compared with the insurance giants such as State Farm Insurance and Allstate; it also had a hard-to-remember name. One way GEICO overcame this weakness was by coming up with a chatty gecko as its mascot, a marketing strategy to help customers remember its name and to associate the name with fun. GEICO also saturated the airwaves with its ads, spending hundreds of millions of dollars on ads a year. The last two parts of a SWOT analysis (opportunities and threats) address factors that are external to a company and mostly beyond its control. Developing an effective marketing

There is no doubt that advertising can provide us with valuable information and options for making our lives easier. On the other hand, the ultimate purpose of advertising is to make money for the advertiser, not to advance truth. Advertising by its very nature is one-sided, persuasive communication. In some instances advertising carries little or no information about the product, instead relying on psychological ploys to create a demand for the product.

The Role of Advertising in the Media

Advertising is the keystone of the mass media. We come into contact more with advertising than with any other specific form of media programming. The average American is exposed to about 250 advertisements a day, or 2 million by the time he or she is 25 years old.[20] Many, if not most, of these ads reach us through the mass media. Even inside movie theaters, which used to be ad-free, we now find ourselves subjected to several minutes of advertisements after the lights dim, followed in some cases by an hour and a half of brand-name products strategically placed throughout the movie itself.

Marketers spend a lot of money identifying audiences for their products and creating ads to appeal to the target audience. Readership in print media is measured by circulation figures, as well as by surveys to find

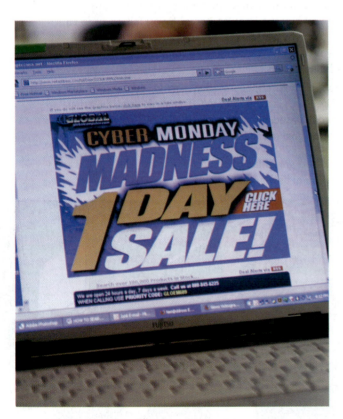

The advent of the Internet has provided marketers with new opportunities for reaching out to consumers.

Hot or Not?

Have you ever changed product loyalty as a result of an ad campaign?

out who is reading what. Media research companies also track radio audiences through the use of diaries that record an individual's listening habits. One of the largest media research companies is Nielsen Media Research, which monitors national television viewing habits using a representative sample of more than 5,000 households and 13,000 people. Through monitoring boxes installed on television sets in these households, Nielsen knows exactly when the televisions are turned on and what program is playing. Nielsen also collects demographic information on each member of participating households. Businesses then use this information to determine which programs have the best audiences for their products.

Through this process, media researchers found that *The Real World* on MTV was one of the most popular programs among young college women. Research also shows not only that young people are more likely than the rest of the population to own cell phones but also that people who watch reality television, such as *The Real World* and *American Idol*, are 34 percent more likely than the general population to switch cellular phone service within the year.[21] Because of this, many of the ads on these types of shows are for cell-phone services.

Internet advertising is also becoming increasingly popular among advertisers. It has the advantage of permitting a more precise targeting of audiences, based on which Web sites people visit. Unlike conventional media advertising, Internet advertising allows two-way communication between the audience and businesses, thus serving as a means of transacting sales and distributing goods, including the downloading of music and video games. The Army National Guard, which is facing recruitment shortfalls, has turned to advertising on the Internet to appeal to 18- to 25-year-olds. Internet surfers who are willing to scroll through the guard's recruitment message are offered free music through iTunes and video game downloads. This advertising strategy has proved successful and has attracted more than 200,000 young people, 9,000 of whom went on to meet face-to-face with a recruiter.[22]

Product Placement

Ads may also be embedded in a television program. Product placement is an advertising strategy in which "a real commercial product is used in fictional media, and the presence of the product is a result of an economic exchange"[23] between the media company and the business that produces the product. Most product placements go unnoticed unless we make a conscious effort to notice them. Coca-Cola,

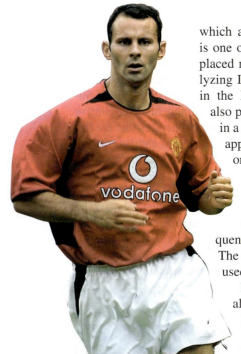

which appears on *American Idol*, is one of the brands that has been placed most frequently (see "Analyzing Images: Product Placement in the Media"). Companies may also pay to have their logos used in a show. The logo for a sports apparel company such as Nike or Wilson Sporting Goods may appear on sports uniforms and equipment in sports broadcasts. Automobile companies frequently use product placement. The television series *X Files* used Fords.

Product placement has also caught on in movies. *The Matrix Reloaded* has a highway scene in which every car was made by General Motors. The sales of Reese's Pieces increased 60 percent after the product was placed in the 1982 film *E.T.: The Extra-Terrestrial*. *You've Got Mail* was in part an advertisement for America Online. *Spider-Man 3* promoted Burger King. Audi cars were placed in *I, Robot*, while Chrysler 300C was highlighted in *Firewall*. Pepsi was pushed as the drink of choice in both *Alien vs. Predator* and *Home Alone*. Apple Computer has used product placement for more than 20 years, appearing in hit films such as *Star Trek IV: The Voyage Home*, *Men in Black*, *Independence Day*, and *Fever Pitch*, as well as in children's movies such as *Sleepover*. Hasbro toy action figures were featured in *Small Soldiers* and *Toy Story*.

Some viewers and media corporations prefer product placement rather than commercials because it doesn't take time away from the programming. Sponsors are also looking more to product placement because many more homes now have DVRs (digital video recorders) that allow viewers to record television shows and movies and skip the ads.

Much of
by info
that can
manipul
nor wou
tisemen
our eme
laden l
informa
to a rea
vice. A
informa
use of
on the
ing. H
the im

Analyzing Images

PRODUCT PLACEMENT IN THE MEDIA   Product placement on Fox television show *American Idol*: Judges Simon Cowell, Paula Abdul, and Randy Jackson shown with their "favorite" beverage.

DISCUSSION QUESTIONS

1. *Discuss the effectiveness of product placement in the photo. Discuss also the extent to which product placements rely on fallacious thinking.*

2. *Imagine that you're an advertising consultant for a show such as* American Idol, *whose target audience is primarily young people. You've been asked to come up with an advertising strategy for an MP3 player. Discuss which strategies, including product placement or separate commercials, would be most effective in getting the attention of the target audience and why.*

The organiz...
placement, arg...
deceptive. Unli...
out, there is n...
ments.[24] In add...
control over wl...
the placements...
ming, as are tr...

Television vie...
school childre...
1,000 hours ...
she spends in...
sion commerc...

Young childre...
....

Rhetorical Devices and Misleading Language

Although the FTC forbids outright deception in advertising, it does permit the use of rhetorical devices. *Euphemisms,* in particular, abound in advertising. In real estate ads, a small house or apartment is "cozy," "quaint," or "compact," while old houses are "charming" or "full of character." A software product is a "solution" and a low-cost item is "economical" or "a great value."

The rhetorical device of *hyperbole*, or exaggeration of claims regarding a particular product, is considered acceptable in the advertising industry as well. NBC's claim that it was "Must See TV" and General Food's assertion that Wheaties is "the Breakfast of Champions" are examples of hyperbole.

In addition, ads frequently contain emotive words and phrases, such as *joystick, fresh, miracle, light,* or *alive with pleasure,* to evoke positive feelings that will become associated with the product. For example, Salton later made a smaller grill that they called the "Lean Mean Fat Reducing Machine," creating the impression that you can lose weight if you use this grill.

Images and slogans are also used to create a feel-good situation without telling us much about the product. Slogans such as "I love what you do for me, Toyota" and Sprite's "Obey your thirst" convey no actual information about these brands. The use of emotive words and phrases sometimes borders on deception. In 2003, Philip Morris was found guilty of consumer fraud for the use of the term *light* in its ads, which gave the false impression that "light" cigarettes were less harmful or safer than other cigarettes.

Another advertising tactic is the use of vague, ambiguous, or obscure language. Words such as *help, can be,* and *up to* are sometimes so vague that they are meaningless. A claim that we can save "up to 50 percent" does not exclude the possibility that we may save nothing or may even pay more than we would for a similar product from a different brand. The use of obscure or technical terms can also be confusing to the consumer. For example, what is a "fixed rate" when it comes to a loan or mortgage, especially when the ad states in tiny letters at the bottom that the rates are subject to daily change?

Faulty and Weak Arguments

Ads may try to persuade us to buy their product by presenting an inductive argument using an analogy in which they compare their product to something positive or powerful. In some cases, this analogy is weak or false. Take the slogan "Chevy: Like a rock." In what ways is a Chevy like a rock? We certainly can't drive a rock. Also, rocks are free and last for millennia without needing maintenance on our part. In fact, there are few relevant similarities between a vehicle and a rock.

Some ads may appear to be logical arguments when in fact, key information is missing or statistics are misrepresented. For example, the pharmaceutical company Glaxo-SmithKline ran a magazine ad that appears to be using an inductive argument to oppose Congress's legalizing the importation of drugs from other countries. However, some of the premises are missing. The ad states: "Experts say 10% of the world's drug supply is counterfeit. Can we be sure we import the 90% that isn't?" The ad ends by inviting the reader to "do your homework. Do the math. And see if drug importation adds up for you." However, the ad doesn't provide all the information we need to do the math. The statistics in the two premises, while accurate, are misleading to the uncritical reader because they convey

Beautifully **unexpected**

IMPORTED
PRODUCT OF THAILAND

SABAI
Wine Spritzer
with Pomegranate

Available in Sainsbury's, Tesco
and bars nationwide
www.sabaispritzer.com
www.drinkaware.co.uk

AD FOR SABAI WINE SPRITZER   This sultry ad appeared in a magazine geared for the general public.

DISCUSSION QUESTIONS

1. *What audience do you think this ad is geared toward? Explain.*

2. *What did you feel and what thoughts came to your mind when you first saw this ad? What rhetorical devices, fallacies, and/or images are being used by the advertisement to evoke these thoughts and feelings in the viewer?*

3. *Discuss the relevance of the ad to the actual product being promoted. Is the ad effective? Did it make you feel more likely to buy the product? Explain why or why not.*

the impression that imported drugs are more likely to be counterfeits. Before we can draw any conclusion about the relative safety of the domestic drug supply, we need a third premise providing information on the percentage of counterfeit drugs produced in this country, as well as those coming from countries such as Canada.[33] Indeed, while the World Health Organization estimates that 10 percent of the world's drug supply is counterfeit, the organization also points out that *most* of the counterfeit drugs are from developing nations. This ad also uses scare tactics as well as the *one of us/one of them* cognitive error by counting on the reader to assume that counterfeit drugs are only a problem in *other* countries, not in *our* country (although this claim is never actually made in the ad).

In some ads, generalizations are made on the basis of statistics without having a control or comparison group or without providing information about how a sample was selected. An ad for Tempur-Pedic mattresses states: "Our sleep technology is recognized by NASA, raved about by the media, recommended worldwide by no less than 25,000 medical professionals." To start with, we have an ambiguous term—*medical professional*. Does it include only physicians and registered nurses? How about chiropractors and massage therapists? Or nurses' aides and hospital orderlies? How large was their sample, and how was it chosen? There are 600,000 physicians in the United States and 2.3 million registered nurses. If we include only these two groups in the category of medical professionals and 25,000 of them recommend Tempur-Pedic, does this mean that 99 percent of medical professionals do *not* recommend Tempur-Pedic mattresses?

A Critique of Advertising

Critics claim that advertising is damaging to society. The fallacies and rhetorical devices used in advertising, they argue, distort consumer thinking and create markets for nonessential goods and services, thereby contributing to a shallow, materialistic mind-set. As ads become increasingly sophisticated and persuasive, more and more of us are going into debt to pay for lifestyles we can't afford. Advertisements can also make people feel they are to blame if they fall short of the ideals portrayed in advertisements.

Another questionable advertising practice is that of targeting minorities and poorer people here and in other countries. Magazines such as *Ebony* and *Latina* have twice as many ads for junk food, cigarettes, and alcohol and one-fourth as many ads for health-promoting products, compared to magazines read primarily by white women such as *Good Housekeeping*.[34] In addition, with more people giving up smoking in developed countries, tobacco companies are stepping up marketing efforts in developing countries, particularly those in Southeast Asia.

Advertising for products such as tobacco and alcohol also encourages addictive behavior. Virginia Slims ads, for example, have been credited with contributing to the increase in young female smokers. Studies have also found a direct correlation between exposure to advertisements for alcohol and how much a person drinks.[35]

Finally, critics point out that advertising is expensive and increases the prices of consumer goods and services, for some products by as much as 30 to 40 percent.[36] Furthermore, the ability of big corporations to spend large sums of money on advertising gives them a huge advantage over smaller companies. Thus, advertising contributes to the decline of small, local businesses and the rise of big business and monopolies.

Defenders of advertising respond that rather than *creating* cultural values, such as materialism, ads merely *reflect* those values. In response to the charge that ads are misleading, they point out that the government protects consumers from deceptive advertising practices. Some people may be

Many ads for products such as alcohol, cigarettes, and junk food target minorities and poorer people.

taken in by persuasive ads, but most reasonable people are able to use their judgment in interpreting these ads.

In addition, if advertising is sometimes misleading or persuades people to buy things they don't really want, this is offset by the information that advertising does provide consumers so that they can make better-informed decisions. Consumers also have other sources of information, particularly through the Internet, media, and such publications as *Consumer Reports*, about products and the market. Placing restrictions on advertising entails placing restrictions on people's freedom of speech. The harms of restricting freedom of speech in the form of advertising in order to protect gullible consumers outweigh any benefits of censoring advertising, say the defenders of unrestricted advertising.[37]

In response to the argument that advertising puts small businesses at a disadvantage, defenders of advertising argue that restricting large corporations' freedom of speech to protect local businesses will lead to a decline in the quality of products and services. In a free-market society, they say, the best businesses will rise to the top. They respond to complaints about the high cost of advertising by saying that without advertising, production costs in many cases would be higher, since marketers could not address a mass market. Finally, it is argued that advertising gives media the financial funding it needs, thus allowing it to be free of government interference.

Whatever position we take regarding advertising, there is no doubt that it has more influence on our buying habits and beliefs than most of us are willing to admit. Because of this, we need to be continually vigilant in using our critical-thinking skills to evaluate advertising messages. The presence of misleading language, fallacies, and rhetorical devices in an ad is not always obvious. One of the main barriers that keeps us from critically analyzing advertisements is self-serving bias and the assumption that we're more rational and smarter than most people. Recognizing our own shortcomings and learning about strategies used by advertisers so we are able to recognize them will make us less likely to fall for manipulative advertising.

> Advertising is expensive and increases the prices of consumer goods and services, for some products by as much as 30 to 40 percent.

to advertising to physicians and other medical professionals? Do mass media ads encourage people to overmedicate themselves or rely on medicine instead of lifestyle changes to solve their health problems? Support your answers.

5. Discuss how ads use fallacies and rhetoric to get a consumer to buy a product. Bring in three different ads to illustrate your answer.

6. Think of the last time you went out and bought something after seeing it in an advertisement. What in the ad convinced you to purchase the product? Were you satisfied with your purchase? Explain why or why not.

7. *Journal Exercise.* Write a journal entry about advertising in the media. Discuss as a class some of the strategies, fallacies, and rhetorical devices used by advertisers and what you might do to make yourself less susceptible to them.

1. What strategies are used in marketing research and marketing?
   - Marketing research strategies include discovering consumers' "hot buttons" and the use of surveys, focus groups, and observation. Marketing strategies include targeting advertisements to specific audiences, placement of goods on certain shelves in stores, and application of the SWOT model to determine a company's marketing strengths and weaknesses as well as opportunities and threats.

2. How does marketing and advertising affect the consumer?
   - Advertising informs consumers of products and services that can improve our lives. But advertising can promote materialism by creating markets for nonessential goods and services. The media is also affected by the market, since the market needs advertisers for financial support.

3. How can we as consumers be more aware of fallacies and rhetorical devices used in advertising?
   - Many ads rely on fallacies and rhetoric rather than credible information and rational argumentation. By being aware of fallacies such as scare tactics, popular appeal, snob appeal, and inappropriate appeal to authority, we will be less likely to accept fallacious arguments about a product. Awareness of rhetorical devices such as hyperbole and the use of euphemisms will also help us to not be fooled by these persuasive tools.

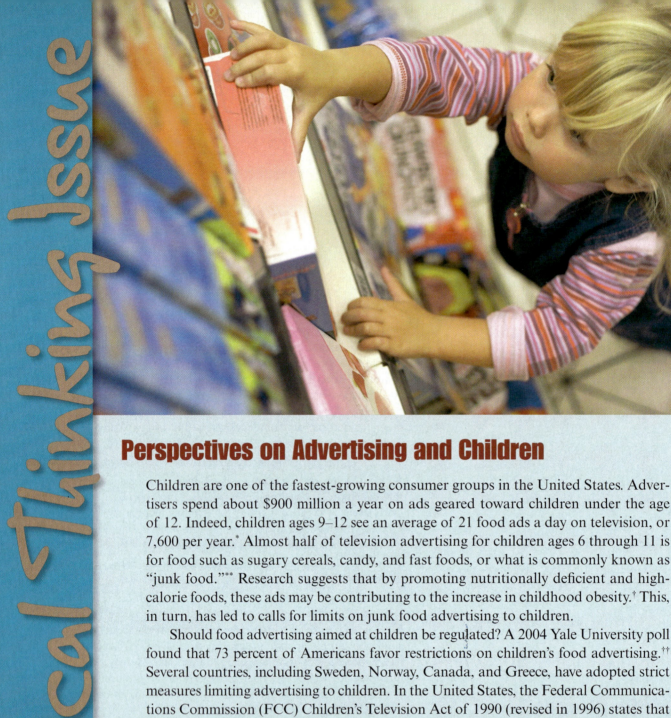

Perspectives on Advertising and Children

Children are one of the fastest-growing consumer groups in the United States. Advertisers spend about $900 million a year on ads geared toward children under the age of 12. Indeed, children ages 9–12 see an average of 21 food ads a day on television, or 7,600 per year.* Almost half of television advertising for children ages 6 through 11 is for food such as sugary cereals, candy, and fast foods, or what is commonly known as "junk food."** Research suggests that by promoting nutritionally deficient and high-calorie foods, these ads may be contributing to the increase in childhood obesity.† This, in turn, has led to calls for limits on junk food advertising to children.

Should food advertising aimed at children be regulated? A 2004 Yale University poll found that 73 percent of Americans favor restrictions on children's food advertising.†† Several countries, including Sweden, Norway, Canada, and Greece, have adopted strict measures limiting advertising to children. In the United States, the Federal Communications Commission (FCC) Children's Television Act of 1990 (revised in 1996) states that broadcasters are a "public fiduciary" who are obligated to serve the educational needs of children and to limit the amount of advertising during children's programs.

However, the content of advertising is generally regarded as protected by a business's First Amendment right to freedom of speech. According to this view, any regulation of content should be voluntary.§ This perspective is defended by Robert Liodice in the second essay in this section as well as by the Children's Advertising Review Unit

---

*James U. McNeal, *The Kids Market: Myths and Realities* (Ithaca, NY: Paramount Market Publishing, 1999).

**"TV Ads Market Junk Food to Kids, New Study Finds," http://www.news.uiuc.edu/news/05/0824junkfood.html.

†The National Academies news release, "Food Marketing Aimed at Kids Influences Nutritional Choices," December 6, 2005.

††Institute of Medicine, "Preventing Childhood Obesity: Health in the Balance," 2005, http://www.iom.edu.

§For more on First Amendment issues and advertising, see Martin H. Redish, "Tobacco Advertising and the First Amendment," *Iowa Law Review,* Vol. 81, March 1996, p. 589.

(CARU), a division of the Council of Better Business Bureaus. CARU's guidelines call for self-regulation by children's advertisers rather than legal regulations.[††]

Not everyone agrees with this voluntary approach when it comes to children's food advertising. An Institute of Medicine (IOM) study on food marketing calls for a law to limit advertising of unhealthy food to children on both broadcast and cable television if the industry does not take voluntary action to do so. The Center for Science in the Public Interest (CSPI) also supports legal regulation of children's advertising. In 2006, the CSPI, along with other advocacy groups and concerned parents, filed a lawsuit against Kellogg and the media giant Viacom (and its subsidiary Nickelodeon) for their roles in advertising sugared cereals on children's television. CSPI argued that certain advertising tactics should be banned because they are irresponsible and contribute to childhood obesity. In response Nickelodeon, in 2007, agreed not to license its cartoon characters for use in advertising unhealthy foods. As of September 2008, 11 large companies—including Kellogg, Kraft, McDonalds, and PepsiCo—have agreed to limit junk food advertising to children. Their progress in doing so is being closely monitored by the FCC. Whether voluntary self-regulation is sufficient remains to be seen.

In the following two readings by Wootan and Liodice we'll examine arguments both for and against the legal regulation of "junk" food advertising to children.

Regulating Food Advertising to Children

MARGO G. WOOTAN

Margo G. Wootan, DSc, is director of nutrition policy for the Center for Science in the Public Interest, a nonprofit organization in Washington, D.C. In her reading she describes the CSPI guidelines and explains why the CSPI supports legislation to regulate food advertising to children.[*]

Guidelines for Responsible Food Marketing to Children

These *Guidelines for Responsible Food Marketing to Children*[**] are for food manufacturers, restaurants, supermarkets, television and radio stations, movie studios, magazines, public relations and advertising agencies, schools, toy and video game manufacturers, organizers of sporting or children's events, and others who manufacture, sell, market, advertise, or otherwise promote food to children. The *Guidelines* provide criteria for marketing food to children in a manner that does not undermine children's diets or harm their health. We hope the *Guidelines* will be helpful to parents, school officials, legislators, community and health organizations, and others who are seeking to improve children's diets.

Over the last 20 years, the rates of obesity have doubled in children and tripled in teens. Even for children at a healthy weight, few (only 2%) eat a nutritious diet as defined by the U.S. Department of Agriculture. Currently, children's diets are too high in calories, saturated and trans fats, refined sugars, and salt and too low in fruits, vegetables, whole grains, and calcium. This increases their risk of heart disease, cancer, diabetes, osteoporosis, and other serious and costly diseases.

Although children's food choices are affected by many factors, food marketing plays a key role. Studies show that food marketing attracts children's attention, influences their food choices, and prompts them to request that their parents purchase products.

Parents bear the primary responsibility for feeding their children. However, getting children to eat a healthful diet would be much easier for parents if they did not have to contend with billions of dollars' worth of sophisticated marketing for low-nutrition foods.

Parental authority is undermined by wide discrepancies between what parents tell their children is healthful to eat and what marketing promotes as desirable to eat. In addition, while many parents have limited proficiency in nutrition, companies have extensive expertise in persuasive techniques. Companies also have resources to influence children's food choices that parents do not have, such as cartoon characters, contests, celebrities, and toy giveaways.

The *Guidelines for Responsible Food Marketing to Children* apply to children of all ages (less than 18 years of age). Society provides special protections for children, including measures to protect their health, such as requiring use of car safety seats or prohibiting them from buying cigarettes or alcoholic beverages. However, even in the absence of legislative or regulatory requirements, marketers should act responsibly and not urge children to eat foods that could harm their health.

[††]For CARU's guidelines, go to http://www.caru.org/guidelines/guidelines.pdf.

[*]Margo G. Wootan, "Guidelines for Responsible Food Marketing to Children," January 6, 2006. Center for Science in the Public Interest (CSPI).

[**] January 2005; second printing, January 2006. The full *Guidelines for Responsible Food Marketing to Children* are available online (free of charge) at http://www.cspinet.org/marketingguidelines.pdf.

Nutrition Guidelines

Responsible food marketing to children must address not only *how* food is marketed but also *which* foods are marketed to kids. Uniquely, the *Guidelines for Responsible Food Marketing to Children* set criteria for which foods are appropriate to market to children.

Ideally, companies would market to children only the most healthful foods and beverages, especially those that are typically underconsumed, such as fruits, vegetables, whole grains, and low-fat dairy products.

However, nutrition criteria that would allow only marketing of those foods seem unrealistically restrictive. Instead, we recommend a compromise approach. These *Guidelines* set criteria that allow for the marketing of products that may not be nutritionally ideal but that provide some positive nutritional benefit and that could help children meet the *Dietary Guidelines for Americans*.

Some marketing efforts do not promote individual products but instead promote a line of products, one brand within a company, or a whole company. For example, a campaign might encourage children to go to a particular restaurant without marketing a specific menu item. A company logo or spokes-character featured on a hat or Web site might promote a whole line of products. Companies should not conduct general brand marketing aimed at children for brands under which more than half of the products are of poor nutritional quality, as defined below. If multiple products are shown in an advertisement, if one product does not meet the nutrition criteria below, then the advertisement is considered to promote foods of poor nutritional quality.

Beverages

Low-nutrition beverages (as defined below) should not be marketed to children.

Nutritious/Healthful Beverages

- Water and seltzer without added sweeteners

- Beverages that contain at least 50 percent juice and that do not contain added sweeteners

- Low-fat and fat-free milk, including flavored milks and calcium-fortified soy and rice beverages

Low-Nutrition Beverages

- Soft drinks, sports drinks, and sweetened iced teas

- Fruit-based drinks that contain less than 50 percent juice or that contain added sweeteners

- Drinks containing caffeine (except low-fat and fat-free chocolate milk, which contain trivial amounts of caffeine)

Foods

Foods marketed to children should meet all of the following criteria (nutritionally poor choices or low-nutrition foods are those that do not meet the criteria):

Nutrient	Criteria
Fat	No more than 35% of total calories, excluding nuts, seeds, and peanut or other nut butters
Saturated plus trans fat	No more than 10% of calories
Added sugars	Less than 35% of added sugars by weight (added sugars exclude naturally occurring sugars from fruit, vegetable, and dairy ingredients)
Sodium	No more than: 1. 230 mg per serving of chips, crackers, cheeses, baked goods, French fries, and other snack items 2. 480 mg per serving for cereals, soups, pastas, and meats 3. 600 mg for pizza, sandwiches, and main dishes 4. 770 mg for meals
Nutrient content	Contains one or more of the following: 1. 10% of the DRI (dietary reference intake) of (naturally occurring/without fortification) vitamins A, C, or E; calcium; magnesium; potassium; iron; or fiber 2. Half a serving of fruit or vegetable 3. 51% or more (by weight) whole-grain ingredients

Portion Size Limits for Foods and Beverages

Individual items	No larger than the standard serving size used for nutrition facts labels (except for fruits and vegetables, which are exempt from portion size limits)
Meals	No more than one-third of the daily calorie requirement for the average child in the age range targeted by the marketing

Marketing Techniques

When marketing foods to children, companies should

Product Characteristics and Overall Messages

- *Support parents' efforts* to serve as the gatekeepers of sound nutrition for their children and not undermine parental authority. Marketers should not encourage children to nag their parents to buy low-nutrition foods.

- Depict and package/serve food in *reasonable portion sizes and not encourage overeating* directly or indirectly.

- *Develop new products* that help children eat healthfully, especially with regard to nutrient density, energy density, and portion size.

- *Reformulate* products to improve their nutritional quality, including adding more fruits, vegetables, and whole grains, and reducing portion sizes, calories, sodium, refined sugars, and saturated and trans fats.

- *Expand efforts to promote healthy eating habits* consistent with the *Dietary Guidelines for Americans* and to promote *healthful products*, such as fruits, vegetables, whole grains, and low-fat milk. Do not portray healthful foods negatively.

Specific Marketing Techniques and Incentives

- Should not advertise nutritionally poor choices during *television* shows (1) with more than 15% of the audience under age 12; (2) for which children are identified as the target audience by the television station, entertainment company, or movie studio; or (3) that are kid-oriented cartoons.

- Not use *product or brand placements*.

- Only offer *premiums and incentives* with foods, meals, and brands that meet the nutrition criteria described above.

- Use/allow *licensing agreements or cross-promotions* (such as with movies, television programs, or video games) or use *cartoon/fictional characters or celebrities* from television, movies, music, or sports to market to children only those foods that meet the above nutrition criteria. This includes depictions on food packages, in ads, as premiums, and for in-store promotions.

- Not put logos, brand names, spokes-characters, product names, or other marketing for low-nutrition foods/brands on baby bottles, children's apparel, books, toys, dishware, or other *merchandise* made specifically for children.

- Incorporate into *games* (such as board, Internet, or video games), toys, or books only those products and brands that meet the nutrition criteria.

- Use *sponsorship* of sporting, school, and other events for children only with brands and foods that meet the above nutrition criteria.

- Not exploit children's natural tendency to play by *building entertainment value into low-nutrition foods.*

Additional Guidance for Schools

- Schools are a unique setting. Companies should *support healthy eating in schools and not market, sell, or give away low-nutrition foods or brands anywhere on school campuses,* including through logos, brand names, spokes-characters, product names, or other product marketing on/in vending machines; books, curricula, and other educational materials; school supplies; posters; textbook covers; and school property such as scoreboards, signs, athletic fields, buses, and buildings; educational incentive programs that provide food as a reward (for example, earning a coupon for a free pizza after reading a certain number of books); incentive programs that provide schools with money or school supplies when families buy a company's food products; in-school television, such as Channel One; direct sale of low-nutrition foods; and school fund-raising activities.

- Should *not mislead children regarding the emotional, social, or health benefits of a product or exploit children's developmental vulnerabilities and emotions* to market any food.

QUESTIONS

1. What is the current political environment regarding television advertising aimed at children?

2. According to Wootan, why can't we expect parents alone to regulate their children's eating habits?

3. Why are children persuaded by media advertising for unhealthy foods?

4. What are CSPI's guidelines regarding the marketing of food to children, and how does CSPI justify these guidelines?

5. What marketing strategies used by advertisers does CSPI argue should be restricted, and why?

Advertising and Freedom of Speech: Beware of the Food Nanny

ROBERT LIODICE

Robert Liodice is the president and CEO of the Association of National Advertisers. In this blog, he responds to the guidelines issued by CSPI, arguing that they are a violation of the right to freedom of speech and the free exchange of information.* Liodice also contends that the guidelines are based on misinformation about food advertising and children's television viewing.

Free speech is the most important and fundamental right we have as Americans. It is the foundation for the free exchange of ideas and ideals that drives the lifestyles and

---

* Robert Liodice, "Advertising and Freedom of Speech: Beware of the Food Nanny," January 24, 2005, http://anablogs.com/liodice/2005/01/america-free_sp.html.

time of the day or night. Magazines such as *Ski*, *Wired*, *Saveur*, *Islands,* and *Internet World*, as well as many radio stations, are niche media geared toward particular lifestyles or ethnic groups.

In addition, more Americans today are choosing what to listen to or watch on the basis of their political views. Conservative critics accuse the news media of having a liberal bias, a bias that has been confirmed by studies.[3] The majority of the news media outlets, for instance, have in the past supported Democratic presidential candidates, abortion rights, stricter environmental regulations, and cuts in military spending. During the 2008 presidential elections, for instance, the media, for the most part, supported Senator Obama.

At the same time that news media options are proliferating, a select few large corporations are controlling the news media. In 1983, fifty corporations controlled the majority of the news media in the United States. By the end of 2006, only nine corporations—AOL TimeWarner, Disney, Rupert Murdoch's News Corporation, Bertelsmann of Germany, TCI, General Electric, Sony, Seagram, and Viacom (renamed CBS Corporation in 2006)—owned most of the U.S. news media industry.[4] Ben Bagdikian, author of *The New Media Monopoly* (2004), suggests that rather than promoting diversity and choice, these media giants act as a cartel, cooperating with each other to promote greed and conservative political values.[5] For example, Disney's corporate values are reflected in programs and movies that promote traditional family values and gender stereotypes, as well as in advertising of its own products, such as toys, clothing, family cruises, and theme parks. The

Hot or Not?

Does the fact that only a select number of corporations control the media affect the quality and objectivity of the media?

content of a television show, magazine, or newspaper, consequently, is dictated to a large extent by the interests and values of its corporate owner.

In addition to influencing the public through their productions, news media corporations also try to influence public policy directly, by donating millions of dollars annually to congressional campaigns and tens of millions more to lobbying efforts.[6] For example, television, radio, and wireless Internet all rely on airway radio frequencies to send and receive messages. Media lobbyists are trying to persuade Congress to privatize these airways, which are currently regulated by the government through the FCC. This pressure on the FCC has contributed to a trend toward government deregulation over the past few decades.

Beyond the media corporations that control the airways, other businesses influence the public through advertising in the mass media. Businesses pay media corporations for advertising time on TV or radio or for ad space in newspapers and magazines and on Web sites. Mass media corporations could not survive without the financial backing of other large corporations. Because advertisers pay media corporations, the public can watch broadcast television and listen to the radio for "free." In return for "free" programs, viewers are subjected to ads. If a show does not hold our attention or a magazine does not sell enough copies, sponsors will withdraw their ads, media corporations will lose money, and sooner or later the show or magazine will be dropped. Thus, the need to keep advertisers is the primary concern of media corporations.

The 2007 purchase of the Wall Street Journal *along with several small New England newspapers by Australian-born global news mogul Rupert Murdoch, who also owns the Fox News Channel, has led to concerns of a move toward a partisan conservative position in news coverage.*

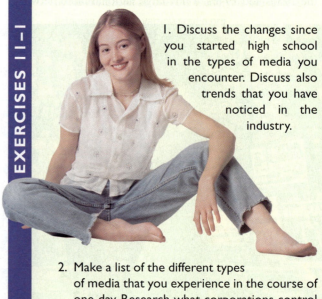

EXERCISES 11–1

1. Discuss the changes since you started high school in the types of media you encounter. Discuss also trends that you have noticed in the industry.

2. Make a list of the different types of media that you experience in the course of one day. Research what corporations control the forms of media that you are exposed to most. Share your findings with the class. How much overlap is there between your answers and those of others in the class?

THE NEWS MEDIA

Seventy-eight percent of Americans get their news mainly from television news broadcasts. Although this number has remained relatively stable since the 1990s, the number of people relying on the Internet for news has increased sharply. Meanwhile the influence of newspapers and news magazines as a source of news is declining, as the Internet siphons off their audiences and advertisers.[7] According to the Project for Excellence in Journalism, between 2000 and 2007 the size of editorial staffs at American newspapers decreased by about 10 percent, and the number is continuing to decline. News magazines have been hit even harder. In 2005 and 2006 alone, *Time* magazine had to cut its news staff by 14 percent.

Another change in the past few decades has been a trend away from reporting government and foreign affairs and toward reporting entertainment, lifestyle, and celebrity-scandal news.[8] Thus, while Americans have an increasing number of news sources, they are no more informed than they were two decades ago and, in some cases, they are less informed. A poll by the Pew Research Center reported that in 1989, 74 percent of Americans could identify the vice president, whereas in their 2007 poll only 69 percent could do so. Americans are also becoming more skeptical about the reliability of the news coverage as it leans more toward "infotainment" than information.

Credibility of News Coverage

Almost invariably, the news media claim to present objective as well as truthful coverage of local, national, and international events and developments. In addition to keeping us informed, the news media has played a key role in exposing corporate and government scandal. The exposé of John D. Rockefeller and his oil monopoly by editor and journalist Ida Tarbell (1857–1944) resulted in a federal investigation and the Supreme Court's eventual breakup in 1911 of Standard Oil. In the early 1970s, Bob Woodward and Carl Bernstein of the *Washington Post* were instrumental in exposing the 1972 Watergate scandal, which led to President Nixon's resignation in 1974. And during and after Hurricane Katrina in 2005, the news networks brought to the nation's attention the lack of government preparedness for major natural disasters, as well as the extent of institutional racism that remains in the United States. These examples illustrate the power of the news media to convey important information to the public.

Singer Kanye West strayed from his script during an NBC Disaster Relief special and launched a vicious attack of then President George Bush's response to the Hurricane Katrina disaster. He was cut off by NBC executives after he stated that "George Bush doesn't care about black people."

Despite the many valuable services provided by the news media, many Americans believe that "media makes news rather than just report it."[9] In 1985, a Pew Research Center survey found that only 56 percent of Americans felt that the news organizations usually got their facts straight. By 2002, this figure had dropped to 35 percent, underscoring a growing lack of public trust in the news media.

> In 1985, a Pew Research Center survey found that only 56 percent of Americans felt that the news organizations usually got their facts straight. By 2002, this figure had dropped to 35 percent, underscoring a growing lack of public trust in the news media.

Like other types of mass media, the goal of the news media is not simply to inform and educate the public about critical issues but also to select stories that will appeal to a large number of people and to present the news in a way that keeps us tuned in so that we will view the commercials.

Sensationalism and the News as Entertainment

News stories are often selected because of their entertainment value rather than their newsworthiness. Most people prefer heartwarming, true-crime, or disaster stories over critical analysis of national and international issues. Therefore, excessive amounts of time and space, including the front pages and headlines of newspapers, may be devoted to stories about daring rescues, celebrity scandals, kidnapped children, airplane crashes, natural disasters, and gruesome murders.

Newscasters and journalists play on our human tendency to engage in the memorable-events cognitive error, in which our mind exaggerates the importance of sensational—and usually gruesome—events, to hold the audience's attention. For example, after the 1999 Columbine High School shootings in Colorado, in which fourteen people were killed, high-profile stories on school shootings left many people with the false impression that there was an epidemic of such shootings

Not only are viewers or readers usually given little insight into issues but also visual images and speakers' comments may be taken out of context or important information may be omitted for the sake of "brevity." Captions used with photos can also be misleading and inadvertently promote racism and other negative stereotypes, as you can see in "Analyzing Images: Stereotypes and Racism in the News Media." In these cases, we are often left not knowing the original context of an image or the intent of a speaker.

Did You Know

The amount of time a typical half-hour local newscast devotes to U.S. foreign policy, including the war in Iraq, is only 38 seconds. The amount of time that it spends on sports and weather, in contrast, averages 6 minutes and 21 seconds.

During the 2000 presidential elections, the team of Republican nominee George W. Bush came up with a political commercial mocking what it said was Vice President Al Gore's claim of having invented the Internet. Although the Republican Party never aired the commercial because it was inaccurate, the story that Gore claimed to have invented the Internet was snatched up by the news media—which never bothered to check the original source of Gore's statement or the context in which it was uttered. In fact, Gore never claimed that he invented the Internet. Instead, he had said in a 1999 interview that "during my service in the United States Congress, I took the initiative in creating the Internet."[12] The context of the comment was regarding his work, not as a scientist or inventor, but as a senator and vice president in actively promoting the development of the Internet and in helping the inventors of the Internet get it to the point where it is today.

Because of time limitations, editors and newscasters must decide which stories to use and which to disregard or shorten. News stories also have to hold the attention of the audience, who may be more interested in sports and weather than in international or national news. This is particularly true with television newscasts. The amount of time that a typical half-hour local newscast devotes to U.S. foreign policy, including the war in Iraq, is only 38 seconds. The amount of time that it spends on sports and weather, in contrast, averages 6 minutes and 21 seconds.[13]

Because of budget restrictions and the need to air a breaking story before other stations do in order to maintain ratings, the news media often relies on information from government or corporate press conferences and press releases rather than do its own investigative reporting (which can be very expensive and time-consuming). However, information from press releases may be presented in an oversimplified and biased manner to bolster the image of those giving the press conference. On the basis of information in a government press release in 2002–2003, during the buildup to the invasion of Iraq, the American media reported, without ever fully investigating the story, that the United States had found mobile laboratories for creating biological weapons in Iraq. As it turned out, that information was incorrect and is now believed to have been a case of disinformation deliberately disseminated by people in the U.S. administration to build public support for the invasion of Iraq.

In addition to issuing press releases, government officials may call on selected journalists during press conferences and ignore others who might ask unwanted questions. In addition, follow-up questions by other journalists may not be allowed. To be one of the favored journalists, a reporter must be careful not to offend government sources or corporate backers. Thus journalists need to think twice about critiquing their sources or printing or airing a story that might offend the hand that feeds them.

In the news coverage following Hurricane Katrina, the caption for an Associated Press (AP) photo (top left) showing a black man wading through the flood waters carrying goods from a store read, "A young man walks through chest-deep flood water after looting a grocery store in New Orleans, Louisiana," whereas the caption for an AP photo (bottom left) of two white people wading through the flood waters carrying goods said, "Two residents wade through chest-deep water after finding bread and soda from a local grocery after Hurricane Katrina came through their area in New Orleans, Louisiana." In other words, white people "find," whereas black people "loot."

Analyzing Images

STEREOTYPES AND RACISM IN THE NEWS MEDIA In addition to using images and quotes out of context, the news media can inadvertently manipulate viewers' perceptions through the use of descriptive language. In the news coverage after Hurricane Katrina in 2005, several readers complained that the captions for the two pictures shown here of people wading through the floodwaters carrying goods from a store showed racial bias.

DISCUSSION QUESTIONS

1. Discuss how, if at all, the two photo captions show racial bias.

2. Bring in examples of photos with captions from magazines and newspapers. Discuss whether the captions are written in a biased fashion. If they are, explain why they are biased and rewrite them using neutral language.

Journalists have also accepted money from political sources to promote particular political agendas—a practice known as "pay to sway." United Press International syndicated columnist Maggie Gallagher was paid more than $40,000 in federal funding from the Department of Health and Human Services to promote in her columns the Marriage Protection Amendment, which would limit marriage to a man and a woman. Her columns ran in newspapers such as the *New York Times*, the *Wall Street Journal*, and the *Washington Post*.[14] Columnist Armstrong Williams was paid $240,000 by the Department of Education to advocate for President George W. Bush's educational initiatives such as No Child Left Behind. Incidents such as these, along with the control government exerts over what information—or misinformation—will be released to the press, raises questions about the ability of the press to play the role of watchdog over government.

Former White House press secretary Tony Snow (1955–2008) briefing the press.

Politically motivated government sources may also leak sensitive news to the press. In 2003, former U.S. ambassador Joseph C. Wilson IV told the press that the Bush administration had distorted intelligence on Iraq's suspected weapons of mass destruction program to justify the war. Angered by the accusations, Lewis "Scooter" Libby, Vice President Dick Cheney's chief of staff—some allege under orders from a higher source—leaked the name of Wilson's wife, Valerie Plame, an undercover CIA operative, to the press, thus jeopardizing her position and putting her at risk from foreign sources with whom she had been dealing.

> United Press International syndicated columnist Maggie Gallagher was paid more than $40,000 in federal funding from the Department of Health and Human Services to promote in her columns the Marriage Protection Amendment, which would limit marriage to a man and a woman.

More recently, a former National Security Agency officer leaked information to the press about an illegal eavesdropping program that allows the agency to monitor phone calls to and from the United States without a warrant if one of the parties is suspected of being linked to a terrorist organization. This disclosure set off a maelstrom of charges that the White House was overstepping its power in spying on Americans.

Confirmation Bias

The increased number of news sources and the need to attract and hold an audience have led the various news media to target particular audiences by tailoring their reporting. Simply by choosing which sources of information to use or which experts to interview, the news media can compromise objectivity and bias the reporting.

The Pew Research Center has found that the news audience is becoming more and more polarized and "politicized."[15] Those who watch Fox News, a conservative news outlet, tend to be Republicans and conservatives, while Democrats and independents tend to prefer CNN. In line with this, a 2005 ABC News–*Washington Post* poll found that 67 percent of the viewers of Fox believed that there were links between al-Qaeda and Saddam Hussein, as opposed to 16 percent of people who got their news from National Public Radio, the network with a liberal leaning. This tendency to choose our news sources on the basis of our political leanings contributes to confirmation bias. Rather than providing us with new information and challenging our preconceptions, the news show simply confirms our previously held views and biases, thus impeding our growth as critical thinkers.

Even if newscasters report the information as they get it and do not give their opinions, it does not mean they are being objective or that the news stories they choose to report are the most important ones in terms of serving the public interests. As critical thinkers, we cannot assume that the news media is presenting an unbiased and balanced coverage of an issue or event. Instead, we need to ask about the reliability and credibility of the sources of the information before accepting a news story as accurate. We also need to keep in mind that the news being reported is to a large extent determined by the need to attract and keep advertisers and to hold the interest of the audience.

1. Where do you get most of your news? Why do you use this source for your news? Do you consider the source's reporting to be accurate and comprehensive? Have you always used this news source? If not, why did you change? Explain.

2. The news media prefers to report on memorable events, such as disasters, kidnappings, and killings, rather than covering ongoing issues. Discuss the effect of this type of reporting on how you and others live your daily lives.

3. Working in small groups, list the five or six most important current events. Where did you hear about them, and what did you learn? Was the coverage sufficient? Is there any disagreement in the group about what happened or the interpretation of what happened? If so, discuss why the discrepancy exists.

4. Make a list of recent and upcoming events on your campus, as well as other events and issues that might be of interest to students on your campus. Working in small groups, put together a layout for a two-page campus newspaper. Discuss the criteria you used in deciding how much space should be given to each story and which stories should go on which page and where on that page. For example, was your primary goal to sell newspapers, grab the reader's attention, or to be accurate and unbiased?

5. Where do we draw the line between the media serving a public good and the media simply engaging in sensationalism? Did the press overstep its ethical boundaries in publishing the information on the federal government's warrantless surveillance program—a move that the White House argued imperils our national security? How about revealing the name of CIA operative Valerie Plame? Construct an argument to support your conclusion.

6. Select a current event. Compare how this story was covered on a broadcast network, a cable network, one newspaper, and an Internet service provider such as AOL or MSN.

SCIENCE REPORTING

While most of us are skeptical of what we see on television or read in the newspaper, a Yale University study found the opposite to be true when it comes to stories about scientific findings and hypotheses. We tend to trust that such information is true simply because what we are reading is called "science." However, this trust is sometimes misplaced.

Misrepresentation of Scientific Findings

Most reporters are not trained in science and sometimes make mistakes in reporting the results of scientific studies. Reporters may also intentionally distort scientific findings to attract a greater audience. In 1986, *Newsweek* featured a cover story entitled "Too Late for Prince Charming?" which was based on a scientific study on marriage patterns in the United States carried out by Yale and Harvard sociologists. According to the study, a single 35-year-old white, college-educated woman had only a 5 percent chance of getting married, whereas a 40-year-old woman had a 2.6 percent chance. The *Newsweek* article reported that "forty-year-olds are more likely to be killed by a terrorist; they have a minuscule 2.6 percent probability of tying the knot."

The part on the terrorist was not in the original study but was a bit of hyperbole added by the reporter for sensationalism and shock value. Furthermore, the reporter never checked the findings of the study against other surveys and studies. In fact, according to the U.S. Census Bureau, in 1986 the chance that a forty-year-old woman—even a white, college-educated woman—would eventually marry was much higher, at 23 percent for the general population. Nevertheless the *Newsweek* article had a profound impact

The media may distort scientific findings for the sake of sensationalism, as happened in a 1986 story about a 40-year-old woman's chance of getting married.

on Americans and created a sense of anxiety and loss of confidence among educated, older women who had hoped someday to get married, illustrating the control that the news media has over our thoughts and feelings.

Scientific findings may also be sensationalized or misrepresented in the media when they present hypotheses as factual findings rather than as hunches or assumptions. In 2003 astronomers discovered a large asteroid—asteroid 2003 QQ47. Scientists estimated that there was just under a 1-in-a-million chance that this asteroid would hit the Earth in 2014. The media immediately picked up the story, with some hyping it with headlines such as "Armageddon Set for March 21, 2014" and "Earth Is Doomed."

Another source of media bias is the interpretation of scientific findings in light of cultural norms and the reporters' own biases, including racial and sex biases. In reports on human evolution, Cro-Magnon man, our direct ancestor, used to be generally depicted as fair-skinned, blond, and inventive, whereas Neanderthal man is depicted as a dark-skinned, black-haired, brutish caveman. In fact, we don't know the skin and hair coloring of either group of early humans. Sex bias is also evident in some science shows. In a 2006 Discovery Channel report, *The Rise of Man*,[16] bias was evident in more than just the title of the show. Men were consistently portrayed as being in the forefront of human evolution, the discovery of fire, the creation of tools, agriculture, and art, with women playing only a very marginal role. In actual fact, scientists don't know whether men or women made these discoveries and advances. Rather, it was the media that imposed this bias.

Reporters may simplify a scientific report or report findings in a way to maximize their impact and attract audience interest. For instance, a study conducted by Harvard researchers on the effects of intercessory prayer (prayer offered on behalf of another person) on healing in cardiac-bypass patients[17] was reported in the *Los Angeles Times* under the headline "Largest Study of Prayer to Date Finds It Has No Power to Heal."[18] However, this headline is misleading because the study was only about a very specific type of prayer—intercessory prayer by a group of strangers. It did not study the effect of prayer by the patients themselves or of prayer by friends and relatives on behalf of the patients. (For a summary of the prayer study and an evaluation of the experiment design, see Chapter 12, page 391.)

In addition, the media may report scientific research in a manner that emphasizes its con-

troversial aspects. For example, when reporting on stem-cell research, the media generally focus on the use of embryonic stem cells, ignoring research findings using stem cells that don't come from embryos. Thus, the public is left with the impression that stem-cell research relies on aborted embryos.

Government Influence and Bias

Since many reporters rely on press releases, science reporting may be biased in favor of government policy and the interests of big corporations. In the 1980s there was a growing concern among the public about the damaging effects of dioxin. Dioxin is a highly lethal chemical that was used in herbicides such as Agent Orange, a defoliant dumped on jungles during the Vietnam War to destroy vegetation and deprive enemy fighters of hiding places. It is also the byproduct of some industrial chemical processes. In 1991 the *New York Times* featured a story that was based on government reports and was headlined "U.S. Officials Say Dangers of Dioxin Were Exaggerated."[19] The article stated that exposure to dioxin "is now considered by some experts to be no more risky than spending a week sunbathing." Some of the facts presented in the article were false; dioxin is far more toxic than sunbathing, but the reporter did not do enough research to unearth this fact.

In cases where scientific research is government funded, pressure may be brought to bear on scientists to report findings to the public in a way that is consistent with a political agenda. The White House has intervened to weaken and even delete sections in reports by Environmental Protection Agency scientists regarding the extent of global warming and the role of industry in creating or accelerating global climate change. In 2004, NASA scientist James Hansen, one of the world's leading researchers on global warming, went public about the White House editing his and other scientists' reports and placing restrictions on people

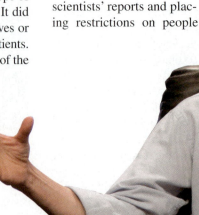

James Hansen, one of the leading researchers on global warming.

he could talk to. Because the media relies primarily on press releases, rather than doing its own investigative reporting, the extent of global warming was underreported in the media for many years.

Evaluating Scientific Reports

Unlike general news reports, for which we generally do not have access to the primary sources, with science reporting we can often assess a story's credibility by looking up the original source of the scientific study. In evaluating a scientific report in the mass media, the first step is to determine who is making the claim. Is it the reporter, or is the reporter citing a scientist or other expert in the field? In addition, is the reporter using direct quotes, or is the reporter paraphrasing or embellishing on what the

Unlike general news reporting which is done by journalists who aren't usually experts in the subjects that they are relaying to the public, scientific reports are often broadcast to the public by the actual scientists who made the discoveries, in order to ensure accuracy.

scientists found, as in the 1986 *Newsweek* report on single women and marriage?

What are the credentials of the source(s) cited by the media? Is he or she associated with a respected university, research lab, or other credible organization? Or is the source someone with little or no background in the field of science under discussion—a religious leader, an actress, a novelist, a politician, or an astrologer? In addition, we should ask about the credentials of the reporter. The source may be credible; however, the reporter may lack the necessary scientific background to accurately summarize the findings or make interpretations of the findings.

A comprehensive scientific report should name the scientific journal in which the study or article first appeared. Is it a respectable scientific journal? That is, does it require peer reviews—confirmation of the research results by other qualified scientists—before it publishes an important find-

ing? If you have any questions about the report, many of these journals are now available in the library or in library online databases. Also, to gain a more balanced perspective, look at how other people who are experts in this field are reacting to the scientific findings. For example, are scientists more concerned about global warming than media reports suggest?

Finally, ask yourself if the media report itself is biased. Does the reporter or the media that he or she represents have a particular political agenda that would cause the reporter to exaggerate certain aspects of the scientific report and downplay or ignore others? Remember, the reporter not only needs to attract the largest audience possible but also needs to avoid offending his or her employer and other powerful interests.

In summary, scientific findings are sometimes misreported or distorted by the media. Reporters may lack the necessary training to accurately summarize a scientific study. In addition, some media outlets have a tendency to sensationalize findings by overemphasizing certain aspects of scientific research and ignoring others, or by masquerading speculation or opinions as facts. Outside interests such as the government and businesses can also influence how scientific findings are reported. As critical thinkers we need to be mindful of these problems when interpreting science reports in the mass media. We'll be looking more at evaluating scientific hypotheses and research in Chapter 12.

EXERCISES 11-3

1. Select a current issue such as global warming, stem-cell research, or sex differences in scientific ability. Discuss what you have learned from the media regarding these issues. Do people in the class have different or conflicting information? What was the media source of their information? Discuss possible explanations for the discrepancies in students' understanding of the scientific issue.

2. Examine the following science headlines. Discuss what tactics are being used to get your attention. From just looking at the headline, state what you think the story is about.
   a. " 'Conclusive Evidence' for Martian Life" (BBC News Online, 2001)
   b. "U.S. Bird Flu Study Predicts Millions of Deaths, Billions in Cost" (San Francisco Chronicle, May 4, 2006)
   c. "Study: Cutting, Self-Abuse Common Among College Students" (FoxNews.com, June 5, 2006)
   d. "Happiness Is Controlled by Your Genes" (The Guardian [UK], July 9, 2004)
   e. "Harvard Scientists Join Human Cloning Race" (MSNBC, June 6, 2006)
   f. "Warning: Medical Websites Damage Your Health" (The Independent, [UK], October 4, 2001)
   g. "UFO Streaks Through Martian Sky" (BBC News Online, March 18, 2004)

3. Working in small groups, write two paragraphs for your local newspaper summarizing the findings of a study in a scientific journal provided by your instructor. Share your paragraphs with others in the class. Evaluate the accuracy of each other's reports. If there was bias or misrepresentation, discuss possible sources of this bias.

4. Look for an article in the mass media, or a news video clip, that reports the results of a scientific study. Find a copy of the original scientific article written by the scientist(s) who did the study. How accurately did the mass media report the study? If the media report was not accurate, discuss why the media might have misrepresented the story.

THE INTERNET

The 1990s were dubbed the "decade of the Internet," with an explosive growth of the Web, e-mail, and electronic commerce. Internet use has almost tripled in the United States since 2000. As of 2008, more than 1.4 billion people worldwide were Internet users, including 73.6 percent of North Americans, 48.1 percent of Europeans, and 15.3 percent of Asians, with the most rapid growth in Internet use occurring in Africa and the Middle East.[20] The pervasive impact of the Internet on global communication and our everyday lives can hardly be overestimated.

Impact of the Internet on Daily Life

Hot or Not?

What do you think is a healthy or reasonable amount of time to spend on the Internet each day?

Internet users in the United States spend an average of 3 hours a day online.[21] According to the fall 2007 American Freshman Survey, college freshmen are now spending more time surfing the Web than studying.[22] People can shop, do their banking, purchase concert or movie tickets, carry out research, play games, gamble, download music, and even earn a college degree without leaving the comfort of their homes. For more on the issue of online gambling among college students, see Chapter 4, pages 114–115.

In addition to creating new career possibilities such as software engineer,* the Internet allows students and other job seekers to find out what job opportunities are available and to post their résumés online.[23] We now can get all our news, watch movies, and read books over the Internet, which may make other forms of the mass media—including television, radio, and printed books—obsolete. Because of the pervasive and growing influence of the Internet on our lives and decisions, it is important that we learn to think critically about what we see, hear, and post on the Internet. In Chapter 4, we examined different criteria for evaluating Internet resources when doing research on the Internet. In the following pages, we will look at the impact of the Internet on our social and political lives.

Social Networking

The Internet is affecting daily life by reshaping social dynamics among young people. Social networking sites such as MySpace, Facebook, and Friendster are growing at a phenomenal rate. These sites rely heavily on messages, photos, stories, personal journals, and music, which users post and other users view. MySpace, the most popular of these Web sites, has more than 100 million members worldwide—mostly high school and college students.[24] According to the *American Freshman National Norms for Fall 2007*, 86 percent of college freshmen spent time each week on social networking sites, with 19 percent spending more than 6 hours a week on the sites.[25]

Wanting to communicate with others is certainly worthwhile. However, good communication skills require discernment and thinking beforehand about what message we are sending: What information is being conveyed by the messages we post? What attitudes and feelings are being communicated, both by our verbal and nonverbal/graphic postings?

For example, some of the profiles on social networking sites contain lewd photographs of students or photographs of students engaging in such illegal activities as smoking marijuana, as well as derogatory remarks about professors and other people. This raises serious questions about the judgment and critical-thinking skills of some of the young people who put their profiles on the sites. While such postings may have been intended to send a message to our peers that we are a lot of fun or can stand up to authority, these messages may be misinterpreted by a college administrator or potential employer as suggesting that we are irresponsible and mean-spirited.

When posting a message, we need to consider who are the potential recipients, both intended and unintended, of our message. Although Facebook and MySpace were designed primarily for college students and give users a lot of control over who can visit their site, the Internet is a form of mass media. As such, it is available to the public. Indeed, Facebook has recently become available to anyone, and more than half of its 64 million users are now off-campus. During the 2008 elections Obama supporters used social networks to encourage young people to get out and vote for their candidate.

Many students assume that their profiles are private. Several college students have been expelled for posting disparaging remarks about professors, racist comments, or threats to kill someone.[26] More and more employers are looking at the profiles of job applicants on these sites as part of a background check, sometimes to the detriment of the college-graduate job-seekers. By not thinking critically before posting a message, these students may place obstacles in the way of achieving their life goals. The police are also looking to personal content social networking sites as a law enforcement tool. A photo on his Facebook page of

---

*For more information on technology jobs, go to the Web site of the U.S. Department of Labor Bureau Labor Statistics: http://stats.bls.gov/oco042.htm.

Bryant College junior Joshua Lipton dressed as a prison inmate and mockingly sticking out his tongue, just days after he had slammed into two cars seriously injuring one of the drivers, was used as evidence of his lack of remorse in his trial and sentencing. Lipton's blood alcohol was more than twice the legal limit at the time of the accident.[27]

As critical thinkers, you need to do your research about social networking sites and how to use them. You also need to think twice before making a posting. What may seem like a joke or just having fun can end up getting a person expelled from college or denied a coveted job interview.

The Internet as "The Great Equalizer"

Since it is so accessible, the Internet has been hailed as "the great equalizer," as "the most participatory form of mass speech yet developed," and as "the best advancement in democracy since universal suffrage."[28] During the 2008 elections, blogs such as www.presidentblog2008.com/ played an important role in dissemination and discussion of information about the candidates and their positions. A free and open flow of information is important in a healthy democracy. Unlike traditional mass media, which is controlled by a handful of large corporations, there is no centralized control of the Internet. In addition, unlike television, which is one-way communication, the Internet is open and accessible to all people. Anyone who has access to the Internet can exchange ideas and post information that is available to people around the world. In his book *The Assault on Reason*, former Vice President Al Gore writes that

> The Internet is perhaps the greatest source of hope for reestablishing an open communicative environment in which the conversation of democracy can flourish. . . . The Internet is not just another platform for disseminating the truth. It's a platform of pursuing the truth, and the decentralized creation and distribution of ideas . . .[29]

With increased opportunity comes increased responsibility for us as critical thinkers and participants in a democratic society. Unlike most real-time conversations and discussions, exchanging ideas on the Internet allows us time to critically analyze and research the credibility of the premises used in other people's arguments, as well as to develop a response or counterargument that is both logical and backed up by credible sources.

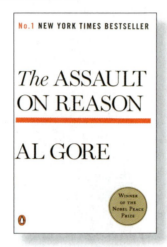

The Internet also has the potential to reverse the growing economic gap between those who enroll in college and those who do not.[30] One of the recent cost-saving developments in higher education is the use of online courses, along with interactive online group study and discussion. The tuition at an online university, for example, can be less than half that of the average private college.[31] The Internet has the potential to make a higher education accessible not only to more low-income families but also to a greater range of people, including long-distance learners and

> The Internet has the potential to make a higher education accessible not only to more low-income families but also to a greater range of people, including long-distance learners and those who are unable to attend classes on campus because of health issues or work or family obligations.

those who are unable to attend classes on campus because of health issues or work or family obligations.

The Internet has greatly leveled the playing field when it comes to learning, sharing, and discussing ideas—but on the downside, the Internet has also created new opportunities for invasions of privacy, harassment, fraud, and terrorism. As critical thinkers we need to do our research and be knowledgeable regarding the risks involved in Internet use. Unscrupulous people can steal our personal information, such as our credit card or Social Security numbers, from Internet databases. Hackers, or even worse—cyberterrorists—can sabotage or alter business, educational, and government records. In addition, Internet technology can be used to distribute damaging computer viruses or to send harassing or fraudulent e-mails to millions of people at one time. Finally, as we noted in Chapter 4, the Internet is replete with sites that are disreputable or biased. Anyone who wants to can set up a Web site. Chat rooms and personal Web sites in particular often have a biased agenda or view they want to promote. Because of this, as critical thinkers we need to be especially cautious when using information from the Internet unless it is from a credible source.

Misuse of the Internet: Pornography and Plagiarism

The proliferation of Internet technology over the past decade has raised the question of whether rules regarding freedom of speech in the media should apply to Internet speech, including obscenity and pornography. In 2007, there were 4.2 million pornographic Web sites (12 percent of total sites). Pornography is a multibillion-dollar enterprise and one of the fastest-growing businesses on the Internet.[32] Twenty-five percent of all search engine requests are for pornography. Unfortunately, many people do not rationally consider the possible repercussions, both on their family life and their career, of visiting these Web sites. For example, 20 percent of men admit to viewing pornography online at work.[33] In some cases, they have lost their jobs because of this. See "Critical Thinking in Action: Over Your Shoulder: Monitoring Employees' Internet Use."

As parents or potential parents, we should research and consider the potential impact of the Internet on our children. The easy availability of the Internet means that children can access it at home. An estimated 90 percent of children between the ages of 8 and 16 have viewed pornography online. The largest consumers of Internet pornography are teenagers, with 80 percent of 15- to 17-year-olds having had multiple exposures to hard-core pornography.[34] Parents can regulate the time children watch a television show or keep pornographic literature out of the house, but Internet pornography is available to children 24 hours a day at the click of a button. To address these potential problems, we need to engage in creative critical thinking to come up with effective solutions.

Plagiarism has also raised concerns about misuse of the Internet. Studies suggest that 40 percent of college students have plagiarized material or bought papers online.[35] Although some people mistakenly assume that the presence of something on the Internet makes it public property and available for anyone to use, others copy from the Internet because they think they can get away with it. Educators are increasingly using plagiarism-detection software and Web sites such as TurnItIn.com to catch student plagiarists. While many educators believe that easy access to information provided by the Internet is partly to blame,[36] the ultimate responsibility lies with the plagiarist. Plagiarism involves not only deception but also an inability or unwillingness on the part of the plagiarist to think for himor herself and to develop his or her critical-thinking skills.

Computers and the Internet have transformed media technology and greatly increased our access to information. Like any new technology, however, the Internet needs to be used with discernment—capitalizing on its strengths and opportunities while avoiding its pitfalls.

Hot or Not?

Does the Internet encourage student plagiarism?

Experiencing the Media

The three-tier model of thinking—experience, interpretation, and analysis—can be used in fostering media literacy skills. (For a review of the three-tier model, see Chapter 1, pages 5–6.) In applying this model, the first step is to develop an awareness of the *experience* of the media in your life.

Most people have no idea how much time they actually spend tuned into the media. A study in which researchers observed and recorded media use by adults found that actual media use was double that reported by standard questionnaires or phone survey methods.[41] If you think that the media doesn't play much of a role in your own life, keep a tally of the television and radio shows you tune into, the newspapers and magazines you read, and Internet sites you visit in a typical day. You'll probably be surprised at the amount of time you spend on the media.

Experience also involves understanding the process involved in creating media messages. Who created each message, and what was the creator's goal? For example, is the article you are reading or the show you are watching intended to be factual—or is it primarily intended as entertainment? Sometimes the two are mixed, as in talk shows, such as the *Jerry Springer Show* or news satires such as *The Daily Show with Jon Stewart* on Comedy Central. Even reputable news sources, as we noted earlier, can present news in a misleading manner because of the need to hold and entertain an audience.

Also ask yourself what issues are being addressed. Write a summary of the message(s) using nonemotive language. There might be several messages or bites of news, information, or entertainment. Note the images used, including the set and appearance of the commentators, performers, or guests on the show—their sex, race, ethnicity, and so forth. Note also the use of music and graphics: Are they upbeat, soothing, inspiring, edgy, gloomy, or ominous? Note as well the amount of time or space devoted to advertisements. What products are being advertised, and how do these products reinforce the message?

Interpreting Media Messages

Once you have collected all your facts, the next step is *interpretation*, or trying to make sense of the experiences. What values and points of view are being expressed in the program's message? Describe your reaction or interpretation of the message or particular show or article. Examine your reaction. Why did it make you feel this way? What effect did the language, music, and visuals have on you? Are there certain media individuals you identified with or felt positive toward and others who evoke a negative reaction? What prompted your reactions?

You might have enjoyed the *Daily Show* on Comedy Central because of the way Jon Stewart pokes fun at conservatives, or *Las Vegas* on NBC because many of the main characters were beautiful young women, or *24* on Fox because of all the exciting action scenes. What do these reactions say about you and how you interpret the world around you, as well as your particular biases and types of resistance? Do you watch only those shows that confirm your political and social worldview and avoid those that don't? If so, you might try to expand your media habits to

Some television shows, such as The Daily Show, combine news and entertainment.

include more programs that have messages that differ from your views.

Only watching programs that confirm your worldview contributes to confirmation bias and narrow-mindedness. To overcome this bias, watch or read coverage of the same issue or news event on a different channel or in a different magazine or newspaper. Once again, apply the three-tier model of thinking, noting your interpretation of the experience and then critically analyzing your interpretation. Expanding your range of media experiences can help you overcome narrow-mindedness.

In interpreting media from the perspective of a critical thinker, it is important to take into account diverse points of view, without assuming that yours is the correct or only interpretation. Don't assume that everyone agrees with your interpretation or with the messages being promoted by your favorite shows. Other people may interpret a media message entirely differently. Ask other people what they thought about a particular show or article. For example, Jon Stewart's show may be interpreted by someone else as disrespectful and anti-American. Another viewer may see the beautiful young women on *Las Vegas*

son and analysis of the issue. On the other hand, emotional reactions such as anger or contempt may be indicative of underlying prejudices or distorted worldviews.

In doing an analysis, keep in mind that this process is most productive when it is done collectively, since we each bring different experiences and interpretations to a message. As you begin the process of analysis, note any resistance on your part if your interpretations are challenged. For example, do you roll your eyes or get annoyed if someone suggests that certain shows or magazines are degrading to women?

In analyzing a media message, identify the purpose or conclusion of the message. How does the message contribute to making us better informed about events, issues, and scientific findings? Is the message backed by good reasoning and facts, or is it based on rhetorical devices and fallacious arguments? To what extent is the portrayal of events or developments biased or sensationalized? Does the media presentation contribute to stereotypes and materialism in our culture, or to poor self-esteem and fear of crime? How about our concepts of what is morally right and wrong? Analysis may require research on your part. Does pornography in the media harm women? Are people who view violence in the media more likely to act violently? What is the effect of the media on children?

The mass media plays an essential role in a democracy because it keeps us informed about issues and events. Indeed, the news media is sometimes called the fourth branch of government because it acts as a check on the executive, judicial, and legislative branches. On the other hand, because the mass media depends on business advertising for financial support, it may be more concerned with holding the audience's attention than with providing information on important issues and scientific developments. As critical thinkers, we need to develop media literacy so that we can understand the influence of the media on our lives and have the skills to critically analyze its messages.

HIGHLIGHTS

ANALYZING MEDIA MESSAGES

- What type of media do you use, and how often?

- Who created the message?

- What is the purpose of the message?

- What techniques are used to attract and hold your attention?

- What values and points of view are represented in the message?

- What was your reaction to the message?

- Why did the message make you feel this way?

- Is your interpretation of the message reasonable and well informed?

- How might different people interpret the message?

- Is the message biased?

- Is the message backed by good reasoning and facts?

- What are the possible effects of the message on individuals and society?

as degrading to women or setting up impossible standards of beauty for women. And the exciting action scenes in *24* may be interpreted by another person as a reflection of rampant crime in our culture. Remember, at this point you are just making a list of interpretations, not evaluating them. Some of our interpretations may be well founded; others may be based merely on our opinions or personal feelings and prejudices, as you will discover when you carry out an analysis.

The third step entails carrying out a critical *analysis* of your interpretations. Analysis often begins by asking a question. You may use your reaction to a particular media message as a starting point in your analysis by asking, "Why did this show or article make me feel this way?" Emotional reactions such as sympathy or moral outrage may be quite appropriate if they are balanced by rea-

EXERCISES 11-5

1. Working in small groups, select a television or radio show that everyone, or almost everyone, has seen or heard. Using the three-tier model of thinking, write down what type of show it is (for example, news, comedy, documentary, reality show, drama, or sitcom) and a summary of the show. Next, make a list of the different interpretations students in your group have of the show. Finally, carry out a critical analysis of the interpretations, noting which ones are most reasonable.

2. Discuss ways in which your media experiences reinforce your existing worldviews and values as well as ways in which they challenge or expand your views. Be specific.

3. Working in pairs or small groups, critically analyze each others' answers to the questions posed earlier in the chapter.

4. Select a show, Web site or magazine that you've never watched or read because it conflicts with your worldview. Critically analyze it using the three-tier model.

5. Referring back to Exercise 7 on page 359, critically analyze the social networking site using your media literacy skills.

6. Select a television show, newspaper, or magazine that you would not ordinarily watch or read because it doesn't fit with your personal beliefs. As you experience it, note the types of resistance you may feel and what messages prompt the resistance. Does being aware of your use of resistance help you to overcome it and be more open to rationally analyzing the messages rather than simply dismissing them? Use specific examples to illustrate your answer.

Think AGAIN >>

1. What is the relationship between mass media and big business in the United States?

   • Much of mass media today is controlled by a few large corporations. In addition, big business influences what appears in the media, since to receive advertising revenue, the media generally needs to promote, or at least not contradict, the values of their sponsor.

2. What are some of the limitations of the news media?

   • With an increasing selection of news sources, including the Internet, people are tending to select news outlets that are consistent with their own worldviews. To attract and keep an audience, news stories are often selected because of their entertainment value and sensationalism rather than their newsworthiness or in-depth analysis of important national and international issues.

3. In what ways has the Internet changed our lives?

   • The Internet is becoming the primary source of news and information for many Americans. It is also used in job searches, for posting information, and for communication and social interaction.

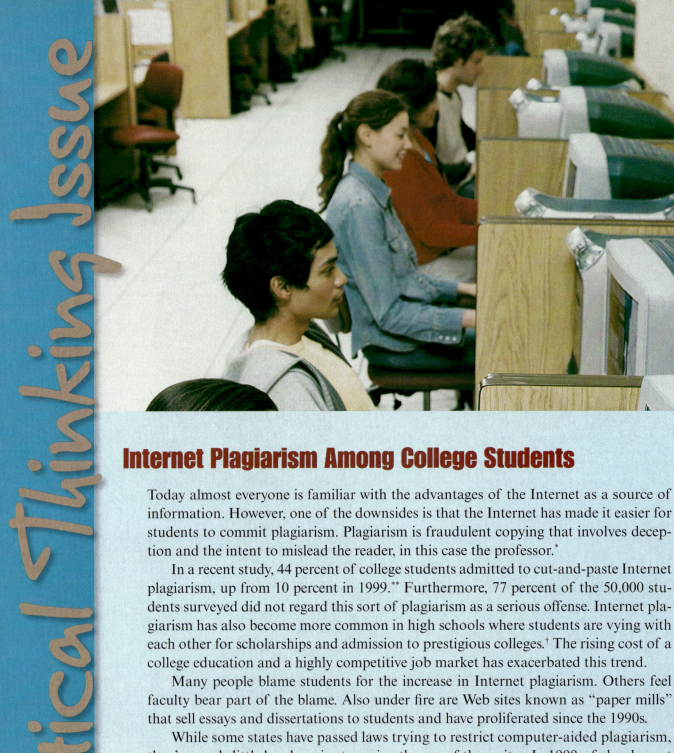

Internet Plagiarism Among College Students

Today almost everyone is familiar with the advantages of the Internet as a source of information. However, one of the downsides is that the Internet has made it easier for students to commit plagiarism. Plagiarism is fraudulent copying that involves deception and the intent to mislead the reader, in this case the professor.[*]

In a recent study, 44 percent of college students admitted to cut-and-paste Internet plagiarism, up from 10 percent in 1999.[**] Furthermore, 77 percent of the 50,000 students surveyed did not regard this sort of plagiarism as a serious offense. Internet plagiarism has also become more common in high schools where students are vying with each other for scholarships and admission to prestigious colleges.[†] The rising cost of a college education and a highly competitive job market has exacerbated this trend.

Many people blame students for the increase in Internet plagiarism. Others feel faculty bear part of the blame. Also under fire are Web sites known as "paper mills" that sell essays and dissertations to students and have proliferated since the 1990s.

While some states have passed laws trying to restrict computer-aided plagiarism, they've made little headway in stemming the use of these sites. In 1999 a federal court rejected a lawsuit brought by Boston University against five companies that sold term papers on the Internet. Defenders of paper mills argue that legal attempts to restrict the exchange of scholarly material would be a violation of the First Amendment freedom of speech.

The development of antiplagiarism software has also made it easier for teachers to find out if a student paper has been plagiarized. TurnItIn.com, a Web site that serves

[*]For a more extensive discussion of the definition of plagiarism, see Richard A. Posner, *The Little Book of Plagiarism* (New York: Pantheon Books, 2007).

[**]http://www.academicintegrity.org/cal%5fresearch.asp.

[†]See David Callahan, *The Cheating Culture: Why More Americans Are Doing Wrong to Get Ahead* (Orlando, FL: Harcourt Books, 2004), Chapter 7.

thousands of educational institutions worldwide, receives about 100,000 student papers a day from teachers. TurnItIn.com uploads the papers into its database, a practice whose legality is questionable, and then searches its database and billions of other pages on the Web for matches.[*]

The victims of Internet plagiarism extend beyond the intended reader(s). Other students also suffer, as well as the plagiarist, who receives no direct educational benefit from the assignment. Finally, society is harmed because students learn that cheating pays and carry this attitude over into their careers.

In the following readings, the authors discuss the reasons for and consequences of Internet plagiarism and what steps academic communities might take to curtail it. Brook Sadler argues that plagiarism is wrong and should be severely penalized. Russell Hunt, in contrast, regards Internet plagiarism as an opportunity for the academic community to rethink the traditional model of knowledge that, he argues, encourages plagiarism.

The Wrongs of Internet Plagiarism: Ten Quick Arguments

BROOK J. SADLER

Brook J. Sadler is an assistant professor of philosophy at the University of South Florida. In the following reading, she presents several arguments for why plagiarism is wrong. She also examines reasons why students plagiarize and the negative effects of this practice on the offending student, the academic community, and society in general. She concludes that it is important for colleges to have a strict policy regarding plagiarism and to enforce penalties against students who plagiarize.

What is wrong with plagiarism?

. . . First, plagiarism, regardless of the copyright issue, can be viewed as a type of theft: the taking of someone else's property and using it as one's own. . . . But this explanation will not apply when, for instance, the roommate has volunteered to give away her own work or when the paper was purchased online.

Second, plagiarism involves the intent to deceive. . . . The professor's activity in grading is one that is predicated on academic honesty; when students knowingly deceive professors about their work, they enlist professors in an activity to which professors would not consent were they fully informed.

Third, plagiarism violates the trust upon which higher education is established. Students trust that professors will do their best to give them an honest education—not unduly biased, not misrepresenting the facts, not deliberately omitting relevant evidence, not distorting the findings of research in the field, not grading students' work on the basis of prejudice, personal feeling, or arbitrary criteria. As we are aware, of course, not all professors maintain their part of this trust, and that is wrong. But students also have a part to play in maintaining trust. Professors give time and energy to educating students on the presumption that students are open *to being educated*. When a student commits any form of academic dishonesty, he or she is shutting down the possibility of being educated; the student does

not learn from the effort required to produce the work on her own, nor from the constructive feedback the professor gives in grading the assignment. . . . The professor's comments cannot really reach the individual student to provoke new avenues of reflection, to inspire improvement, or to assist in identifying her particular weaknesses as a writer and offer her the instruction necessary to overcome them. Plagiarism has a gravely dispiriting effect on professors who care about teaching. . . . The trust that underwrites education, especially university education, is disrupted, even annihilated, by academic dishonesty.

Fourth, plagiarism is unfair to other students in the class. Especially when the source of the plagiarism is a professional research paper, the plagiarized paper may be much better than the work produced by the other students in the class. If a professor does not detect the plagiarism, the fact that the plagiarized paper is of higher quality than others throws off a professor's sense of her students' capabilities regarding the material covered by the assignment. It makes the work of honest students appear comparatively weak. This has two detrimental effects. One is that it may alter a professor's grade scale, disadvantaging honest students. . . . The second detrimental effect is that plagiarism makes it difficult for a professor to assess the effectiveness of her instruction. . . . Thus, plagiarism undermines the professor's effort to mold her instruction to students' actual abilities and does an injustice to other students who stand to benefit from that instruction.

Fifth, a student who plagiarizes does not benefit from the process of struggling with the material on her own. She does not truly learn the material or engage the assignment.

[*]Erik W. Robelen, "Online Anti-Plagiarism Service Sets off Court Fight," *Education Week*, Vol. 26, Issue 36, May 9, 2007. pp. 16–17.

on keeping their GPA up to some arbitrary scratch). An even more central consideration is the way the existence of plagiarism itself challenges the way the university structures its system of incentives and rewards, as a zero-sum game, with a limited number of winners.

University itself, as our profession has structured it, is the most effective possible situation for encouraging plagiarism and cheating. If I wanted to learn how to play the guitar, or improve my golf swing, or write HTML, "cheating" would be the last thing that would ever occur to me. It would be utterly irrelevant to the situation. On the other hand, if I wanted a *certificate* saying that I could pick a jig, play a round in under 80, or produce a slick Web page (and never expected actually to perform the activity in question), I might well consider cheating (and consider it primarily a moral problem). This is the situation we've built for our students: a system in which the only incentives or motives anyone cares about are marks, credits, and certificates. . . . When students say—as they regularly do—"Why should I do this if it's not marked?" or "Why should I do this well if it's not graded?" or even "I understand that I should do this, but you're not marking it, and my other professors are marking what I do for them," they're saying exactly what educational institutions have been highly successful at teaching them to say.

They're learning exactly the same thing, with a different spin, when we tell them that plagiarism is a moral issue. We're saying that the only reason you might choose not to do it is a moral one. But think about it: if you wanted to build a deck and were taking a class to learn how to do it, your decision not to cheat would not be based on moral considerations.

3. **The model of knowledge held by almost all students, and by many faculty—the tacit assumption that knowledge is stored information and that skills are isolated, asocial faculties—is challenged by this, and that's a good thing**. When we judge essays by what they contain and how logically it's organized (and how grammatically it's presented) we miss the most important fact about written texts, which is that they are rhetorical moves in scholarly and social enterprises. In recent years there have been periodic assaults on what Paolo Freire called "the banking model" of education. . . . Partisans of active learning, of problem- and project-based learning, of cooperative learning, and of many other "radical" educational initiatives, all contend that information and ideas are not inert masses to be shifted and copied in much the way two computers exchange packages of information, but rather need to he continuously reformatted, reconstituted, restructured, reshaped and reinvented, and exchanged in new forms—not only as learning processes but as the social basis of the intellectual enterprise. A model

of the educational enterprise which presumes that knowledge comes in packages. . . invites learners to think of what they're doing as importing prepackaged nuggets of information into their texts and their minds.

Similarly, a model which assumes that a skill like "writing the academic essay" is an ability which can be demonstrated on demand, quite apart from any authentic rhetorical situation, actual question, or expectation of effect (or definition of what the "academic essay" actually *is*), virtually prohibits students from recognizing that all writing is shaped by rhetorical context and situation, and thus renders them tone-deaf to the shifts in register and diction which make so much plagiarized undergraduate text instantly recognizable. . . .

4. But there's a reason to welcome this challenge that's far more important than any of these—more important, even, than the way the revolutionary volatility of text mediated by photocopying and electronic files have assaulted traditional assumptions of intellectual property and copyright by distributing the *power* to copy beyond those who have the *right* to copy. It's this: **by facing this challenge we will be forced to help our students learn what I believe to be the most important thing they can learn at university: just how the intellectual enterprise of scholarship and research really works**. Traditionally, when we explain to students why plagiarism is bad and what their motives should be for properly citing and crediting their sources, we present them in terms of a model of how texts work in the process of sharing ideas and information which is profoundly different from how they actually work outside of classroom-based writing, and profoundly destructive to their understanding of the assumptions and methods of scholarship. . . .

Scholars—writers generally—use citations for many things: they establish their own *bona fides* and, currency, they advertise their alliances, they bring work to the attention of their reader, they assert ties of collegiality, they exemplify contending positions or define nuances of difference among competing theories or ideas. They do not use them to defend themselves against potential allegations of plagiarism.

The clearest difference between the way undergraduate students, writing essays, cite and quote and the way scholars do it in public is this: typically, the scholars are achieving something positive; the students are avoiding something negative.

The conclusion we're driven to, then, is this: offering lessons and courses and workshops on "avoiding plagiarism"—indeed, posing plagiarism as a problem at all—begins at the wrong end of the stick. It might usefully be analogized to looking for a good way to teach the infield fly rule to people who have no clear idea what baseball is.

1. How do most people in postsecondary education view the information technology revolution, and what are their assumptions regarding their concern?

2. In what ways does the issue of Internet plagiarism present a challenge to academia's current system of rewards?

3. What is the difference between the way scholars and college undergraduates use quotes and citations?

4. How do most faculty members respond to the issue of Internet plagiarism?

5. What is the old model of knowledge, and why does Internet plagiarism challenge this model?

6. Why is Hunt happy about Internet plagiarism?

Think >> AND DISCUSS

1. Critically analyze the responses of both Sadler and Hunt to the issue of Internet plagiarism. Which person presents the best argument? Support your answer.

2. Have you or someone you know ever plagiarized or been tempted to plagiarize from the Internet? Explain what motivated you or the other person. Which response to the issue of plagiarism, that of Sadler or that of Hunt, would make a student less likely to consider plagiarizing?

3. In *The Little Book of Plagiarism*, Richard Posner maintains that students who plagiarize are also victims since they derive no direct educational benefit from the assignment. On the other hand, these students receive indirect benefits in terms of better grades and improved career opportunities. Imagine a student who is considering purchasing an essay from the Internet because she has a heavy academic workload and does not have the time to research and write an essay. She also needs a good grade in the course to get into graduate school. Referring to Chapter 9, pages 289–290, discuss how a utilitarian might advise the student.

4. MasterPapers.com provides a "custom essay, term paper and dissertation writing service." The site states:

> Experience your academic career to the fullest—exactly the way you want it! ... Our company is perfectly aware that a number of tutors do not appreciate when their students resort to essay writing services for help. We strongly believe that professional and legitimate research paper writing services do not hamper students [sic] progress in any way, while the contemporary academic environment often leaves them absolutely no choice but to take advantage of our help.

Critically analyze the argument by MasterPapers.com that using a writing service is justified because (1) it does not interfere with students' progress, and (2) the current academic atmosphere sometimes leaves students no other choice. Discuss how Sadler and Hunt might each respond to the argument.

5. In the United States and most Western nations, published information is regarded as belonging to a particular person. But in some cultures, such as much of India, people regard information on the Internet as communal property that's free for the taking. Given this difference in cultural values, discuss how professors should respond if they find that a student from another cultural background has plagiarized an essay.

6. Some colleges reject plagiarism software and Web sites, such as TurnItIn.com, and instead prefer to use an honor code or lecture their students about the evils of plagiarism. Are these approaches naïve as some claim?[*] Discuss your answer in light of your answer to question 2.

7. The advent of the Internet allows students to query specialized Web sites. Miriam Schulman, the manager of a Web site for Santa Clara University's Markkula Center for Applied Ethics, receives many requests from students seeking answers to questions that, she says, are "essentially homework assignments pasted into an e-mail."[**] How should these Web sites respond to these requests from students? Are these types of requests plagiarism, or are they Web-based research? Support your answer.

---

[*]Richard A. Posner, *The Little Book of Plagiarism* (New York: Pantheon Books, 2007), pp. 82–83.
[**]Miriam Schulman, "I Have a Question," *Santa Clara Magazine,* fall 2004; available from http://www.scu.edu/scm/fall2004/research.cfm.

12

SCIENCE

Sea levels have risen 4 to 10 inches in the last hundred years because of global warming, according to the United Nations Environment Programme, and they are continuing to rise.[1] In the past few decades, global warming has accelerated. The hottest 11 years on record since we began recording the temperature in 1850 have occurred in the last 13 years.[2] January 2006 was one of the warmest ever recorded in the United States, with temperatures averaging 8.5°F above the norm of 31°F for the years 1895 through 2005.[3]

In 2002, a piece of the Antarctic ice shelf the size of Rhode Island broke off and fell into the ocean. If the West Antarctic ice sheet were to completely melt—a process that has begun and is occurring at a much faster rate

Think
FIRST >>

- What is the scientific method?
- How does science differ from pseudoscience?
- What are some of the different types of scientific experiments and research methods?

than previously predicted by scientists—the sea level could rise by as much as 30 inches by 2050.[4] In other words, if these trends continue, by the time today's typical college freshman retires, most of the world's coastal cities and communities will be under water.[5]

Rising sea levels will also contribute to land erosion, as well as to the salinization of freshwater and agricultural land in low-lying areas, thus disrupting our food and water supply.[6] In addition, major storms are predicted to increase in number and intensity, while the warmer climate will ensure that infectious diseases, especially such tropical diseases as malaria, will flourish in places like the southern United States.[7]

An alternative, though much less likely, scenario is portrayed in the 2004 sci-fi film *The Day After Tomorrow:* that climate change will cause ocean currents to shift (as they have done in the past), catapulting Earth into another ice age.

Some scientific research on global warming and other natural processes is more rigorous and better at explaining and predicting phenomena than other research. As critical thinkers, we need to be able to interpret and evaluate science stories in the news media, as well as research reports in scientific journals. We need to decide not only whether they are worth considering but also how scientific findings can be applied to our lives and to public policy. Even more basic to this process is the capacity to think critically about science itself as a method for discovering truth.

In this chapter we'll

- Learn about the history of science

- Identify and critically analyze the assumptions underlying science

- Study the scientific method

- Learn how to evaluate scientific explanations

- Distinguish between science and pseudoscience

- Learn about the different types of scientific experiments and how to evaluate them

- Look at ethical concerns in scientific experimentation

- Examine Thomas Kuhn's theory of normal science and paradigm shifts

WHAT IS SCIENCE?

Science rests on reasoning that moves from observable, measurable facts (usually called *data* by scientists) to testable explanations for those facts. The task of scientists is to discover, observe, and collect facts in a systematic manner and to explain relationships among data. To determine whether their explanations are sound, scientists formulate and test hypotheses. We'll be looking more at the method used by scientists in the section of this chapter entitled "The Scientific Method."

Modern science has a profound impact on our lives. Because it is so pervasive in our culture, we tend to assume that science is the natural method for obtaining knowledge about the world. In this section, we'll examine the development of modern science, as well as some of the assumptions underlying science.

The Scientific Revolution

Prior to the seventeenth century, the teachings of Christianity, and in particular those of the Catholic Church, were regarded as the final source of truth in Western Europe. Nicolaus Copernicus (1473–1543), a Polish astronomer, launched the scientific revolution with his assertion that the sun, not the Earth, is the center of the universe. Most historians, however, recognize English philosopher and statesman Sir Francis Bacon (1561–1626), who systematized the scientific method, as the father of modern science. In his *Novum Organum* (1620), Bacon put forth a method based on direct observation for discovering truths about the world. Bacon's scientific method, which begins with carrying out systematic observations about the world and using testing and experimentation to draw inferences that are based on these observations, has been tremendously successful in advancing our knowledge about the world and our ability to manipulate nature.

> **science** The use of reason to move from observable, measurable facts to hypotheses to testable explanations for those facts.
>
> **empiricism** The belief that our physical senses are the primary source of knowledge.

Assumptions Underlying Science

Science is the primary way and, indeed, is often considered the natural way in Western culture of perceiving and interpreting reality. However, it is important to keep in mind that science is a system created by humans and, as such, is based on a particular worldview or set of assumptions.

Empiricism. **Empiricism**, the belief that our physical senses are the primary source of knowledge, is one of the most basic assumptions of science. Scientists consider the empirical method the only reliable method for obtaining knowledge. Consequently, the more data and observations that scientists accumulate over the generations, the greater is science's ability to correctly explain the workings of nature.

Objectivity. A related assumption underlying modern science is **objectivity**, the belief that we can observe and study the physical world "out there" as an object outside of us without bias on the part of the scientist/observer. Because the world is objective and independent of the individual observer, the presumption is that systematic observation will lead to agreement among scientists. This assumption has been called into question by quantum physics, which has found that the mere act of observing a quantum event changes it.

Although early empiricists (including Bacon) thought that objectivity was achievable, most scientists now also acknowledge that past social experiences, as well as inborn cognitive and perceptual errors, can influence how even the best-trained scientists perceive the world. For example, as we noted in Chapter 4, we have a tendency to see order in random phenomena. One of the most famous examples of this type of error was the Martian canals, which many astronomers continued to believe in until 1965, when the space probe *Mariner 4* flew close to Mars and took photos of the planet's surface. No canals showed up in the photos. It turned out that the "canals" were a combination of an optical illusion and our brain's tendency to impose order on random data, as well as the expectation on the part of scientists that canals existed on Mars.

Despite the fact that complete objectivity is unattainable, it remains the ideal. Scientists strive as much as possible to be aware of their biases, to be objective in their observations, and to be precise in their use of language.

Hot or Not?

Is science the best tool for learning about the world?

> **objectivity** The assumption that we can observe and study the physical world without any observer bias.
>
> **materialism** The belief that everything in the universe is composed of physical matter.
>
> **dualism** The belief that there are two substances—the physical and the nonphysical.

Materialism. With the doctrine known as **materialism**, empiricism goes one step further. Scientific materialists argue that *everything* in the universe is physical matter. (*Materialism* in this sense has nothing to do with being obsessed with acquiring money, consumer goods, and other "material things.") Although some scientists believe that there is an independent nonmaterial or spiritual realm—a philosophical position known as **dualism**—materialism is the working assumption of most scientists. According to scientific materialism, perceptions, thoughts, and emotions can all be reduced to descriptions of physical systems, such as brain waves or stimulus and response. There is no need to bring into scientific descriptions and explanations extraneous, nonmaterial concepts such as a conscious mental life. Because of its materialistic roots, science has made little, if any, progress in explaining how matter is or can become conscious.

Predictability. Scientists have traditionally assumed that the physical world is *orderly and predictable*. The universe consists of interconnected causal relationships that are intelligible to the human mind and that can be discovered through systematic observation and inductive reasoning. As with objectivity, this assumption has been called into question by quantum theory and the Heisenberg uncertainty principle, which states that it is impossible to predict both the position and momentum of a particle simultaneously, even under ideal conditions of measurement.

Unity. Associated with the traditional belief in predictability is the assumption that there is an *underlying unity of the universe*, or a unified dynamic structure that is present in all phenomena. These unified structures can be translated into scientific laws that are universally applicable. Indeed, Albert Einstein devoted considerable effort during his lifetime in search of a grand unification principle, a search that to date has been unfruitful.

Limitations of Science

Despite its obvious strengths in enabling us to build a body of knowledge about the natural world, science has some limitations. One of these, at least from a philosophical viewpoint, is that it uses the existence of a physical world as its starting point. But as the seventeenth-century French philosopher René Descartes noted, we only have an idea in

HIGHLIGHTS

ASSUMPTIONS OF SCIENCE:

- **Empiricism:** Sensory experience is the source of truth.
- **Objectivity:** We can study the physical world without bias.
- **Materialism:** Everything in the universe is made up of physical matter.
- **Predictability:** The universe is made up of interconnected causal relationships.
- **Unity:** The universe has an underlying unified dynamic structure.

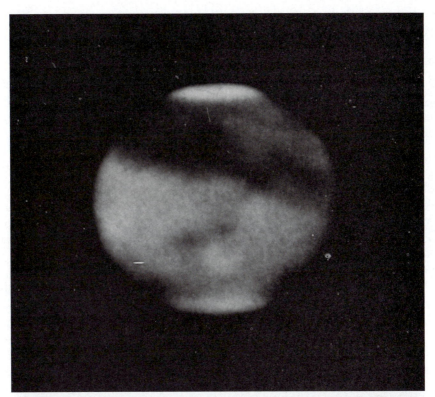

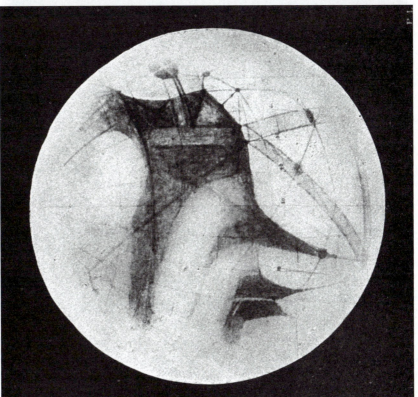

THE "CANALS" OF MARS
DISCUSSION QUESTIONS

1. *Discuss how language shapes your expectations and observations of natural phenomena, as occurred with the "canals" of Mars. Use specific examples to illustrate your answer.*

2. *Think of a time when you drew an incorrect conclusion on the basis of observation alone. How did you discover that your observation mislead you? What role did scientific knowledge play in correcting your misperception?*

Analyzing Images

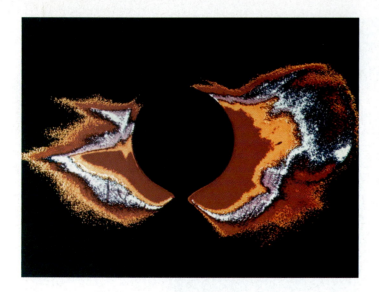

Quantum mechanics in particular challenges the idea of an ultimately predictable, determinist, material reality, suggesting that there are forces at play in the universe other than strictly physical causal laws. Because of this, Stanley Klein, physicist and visual sciences faculty member at the University of California, Berkeley, suggests that quantum mechanics provides a bridge for dialogue between science and religion.[9]

Science and Religion

There are four basic positions regarding the relationship between science and religion: (1) science always trumps religion when there is a conflict; (2) religion always trumps science when there is a conflict; (3) science and religion operate in two separate and mutually exclusive realities; and (4) science and religion are concerned with the same reality and are compatible and complementary.

Most scientists and Western philosophers adopt the position that science always trumps religion when there is a conflict between them. This attitude has created antagonism between science and religion, especially fundamentalist religions. Many conservative Christians, for example, believe that the Bible is the literal and infallible word of God not only in the religious sphere but also in science. Indeed, the American public's belief in evolution has never been measured at more than 51 percent in any Gallup Poll taken since 1982, with only 14 percent of Americans believing in scientific evolution unguided by the hand of God. In other words, the majority of Americans believe that Darwin's theory of evolution is wrong, and many, if not most, accept some version of creationism.

People who adopt the third position, such as Judge John E. Jones (see "Critical-Thinking Issue: Evolution Versus Intelligent Design"), deny that there is a conflict. They argue instead that science and religion each deal with separate and mutually exclusive realms. Science deals with the objective, empirical reality; religion is concerned with values and a subjective, spiritual reality. Science asks how and what; religion asks why. According to this view, we can accept evolution, for example, without relinquishing our religious convictions regarding the special creation of human beings in the image of God, since ensoulment is a process that occurs in the spiritual realm. This view is reflected in Pope John Paul II's 1996 "Message to Pontifical Academy of Sciences."

One of the problems with this approach is that in some cases science and religion make claims about the same phenomenon, whether it is the origin of human life, the effect of prayer on healing, or the occurrence of the Biblical Great Flood. When these claims are in conflict, logically they cannot both be true.

our mind of a world outside of us—not direct evidence that the world "out there" actually exists.[8] In other words, the very starting point of science—the existence of a physical world—cannot be empirically proven!

Empiricism and the use of sensory experience as the foundation of science also limits science to observable, shared phenomena. However, there are many aspects of the physical world—such as dark energy and dark matter, certain electromagnetic waves, and subatomic particles—that are imperceptible to human senses and to the scientific instruments that are designed to function as extensions of our senses. In addition, according to string theorists, physicists who use mathematical reasoning, there are at least nine dimensions, not just three, that our brain is able to perceive and process.

Furthermore, the assumption that the universe is orderly and predictable has been called into question by quantum mechanics. Some philosophers, such as David Hume and Immanuel Kant, argue that observation alone, no matter how many times we observe one event to follow another, cannot logically establish a necessary causal connectedness between the two events. Kant in particular maintained that causality is a property of our mind, not of the outside world.* In addition, observation alone is insufficient to reveal any underlying unity or structure of nature, if in fact there is one. In other words, how we experience reality is dependent on the structure of our brains, which organize and give meaning to input from our senses.

> . . .how we experience reality is dependent on the structure of our brains, which organize and give meaning to input from our senses.

*For a review of Kant's theory of the mind and critique of empiricism, see Chapter 4, pages 99–100.

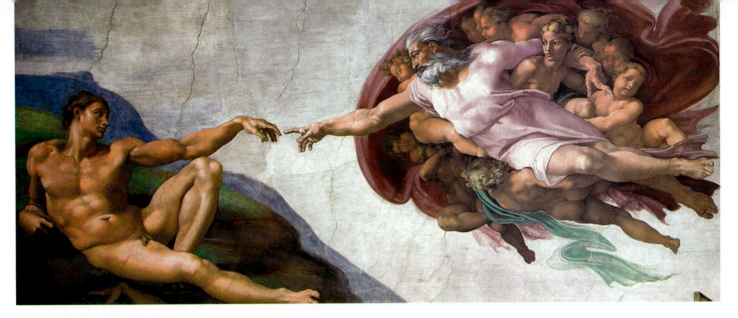

Michelangelo's rendition of the Genesis story of "The Creation of Man."

According to the fourth view, science and religion are dealing with the same reality and, as such, are compatible. This view is found in Judaism, Hinduism, Islam,[10] and in some mainstream Protestant denominations. If scripture conflicts with the claims of science, then scripture should be reinterpreted. For example, the creation story in Genesis should be seen as a metaphor rather than taken literally. British biophysical chemist and Anglican clergyman Arthur Peacocke supports this approach. Religion and science, he argues, are both dealing with the same reality. However, they focus on different aspects of that reality. As such, they must always "be ultimately converging. . . . The scientific and theological enterprises [are] interacting and mutually illuminating approaches to reality."[11] Therefore, science and religion should use information from each other to broaden each of their own perspectives on reality.

Though scientists often reject religious explanations for natural phenomena, there are strands of religious belief in science. The Judeo-Christian view that God gave humans dominion over the world legitimates the use of science to control and alter nature for our benefit. In addition, anthropocentrism—the assumption that humans are the central reality in the universe and are qualitatively different from other animals—allows scientists to confine and use other animals in research and experiments as a means to better the lives of humans. Some scientists take anthropocentricism even further and argue that the universe exists so that conscious human life would have a place to arise—a doctrine known as the anthropic principle.[12]

Although science is grounded in a set of unproven assumptions, this does not mean that science is invalid or even that these assumptions are false. Instead, we need to keep in mind that science has limitations in addition to its strengths. As we already noted, science has been extremely successful in uncovering many of the mysteries of the universe. Science has also been responsible for producing new technology for improving our lives.

EXERCISES 12-1

1. It has been said that science has become the religion of the twentieth and early twenty-first centuries. What do you think this means? Do you agree? Support your answers.

2. Is science just one way of viewing or experiencing the world or reality? If not, what are some other ways? Are these ways more or less valid than science?

3. If you depended on observation with the naked eye alone, what would you most likely conclude about the relationship of the Sun and the Earth? Discuss how religious assumptions at the time of Copernicus reinforced this observation.

4. In small groups, discuss the assumption of anthropocentrism in science, as well as the applications of this assumption. Discuss whether this assumption is justified or if scientists should refrain from practices that exploit other animals and so-called natural resources to benefit humans.

5. Discuss Peacocke's claim that religion and science complement each other. Is his position reasonable? Support your answer.

6. Compare the assumptions of science as a means of discovering the truth with a belief in faith in God (fidelism) as a means of discovering the truth.

EXERCISES 12-1 cont.

7. Inventor and computer scientist Raymond Kurzweil rejects the assumption that only "God" or "natural forces" can create new life forms. He argues that the creation of AI by humans may be a natural step in evolution. Review his reading from his book *Artificial Intelligence and Evolution* in Chapter 2 on pages 58–59. Write a two-page essay addressing the following questions: Which of the assumptions of science does Kurzweil reject? Is his rejection of these assumptions reasonable or unreasonable? How did you first react when you came across an argument that ran counter to the assumptions of science? Why did you react this way? Support your answers.

THE SCIENTIFIC METHOD

scientific method A process involving the rigorous, systematic application of observation and experimentation.

A National Science Foundation study found that although most Americans realize that almost everything in their lives is the result of scientific research, 70 percent of those surveyed had no understanding of the scientific process or method. The **scientific method** involves the identification of a problem and the rigorous, systematic application of observation and experimentation in testing an explanation for the problem.

As such, it is similar to the three levels of thinking—experience, interpretation, and analysis—that we studied in Chapter 1. Alone, experience or sensory data tell us nothing. It has to be interpreted in light of existing scientific knowledge and theories (analysis). Like the three levels of thinking, the scientific method is dynamic and recursive rather than linear, with analysis returning to observation to check for consistency, and interpretation being revised in light of further analysis and observation.

Experimentation/Testing (Analysis)

↑ ↓

Hypothesis (Interpretation)

↑ ↓

Observation (Experience)

The scientific method includes specific steps to guide a scientist through this process of systematically analyzing his or her observations. Although there is some variation in the steps between the different scientific disciplines, the steps basically are as follows: (1) identifying the prob-lem, (2) developing a hypothesis, (3) gathering additional information and refining the hypothesis, (4) testing the hypothesis, and (5) evaluating the results of the tests or experiments. We'll examine each of these steps in turn in this section.

1. Identify the Problem

The scientific method begins with the identification of a problem for investigation. This requires good observation skills, an inquisitive mind, and the ability to ask the right questions. Biologist Russell Hill, in his study of athletes on British soccer teams, observed that the teams that wore red uniforms seemed to win more often. He asked the question: Might there be a causal relationship at work?[13]

A problem may also arise as the result of previous work in the field. The Human Genome Project developed out of previous genetic research, including Watson and Crick's 1953 discovery of the structure of DNA. Or a problem may be brought to the attention of a scientist by a politician, by a government agency, or by concerned citizens. In the fall of 2006, beekeepers in both North America and Europe began noticing that their honeybees were disappearing. Entomologists are still working on the problem.

2. Develop an Initial Hypothesis

Once a problem has been identified, the next step in the scientific method is to develop a working hypothesis. A **hypothesis** is basically an educated guess—a proposed explanation for a particular set of phenomena,

hypothesis A proposed explanation for a particular set of phenomena.

which can serve as a starting point for further investigation. Several hypotheses have been put forth regarding the cause of the collapse of the honeybee colonies. Some researchers hypothesize that the use of insecticides known as neonic-otinoids are responsible. Others think a pathogen or fungus may be killing the bees. Still others suggest that radiation from cell phones may be interfering with honeybee navigation, a hypothesis that has since been dismissed.[14]

Hypotheses are put forth tentatively and may be changed on the basis of further observation. A scientific theory, on the other hand, is usually more complex and supported by previous work in the field. The U.S. National Academy of Sciences defines a **scientific theory** as "a well-substantiated explanation of some aspect of the natural world that can incorporate facts, laws, inferences, and tested hypotheses." However, because the scientific method is inductive, scientists can never prove with absolute certainty that a theory or a hypothesis is true. Richard Feynman (1918–1988), American physicist and Nobel Prize winner for his work in quantum electrodynamics, once said, "If you thought that science was certain—well, that is just an error on your part." Scientists may have great confidence in certain conclusions, such as the theory of evolution, but they can never have absolute certainty.

> **scientific theory** An explanation for some aspect of the natural world based on well-substantiated facts, laws, inferences, and tested hypotheses.

A well-formulated hypothesis uses precise language with key terms clearly defined. The scientific definition of a term is generally a theoretical or operational definition. Operational definitions provide precise measures that can be used in data collection, interpretation, and testing.* For example, meteorologists studying weather and climate changes define El Niño as an oceanic condition where the temperature continues at +0.5°C or higher, averaged over 3 or more consecutive months.[15] If a hypothesis introduces a new term, a stipulative definition must be provided.

A scientific hypothesis should provide a testable explanation for the problem being investigated. To facilitate this, hypotheses are often formulated as hypothetical ("If . . . then . . .") propositions. Writing Hill's soccer hypothesis as a hypothetical proposition, we have: If a team is wearing red (Antecedent), then the team is more likely to win the game than is a team wearing blue (Consequent).

> If A, then C.
> A.
> Therefore, C.

In this case we have a *modus ponens* argument.** Does the consequent or conclusion—"the team is more likely to win the game than is a team wearing blue"—regularly follow the antecedent—"a team is wearing red"? If it does follow, then the first premise (the hypothesis) is true and the hypothesis is worth further testing. If it does not follow, then the first premise (the hypothesis) is false and the hypothesis should be discarded. We'll look at additional criteria for evaluating scientific explanations later in this chapter.

3. Gather Additional Information and Refine the Hypothesis

Since we cannot possibly take in all the sensory data coming at us, hypotheses are used to guide and focus the collection of additional information. Without a hypothesis to guide our observations, we don't know what is relevant and what to ignore.

Scientific observation may be direct or indirect. To aid their senses and to minimize observer bias and cognitive and perceptual errors, scientists use instruments such as microscopes, telescopes, tape recorders, and stethoscopes.

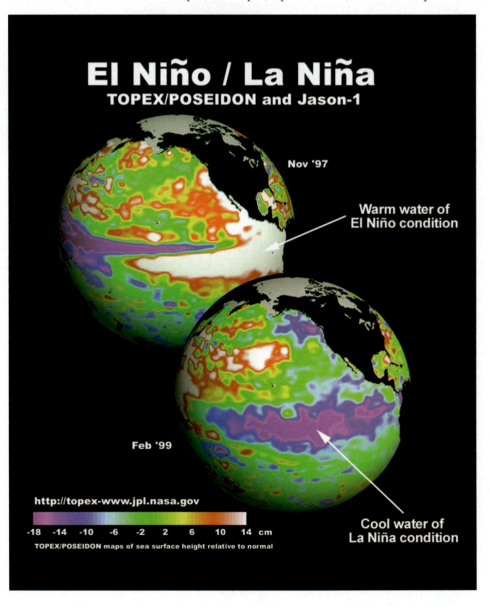

*For a review of the different types of definitions, see Chapter 3, pages 71–74.

**For a review of hypothetical reasoning, see Chapter 8, pages 249–253.

Almost all astronomical discoveries today are carried out by means of computerized cameras that do the "looking" through the telescopes, while astronomers study the photographs from their computers rather than in an observatory. Scientists also use measuring devices, such as thermometers, clocks, and scales, to supplement observation.

The initial hypothesis may be modified on the basis of further observation. Since we can never be certain that our hypothesis is correct, collecting information is an ongoing process in science. It is vital during this step in the scientific method that scientists strive to be as objective as possible and systematically record their observations without bias.

It may be only after an examination of their observations that scientists notice an unexpected pattern. For example, when Charles Darwin as a young man of 22 traveled aboard a British naval vessel, the HMS *Beagle*, as the ship's naturalist, he collected specimens and took abundant notes on the flora and fauna of the Galapagos Islands. However, it wasn't until after he returned to England that he noticed patterns and from these, years later, developed his theory of evolution.

In collecting information, scientists avoid anecdotal and hearsay evidence. They are skeptical and do not accept at face value what people tell them, unless they have compelling firsthand evidence

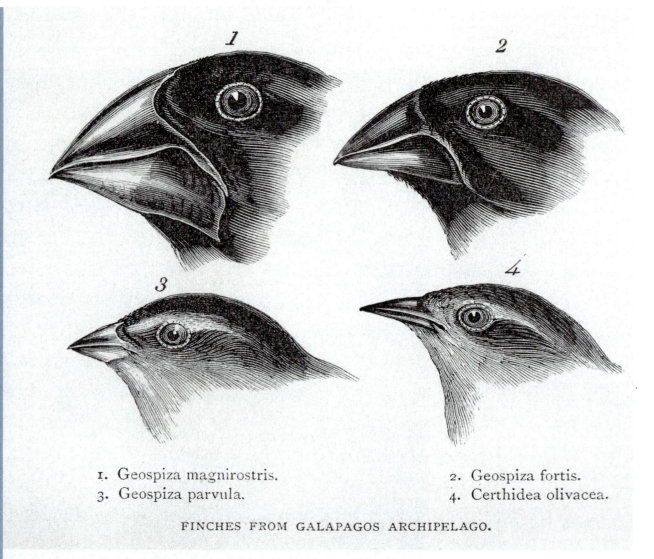

1. Geospiza magnirostris.
3. Geospiza parvula.
2. Geospiza fortis.
4. Certhidea olivacea.

FINCHES FROM GALAPAGOS ARCHIPELAGO.

Analyzing Images

DARWIN'S DRAWINGS OF GALAPAGOS ISLAND FINCH BEAKS

DISCUSSION QUESTIONS

1. *Look at the drawings and come up with a list of possible explanations for the differences in the beaks of the finches.*

2. *Review the list of critical-thinking skills on page 394. Discuss the role that these skills played in Darwin's formulation of his theory of evolution.*

that what is being said is true. For example, as we learned in Chapter 7, people have a tendency to tell an interviewer what makes them look good or what they think the interviewer wants to hear.

Margaret Mead lived with Samoan villagers to conduct observational study to prove her theory that adolescence in simpler cultures was more carefree for girls than in Western society. She is shown here, many years later, being interviewed about claims that some of the information she received was false.

As a graduate student in anthropology, Margaret Mead (1901–1978) was interested in finding out whether the troubles that plague adolescence in our culture are also found in so-called primitive or simpler cultures. Her hypothesis was that in these cultures, adolescence would present a different, less troubled, picture. To gather data on her hypothesis, Mead lived with, observed, and interviewed sixty-eight young women, ages 9 to 20, in a small village in Samoa, an island in the South Pacific. On the basis of her interviews, she concluded that Samoan girls experienced a carefree adolescence and engaged in casual sex from an early age, a finding that shocked many Westerners (and enthralled many Western teens and college students).[16] Many years later, the now-elderly Samoan women who had been interviewed by Mead confessed that they had lied to her, mainly as a joke. In this case, Mead's attachment to her hypothesis and her reliance on anecdotal evidence biased the way she gathered her information.

Scientists cannot rely on observations alone to determine whether a particular hypothesis is correct or is the best explanation of a phenomenon. Observations may be incomplete or biased because of poor collection methods, social expectations, or cognitive and perceptual errors. Instruments themselves may also be biased, since it is human inventors who determine what the instruments measure. For example, in the search for new life forms, both on Earth and beyond the Earth, scientists use instruments that measure the presence of DNA in soil, water, rock, and atmospheric samples. However, it is possible—even probable—that non-DNA life forms exist (or once existed), such as those based on RNA.[17]

4. Test the Hypothesis

After completing the observations and data collection and refining the hypothesis, the next step in the scientific method is to test the hypothesis. Russell Hill and his fellow scientist Robert Barton tested the hypothesis about the relationship between a team's uniform color and winning by carrying out a study of team events at the 2004 Olympics.

Testing may also be done in a laboratory using a controlled experiment. To determine the effectiveness of a vaccine made from anthrax germs, Louis Pasteur designed an experiment in which he inoculated twenty-five animals with the vaccine. He also had a control group of twenty-five animals that did not receive the vaccine. Through scientific experimentation, he found that the vaccine was effective against anthrax. We'll be studying experimental design in more detail later in this chapter.

Testing a new hypothesis may take time if it depends on direct testing of empirical evidence that doesn't occur very often. For example, Einstein's theory of relativity predicted that the Sun's gravitational pull would bend starlight. However, to test this prediction, scientists had to wait several years, until (in 1919) a total eclipse of the sun occurred. It may also take several years to thoroughly test a hypothesis. The Minnesota Twin Family Study is a longitudinal study begun in 1983 conducted to identify the genetic and environmental influences on psychological development.[18] Researchers are following the development of more than 8,000 pairs of twins and their families.

By carefully comparing traits in identical twins with those in fraternal twins, the researchers have been able to determine, for example, that about 40 percent of the variation in religious behavior, such as praying and attending religious services, is due to genetic rather than environmental factors.[19] The study is ongoing.

Testing and experimentation is a critical step in the scientific method, since some hypotheses that we assume to be true are, in fact, poorly supported and fall apart when tested. The more testing confirms one's hypothesis, the more confidence we can feel that the hypothesis is *probably* true. However, as we noted earlier, we will never be able to be absolutely certain that it is true.

The scientific method is ongoing. Old hypotheses and theories may be revised or discarded in light of new evidence or be replaced by hypotheses with greater explanatory power. But keep in mind that for scientists, *any* theory, including those as well accepted as Darwin's theory of evolution or Einstein's theory of relativity, is always subject to replacement if new data contradicts it. In the next section we'll be examining some of the criteria used for evaluating scientific explanations.

5. Evaluate the Hypothesis on the Basis of Testing or Experimental Results

The last step in the scientific method is to evaluate the hypothesis on the basis of the results of testing and experimentation. If the results or findings do not support the hypothesis, then scientists reject it and go back to step 2, come up with a new hypothesis, and repeat the process. We'll be learning how to interpret experimental results in the section "Evaluating an Experimental Design."

HIGHLIGHTS

THE SCIENTIFIC METHOD

1. Identify the problem
2. Develop an initial hypothesis
3. Gather additional information and refine the hypothesis
4. Test the hypothesis
5. Evaluate the hypothesis on the basis of results of testing or experimentation

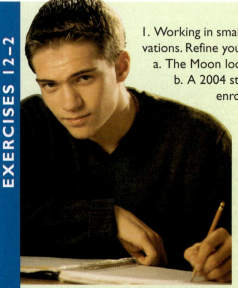

EXERCISES 12–2

1. Working in small groups, come up with hypotheses to explain each of the following observations. Refine your hypotheses on the basis of feedback from the class.
   a. The Moon looks larger when it is on the horizon than when it is high in the sky.
   b. A 2004 study found that more than 6,000 American students are currently enrolled at Canadian colleges—up from about 2,500 in 1998.[20]
   c. Since the 1950s, tens of thousands of people claim to have seen UFOs.
   d. Women are significantly underrepresented in senior faculty positions in science and math departments at Ivy League colleges. In addition, when *Scientific American* published its list of the fifty greatest scientific achievements for 2005, only one woman scientist was included.
   e. One out of eight babies in the United States is born at least 3 weeks before the due date. This represents a 27 percent increase since 1980.[21]
   f. Left-handed people die an average of 9 years earlier than the general population.[22]
   g. Married people live about 3 years longer, on the average, than unmarried people.[23]

2. Select three of your hypotheses from the previous exercise and discuss what preliminary observations you might carry out to gather more information about them. Modify or refine your initial hypotheses on the basis of your observations and new information.

3. Select one of your hypotheses from question 2. Word the hypothesis in the form of a hypothetical argument. Discuss how you might test your hypothesis.

4. "The real purpose of [the] scientific method," writes Robert Pirsig, author of *Zen and the Art of Motorcycle Maintenance*, "is to make sure Nature hasn't misled you into thinking you know something you actually don't know." What do you think he meant by this? Relate your answer to the study of informal fallacies in Chapter 5 and the study of cognitive, perceptual, and social errors in Chapter 4.

5. Select one of your hypotheses from exercise 1. Look online or in scientific journals to see whether these hypotheses are consistent with those accepted by most scientists and whether there is research to back the hypotheses. Report your findings to the class.

6. Think of a problem or question in your life, such as why your car isn't getting better gas mileage, the most efficient way to study for an exam, or whether you should drink less coffee. Write an essay explaining how you would apply the scientific method to coming up with an answer to the problem.

7. Austrian zoologist Konrad Lorenz once gave the following advice: "It is a good morning exercise for a research scientist to discard a pet hypothesis every day before breakfast. It keeps him young."* What are some of your pet hypotheses about your life and the way the world works? Applying the characteristics of a critical thinker found in Chapter 1 on pages 7–12, decide whether you should discard some or all of these hypotheses.

_____

*Quoted in Singh Simon, "How a Big Idea Is Born," *New Scientist,* Vol. 184, Issue 2476, December 4, 2004, p. 23.

EVALUATING SCIENTIFIC HYPOTHESES

Different scientists observing the same phenomenon might come up with different hypotheses or explanations. We've already mentioned a few criteria for a good scientific hypothesis: It should be relevant to the problem under study, use precise language, and provide a testable explanation. Other criteria for evaluating a scientific explanation include consistency, simplicity, falsifiability, and predictive power.

A Good Hypothesis Is Relevant to the Problem Under Study

First of all, a good hypothesis or explanation should be relevant to the problem under study. In other words, it should be related to the phenomenon it is intending to explain. Obviously, we cannot include all observations and facts in a hypothesis. Instead, we need to decide which are relevant to the problem under investigation. Polish chemist Marie Curie (1867–1934), for example, focused specifically on the atomic properties of radium and polonium in coming up with her initial hypothesis about the nature of radioactivity; Hill focused on the color of a sport team's uniform in his hypothesis.

A Good Hypothesis Is Consistent with Well-Established Theories

Science is a system of logically consistent hypotheses or theories. Scientific explanations are preferred if they are consistent with well-established theories in the field—what American historian of science Thomas Kuhn refers to as "normal science." (We'll be studying Kuhn's concepts of normal science and paradigms later in this chapter.) This system forms a paradigm, or particular way of looking at and explaining the world. For example, the new hypothesis that "internal processes in the ocean such as the release of oceanic methane hydrate deposits that exist on the sea floor on continental margins are the primary cause of global warming" is considered a good hypothesis by environmental scientists since it is consistent with the established paradigm that global warming is

Outside the Box

ALBERT EINSTEIN, *Inventor*

One of Albert Einstein's high school teachers told his father: "It doesn't matter what he does—he will never amount to anything." However, young Einstein (1879–1955) was not one to let others' opinions determine the course of his life. A mediocre student in school, he preferred learning on his own and taught himself mathematics and science. Having a curious, creative, and analytical mind, he soon realized the inadequacies of Newtonian physics and by the age of sixteen had already developed the basics of his theory of relativity.

Einstein graduated from the Swiss Federal Polytechnic School at Zurich in 1900 with a degree in physics. Unable to find a teaching position, he accepted a job in the Swiss patent office. In his spare time he continued to work on physics and completed a doctorate in physics in 1905. In the same year he published the papers that introduced his theory of relativity and would later revolutionize physics. His papers were initially met with skepticism and ridicule. However, his theory eventually won support and in 1914 he was offered a professorship at the University of Berlin. In 1921 he won the Nobel Prize for physics.

By the 1930s Einstein, who was a Jew, was high on Hitler's enemy list. He moved to the United States in 1933 and accepted a position at the Institute for Advanced Research at Princeton, New Jersey. Einstein was a humanist and pacifist who saw science in its wider social context. Fearful that Germany was building an atomic bomb, he wrote a letter to President Franklin D. Roosevelt in 1939, urging him to develop the bomb first. He also stressed in his letters to the president that the bomb should never be used on people. He was appalled when the U.S. dropped the atomic bombs on Japan.

After Hiroshima, Einstein became an anti-nuclear and anti-war activist, and a leading figure in the World Government Movement. He was invited to become president of Israel, an offer he declined. During his later years Einstein worked on the construction of a unified field theory in physics, which would reconcile his theory of relativity with the quantum theory, but never succeeded. He died in his sleep in 1955.

DISCUSSION QUESTIONS

1. In what ways might young Einstein's rebelliousness against authority have aided him in remaining open-minded and questioning established scientific paradigms? Relate your answer to your own attitudes toward accepted science.

2. Einstein emphasized the role of the community of scientists, including past scientific discoveries, in problem-solving and scientific progress. Discuss ways in which a collaborative approach and being open to the ideas of others is important in scientific thinking.

3. Do scientists have a moral obligation to refuse to engage in research that might be used to produce destructive technology? Relate your answer to a future career you might be considering. Do you, as a consumer, also have a responsibility not to purchase products based on technologies that may be harmful to people or the environment? Support your answers.

the result of a combination of anthropogenic and natural physical and chemical changes in the Earth. The intelligent design theory, on the other hand, does not meet this criterion because it is inconsistent with the well-established theory of evolution.

However, scientists do not automatically discard explanations that contradict well-established theories, especially if they meet the other criteria for a good explanation. Einstein's theory of relativity, which stated that time and space are relative, was not compatible with Newtonian physics, in which time and space are fixed and absolute. As it turned out, the theory of relativity—bizarre as it first sounded—turned out to be a better explanation of some phenomena. While Newton's theory remains a valid predictor at the level of phenomena that we can detect with our "normal" powers of observation, it fails at extreme conditions, such as those involving the speed of light (186,000 miles per second). Einstein's theory of relativity led to a radical rethinking of physics on the cosmic level.

A Good Hypothesis Is Simple

If rival hypotheses or explanations both satisfy the basic criteria, scientists generally accept the one that is simpler, a logical principle known as Ockham's razor (named for the medieval philosopher William of Ockham). For example, the great majority of scientists reject intelligent design theory because, among other reasons, the theory of evolution is simpler than that of intelligent design. The process of evolution alone, scientists argue, can explain the gradual development of complex organs such as the human eye, beginning with the light-sensitive cells that primitive organisms possess. There is no need to add the idea of an intelligent designer to the process.

On the other hand, there is nothing about the physical world itself that points to a preference for simplicity. Simplicity is a preference on the part of scientists. When there are competing hypotheses, the more complex hypothesis may turn out to be correct. For example, Einstein's theory of relativity failed the test of simplicity. However, it explained certain phenomena better and had more predictive power than the competing and simpler Newtonian theory of absolute space and time.

A Good Hypothesis Is Testable and Falsifiable

A hypothesis or explanation should be presented in a form that is testable and can be replicated by other scientists. In addition to being testable, an explanation must be able to be falsified by a scientific experiment or observation.[24] Since we can never prove that a scientific explanation is true with 100 percent certainty, falsifiability rather than confirmation is used as a test of a good scientific explanation. For example, the hypothesis that "all swans are white" was based on observations of hundreds of thousands of swans, every one of which was white. However, the hypothesis was falsifiable, since it would take only one nonwhite swan to prove it false, which happened when black swans were discovered in Australia. Resistance to falsification is a constant struggle in science because of confirmation bias. A good scientist seeks evidence and carries out experiments that might falsify his or her theory.

On the other hand, theories that are able to accommodate all challenges have a critical weakness, because they cannot be tested for falsity. For example, Sigmund Freud's theories about the Oedipus complex fail the falsifiability criterion since, if a man claims that he does not have this complex, Freudians argue that he has repressed it into his unconscious.* However, unconscious thoughts, by their very nature, are untestable. Therefore, there is no way of falsifying Freud's theory.

A Good Hypothesis Has Predictive Power

Finally, a good hypothesis or explanation has predictive power and can be used to accurately predict and explain the occurrence of similar events. The greater the predictive power, the more fruitful the hypothesis is. A hypothesis is fruitful if it suggests new ideas for future research.

The big bang theory, for example, was able to predict not only that the universe was expanding but also the amount of helium in the universe and the distribution of the galaxies. It alone was also able to explain the existence of microwave background radiation throughout the universe, which was first detected in 1965. Likewise, one of the reasons Einstein's theory of general relativity became so widely accepted was because of its predictive power. His theory of relativity predicted with greater accuracy certain eclipses than did Newton's theory.

Good scientific explanations meet all or most of the criteria that we have described so far. In the subsection that follows, we'll be looking at the differences between scientific explanations or hypotheses and those of pseudoscience.

---

*The Oedipus complex is the theory that young boys have sexual feelings toward their mothers that often involve rivalry with the father for the mother's affection. Freud considered this part of normal development.

Distinguishing Between Scientific and Pseudoscientific Hypotheses

pseudoscience A body of explanations or hypotheses that masquerades as science.

Pseudoscience is a body of explanations or hypotheses that, in an attempt to gain legitimacy, masquerades as science. However, unlike science in which explanations are grounded in the scientific method, including systematic observation, reason, and testing, pseudoscience is based on emotional appeals, superstition, and rhetoric. Astrology,

psychic healing, numerology (the study of numbers, such as one's date of birth or 9/11/2001, to determine their supernatural meaning), tarot card readings, and mind reading are all examples of pseudoscience.

While scientific explanations and hypotheses use precise wording, those of pseudoscience are usually framed in such ambiguous language that it is impossible to determine what would count as verification of the hypothesis. Astrological descriptions, for example, are usually so vague that that they apply to anyone. Because of this, pseudoscientific claims are unfalsifiable.

For the most part, no tests or experiments are carried out to check out the validity of pseudoscientific explanations. When a prediction turns out to be incorrect, no effort is made to find out why or to discover the causal mechanism behind an alleged phenomenon. The few studies that are carried out, such as those on extrasensory perception or ghosts, are generally poorly designed and rarely replicable. When a properly designed scientific experiment fails to find support for the claims of pseudoscience, these experiments are generally dismissed offhand. Pseudoscience may also explain the failure of its explanations to stand up to scientific scrutiny by blaming the subject. For example, it might be said that a person was not healed by a faith healer because he or she did not have enough faith.

Pseudoscientific explanations also fail to meet the criteria of predictability. Most are so broadly worded that just about anything would bear out their predictions. In addition, pseudoscientists rely primarily on anecdotal stories about times when predictions happen to support their claims; they ignore failed predictions. This tactic contributes to the memorable events error. Pseudoscience also takes advantage of cognitive errors in our thinking. For example, premonitions, taken as evidence of extrasensory perception, are actually coincidences based on probability error and on memorable events error.

Not surprisingly, most pseudoscientific predictions are done after the fact. Nostradamus, a sixteenth-century writer of prophecies, is today credited with foreseeing events such as the French Revolution, the rise of Nazism in Germany, and the September 11, 2001, attacks on the World Trade Center. Like the first two prophecies, the one that "predicted" 9/11 was brought to people's attention only *after* the attacks had already occurred.[25]

Because the language used in prophecies tends to be so vague and obscure, it can be manipulated to fit many similar events, as in the following example from Nostradamus that "predicted" 9/11.

> Ennosigee, fire of the center of the earth,
> Shall make an earthquake of the New City,
> Two great rocks shall long time war against each other,
> After that, Arethusa shall color red the fresh water.[26]

Despite its lack of scientific legitimacy, belief in pseudoscience is widespread and has been on the increase since 1990.

One of the most insidious uses of pseudoscience is in scams to get money from gullible people. Each year Americans spend billions of dollars on pseudoscience, which baits us with emotional appeals and promises of miracle cures, happiness, wealth, and the development of extraordinary, occult powers.

Pseudoscience literally means "fake science." To avoid falling for the empty promises of pseudoscience, we need to know how to critically evaluate the claims of pseudoscience, using the criteria listed on page 386. We should also be aware of how cognitive and social errors can distort our thinking and make us vulnerable to the lure of pseudoscience.

Analyzing Images

TEACH BOTH THEORIES... LET THE KIDS DECIDE.

CHEMISTRY — ALCHEMY — PHRENOLOGY — NEUROLOGY — MAGIC $E = MC^2$ PHYSICS — ASTROLOGY — ASTRONOMY — AUTH

8.4.05 THE PHILADELPHIA INQUIRER. UNIVERSAL PRESS SYNDICATE.

SCIENCE VERSUS PSEUDOSCIENCE
DISCUSSION QUESTIONS

1. *For each of the four examples shown in the cartoon above, apply the criteria discussed in the text to determine which of the alternatives, if any, is science and which, if any, is pseudoscience.*

2. *Should pseudosciences be taught in schools and colleges? Discuss ways in which learning about pseudoscience might enhance or impede the development of students' critical-thinking skills.*

EXERCISES 12–3

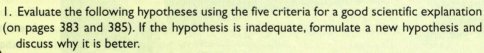

1. Evaluate the following hypotheses using the five criteria for a good scientific explanation (on pages 383 and 385). If the hypothesis is inadequate, formulate a new hypothesis and discuss why it is better.

   a. People who consume diet soda are more likely to gain weight than those who do not.

   b. Kwanda was having trouble with her computer. It would often freeze up when she was using her word processing program. She concluded that the problem must be a computer glitch.

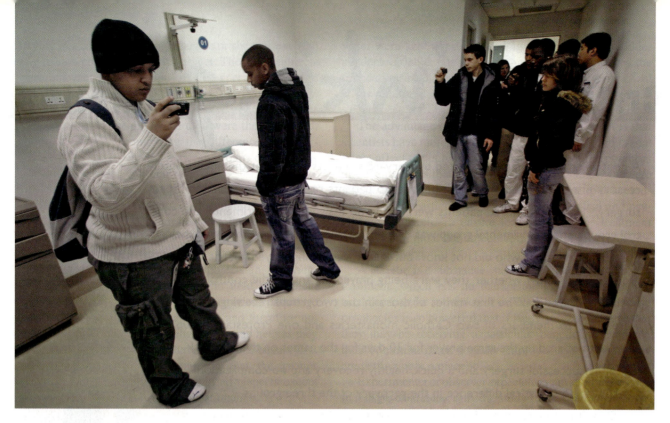

These university students are participating in a single-group experiment in which their observations about healthcare facilities at the university hospital are recorded without any prior information from nurses or doctors about the care given. Then they receive an orientation from healthcare providers and are given another tour and their observations are recorded again.

Single-Group (Pretest–Posttest) Experiments

Instead of using a control group and an experimental group, a single-group experiment uses only one group of study subjects. The variable under investigation is measured by a pretest before the intervention and again with a posttest after the intervention. Generally the same test is used in both the pre- and posttest.

> Single Group:
> Pretest ———→ Treatment ———→ Posttest

For example, in studying the effect of community service on moral reasoning, the Defining Issues Test (DIT)—a test of moral reasoning—is administered to a group of college students before their community service and then again at the end of the semester after they complete the service. It was found that the students score significantly higher on the DIT at the end of the semester.[32] Can we conclude from this that community service (the independent variable) was responsible for the improvement in the scores (the dependent variable)? Not with the same degree of certainty that we could if there was a control group.

One of the weaknesses of the single-group study is that without a control group, it doesn't control for other variables that might be affecting the outcome, such as maturation and familiarity with the test from the pretest. For this reason, single-group studies, because they are easier to set up and administer than studies with control groups, are often used as exploratory experiments, which if the results are promising are followed up with a controlled experiment.

In some research, however, single-group experiments may be preferable to controlled experiments, especially when it is clear that the variable under study is having a significant positive effect on the experimental group. For example, a new cancer drug is being tested on children with leukemia using a controlled experiment. After 3 months it is found that the children taking the new drug are doing significantly better than those taking the placebo. At this point the experimenters have an ethical obligation to stop the controlled experiment and switch to a single-group experimental design in which all the children are receiving the drug. The pretests and posttests on the extent of their leukemia are then compared, rather than the two groups being compared.

Evaluating an Experimental Design

As we noted, there are several types of experiment design. However, good designs all have certain characteristics in common. One of the foremost is being able to *discriminate between different hypotheses*. If the same experimental results can be used to support two competing hypotheses, then the experiment was poorly designed. For example, you decide to conduct an experiment to test your hypothesis that hanging garlic on your front door will keep vampires away. You hang up the garlic and use a hidden camera to record the number of vampire visits during the next month. No vampires come to your house during the month. Does this prove your hypothesis that garlic keeps vampires away? Not necessarily, because the results of your experiment also support the competing hypothesis that vampires don't exist.

A well-designed experiment is also *unbiased*. It uses checks and controls to minimize experimental error, which can result from small sample size, an unrepresentative sample, or subject or experimenter bias. A 1998 study published in the *Lancet*, a British medical journal, suggesting a link between autism and childhood vaccinations was based on testing of only twelve children with autism; there was no control group for comparison. Unfortunately, the media publicized these findings and many parents took them seriously, despite scientists' criticisms of the experimental design and the lack of corroborating evidence.

A third criterion of a good design is that the *measurements of the outcome of the variable under investigation are reliable as well as accurate and precise*. Measurement tools meet the standard of **reliability** if they provide consistency of results over time and when used by different people. An IQ test is reliable if it gives the same results when used by two different experimenters on study subjects and if the results remain consistent when the test is used on the same study subject over a period of time.

> **reliability** The standard in which scientific tools provide consistency of results over time.

An accurate measurement is one that is consistent with other standards used for measuring a phenomenon. An accurate measure of a second in science is "9,192,631,770 periods of the radiation corresponding to the transition between two levels of the ground state of the cesium-133 atom."[33] Measurement should also be precise. Precision depends on the problem under investigation. Days or even years may be a precise enough measurement of time in a study of the effect of global warming on the retreat of glaciers in Alaska. However, we need a more precise definition of time for calculating the timing of chain reactions in nuclear fission, which are measured in milliseconds (thousandths of a second).

Accurate and precise measurements allow the experiment to be *replicated or reproduced* by other scientists. One of the purposes of writing up experiments in a scientific journal is to provide enough details on the experimental design so that other scientists can replicate it—that is, run the same experiment and obtain the same results (see "Critical Thinking in Action: How to Read a Scientific Paper"). Replicability is necessary because the results of one study might have occurred by chance, might have used a faulty sample, or might even have been fabricated. (Well-publicized cases of fraudulent experiments and falsified data have occurred in recent years, notably in biotechnology, where the financial stakes are very high.)

The final criterion is *generalizability*. A well-designed experiment produces results that can be generalized from the sample used in the experiment. An experiment has **external validity** if its results can be accurately generalized to the real world. A problem with generalizability occurs when the sample in a study is not representative of the overall population that it is supposed to represent. Prior to the 1980s, most medical and psychological studies used only white males as study subjects. The rationale behind this was to keep the sample homogeneous, thus minimizing sampling error. However, when scientists generalized the results to all people, they sometimes ran into problems. For example, we have since learned that women wake up earlier from anesthesia than do men—a fact that could have easily led to horrific surgical experiences for female patients. In 1985, the U.S. Food and Drug Administration began requiring clinical trials sponsored by drug manufacturers to include data about sex as well as age and race.

> **external validity** The results of an experiment can be accurately generalized to the real world.

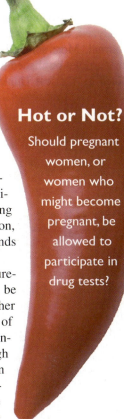

Hot or Not?

Should pregnant women, or women who might become pregnant, be allowed to participate in drug tests?

HIGHLIGHTS

CRITERIA FOR A WELL-DESIGNED EXPERIMENT

- **Discrimination:** The experiment discriminates between conflicting hypotheses

- **Unbiased:** The experiment has checks or uses controls to eliminate the possibility of subject and experimenter bias

- **Measurement:** The measurements used are appropriate and reliable as well as accurate and precise

- **Replicable:** The experiment can be reproduced by other scientists

- **Generality:** The experimental results can be generalized to the population under study

South Korean scientist Hwang Woo-Suk admitted at a 2005 news conference that he had faked the results of his work on cloned embryo stem cells.

publications—the enormous pressure to "publish or perish"—scientists may exaggerate results or be selective in what they choose to report.[34]

South Korean biomedical scientist Hwang Woo-Suk was considered one of the foremost experts in the world in stem-cell research and cloning. In 2004 and 2005, he published two articles in *Science* claiming that he had successfully cloned human embryo stem cells. His achievement was hailed as a major breakthrough in the field. However, some scientists were critical of his work and suspicious of the method used. At a November 2005 news conference, Hwang broke down and admitted that he had made up

> It is up to the community of scientists to employ their critical-thinking skills to analyze the work of other scientists in their field and to expose frauds.

the results, apologizing for his deception and saying, "I was blinded by work and my drive for achievement." As a result of his deception, he has been totally discredited as a professional scientist.

It is up to the community of scientists to employ their critical-thinking skills to analyze the work of other scientists in their field and to expose frauds. Although peer review is an effective process for safeguarding against ethical wrongdoing, procedural errors, and fraud, reviewers tend to reject for publication scientific hypotheses and studies that fall outside the established norms in science. In the next section, we'll be looking at paradigms in normal science.

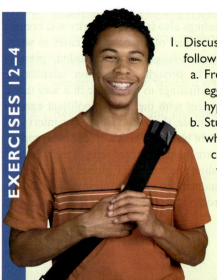

EXERCISES 12–4

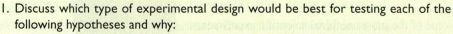

1. Discuss which type of experimental design would be best for testing each of the following hypotheses and why:
   a. Fred noticed that his hens as well as those on the neighboring farm laid more eggs when the children were away at summer camp in June and July. He hypothesized that the children's absence caused the hens to lay more eggs.
   b. Students who drink a cup of coffee before a test perform better than those who do not.
   c. Men are more likely to look at women who have blond hair than women who have brown or black hair.
   d. Taking antibiotics doubles a woman's risk of getting breast cancer.
   e. Computers are conscious.

2. Read the article by Russell Hill and Robert Barton in the May 19, 2005, issue of *Nature*.[35] Evaluate the experimental design used by Hill and Barton in their study of the effect of the color red on winning, as well as the significance of their results. Working in small groups, design an experiment to test Hill's experimental results regarding the relationship between color of team uniform and winning.

3. Millions of men take drugs such as Viagra for impotence, but are these drugs safe? According to a 2005 report, forty-three men who had taken Viagra had developed a form of blindness. The question now facing researchers is: "Was Viagra a causal factor?" The Food and Drug Administration has hired you to come up with a controlled experiment to test this question. Working in small groups, develop an experimental design to test the hypothesis.

4. Discuss the use of placebos in controlled experiments. Is their use immoral because it involves deception? Present a logical argument to support your conclusion.

5. Psychology professors sometimes use their students as subjects in experiments or studies and may even require that students participate as part of their grade in the course. Discuss the ethical issues involved in this practice.

6. Nazi experiments on hypothermia involved submerging prisoners for long periods of time in icy water. Although the experiments resulted in the death of many of the study subjects, they were well-designed experiments that yielded valuable results, which could save the lives of people who have hypothermia. Is it morally acceptable to use the data from these and other Nazi death camp experiments to save the lives of people? Support your answer.

7. Bring in an example of a graph or table from a science journal, textbook, or a Web site. Discuss how the use of visuals makes it easier to understand the significance of the results.

8. Look for an article in the mass media, or a news clip, which reports the results of a scientific study. Find a copy of the original scientific article written by the scientists who did the study. How accurately did the mass media report the study? Looking back at the discussion of mass media in Chapter 11, discuss why the media sometimes distort, either intentionally or unintentionally, scientific findings.

9. What are some of the moral issues involved in (a) stem-cell research or (b) human cloning? Using the process for resolving a moral issue outlined in Chapter 9 (see "Steps for Resolving a Moral Dilemma," page 299), formulate a policy regarding ethical guidelines for experimentation on stem cells or human cloning.

THOMAS KUHN AND SCIENTIFIC PARADIGMS

normal science Scientific research that is based on past achievements and is recognized by most scientists.

paradigm The accepted view of what the world is like and how we should go about studying it.

In his landmark book, *The Structure of Scientific Revolutions* (1962), American physicist and historian of science Thomas Kuhn (1922–1996) challenged the idea that the scientific method is objective and that science is progressive. He argued that science, like other human enterprises, is a social construct—a product of its society. As such, it is biased by social expectations and professional norms that determine what is an acceptable hypothesis.

achievements, achievements that some particular scientific community acknowledges for a time as supplying the foundation of its further practice."[36] Normal science is conveyed in science journals and textbooks.

The achievements of normal science provide paradigms or models for research in the field. A **paradigm** is the accepted view of what the world is like and how we should go about studying it. A paradigm becomes part of normal science if it is both successful in solving problems that scientists are working on and also able to attract a large group of adherents.

Normal Science and Paradigms

Kuhn put forward three key concepts: normal science, paradigms, and scientific revolutions. **Normal science** refers to "research firmly based upon one or more past scientific

Paradigms, according to Kuhn, can influence not only what is considered to be a problem worth studying but also our actual perceptions of a phenomenon. For example, it is a current paradigm in science that consciousness is organically based and therefore will never be emulated by computers or artificial intelligence (AI). Consequently, the majority of scientists perceive the actions or operations of computers, even intelligent ones, in purely mechanical terms.

Although normal science is tremendously successful in generating results and new technology, Kuhn argued that it does not seek novelty. This in turn contributes to confirmation bias. When an anomaly is found, it is often dismissed out of hand, or scientists may try to reconcile it to the existing paradigm. For example, the orbit of Mars was an anomaly that could not be explained by the old geocentric (Earth-centered) paradigm of the universe and hence was ignored for many years by Western scholars until Copernicus.

Scientific Revolutions and Paradigm Shifts

Scientific progress, according to Kuhn, is not strictly linear—that is, it does not proceed in a straight line. A crisis, Kuhn argues, is necessary for the emergence of a new paradigm. If anomalies persist or cannot be explained by the current paradigm, a "crisis" may occur that leads to a rejection of the old paradigm.

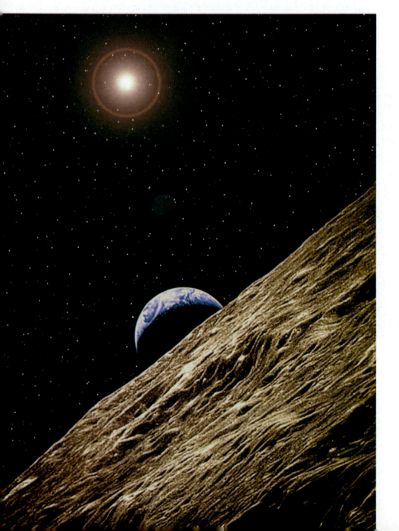

A **scientific revolution**, or paradigm shift, occurs when a new scientific theory is made available to replace a problematic paradigm. Copernicus's theory that the Earth goes around the Sun, Einstein's theory of relativity, German earth scientist

> **scientific revolution** A paradigm shift in which a new scientific theory replaces a problematic paradigm.

Alfred Wegener's tectonic-plate or continental-drift theory, and Darwin's theory of human evolution all represented paradigm shifts in their respective fields.

A paradigm shift requires a new way of looking at the world and may take several decades to complete. It is especially difficult for scientists who have been brought up and worked under the old paradigm to make the shift. Since they have invested years of their lives as well as their professional reputations in proving a particular theory, most will defend it vigorously when challenged, even in the face of contradictory evidence.

Those who fail to conform to the standards of normal science are often ridiculed as frauds, and their research findings get rejected by mainstream scientific journals. When Wegener first proposed the theory of continental drift in 1915, he too was attacked by his fellow scientists. The idea that something as large as a continent could move was considered ludicrous. However, by the early 1960s the evidence for the tectonic-plate and continental-drift theory eventually became so overwhelming that it could no longer be ignored.*

New paradigms generally win adherents from young scientists and people who are new to or outside of the field and are not heavily invested in the old paradigm. For example, Einstein was only 26 when in 1905 he first published his hypothesis regarding relativity.

Kuhn's critique of normal science has been tremendously valuable in making scientists and others more aware of the role that social expectations and confirmation bias play in science. As critical thinkers, we need to be aware of the assumptions and paradigms of normal science and to remain open-minded to hypotheses that might not conform to these norms. In evaluating a new hypothesis, we should apply the criteria discussed in this chapter rather than dismissing the hypothesis because it does not conform to the paradigms to normal science.

---

*When I was a little girl in elementary school, one of my classmates pointed to the world map on the wall and excitedly pointed out that Africa and Europe fit into North and South America like a puzzle, asking if they used to be part of one great continent. I thought that the student made a great point and was quite excited by her "discovery." However, the idea was ridiculed at length by the teacher as preposterous and unscientific (pseudoscience). It wasn't until many years later that continental-drift theory became accepted by most people in the field. This experience, and the importance of keeping an open mind, has always stuck with me.

EXERCISES 12–5

1. Looking back at the list of assumptions at the beginning of this chapter on pages 373–374, discuss how they have shaped the current paradigms in science. Use specific examples.

2. In Chapter 2 we studied AI. Identify at least one hypothesis in this relatively new field that challenges some of the accepted paradigms of normal science. Discuss what scientific findings regarding AI would be most likely to precipitate a scientific revolution and why.

3. What are some of the paradigms guiding medical research? How does acceptance of these paradigms by physicians influence medical treatment? Give specific examples from your own experience as a patient.

4. Discuss, hypothetically, what evidence in the field of human evolution would result in a paradigm shift and giving up the savannah theory for a new paradigm.

Think AGAIN >>

1. What is the scientific method?
   - The scientific method, which was first systematized by Francis Bacon, involves the identification of a problem and the rigorous, systematic application of observation and experimentation in testing an explanation for the problem.

2. How does science differ from pseudoscience?
   - Pseudoscience is a body of explanations or hypotheses that are based on emotional appeals, superstition, and rhetoric rather than scientific observation, reasoning, and testing. Furthermore, unlike scientific hypotheses, those of pseudoscience are often worded so vaguely as to be untestable.

3. What are some of the different types of scientific experiments and research methods?
   - Scientific experiments are carried out under controlled or semicontrolled conditions and involve systematic measurement and statistical analysis of data. Other research methods include observation, surveys, and interviews.

Think >>
AND DISCUSS

1. Using the criteria for evaluating an analogy in an inductive argument listed in Chapter 7, pages 218–219, evaluate the mousetrap analogy used by Behe. Does the analogy support his conclusion regarding irreducible complexity in biology and the existence of an intelligent designer?

2. Was Miller successful in disproving ID and irreducible complexity? Discuss how effective Behe's counterarguments were in responding to Miller's criticisms.

3. Evaluate both the theory of evolution and the theory of intelligent design using the criteria for evaluating a hypothesis listed on page 386. Discuss what evidence or experimental findings might falsify the ID theory/hypothesis. Discuss what evidence or experimental findings might falsify the theory of evolution by natural selection.

4. President George W. Bush, at an August 2005 press conference, endorsed the teaching of ID alongside evolution, stating, "Both sides ought to be properly taught so people can understand what the debate is all about." Along the same lines, Richard Thompson, the lawyer who represented the Dover School Board members during the court hearing, said that the decision to include ID in the science curriculum was about "academic freedom more than anything else." Author and physicist Robert Ehrlich disagrees. He writes that "to require intelligent design to be taught alongside evolution makes as little sense as requiring flat-Earth theory to be taught in science courses, so that students 'can make up their own minds' whether the Earth is round or flat." Discuss whether access to all sides of an argument, even ones that may be mistaken, is important in developing students' critical-thinking skills in science.

5. Some people argue that ID theory is not developed and tested sufficiently yet to be introduced to the public school curriculum and that public schools are not the proper testing ground for untested hypotheses. Instead the case for ID should be made and responded to in universities and scientific journals. Discuss how Thomas Kuhn would most likely respond to this controversy.

6. Zoologist, evolutionist, and atheist Sir Richard Dawkins maintains that religion and evolutionary theory are incompatible. Judge Jones, in his ruling against the Dover School Board, in contrast, concluded that "the theory of evolution . . . in no way conflicts with, nor does it deny the existence of a divine creator." Is the theory of evolution consistent with the existence of a divine creator? Develop an argument to support your answer.

7. A school board in Georgia raised the ire of some members of the community when it added stickers to biology textbooks that stated that "evolution is a theory, not a fact . . . [and] should be approached with an open mind, studied carefully and critically considered."* The court ruled that the stickers had to be removed because the stickers violated the constitutional separation of church and state and that by labeling evolution a theory, it played on the popular definition of *theory* as a hunch, which would confuse students. Do you agree with the ruling? Support your answer.

---

*Jerry Adler, "Doubting Darwin," *Newsweek,* February 7, 2005, p. 46.

Think FIRST >>

- What are the two main types of democracy?
- What are the three branches of government?
- How can citizens get involved in the government process in the United States?

high, it has since waned. In particular, the provisions addressing "domestic terrorism" have met resistance from citizens who feel that the law infringes on their civil liberties.[1]

One of the most controversial provisions of the Patriot Act is Section 215. This provision allows investigators to obtain suspects' library borrowing records, their credit-card records, and their business accounts. It also permits federal agents, without first obtaining a warrant, to install technological tools that intercept and collect information from Internet traffic and to obtain access to stored e-mail. Several colleges have protested the law, arguing that it infringes on academic freedom and privacy rights.[2] At least 7 states and more than 380 cities and counties have passed resolutions opposing the Patriot Act.[3]

Former Vice President Al Gore, in a 2005 speech opposing the renewal of the Patriot Act, accused President Bush of curtailing Americans' civil liberties, shredding the Constitution, and "breaking the law repeatedly and insistently."[4] Defenders of the act, such as former Attorney General Alberto Gonzales, argued that it is essential for national security and fighting terrorism.[5] The Patriot Act was renewed in 2006 for another 4 years. The USA Patriot Improvement and Reauthorization Act expanded the Justice Department's ability to "detect and disrupt" the activities of suspected terrorists. In 2007 the act was extended to allow the government the right to wiretap without Foreign Intelligence Surveillance Act approval. What is the process by which bills, such as the Patriot Act, are enacted into law? What happens if a law violates our civil liberties? How can we, as citizens living in a democracy, use our critical-thinking skills to evaluate public policy and to positively influence the political process? In this chapter we will address some of these questions. Specifically, we will

- Learn about the social contract theory of government and the concept of sovereignty
- Study the development of U.S. democracy

410 • THINK

- Critically evaluate the different types of democracy and their justifications

- Identify and discuss the rights and obligations of citizens in a democracy

- Examine the election process and whether we have a duty to vote

- Learn about the three branches of government—executive, legislative, and judicial

- Learn about the process of making a law and how citizens can participate in the process

- Study the relationship between law and morality

- Examine the use of and logical foundation of rules of evidence and legal precedence in the court system

THE SOCIAL CONTRACT THEORY OF GOVERNMENT

Why should we obey laws? Indeed, why have government and laws in the first place? Shouldn't we be free to make our own decisions? Doesn't government, by imposing constraints and laws on us, compromise our autonomy as critical thinkers and our ability to make rational decisions about our lives?

The State of Nature

state of nature The condition in which people lived prior to the formation of a social contract.

Most political theorists would answer no to the last two questions. They argue that people are better off living under a government than without a government—a condition referred to as a **state of nature**.[6] Although a state of nature may sound like the ideal condition for exercising our freedoms, without a government the strongest people would be able to impose their will on others with no legal restraints to curb their aggression and ambitions.

In the state of nature we would live a life, to use the words of English political philosopher Thomas Hobbes (1588–1679), where there is "continual fear, and danger of violent death; and the life of man, solitary, poor, nasty, brutish and short . . . a constant war of every man with every man."[7] Under such conditions, our everyday deci-

sions would be based primarily on the fallacy of appeal to force or scare tactics rather on than rational discussion and argumentation.

Social Contract Theory

The ideas of English philosopher John Locke (1632–1704) greatly influenced the development of the American government. According to Locke, the primary purpose of forming a government is to protect us in our exercise of our natural rights.[8] Without government, our right to freedom of speech and the right to openly debate controversial ideas, which is so important to critical thinking, would be at grave risk.

Locke thought that our natural rights would best be protected by a government that recognizes the existence of a **social contract**: a voluntary, unanimous agreement among the people in a society to unite as a political community and to obey the laws enacted by the government they select. This social contract is *implicit*. Locke did not claim that some kind of actual contract was ever signed in the distant past. Nevertheless, social-contract theory holds that the people accept the government's **sovereignty**—its exclusive right to exercise political authority—only so long as the government actually protects the people from harm and does not abuse them. A social contract must be mutually beneficial to both citizens and the government; otherwise, there would be no point in our giving up our life in a state of nature to live in a civil society.

John Locke (1632–1704). Locke's political philosophy influenced the development of American government.

social contract A voluntary agreement among the people to unite as a political community.

sovereignty The exclusive right of government to exercise political power.

Thomas Hobbes (1588–1679). Hobbes believed that in a state of nature without government, life would be nasty, brutish, and short.

The United States Constitution, which was written under the influence of Locke's ideas, is an example of a social contract. Its Preamble states:

> We the People of the United States, in Order to form a more perfect Union, establish Justice, insure domestic Tranquility, provide for the common defense, promote the general Welfare, and secure the Blessings of Liberty to ourselves and our Posterity, do ordain and establish this Constitution for the United States of America.

For those of us who were not around when the social contract—the Constitution in this case—was created, Locke argued that the act of remaining in a country and enjoying its benefits constitutes **tacit consent** to abide by the social contract and laws of the country. However, when he put forward his concept of tacit consent, there were still unclaimed areas of the world (at least from the point of

tacit consent The implicit agreement to abide by the laws of a country by remaining there.

view of the Europeans) such as the Americas, where people could move to if they disagreed with or rejected their government. Without this option, tacit consent today no longer has the voluntary quality that it did when Locke was writing, since there is no longer any place where we can go and live without being under some government. In addition, many of us lack the resources to pick up and move to another country, or we may not qualify for immigration status in the country of our choice. In this latter case, since people naturally want the best for themselves and their family, they may opt to illegally immigrate to another country, which raises a whole new set of issues regarding the limits of national sovereignty and the rights of individuals to determine which social contract is the best for themselves and their families.

International Law

Today the world is divided into sovereign nations, each with a defined territory. Individuals who disagree with their government cannot opt to be world citizens, since there is no world government. Although there is a body of law known as international law, which includes the Geneva Conventions and the United Nations Universal Declaration of Human Rights, international law regulates relations between nations rather than between individuals.

In addition, international law presents a dilemma because it conflicts with the concept of absolute national sovereignty. The current United Nations is not a world government but a collection of independent, sovereign nations. Therefore, international laws are not strictly laws in the sense of those issued by the legislatures of sovereign nations. Because the United Nations lacks sovereign power over its member nations, it has no legitimate power to enforce international law and treaties.

Although compliance with international law is voluntary in the absence of a world government with sovereign power, there are consequences for ignoring it. International law, as it now stands, has some force behind it, but that force is all too often that of the "state of nature" rather than that of a social contract. Except for a nation's inclination to obey it, the force of international law usually comes not from logical argumentation but from pressure by other nations that find it in their interest to enforce the law. If a nation refuses to comply, it can face economic incentives, threats, sanctions, or even war by the more powerful nations. In other words, as long as nations retain absolute sovereign power, the nations of the world essentially live in a Hobbesian state of nature, with the more powerful being able to impose their will on weaker nations.

1. Imagine a scenario, such as that on the television show *Lost* or in William Golding's novel *Lord of the Flies*, in which people are living without government and laws. Discuss whether the people in this situation would be better off with or without a government. Support your answer.

2. Analyze the concept of tacit consent. Does it provide sufficient justification for why you are bound to obey the laws of this country? Support your answer.

3. Is there something fundamentally unjust about absolute national sovereignty in a world where there is so much inequality? Do we, as critical thinkers, need to rethink this concept?

4. How should we, as individuals and as a nation, respond to people who immigrate into this country illegally in search of a better life and social contract? Indeed, do people who are living in poverty have a moral obligation, or at least a moral right, to seek a better life for their families by immigrating (if necessary, illegally) to a country where they and their families can enjoy a decent life? Support your answers.

5. Globalization and the increasing economic dependency of nations on each other have made the formation of an international government even more of a critical issue. Is it time that individual nations considered relinquishing some of their sovereignty to a world government in exchange for the benefits and protection of such a government? Evaluate arguments both for and against a world government.

6. Discuss ways in which resistance and narrow-mindedness, both on an individual and a national level, interfere with global security and world peace. Discuss also possible steps we might take for counteracting this type of thinking.

THE DEVELOPMENT OF DEMOCRACY IN THE UNITED STATES

> **legitimate authority** In a democracy, the right to rule given to the government by the people.

In a democracy, the **legitimate authority** of the government comes from the people themselves. In return for the benefits and protection that the government provides, we have a duty to obey the laws because we entered into a voluntary contract—that is, we have given our tacit consent—to live under the government. In a democracy based on a social contract, it is particularly important for us as citizens to be well informed about the government and current issues. Most Americans, unfortunately, are not that knowledgeable about their government. In a 2006 survey, only 1 percent of Americans could name the five freedoms protected by the First Amendment, while 20 percent knew the names of the cartoon Simpson family members.[9]

In the following sections we'll be learning more about how our democracy works and how we as citizens can use our critical-thinking skills to influence the political process.

Representative Democracy: A Safeguard Against the "Tyranny of the Majority"

In a **direct democracy**, all the people directly make laws and govern themselves. In a **representative democracy**, such as the United States, the people turn over this authority to their elected representatives. The founders of our Constitution set up a representative democracy in part because the United States, with its 4 million people (including 1 million slaves) in the late 1780s, was too large for direct democracy. Another reason was the founders' belief that the general public is not in a position to make the best decisions when it comes to public policies and legislation. Not only are most people prone to errors in their thinking and fallacious reasoning but also many of us are misinformed or lack the necessary information to make important policy decisions. Because of this, the majority could end up imposing on the country poorly-thought-out policies and laws that are detrimental to political minorities as well as to the greater good—a scenario known as the **tyranny of the majority**. To counter this, representative democracy entrusts day-to-day political judgments to representatives who are elected by the people because—at least ideally—of these representatives' ability to make rational, well-informed public policy decisions.

The fear of direct democracy and majority rule, coupled with the founding fathers' mistrust of the British monarchy and of any

> **direct democracy** A type of democracy in which all of the people directly make laws and govern themselves.
>
> **representative democracy** A form of democracy in which people turn over their authority to govern to their elected representatives.
>
> **tyranny of the majority** The majority impose their policies and laws on the political minorities.

Calvin Coolidge, president from 1923 to 1929, was known for his wisdom and common sense and was very popular among the people.

populism A belief in the wisdom of the common people and in the equality of all people.

elitism A belief in the rule of "the best people."

government with too much power, has contributed to two distinct and sometimes conflicting assumptions—populism and elitism. **Populism** is the belief in the wisdom and virtue of the common people and the belief in equality of all people. **Elitism**, in contrast, is rule by "the best people" in terms of socioeconomic class, sex, ethnic group, education, and (in the case of a monarchy) royal blood.

The U.S. Constitution was initially more elitist than it currently is. For many decades, the ideals of individual freedom and equality enumerated in the Constitution applied only to white males of European descent. This elitism was challenged by James Madison in his series of essays, called the Federalist Papers, defending the proposed new Constitution (see "Thinking Outside the Box: President James Madison"). Antifederalists, in turn, feared that the Constitution might undermine the more direct self-government that some states enjoyed in the 1780s. American democracy has moved gradually from an elitist model

Thinking

Outside the Box

PRESIDENT JAMES MADISON

James Madison (1751–1836), fourth president of the United States, is known as the "Father of the Constitution." Unlike many of his elitist colleagues, he leaned more toward egalitarianism and listening to the voice of the people. An exemplary critical thinker, he was able to analyze the worldviews and institutions of his time with an unbiased mind, rather than accepting the prevailing majority opinion.

Madison was an outspoken opponent of slavery, arguing that it ran counter to the notion of a republic. He managed, against much resistance, to keep wording accepting slavery out of the Constitution, reasoning that since the South would oppose an outright abolition of slavery, a temporary 20-year compromise was more desirable than slavery forever. This compromise might also have been motivated by the fact that Madison himself was a slaveholder and never emancipated his own slaves, probably because he was in debt and could not maintain his gentleman's lifestyle without slaves. Indeed, it would be more than 75 years after the Constitution was ratified before the Thirteenth Amendment, outlawing the institution of slavery, was passed.

Although Madison was a close advisor to George Washington, he was disturbed by the elitism and growing power of the executive branch of government. He broke with George Washington and aligned himself with Thomas Jefferson, the principal author of the Declaration of Independence and a strong supporter of individual liberty rights. Even though Jefferson himself was a slave owner, he was an opponent of slavery. Madison succeeded Jefferson as president in 1809.

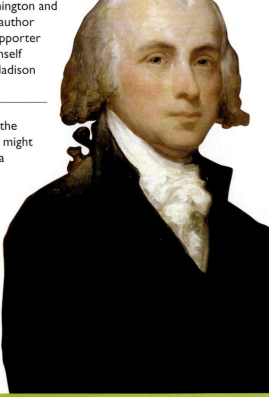

DISCUSSION QUESTIONS

1. Discuss Madison's compromise in excluding the mention of slavery in the Constitution. How might you have resolved the type of moral dilemma facing Madison, particularly if your lifestyle was dependent on maintaining the very practice that you deplored (e.g., products produced by cheap or slave labor from poor nations)? Use a specific example to illustrate your answer.

2. Madison was notable for his ability to see beyond the prevailing political worldview of his time. What are the primary political worldviews of today? Do any of the views violate the democratic principles of equality and justice? If so, discuss what steps might be taken to correct this.

to one of populist democracy with voting rights first being extended to all adult males in 1870 and to women in 1920. In 1978, the Twenty-Sixth Amendment extended the right to vote to 18- to 20-year-olds.

Despite these changes, doublethink—in this case, a simultaneous belief in both elitism and populism—is still evident in modern politics. The belief that political office should be available to all people conflicts with the need for a candidate to have his or her own wealth to finance a run for high office. To use another example, the conscription laws of the Vietnam War era placed a greater burden on people who were poor and uneducated. About 60 percent of eligible men did not serve because they received legal exemptions or deferments because they were in college (or, later, were lucky enough to draw "good" draft-lottery numbers). Other young men, whose parents had political connections, managed to receive assignments to noncombat service in the United States, such as in the reserves of the various military branches. This led to outcries of unfairness and, eventually, to the end of the draft. We'll be studying the issues involved in the draft or military conscription in more depth at the end of the chapter in the "Critical Thinking Issue" readings.

liberal democracy A form of democracy emphasizing liberty of individuals.

federalism A system in which power is divided between the federal and state governments.

separation of powers A system in which three separate branches of government act as a check on one another.

Thomas Jefferson is credited with having said: "A democracy is nothing more than mob rule, where fifty-one percent of the people may take away the rights of the other forty-nine."[10] Because of fear of the tyranny of the majority, the Bill of Rights, or first ten amendments, was added to the Constitution to place certain rights beyond the reach of majority vote and popular opinion. Because of this, in addition to being a representative democracy, the United States is a **liberal democracy** in which the liberties of individuals, including the right to vote, freedom of religion, and freedom of speech, are protected.

To protect citizens from abuses of power by government, the authors of the Constitution built in checks against unlimited power. One of these checks is **federalism**. This is a system of government in which power is divided between a central authority—the federal government—and constituent state governments. Another check is the division of the federal government into three branches: the executive, the legislative, and the judicial. Each of the three branches of government is separate and has authority to act on its own, a principle known as **separation of powers**. To prevent the abuse of power by one branch of government, a system of checks and balances was put in place, giving each branch

some power to block the others' actions. We'll be studying each of the three branches of government in greater depth later in this chapter.

Political campaigns and elections are an important aspect of representative democracy. Through campaigns, we learn about the people who want to represent us, and through elections, we can express our political choices. On the other hand, because elections are held so frequently in the United States, parties and candidates are more likely to focus on policies that bring short-term benefits to the electorate, such as cutting taxes. Long-term policies, such as eliminating poverty, tend to get ignored. As critical thinkers, our responsibility does not end with voting. We must insist that our representatives be held accountable for their decisions, and we need to be able to evaluate government policies critically and respond effectively to challenges such as poverty, global warming, job outsourcing, immigration, and terrorism.

In 2008 Barack Obama ran on a platform of "Change We Need," thus taking advantage of people's dissatisfaction with the Bush administration.

During the 2008 presidential elections, Democratic nominee Barack Obama spent more than half a billion dollars on his campaign, thus far outspending any previous presidential candidate as well as his opponent John McCain. In presidential elections the effect of campaign spending is usually modest, except in very close races. Ninety percent of the variation in the outcome of presidential campaigns is determined before the campaign actually begins, with party affiliation being one of the primary determinants of how a citizen votes.[11]

Although democracy allows citizens to participate in the political process through elections, political campaigns do not always guarantee that the best-qualified people will represent us. Political campaigns are very expensive—a factor that favors candidates who have huge personal fortunes or have won the backing of wealthy contributors, corporations, and interest groups. Campaign spending is a greater problem in congressional campaigns, where the level of spending is one of the primary factors in who wins the election.[12] The distribution of campaign funds in these races tends to be unequal. Incumbents—politicians already in office—generally receive a much larger share of contributions.[13] Candidates who challenge an incumbent usually have to rely heavily on their own personal resources, making a Senate seat feasible only for people who are wealthy or well connected.

Another factor that influences the outcome of an election is the media portrayal of a candidate's image, such as Barack Obama being the face of "change," personal qualities, such as McCain's experience and integrity, and positions on controversial issues. For example, John F. Kennedy's standing in the 1960 presidential race was greatly bolstered by his charismatic presence in his television debates with Richard Nixon, akin to Obama's captivating speeches on the campaign trail in 2007 and 2008.

Beginning with the Kennedy–Nixon contest in 1960, the mass media have dramatically transformed political campaigning. Because of the need to appeal to a large number of viewers, the media, rather than informing citizens and critically analyzing important issues, tend to rely heavily

One of the criticisms of election polls is that voters tend to swing toward the candidate who is ahead in the polls.

Red States vs. Blue States

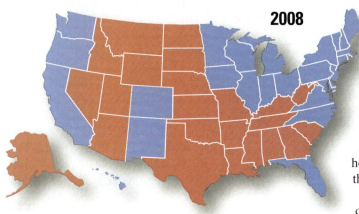

2008

on rhetorical devices and to reinforce positive or negative views of the candidates that people already have. For example, after John McCain's nomination of Alaska governor Sarah Palin for vice president, the liberal media continued to paint her as an underprepared, naive backwoods candidate. To further compound the problem of confirmation bias, most people watch only those news shows and read only those newspapers that confirm their preexisting views of the candidates and parties. Then again, several reputable newspapers and news magazines provide in-depth information on candidates and issues and play an invaluable role in a democracy of keeping the public informed.

The growing role of public opinion polls has also influenced the election process. Although some polls, such as the Gallup Poll, are reputable and unbiased, other polls word their survey questions to produce a desired result rather than accurately measure the views of those being polled. In addition, the availability of polling information makes it easier for candidates to shape their campaigns toward appealing to the majority and to avoid taking unpopular stands. Polling also influences how we vote, since people have a tendency to change their position to conform to that of the majority.

The Internet has the potential to dramatically change democracy by connecting parties, politicians, and citizens in a network of political activity. In 2004, for the first time, the Internet played a significant role in the presidential election, with candidates doing fund-raising and campaigning online. During the 2008 campaign Obama raised several million dollars online, mostly from small contributions.

The Supreme Court of Delaware, in *John Doe v. Patrick Cahill* (2005), described the Internet as "a unique democratization medium unlike anything that has come before." The Internet permits people to express their opinions to thousands through blogs and message boards. It also opens up the possibility of direct voting on candidates and issues from our home or library. We have yet to see how extensively the Internet will transform elections and politics.[14]

One of the primary ways we as citizens participate in a representative democracy is through voting. Despite the crucial role of voting, voter turnout in the United States is one of the lowest among the world's democracies. Only a handful of less-developed nations such as Zambia have a lower turnout.[15]

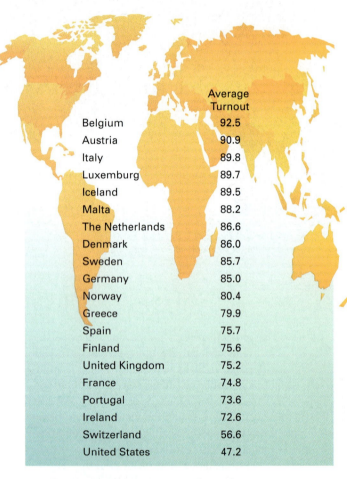

	Average Turnout
Belgium	92.5
Austria	90.9
Italy	89.8
Luxemburg	89.7
Iceland	89.5
Malta	88.2
The Netherlands	86.6
Denmark	86.0
Sweden	85.7
Germany	85.0
Norway	80.4
Greece	79.9
Spain	75.7
Finland	75.6
United Kingdom	75.2
France	74.8
Portugal	73.6
Ireland	72.6
Switzerland	56.6
United States	47.2

Percentage of Voters Worldwide

Did You Know

In the 2004 presidential elections, only 58.3 percent of American citizens eligible to vote actually voted. In non-presidential elections and primaries the turnout is typically even lower.

In the United States responsibility for voting is left up to the individual. The high value placed on personal freedom and liberty rights in American democracy rests on the belief that citizens should be allowed to engage voluntarily in economic and political activities, including voting, without interference from government regulations. In contrast, in some democracies such as Australia, Belgium, and Luxemburg, voting in national elections is mandatory, and thus voter turnout is very high.

Some people who favor mandatory voting question whether our system of voluntary voting in the United States skews our elections toward elitism because of the high positive correlation between voter turnout and educational level and socioeconomic class. Those who don't vote are disproportionately younger people, the economically disadvantaged, people with less formal education, and members of certain ethnic and minority groups. For example, in 2004 only 41.9 percent of people between the ages of eighteen and twenty-four voted, compared to 70.8 percent of those between sixty-five and seventy-five.[16] In addition, only 28 percent of Hispanic citizens voted. Turnout in the 2008 presidential election, at approximately 64.1 percent, was the highest in at least twenty years, in part because of the higher turnout of young, Hispanic, and African-American voters who voted overwhelmingly for Barack Obama.[17] Nevertheless, the youth vote was still lower than that of older voters, with only about 53 percent of people under the age of 30 voting in the election.[18] Opponents of mandatory voting argue that citizens should not be forced to exercise their rights. Forcing people to vote who are not motivated or informed or who do not have the necessary critical-thinking skills for evaluating the various candidates and issues would not contribute to the election of the best-qualified representatives.

As responsible citizens, we need to remain open-minded when making a decision on how we will vote. The information we gather should be accurate and unbiased. We should be alert to faulty reasoning, including fallacies and rhetorical devices, used in political campaigns. We also need to keep in mind that when it comes to stating positions on controversial issues, candidates have a strong incentive, if they want to get elected, to outwardly adopt a position that will appeal to as many voters as possible or to be vague or ambiguous about their position to avoid offending potential supporters.[19]

In summary, according to social-contract theory, the legitimate authority of a government comes from the people. Over the past two centuries, the United States has moved from being an elitist democracy to one based more on populism, or government by the people. Although the Constitution, our social contract, imposes duties on the government to protect individual rights and the social good, we as citizens have an obligation to obey laws and vote in elections. Even failure to vote or to engage in public discussions on critical issues is a form of participation in that it supports the status quo or the most vocal and powerful group.

1. In his book *The Wisdom of Crowds*, James Surowiecki notes that when we calculate the average answer of a large group of people—who are each unaware of the answers the others are giving—the average answer is generally very accurate when it comes to solving cognitive problems, such as guessing how much an ox weighs or how many jelly beans are in a jar. Given this, he asks whether the "wisdom of crowds" would prevail in coming up with solutions for what he calls coordination and cooperative problems of the type we find in the democratic process.[20] In particular, can voters be trusted to elect the candidates who will make the best decisions? How would you answer Surowiecki's question? Discuss how, if at all, the voting process would have to be changed to take advantage of the "wisdom of crowds."

2. The use of public opinion polls to influence policy decisions, where everyone's judgment is considered equally valid whether or not they are an expert, is an example of one of the pitfalls of democracy. Should we put restrictions on the use of polling, or should we give greater weight to the answers of experts? Develop an argument to support your answer.

3. Why is voter turnout lower in the United States than other Western democracies? Should voting in federal elections be mandatory? Discuss reforms you could make or legislation you might pass to improve voter turnout, particularly among young people.

4. Because of the tendency to go along with the majority, some people question the wisdom of publishing preelection polls, since they have the effect of swaying the electorate in favor of the leading candidate. Should preelection polls be banned? Support your answer.

5. To become an American citizen, an immigrant must first pass a test on the history and principles of the U.S. government. Discuss whether passing this test should be a requirement for native-born citizens to be eligible to vote. Relate your answer to the importance of critical-thinking skills for effective participation in democracy.

6. Make a list of ways in which the Internet has made direct democracy possible for the first time in this country's history. Discuss the advantages and disadvantages of moving in the direction of a direct democracy. Present your analysis in the form of an argument.

7. If you are not already registered to vote, go to http://firstgov.gov or to your state's Web site to learn how and where to register. If you are going to a college in a state other than your home state, research in which state you should register.

8. Write an essay presenting an argument on one of the following topics.
   a. Is representative democracy the best form of government?
   b. Should the voting age be lowered (or raised)?

9. If eligible, did you vote in the last presidential, state, and/or local elections? Why or why not? To what extent did polls influence your voting decisions? Relate your answer to your critical-thinking skills.

THE EXECUTIVE BRANCH OF GOVERNMENT

In the United States, the executive branch of the federal government is headed by the president, who is the head of state and the highest government official in the country. In addition to the president and his White House staff, the executive branch of the federal government includes the agencies that carry out much of the work of government.

The Role of the Executive Branch

The executive branch is made up of the president's executive staff, a cabinet, and fifteen executive departments, including the Department of Defense and the Department of Education. The cabinet consists of the vice president and the fifteen department heads. The nominal purpose of the cabinet is to advise the president, although today their primary purpose is running their departments. The executive branch administers government departments and public services, conducts foreign affairs, commands the armed

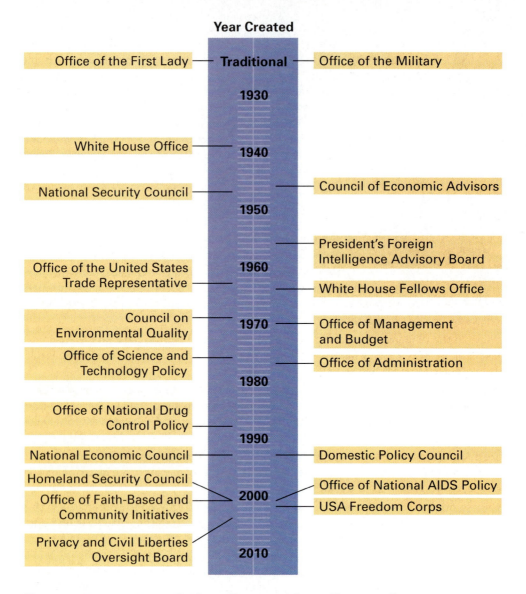

Year Created

Office of the First Lady —	**Traditional** — Office of the Military
	1930
White House Office —	**1940**
National Security Council —	— Council of Economic Advisors
	1950
	— President's Foreign Intelligence Advisory Board
Office of the United States Trade Representative —	**1960**
	— White House Fellows Office
Council on Environmental Quality —	**1970** — Office of Management and Budget
Office of Science and Technology Policy —	— Office of Administration
	1980
Office of National Drug Control Policy —	
	1990
National Economic Council —	— Domestic Policy Council
Homeland Security Council —	— Office of National AIDS Policy
Office of Faith-Based and Community Initiatives —	**2000** — USA Freedom Corps
Privacy and Civil Liberties Oversight Board —	
	2010

Departments of the Executive Branch

forces, and, with the approval of the Senate, appoints federal judges (including Supreme Court justices), ambassadors, and other high-level government officials. The executive branch is also charged with enforcing or executing the law through the administration of prisons, the police force, and the prosecution of criminals in the name of the state (see "Analyzing Images: Police and Law Enforcement").

Executive Orders and National Security

The executive branch of government traditionally has more power in times of war. For this reason, it is especially important during a national crisis or war that we use our critical-thinking skills in evaluating government policy and directives, rather than simply conforming to what the authorities say. During the Civil War, President Lincoln suspended habeas corpus (a procedure that serves as a protection against

being detained or imprisoned illegally). President Woodrow Wilson jailed Socialist and former presidential candidate Eugene V. Debs for protesting the entry into World War I. And, during World War II, Franklin D. Roosevelt had Japanese Americans sent to internment camps (see "Analyzing Images: Japanese American Internment Camps and Executive Order 9066"). These policies, which might or might not have been justified, were all put in place with little protest from citizens. As a check on executive power, Congress passed the Non-Detention Act in 1971, which states that "no citizen shall be imprisoned or otherwise detained by the United States except pursuant to an Act of Congress."

More recently, the George W. Bush administration exercised executive privilege to detain enemy combatants indefinitely and to deny them access to lawyers or courts. The former Bush administration had also expanded its interrogation techniques to include torture and the wiretapping and reading of e-mails of U.S. citizens without first

POLICE AND LAW ENFORCEMENT*

POLICE AND LAW ENFORCEMENT*   Police forces fall under the executive branch of government and are responsible for maintaining law and order. There are several levels of law enforcement services, including the federal police, state police (sometimes called state troopers), county sheriffs, and local police.

No matter at what level of government, police must be able to think quickly and solve novel problems. In a democracy, they need to be aware of citizens' rights and be able to balance these rights against the need for peace and order. In addition, they must be able to quickly identify a problem, break it down, and evaluate alternative solutions, often in a matter of minutes or less, as in the picture in this box.

Because of too many instances of police misconduct, including resorting to scare tactics and intimidation, and the need for better critical-thinking skills, many police forces are now requiring college diplomas or degrees for promotion. The education of police includes decision-making skills in such ambiguous situations as street policing, stress management, leadership, conflict resolution, diversity training, and communication skills, as well as training in law and the values of a democratic society.

DISCUSSION QUESTIONS

1. *Evaluate the picture in this box. Working in small groups, evaluate the problem that it illustrates and come up with possible solutions to it. Remember to have a backup plan in case your initial solution doesn't work. Discuss your solution with the class.*

2. *Discuss an encounter you or someone you know has had with a police officer (e.g., stopped for a traffic violation, asking an officer for directions or assistance). Evaluate the officer's behavior and discuss how it illustrated effective critical-thinking skills (or lack thereof).*

*For more on this subject, see Otwin Marenin, "Police Training for Democracy," *Police Practice and Research,* Vol. 5, Issue 2, May 2004, pp. 107–123.

getting court-approved warrants. Some of these actions are in violation of federal law and in some cases international law, and—say critics—some appear to overstep constitutional guarantees against "unreasonable" search and seizure. Bush justified these actions on the grounds that our nation faces the continuing threat of terrorism and that these activities are necessary to protect national security and effectively fight the war on terror. Opponents argue that Bush exceeded his executive power.

Checks on Executive Power

The danger of executive power is that it can be taken too far, to the point where the violations of individual rights exceed the requirements of national security. The legislature serves as one of the primary checks against excesses of executive power. Congress has to approve any declarations of war (although Congress has not been asked to

JAPANESE AMERICAN INTERNMENT CAMPS AND EXECUTIVE ORDER

9066 On December 7, 1941, during World War II, the Japanese bombed the U.S. military base at Pearl Harbor in Hawaii. Within days, the United States declared war against Japan, Germany, and Italy. On February 19, 1942, President Franklin D. Roosevelt issued Executive Order 9066, declaring that no one of Japanese ancestry could live on the West Coast of the United States.

As a result of this executive order, about 120,000 Japanese American families were forced to give up their jobs, homes, and most of their belongings and were sent to internment camps such as the one in the photo in this box, taken on April 29, 1942, at the Tanforan Assembly Center in San Bruno, California. Some internees spent several years in the camps, behind barbed-wire fences, surrounded by armed guards, and under minimally adequate living conditions. Protests against the internment policy were unsuccessful. In *Korematsu v. the United States* (1944), which contested the government's authority to intern people on the basis of their ancestry, the U.S. Supreme Court sided with the federal government.

In 1988 President Ronald Reagan signed the Civil Liberties Act, which provided a presidential apology and reparation in the form of a payment of $20,000 apiece to internees and other American citizens of Japanese descent who lost their liberty and property as a result of Executive Order 9066.

DISCUSSION QUESTIONS

1. *Using your moral reasoning skills from Chapter 9, discuss whether Executive Order 9066 was morally justified.*

2. *Construct an argument addressing the question of whether there should have been reparations to those affected by the order and, if so, whether the reparation was adequate.*

---

issue a declaration of war since World War II).* In addition, Congress can withhold funding from particular programs it wishes to check and can pass legislation to limit executive power if it feels that the executive branch is overstepping its powers. For example, the Freedom of Information Act (FOIA) was passed by Congress to protect citizens' access to government information. There are several exemptions in the FOIA, however, including unlimited presidential power to withhold information affecting national security.

This exemption has been particularly frustrating to members of the press who feel it interferes with their mandate to keep the public well informed.

> **impeachment** The process by which Congress brings charges against and tries a high-level government official for misconduct.

The final recourse of the legislative branch against abuse of executive power is **impeachment**, the process by which the House of Representatives formally brings charges against a high-level government official and the Senate puts the official on trial and, if it convicts, removes him or her from office.

The judicial branch also has the power to limit or challenge executive power. Several cases came before federal courts challenging former President George W. Bush's

---

* The Korean War (1950–1953) was a United Nations "police action," and the Vietnam War was fought under the Gulf of Tonkin Resolution. In the case of the recent war in Iraq, Congress authorized the use of force rather than issuing an actual declaration of war.

detainment of citizens without the benefit of habeas corpus, particularly the right to have the legality of one's detention assessed by a court. Bush argued that these detainees are not ordinary criminals but "enemy combatants," a term adopted for the purpose of detaining terrorist suspects so that they fall outside the protection of the Non-Detention Act. The Supreme Court disagreed, affirming the right of citizen "enemy combatants" to legal counsel and a court hearing in *Hamdi v. Rumsfeld* (2004). In this ruling, Justice Antonin Scalia wrote: "The very core of liberty secured by our Anglo-Saxon system of separated powers has been freedom from indefinite imprisonment at the will of the Executive."

The media also acts as a check against executive excesses. For this reason, freedom of the press is one of the most carefully guarded rights in a democracy. Indeed, the press has been called the fourth branch of government because of its critical role as a watchdog against government corruption and abuse of power. Large newspapers such as the *New York Times*, the *Los Angeles Times*, the *Wall Street Journal*, and the *Washington Post*—the latter, for example, exposed the Watergate scandal during the Nixon era (1969–1974)—have been particularly significant in keeping us informed about government doings and misdoings and in presenting carefully researched arguments for or against particular policies and decisions.

Finally, we, the citizens, act as an important check against abuse of power. Martin Niemoeller, one of the Protestant leaders in Germany who defied the nation's Nazi rulers, once said:

> First they came for the communists, and I did not speak out—
> because I was not a communist;
> Then they came for the socialists, and I did not speak out—
> because I was not a socialist;
> Then they came for the trade unionists, and I did not speak out—
> because I was not a trade unionist;
> Then they came for the Jews, and I did not speak out—
> because I was not a Jew;
> Then they came for me—
> And there was no one left to speak out for me.

> "The very core of liberty secured by our Anglo-Saxon system of separated powers has been freedom from indefinite imprisonment at the will of the Executive."

The transformation of German democracy in the 1930s into a dictatorship happened in part because people did not speak out loudly enough against abuses by an unscrupulous few, including Adolf Hitler before his rise to power. Although dictatorships thrive on a poorly informed or apathetic public, a healthy democracy requires feedback from an informed and reasonable citizenry. As critical thinkers, we need to be vigilant and well informed; we also need to be willing to protest to our representatives or write to the media if we have good reasons to support our claim that executive power, or the power of any other government branch, is being misused.

1. In *The Republic*, the ancient Greek philosopher Plato argued that philosophers, because they are both wise and reasonable and are not concerned with amassing worldly wealth, would make the best leaders. Do you agree? Describe the qualities of an ideal president or political leader. Is our current system of representative democracy the best way for ensuring that the best people become our leaders? Support your answers.

2. Franklin D. Roosevelt was a very popular president who was elected for four terms. In 1951, the Twenty-Second Amendment to the U.S. Constitution limited a president to two elected terms of office. Discuss whether the Twenty-Second Amendment is desirable for our democracy.

3. Benjamin Franklin once said, "Those who would sacrifice liberty for security deserve neither." What do you think Franklin meant by this? Discuss, as if you were an adviser to the president, what criteria you would use in coming up with balance between the need for security and citizens' liberty rights in the current war on terrorism.

4. Opponents of conscription (the military draft) argue that it is an infringement on individuals' liberty rights. Those who favor conscription, on the other hand, regard military service as a responsibility incurred because of our membership in a democratic political

community. Although conscription may restrict our liberties, they argue that this is offset by the necessity in times of crisis to go to war to protect these liberties and our national security. Using a conscripted army to fight an unpopular war, supporters point out, thus acts as a check against an overzealous executive branch. Discuss these particular arguments for and against conscription.

5. Discuss the practice of racial profiling, in the name of national security, of Arabs and Arab companies who want to operate in the United States. Is the practice justified, or is it discriminatory? Support your answer.

6. In his 1935 novel *It Can't Happen Here*, American writer Sinclair Lewis asked whether an ambitious and unscrupulous politician could use a U.S. presidential election to make himself a dictator as Hitler did in Germany in 1933. Discuss how you would answer Lewis's question.

7. Find examples of the news media acting as a check on presidential power. Share your examples with the class.

8. Citizens are one of the most important checks against abuse of power by the government. Think of an executive policy that you feel strongly about. It could be a presidential policy or a policy developed by one of the fifteen departments of the executive branch. Or it could be a state executive office issue. Research the policy and write a one-page letter presenting a logical argument supporting your position. Send or e-mail the letter to the appropriate government official.

THE LEGISLATIVE BRANCH OF GOVERNMENT

In a democracy we have what is known as the **rule of law**, in which government authority must be exercised in accordance with written laws that have been established through proper procedures. The rule of law protects citizens from the **rule of men**, where members of the ruling class can make arbitrary laws and rules for individual cases.

rule of law The idea that governmental authority must be exercised in accordance with established written laws.

rule of men A system in which members of the ruling class can make arbitrary laws and rules.

The Role of the Legislative Branch

In the United States, Article I of the Constitution created the federal government's legislative branch, Congress, and gave it the power to make laws. Congress consists of two houses: the Senate and the House of Representatives.

During each two-year session of Congress, thousands of bills are introduced. Of these, fewer than 500 will eventually become laws. It can take several years or only a few days for a bill to become a law. The USA Patriot Act was introduced to the House of Representatives on October 23, 2001, and passed through both houses of Congress in only two days with little dissent. In contrast, it took several years for the civil rights legislation of the 1960s to pass, as well as many years to abolish slavery and to enact legislation giving women the right to vote. Most laws are permanent, unless they are overturned by the Supreme Court or changed by Congress. Others, such as the USA Patriot Act and the Endangered Species Act, are valid only for a specified time, and thus Congress has the options of renewing or modifying them or allowing them to lapse.

Congress, the legislative branch of government, enacts laws and acts as a check on executive power.

Citizens and Legislation

Despite barriers to direct participation in the law-making process, there are several ways in which we as citizens can participate in the legislative process.

Lobbying is the practice of private advocacy to influence the government by promoting a point of view that benefits an individual or an organization's goals. Most lobbying in the United States is done by interest groups. Major corporations, trade associations, unions, advocacy groups, and political interest groups have paid lobbyists to promote their interests. There are more than 27,000 registered lobbyists in Washington—that is, more than 50 lobbyists for each legislator in Congress.[21]

lobbying The practice of private advocacy to influence the government.

Since the civil rights movement of the 1960s, there has been a huge increase in the number of public-interest groups and single-issue advocacy groups. Two of the most influential public-interest groups are Common Cause, which lobbies for a wide range of causes including improved government ethics and government reform, and Public Citizen, a collection of advocacy groups headed by Ralph Nader that lobby for a variety of causes including consumer safety, the environment, and regulatory reform. The Center on Conscience & War, in contrast, is a single-issue advocacy group that focuses its lobbying efforts on expanding legal protection for conscientious objectors and protesting proposed bills such as the Universal National Service Act (2007), which would reinstate the draft or military conscription (see "Critical-Thinking Issues: Military Conscription and the Universal National Service Act").

Lobbying is protected under the First Amendment, which states that "Congress shall make no law . . . prohibiting the free exercise thereof; or abridging the freedom . . . to petition the Government for a redress of grievances." The framers of the Constitution believed that lobbying by public and private interest groups encourages full competition among interest groups. Lobbying also benefits the political system by providing information and expertise on particular issues and bills, by explaining difficult subjects in understandable language, and by speaking for various economic, business, and citizen interests.

Critics of lobbying argue that lobbying groups, especially those financed by large corporations and business interests, such as the tobacco, pharmaceutical, and petroleum industries, exert undue influence over government. This becomes particularly a problem when these lobbying groups, rather than relying on rational arguments and credible evidence to make their points, also try to influence legislators by giving gifts, providing entertainment, and making campaign contributions to candidates and parties. Some of the public-interest groups are lobbying to get these practices outlawed or at least limited.

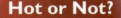

Hot or Not?

Do lobbyists undermine the basic principles and goals of democracy?

Ralph Nader, head of Public Citizen, which lobbies for consumer safety, the environment, and regulatory reform.

As individual citizens we can influence the legislative process by contacting our legislators regarding a particular bill or about an issue for which we think there should be legislation. If you are not sure who your members of Congress are, go to http://www.govtrack.us/congress/findyourreps.xpd and type in your ZIP code. The page has direct e-mail links to your two senators and your representative and also allows you to monitor their legislative activities. The Web site http://www.congress.org provides information on your legislators, assists you in registering to vote, posts action alerts regarding legislation, and forwards your e-mail to your legislators. Individual states also have Web sites with names and links to your state representatives.

Before contacting your representative at the federal or state level, you first need to be knowledgeable about the proposed legislation or issue. The Legislative Information System Web sites (http://www.senate.gov and http://www.house.gov) contain up-to-date information on all the bills pending in each chamber of Congress. Because there are so many bills under consideration at one time, it is generally most efficient to focus on an area of public policy that is of interest to you. For names of federal and state agencies associated with the issues that interest you, the best place to start is http://www.firstgov.gov. This Web site has a list of the U.S. government Web sites, information about government resources and services, and the names of, links to, and e-mail addresses of U.S. senators and representatives, state legislators, and the White House.

If there is a particular issue that interests you, you can also join a citizen advocacy or watchdog organization, such as the Sierra Club, Amnesty International USA, or the National Rifle Association, that tracks legislation regarding particular issues. This approach has the advantage of having a reputable citizen's group doing the research on pending bills for you and keeping you up-to-date. Most of these organizations will also let you know, generally through an e-mail list, when it is important for you to contact your legislators regarding a relevant bill.

Putting together an effective argument requires good analytical skills as well as knowledge of the legislative process. Being well informed also requires that you remain open-minded, cultivate a healthy skepticism, and be able to identify fallacies, faulty reasoning, and rhetorical devices. Obviously, the sounder and more cogent your argument and the more complete your research, the more likely you are to get a positive response.

Some states have initiative and referendum laws that allow citizens to directly vote on issues. **Initiatives** include laws or constitutional amendments proposed by citizens. Writing an initiative requires a lot of research and getting feedback from experts and constituents who will be affected by the initiative. This process also requires collecting enough signatures on a petition to have the initiative added to the ballot. **Referenda** are similar to initiatives, but they are put on the ballot by state legislators.

initiatives Laws or constitutional amendments proposed by citizens.

referenda Laws or constitutional amendments put on the ballot by state legislators.

Some people applaud initiatives and referenda because they are forms of direct democracy, but opponents argue that they are subject to the whims of the majority—the fallacy of popular appeal—rather than the reasoned judgment of more informed representatives. Another criticism is that the availability of only two options—yes or no—on initiatives and referenda dealing with complex issues creates a false dilemma for the voter. Still another objection is that today enormous amounts of money are needed to wage an initiative or referendum campaign, particularly in a vast state like California (where these campaigns are frequently used), allowing major interest groups and large corporations to dominate the process.

If you like hands-on experience and want a chance to hone your critical-thinking skills, there are many opportunities for college students to serve as interns in a government department or to do volunteer work with a political campaign or a lobbying or public-interest group. For example, each semester about 400 students from around the country participate in the Washington Semester Program. This internship involves spending a semester in Washing-

Students arriving to participate in a Washington Semester Program at American University, in Washington, D.C. Students volunteer to work hands-on in a government department or on a political campaign.

Hundreds of African-American sanitation workers protesting unfair and inhumane work conditions, Memphis, Tennessee, 1968.

ton, D.C., and participating in a full-credit program offered through American University, credits that you can transfer back to your home college. (For more information, go to http://www.washingtonsemester.com.) State and local governments also offer internships in locations such as the governor's office, state legislature, city government, and the public defender's office. Many of these internships offer stipends, and some offer living quarters.

Unjust Laws and Civil Disobedience

Although there is a difference between "moral laws" and "legal laws," in a democracy we expect that laws should be just and not violate universal moral principles. Some laws—such as which side of the street to drive on or the deadline for filing income tax returns—have little to do with morality. The primary purpose of criminal law, on the other hand, is to make offenses against morality—such as murder, rape, stealing, extortion, and blackmail—illegal.

Behaviors that are immoral because of the harm they cause others are generally considered the province of criminal law. However, behaviors that are harmful to ourselves, such as smoking cigarettes, personally using (but not selling) marijuana, and motorcycling without a helmet are in a morally gray area. **Libertarians**—who oppose any government restrains on individual freedom—argue that we have a liberty right to engage in activities that

libertarian A person who opposes any government restraints on individual freedom.

might harm us as long as doing so doesn't harm others. Critics of libertarianism respond that in society there is no such thing as an individual action that does not affect others. (For example, say critics, if we ride a motorcycle without a helmet and as a result sustain a permanent brain injury, we are saddling society with the cost of caring for us for the rest of our lives, as well as depriving society of the benefit of our talents and skills.)

Responsible citizenship requires that we be aware of the basic moral principles and rights, described in Chapter 9, and not simply go along with what our culture says is right.[22] We should be able to develop arguments that balance both prescriptive and descriptive premises in supporting or rejecting particular laws and policies on issues such as conscription, capital punishment, same-sex marriage, and hate speech. Some moral offenses, such as engaging in hate speech or being rude to our parents and friends, are not illegal, since the negative consequences of making these actions illegal, in terms of restrictions on our liberty rights and freedom of speech, outweigh the benefits. Instead, we usually depend on family or peers to regulate this type of offensive behavior.

Although we may face cultural censure if we break a moral norm, only legal claims carry the weight of official punishment or fines. Unfortunately, not all laws are just. A law that is discriminatory, degrading to humans, or a violation of our basic freedoms may be an unjust or immoral law. For example, the Jim Crow laws that legalized segregation and other forms of discrimination against African Americans in the South were unjust laws. In Chapter 9, we learned that when there is a conflict between a moral and a nonmoral concern, including what the law states, morality takes priority. This may require that we engage in legal protest against the unjust law or, if that is not effective, in civil disobedience.

Civil disobedience is the active, nonviolent refusal to obey a law that is deemed to be an unjust law for the purpose of trying to bring about a change in legislation or government policy. During the civil rights movement, Rosa Parks employed civil dis-

> **civil disobedience** The active, nonviolent refusal to obey a law that is deemed unjust.

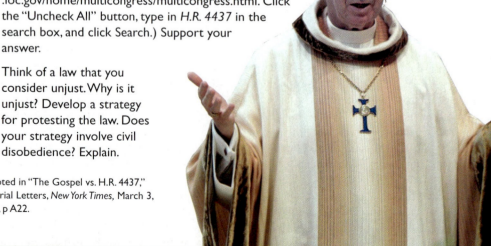

Thinking

Outside the Box

CARDINAL ROGER MAHONY

Roger Mahony was ordained into the priesthood in 1962. For several years he taught social work at California State University, Fresno. He also worked with the United Fruit Workers and growers to help them resolve labor disputes. In 1985 Mahony was named archbishop of the Roman Catholic Archdiocese of Los Angeles, the nation's largest archdiocese. Six years later he was elevated to cardinal. One of the missions of the archdiocese and its 288 parishes is to provide assistance to those in need—no questions asked. In a diocese where the majority of parishioners are Latino, the church is often the last resort for both legal and undocumented immigrants in need.

In 2005 a bill—the Border Protection, Antiterrorism, and Illegal Immigration Control Act (H.R. 4437)—was passed by the House of Representatives that would made it illegal to provide assistance to undocumented immigrants, including charitable acts such as serving them in a soup kitchen. Cardinal Mahony protested, arguing that it is not the place of the government to criminalize the charitable work of private organizations such as churches, since doing so would violate a higher authority than Congress. In particular, he contended, the bill conflicted with the Bible's command for us to "attend to the last, littlest, lowest and least in society."*

Mahony called for the priests and parishioners of his archdiocese to disobey the law, to continue to help undocumented immigrants in need, and to be ready to engage in civil disobedience should the bill become law. Millions of Americans also engaged in public protests against the act, which later failed to pass the Senate. The Comprehensive Immigration Reform Act of 2007 also failed to become law.

DISCUSSION QUESTIONS

1. Do you agree with Cardinal Mahony that H.R. 4437 is unjust? (To read the entire bill, go to http://thomas.loc.gov/home/multicongress/multicongress.html. Click the "Uncheck All" button, type in *H.R. 4437* in the search box, and click Search.) Support your answer.

2. Think of a law that you consider unjust. Why is it unjust? Develop a strategy for protesting the law. Does your strategy involve civil disobedience? Explain.

*Quoted in "The Gospel vs. H.R. 4437," Editorial Letters, *New York Times*, March 3, 2006, p A22.

obedience by sitting in the part of a Montgomery, Alabama, city bus that was by law designated "White only." Civil disobedience was also used during the 1930s and 1940s by the nonviolent resistance movement in India against British colonialism, as well as in later struggles against apartheid in South Africa and for democracy in China. Since the early nineteenth century, Americans have engaged in civil disobedience by helping runaway slaves, resisting unjust wars, protesting segregation, refusing to comply with military conscription, freeing animals from laboratories, protesting both abortion and lack of access to abortion, and staging sit-ins to object to the use of college funds to support apartheid.

In 1846, American writer and great critical thinker Henry David Thoreau went to jail rather than pay a state tax in support of the Mexican-American War, which he opposed as an unjust war intended to expand the slave states. Although his protest was short-lived (against his wishes, his friend Ralph Waldo Emerson paid the fine and got him released the next day), this was one of the first significant acts of civil disobedience in American history. In 1849, publishing his essay "Civil Disobedience," Thoreau outlined four criteria for an action to be considered civil disobedience. First, we should use only moral and nonviolent means to achieve our goals. These methods include boycotting, illegal picketing, and nonviolent resistance. Second, we should first try to bring about a change in the unjust law through legal means such as writing letters to the editor or lobbying our senators and representatives in Congress. Third, we must be open and public about our illegal actions. If no one knows we are breaking the law, then our actions are unlikely to bring about any changes in the law. Fourth, we should be willing to accept the consequences of our actions. These might include imprisonment, fines, deportation, loss of a job, or social disapproval.

In 1846, American writer and great critical thinker Henry David Thoreau went to jail rather than pay a state tax in support of the Mexican-American War, which he opposed as an unjust war intended to expand the slave states.

Engaging in civil disobedience requires that we carefully and logically think through our position from all perspectives. Rather than resorting to fallacies and rhetorical devices, we need to be prepared to use well-reasoned arguments and assertive communication.

Before making a decision to use civil disobedience—which could land us in jail or worse—we need to step back and critically analyze the situation and come up with the most effective strategy for protesting a law. This strategy may or may not involve civil disobedience. Some people may protest an unjust law by leaving the country. During the Vietnam War, about 90,000 so-called draft dodgers immigrated to Canada, and many of them still live there. However, because they chose not to remain in the United States and make their protest public, as did a much smaller number of draft resistors who stayed here and ended up in jail, they were not engaging in civil disobedience.

In summary, in the United States lawmaking belongs to the legislature. There are several ways in which we as citizens can participate in the lawmaking process. This includes directly contacting legislators, lobbying, volunteering, interning, and getting an initiative on the ballot. When we consider a particular law to be unjust, we can protest the law or engage in civil disobedience.

HIGHLIGHTS

THOREAU'S FOUR CRITERIA FOR CIVIL DISOBEDIENCE

1. Use only moral and nonviolent means to achieve our goals.

2. First make an effort to bring about change through legal means.

3. Be open and public about our actions.

4. Be willing to accept the consequences of our actions.

1. The House of Representatives was created to represent the interests of ordinary people. However, is the House truly representative? Would the interests of the public be better served by selecting representatives through a lottery-based system, such as we use in calling citizens for jury duty, so that it is a random sample of American people? Present an argument to support your answer.

2. Working in small groups, write an initiative for legislation relating to a current issue on your campus such as free-speech zones or affirmative action. Have the class vote on and critique each of the initiatives.

3. Develop an argument addressing the question of whether there should be laws against one or more of the following: lying, adultery, nude bathing on public beaches, hate speech, smoking. Discuss your conclusion with the class and, if appropriate, modify your argument.

4. Discuss the justifications for (or against) laws that do the following:
   a. Allow children of undocumented immigrants to attend state colleges at in-state tuition rates
   b. Allow undocumented immigrants living and working in the United States to apply for residency status
   c. Legalize same-sex marriage
   d. Outlaw abortion except to save the life of the mother
   e. Decriminalize prostitution
   f. Decriminalize marijuana
   g. Make voting mandatory in federal elections
   h. Outlaw downloading music from the Internet

5. Although the United States is committed to capitalism and free enterprise, there are many areas of business—such as employment practices, copyright, fair competition, and environmental pollution—that are regulated by government. It is estimated that it costs businesses about $700 billion a year to comply with these laws and regulations.[23] Should the government regulate business less or more than it currently does? Discuss the benefits and drawbacks of government regulation of American businesses in the global economy.

6. Billions of dollars are spent every year on lobbying. In 2003, for example, $300 million was spent on healthcare lobbying alone. Should the amount of money an organization or business, such as a pharmaceutical company, can spend on lobbying and donations to candidates' campaigns be limited? Or does placing limits on lobbying violate the First Amendment? Support your answers.

7. Howard Zinn, an American historian, political theorist, and educator, writes about our capitalist society: "The role of law does not do away with the unequal distribution of wealth and power, but reinforces that inequality with the authority of law. It allocates wealth and poverty . . . in such complicated and indirect ways as to leave the victims bewildered." Do you agree with Zinn? Support your answer using specific examples.

8. You have just received a notice from the Selective Service System conscripting you to serve in a war that you believe is unjust. However, the SSS has rejected your petition for conscientious objector status. Discuss what you would do. Relate your answer to this chapter's section on civil disobedience.

9. Go to http://thomas.loc.gov/ and click on the "Bills, Resolutions" link. Identify a bill that is of interest to you and answer the following questions: (a) What is the bill (write a one- or two-paragraph summary of the bill)? (b) Who is sponsoring the bill? (c) Where is the bill being sponsored (which house)? (d) When is it being heard in committee or voted on?

10. Select an issue, such as clean air, stem-cell research, homelessness, immigration, conscription, or fair trade. Do an Internet search on lobbying and citizen advocacy groups that are focused on the issue. List steps that you might take, as a citizen, to influence the legislative process on this issue.

11. C-SPAN and C-SPAN2 televise live the proceedings of the House of Representatives and the Senate. Spend an hour watching either channel. Write a few paragraphs describing what you learned about the working of the legislature and how it differed, if at all, from your expectations.

12. Using the bill you selected in question 9 of this set of exercises, write a one- to two-page letter to one of your legislators using sound arguments regarding your position on the bill, as well as changes, if any, you would like to see in the bill (if it still has to go to committee) and how you would like your legislator to vote (if it is going to one of the houses for a vote). Send the letter to your legislator, either by e-mail or regular mail.

13. Suppose one of your state legislators is proposing a bill that would lower the drinking age in your state from 21 to 18. Research the issue and write an argument to send to the legislator, either in support of or in opposition to the bill.

THE JUDICIAL BRANCH OF GOVERNMENT

Article III of the U.S. Constitution created the federal government's judicial branch. The Founding Fathers considered the judicial branch—the court systems—to be the least dangerous branch of government, since the justices (judges) are usually appointed and serve for life. Because of this, the justices are not subject to pressure from the majority in the way elected officials are. The founders also recognized that judges need protection from political pressure by elected officials.

The Role of the Judicial Branch

While legislators consider what the law should be, the judicial branch asks when the law should be applied and how it should be interpreted. Courts also have the power to impose sentences in criminal cases and to award damages in civil trials. The judicial branch does not have the power to enforce laws or sentences. Instead, it relies on the executive branch of government to enforce its decisions. For example, following the U.S. Supreme Court's decision in *Brown v. Board of Education* (1954), which overturned laws permitting or requiring school segregation based on race, law enforcement agencies had to be called in to implement integration in several school districts. Several times during the 1950s and 1960s, Presidents Dwight D. Eisenhower and John F. Kennedy had to use federal troops to enforce compliance with desegregation orders.

> . . . in 1989 Congress passed the Flag Protection Act, which criminalized anyone who knowingly defaces an American flag.

The U.S. Supreme Court is the highest court in the land. The role of the Supreme Court is to evaluate the law and strike down any law, federal or state, that it determines to be unconstitutional. This is known as the power of **judicial review**. The Supreme Court also acts as a check on executive and congressional power. For example, in 1989 Congress passed the Flag Protection Act, which criminalized anyone who knowingly defaces an American flag. Protestors argued that the act violated their First Amendment right to freedom of speech. The U.S. Supreme Court agreed and, in *United States v. Eichman* (1990), struck down the act as unconstitutional.

> **judicial review** The power given to the Supreme Court to strike down any law that it deems to be unconstitutional.

The U.S. Supreme Court Justices. Chief Justice John Roberts (center, bottom row) was appointed to the Court in 2005 by the Bush administration.

Rules of Evidence

One distinctive feature of our judicial system is that we conduct cases by pitting two sides against each other. In civil cases, one party sues another over a dispute; in criminal cases, the government (representing the people) confronts a criminal defendant accused of breaking the law. Because our system is based on an adversarial model, the judicial procedure is governed by strict **rules of evidence**. The purpose of these rules is to ensure "fairness in the administration of law . . . and the promotion of growth and development of the law of evidence to the end that the truth may be ascertained and proceedings justly determined."[24]

The rules of evidence prohibit the use of claims based on fallacious and faulty reasoning. Personal attacks (the ad hominem fallacy), which tend to be prevalent in an adversarial model, are specifically prohibited. Statements about the character of a person or witness that are not related to the truthfulness of and qualification of the person to be a witness are generally inadmissible in federal and state courts. In addition, witnesses may not testify about a matter unless it can be shown that they have personal knowledge of the matter or are credible experts in the field. Hearsay evidence is forbidden, except in some cases where a witness is unavailable to testify (see "Analyzing Images: The Salem Witchcraft Trials").

Analyzing Images

THE SALEM WITCHCRAFT TRIALS The rules of evidence were established by the judiciary to prevent court proceedings from degenerating into unfounded accusations, where public opinion and hysteria is substituted for credible evidence, as happened in the 1692 witchcraft trials in Salem, Massachusetts. Judge William Stoughton, who was a clergyman with no training in law, presided over the trials. Nineteen people, mostly women, were sentenced to death for witchcraft on the basis of the most flimsy evidence, and most were executed. Only one person was found innocent.

In his denunciation of the Salem court proceedings, Boston clergyman Increase Mather wrote that "It is better that ten suspected witches should escape than that the innocent person should be condemned." Although Mather, a leading Puritan intellectual, still believed in the existence of witches, he also felt that human beings were unable to detect them through judicial means. The impropriety of the Salem witch trials had a profound influence on the development of the American judicial system. The public outrage elicited by these trials brought an end to the Puritans' control of the courts in Massachusetts and are reflected in the "innocent until proven guilty" philosophy of today's court system.

DISCUSSION QUESTIONS

1. Discuss how the application of the rules of evidence might have affected the outcome of the Salem witch trials in colonial America.

2. Think of a time when you mistakenly accused someone, or were accused yourself, of a wrongdoing. Discuss how applying the rules of evidence might have helped you, or the person who accused you, to make a better and fairer decision.

It is the role of the judge to determine whether the evidence at trial is admissible, to impose reason on a dispute, to instruct the jury regarding the rules of evidence, and to reach a decision that is both fair and enforceable under the law. The effectiveness of lawyers and judges in a court of law depends on their ability to construct and understand arguments. Judges, in particular, need to be proficient in interpreting arguments and judging how sound and convincing an argument is.

Because jurors may be biased or prone to cognitive errors and faulty reasoning, a court cannot rely on the jurors alone to decide a case. If the judge believes that a lawyer in the case has tried to influence the jurors through faulty reasoning, the judge can instruct the jurors to ignore certain testimony in reaching their conclusion. If the judge believes that the jury has made a decision that violates the rules of evidence or cannot be supported under the law, the judge may even overrule the jury's decision.

Legal Reasoning and the Doctrine of Legal Precedent

Legal reasoning makes use of the same types of deductive and inductive logical arguments that we use in our everyday life. Legal reasoning frequently involves inductive arguments using analogies. These analogies take the form of an appeal to precedents. In the American judicial system, there is an expectation that a judge will respond in a manner that is consistent with how a previous case was decided by a higher court in the same jurisdiction, even though court rulings are not actually laws. Legal precedents form what is known as **common law** and, in some cases, go back to medieval England. Unlike laws or constitutional amendments, which come from the legislative branch of government, common law is a system of case-based law that is derived from judges' decisions over the centuries.

Legal precedence is important because in a just society laws should be applied in a consistent and fair manner. According to the **doctrine of legal precedent**, if previous legal cases are similar in relevant ways to the current case, then the current case should be decided in the same way. However, because precedents are based on analogies or inductive logic, they are never definitive, merely stronger or weaker. Nor are they binding on Congress. In some cases, decisions based on precedents may be overturned in later rulings.

The first step in determining whether there is a legal precedent is to prepare a **case brief**. This involves researching the case under consideration and summarizing its rel-

> **common law** A system of case-based law that is derived from judges' decisions over the centuries.
>
> **doctrine of legal precedent** The idea that legal cases should be decided in the same way as previous, similar legal cases.
>
> **case brief** Researching the case under consideration and summarizing its relevant details.

HIGHLIGHTS

LEGAL PRECEDENCE

To determine if a previous case provides legal precedents:

1. **Research the present case.** Study the relevant details and issues of the case being contested.
2. **Examine possible precedents.** Find other cases (court decisions) that are similar to your case.
3. **Identify shared general principles.** Look for principles that apply both to your case and to the precedent(s).
4. **Evaluate the analogy.** Determine how strong and relevant the similarities are and if there are relevant dissimilarities.

---

evant details. After a list of relevant details is compiled, a search for other similar court decisions addressing the same general principle(s)—for example, privacy rights or eminent domain—is conducted. The final step is to evaluate the analogy. What are the relevant similarities? How strong are these similarities? How can your case be distinguished? Are there relevant dissimilarities that might weaken the analogy? What was the ruling in each of the cases? Does the current case warrant the same decision?

For example, in *Good News Club et al. v. Milford Central School* (2001), the U.S. Supreme Court ruled that the First Amendment prohibition on the establishment of religion required the high school to exclude the Christian Good News Club from its facilities. They based their decision on the similarities between this case and two earlier landmark cases, *Everson v. Board of Education* (1947) and *Illinois ex rel. McCollum v. Board of Education* (1948). Both earlier cases applied to public education Thomas Jefferson's metaphor of a "wall of separation between church and state."[25] On the basis of these earlier rulings, which drew a separation between religion and public institutions, the court concluded that religious organizations should be kept separate from public schools.

Precedents are ordinarily authoritative on later court decisions, unless it can be shown that a previous decision differs in some relevant way or that it was wrongly decided. To be valid, precedents must be based on reason and justice. Legal precedents are not binding on the courts if they violate the principle of justice. For example, the U.S. Supreme Court's *Dred Scott v. Sanford* decision of 1857 upheld laws that defined slaves as property, and the court's majority argued that "the right of property in a slave is distinctly and expressly affirmed in the Constitution." However, because this ruling violated the principle of justice, it was not binding in later cases; indeed, in 1865 the Thirteenth Amendment, banning slavery, was added to the U.S. Constitution.

In some cases there are no precedents. This often happens with cases involving the use of new technologies. For example, does downloading, or prohibiting downloading, from the Internet violate the First Amendment right to freedom of speech? Does electronic wiretapping violate the protection "against unreasonable searches and seizures" clause in the Fourth Amendment?

Because the Constitution is more than 200 years old, it is difficult to know how to interpret the constitutionality of some of the newly created laws. The provisions in the Constitution were made so long ago, before the advent of modern technology, that it is difficult to know how to apply these provisions to today's issues. For example, does the equal-protection clause of the Fourteenth Amendment protect a woman's legal right to have an abortion? Does the Second Amendment, which was written in 1791, guarantee the right of individual citizens to own automatic weapons?* Issues such as these raise the question of whether portions of the Constitution are too outdated and should be amended.

Although the Supreme Court does not use juries to decide cases, as do most lower courts (but not courts of appeals), citizens and citizen groups whose interest may be affected by the outcome of a case may file an amicus curiae, or "friend of the court," brief. An amicus curiae brief presents arguments for a particular position on a case or brings to the court's attention matters or evidence that have not yet been considered.

Jury Duty

In the United States, unlike many other countries, jurors play an important role in the judicial system. One of the fundamental rights guaranteed by the Sixth Amendment of the Constitution is the right of citizens to a trial by an impartial jury of their peers. To serve on a jury, a person must be a U.S. citizen and at least 18 years old. The court selects potential jurors by randomly choosing names from voter lists or combined voter and driver lists. Because random selection is required for there to be an unbiased sample, people may not volunteer for jury duty. Some people are called for jury duty several times during their lives; others are never called. For more information on jury duty and how the court system works, go to http://www .uscourts.gov/faq.html or http://www.pagerealm.com/jury/ index.html

Good critical-thinking skills are crucial for an effective juror. A Canadian study found that people who are most advanced in their ability to engage in legal reasoning are

best prepared for jury duty. These people also tend to dominate jury deliberations, thus encouraging the other jurors to engage in critical thinking and providing a positive influence on their views and analysis of the case.[26] Serving on a jury, in other words, has the potential to improve our critical-thinking skills. In addition to being challenged by interesting cases and exposed to the arguments of other jurors who may be better than we are at critical thinking, jurors receive instruction from the court justices, who are trained in critical thinking about the rules of evidence.

The judicial branch of government is concerned with how law should be interpreted. The judicial procedure is governed by rules of evidence and legal precedence, which involves inductive reasoning by analogy. One of the ways citizens participate in the judicial system is through jury service.

EXERCISES 13-5

1. Someone in your class has been cheating on exams. A slip of paper with test answers has been found on the floor of the classroom near the desk of a student who has subsequently been accused of cheating. Carry out a mock trial using the rules of evidence. Appoint a defendant, a judge, and lawyers for the defense and prosecution. The rest of the class will serve as the jury.

2. In 1982 the Supreme Court ruled that states must educate undocumented immigrants through the twelfth grade, arguing that children of undocumented immigrants need an education to be able to participate economi-

---

*Amendment II states: "A well regulated Militia, being necesary to the security of a free State, the right of the people to keep and bear Arms, shall not be infringed."

cally in society. However, the court said nothing about education at the college level. Should undocumented immigrants who are residents of a state and have been educated in the public schools be eligible for in-state tuition at the state colleges? Support your argument.

3. Imagine that you have been appointed to a committee to review the Constitution and make suggestions for its revision regarding new technology and issues that are currently facing the Supreme Court. Discuss what revisions you would recommend, and why.

4. The LSAT (Law School Admission Test) is a required exam for entrance to most U.S. law schools. Because of the importance of effective critical-thinking and logic skills in the practice of law, two of the five sections on the LSAT are devoted to testing these skills. Go to http://www.lsat-center.com/sampletest1.html and take the sample LSAT test in reasoning. Check your answers against the correct answers and explanations. Discuss how the questions engaged your critical-thinking skills.

5. Go to http://www.uscourts.gov/outreach/topics/habeascorpus-rasulbush.htm. Read the argument put forth in the *Rasul v. Bush* case by both Rasul's legal team and former President George W. Bush's lawyers regarding the issue of balancing liberties and national security in withholding the identities and nationalities of approximately 490 terrorist suspect detainees at Guantanamo Bay in Cuba. Which team makes the best arguments? Support your answers.

6. Watch a case being tried on Court TV or another station that televises actual court cases. Note how the court procedures conform to the rules of evidence. What steps did the judge take to enforce the rules if the lawyers or jury didn't heed them?

7. Watch the movie *12 Angry Men*, starring Henry Fonda as one of the jurors. Evaluate the Fonda character's critical-thinking skills as a juror. Discuss ways in which critical-thinking skills are important for both jurors and lawyers.

8. Referring to the "Critical-Thinking Issues: Perspective on Free-Speech Zones on College Campuses" at the end of Chapter 3, imagine that you are a Supreme Court justice and that FIRE (Freedom for Individual Rights in Education) has brought a case before the court challenging the constitutionality of restricting controversial speech on college campuses to free-speech zones. Research possible precedents for the case. Write a short essay analyzing the analogies between these cases and the FIRE case. Discuss whether these cases provide a solid legal precedent for deciding for or against restricting controversial speech to free-speech zones on campuses and, if so, whether the precedents were just and should apply in this case.

9. Look back at a time when you got into a dispute with a friend or family member. How did you resolve the dispute? Were you satisfied with the resolution? How might applying the rules of evidence have made achievement of a satisfactory resolution easier?

10. President Dwight D. Eisenhower once said, "Politics should be the part-time profession of every American." Looking back through this chapter, examine the different ways you might participate in politics. Write a two-page essay describing at least two specific ways in which you might make politics your part-time profession, whether at the local, state, national, or international level.

Think AGAIN >>

1. What are the two main types of democracy?
   - In a direct democracy, all of the people directly make laws and govern themselves. In a representative democracy, such as that in the United States, the people turn over this authority to their elected representatives.

2. What are the three branches of government?
   - The three branches of government in the United States are the executive, legislative, and judicial.

3. How can citizens get involved in the governmental process in the United States?
   - Citizens can get involved through participating in a political campaign, voting in elections, lobbying legislators, joining advocacy groups, serving as interns in government departments, serving on juries, and engaging in civil disobedience to protest unjust laws.

Military Conscription and the Universal National Service Act (2007)

Most nations do not have conscription—also known as the draft. Americans have a long history of ambivalence about military conscription. Those who oppose it argue that conscription violates our liberty rights and lowers the quality and motivation of the military. They also argue that conscription, at least as it has been instituted in the past, is discriminatory, since it places an unfair burden on poorer, young men. Those who favor conscription regard military service as a responsibility incurred because of our membership in the political community. While conscription may restrict our liberties, this is offset by the necessity in times of crisis to go to war to protect these liberties. In addition, a conscripted army, as existed during the Vietnam War, is more reluctant to fight an unpopular war and thus acts as a check against an overzealous administration or professional army.

In 1863, Congress passed the Union Conscription Act, through which all able-bodied men between the ages of 20 and 45 could be drafted into the military. The act allowed men to hire a substitute or pay a commutation fee of $300. Draft riots broke out in working-class sections of New York City protesting the unfairness of the act as well as the war itself.*

The Selective Service Act was passed in 1917 during World War I. Conscription was regarded by the administration as the most equitable and efficient way to raise military forces during wartime. To avoid the charge of unfairness, the law prohibited substitutions and enlistment fees. In addition, conscientious objectors were allowed to

*The draft riots are the subject of the Martin Scorsese movie *Gangs of New York* (2002).

choose noncombat service. Despite these improvements, there was an outcry against the draft on the grounds that it imposed "involuntary servitude" and as such was a violation of the Thirteenth Amendment, which had outlawed slavery. In 1918, the U.S. Supreme Court ruled that conscription was constitutional as well as a "supreme and noble duty."[**]

Conscription was again reintroduced in 1940 during World War II. In 1941 the ages of eligibility were extended to 18 to 38. During this time about 10 million men were drafted through the Selective Service System (SSS). The draft continued, with only a few breaks, until 1973, despite fierce protests from pacifists and others. During the Korean War, 1.5 million men were drafted.

In 1969, the draft was reinstituted during the Vietnam War using a lottery system. Of the men who were of eligible age, about 60 percent did not serve because they received legal exemptions or deferments because they were in college, which lead to cries of unfairness. About 90,000 law-breaking draft dodgers fled to Canada, where they were welcomed as immigrants. The draft ended in 1973, and the SSS was put on "deep standby" until 1980, when compulsory draft registration was reinstated in reaction to the Soviet invasion of Afghanistan requiring young men between the ages of 18 and 25 to register for military service with the SSS. At that time, the question of drafting women was raised. However, the Department of Defense believed that women should not be included in registration because they were not allowed to serve in ground combat assignments.

In 2003, the Universal National Service Act was introduced in Congress in response to the strain being placed on the professional military by the war in Iraq. The Bush administration and the Department of Defense are both opposed to the act and reinstating the draft, preferring to rely on a volunteer military. The act was rewritten and reintroduced in 2005, 2006, and 2007. President Barack Obama, who was a senator at the time, voted in favor of the bill. If the act eventually passes, it would reinstate conscription, making it "the obligation of every citizen [male and female] of the United States, and every other person residing in the United States, who is between the ages of 18 and 42 to perform a period of [two years] of national service." Deferments would be granted to full-time high school students younger than 20 and exemptions given for extreme hardship or physical or mental disability as well as for those who have "served honorably in the military for at least six months." People who are conscientious objectors to combat or war on ethical or religious grounds would be assigned to either noncombat or national civilian service.

In the following readings, U.S. Representatives Charles Rangel and Ron Paul debate the merits of the Universal National Service Act and reinstituting the draft.

[**] *Aver v. United States,* 245 U.S. 336 (1918).

Reinstating the Military Draft[*]

CONGRESSMAN CHARLES RANGEL

Charles Rangel of New York has been a Democratic member of the U.S. House of Representatives since 1971. During his tenure Rangel, a sponsor of the Universal National Service Act, has repeatedly called for government to reinstate the draft. In the following reading, Rangel argues that relying on a voluntary military is unjust since it places an undue burden on a small group of people rather than distributing the task of defending the country equitably across all economic classes.

I have reintroduced my bill to reinstate the draft, not because I support the war in Iraq or the President's plan to escalate the conflict. The reason is my belief that if Americans are to be placed in harm's way, all of us, from every income group and position in society, must share the burden of war.

[*]Charles Rangel, "Reinstating the Military Draft," from "Congressman Rangel Introduces New Bill to Reinstate the Military Draft," U.S. House of Representatives press release, January 11, 2007.

That has not been the case so far. The overwhelming majority of our troops fighting in Iraq are young men and women who have chosen to enlist because military service is an economic opportunity. They are motivated by enlistment bonuses up to $40,000 and additional thousands in scholarships to attend college. They are from urban and rural communities where there is high unemployment and few opportunities to pursue the American Dream. My colleague, Congressman Ike Skelton, has confirmed that fact while pointing out the patriotism of these young men and women, and I agree with him.

It is time that all Americans—including the wealthy—be given the opportunity to prove their patriotism as well, by saluting when the flag goes up and defending their country in wartime. A military draft would ensure that.

My bill requires that, during wartime, all legal residents of the U.S. between the ages of 18 and 42 would be subject to a military draft, with the number determined by the President. No deferments would be allowed beyond the completion of high school, up to age 20, except for conscientious objectors or those with health problems. A permanent provision of the bill mandates that those not needed by the military be required to perform two years of civilian service in our sea and airports, schools, hospitals, and other facilities.

I don't see how anyone who supports the War in Iraq would not support reinstatement of the draft.

The President [Bush] announced last night his intention to send an additional 21,000 U.S. troops to Iraq. The military is at the breaking point with more than 50 percent of our combat troops already deployed in Iraq. The question is: where will the additional troops—including those that may follow if the war is escalated further—come from?

The 21,000 soldiers that the President was talking about will not be fresh troops. Many of them are already on the ground in Iraq and will have their deployments extended. Almost 250,000 of the troops currently deployed in Iraq have served more than one tour, and some have been deployed as many as six times.

Since the start of the war, more than 14,000 discharged army veterans—members of the Individual Ready Reserve—have been called back from their jobs and families to serve in Iraq. Thousands have had their tours extended under so-called stop-loss orders.

The forced, repeated deployments of nominally volunteer troops not only violates the spirit of the contract with these soldiers, it is a cruel and unfair erosion of the principle of shared sacrifice which has been totally absent in the prosecution of this war.

Last night President Bush warned the nation that we are in for further sacrifices in Iraq. But the truth is, the sacrifice is being borne exclusively by the 1 million-plus troops who have served, and their families. Three thousand have made the ultimate sacrifice and 22,000 have been wounded and maimed.

The rest of us have not been called upon to make any sacrifice at all. It is the first time in an American war in which the populace has not even been asked to bear the burden of the war's cost. Fighting this war with borrowed money, we are leaving our children and their children to pick up the check that as of now is roughly $500 billion, and counting.

QUESTIONS

1. Why has Rangel reintroduced the Universal National Service Act?

2. What role does the war in Iraq play in his reasoning?

3. According to Rangel, what are the primary motivations now for young people to enlist in the military?

4. What are the basic components of Rangel's bill?

5. How does Rangel respond to people who oppose a national service act?

Conscription: The Terrible Price of War**   CONGRESSMAN RON PAUL

Republican Ron Paul of Texas has been a member of the U.S. House of Representatives since 1996. A physician by training, Paul was a flight surgeon in the U.S. Air Force between 1963 and 1968. Paul is an advocate of limited Constitutional government. In the following reading, Paul argues against conscription on the grounds that most wars cause senseless suffering and that conscription of young people is discriminatory and constitutes forced servitude.

The ultimate cost of war is almost always the loss of liberty. True defensive wars and revolutionary wars against tyrants may preserve or establish a free society, as did our war against the British. But these wars are rare. Most wars are unnecessary, dangerous, and cause senseless suffering with

---

**Ron Paul, "Conscription: The Terrible Price of War," *Congressional Record*, November 21, 2003.

little being gained. The result of most conflicts throughout the ages has been loss of liberty and life on both sides. The current war in which we find ourselves clearly qualifies as one of those unnecessary and dangerous wars. To get the people to support ill-conceived wars, the nation's leaders employ grand schemes of deception.

Woodrow Wilson orchestrated our entry into World War I by first promising during the election of 1916 to keep us out of the European conflict, then a few months later pressuring and maneuvering Congress into declaring war against Germany. Whether it was the Spanish American War before that or all the wars since, U.S. presidents have deceived the people to gain popular support for ill-conceived military ventures. . . .

When it comes to war, the principle of deception lives on. The plan for "universal liability to serve" once again is raising its ugly head. The dollar cost of the current war is already staggering, yet plans are being made to drastically expand the human cost by forcing conscription on the young men (and maybe women) who have no ax to grind with the Iraqi people and want no part of this fight.

Hundreds of Americans have already been killed, and thousands more wounded and crippled, while thousands of others will experience new and deadly war related illnesses not yet identified.

We were told we had to support this pre-emptive war against Iraq because Saddam Hussein had weapons of mass destruction (and to confront al Qaeda). It was said our national security depended on it. But all these dangers were found not to exist in Iraq. It was implied that lack of support for this Iraqi invasion was un-American and unpatriotic.

Since the original reasons for the war never existed, it is now claimed that we're there to make Iraq a western-style democracy and to spread western values. . . .

The current quagmire prompts calls from many for escalation, with more troops being sent to Iraq. Many of our reservists and National Guardsmen cannot wait to get out and have no plans to re-enlist. The odds are that our policy of foreign intervention, which has been with us for many decades, is not likely to soon change. The dilemma of how to win an un-winnable war is the issue begging for an answer.

To get more troops, the draft will likely be reinstated. The implicit prohibition of "involuntary servitude" under the 13th Amendment to the Constitution has already been ignored many times, so few will challenge the constitutionality of the coming draft.

Unpopular wars invite conscription. Volunteers disappear, as well they should. A truly defensive just war prompts popular support. A conscripted, unhappy soldier is better off on the long run than the slaves of old since the "enslavement" is only temporary. But in the short run the draft may well turn out to be more deadly and degrading, as one is forced to commit life and limb to a less than worthy cause—like teaching democracy to unwilling and angry Arabs. Slaves were safer in that their owners had an economic interest in protecting their lives. Endangering the lives of our soldiers is acceptable policy, and that's why they are needed. Too often, though, our men and women who are exposed to the hostilities of war and welcomed initially are easily forgotten after the fighting ends. Soon afterward, the injured and the sick are ignored and forgotten.

It is said we go about the world waging war to promote peace, and yet the price paid is rarely weighed against the failed efforts to make the world a better place. Justifying conscription to promote the cause of liberty is one of the most bizarre notions ever conceived by man! Forced servitude, with the risk of death and serious injury as a price to live free, makes no sense. What right does anyone have to sacrifice the lives of others for some cause of questionable value? Even if well motivated it can't justify using force on uninterested persons.

It's said that the 18-year-old owes it to his country. Hogwash! It just as easily could be argued that a 50-year-old chicken-hawk, who promotes war and places the danger on innocent young people, owes a heck of a lot more to the country than the 18-year-old being denied his liberty for a cause that has no justification.

All drafts are unfair. All 18- and 19-year-olds are never drafted. By its very nature a draft must be discriminatory. All drafts hit the most vulnerable young people, as the elites learn quickly how to avoid the risks of combat.

The dollar cost of war and the economic hardship is great in all wars and cannot be minimized. War is never economically beneficial except for those in position to profit from war expenditures. The great tragedy of war is the careless disregard for civil liberties of our own people. Abuses of German and Japanese Americans in World War I and World War II are well known.

But the real sacrifice comes with conscription—forcing a small number of young vulnerable citizens to fight the wars that older men and women, who seek glory in military victory without themselves being exposed to danger, promote. These are wars with neither purpose nor moral justification, and too often not even declared by the Congress.

Without conscription, unpopular wars are much more difficult to fight. Once the draft was undermined in the 1960s and early 1970s, the Vietnam War came to an end. But most importantly, liberty cannot be preserved by tyranny. A free society must always resort to volunteers. Tyrants thinks nothing of forcing men to fight and serve in wrongheaded wars; a true fight for survival and defense of America would elicit, I'm sure, the assistance of every able-bodied man and woman. This is not the case for wars of mischief far away from home in which we so often have found ourselves in the past century.

One of the worst votes that an elected official could ever cast would be to institute a military draft to fight an illegal war, if that individual himself maneuvered to avoid military service. But avoiding the draft on principle qualifies oneself to work hard to avoid all unnecessary war and oppose the draft for all others.

A government that is willing to enslave a portion of its people to fight an unjust war can never be trusted to protect the liberties of its own citizens. The ends can never justify the means, no matter what the Neo-cons say.

1. According to Paul, what is the ultimate cost of most wars?

2. What does Paul mean when he says that "when it comes to war, the principle of deception lives on"?

3. According to Paul, why do unpopular wars invite conscription, whereas truly defensive and just wars do not?

4. Why is conscription, by its very nature, discriminatory?

5. On what grounds does Paul make a comparison between slavery and conscription?

Think
AND DISCUSS >>

1. Evaluate the arguments by Rangel and Paul regarding reinstating conscription. Which person makes the best argument? Support your answer.

2. Research suggests that democracies with conscripted armies are more cautious about going to war and experience fewer combat casualties than democracies with volunteer or professional armies.[*] If this is the case, discuss whether this justifies bringing back conscription in the United States. Discuss also how both Rangel and Paul would most likely respond to this question.

3. Discuss whether women should be conscripted to serve in the military and in combat duty in particular. If so, should exceptions be made for women who are pregnant, as well as for women (and men) who are the primary caretakers of young children? Develop an argument supporting your position.

4. The 2003 Universal National Service Act required men and women between 18 and 26 to perform national service. This has since been changed to ages 18 to 42. Discuss whether this change eliminates the charge that conscription is unfair because it is based on age discrimination.

---

[*]Joseph Paul Vasquez III, "Shouldering the Soldiering: Democracy, Conscription, and Military Casualties," *Journal of Conflict Resolution,* Vol. 49, Issue 6, December 2005, pp. 849–873.

5. Young people are far more opposed than older people to conscription, with 84% of people between the ages of 18 and 34 being opposed to a draft, compared with only 59% of people older than 55 being opposed.[**] Does forcing young people who are opposed to conscription to serve constitute "involuntary servitude" and thus violate the Thirteenth Amendment to the Constitution?

6. You have just received a notice from the SSS conscripting you to serve in a war that you believe is unjust. However, the SSS has rejected your petition for conscientious objector status. Discuss what you would do. Relate your answer to the section in this chapter on civil disobedience.

7. President Ronald Reagan opposed the draft on the grounds that it "rests on the assumption that your kids belong to the state. If we buy that assumption then it is the state—not the parents, the community, the religious institutions or teachers—to decide who shall have what values and who shall do what work, when, where and how in our society. That assumption isn't a new one. The Nazis thought it was a great idea."[†] Evaluate Reagan's argument.

[**]Survey USA News Poll #6000, June 27, 2005.

[†]For more on Reagan's views on the draft, see Ronald Reagan, "The Coerciveness of National Service," *Human Events,* April 1979, page 11.

Answers to Selected Exercises in the Text

3 Language

EXERCISES 3-1

14. **a.** Informative
    b. Expressive
    c. Ceremonial
    d. Expressive and informative
    e. Directive
    f. Expressive
    g. Informative and expressive
    h. Directive and informative
    i. Ceremonial

EXERCISES 3-2

3. **a.** Theoretical (operational)
   b. Theoretical
   c. Lexical
   d. Precising
   e. Theoretical
   f. Persuasive
   g. Lexical
   h. Precising
   i. Persuasive

EXERCISES 3-3

1. **a.** Figurative language
   b. Good definition
   c. Too narrow since some restaurants are cafeterias and too broad since there are other places on campus, such as fast-food restaurants, where students can eat their meals.
   d. Emotive definition intended to evoke a negative feeling toward marriage.
   e. Circular
   f. Both too broad and too narrow.
   g. Obscure definition when used for policymakers and the public.
   h. Figurative language
   i. Too broad; cats and parakeets are household pets.
   j. Emotive language
   k. Too narrow. Students can also attend high school or adult education classes.
   l. Figurative language
   m. Good definition; it contains all and only the essential attributes of the term *teenager*.
   n. Obscure language

3. **a.** Disagreement in fact
   b. Verbal dispute; the key term "sovereign nation" is being used differently by each person.
   c. Verbal dispute; the first person is using the term "right" as a moral right, while the second person is defining "right" in terms of legal rights.
   d. Verbal dispute; the first person is using the term "girl" to mean women, whereas the second person is using the term "girl" to mean female child.
   e. Factual dispute over the law regarding meaning of DWI.

f. Verbal dispute; both people are using different definitions of "best teacher."

EXERCISES 3-5

3. **a.** Euphemism
   b. Doublethink
   c. Sarcasm
   d. Hyperbole
   e. Euphemism
   f. Emotively loaded language
   g. Dysphemism
   h. Sarcasm
   i. Euphemism
   j. Sarcasm
   k. Hyperbole
   l. Sarcasm

5 Informal Fallacies

EXERCISES 5-2

1. **a.** equivocation on "arguments"
   b. division
   c. accent
   d. division
   e. accent
   f. equivocation on "bad"
   g. amphiboly
   h. equivocation on "men"
   i. division
   j. amphiboly—does Bush mean love of their profession or love of women?
   k. division
   l. equivocation on "equal"

EXERCISES 5-3

1. **a.** ignorance
   b. red herring
   c. appeal to force
   d. straw man
   e. hasty generalization
   f. red herring
   g. appeal to force
   h. hasty generalization
   i. personal attack
   j. no fallacy
   k. popular appeal
   l. red herring
   m. ignorance
   n. appeal to pity
   o. appeal to force
   p. no fallacy
   q. personal attack
   r. appeal to pity
   s. personal attack
   t. no fallacy—we should worry about our computer's security

1. **a.** slippery slope
   b. loaded question
   c. naturalistic
   d. loaded question—you may have a dime to spare but don't want to give it to a panhandler
   e. appeal to inappropriate authority
   f. no fallacy—meteorologists are authorities on weather-related conditions
   g. loaded question—assumes that restricting abortion will lead to increase in deaths among women
   h. slippery slope
   i. appeal to inappropriate authority
   j. naturalistic
   k. begging the question
   l. false dilemma
   m. appeal to inappropriate authority
   n. begging the question
   o. questionable cause
   p. loaded question—a person may believe in gender equality and at the same time be opposed to the draft for both men and women
   q. slippery slope

6 Recognizing, Analyzing, and Constructing Arguments

1. **a.** For example: Should there be free speech zones on campuses? Should the administration have the power to censor material in student-run newspapers? Do students have the right to boo unpopular guest speakers on campus so they can't be heard? Should colleges censure politically incorrect speech or hate speech?
   b. For example: What, if any, are the effects of genetically engineered food on our health? What is the effect on the environment? Do we have a right to genetically modify food, or is it morally unacceptable to tamper with nature and creation of new species?
   c. For example: Is sex outside of marriage morally permissible or desirable? Should college administrations provide dorms that allow cohabitation? What are the effects of cohabitation on future relationships?
   d. For example: copyright theft, individual freedoms, the Internet as public domain.
   e. For example: What are the causes of global warming? What is the primary cause—human activities, or solar activity, or something else? How does each of us contribute to global warming? What are the effects of global warming on the environment and humans? Do we have a moral obligation to make changes in our lifestyle? What is the government's responsibility for legislating lifestyle changes, including energy consumption?
   f. For example: What is the current legislation and is it fair? Do the current laws violate our liberty rights? What are the health risks of marijuana? What is the effect of marijuana on academic performance? What have the effects been in other countries of decriminalizing marijuana? What legislation regarding marijuana use would be most just?
   g. For example: Does prayer in schools violate the separation of church and state? Should we have separation of church and state? Does prohibiting prayers violate our freedom of speech? What is "prayer" (for example, is a period of silence "prayer")?
   h. For example: Is this because of gender discrimination in hiring? Are there gender differences in college major and job preference and, if so, what is the cause? Should we have affirmative action in hiring faculty? What is the responsibility of colleges to redress pass discrimination?

2. **a.** For example: Who should be responsible for paying for higher education—the individual or the state? Does raising tuition constitute discrimination against poorer families? What is the effect of having to work to pay for college on students' academic performance?
   b. For example: Should colleges provide housing for cohabiting students? Is cohabitation desirable?
   c. For example: Who has the responsibility to pay for pharmaceutical drugs? Should we have nationalized medical coverage? Does our current system discriminate against the poor? What responsibility, if any, do doctors have to make sure their patients are taking their prescribed medications?
   d. For example: Should special interest groups be allowed to promote their views on college campuses? Do we have a moral obligation not to eat animals? What is the best way to reach college students with a message, given their level of cognitive development?
   e. For example: Did China have a right to take over Tibet? Do we have a moral obligation to assist in liberating Tibet? What moral obligations does an occupying country have to the residents of the occupied country? How should people of an occupied country respond to an occupying force?
   f. For example: Do we as individuals have a moral responsibility to vote? Should voting be mandatory in the United States?

2. **a.** Not a proposition. This is simply an expressive of emotion.
   b. Proposition. It conveys information about the speaker's feelings. The person may or may not be telling the truth.
   c. Proposition
   d. Not a proposition. It is a directive statement that conveys no information.
   e. A proposition. This is a descriptive statement that can be either true or false.
   f. This is not a proposition since it is a directive statement.
   g. A proposition. This is a prescriptive premise. This proposition could also be a conclusion or subconclusion in an argument depending on the issue under discussion.
   h. A proposition, albeit a false one.
   i. A proposition. This is a lexical definition and, therefore, can be either true or false.
   j. Not a proposition.
   k. A proposition.

3. a. Descriptive
   b. Definition
   c. Descriptive
   d. Prescriptive
   e. Analogy
   f. Prescriptive
   g. Analogy
   h. Definition
   i. Descriptive

5. a. Explanation
   b. Conditional statement
   c. Argument
   d. Explanation
   e. Conditional statement
   f. Explanation
   g. Explanation
   h. Conditional statement
   i. Explanation
   j. Argument
   k. Conditional statement

EXERCISES 6-4

1. a. (1) [Be an optimist.] (2) [*There is not much use being anything else.*]

   b. (1) [Computers may soon fade into the background] since (2) [*most people prefer portable handheld devices*] as well as (3) [*ones that turn on instantly*].

   c. (1) [*The right to vote is the very core of democracy.*] (2) [We cannot allow public apathy and political manipulation to undermine it.]

   d. (1) [Drinking alcohol is stupid.] (2) [*Alcohol has no taste at all, it's just a burning sensation.*] (3) [*You don't drink to have a good time,*] (4) [you drink to forget a bad time.]

   e. (1) [*The magnitude of devastation from the [2004] tsunami has exposed the limits of scientific knowledge*] and (2) [*the lack of cooperation among nations in using sophisticated tools to prevent human suffering*]. . . (3) [*Had there been a global tsunami-warning network in place, the death and suffering of tens of thousands could have been avoided*]. . . (4) [The international community must develop a global early-warning system to inform people of any looming threat.]"[1]

   f. (1) [*Lack of experience,*] (2) [*excessive speed,*] and (3) [*tailgating are three of the most frequent causes of automobile accidents*]. For these reasons (4) [we should raise the driving age to 18] since (5) [*older drivers might be more experienced*] and (6) [*have better judgment*]. NOTE: In this argument the first three premises all end with "is a frequent cause of automobile accidents," although this is only stated once at the end of the sentence. Also the phrase "older drivers might be" also goes with both premises (5) and (6).

g. (1) [All college students should routinely be tested for HIV, the virus that causes AIDS.] (2) [*Half of the people who carry the virus don't know they have it.*] (3) [*The HIV virus is transmitted primarily through sexual contact.*] (4) [*Not only are most college students sexually active*], (5) [*they also have multiple partners.*]

3. a. (1) "[It is impossible to exaggerate the impact that Islam has on Saudi culture] since (2) [*religion is the dominant thread that permeates every level of society.*]"

b. (1) [God does not exist.] (2) [*There is much evil and suffering in the world.*] (3) [A good and loving God would not permit so much evil.]

c. (1) [*our youngest voting-age group has grown accustomed to a wide array of options when making consumer choices,*] and (2) [*will naturally expect the same with their Social Security accounts.*] (3) ['Reform' of Social Security in the form of partial privatization sounds practically inevitable.]

d. (1) [We should not buy a new car for Jack for his graduation.] (2) [*Jack is irresponsible*] because (3) [he doesn't care for the things he already owns.] Also, (4) [*we don't have enough money to buy him a new car.*]

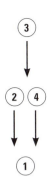

e. (1) "[*An unbalanced diet can depress serotonin levels—and bingo, you're a grouch!*] (2) *Too much alcohol unbalances our diet.* (3) [*Alcohol gives serotonin a temporary bump but then dramatically lowers it,*] (4) [so it pays to go easy on the sauce.]"

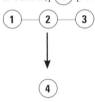

f. (1) [*Freedom to decide what we do in our lives, as long as we're not harming others, is a basic right in our country.*] Therefore, (2) [motorcyclists should not be required by law to wear helmets] because (3) [*those who don't are not harming anyone else.*]

g. (1) "[There's a need for more part-time or job-sharing work.] (2) [*Most mothers of young children who choose to leave full-time careers and stay home with their children find enormous delights in being at home with their children*], not to mention (3) [*the enormous relief of no longer worrying about shortchanging their kids.*] On the other hand, (4) [*women who step out of their careers can find the loss of identity even tougher then the loss of income.*]"

h. (1) [*The toughest part of buying life insurance is determining how much you need,*] since (2) [*everyone's financial circumstances and goals are different.*] (3) [The best way to determine your life

insurance needs is to have a State Farm Insurance professional conduct what's called a Financial Needs Analysis.]

i. (1) ["In schools, we should give equal time with Darwinism to theories of intelligent design or creationism.] (2) [*Darwin's theory of evolution is a theory, not a fact.*] (3) [*The origin of life, the diversity of species and even the structure of organs like the eye are so bewilderingly complex that they can only be the handiwork of a higher intelligence.*"]

j. (1) [You shouldn't bother trying out for that internship] because (2) [*you won't get it.*] (3) [*The company only wants students who are business majors.*] (4) [*You aren't a business major.*] (5) Besides, [*the company isn't on a bus line and you don't own a car.*]

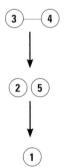

k. (1) [The BlackBerry handheld from T-Mobile is all you need to stay in touch wherever you go.] (2) [*It's a tri-band phone, so you can use it to make calls both here and overseas.*] What's more, (3) [*you can add unlimited BlackBerry e-mail and unlimited Internet access to your wireless calling plan for just $29.95 a month.*] (4) [*Meaning, you can get out of the office and start getting some work done.*]

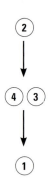

l. ① [*I saw Bob coming out of Mark's dorm room at 2 a.m.*] ② [*Mark reported his cell phone stolen the next morning.*] ③ [*Bob was caught stealing from a student's room once before.*] I think the evidence speaks for itself. . . ④ [Bob in all likelihood stole Mark's cell phone.]

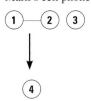

EXERCISES 6-5

1. a. The argument needs a premise linking illegal immigrants to loss of jobs for Americans.

b. Acceptance of the argument depends on how good students think the analogy is. Also, what about people who choose not to drive (perhaps because they live in New York City) or who have a physical disability, such as blindness, that prevents them from driving—are they all unsuited to be parents?

c. This argument is weak since the single premise focuses only on one particular aspect of fraternities.

d. We need evidence to support the first premise. Since we cannot get inside Rex's head, it is difficult to support the conclusion. Rex might also growl out of jealousy.

e. Good argument.

f. The premise in the argument is irrelevant. It commits the red herring fallacy.

g. Not everyone will agree with how *God* is defined in the premises. It is best to first get agreement on the key terms before proceeding.

h. The word *troublemaker* is ambiguous.

2. a. There is an unstated premise: "Michael Jackson is a child molester." However, the case against Jackson is weak and he has since been acquitted of the charge. Therefore, the argument is weak.

b. The unstated premise is "Single mothers do not perform well in premed programs." Stating the premise would strengthen the argument, if facts support it. Otherwise, it would weaken the argument.

c. The missing premise is "Students who have a parent who is a physician will do well in a premed program." This premise needs to be added and researched in order to have a strong argument.

d. It's not clear what the missing premise is here. The speaker could be assuming that Clinton is a well-qualified candidate, that Clinton is a poor speaker,

or perhaps that Americans would not elect a female president.

e. The unstated premise is "Friskie is a cat."

f. The unstated premise is "People who are abused as children are more likely to become child abusers themselves when they grow up." The premise is not supported by evidence since the causal relationship is weak.

7 Inductive Arguments

EXERCISES 7-1

2. a. Inductive
b. Inductive
c. Deductive
d. Inductive
e. Neither; this is an explanation
f. Inductive
g. Deductive
h. Inductive
i. Deductive

EXERCISES 7-2

1. a. Slanted to elicit a positive response.

b. Poor question. Because of self-serving bias almost everyone will answer "yes."

c. Good question from the 2003 Gallup Poll. The question uses neutral language and explains the key term "marriage."

d. Loaded question. It assumes that the U.S. should have only one official language. However, several nations, including Canada, have more than one official language.

e. Slanted to elicit a "no" response.

f. Loaded; privatizing Social Security may not place benefits of future retirees at risk.

g. False dilemma. There are other alternatives such as charging them out-of-state tuition.

3. a. Good use of generalization

b. Conclusion goes beyond the premises. We can only conclude that Rex very likely will bark at strangers.

c. Good application of generalization to a specific case.

d. Hasty generalization based on too small a sample.

e. Poor generalization based on an outdated sample.

f. False premise based on confirmation bias. We remember the times when toast falls butter-side down because it inconveniences us more. However, studies show that toast only falls butter-side down about half the time.

g. Unrepresentative sample. Fraternity members are more likely than students who aren't members of fraternities to drink alcohol.

h. Hasty generalization based on an unrepresentative sample.

i. Outdated sample. It's much harder for new graduates to find good jobs now.

j. Biased sample because only physicians were polled and also because of the self-serving error.

k. Biased sample and missing premise. We don't know the average size of a dog living in the United States.

l. Sample is too small.

EXERCISES 7-3

3. a. Weak analogy since the president does not pretend he wrote the speeches, only that he provided the ideas.

b. Strong analogy if we think our pets do have inherent moral value as do humans. Weak if we believe pets do not.

c. Premise doesn't support the conclusion. One might also conclude that alcohol should be illegal since marijuana is.

d. Weak analogy since hate speech does not normally result in physical harm and death.

e. Probably a weak analogy because of dissimilarities between the two wars.

f. Weak analogy; not being able to dance is not addictive as is smoking.

g. Weak analogy since tuberculosis can be spread by airborne particles whereas AIDS cannot be spread through casual contact.

h. Weak analogy; buyers presumably are informed about the product choices, whereas students are coming to class to gain rather than act on information.

i. Perhaps a weak analogy. Herbert A. Simon, Nobel Prize winner and "father of artificial intelligence," argues that this is an incorrect analogy. Computers are not merely pretending to think; they do think. They process real input and produce a real solution based on the input. Intelligent computers also perform transformations on the problems and solutions, and come up with creative solutions, just as the human mind does.

j. Weak analogy between human body and something mechanical since humans are presumably more than their physical bodies. Unlike automobiles, as autonomous beings we can participate in decisions regarding our treatment.

k. Good analogy if one believes that other species have moral value and rights; otherwise, a weak analogy.

EXERCISES 7-4

1. a. This is a causal relationship since older couples are more likely to use fertility treatment, which results in more multiple births.

b. A negative correlation

c. This may be a causal connection, or it may be a correlation due to a third factor. Being a member of a supportive group or family, whether or not it is religious, is a contributing cause of happiness.

d. A causal relationship

e. This could be a causal relationship or it could be a correlation. They might both have the flu and eating at the sushi bar has nothing to do with their nausea.

f. This is probably a causal relationship. However, to be confident that it is, we would have to determine what causal mechanism was at work, such as animals being able to sense ground vibrations signaling the approach of the tsunami.

3. a. Fallacy of questionable cause. There is a positive correlation between being in bed and time of death because of a third factor—very ill people are more likely to be bedridden.

b. A good argument. It does not go beyond the premises but simply states that discrimination is a contributing cause.

c. The premises are not strong enough to support the conclusion. It is not clear whether there is a causal relationship or simply a correlation between marijuana use and depression and other mental disorders.

d. Poor argument based on the cognitive error of believing we are more in control than we are. While employees tend to believe their presence is necessary to the smooth running of the workplace, employers feel the opposite, preferring that sick employees stay home rather than coming to work and infecting others.

e. Outdated data. Marijuana today is generally much more potent.

f. Fallacy of ignorance. Even though the existence of aliens has not been proved, we cannot conclude from this that aliens do not exist.

g. Good argument. This causal relationship is supported by numerous studies.

h. Most likely, simply a positive correlation. The real cause is probably the opportunity to relax and have a good time.

i. Fallacy of questionable cause based on the memorable events cognitive error.

j. Although there is a high positive correlation between marijuana use and later use of cocaine, the causal relationship is unclear. Later marijuana use could be due to other causal factors such as easy access to drugs or peer pressure to use drugs. The speaker is also committing the slippery slope fallacy by exaggerating the potential effects of trying marijuana.

k. The slippery slope fallacy. It is unlikely that hikers throwing out food can even come close to satisfying the year-round nutritional needs of all the wildlife living in these mountains. However, if there is a dramatic increase in the number of future hikers who throw their perishable garbage into the woods, this might no longer be a fallacy.

8 Deductive Arguments

EXERCISES 8-1

3. a. Invalid (e.g., substitute "high school dropouts" for "women")

b. Invalid hypothetical syllogism

c. Invalid. Substitute "men" for "college students"

d. Invalid. Substitute "tree" for "orchid"

e. Invalid hypothetical syllogism.

4. a. Unsound—The second premise is false.

b. Sound—Both premises are true.

c. Unsound—the first premise is false. The conclusion just happens to be true.

d. Unsound—The second premise is false. Mexico is not in South America, as many people incorrectly assume. Instead Mexico is classified by geographers as part of North America. This is a good example of the importance of verifying the truth of the premises in determining if a valid argument is also sound.

e. Sound. Both premises are true.

EXERCISES 8-2

1. a. Disjunctive syllogism—a type of argument by elimination.

b. Argument by definition. In the United States, all psychiatrists, by definition, are MDs—that is, physicians.

c. Argument based on mathematics.

d. Disjunctive syllogism—a type of argument by elimination.

e. Argument based on mathematics.

f. This is an inductive argument since the premises only tell us where Mary *might* be. It has not eliminated other possibilities, such as Mary being at home.

g. Argument based on definition.

h. Disjunctive syllogism—a type of argument by elimination.

i. Argument based on mathematics.

j. Inductive argument based on analogy.

k. Argument by elimination.

l. Inductive generalization using statistics.

m. A disjunctive syllogism.

n. Argument based on mathematics.

3. It's true that one cat, with the exception of a Manx, has one more tail than no cats. The problem lies in the treatment of "no cat" as an actual being which actually has twelve tails. In fact, if there is no cat, there is no tail (he has committed the fallacy of amphiboly). Once this is straightened out, using an argument based on mathematics, it follows that an actual cat does have one more tail than a nonexistent cat—which, because it is nonexistent, has zero tails.

4. This problem involves the use of argument by elimination. Mike has the grape juice, Amy the Pepsi, Brian the Coke, Lisa the iced tea, and Bill the 7-Up.

5. Note that in deductive arguments the premises are usually dependent, working together to support the conclusion.

EXERCISES 8-3

1. a. *Modus tollens* argument. Unstated conclusion: Sam did not enlist in the Army.

b. *Modus ponens* argument with an unstated conclusion—"I'm going to leave you."

c. *Modus tollens* argument with an unstated conclusion—"It rained today."

d. Chain argument. Unstated conclusion: Therefore, if I call Lisa, she might notice me more around campus.

e. *Modus ponens* argument. Unstated conclusion: "I have to get a job."

f. *Modus tollens* argument. The second premise can be interpreted as: "Bush is not moving quickly to the center." The unstated conclusion is "Therefore, Bush does not want to secure his legacy and defy expectations."

g. Chain argument with two missing second premises: "If I complete my major in accounting, then I'll be able to graduate from college. If I graduate from college then I'll be able to apply to do an MBA in accounting."

h. A *modus ponens* argument with an unstated conclusion: "Therefore, Seattle will save several thousands of gallons of fuel annually."

2. a. A valid *modus tollens* argument. The conclusion is stated at the beginning of the argument followed by the conditional premises.

b. This is a valid *modus ponens* argument.

c. This is an unsound argument. Although the form of the argument is valid, the first premise is false. With proper medical care, children born with AIDS can live into their teens and perhaps longer.

d. A valid chain argument

e. This argument is invalid because the second premise denies the antecedent.

f. A valid *modus ponens* argument—and an example of the importance of thinking before you speak.

g. An invalid *modus tollens* argument since the second premise denies the antecedent of the first premise, rather than the consequent.

h. Valid *modus ponens* argument.

i. Valid *modus ponens* argument.

j. Valid *modus ponens* argument. However, the argument is unsound, since it assumes incorrectly that all people born under the astrological sign Leo are brave.

k. Valid chain argument.

EXERCISES 8-4

1. a. Universal affirmative.

b. Particular affirmative.

c. Universal negative.

d. Particular affirmative.

e. Particular negative.

f. Universal negative

g. Universal affirmative

h. Particular affirmative

i. Particular negative

j. Universal affirmative

2. Using Venn diagrams, determine which of the following syllogisms are valid and which are invalid.

a. All (published authors) are (writers).

Some (writers) are (professors).

Therefore, some (professors) are (published authors).

Invalid Argument

b. Some (scholars) are not (geniuses).

Some (scholars) are (football players).

Therefore, some (football players) are not (geniuses).

Invalid Argument

c. Some (Latinos) are (Republicans).

All (Republicans) are (American citizens).

Therefore, some (American citizens) are not (Latinos).

Invalid Argument

P   M
d. All (members of fraternities) are (male).

S   M
Some (college students) are not (males).

S   P
Therefore, some (college students) are not (members of fraternities).

Valid Argument

M   P
e. No (Republican presidential candidates) are (women).

M
Some (Republican presidential candidates) are
S
(senators).

S   P
Therefore, some (senators) are not (women).

Valid Argument

M   P
f. Some (UFO sightings) are (hallucinations).

M   S
Some (UFO sightings) are (sightings of airplanes).

S
Therefore, (some sightings of airplanes) are
P
(hallucinations).

Invalid Argument

M
g. No (nations that allow capital punishment) are
P
(members of the European Union).

S   M
No (European nations) are (nations that allow capital punishment).

S   P
Therefore, all (European nations) are (members of the European Union).

Invalid Argument

P   M
h. Some (Olympic athletes) are (professional athletes).

S   M
No (high school cheerleaders) are (professional athletes).

S   P
Therefore, no (high school cheerleaders) are (Olympic athletes).

Invalid Argument

EXERCISES 8-5

M   P
1. a. No (beings created in the image of God) are (beings whose lives should be destroyed).

S   M
All (men) are (beings created in the image of God).

S   P
Therefore, no (men) are (beings whose lives should be destroyed).

Valid Argument

M   P
b. Some (people who do volunteer work) are (people who are civic-minded).

S   M
Some (college students) are (people who do volunteer work).

S   P
Therefore, some (college students) are (people who are civic-minded).

Invalid Argument

M   P
c. No (college roommates of mine) are (people who go on to use hard drugs).

M   S
All (college roommates of mine) are (people who smoked marijuana).

S
Therefore, some (people who smoked marijuana) are
P
not (people who go on to use hard drugs).

Invalid Argument

d. The four terms in this argument can be reduced to three by using *not Democrats* for *Republican*. The argument can be written in standard form as follows:

M   P
Some (Cubans) are not (Democrats).
M   S
All (Cubans) are (Hispanics).
S   P
Therefore, some (Hispanics) are not (Democrats).

Valid Argument

e. There is an unstated major premise: "No heterosexuals are people who are gay or lesbian." The argument can be written in standard form as follows:

P   M
No (heterosexuals) are (people who are gay or lesbian).

S   M
Some (parents) are (people who are gay or lesbian).

S   P
Therefore, some (parents) are not (heterosexuals).

Valid Argument

M   P
f. Some (teams wearing blue uniforms) are (teams that will win).

S   M
All (teams named Blue Jays) are (teams wearing blue uniforms).

$$S \qquad\qquad P$$

Therefore, all (teams named Blue Jays) are (teams that will win).

Invalid Argument

M

g. Some (abnormal weather patterns we've been

P

experiencing in the past decade) are (the result of global warming).

M

Some (abnormal weather patterns we've been

S

experiencing in the past decade) are (droughts and heat spells).

$$S \qquad\qquad P$$

Therefore, some (droughts and heat spells) are (the result of global warming).

Invalid Argument

M

P \qquad\qquad M

h. No (liberals) are (people who favor free speech zones on campus).

M

Some (people who favor free speech zones on

S

campus) are (college professors).

$$S \qquad\qquad P$$

Therefore, some (college professors) are not (liberals).

Valid Argument

M

9 Ethics and Moral Reasoning

EXERCISES 9-3

2. An ethical subjectivist would have to reply that, if a person watching Word being bludgeoned to death felt like watching and even cheering the attacker, then this was the right thing for him or her to do. And if the attacker felt it was morally acceptable to beat another person to death because she dented his fender, then it *was* morally right, and perhaps morally obligatory, for him to do so.

6. Sample answer: Premise 1: If cultural relativism is true (morality is nothing more than cultural customs), then people who oppose cultural customs or break laws in protest, such as Gandhi, Elizabeth Cady Stanton, and Martin Luther King, Jr., are immoral people. Premise 2: Cultural relativism is true. Conclusion: Therefore, people who oppose and break cultural norms, such as Gandhi, Stanton, and King, are immoral people.

EXERCISES 9-4

1. For example: Should college students be drafted? Should women be drafted? How about parents of young children?

EXERCISES 9-5

1. a. Prescriptive
b. Descriptive

c. Descriptive
d. Definition
e. Prescriptive
f. Descriptive
g. Descriptive premise with a sub-conclusion
h. Prescriptive

3. a. Missing prescriptive premise: The law is a moral and just law.
b. This argument contains the naturalistic fallacy.
c. Unstated premise: "We have a duty of self-improvement." Otherwise, this is a good inductive argument based on generalization.
d. Missing premise: The duty of justice entails equality. A relationship where one partner has power over the other is by its nature unequal. If you accept this premise, this is a good argument.
e. Unsound argument: It contains a false premise. People who marry in their twenties have the lowest divorce rates. Divorce rates start climbing for people who marry after age thirty-five. [2]
f. Good deductive argument if you accept the second premise. However, it might be stronger, depending on the audience, if the term "sentient" was defined.
g. Missing premise and fallacy of popular appeal: The unstated prescriptive premise makes the questionable claim that morality is determined by what the majority of people in a culture think is moral.
h. The first sentence is the conclusion and the last sentence a descriptive premise. The unstated prescriptive premise(s) are: 1) A person has a right to practice their religion, and 2) This right entails a duty on the part of the campus to provide the means (kosher meals) for students to practice their religion. The second premise is controversial because it assumes that there is also a welfare right involved—that is, that the college has a *duty* to provide kosher meals for Orthodox and other observant Jewish students.

10 Marketing and Advertising

EXERCISES 10-2

2. Examples might include the use of fallacies rather than rational arguments in marketing a candidate, as well as the unequal access to campaign funds, which would give an advantage to the candidate with the most money.

EXERCISES 10-3

2. Relate this to the importance of mindfulness and attentiveness in critical thinking. See Chapter 1.

7. Issues include invasion of privacy and the exposure of other onlookers, such as children, to inappropriate ads.

EXERCISES 10-4

1. a. A false analogy—the similarities between the regularity of the sun rising and Metropolitan Life are superficial at best.
b. Fallacy of popular appeal
c. Scare tactics
d. Obscure technical language. The term "fully vested" is not defined in the ad.

e. Snob appeal. This ad plays into the self-serving bias that we are in control and will maintain our independence even in the military.

f. Equivocation on the term *nut*. Many unconsciously believe that eating this candy bar will make you feel pleasantly "nutty" or zany.

g. Ambiguous. Can we drive an Avalon to another galaxy?

h. Comparison information is missing. This ad gives the impression that Verizon has a broader range than other cell phone providers without presenting any information to substantiate this claim.

i. Hyperbole

j. Euphemism for "use your credit card to buy what makes you happy." The word *richly* is emotively loaded, calling attention to the benefits of credit card use rather than the debts incurred.

k. Inappropriate appeal to authority. She's an actress, not an authority on mobile phones.

l. Hyperbole

m. Popular appeal: association of the vacuum cleaner with being a good American. To reinforce this patriotic message, the person shown beside the vacuum cleaner is wearing a tie with the American flag on it.

n. "Last up to" is ambiguous. Do the pills last this long most of the time or only in rare cases?

o. Incomplete statistics. No source is cited for the statistics or explanation given of how the sample was selected. Nor is *exercise* ever defined in the ad.

2. Ads generally promote the non-moral values of wealth, status, competition, popularity, beauty, and youth.

11 Mass Media

EXERCISES 11-3

2. a. The headline is misleading and based on the fallacy of hasty generalization. The new story is about a tiny crystal of magnetite found in a meteorite that scientists believe originated on Mars. Magnetite crystals are formed by bacteria here on Earth. However, the evidence for life on Mars is far from conclusive. It is possible the meteorite was contaminated after it landed on Earth or that the crystals formed under high heat when the meteorite passed through the Earth's atmosphere.

b. Headline based on a report released by scientists outlining possible scenarios that could happen, if a bird flu pandemic were to hit the United States. It was not a prediction. The headline uses sensationalism to catch the audience's attention.

c. This headline is misleading. It gives the impression that at least half of college students are engaging in these practices and that they are more prone to these practices than are other people. In fact, the study from the *Journal of Pediatrics* that the news article is reporting was based on an Internet survey of Cornell and Princeton students in which 17 percent reported engaging in these practices. This percentage is about the same as that for teenagers and young adults in the general population.

d. The headline is a distortion of the scientific findings. In fact, the word *happiness* does not even appear in the story that appeared in the journal *Science* about the discovery by scientists of a genetic mechanism which influences serotonin level in the brain and may explain why some people are more susceptible to debilitating psychiatric disorders.

e. This headline relies on sensationalism and the appearance of controversy. By omitting human embryonic stem cells, the headline leaves readers with the erroneous impression that Harvard scientists are cloning real live humans.

f. This headline uses hyperbole and distortion, implying that the findings apply to the general population. In fact, the article is about a small group of people known as "cyberchondriacs" who use the Web for self-diagnosis and to garner information on disorders in order to convince their physicians they have illnesses that they don't really have.

g. This headline commits the fallacy of equivocation on "UFO" in order to capture readers' attention. The "unidentified flying object" spotted by the U.S. Mars rover Spirit is thought by NASA to have been a meteor or old orbiting spacecraft that had been sent to Mars thirty years ago.

12 Science

EXERCISES 12-1

1. For example, there is a common attitude that science is not to be questioned. People who question science are often ridiculed and seen as "heretics" engaging in pseudoscience. Also, science is often seen as the source of truth and as our salvation or the solution to humans' problems.

EXERCISES 12-2

1. a. Possible hypotheses: "It's an illusion based on a perceptual error," "The Moon is closer to the Earth when it is on the horizon," and "The Earth's atmosphere makes the Moon look bigger when it's near the horizon."

b. Possible hypotheses: "Canadians are becoming better at marketing their universities to Americans," "The tuition at Canadian colleges is lower and therefore more attractive to American students," and "Young Americans are more disillusioned with the United States since we invaded Iraq and are moving to Canada."

c. Possible hypotheses: "The sightings are a collective delusion based on social expectations," "People who claim to have seen UFOs are making up the stories in order to get attention," and "Some of the sightings are of actual UFOs."

d. Possible hypotheses: "Women have less innate ability than men at science and math," "Women have child-minding duties that keep them from working the long hours necessary for promotion," and "Women are being held back because of gender discrimination."

e. Possible hypotheses: "More teenagers are having babies and they tend to deliver earlier," "Fewer women are getting proper prenatal care," "There is a growing number of multiple births—twins, triplets, or more—and multiple births tend to have a shorter gestation period."

f. Possible hypotheses: "Left-handed people are more accident-prone because we live in a world made for right-handed people," and "Left-handedness is associated with certain innate health problems that contribute to a shorter life span."

g. Possible hypotheses: "Married people are more likely to have a higher combined income and thus better health care," "Healthy people are more likely to get married," "Married people are more likely to have children to care for them in their old age," and "Married people are happier than single people and happier people live longer."

EXERCISES 12-3

1. a. Good hypothesis. Ask students, if this hypothesis turns out to be true based on observation and testing, to come up with a new hypothesis regarding an explanation of this phenomenon.

b. Poor hypothesis: What exactly is a "computer glitch"? She needs to operationalize the definition before the hypothesis can be tested.

c. Poor hypothesis. It cannot be evaluated scientifically because there is no way to prove that God was *not* responsible for Hurricane Katrina and, therefore, there is no way to falsify the hypothesis.

d. A good hypothesis. This hypothesis is based on the observation that 90 percent of heroin users used marijuana before becoming addicted to heroin. However, the hypothesis may be false. It's possible that there are environmental and/or genetic variables that play a key causal role in both heroin and marijuana use.

e. Poor hypothesis: It is untestable because of the vague wording. What is meant by "fun"? How do we measure whether other animals are having "fun" while engaging in sex?

f. Unfalsifiable hypothesis. The philosophical theory of determinism is unfalsifiable: the person putting forward the hypothesis can always claim that we were unable to predict a particular event because there must be causes that we don't know about.

g. Good hypothesis

h. Poor hypothesis. The word "best" would have to be operationalized in order for it to be tested. What do we mean by "best"? If a person replies, "Whatever happens," he or she is engaging in circular reasoning.

i. Good hypothesis

j. Poor hypothesis. Because of its vagueness, it has no predictive power.

EXERCISES 12-4

1. a. This could be done by a field experiment in which the two families stagger the dates that their children go to summer camp. The egg-laying rate of the two farms could then be compared. What they would find is that the confounding variable is length of daylight, which is correlated to both the timing of the children's summer camp and the number of eggs the hens from each farm are laying.

b. This could be done as a controlled laboratory experiment using an experimental and a control group. Decaf coffee could be used as the placebo.

c. This could done as a controlled experiment in which men were shown pictures of both blond and non-blond women. What constitutes "blond" would have to be given an operational definition. The color of the hair on each woman should be changed for different subjects to control for other variables such as face and place of each woman in the picture. To minimize experimenter bias, a video camera should be used to record how long each subject looked at each woman in the picture.

d. Need to do a controlled experiment with a randomly selected experimental and control group. A field experiment is not sufficient here, since taking antibiotics is sometimes related to having a disease, which would confound the study.

e. To test this, students first need to come up with an operational definition of consciousness. They then have to develop a test, such as the Turing test, to test for the presence of consciousness in intelligent computers. This may be done by conversing with a Chatbot and determining whether or not the computer met the students' definition of consciousness.

2. Hill and Barton found that nineteen of the twenty-nine classes or sporting events observed had more red winners, while only six had more blue winners. The difference was significant at $p \leq 0.015$ (98.5% confidence level). However, they used a field experiment so there may have been confounding variables that were not controlled for. In addition, the experimental design limited the generalizability of the results to a particular type of contact sporting event. Finally, the results were only significant for male athletes. In addition to a good experimental design that overcomes some of the flaws in Hill's naturalistic experimental design, students need to consider the feasibility of actually conducting the experiment on their campus.

3. Examples of one or two of these paradigms are: 1) Humans are a machine that can fixed by mechanical interventions such as surgery or a pill, and 2) Death is bad and to be avoided as long as possible.

4. The first requirement would be another hypothesis to take the place of the Old Savannah paradigm. The second requirement would be that the new hypothesis is better at explaining the evidence. This evidence, in the case of Aquatic Ape Hypothesis (the hypothesis that the human species evolved as an aquatic or wading ape in a time when the Earth was warm and water level much higher than it is today) might include finding human fossil remains in areas that were covered by shallow water or lagoons at the time our ancestors evolved into bipeds. (For more information, refer students to Elaine Morgan, *The Aquatic Ape Hypothesis*, 1997. www.wikipedia.com also has a nice critique of the hypothesis.)

[1] Letter to the Editor, *Time*, January 31, 2005, p. 13.

[2] Andrew J. Cherlin, *Public and Private Families* (New York: McGraw-Hill, 2002).

A

accent The meaning of an argument changes depending on which word or phrase in it is emphasized.

ad hominem fallacy Instead of presenting a counterargument, we attack the character of the person who made the argument.

affective The emotional aspect of conscience that motivates us to act.

agnostic A person who believes that the existence of God is ultimately unknowable.

amphiboly An argument contains a grammatical mistake which allows more than one conclusion to be drawn.

analogical premise A premise containing an analogy or comparison between similar events or things.

analogy A comparison between two or more similar events or things.

anecdotal evidence Evidence based on personal testimonies.

anthropocentrism The belief that humans are the central or most significant entity of the universe can blind people, including scientists, to the capabilities of other animals.

appeal to force (scare tactics) The use or threat of force in an attempt to get another person to accept a conclusion as correct.

appeal to ignorance The claim that something is true simply because no one has proven it false, or that something is false simply because no one has proven it true.

appeal to pity Pity is evoked in an argument when pity is irrelevant to the conclusion.

argument Reasoning that is made up of two or more propositions, one of which is supported by the others.

argument based on mathematics A deductive argument in which the conclusion depends on a mathematical calculation.

argument by elimination A deductive argument that rules out different possibilities until only one remains.

argument from definition A deductive argument in which the conclusion is true because it is based on a key term in a definition.

argument from design An argument for the existence of God based on an analogy between man-made objects and natural objects.

artificial intelligence The study of the computations that make it possible for machines to perceive, reason, and act.

atheist A person who does not believe in the existence of a personal God.

B

begging the question The conclusion of an argument is simply a rewording of a premise.

business An organization that makes a profit by providing goods and services to customers.

C

care perspective The emphasis in moral development and reasoning on context and relationships.

case brief Researching the case under consideration and summarizing its relevant details.

categorical imperative Kant's fundamental moral principle that helps to determine what our duty is.

categorical syllogism A deductive argument with two premises and three terms, each of which occurs exactly twice in two of the three propositions.

causal argument An argument that claims something is (or is not) the cause of something else.

cause An event that brings about a change or effect.

ceremonial language Language used in particular prescribed formal circumstances.

chain arguments A type of hypothetical argument with three or more conditional premises linked together.

civil disobedience The active, nonviolent refusal to obey a law that is deemed unjust.

cognitive dissonance A sense of disorientation which occurs in situations where new ideas directly conflict with a person's worldview.

common law A system of case-based law that is derived from judges' decisions over the centuries.

compassion Sympathy in action.

conclusion The proposition in an argument that is supported on the basis of other propositions.

conditional statement An "If ... then ..." statement.

confidence level The percentage by which a scientist can be confident in generalizing the results of an experiment to a population.

confirmation bias The tendency to look only for evidence that supports our assumptions.

confounding variable A fact that is not accounted for or controlled by the experimental design.

connotative meaning The meaning of a word or phrase that is based on past personal experiences or associations.

conscience A source of knowledge that provides us with knowledge about what is right and wrong.

conventional stages Stage of moral development in which people look to others for moral guidelines.

correlation When two events occur together regularly at rates higher than probability.

cost–benefit analysis A process where the harmful effects of an action are weighed against the benefits.

controlled experiment An experiment in which the sample is randomly divided into an experimental and a control group.

critical rationalism The belief that faith is based on direct revelation of God and that there should no logical inconsistencies between revelation and reason.

cultural relativism People look to societal norms for what is morally right and wrong.

critical thinking A collection of skills we use every day that are necessary for our full intellectual and personal development.

cyborg Humans who are partially computerized.

D

deductive argument An argument that claims its conclusion necessarily follows from the premises.

democracy A form of government in which the highest power in the state is invested in the people and exercised directly by them or, as is generally the case in modern democracies, by their elected officials.

denotative meaning The meaning of a word or phrase that expresses the properties of the object.

deontology The ethics of duty.

dependent variable The fact in a controlled experiment that changes in response to the manipulation.

descriptive premise A premise that is based on empirical facts.

diffusion of responsibility The tendency, when in a large group, to regard a problem as belonging to someone else.

direct democracy A type of democracy in which all of the people directly make laws and govern themselves.

directive language Language used to direct or influence actions.

disjunctive syllogism A type of deductive argument by elimination in which the premises present only two alternatives.

doctrine of legal precedent The idea that legal cases should be decided in the same way as previous, similar legal cases.

double-blind study A controlled experiment in which neither study subjects nor experimenters know which group the study subjects are in.

doublethink Involves holding two contradictory views at the same time and believing both to be true.

dualism The belief that there are two substances—the physical and the nonphysical.

dysphemism A word or phrase chosen to produce a negative effect.

E

egocentrism The belief that the self or individual is the center of all things.

elitism A belief in the rule of "the best people."

emotional intelligence The ability to perceive accurately, appraise and express emotion.

emotive language Language that is purposely chosen to elicit a certain emotional impact.

empathy (sympathy) The capacity to enter into and understand the emotions of others.

empirical fact A fact based on scientific observation and the evidence of our five senses.

empiricism The belief that our physical senses are the primary source of knowledge.

empiricist One who believes that we discover truth primarily through our physical senses.

equivocation A key term in an argument changes meaning during the course of the argument.

escalation of commitment The overcommitment of marketing to a particular answer.

ethical subjectivist One who believes that morality is nothing more than personal opinion or feelings.

ethnocentrism The belief in the inherent superiority of one's own group and culture is characterized by suspicion and a lack of understanding about other cultures.

euphemism The replacement of a term that has a negative association by a neutral or positive term.

evidence Reasons for believing that a statement or claim is true or probably true.

experimental material The group or class of objects or subjects that is being studied in an experiment.

explanation A statement about why or how something is the case.

expressive language Language that communicates feelings and attitudes.

external validity The results of an experiment can be accurately generalized to the real world.

F

faith Belief, trust, and obedience to a religious deity.

fallacy A faulty argument that at first appears to be correct.

fallacy of ambiguity Arguments that have ambiguous phrases or sloppy grammatical structure.

fallacy of division An erroneous inference from the characteristics of an entire set or group about a member of that group or set.

fallacy of hasty generalization A generalization made from a sample that is too small or biased.

fallacy of relevance The premise is logically irrelevant, or unrelated, to the conclusion.

false dilemma Responses to complex issues are reduced to an either–or choice.

false memory syndrome The recalling of events that never happened.

federalism A system in which power is divided between the federal and state governments.

fideism The belief that the divine is revealed through faith and does not require reason.

form The pattern of reasoning in a deductive argument.

formal fallacy A type of mistaken reasoning in which the form of an argument itself is invalid.

G

gambler's error The belief that a previous event affects the probability in a random event.

generalization Drawing a conclusion about a certain characteristic of a population based on a sample from it.

H

hasty generalization A generalization is made from a sample that is too small or biased.

hearsay Evidence that is heard by one person and then repeated to another.

helper's high The feeling that occurs when we help other people.

hyperbole A rhetorical device that uses an exaggeration.

hypothesis A proposed explanation for a particular set of phenomena.

hypothetical syllogism A deductive argument that contains two premises, at least one of which is a conditional statement.

I

impeachment The process by which Congress brings charges against and tries a high-level government official for misconduct.

inappropriate appeal to authority We look to an authority in a field other than that under investigation.

independent variable The factor in a controlled experiment that is being manipulated.

inductive argument An argument that only claims that its conclusion probably follows from the premise.

informal fallacy A type of mistaken reasoning that occurs when an argument is psychologically or emotionally persuasive but logically incorrect.

informative language Language that is either true or false.

initiatives Laws or constitutional amendments proposed by citizens.

issue An ill-defined complex of problems involving a controversy or uncertainty.

J

judicial review The power given to the Supreme Court to strike down any law that it deems to be unconstitutional.

justice perspective The emphasis on duty and principles in moral reasoning.

K

knowledge Information which we believe to be true and for which we have justification or evidence.

L

language A system of communication that involves a set of arbitrary symbols.

legitimate authority In a democracy, the right to rule given to the government by the people.

legitimate interests Interests that do not violate others' similar and equal interests.

lexical definition The commonly used dictionary definition.

liberal democracy A form of democracy emphasizing liberty of individuals.

libertarian A person who opposes any government restraints on individual freedom.

liberty rights The right to be left alone to pursue our legitimate interests.

loaded question A fallacy that assumes a particular answer to another unasked question.

lobbying The practice of private advocacy to influence the government.

logic The study of the methods and principles used to distinguish correct or good arguments from poor arguments.

M

major premise The premise in a categorical syllogism that contains the predicate term.

major term The predicate (P) term in a categorical syllogism.

margin of error The chance that the results of an experiment are based on random variation in the sample.

marketing research Identifying a target market and finding out if it matches customer desires.

mass media Forms of communication that are designed to reach and influence very large audiences.

materialism The belief that everything in the universe is composed of physical matter.

mature care ethics The stage of moral development in which people are able to balance their needs and those of others.

media literacy The ability to understand and critically analyze the influence of the mass media.

memorable-events error A cognitive error that involves our ability to vividly remember outstanding events.

meta-analysis The statistical analysis of the results of several similar experiments.

metaphor A descriptive type of analogy, frequently found in literature.

method of belief A method of critical analysis in which we suspend our doubts and biases and remain genuinely open to what people with opposing views are saying.

method of doubt A method of critical analysis in which we put aside our preconceived ideas and beliefs and begin from a position of skepticism.

middle term In a categorical syllogism, the term is the one that appears once in each of the premises.

minor premise The premise in a categorical syllogism that contains the subject term.

minor term The subject (S) term in a categorical syllogism.

modus ponens A hypothetical syllogism in which the antecedent premise is affirmed by the consequent premise.

modus tollens A hypothetical syllogism in which the antecedent premise is denied by the consequent premise.

moral dilemma A situation in which there is a conflict between moral values.

moral outrage Indignation in the presence of an injustice or violation of moral decency.

moral reasoning Used when a decision is made about what we ought or ought not to do.

moral sensitivity The awareness of how our actions affect others.

moral sentiments Emotions that alert us to moral situations and motivate us to do what is right.

moral tragedy This occurs when we make a moral decision that is later regretted.

moral values Values that benefit oneself and others and are worthwhile for their own sake.

N

naturalist fallacy A fallacy based on the assumption that what is natural is good.

negative correlation When the occurrence of one event increases as the other decreases.

niche media Forms of communication geared to a narrowly defined audience.

nonmoral (instrumental) values Values that are goal oriented—a means to an end to be achieved.

normal science Scientific research that is based on past achievements and is recognized by most scientists.

O

objectivity The assumption that we can observe and study the physical world without any observer bias.

operational definition A definition with a standardized measure for use in data collection and interpretation.

opinion A belief based solely on personal feelings rather than on reason or facts.

P

paradigm The accepted view of what the world is like and how we should go about studying it.

persuasive definition A definition used as a means to influence others to accept our view.

placebo A substance used in experiments that has no therapeutic effect.

poll A type of survey that involves collecting information from a sample group of people.

popular appeal An appeal to popular opinion to gain support for our conclusion.

populism A belief in the wisdom of the common people and in the equality of all people.

positive correlation The incidence of one event increases when the second one increases.

postconventional stages Stage in which people make moral decisions on the basis of universal moral principals.

precising definition A definition used to reduce vagueness that goes beyond the ordinary lexical definition.

preconventional stages Stage of moral development in which morality is defined egotistically.

predicate term In a categorical syllogism, the term that appears second in the conclusion.

premise A proposition in an argument that supports the conclusion.

prescriptive premise A premise in an argument containing a value statement.

prima facie duty Moral duty that is binding unless overridden by a more compelling moral duty.

principle of utility (greatest happiness principle) The most moral action is that which brings about the greatest happiness or pleasure and the least amount of pain for the greatest number.

probability error Misunderstanding the probability or chances of an event by a huge margin.

profit The money left over after all expenses are paid.

proposition A statement that expresses a complete thought and can be either true or false.

pseudoscience A body of explanations or hypotheses that masquerades as science.

push poll A poll that starts by presenting the pollsters' views before asking for a response.

Q

qualifier A term such as *all*, *no*, or *not*, which indicates whether a proposition is affirmative or negative.

quality Whether a categorical proposition is positive or negative.

quantity Whether a categorical proposition is universal or particular.

questionable cause (post hoc) A person assumes, without sufficient evidence, that one thing is the cause of another.

R

random sampling Every member of the population has an equal chance of becoming part of the sample.

rationalism The belief that religion should be consistent with reason and evidence.

rationalist One who claims that most human knowledge comes through reason.

reason The process of supporting a claim or conclusion on the basis of evidence.

red herring fallacy A response is directed toward a conclusion that is different from that proposed by the original argument.

referenda Laws or constitutional amendments put on the ballot by state legislators.

reliability The standard in which scientific tools provide consistency of results over time.

representative democracy A form of democracy in which people turn over their authority to govern to their elected representatives.

representative sample A sample that is similar to the larger population from which it was drawn.

research methodology A systematic approach in science to gathering and analyzing information.

resentment A type of moral outrage that occurs when we ourselves are treated unjustly.

rhetoric The defense of a particular position usually without adequate consideration of opposing evidence in order to win people over to one's position.

rhetorical devices The use of euphemisms, dysphemisms, hyperbole, and sarcasm to manipulate and persuade.

rule of law The idea that governmental authority must be exercised in accordance with established written laws.

rule of men A system in which members of the ruling class can make arbitrary laws and rules.

rules of evidence A set of rules that ensure fairness in the administration of law.

S

sampling Selecting some members of a group and making generalizations about the whole population on the basis of their characteristics.

sarcasm The use of ridicule, insults, taunting, and/or caustic irony.

science The use of reason to move from observable, measurable facts to hypotheses to testable explanations for those facts.

scientific experiment Research carried out under controlled or semicontrolled conditions.

scientific method A process involving the rigorous, systematic application of observation and experimentation.

scientific revolution A paradigm shift in which a new scientific theory replaces a problematic paradigm.

scientific theory An explanation for some aspect of the natural world based on well-substantiated facts, laws, inferences, and tested hypotheses.

self-selected sample A sample where only the people most interested in the poll or survey participate.

separation of powers A system in which three separate branches of government act as a check on one another.

shame A feeling resulting from the violation of a social norm.

single-blind study A controlled experiment in which only the experimenter knows which study subjects are in which group.

slanted question A question that is written to elicit a particular response.

slippery slope The faulty assumption that if certain actions are permitted, then all actions of this type will soon be permissible.

social contract A voluntary agreement among the people to unite as a political community.

social dissonance A sense of disorientation which occurs when the social behavior and norms of others conflicts with a person's worldview.

sound A deductive argument that is valid and that has true premises.

sovereignty The exclusive right of government to exercise political power.

state of nature The condition in which people lived prior to the formation of a social contract.

stereotyping Labeling people based on their membership in a group.

stipulative definition A definition given to a new term or a new combination of old terms.

strategic plan A method by which an organization deploys its resources to realize a goal.

straw man fallacy An opponent's argument is distorted or misrepresented in order to make it easier to refute.

subject term In a categorical syllogism, the term that appears first in the conclusion.

SWOT model Used to analyze a company's strengths, weaknesses, external opportunities, and threats.

syllogism A deductive argument presented in the form of two supporting premises and a conclusion.

T

tacit consent The implicit agreement to abide by the laws of a country by remaining there.

theoretical definition A type of precising definition explaining a term's nature.

Turing test A means of determining if artificial intelligence is conscious, self-directed intelligence.

tyranny of the majority The majority impose their policies and laws on the political minorities.

U

unwarranted assumption A fallacious argument that contains an assumption that is not supported by evidence.

utilitarian calculus Used to determine the best course of action or policy by calculating the total amount of pleasure and pain caused by that action.

utilitarianism A moral philosophy in which actions are evaluated based on their consequences.

V

valid A deductive argument where the form is such that the conclusion must be true if the premises are assumed to be true.

Venn diagram A visual representation of a categorical syllogism used to determine the validity of the syllogism.

virtue ethics Moral theories that emphasize character over right actions.

W

welfare rights The right to receive certain social goods that are essential to our well-being.

Chapter 1

1. Stanley Milgram, *Obedience to Authority* (New York: Harper & Row, 1974).

2. See Zimbardo, P. G. "The Power and Pathology of Imprisonment." *Congressional Record*. (Serial No. 15, October 25, 1975).

3. Ibid, p. 22.

4. For an excellent summary and analysis of the Milgram study, see John Sabini and Maury Silver, "Critical Thinking and Obedience to Authority," *National Forum: The Phi Kappa Phi Journal*, winter 1985, pp. 13–17.

5. Irving Copi, *Symbolic Logic* (New York: Macmillan, 1954), p. 1.

6. Ron Catrell, Fred A. Young, and Bradley C. Martin, "Antibiotic Prescribing in Ambulatory Care Settings for Adults with Colds, Upper Respiratory Tract Infections and Bronchitis," *Clinical Therapeutics*, Vol. 24, Issue 1, January 2002, pp. 170–182.

7. See "Extending the Cure: Policy Responses to the Growing Threat of Antibiotic Resistance," Robert Wood Johnson Foundation, March 2007.

8. "Trends in Reportable Sexually Transmitted Diseases in the United States, 2005," Centers for Disease Control and Prevention, December 2006.

9. William G. Perry, *Forms of Intellectual and Ethical Development in College Years: A Scheme* (New York: Holt, Rinehart and Winston, 1970).

10. See Milgram study on pages 1–2.

11. Chau-Kiu Cheung, Elisabeth Rudowicz, Anna S.F. Kwan, and Xiao Dong Yue, "Assessing University Students' General and Specific Critical Thinking," *College Student Journal*, December 2002, Vol. 36, Issue 4, pp. 504–525.

12. Charles E. Murray, "Financial Fraud Targets Youth," *Washington Times*, August 8, 2004; "The Demographics of Identity Fraud," April 2006. A Publication of Javeline Strategy & Research. http://www.javelinstrategy.com

13. David Burns, *Feeling Good: The New Mood Therapy* (New York: Signet, New American Library, 1980), p. 47.

14. Dwight Boyd, "The Problem of Sophomoritis: An Educational Proposal," *Journal of Moral Education*, Vol. 6, Issue 1, October 1976, pp. 36–42.

15. Stephen A. Satris, "Student Relativism," *Teaching Philosophy*, September 1986, pp. 193–200.

16. National Assessment of College Student Learning: 1995, pp. 15–16.

17. René Descartes, "Discourse on the Method of Rightly Conducting One's Reason and Seeking the Truth in the Sciences," in *The Philosophical Writings of Descartes*, eds. John Cottingham, Robert Stoothoff, and Dugald Murdoch (Cambridge, England: Cambridge University Press, 1985), p. 120.

18. Bradley J. Fisher and Diana K. Specht, "Successful Aging and Creativity in Later Life," *Journal of Aging Studies*, Vol. 13, Issue 4, winter 1999, p. 458.

19. Kimberly Palmer, "Creativity on Demand," *U.S. News & World Report*, April 30, 2007, p. EE2.

20. Shunryu Suzuki, *Zen Mind, Beginner's Mind* (New York, Weatherhill, 1989), pp. 13–14 and 21.

21. Sharon Begley, *Train Your Mind, Change Your Brain* (New York: Ballantine Books, 2007.)

22. "Transcendental Meditation in the Workplace," 1999, www:tmscotland.org/popup/businesses.html.

23. Evelyn Fox Keller, *Gender and Science* (New Haven, CT: Yale University Press, 1985).

24. W. Steward Wallace, "Military History," *The Encyclopedia of Canada*, Vol. 3 (Toronto: University Associates of Canada, 1948), pp. 171–172.

25. Michael D. Yapko, PhD, "The Art of Avoiding Depression: Skills and Knowledge You'll Need to Prevent Depression," *Psychology Today*, May 1, 1997; Michael D. Yapki, *Breaking the Patterns of Depression* (New York: Doubleday Publishing, 1988). For further references on the role of faulty reasoning in depression, see "Cognitive Therapy for Depression," http://psychologyinfo.com/depression/cognitive.htm

26. American College Health Association, *National Health Assessment: Spring 2003* (Baltimore: AMCH, 2003). See also Daniel McGinn and Ron DePasquale, "Taking Depression On," *Newsweek*, August 23, 2004, p. 59.

27. W. Irwin and G. Bassham, "Depression, Informal Fallacies, and Cognitive Therapy: The Critical Thinking Cure," *Inquiry: Critical Thinking Across the Disciplines*, 2002, Vol. 21, pp. 15–21, and Tom Gilbert, "Some Reflections on Critical Thinking and Mental Health," *Teaching Philosophy*, Vol. 26, Issue 4, December 2003, pp. 333–349.

28. John Rawls, *A Theory of Justice* (Cambridge, MA: Harvard University Press, 1971), pp. 408–409.

29. Cooperative Institute Research Program, *The American Freshman National Norms for Fall 2004*, Higher Education Research Institute, University of California, December 2004.

30. For more on the Myers-Briggs test, see Paul D. Tieger and Barbara Barron-Teiger, *Do What You Are: Discover the Perfect Career for You Through the Secrets of Personality Type* (Boston: Little, Brown, 1992) and David Keirsey and Marilyn Bates, *Please Understand Me: Character and Temperament Types* (Del Mar, CA: Prometheus Nemesis Books, 1984).

31. Michael D. Yapko, PhD, "The Art of Avoiding Depression: Skills and Knowledge You'll Need to Prevent Depression," *Psychology Today*, May 1, 1997, and Richard Paul, "Critical Thinking: Basic Question and Answers," *Think* (April 1992).

32. M. McLaughlin, "Embedded Identities: Enabling Balance in Urban Contexts," in S. B. Heath and W. W. McLaughlin, eds., *Identity and Inner-City Youth: Beyond Ethnicity and Gender* (New York: Teachers College Press, 1993), p. 54.

33. Allen N. Mendler, *Smiling at Yourself: Educating Young Children About Stress and Self-Esteem* (Santa Cruz, CA: Network, 1990), p. xvi.

34. Letter to David Harding (1824).

35. Einstein came in second. See Walter Isaacson, *Einstein: His Life and Universe* (New York: Simon and Schuster, 2007).

36. Daryl G. Smith and Natalie B. Schonfeld, "The Benefits of Diversity: What the Research Tells Us," *About Campus*, November-December 2000, p. 21.

37. Daryl G. Smith and Natalie B. Schonfeld, "The Benefits of Diversity: What the Research Tells Us," *About Campus*, November-December 2000, p. 19.

38. Immanuel Kant, "Proper Self-Esteem," in *Lectures on Ethics* (Indianapolis: Hackett, 1775–1780/1963), p. 127.

39. Raymond V. Raehn, "The Historical Roots of Political Correctness," *Altermedia Scotland*, June 29, 2004. http://scot.altermedia.info/index.php?p=568

40. Al Gore, *The Assault on Reason* (New York: Penguin Press, 2007), p. 11.

41. "The Real Meaning Behind Horowitz Advertisement," Op-Ed, *Brown Daily Herald* Vol. 139, no. 93, 2001 http://www.browndailyherald.com.

42. See *CIA World Factbook* 2005, and www.prisonpolicy.org/graphs/index/shtml.

43. http://www.cdc.gov/ncipc/factsheets/drving.htm.

44. L. F. Ivanhoe, "Future World Oil Supplies: There is a Finite Limit." http://dieoff.org/page 88.htm.

45. Quoted on Bill Moyers's 1990 PBS broadcast of Pierre Sauvage's 1989 television documentary *Weapons of the Spirit*.

46. Elise J. West, "Perry's Legacy: Models of Epistemological Development," *Journal of Adult Development*, Vol. 11, Issue 2, April 2004, p. 62.

47. Ibid, p. 61.

48. Anne Harrigan and Virginia Vincenti, "Developing Higher-Order Thinking Through an Intercultural Assignment," *College Teaching*, Vol. 52, Issue 3, p. 117.

49. For a copy of the report go to http://info.worldbank.org/governance/wgi2007/

50. A. H. Martin, "An Experimental Study of the Factors and Types of Voluntary Choice," *Archives of Psychology*, 1922, Vol. 51, pp. 40–41.

51. Peggy Orenstein, *Schoolgirls: Young Women, Self-Esteem, and the Confidence Gap* (New York: Doubleday, American Association of University Women, 1994).

52. Alice Domar and Lynda Wright, "Could You Harbor Unconscious Prejudice?" *Health*, July/August 2004, Vol. 18, Issue 6, p. 139.

53. Tim Driver, "How Men and Women Use Their Time," Salary.com, Inc.

54. Leon Festinger, *A Theory of Cognitive Dissonance* (Stanford, CA: Stanford University Press, 1957), pp. 120–121.

55. John Leach, "Why People 'Freeze' in an Emergency: Temporal and Cognitive Constraints on Survival Responses," *Aviation, Space, and Environmental Medicine*, June 2004, Vol. 75, Issue 6, pp. 539–542.

56. Quoted in Amanda Ripley, "How to Get Out Alive," *Time*, May 2, 2005, p. 62.

57. Zehra R. Peynircioglu, Jennifer L. W. Thompson, and Terri B. Tanielian, "Improvement Strategies in Free-Throw Shooting and Grip-Strength Tasks," *Journal of General Psychology*, April 2000, Vol. 127, Issue 2, pp. 145–156.

58. Analogy used in a speech. Quoted in Douglas Adams, *The Salmon of Doubt: Hitchhiking the Galaxy One Last Time* (London: Macmillan, 2002).

Chapter 2

1. Fyodor Dostoyevsky, *Crime and Punishment*, trans. by Jessie Coulson (Oxford University Press, 1953). For an online edition of the novel, go to http://www.bartleby.com/318/

2. This logic problem is based on one from Gregory Bassham et al., *Critical Thinking* (New York, McGraw-Hill, 2005), p. 56.

3. Quoted in S. F. Spontzis, *Morals, Reason, and Animals* (Philadelphia: Temple University Press, 1987), p. 33.

4. Clive D. L. Wynne, *Do Animals Think?* (Princeton, NJ: Princeton University Press, 2004).

5. Temple Grandin, Matthew Peterson, and Gordon L. Shaw, "Spatial-temporal versus language-analytical reasoning: the role of music training," *Arts Education Policy Review*, July-August 1998, vol. 99, no. 6, pp. 11–14.

6. See Jonathan Barnes, *Articles on Aristotle: Ethics and Politics* (Duckworth, 1977).

7. For other examples of this type of thinking, see Jean-Jacques Rousseau's *Emile* (1762), Hegel's *Philosophy of Right* (1872), and Friedrich Nietzsche's *Beyond Good and Evil*, Part VII (1886).

8. Austin W. Astin et al., *The American Freshman: Thirty-Five Year Trends* (Los Angeles: Cooperative Institutional Research Program, University of California), p. 11.

9. Naomi Schaefer Riley, "Sarah Palin Feminism," *Wall Street Journal*, Sept. 5, 2008.

10. See Steven Goldberg, "The Logic of Patriarchy," in *Fads and Fallacies in the Social Sciences* (Amherst, NY: Humanity Books, 2003), pp. 93–108.

11. For more on research on sex differences, see Kingsley Browne, *Biology at Work: Rethinking Sexual Equality* (New Brunswick, NJ: Rutgers University Press, 2002); Anne Fausto-Sterling, *Sexing the Body: Gender Politics and the Construction of Sexuality* (New York: Basic Books, 2000); Melissa Hines, *Brain Gender* (New York: Oxford University Press, 2004); Steven Rhoads, *Taking Sex Differences Seriously* (San Francisco: Encounter Books, 2004); Leonard Sax, *Why Gender Matters: What Parents and Teachers Need to Know About the Emerging Science of Sex Differences* (New York: Doubleday, 2005).

12. "Over 30 and Over the Hill," *The Economist*, Vol. 371, Issue 8381, June 26, 2004, p. 60.

13. See Bruce Bower, "A Thoughtful Angle on Dreaming," *Science News*, June 2, 1990, Vol. 137, Issue 22, p. 348.

14. Quoted in Barbara Kantrowitz and Karen Springen, "What Dreams Are Made Of," *Newsweek*, August 9, 2004, p. 44.

15. J. L. McClelland, "Toward a Pragmatic Connectionism." In P. Baumgartner and S. Payr, eds., *Speaking Minds: Interviews with Twenty Eminent Cognitive Scientists* (Princeton, NJ: Princeton University Press, 1995), p. 141.

16. Deidre Barrett, *The Committee of Sleep: How Artists, Scientists and Athletes Use Their Dreams for Creative Problem Solving* (New York: Crown/Random House, 2001).

17. Mark Nelson, "Sleep On It: Solving Business Problems," *Nation's Business*, December 1987, Vol. 75, Issue 12, pp. 72–73.

18. Thea Singer, "Your Brain on Innovation," *Inc.*, September 2002, Vol. 24, Issue 9. http://www.inc.com/magazine/20020901/24544.html

19. For more information on the role of sleep and dreams in solving problems and reducing stress, read Eric Maisel's book *Sleep Thinking* (Avon, MA: Adams Media Corp. 2001).

20. Reuven Bar-Levav, *Thinking in the Shadow of Feelings* (New York: Simon & Schuster, 1988), p. 20.

21. "Over 30 and Over the Hill," *The Economist*, Vol. 371, Issue 8381, June 26, 2004, p. 60.

22. This exercise is adapted from Daniel Rigney, "What If You Could Be Instantly Smarter? A Thought Experiment," *The Futurist*, Vol. 38, Issue 2, March-April 2004, pp. 34–36.

23. Barbara J. Thayer-Bacon, "Feminism and Critical Thinking," in Joe L. Kincheloe and Danny Weil, *Critical Thinking and Learning: An Encyclopedia for Parents and Teachers* (Westport, CT: Greenwood Press, 2004), p. 280.

24. *Random House Webster's College Dictionary* (New York, Random House, 2001).

25. Reuver Bar-Levav, *Thinking in the Shadow of Feelings* (New York: Touchstone Book, 1988), p. 116.

26. W. J. Ndaba, "The Challenge to African Philosophy," http://singh.reshma.tripod.com/alternation/alternation6_1/12JNDABA.htm

27. Edward R. Howe, "Secondary Teachers Conceptions of Critical Thinking in Canada and Japan: A Comparative Study," *Teacher and Teaching*, Vol. 10, Issue 5, November 2004, pp. 505–525.

28. Janette Warwick and Ted Nettelbeck, "Emotional Intelligence Is . . . ?" *Personality and Individual Differences*, Vol. 37, Issue 5, October 2004, pp. 1091–1100.

29. J. D. Mayer and P. Salovey, "What Is Emotional Intelligence," in P. Salovey and D. J. Sluyter, eds., *Emotional Development and Emotional Intelligence: Educational Implications* (Basic Books: New York, 1997), p. 10.

30. Al Gore, *The Assault on Reason* (New York: Penguin Press, 2007), pp. 154–155.

31. For more on the importance of emotional intelligence in everyday life, see David Goleman's *Emotional Intelligence: Why It Can Matter More Than IQ* (1995).

32. Delores Gallo, "Educating for Empathy, Reason, and Imagination," in Kerry S. Walters, ed., *Re-Thinking Reason: New Perspectives in Critical Thinking* (Albany, NY: State University of New York Press, 1994), p. 56.

33. Matthew P. Walker, Conor Liston, J. Allan Hobson, and Robert Stickgold, "Cognitive Flexibility Across the Sleep-Wake Cycle: REM-Sleep Enhancement of Anagram Problem Solving," *Cognitive Brain Research*, Vol. 14, Issue 3, November 2002, pp. 317.

34. Nel Noddings, *Caring: A Feminine Approach to Ethics and Moral Education* (Berkeley: University of California Press, 1984).

35. Kerry S. Walters, "Critical Thinking, Rationality, and the Vulcanization of Students," in Kerry S. Walters, ed., *Re-Thinking Reason: New Perspectives in Critical Thinking* (Albany, NY: State University of New York Press, 1994), pp. 61–63.

36. W. J. Ndaba, "The Challenge to African Philosophy," http://singh.reshma.tripod.com/alternation/alternation6_1/12JNDABA.htm

37. Patrick Henry Winston, *Artificial Intelligence*, 3rd ed. (Reading, MA: Addison-Wesley Publishing Co., 1993).

38. For more on the Turing test, go to http://www.turing.org.uk.

39. See http://newsvote.bbc.co.uk/2/hi/uk_news/magazine/3503465.stm and Charles W. Bailey, Jr., *Truly Intelligent Computers* (Library & Information Technology Association, 1992), http://www.cni.org/pub/LITA/Think/Bailey.html

40. Ray Kurzweil, *The Age of Spiritual Machines: When Computers Exceed Human Intelligence* (New York: Viking, 1999), p. 4.

41. Herbert A. Simon, "Machines as Mind," in Kenneth M. Ford, Clark Glymour, and Patrick J. Hayes, eds., *Android Epistemology* (Menlo Park, CA: AAAI Press, 1995), p. 36.

42. See Roger Penrose's *The Emperor's New Mind* (Oxford University Press, 1989) and *Shadows of the Mind* (Oxford University Press, 1994).

43. Steven Pinker, "Using Our Minds to Help Heal Ourselves," *Newsweek*, September 27, 2004.

44. Margaret A. Boden, "Could a Robot Be Creative?" in Kenneth M. Ford, Clark Glymour, and Patrick J. Hayes, eds., *Android Epistemology* (Menlo Park, CA: AAAI Press, 1995), pp. 69–70.

45. For a more in-depth coverage of this topic, refer to Paul Helm, ed., *Faith and Reason* (Oxford, Oxford University Press, 1999).

46. Quoted in Brian Kolodiejchuk, *Mother Teresa: Come Be My Light* (New York: Doubleday, 2007).

47. For more on the work and writings of Billy Graham, go to http://www.billygraham.org/

48. For an example of fideism, read Danish existentialist Søren Kierkegaard's "Concluding Unscientific Postscript to the *Philosophical Fragments*."

49. Richard Dawkins, "Viruses of the Mind." In Paul Kurtz and Timothy J. Madigan, *Challenges to Enlightenment: In Defense of Reason and Science* (Buffalo, NY: Prometheus Books, 1994), p. 197.

50. Dean Hamer, *The God Gene: How Faith Is Hardwired into Our Genes* (New York: Doubleday, 2004).

51. Jeffrey Kluger, "Is God in Our Genes?" *Time*, October 25, 2004, p. 68.

52. Lippman Bodoff, "Was Abraham Ready to Kill His Son?" in Hershel Shanks, ed., *Abraham and Family: New Insights into the Patriarchal Narratives* (Washington, D.C.: Biblical Archaeology Society, 2000).

53. For more on this argument, see colonial American theologian Jonathan Edward's sermon on "Reason No Substitute for Revelation," in Paul Helm, ed., *Faith and Reason* (Oxford, Oxford University Press, 1999), pp. 221–222.

54. Keith A. Roberts, *Religion in Sociological Perspective* (Homewood, IL: Dorsey Press, 1984), p. 62.

55. Jeff Chu, "Faith and Frat Boys," *Time*, May 9, 2005, p. 49.

56. Cited in "College Students Losing Faith?" *A Chronicle of the Christian Faith*, August 24, 2004. http://www.inthefaith.com/2004/08/24/college-students-losing-faith/

57. http://www.worldnetdaily.com/news/article.asp?ARTICLE_ID=34540

58. For more on this controversy, see John L. McCarthy and Hubert L. Dreyfus, "What Computers Still Can't Do," *Artificial Intelligence*, Vol. 80, nos. 1–2, pp. 143–150, and Hubert L. Dreyfus, "Response to My Critics," *Artificial Intelligence*, Vol. 80, nos. 1–2, pp. 171–191.

59. Ray Kurzweil, *The Age of Spiritual Machines* (New York: Penguin, 1999), pp. 5, 14, 45–47, 149–153.

60. Noreen Herzfeld, *In Our Image: Artificial Intelligence and the Human Spirit* (Minneapolis: Fortress Press, 2002), pp. 1, 5–7, 71–74, 75.

Chapter 3

1. Noam Chomsky, *On Language and Nature* (Cambridge, UK: Cambridge University Press, 2002). See also Mark C. Baker, *The Atoms of Language: The Mind's Hidden Rules of Grammar* (New York: Basic Books, 2001).

2. Geoffrey Sampson, *The 'Language Instinct' Debate* (London: Continuum International, 2005).

3. "Language," *The Columbia Encyclopedia*, 6th ed. (New York: Columbia University Press, 2000), p. 22073.

4. Veanne N. Anderson, Dorothy Simpson-Taylor, and Douglas J. Herrmann, "Gender, Age, and Rape: Supportive Rules," *Sex Roles: A Journal of Research*, Vol. 50, Issue 1, January 2004, pp. 77–90.

5. Lindsley Smith, "Juror Assessment of Veracity, Deception, and Credibility" (for publication), http://www.uark.edu/depts/comminfo/CLR/smith1.html

6. Estes Thompson, " 'Moral Call' Led Soldier to Expose Prison Abuse," http://aolsvc.news.aol.com/news/article.adp?id=20040803033109990001

7. Sarah Childress, "A New Controversy in the Fetal-Rights Wars," *Newsweek*, March 29, 2004, p. 7.

8. All passages are from *The New English Bible* (New York: Cambridge University Press, 1972).

9. For more on the development of the English language, see David Wilton, "A (Very) Brief History of the English Language," http://www.wordorigins.org/index.php/site/comments/a_very_brief_history_of_the_english_language3/

10. This exercise is from Clive Wynne's book *Do Animals Think?* (Princeton, NJ: Princeton University Press, 2004), p. 108.

11. Mary Daly, *Beyond God the Father* (Boston: Beacon Press, 1985).

12. Lois Pineau, "Date Rape: A Feminist Analysis," *Law and Philosophy*, Vol. 8, 1989, pp. 217–243.

13. "General Information about Learning Disabilities," Fact Sheet Number 7 (FS7), 1997. http://www.kidsource.com/NICHCY/learning_disabilities.html

14. Prior HHS Poverty Guidelines and Federal Register References, U.S. Department of Health & Human Services, 2001, http://aspe.hhs.gov/poverty/08computations.shtml

15. Chapter 48 of the Texas Statutes Human Resources Code, http://tlo2.tlc.state.tx.us/statutes/docs/HR/content/pdf/hr.002.00.000048.00.pdf

16. http://www.answers.com/topic/community-college

17. Samuel Johnson, *Dictionary of the English Language*, 1755.

18. Chris Mooney, "Emotional Rescue," *Seed Magazine*, May/June 2007, pp. 26–28.

19. *Random House Webster's College Dictionary* (New York: Random House, 2001), pp. 1253–1254.

20. Cherrie Moraga, *Loving the War Years* (Boston: South End Press, 1983).

21. http://www.gutenberg.org/files/12242/12242-h/12242-h.htm

22. Shelly L. Gable, Harry T. Reis, and Geraldine Downey, "He Said, She Said: A Quasi-Signal Detection Analysis of Daily Interactions Between Close Relationship Partners," *Psychological Science*, Vol. 14, Issue 2, March 2003, p. 102.

23. Diana K. Ivy and Phil Backlund, *GenderSpeak: Personal Effectiveness in Gender Communication*, 3rd ed. (Boston: McGraw-Hill, 2004), p. 211.

24. Deborah Tannen, *You Just Don't Understand: Women and Men in Communication* (New York: Morrow, 1990), p. 42.

25. Amy Clements, "Study Confirms Males/Females Use Different Parts of Brain in Language and Visuospatial Tasks," *Brain and Language*, Vol. 98, August 2006, pp. 150–158.

26. For a debate on this issue, go to http://www.pbs.org/thinktank/transcript216.html

27. Jean Chatzky, "Wheel and Deals," *Time*, October 18, 2004, p. 94.

28. Michelle LeBaron, "Culture-Based Negotiation Styles," Intractable Conflict Knowledge Base Project, University of Colorado, 2003, http://www.beyondintractability.org/m/culture_negotiation.jsp

29. Phil Williams and Veronica Duncan, "Different Communication Styles May Be at Root of Many Problems Between African American Males and Females," University of Georgia News Bureau, October 8, 1998, http://www.uga.edu/columns/101998/campnews3.html

30. Mark P. Orbe, "Remember, It's Always Their Ball: Descriptions of African American Male Communication," *Communication Quarterly*, Vol. 42, Issue 3, summer 1994, pp. 287–300.

31. Li-Jun Ji, Zhiyong Zhang, and Richard E. Nisbett. "Is It Culture or Is It Language? Examination of Language Effects in Cross-Cultural Research on Categorization," *Journal of Personality and Social Psychology*, Vol. 87, Issue 1, July 2004, PsychARTICLES, http://content.apa.org/journals/psp/87/1/57.html, p. 2.

32. AnneMarie Pajewski, Ph.D., and Luis Enriquez, B.S., Teaching from a Hispanic Perspective: A Handbook for Non-Hispanic Adult Educators (Phoenix, AZ: Arizona Adult Literacy and Technology Resource Center, 96), http://www.literacynet.org/lp/hperspectives/hispcult.html

33. Ibid.

34. For more information on fashion as language, see Stuart Hall, *Representation: Cultural Representations and Signifying Practices* (London: Sage Publications, 1997), p. 37.

35. Daniel Okrent, "The War of the Words: A Dispatch from the Front Lines," *New York Times*, March 6, 2005.

36. Amber Gudikunst, "The Heated Debate over Stem Cell Research," Letter to the editor, *Newsweek*, Nov. 8, 2004, p. 16.

37. "Tourism: Do Slogans Sell?" *Newsweek*, August 30, 2004, p. 9.

38. Phil Cox, "The Disputation of Hate: Speech Codes, Pluralism, and Academic Freedoms," *Social Theory and Practice*, Vol. 21, Issue 1, 1995, p. 113.

39. George Orwell, *Nineteen Eighty-Four* (New York: New American Library, 1949), pp. 176–177.

40. Gallup poll, 2002, p. 45.

41. "Gay Marriage in Oregon," Letters to the editor, *Newsweek*

42. March 22, 2004, p. 45.

43. Bernard N. Nathanson and Richard N. Ostling, *Aborting America* (Garden City, NY: Doubleday, 1979), p. 193.

44. Mark G. Frank and Thomas Hugh Feeley, "To Catch a Liar: Challenges for Research in Lie Detection Training," *Journal of Applied Communication Research*, Vol. 31, Issue 1, February 2003, p. 60.

45. Nationally televised speech by President Clinton, CNN, August 17, 1998.

46. Denis Boyles, "A Guide to Everything that Matters." AARP, September/October 2004, p. 108.

47. Mark G. Frank and Thomas Hugh Feeley, "To Catch a Liar: Challenges for Research in Lie Detection Training," *Journal of Applied Communication Research*, Vol. 31, Issue 1, February 2003, p. 59.

48. Carrie Lock, "Deception Detection," *Science News*, Vol. 166, Issue 5, July 13, 2004, p. 72.

49. Frederic Golden, "Face the Music: How New Computers Catch Deceit," *Time Europe*, March 13, 2000, Vol. 155, no. 10, p. 46.

50. Eve Conant, Arian Campo-Flores and John Barry, "I Mean, Raise Pure Hell," *Newsweek*, October 25, 2004, p. 57.

51. Richard H. Escobales, Jr., "The Heated Debate over Stem Cell Research," Letter to the editor, Newsweek, Nov. 8, 2004, p. 16.

52. David Ansen, "Not So Great," *Newsweek*, November 29, 2004, p. 60.

53. Sarah Childress and Dirk Johnson, "The Hot Sound of Hate," *Newsweek*, November 29, 2004, p. 30.

54. Marvin Olasky, "Blue-State Philosopher," *World*, November 27, 2004, p. 34.

55. Michael D. Lemonick, "In Search of Sleep," *Newsweek*, September 27, 2004, p. 44.

56. Headline from the *Weekly World News*, March 22, 2004, p. 10.

57. Brooke Noel Moore and Richard Parker, *Critical Thinking* (New York: McGraw-Hill, 2004), p. 144.

58. Headline from the March 22, 2004, *Weekly World News*, pp. 26–27.

59. James Rhodes, "An Insult to Churchill?" Letter to the editor, *Time*, March 29, 2004, pp. 16.

60. James Geary, "Deceitful Minds: The Awful Truth about Lying," *Time Europe*, March 13, 2000, Vol. 155, Issue 10. http://www.time.com/time/europe/magazine/2000/313/deceit.html

61. "Political correctness squelching campus speech," Associated Press, October 30, 2003. Reprinted at http://www.firstamendmentcenter.org/news.aspx?id=12145

62. Christian Mignot, "Lawsuits, Debate Intensify over University 'Free Speech Zones,'" *Daily Bruin (UCLA)*, October 1, 2002.

63. Ibid. Reprinted at http://www.thefire.org/index.php/article/5318.html

64. "Campus Speech Rules Scrutinized by Courts, Students, Advocates: Opponents Say Policies Violate First Amendment Right to Protest and Distribute Material," *College Censorship*, Vol. XXI, Issue 1, Winter 2002–2003, p. 6.

65. West Virginia University, "Policy on Free Speech Activity." *Student Handbook, The Mountie*, February 2002, pp. 17–18.

66. Greg Lukianoff, Foundation for Individual Rights in Education, letter to David Hardesty, president of West Virginia University, February 11, 2002.

67. Robert J. Scott, "Reasonable Limits Are Good," *USA Today*, May 27, 2003, p. 14a.

Chapter 4

1. See John Grisham's novel *The Innocent Man* for an excellent description of this type of "evidence" collecting.

2. For more on string theory, see Brian Greene, *The Elegant Universe: Superstrings, Hidden Dimensions, and the Quest for the Ultimate Theory* (New York: W.W. Norton, 2003), or go to: http://superstringtheory.com/basics/

3. U. Neisser and H. Harsch, "Phantom flashbulbs: False recollection of hearing the news about *Challenger*." In E. Winograd & U. Neisser, eds., *Affect and Accuracy in Recall: Studies of "Flashbulb Memories"* (New York: Cambridge University Press, 1992).

4. Elizabeth F. Loftus and John Palmer, "Reconstruction of Automobile Destruction," *Journal of Verbal Learning and Verbal Behavior*, Vol. 13, 1974, pp. 585–589.

5. Gary Wells, Iowa State University, quoted at http://www.truthinjustice.org/witness.htm

6. Elizabeth Loftus, "Our Changeable Memories: Legal and Practical Implications," *Nature Reviews*, Vol. 4, March 2003, pp. 231–234.

7. I.E. Hyman, T.H. Husband and I.J. Billings (1995). "False Memories of Childhood Experiences," *Applied Cognitive Psychology*, Vol. 9, 1995, pp. 181–197.

8. Elizabeth Loftus, "Creating False Memories," *Scientific American*, Vol. 277, 1997, pp. 70–75.

9. For a summary of studies on the effect of marijuana, see http://www.gdcada.org/statistics/marijuana.htm. For more specifics on the effects of marijuana and alcohol on driving, go to the National Highway Traffic Safety Administration Web site at http://www.nhtsa.dot.gov/people/outreach/safesobr/15qp/web/iddrug.html

10. Diane Feskanich, Walter C. Willett, Meir J. Stampfer, and Graham A. Colditz, "Milk, Dietary Calcium, and Bone Fractures in Women: A 12-Year Prospective Study," *American Journal of Public Health*, Vol. 87, Issue 6, June 1997, pp. 992–997.

11. Michael Isikoff, Andrew Murr, Eric Pape, and Mike Elkin, "Mysterious Fingerprint," *Newsweek*, May 31, 2004, p. 8.

12. J. Cocker, "Biased Questions in Judgment of Covariation Studies," *Personality and Social Psychology Bulletin*, Vol. 8, June 1982, pp. 214–220.

13. Thomas Gilovich, *How We Know What Isn't So* (New York: Free Press, 1991), p. 54.

14. Michael Sherman, "The Political Brain," *Scientific American*, July 2006, p. 36.

15. See http://www.danbrown.com/novels/davinci_code/faqs.html

16. National Advisory Mental Health Council, "Basic Behavioral Science Research for Mental Health Thought and Communication," *American Psychologist*, March 1996, Vol. 51(3), p. 181.

17. See Theodore Schick, Jr., and Lewis Vaughn, *How to Think About Weird Things*, 4th ed. (New York: McGraw-Hill, 2005), pp. 51–52.

18. Joe Kline, "Listen to What Katrina is Saying," *Newsweek*, September 12, 2005, p. 27.

19. J. Liu and S. A. Siegelbaum, "Change of Pore Helix Conformation State Upon Opening of Cyclic Nucleotide-Gated Channels," *Neuron*, Vol. 28, 2000, pp. 899–909.

20. Curtis White, *The Middle Mind* (San Francisco, CA: HarperCollins, 2003), pp. 105–106.

21. Donn C. Young and Erinn M. Hade, "Holidays, Birthdays, and Postponement of Cancer Death," *Journal of the American Medical Association*, Vol. 292, Issue 24, December 29, 2004, pp. 3012–3016.

22. Rodger Dole, "Lady Luck," *Scientific American*, April 2006, p. 30.

23. Robert Ladouceur, "Gambling: The Hidden Addiction," *Canadian Journal of Psychiatry*, Vol. 49, Issue 8, August 2004, pp. 501–503.

24. "Numbers," *Time*, March 21, 2005, p. 20.

25. Edward S. Kubany, "Thinking Errors, Faulty Conclusion, and Cognitive Therapy for Trauma-Related Guilt," *NCP Clinical Quarterly*, Vol. 7, Issue 1, winter 1997. http://www.cbt.ca/trauma-related_guilt.htm

26. Pew Charitable Trusts, "Social Trends Poll: Americans See Weight Problems Everywhere But in the Mirror," April 11, 2006.

27. Douglas T. Kenrick, Steven L. Neuberg, and Robert B. Cialdini, *Social Psychology: Unraveling the Mystery*, 3rd ed. (Boston: Pearson Education, 2005), p. 84.

28. Amy Joyce, "We All Experience Office Conflict, But It's Never Our Fault," *Providence Sunday Journal*, June 13, 2004, p. H3.

29. Carol Tavris and Elliot Aronson, *Mistakes Were Made (But Not By Me): Why We Justify Foolish Beliefs, Bad Decisions, and Hurtful Acts* (New York: Harcourt, 2007).

30. Douglas T. Kenrick, Steven L. Neuberg, Robert B. Cialdini, *Social Psychology: Unraveling the Mystery*, 3rd ed. (Boston: Pearson Education, 2005), p. 84.

31. Pat Croskerry, "The Importance of Cognitive Errors in Diagnosis and Strategies to Minimize Them," *Academic Medicine*, Vol. 78, Issue 8, August 2003, pp. 775–780, and Ruthanna Gordon and Nancy Franklin, "Cognitive Underpinnings of Diagnostic Error," *Academic Medicine*, Vol. 78, Issue 8, August 2003, p. 782.

32. Ian I. Mitroff and Harold A. Linstone, *The Unbounded Mind: Breaking the Chains of Traditional Business Thinking* (New York: Oxford University Press, 1993), p. 94.

33. Tiffany A. Ito, Krystal W. Chiao, Patricia G. Devine, Tyler S. Lorig, and John T. Cacioppo, "The Influence of Facial Feedback on Racial Bias," *Psychological Science*, Vol. 17, Issue 3, 2006, pp. 256–261.

34. Sally Lehrman, "The Implicit Prejudice," *Scientific American*, June 2006, pp. 32–34.

35. "Noise Like an Airplane. Fire Island Surfman Heard It in the Air: Sure It Was Not Geese," *Boston Herald*, December 13, 1909, p. 1.

36. "Thousands See Big Airship over Worcester," *Boston Journal*, December 23, 1909, p. 1.

37. Robert E. Bartholomew and Benjamin Radford, *Hoaxes, Myths, and Manias: Why We Need Critical Thinking* (Amherst, NY: Prometheus Books, 2003), p. 210.

38. Joy D. Osofky, "Prevalence of Children's Exposure to Domestic Violence and Child Maltreatment: Implications for Prevention and Intervention," *Clinical Child and Family Psychology Review*, Vol. 6, Issue 3, Sept. 2003, pp. 161–170. See also the work of Dr. Richard Gelles.

39. Solomon Asch, "Effects of Group Pressure upon the Modification and Distortion of Judgments," in Harold Guetzkow, *Groups, Leadership and Men* (New York: Russell and Russell, 1963), pp. 177–190.

40. Ian I. Mitroff and Harold A. Linstone, *The Unbounded Mind: Breaking the Chains of Traditional Business Thinking* (New York: Oxford University Press, 1993), p. 23.

41. "LifeEtc.," *AARP Magazine*, September/October 2004, p.110.

42. Edward U. Condon, *Scientific Study of Unidentified Flying Objects* (Boulder, CO: Regents of the University of Colorado, 1969).

43. J. Allen Hynek, *The UFO Experience: A Scientific Inquiry*. (New York: Marlowe, 1972), pp. 214–222, 226–227.

44. Royston Paynter, "Physical Evidence and UFOs," http://www.geocities.com/Area51/Corridor/8148/physical.html, 1996

45. For more on string theory, see Brian Greene, *The Elegant Universe: Superstrings, Hidden Dimensions, and the Quest for the Ultimate Theory* (New York: W.W. Norton, 2003), or go to http://super-stringtheory.com/basics/

Chapter 5

1. Lynette Clemetson, "The Alarming Growth of Campus Cults," *Newsweek*, August 1999, p. 35.

2. Bates College Office of the Chaplain, "A Word about Cults," 1997.

3. Bates College Office of the Chaplain, "A Word about Cults," 1997.

4. Laura Withers, "Students Susceptible to Cults' Lures," *The Post* (online edition), Ohio University, February 15, 2002.

5. From "The Battle Over Terri Schiavo," *AOL News*, March 27, 2005.

6. "Ignorance and Fear Trump Kids' Health," *U.S. News & World Report*, March 12, 2007, p. 21.

7. Arthur Jensen, "How Much Can We Boost IQ and Scholastic Achievement?" *Harvard Educational Review* 39, winter 1969, pp. 1–23.

8. See John Cloud, "Ms. Right," *Time*, April 25, 2005, pp. 32–41.

9. Austin W. Astin et al., *The American Freshman, Thirty-Five Year Trends, 1966–2001* (Los Angeles, CA: Higher Education Research Institute, University of California, 2002), p. 30.

10. Brian Burrell, *Postcards from the Brain Museum: The Improbable Search for Meaning in the Matter of Famous Minds* (New York: Broadway Books, 2005).

11. Philip Terzian, "A Self-Inflicted Wound," *Providence Sunday Journal*, May 9, 2004, p. 19.

12. Quoted in Mike Billips, "Confronting a Scandal's Debris," *Time*, May 24, 2004, p. 50.

13. Harold A. Herzog, "Conflicts of Interest: Kittens and Boa Constrictors, Pets and Research," *American Psychologist*, Vol. 46, Issue 3, 1991, pp. 246–248.

14. Jonathan Alter, "We're Dodging the Draft Issue," *Newsweek*, October 4, 2004, p. 39.

15. Argument paraphrased from Francis Fukuyama, *Our Posthuman Future: Consequences of the Biotechnology Revolution* (New York: Picador, 2002), pp. 169–170.

16. "10 Questions for Rush Limbaugh," *Time*, June 7, 2004, p. 17.

17. Hazel Erskine, "The Polls: Politics and Law and Order," *Public Opinion Quarterly*, Vol. 38, Issue 4, winter 1974–1975, pp. 623–634.

18. Quote in "Notebook," *Time*, April 19, 2004, p. 19.

19. See Dan Shaughnessy, *The Curse of the Bambino* (New York: Penguin Putnam, 1990).

26. This example is based on a real-life case. I—the author—had both my children as a young undergraduate in Australia. In Australia, students who attained a certain grade point average in their first year of college were given a scholarship that paid all their tuition plus a small living allowance. I attained that average, but was denied a scholarship. Fortunately, I was motivated by my moral outrage at being unjustly treated to send a complaint to the federal government. As a result, I got the scholarship, including all the back payments I was due.

27. http://health.discovery.com/centers/loverelationships/articles/divorce.html

28. See Centers for Disease Control abortion surveillance data at http://www.cdc.gov/mmwr/preview/mmwrhtml/ss5511a1.htm. For a summary of statistics on abortion, go to http://www.religioustolerance.org/abo_fact2.htm

29. For the complete text of the *Roe v. Wade* ruling, go to http://laws.findlaw.com/us/410/113.html

30. For the latest polling results, go to www.pollingreport.com/abortion.htm

31. Judith Jarvis Thomson, "A Defense of Abortion," *Philosophy and Public Affairs*, Vol. 1, Issue 1, 1971, pp. 47–66.

32. For more on the issue of fathers' rights and obligations, see Stephen Hales, "Abortion and Fathers' Rights," in James M. Humber and Robert F. Almeder, eds., *Reproduction, Technology, and Rights* (Totowa, NJ: Humana Press, 1996), pp. 5–26.

Chapter 10

1. Ramin Setoodeh, "Caveman Chic," *Newsweek*, April 9, 2007, p. 50.

2. Matthew Creamer, "Southwest Rings $20M in Fares with Killer Application," *Advertising Age*, Vol. 76, Issue 28, July 11, 2005, p. 88.

3. Eileen C. Shapiro, *The Seven Deadly Sins of Business* (Oxford, UK; Capstone Publishing Ltd., 1998).

4. For more on the U.S. car industry, read Maryann Keller's book on General Motors, *Rude Awakenings: The Rise, Fall, and Struggle for Recovery of General Motors* (New York: William Morrow, 1989).

5. Shapiro, *Seven Deadly Sins*, pp. 180–181.

6. See "Geo Gaffes," *BrandWeek*, Vol. 39, Issue 8, February 23, 1996.

7. Shapiro, *Seven Deadly Sins*, p. 2.

8. Frederick Betz, "Strategic Business Models," *Engineering Management Journal*, Vol. 14, Issue 1, May 2002, p. 21.

9. William Cook, Jr., *Strategics: The Art and Science of Holistic Strategy* (Westport, CT: Quorum Books, 2000), p. 124.

10. http://walmartstores.com/FACTS

11. Doron Levin, "Toyota Rise Plus for U.S. Economy," *Bloomberg News*, April 27, 2007.

12. Owen Matthews, "How the West Came to Run Islamic Banks," *Newsweek*, October 31, 2005, p. E30.

13. Sean Gregory, "The Arte of Baseball," *Time*, June 2005, pp. A33–A34.

14. Brian Padden, "Can an American Auto Industry Town Regain Past Prosperity?" *Voice of America*, April 26, 2007, http://www.voanews.com/english/2007-04-26-voa57.cfm

15. http://www.lego.com/eng/info/default.asp?page=pressdetail&contentid=12504&countrycode-2057

16. Julie Kirkwood, "What's in a Name?" *The Eagle-Tribune*, September 1, 2003, www.igorinternational.com/press/eagletrib-drug-names.php

17. Casey Clapper, "Reaching Customers with the Touch of a Button," *Aftermarket Business*, September 2005, p. 10.

18. Darren W. Dahl, Heather Honea, and Rajesh Manchanda, "Three Rs of Interpersonal Consumer Guilt: Relationships, Reciprocity, Reparation," *Journal of Consumer Psychology*, Vol. 15, Issue 4, 2005, pp. 307–315.

19. http://www.newdream.org/kids/poll.php

20. Michael H. Meson, Courtland L. Bovée, and John V. Thill, *Business Today*, 10th ed. (Upper Saddle River, NJ: Prentice Hall, 2002), p. 403.

21. "Nielson to Measure the Mobile Media Consumer," June 6, 2007 http://www.nielsen.com/media/2007/pr_07060.html

22. Dan Ephron, "The Pizza Offensive," *Newsweek*, May 29, 2006, p. 30.

23. "Product Placement," BusinessDictionary.com. Available at http://www.businessdictionary.com/definition/product-placement.html

24. See http://www.commercialalert.org/issues/culture/product-placement.

25. "Watch What Your Kids Watch," *Mediawise*, Vol. 10, 2005.

26. http://www.tvturnoff.org/

27. Elizabeth S. Moore, "Children and the Changing World of Advertising," *Journal of Business Ethics*, Vol. 52, Issue 2, 2004, pp. 161–167.

28. Jonathan Freedland, "The Onslaught," *Guardian*, October 25, 2005. See http://www.guardian.co.uk/media/2005/oct/25/advertising/food.

29. Rebecca A. Clay, "Advertising to Children: Is It Ethical?" *Monitor on Psychology*, Vol. 31, Issue 8, September 2000. See http://www.apa.org/monitor/sep00/advertising.html.

30. Dan Acuff, "Taking the Guesswork out of Responsible Marketing," *Young Consumers*, Quarter 3, 2005, p. 68.

31. "Children, Health and Advertising: Issue Briefs" (Studio City, CA: Mediascope Press, 2000). For more on tobacco advertising to children and a summary of the Masters Settlement Agreement with the six largest tobacco companies, see David Hudson, Jr., "Tobacco Ads," at http://www.firstamendmentcenter.org/speech/advertising/topic.aspx?topic=tobacco_alcohol.

32. Todd House and Tim Loughran, "Cash Flow Is King? Cognitive Errors by Investors," *Journal of Psychology & Financial Markets*, Vol. 1, Issue 2/3, 2000, pp. 161–175.

33. For more information on the FDA's proposed initiative for curbing counterfeit prescription drugs, go to http://findarticles.com/p/articles/mi_m1370/is_/ai_109906674.

34. "Doctor's Orders: Bad Health for Sale: Does Advertising Hit Minorities Harder?" *Time*, August 29, 2005, p. 75. Available at http://www.time.com/time/magazine/article/0,9171,1096508,00.html.

35. "Children, Health and Advertising: Issue Briefs" (Studio City, CA: Mediascope Press, 2000).

36. Paul W. Farris and David J. Reibstein, "Consumer Prices and Advertising." In *Blackwell Encyclopedia of Business: Ethics*, 2nd ed. (Oxford, UK: Blackwell Publishers, 2005), p. 107.

37. For more on the issue of freedom of speech and advertising, see Martin H. Redish, "Tobacco Advertising and the First Amendment," *Iowa Law Review*, Vol. 81, March 1996.

38. *Advertising Week* New York City results: September 20–24, 2004.

39. "Keeping Well, at a Cost," *Newsweek*. Vol. 144, Issue 15, Oct. 11, 2004, pp. 20. Letters, Michael R. Heyman. Roseburg, Ore.

Chapter 11

1. Jim Martyka, "College Station Gives 'Average' Iraqi Voices Global Reach," *Associated Collegiate Press*, February 23, 2006. Available at http://www.studentpress.org/acp/trends/~warnews.html

2. Leela de Kretser and Lorena Mongelli, "Mesmerized by the Media—We're Obsessive Watchers, Listeners and Readers," *The New York Post*, Dec. 15, 2006, p. 35.

3. "Media Bias Is Real, Finds UCLA Political Scientist," *UCLA News*, December 14, 2005. Available at http://newsroom.ucla.edu/portal/ucla/Media-Bias-Is-Real-Finds-UCLA-6664.aspx

4. http://www.globalissues.org/HumanRights/Media/Corporations/Owners.asp

5. Ben Bagdikian, *The New Media Monopoly* (Boston: Beacon Press, 2004).

6. Ben Clark, "Power Surge," *San Francisco Bay Guardian*, September 20, 2000. Available at http://www.sfbg.com

7. "More Americans Get Political News from Internet," *IT-Observer*. March 2005. Also see Brendan MacGuire, "Television Network News

Coverage of Corporate Crime from 1970–2000," *Western Criminology Review*, Vol. 3, Issue 2, 2002. Available at http://wcr.sonoma.edu/v3n2/maguire.html

8. "Changing Definitions of News," March 6, 1998.

9. Robert J. Samuelson, "Picking Sides for the News," *Newsweek*, June 28, 2004, p. 37.

10. "The Gender Gap: Women Are Still Missing as Sources for Journalists," Project for Excellence in Journalism, May 23, 2005. Available at http://www.journalism.org/node/141

11. Jennifer Barrett, "New Secrets for Youthful Skin," *Newsweek*, April 24, 2006, pp. 74–76.

12. "Inventing the Internet. Did Al Gore Invent the Internet?" http://www.perkel.com/politics/gore/internet.htm

13. "Numbers," *Time*, February 28, 2005, p. 24.

14. Media Matters for America, "Media Watchdog, Government Ethics and Advocacy Groups Call for Action on 'Pay-Sway' Scandal," January 27, 2005. See http://mediamatters.org/items/200501270003

15. Andrew Kohut, "The Biennial Pew Media Survey: How News Habits Changed in 2004," http://www.brookings.edu/events/2004/0608media.aspx

16. Aired June 1, 2006.

17. H. Benson, J. A. Dusek, J. B. Sherwood et al., "Study of the Therapeutic Effects of Intercessory Prayer (STEP) in Cardiac Bypass Patients: A Multicenter Randomized Trial of Uncertainty and Certainty of Receiving Intercessory Prayer," *American Heart Journal*, Vol. 151, Issue 4: pp. 762–764, April 15, 2006.

18. Quotes from Denise Gellene and Thomas H. Maugh II, "Largest Study of Prayer to Date Finds It Has No Power to Heal," *Los Angeles Times*, March 31, 2006.

19. K. Scheider, "U.S. Officials Say Dangers of Dioxin Were Exaggerated," *New York Times*, August 5, 1991, p. 1.

20. "Internet Usage Statistics," 2007. http://www.internetworldstats.com

21. "Numbers," *Time*, January 10, 2005, p. 19.

22. "The American Freshman: National Norms for 2002." http://www.gseis.ucla.edu/heri/heri/html

23. http://money.cnn.com/magazines/moneymag/bestjobs/top50/index.html

24. Karine Joly, "Facebook, MySpace, and Co.," April 2007, p. 71. Available at http://www.universitybusiness.com/viewarticle.aspx?articleid=735&p=2

25. Janet Kornblum and Mary Beth Marklein, "What You Say Online Could Haunt You," *USA Today*, March 8, 2006.

26. Edward Fitzpatrick, "Fallout from Facebook is Forever," *The Providence Sunday Journal*, October 5, 2008, p. A1.

27. Reid Goldsborough, "Free Speech in Cyberspace—Both a Privilege and a Burden," *Community College Week*, Vol. 12, Issue 1, August 23, 1999, p. 27.

28. Al Gore, *The Assault on Reason* (New York: Penguin Press, 2007), p. 260.

29. "Losing Ground," (San Jose, CA: National Center for Public Policy and Higher Education, 2002). http://www.highereducation.org/reports/losing_ground/ar2.shtml

30. See www.universityofphoenix.com

31. Jerry Ropelato, "Internet Pornography Statistics," *Internet Filter Review*, 2007. http://internet-filter-review.toptenreviews.com/internet-pornography-statistics.html

32. Ibid.

33. Ibid.

34. Brian Hansen, "Is the Internet Causing More Students to Copy?" *CQ Researcher*, Vol. 13, No. 32, September 19, 2003.

35. Ibid.

36. Eric Hoover, "Here's Looking at You, Kid: Study Says Many Students are Narcissists," *Chronicle of Higher Education*, Vol. 53, Issue 27, March 9, 2007.

37. Peter Gumbel, "How the U.S. Is Getting Beat in Online Gambling," *Time* Bonus Edition, December 2005, pp. A1–A6.

38. George S. McClellan, "What Colleges Can Do about Student Gambling," *Chronicle of Higher Education*, 3/7/08. vol. 54, Issue 26, pp. A33–35.

39. Wendy Koch, "It's Always Poker Night on Campus," *USA Today*, December 23, 2005. Available at http://www.usatoday.com/news/nation/2005-12-22-gamble-college_x.htm

40. "People use media twice as much as they think they do," http://www.bsu.edu/icommunication/news/stories/february/2_25_03.html

Chapter 12

1. United Nations Environmental Programme, "Sea Level Rise Due to Global Warming." http://www.grida.no/climate/vital/19.htm

2. Tom Mosakowski, "2008 Will Be Among the Ten Hottest Years on Record." http://www.naturalnews.com/022658.html

3. American Meteorological Society, "NOAA: January 2006 Warmest on Record for Us," http://www.ametsoc.org/AMSNews/news0407.html

4. For more statistics, go to the U.S. Environmental Protection Agency Web site on global warming at http://epa.gov/climatechange/index.html.

5. United Nations Environmental Programme, "Sea Level Rise Due to Global Warming." http://www.grida.no/climate/vital/19.html.

6. For more information on the impact of global warming see the UN Environmental Programme website as well as the U.S. Environmental Protection Agency website on global warming at http://yosemite.epa.gov/oar/globalwarming.nsf/content/index.html.

7. Dushana Yoganathan and William N. Rom, "Medical Aspects of Global Warming," *American Journal of Industrial Medicine*, Vol. 40, Issue 2, 2001, pp. 199–201.

8. For a review of Descartes' position of epistemological skepticism see Chapter 1, pages 8–9.

9. Stanley Klein, "Quantum Mechanics as Science–Religion Bridge," 2002. http://cornea.berkeley.edu/pubs/158.pdf

10. For a summary of the Islamic position on science, see Todd Pitock, "Science and Islam," *Discover*, July 2007, pp. 36–45.

11. Arthur Peacocke, *Intimations of Reality: Realism in Science and Religion* (Notre Dame: University of Notre Dame Press, 1984), p. 51.

12. John D. Barrow, Frank J. Tipler, and John A. Wheeler, *The Anthropic Cosmological Principle* (New York: Oxford University Press, 1988).

13. See Russell A. Hill and Robert A. Barton, "Psychology Enhances Human Performance in Contests," *Nature*, Vol. 435, May 19, 2005, p. 293.

14. Josie Glausiusz, "Can We Bring Back the Vanishing Bees Before It's Too Late?" *Discover*, July 2007, p. 32.

15. B. Nyenzi and P. F. Lefale, "El Niño Southern Oscillation (ENSO) and Global Warming," *Advances in Geosciences*, Vol. 6, January 2006, pp. 95–101.

16. See Margaret Mead, *Coming of Age in Samoa* (New York, W. Morrow & Company, 1928).

17. Carl Zimmer, "Aliens Among Us: Do We Share Our Planet with Alternative Forms of Life?" *Discover*, July 2007, pp. 62–65.

18. http://www.psych.umn.edu/psylabs/mtfs/default.htm

19. For their operational definition of *religiousness*, see Laura Koenig et al., "Genetic and Environmental Influences on Religiousness: Findings for Retrospective and Current Religiousness Ratings," *Journal of Personality*, Vol. 73, Issue 2, April 2005, pp. 471–488.

20. Pat Wingert, "Blame Canada for This Brain Drain," *Newsweek*, April 19, 2004. Available at http://www.newsweek.com/id/53749

21. Christine Gorman, "Born Too Soon," *Time*, October 18, 2004, pp. 73–74.

22. Stanley Coren, PhD, *The Left-Handed Syndrome: The Causes and Consequences of Left-Handedness* (New York: Simon & Schuster, 1992).

23. "Healthbeat," *Newsweek*, January 17, 2005, p. 69.

24. For more on the concept of falsifiability, see Karl Popper, *The Logic of Scientific Discovery* (New York: Basic Books, 1959).

25. For a list of these predictions, go to http://farshores.org/dy09.htm

26. http://en.wikipedia.org/wiki/Nostradamus

27. "Most American Believe in Ghosts: Survey Shows _ Accept Astrology, 1/4 Reincarnation." *World Net Daily*, February 27, 2003. Data from a January 2003 Harris Poll.

28. See Megan Mansell Williams, "Should Losers Wear Red?" *Discover*, August 2005, p. 11.

29. For a review of sampling methods, see Chapter 7, pp. 206–209.

30. Sharon Begley, "Just Say No—to Bad Science," *Newsweek*, May 7, 2007, p. 57.

31. Daniel M. Wegner and William D. Crano, "Racial Factors in Helping Behavior: An Unobtrusive Field Experiment," *Journal of Personality and Social Psychology*, Vol. 32, No. 5, 1975, pp. 901–905. Available at http://www.wjh.harvard.edu/~wegner/pdfs/Wegner%20&%20Crano%201975.pdf

32. Judith A. Boss, "The effect of community service work on the moral development of college ethics students." *Journal of Moral Education*, Vol. 23, Issue 2, 1994, pp. 183–198.

33. Robert Barnhart, *The American Heritage Dictionary of Science* (Boston: Houghton Mifflin), p. 582.

34. See John Ioannidis, "Contradicted and Initially Stronger Effects in Highly Cited Clinical Research," *Journal of the American Medical Association*, Vol. 294, 2005, pp. 218–228, and Joao Medeiros, "Dirty Little Secret," *Seed*, May/June 2007, p. 20.

35. Russell A. Hill and Robert A. Barton, "Psychology: Red Enhances Human Performance in Contests," *Nature*, Vol. 435, May 19, 2005, p. 293.

36. Thomas Kuhn, *The Structure of Scientific Revolutions* (Chicago: University of Chicago Press, 1962), p. 10.

Chapter 13

1. Richard Wolffe and Holly Bailey, "The Presidency: Now, Time to Dig Out," *Newsweek*, January 2, 2006, p. 12.

2. Scott Carlson and Andrea L. Foster, "Colleges Fear Anti-Terrorism Law Could Turn Them into Big Brother," *Chronicle of Higher Education*, March 1, 2002, p. A31.

3. Charles C. Haynes, "The Sun May Be Setting on Patriot Act's Section 215," *Providence Sunday Journal*, June 26, 2005, p. D2.

4. Quoted in Byron York, "Off Course," *National Review*," February 13, 2006, p. 20.

5. See "Ask the White House," http://www.whitehouse.gov/ask/

6. The state of nature is purely hypothetical, since all known human societies have at least a rudimentary form of government.

7. Thomas Hobbes, *Leviathan* (1651), Chapter VIII.

8. John Locke, *Two Treatises of Government*, 1699.

9. The survey was conducted by the McCormick Tribune Freedom Museum. See "Poll: Simpson Better Known Than 1st Amendment," *Providence Sunday Journal*, March 5, 2006, p. D5.

10. UVE EText Jefferson Digital Archive: Thomas Jefferson on Politics and Government, "Majority Rule," http://etext.lib.virginia.edu/jefferson/quotations/jeff0500.htm

11. Gary C. Jacobson, *Money in Congressional Elections; The Politics of Congressional Elections*, 5th ed. (New York: Longman Publishers, 2001).

12. George R. Will, "An Election Breakwater," *Newsweek*, February 27, 2006, p. 68.

13. Daron R. Shaw, "The Effect of TV Ads and Candidate Appearances on Statewide Presidential Votes, 1988–1996," *American Political Science Review*, Vol. 93, June 1999, pp. 345–362.

14. Anita Fore, "Battle in the Blogosphere: *John Doe v. Patrick Cahill*," *Authors Guild Bulletin*, Winter 2006, p. 10.

15. John W. Dean, "Is It Time to Consider Mandatory Voting Laws?" *FindLaw Legal News and Commentary*, February 28, 2003.

16. U.S. Census Bureau, Current Population Survey, November 2004.

17. U.S. Census Bureau, Current Population Survey, November 2004.

18. Alan Abramowitz, *Voice of the People: Elections and Voting in the United States* (Boston: McGraw-Hill, 2004), pp. 184–185.

19. James Surowiecki, *The Wisdom of Crowds* (New York: Doubleday, 2004), pp. 268–271.

20. Jan Witold Baran, "Can I Lobby You?" *Washington Post*, January 8, 2006, p. B01.

21. For a review of cultural relativism and how this relates to the stages of moral reasoning, see Chapter 9, pages 286–287.

22. Michael H. Mescon, Courtland L. Bovée, and John V. Thill, *Business Today*, tenth edition (Upper Saddle River, NJ: Prentice Hall, 2002), p. 510.

23. The complete *Federal Rules of Evidence* are available at http://uscourts.gov/rules/

24. For more on this case, go to http://www.findlaw.com

25. Ken J. Rotenberg and Mike J. Hurlbert, "Legal Reasoning and Jury Deliberations," *Journal of Social Psychology*, August 1992, Vol. 132, Issue 4, pp. 543–544.

PHOTOS

Chapter 1

Opener: © Solus-Veer/Corbis; **p. 2:** © 1965 by Stanley Milgram. From the film OBEDIENCE, distributed by Penn State, Media Sales; **p. 3:** © The Gallery Collection/Corbis; **p. 7:** © Digital Vision/Getty; **p. 8:** © Hulton Archive/Getty; **p. 9:** © Mario Tama/Getty; **p. 10 (top):** PRNewsFoto/ Apple; **p. 10 (bottom):** © Bettmann/Corbis; **p. 11:** © Hans Neleman/Stone/Getty; **p. 12:** © Banana Stock/JupiterImages; **p. 14:** © Jeff Sherman/Taxi/Getty; **p. 15:** © Bettmann/Corbis; **p. 16:** AP Photo; **p. 18:** AP Photo/Jeff Widener; **p. 19:** © Digital Vision/SuperStock; **p. 21:** © Stockbyte/Getty; **p. 23:** © Medioimages/Photodisc/Getty; **p. 24:** © David Silverman/Getty; **p. 25:** © Greg Wahl-Stephens/Getty; **p. 26:** © Michael Poehlman/The Image Bank/Getty; **p. 27:** © Corbis; **p. 29:** © Moodboard/ Corbis; **p. 30:** © Bill Pugliano/Getty

Chapter 2

Opener: © Digital Vision/Getty; **p. 36:** © Gabe Palmer/Zefa/Corbis; **p. 36 (top, left):** © Tracy Hebden/iStock; **p. 36 (top, right):** © Sebastian Vera/ iStock; **p. 37 (bottom, right):** © Digital Archive Japan/Alamy; **p. 39:** © Nancy Kaszerman/ZUMA Press; **p. 40:** © Daniel Kopton/Corbis; **p. 41:** © Stockbyte/Getty; **p. 43 (left):** © Pixland/Jupiterimages; **p. 43 (second):** © Eastcott-Momatiuk/The Image Works; **p. 43 (third):** © Westend61/Getty; **p. 43 (fourth):** AP/Image Source; **p. 43 (right):** © Photodisc/Getty; **p. 45:** © Don Cravens//Time Life Pictures/Getty; **p. 46:** © Photodisc/SuperStock; **p. 47:** © Photodisc Collection/Getty; **p. 50:** © Photodisc/SuperStock; **p. 51:** © Tim Graham/Getty; **p. 54:** © Chris Ware/The Image Works; **p. 55:** © Key Color/Jupiter Images; **p. 56:** © Photographers Choice RF/SuperStock; **p. 57:** © George Steinmetz/Corbis

Chapter 3

Opener: © Judith Haeusler/Cultura/Getty; **p. 66:** © Elva Dorn/Alamy; **p. 67:** © Bettmann/Corbis; **p. 68:** © Scott Camazine/Photo Researchers, Inc.; **p. 69:** AP Photo/Pool, Al Golub; **p. 70:** © Amos Morgan/Getty; **p. 71:** © G.K. & Vikki Hart/Getty; **p. 72:** © Corbis; **p. 73:** © Stockdisc/PunchStock; **p. 75:** © Comstock/Picture Quest; **p. 76:** © Ingram Publishing/Alamy; **p. 77:** © Corbis; **p. 80:** © Bananastock/Jupiter Images; **p. 81 (left):** © Getty; **p. 81 (right):** © Getty; **p. 82:** © Jim Watson/AFP/Getty; **p. 83 (top):** © PureStock/Jupiter Images; **p. 83 (bottom):** © Peter DazeleyPhotographer's Choice RF/Getty; **p. 84:** © Photodisc/PunchStock; **p. 85:** © Chris Jackson/ Getty; **p. 86:** © Ottmar Bierwagen; **p. 87 (top):** © Ben Sklar/Getty; **p. 87 (bottom):** © Look Twice/Alamy; **p. 89 (top, left):** © Veer; **p. 89 (top, right):** © Image Source Black; **p. 89 (bottom):** © John Boyki/Stock Connection Distribution/Alamy; **p. 90:** © Amos Morgan/Getty; **p. 91:** © CMCD/Getty; **p. 92:** © Ottmar Bierwagen

Chapter 4

Opener: © Blue Syndicate/Corbis; **p. 98:** © Bettmann/Corbis; **p. 100 (top):** © Stockbyte/Getty; **p. 100 (bottom):** © Kimura/Getty; **p. 101:** © Stefan Zaklin/Getty; **p. 103:** © Andersen Ross/Blend Images/Corbis; **p. 104 (top):** © Business Wire via Getty; **p. 104 (bottom):** © Jemal Countess/WireImage; **p. 105:** © Hank Walker/Time & Life Pictures/Getty; **p. 106:** © Kaskad Film/ITAR-TASS/Corbis; **p. 108:** © Comstock/PictureQuest; **p. 109:** © Paramount Pictures/Getty; **p. 110:** © Phil Degginger/Alamy; **p. 111:** © Science Museum/SSPL/The Image Works; **p. 112:** © Scott Camazine/Alamy; **p. 113:** © Photodisc/Getty; **p. 114:** © Gary Walts/Syracuse Newspapers/The Image Works; **p. 115 (top):** © Hitoshi Nishimura/Taxi Japan/Getty; **p. 115 (bottom):** © William Thomas Cain/Getty; **p. 116 (top):** © Photodisc/Getty; **p. 116 (bottom):** © Alvis Upitis/Getty; **p. 117:** © PhotoAlto/PictureQuest; **p. 118:** © Corbis; **p. 119:** © Mary Evans Picture Library/The Image Works; **p. 120:** © Dynamicgraphics/JupiterImages; **p. 121:** © V&W/The Image Works; **p. 122:** © North Wind Picture Archives/Alamy; **p. 123:** William Vandivert, Scientific American, November 1955, Vol. 193, Issue 5, pp. 31-35.; **p. 125 (top):** © Moodboard/Corbis; **p. 125 (bottom):** © Comstock/PunchStock; **p. 126:** © James Porto/Taxi/Getty

Chapter 5

Opener: © Reuters/Corbis; **p. 136:** © Rob Howard/Corbis; **p. 137:** © Matt May/Getty; **p. 138 (top):** © Gilbert Carrasquillo/FilmMagic/Getty; **p. 138 (bottom):** © Photodisc/PunchStock; **p. 140:** © Corbis; **p. 142:** © Mary Evans Picture Library/Alamy; **p. 143:** © Sonda Dawes/The Image Works; **p. 144:** © Brand X Pictures; **p. 145:** Courtesy of The Advertising Archives; **p. 146:** AP Photo/ABC, Andrew Eccles; **p. 148 (top):** © Jun Sato/ WireImage/Getty; **p. 148 (bottom):** © Weinstein Company/Photofest; **p. 149:** © SSPL/The Image Works; **p. 150:** © Digital Vision/SuperStock; **p. 152:** © Jessica Leigh-Pool/Getty; **p. 153:** © Corbis; **p. 154 (top):** © Kim Komenich//Time Life Pictures/Getty; **p. 154 (bottom):** Library of Congress Prints & Photographs Division [LC-DIG-ggbain-32385]; **p. 157 (top):** © Larry Kolvoord/ The Image Works; **p. 157 (bottom):** © Amos Morgan/ Getty; **p. 159:** © Ryan McVay/Getty; **p. 160:** © Comstock/PictureQuest; **p. 161:** © Stockbyte/PunchStock; **p. 162:** Department of Defense photo by Sgt. David Foley, U.S. Army

Chapter 6

Opener: © Stefan Zaklin/epa/Corbis; **p. 168:** © Hulton Archive/Getty; **p. 169:** © Alberto Coto/Taxi/Getty; **p. 170 (top):** © Bettmann/Corbis; **p. 171:** Library of Congress Prints & Photographs Divison [LC-USZ62-13016]; **p. 173 (top):** AP Photo/Jeff Chiu; **p. 174:** © Getty/Digital Vision; **p. 175:** © Lightroom Photos/Topham/The Image Works; **p. 176:** © CMCD/Getty; **p. 177:** © BananaStock/PictureQuest; **p. 181:** © Neil Jacobs/Getty; **p. 182:** © Alex Wong/Getty; **p. 184:** © 2005 Comstock Images, JupiterImages Corporation; **p. 187 (top):** © James Leynse/Corbis; **p. 189:** © PhotoAlto/ PunchStock; **p. 192:** © Banana Stock/JupiterImages; **p. 195:** © Corbis; **p. 196:** © Gabriel Bouys/AFP/Getty

Chapter 7

Opener: © Fred Paul/Getty; **p. 205 (top):** © Punchstock; **p. 205 (bottom):** © Amos Morgan/Getty; **p. 207:** © Bob Daemmrich/The Image Works; **p. 209:** © F. Micelotta/American Idol 2008/Getty for Fox; **p. 210:** © Keystone/Getty; **p. 214 (top):** © Patrick Baz/AFP/Getty; **p. 214 (bottom):** © SuperStock; **p. 216 (top):** © Urs Kuester/Photonica; **p. 216 (bottom):** Library of Congress, Prints and Photographs Division [LC-USZC4-3616]; **p. 217 (top):** © The Bridgeman Art Library/Getty; **p. 218:** © John Tenniel/ The Bridgeman Art Library/Getty; **p. 219:** © Warner Bros./Dreamworks/ Photofest; **p. 220:** © Comstock/PunchStock; **p. 222:** © Scott Gries/Getty; **p. 223 (top):** AP Photo; **p. 223 (bottom):** © Don Farrall/Photodisc/Getty; **p. 224:** © Michael A. Keller/Zefa/Corbis; **p. 225 (inset):** © Comstock/Alamy; **p. 225:** © Gandee Vasan/Stone/Getty; **p. 227:** © Amos Morgan/Getty; **p. 228:** © Veer; **p. 230:** © CMSP/Science Faction/Getty

Chapter 8

Opener: © Zigy Kaluzny-Charles Thatcher/Stone/Getty; **p. 240:** © Alfred Gescheidt/Stone/Getty; **p. 242 (top):** © Christopher Gould/Photographer's Choice; **p. 242 (bottom):** © Corbis; **p. 244:** © Lawrence Schwartzwald /Sygma/Corbis; **p. 245 (top):** © Mike Kemp/Rubberball Productions/Getty; **p. 245 (bottom):** © Justin Sullivan/Getty; **p. 246 (top):** NASA; **p. 246 (bottom):** © Justin Sullivan/Getty; **p. 247:** © Ian Mckinnell/Photographer's Choice RR/Getty; **p. 248:** © Comstock/PictureQuest; **p. 250:** © Brand X Pictures/PunchStock; **p. 251:** © Frederick M. Brown/Getty; **p. 253:** © CMCD/Getty; **p. 256:** © Corbis; **p. 259:** © Geoff Dann/Dorling Kindersley/Getty; **p. 261:** © Veer; **p. 262:** © David Leeson/Dallas Morning News/The Image Works

Chapter 9

Opener: © Albert Ferreira/Reuters/Corbis; **p. 274:** © George Napolitano/ WireImage/Getty; **p. 275:** © Stock Montage/Hulton Archive/Getty; **p. 277:** © Paul Burns/Photodisc/Getty; **p. 278:** © Don Cravens/Time & Life Pictures/Getty; **p. 280 (top):** © Nick White/Getty; **p. 280 (bottom):** © Lee Lockwood/Time & Life Pictures/Getty; **p. 282 (top):** © Michael Quan/ ZUMA Press via Newscom; **p. 282 (bottom):** © Andrew Lichtenstein/The Image Works; **p. 283:** AP Photo; **p. 286:** © Bettmann/Corbis; **p. 287:** © Imagno/Getty; **p. 289:** Photo via Newscom; **p. 290:** © Kean Collection/ Getty; **p. 292:** © Corbis; **p. 293:** © Corbis; **p. 294:** © CMCD/Getty; **p. 296:** © Ron Sachs/CNP/Corbis; **p. 297:** © Comstock/Corbis; **p. 298:** © Ralph Lee Hopkins/National Geographic/Getty; **p. 302:** © Jim West/Alamy

Chapter 10

Opener: © Tim Hall/Getty; **p. 312:** Courtesy of Geico, Inc.; **p. 313:** © Tibor Bozi/Corbis; **p. 314:** © Topham/The Image Works; **p. 315:** © Rommel Pecson/The Image Works; **p. 317:** © Gilles Mingasson/Getty; **p. 318:** © Stephen Dunn/Getty; **p. 319 (top):** © Peter Hvizdak/The Image Works; **p. 319 (McDonalds):** © Bo Zaunders/Corbis; **p. 319 (Geek Squad):** AP Photo/Dino Vournas; **p. 320:** © Suzanne Opton/Time & Life Pictures/ Getty; **p. 321 (bottom):** © Image Source/Getty; **p. 322:** © Robyn Beck/ AFP/Getty; **p. 323 (top):** © Professional Sport/Topham/The Image Works; **p. 323 (bottom):** AP Photo/Kevork Djansezian; **p. 324:** © Banana Stock, - All Rights Reserved; **p. 326 (top):** Image courtesy of The Advertising Archives; **p. 326 (bottom):** © Ferdaus Shamim/WireImage/Getty; **p. 327:** Image courtesy of The Advertising Archives; **p. 329:** Image courtesy of The Advertising Archives; **p. 330 (left):** © Rachel Epstein/The Image Works; **p. 330 (right):** © Rommel Pecson/ The Image Works; **p. 334:** © image100/Corbis

Chapter 11

Opener: © Rick Gershon/Getty Images; **p. 342:** Courtesy of Swarthmore College; **p. 343 (left):** © Michael Reynolds/epa/Corbis; **p. 344 (left):** © Max Mumby/FNP/Topham/The Image Works; **p. 345:** © Dana Edelson/NBC via Getty; **p. 346 (top):** © David Howells/Corbis; **p. 346 (bottom):** © Monika Graff/The Image Works; **p. 347:** © Bettmann/Corbis; **p. 348:** © Bob Daemmrich/The Image Works; **p. 349 (top):** AP Photo/Dave Martin; **p. 349 (bottom):** © Chris Graythen/Getty; **p. 350:** © Jim Watson/AFP/Getty; **p. 351 (bottom):** © Fabio Cardoso/Corbis; **p. 352 (top):** © Time Life Pictures/ Mansell/Time Life Pictures/Getty; **p. 352 (bottom):** © Jordin Althaus/ WireImage/Getty; **p. 353:** © Matthew Cavanaugh/epa/Corbis; **p. 354 (bottom):** © THERENCE KOH/AFP/Getty; **p. 355:** © Chris Jackson/Getty; **p. 356:** © Studio 101/Alamy; **p. 357:** © vario images GmbH & Co.KG/ Alamy; **p. 358:** © Asia Images Group/PictureIndia/Getty; **p. 360:** © Frank Micelotta/Getty for Comedy Central; **p. 363:** © PhotoAlto/PunchStock

Chapter 12

Opener: © Steve McAlister/Getty; **p. 372:** © Digital Vision/Getty; **p. 373 (left):** © Jean-Leon Huens/National Geographic/Getty; **p. 373 (right):** © John Wang/Getty; **p. 375 (top):** Photo by Earl Slipher. Courtesy of Lowell Observatory.; **p. 375 (bottom):** © World History/Topham/The Image Works; **p. 376:** © NASA/SSPL/The Image Works; **p. 377 (top):** © Jim

Zuckerman/Corbis; **p. 378:** © Ted Spiegel/Corbis; **p. 379:** © JPL/NASA; **p. 380 (top):** © Comstock/Alamy; **p. 380** (bottom): © Mary Evans Picture Library/The Image Works; **p. 381 (top):** © Arthur Swoger/Archive Photos/ Getty; **p. 381** (bottom): © Barbara Penoyar/Getty; **p. 383:** © Bettmann/ Corbis; **p. 384:** Library of Congress Prints and Photographs Division [LC-DIG-ggbain-32094]; **p. 385:** © Simon Wilkinson/Riser/Getty; **p. 386** (left): © Charles Walker/Topfoto/The Image Works; **p. 386** (right): © Photo12/The Image Works; **p. 388:** © Karl Ammann/Corbis; **p. 389:** © Mario Beauregard/Corbis; **p. 390:** © Oxford Science Archive/Heritage-Images/The Image Works; **p. 391:** © Thinkstock/PunchStock; **p. 392:** © Peter Parks/AFP/Getty; **p. 395:** © Bettmann/Corbis; **p. 396 (top):** © You Sung-Ho/Reuters/Corbis; **p. 397:** © Studio 101/Alamy; **p. 398:** © Brand X Pictures/PunchStock; **p. 400:** © Tom Brakefield/Getty

Chapter 13

Opener: © Jonathan Ernst/Reuters/Corbis; **p. 410:** © Sean Adair/Reuters/ Corbis; **p. 411 (top):** © Bettmann/Corbis; **p. 411** (bottom): © The Print Collector/Heritage/The Image Works; **p. 412:** © Joseph Sohm; Visions of America/Corbis; **p. 413 (top):** © Digital Archive Japan/Alamy; **p. 414:** © Popperfoto/Getty; **p. 415:** © Roger-Viollet/The Image Works; **p. 416:** © Ethan Miller/Getty; **p. 417:** © Shawn Thew/epa/Corbis; **p. 421:** © Justin Sullivan/Getty; **p. 422:** © Seattle Post-Intelligencer Collection; Museum of History and Industry/Corbis; **p. 423** (bottom): © Dmitri Kessel//Time Life Pictures/Getty; **p. 424:** © Bettmann/Corbis; **p. 425:** © Peter Silva/ZUMA/ Corbis; **p. 426:** © ROBYN BECK/AFP/Getty; **p. 427:** © Rolls Press/ Popperfoto/Getty; **p. 428:** AP Photo/Reed Saxon; **p. 429:** © Antar Dayal/ Illustration Works/Getty; **p. 431 (top):** © Hisham F. Ibrahim/Getty; **p. 431** (bottom): © Mark Wilson/Getty; **p. 432:** © After Frederick Coffay Yohn/ The Bridgeman Art Library/Getty; **p. 434 (top):** © Tim Pannell/Corbis; **p. 436:** © Peter Hvizdak/The Image Works

All spot photos not listed are from the McGraw-Hill Digital Asset Library.

Text Credits

p. i From top to bottom: Harris Poll, June 17-21, 2005; Fox News/Opinion Dynamics Poll, Jan 30-31, 2007; CNN/Essence Magazine/Opinion Research Corporation Poll, March 26-April 2, 2008; VCU Life Sciences Survey, September 3-26, 2003; ABC News Poll, Jan 25-29, 2008; Fox News/Opinion Dynamics Poll, Sept. 23-24, 2003; CBS News/NY Times Poll, April 20-24, 2007; Fox News/Opinion Dynamics Poll, Sept. 23-24, 2003.

p. 5, CALVIN AND HOBBES © Watterson. Distributed by Universal Press Syndicate, Inc. Reprinted with permission. All rights reserved.

p. 6 (figure), Cognitive Development in College Students, adapted from Ron Sheese and Helen Radovanovic, W.G. Perry's Model of Intellectual and Ethical Development: Implications of Recent Research for the Education and Counseling of Young Adults (paper presented at the Annual Meeting of the Canadian Psychological Association, Ottawa, Ontario, June 1984). Used by permission of Ron Sheese, York University, Toronto.

p. 22 (figure), From John Rourke, *International Politics on the World Stage, Eleventh Edition.* Copyright © 2007. Reprinted by permission of The McGraw-Hill Companies, Inc.

p. 22, CALVIN AND HOBBES © Watterson. Distributed by Universal Press Syndicate, Inc. Reprinted with permission. All rights reserved.

p. 26, From Richard T. Schaefer, *Sociology, Tenth Edition.* Copyright © 2005. Reprinted by permission of The McGraw-Hill Companies, Inc.

p. 31, Nancy Cantor, excerpt from Affirmative Action and Higher Education: Before and After the Supreme Court Rulings on the Michigan Cases, from *The Chicago Tribune* (January 28, 2003). Copyright © 2003. Reprinted with the permission of Nancy Cantor.

p. 42, Definition for Emotion, from *Random House Webster's College Dictionary.* Reprinted with the permission of Random House, Inc.

p. 48, Reprinted with the permission of Ray Kurzweil.

p. 45-48, Ray Kurzweil, excerpts from *The Age of Spiritual Machines: When Computers Exceed Human Intelligence.* Copyright © 1999 by Ray Kurzweil. Reprinted with the permission of Ray Kurzweil.

pp. 59-60, Noreen L. Herzfeld, excerpts from *In Our Image: Artificial Intelligence and the Human Spirit.* Copyright © 2002 by Fortress Press. Reprinted with the permission of Augsburg Fortress Publishers.

p. 73, New words for the 1970s, 1980s, and 1990s from *Random House Webster's College Dictionary.* Copyright © by Random House, Inc. Used by permission of Random House, Inc.

p. 76, Definition for a sound, from Random House Webster's College Dictionary. Copyright © by Random House, Inc. Used by permission of Random House, Inc.

p. 79, From Donald A. Cadogan, How Self-Assertive Are You? (1990), ww.oaktreecounseling.com/assrtquz.htm. Reprinted with the permission of Donald A. Cadogan.

p. 86, Copyright © 1999 by M. Cooper. All rights reserved.

pp. 93-94, Greg Lukianoff, excerpt from a letter to David Hardesty, President of West Virginia University (February 11, 2002). Reprinted with the permission of Greg Lukianoff.

p. 94, Robert J. Scott, Reasonable Limits Are Good, from *USA Today* (May 27, 2003). Reprinted with the permission of Robert J. Scott.

pp. 127-128, Edward U. Condon, excerpts from Section I: Conclusions and Recommendations, from *Scientific Study of Unidentified Flying Objects.* Copyright © 1968 by The Regents of the University of Colorado. Reprinted with the permission of The Regents of the University of Colorado.

pp. 128-129, J. Allen Hynek, excerpts from *The UFO Experience: A Scientific Inquiry.* Reprinted with the permission of Perseus Books Group.

p. 130, Royston Paynter, Physical Evidence. Reprinted with the permission of Royston Paynter.

p. 137, Copyright © Wm. Hoest Enterprises, Inc. All rights reserved.

p. 155, STEVE BENSON reprinted by permission of Newspaper Enterprise Association, Inc.

pp. 164-165, Dave Koehler, excerpt from Fallacies and War: Misleading a Nervous America to the Wrong Conclusion, from www.phillyburbs.com (February 28, 2003). Reprinted with the permission of David Koehler, PhillyBurbs.com.

p. 171, Vegan Spam, excerpt from Adopt a College Program, Launched from *Vegan Spam* (September 1, 2003). Reprinted with the permission of Vegan Outreach.

p. 179, Reprinted with the permission of the American Civil Liberties Union.

p. 186, The Far Side® by Gary Larson © 1988 FarWorks, Inc. All Rights Reserved. The Far Side® and the Larson® signature are registered trademarks of FarWorks, Inc. Used with permission.

p. 189, Reprinted with the permission of Sidney Harris, www. sciencecartoonsplus.com.

pp. 190-191, James Rachels, excerpts from Active and Passive Euthanasia, from *New England Journal of Medicine* 292 (1975). Copyright © 1975 by The Massachusetts Medical Society. Reprinted with the permission of *The New England Journal of Medicine.* All rights reserved..

pp. 197-198, Michael Nava and Robert Davidoff, excerpt from The Case for Gay Marriage, from *Created Equal: Why Gay Rights Matter to America.* Copyright © 1994 by Michael Nava and Robert Davidoff. Reprinted with the permission of St. Martin's Press.

pp. 199-200, Robert Sokolowski, excerpts from The Threat of Same-Sex Marriage from *America* 190-19 (June 7, 2004). Copyright © 2004. All rights reserved. Reprinted with the permission of America Press.

p. 213, Copyright © John Pritchett. Reprinted by permission.

p. 233, Reprinted with the permission of Professor J. F. Heron.

pp. 231-233, Karen P. Tandy, excerpts from Marijuana: The Myths Are Killing Us, from *Police Chief* (March 2005). Copyright © by the International Association of Chiefs of Police. Reprinted with the permission of the International Association of Chiefs of Police.

pp. 233-234, Paul Armentano, Cannabis, Health and Context: The Case for Regulation. Reprinted with the permission of Paul Armentano.

pp. 235-236, Wayne Hall, excerpts from The Cannabis Policy Debate: Finding a Way Forward, from *Canadian Medical Association Journal / Journal de L'Association Medicale Canadienne* 162.12 (June 13, 2000): 1690-1692. Copyright © 2000 by the CMA Media, Inc. Reprinted with the permission of the publisher.

pp. 244-246, Edward van den Haag, The Ultimate Punishment: A Defense of Capital Punishment, from *The Harvard Law Review* 99 (1986): 1662-1669. Copyright © 1986 by The Harvard Law Review Association. Reprinted with the permission of The Harvard Law Review via Copyright Clearance Center.

pp. 266-269, Copyright © European Communities.Reprinted with permission.

p. 276, From Judith Boss, *Ethics for Life, Fourth Edition.* Copyright © 2008. Reprinted by permission of The McGraw-Hill Companies, Inc.

p. 295, CALVIN AND HOBBES © Watterson. Distributed by Universal Press Syndicate, Inc. Reprinted with permission. All rights reserved.

pp. 304-307, Judith Jarvis Thompson, excerpts from A Defense of Abortion, from *Philosophy and Public Affairs* 1.1 (1971): 47-66. Copyright © 1971. Reprinted with the permission of Blackwell Publishers, Ltd.

pp. 307-309, Serrin M. Foster, Refuse to Choose: Women Deserve Better than Abortion. Reprinted with the permission of Serrin M. Foster.

p. 315, CATHY © Cathy Guisewite. Distributed by Universal Press Syndicate, Inc. Reprinted with permission. All rights reserved.

p. 317, Based on www.businessballs.com/swotanalysisfreetemplate.htm

pp. 335-337, Center for Science in the Public Interest, excerpt from *Guidelines for Responsible Food Marketing to Children* (January 2005), www.cspinet. org/marketingguidelines.pdf. Reprinted by permission.

pp. 337-339, Robert Liodice, America = Free Speech--Whether We Like It or Not, (January 24, 2005), http://ana.blogs.com/liodice/2005/01/america_ free_sp.html. Reprinted by permission.

p. 365-366, Brook J. Sadler, excerpt from The Wrongs of Plagiarism: Ten Quick Arguments, from *Teaching Philosophy* 30:3 (September 2007): 283-294. Reprinted with the permission of the Philosophy Documentation Center.

pp. 367-368, Russell Hunt, excerpts from Four Reasons to Be Happy about Internet Plagiarism, from *Teaching Perspectives* 5 (December 2002):1-5. Reprinted with the permission of the author.

p. 379, Courtesy of NASA/JPL/Caltech.

p. 387, Philadelphia Inquirer/Universal Press Syndicate, Inc. Reprinted with permission.All rights reserved.

pp. 401-403, Michael Behe, Ph.D., excerpt from Irreducible Complexity: Obstacle to Darwinian Evolution, in *Debating Design: From Darwin to DNA,* edited by W.A. Dembski and M. Ruse. Copyright © 2004, 2006 by Cambridge University Press. Reprinted with the permission of Cambridge University Press.

pp. 403-405, Kenneth R. Miller, excerpt from Answering the Biochemical Argument from Design, in Neil Manson, *God and Design: The Teleological Argument and Modern Science.* Copyright © 2003. Reprinted with the permission of Kenneth R. Miller.

p. 418, From Thomas E. Patterson, *American Democracy, Eighth Edition.* Copyright © 2008. Reprinted by permission of The McGraw-Hill Companies, Inc.

p. 420, From Thomas E. Patterson, *We the People: A Concise Introduction to American Politics, Seventh Edition.* Copyright © 2008. Reprinted by permission of The McGraw-Hill Companies, Inc.